MASONRY DEFINED

A Liberal Masonic Education Every Mason Should Have
Compiled from the Writings of Albert G. Mackey
and Many Other Eminent Authorities
Revised and Enlarged

"The average Mason, after taking his degrees in Masonry, immediately asks himself what it all means. Few Masons have, or will take, the time to make an exhaustive study of Masonry. It is to this class of busy Masons this work will make an especial appeal. We have culled from the writings of many eminent Masonic scholars the 'meat' of the subject, and present it in such form that the busy Mason can get what he wants without the necessity of extensive reading or study. No Mason can acquire in a few days or months, or even years, all there is in Masonry. Everything in Masonry has a beautiful meaning if rightly understood, and everything done in the ritual work is meant to teach a distinct moral lesson. Masonry would die out in five years if it had to depend upon about 85% of the membership. It is the small minority—the really interested Masons—who have kept and are keeping the order alive today."

Volume 2

E. R. Johnston

835—How does the word sacred apply to Masonry?

Sacred. We call that sacred which is separated from common things, and dedicated either entirely or partially to the Most High. The ideas of truth and virtue, the feeling of a pure love and friendship are sacred for they elevate us above common things and lead to God. The tenor of sacred thought and feelings is towards religion, and therefore all things are sacred which are peculiarly dedicated to religious services, and carefully guarded from being applied to profane uses, or which, by means of their religious importance and value, are especially honored and considered indispensable to our spiritual and moral welfare. According to these ideas of what is sacred, the Freemason can call his work sacred, and every brother must acknowledge it to be so. Our labors being separated from the outward world, and founded upon truth and virtue, require brotherly love and philanthropy, and always elevate the spirit to the Great Architect of the Universe. But true inward sanctity every brother must have in his own breast, and not have it to seek in the degrees of the Order.

836—What is the legendary Sacred Lodge?

Sacred Lodge. Over the sacred lodge presided Solomon, the greatest of kings, and the wisest of men: Hiram, the great and learned king of Tyre; and Hiram Abif, the widow's son, of the tribe of Napthali. It was held in the bowels of the sacred Mount Moriah, under the part whereon was erected the sanctum sanctorum or Holy of Holies. On this mount it was where Abraham confirmed his faith by his readiness to offer up his only son Isaac. Here it was where David offered that acceptable sacrifice on the threshing-floor of Aman, by which the anger of the Lord was appeased. Here it was where the Lord delivered to David in a dream, the plan of the glorious temple, afterwards erected by our noble Grand Master, King Solomon. And lastly, here it was where he declared he would establish his sacred name and word, which should never pass away; and for these reasons, this was justly styled the Sacred Lodge.

837—When did the first three degrees receive the name of St. John's Masonry?

St. John's Masonry. Originally there was only one kind of Freemasonry. But when the Scottish and other higher degrees were introduced, the three first degrees received the name of the St. John's Masonry.

838—Who was St. John the Baptist?

St. John the Baptist. He was the forerunner of Jesus, a son of the Jewish priest Zacharias and of Elizabeth, who, as a zealous judge of morality and undaunted preacher of repentance, obtained great celebrity, first in his native country, then in the mountains of Judea, and afterwards among the whole nation. His simple and abstemious manner of living contributed much to his fame, and especially the peculiar purification or consecration by baptism in a river bath, which he introduced as a symbol of that moral purity which he so zealously inculcated. Jesus allowed himself to be baptized by him, and from that time forward John said unto his disciples, that he was certainly the Messiah. The frank earnestness and the great fame with which he preached even in Galilee, soon brought upon him the suspicion and hatred of the court of Tetrarch Antipas, or King Herod, who imprisoned him, and on the 29th August, in the thirty-second or thirty-third year of his life, caused him to be beheaded. The 24th June, his birthday, is dedicated to his memory through all Christendom. The patron saint of the Freemasons' brotherhood was formerly not St. John the Baptist, but St. John the Evangelist, whose festival they celebrated the 27th December, upon which day they hold their general assembly, probably induced thereto because at this season of the year the members could be better spared from their business or profession. For this reason also they chose for their quarterly festivals, the Annunciation of the Virgin Mary, Michaelmas, and the festival of St. John the Baptist, which last festival, on account of the better weather and other circumstances having been found to be more convenient for the yearly assembly, was often appointed for the time on which it should be held, so that it has now become nearly general. Many British lodges still celebrate the 27th December, and call it the minor St. John's day.

839—Who was St. John the Evangelist?

St. John the Evangelist. St. John the Evangelist and Apostle of Jesus, was born in Bethsaida, in Galilee, a son of Zebedee, and a disciple of Jesus, who loved him because he distinguished himself by his gentleness and humility. After the ascension of Jesus, he preached the gospel principally in Asia Minor and at Ephesus, where it is probable that he died in a good old age. He was a man of great energy and poetic fire and life; in his early years somewhat haughty and intolerant, but afterwards an example of love. We have a gospel or biography of Jesus by him, and three of the epistles also bear his name. The Gospel of St. John is especially important to the Freemason, for he preached love, and his book certainly contains all the fundamental doctrines of Freemasonry. As a Freemason ought never to forget that he has laid his hand upon the gospel of St. John, so should he never cease to love his brethren according to the doctrine of love contained in that sacred book. Many lodges celebrate his anniversary, the 27th December.

840—On what days occur the feasts of the two Saints John?

Saints John, Festivals of. The 24th of June is consecrated to Saint John the Baptist, and the 27th of December to Saint John the Evangelist. It is the duty of Masons to assemble on these days, and by a solemn invocation of the past, renew the ties and strengthen the fraternal bonds that bind the present to the brotherhood of the olden time.

841—What was the Lodge of Saints John?

Saints John Lodges. Masonic tradition has it that the primitive or Mother Lodge was held at Jerusalem, and dedicated to St. John the Baptist, and then to St. John the Evangelist, and finally to both. This Lodge therefore was called the "Lodge of the Holy Saints John of Jerusalem." From this Lodge all other Lodges are figuratively supposed to descend.

842—Of what is salt the emblem?

Salt. In the Helvetian ceremonies of Masonry, salt is added to the corn, wine and oil, because it was a symbol of the wisdom and learning which characterize Masons' lodges. Pierius makes it an emblem of hospitality and friendship, and also of fidelity. In the Scriptures, salt is considered as a symbol of perpetuity and incorruption, and used as a covenant. The formula used by our ancient brethren, when salt was sprinkled on the foundation-stone of a new lodge was, "May this undertaking, contrived by wisdom, be executed in strength and adorned with beauty, so that it may be a house where peace, harmony, and brotherly love shall perpetually reign."

843—What part of the Temple was called the Sanctuary?

Sanctuary. That part of the Temple at Jerusalem which was the most secret and most retired; in which was the ark of the covenant, and wherein none but the High-Priest might enter, and he only once a year, on the day of holy expiation. The same name was also given to the most sacred part of the Tabernacle, set up in the Wilderness, which remained until some time after the building of the Temple.

844—Of what is the color scarlet emblematic?

Scarlet. This rich and beautiful color is emblematical of fervency and zeal. It is the appropriate color of the Royal Arch degree; and admonishes us that we should be fervent in the exercise of our devotions to God, and zealous in our endeavors to promote the happiness of man.

845—As a science what does Freemasonry embrace?

Science. Freemasonry is a science not to be confined to a few Israelitic traditions learned by heart, as a school-boy learns his lessons; it is a science which embraces everything useful to man; it corrects the heart and prepares it to receive the mild impressions of the divine code; its moral injunctions, if duly weighed and properly applied, never fail to form its disciples into good members of society. It opens a progressive field for inquiry, and ought never to be driven into narrow bounds by the enactment of a law, saying, thus far will we allow you to go, and no farther, under the penalty of exclusion from its universality.

846—What passages of scripture are most appropriate for reading in Lodge?

Scriptures, Reading of the. By an ancient usage of the Craft, the Book of the Law is always spread open in the lodges. There is in this, as in everything else that is Masonic, an appropriate symbolism. The Book of the Law is the Great Light of Masonry. To close it would be to intercept the rays of divine light which emanate from it, and hence it is spread open, to indicate that the lodge is not in darkness, but under the influence of its illuminating power. Masons in this respect obey the suggestion of the Divine Founder of the Christian religion, "Neither do men light a candle and put it under a bushel, but on a candlestick; and it giveth light unto all that are of the house." A closed book, a sealed book, indicates that its contents are secret; and a book or roll folded up was the symbol, says Wemyss, of a law abrogated, or of a thing of no further use. Hence, as the reverse of all this, the Book of Law is opened in our lodges, to teach us that its contents are to be studied, that the law which it inculcates is still in force, and is to be "the rule and guide of our conduct."

But the Book of the Law is not opened at random. In each degree there are appropriate passages, whose allusion to the design of the degree, or to some part of its ritual, makes it expedient that the book should be opened upon those passages.

Masonic usage has not always been constant, nor is it now universal in relation to what particular passage shall be unfolded in each degree. The custom in this country, at least since the publication of Webb's *Monitor,* has been very uniform, and is as follows:

In the first degree, the Bible is opened at Psalm cxxxiii., an eloquent description of the beauty of brotherly love, and hence most appropriate as the illustration of a society whose existence is dependent on that noble principle. In the second degree the passage adopted is Amos vii. 7, 8, in which the allusion is evidently to the plumb-line, an important emblem of that degree. In the third degree the Bible is opened at Ecclesiastes xii. 1-7, in which the description of old age and death is appropriately applied to the sacred object of this degree.

But, as has been said, the choice of these passages has not always been the same. At different periods various passages have been selected, but always with great appropriateness, as may be seen from the following sketch.

Formerly, the Book of the Law was opened in the first degree at the 22d chapter of Genesis, which gives an account of Abraham's intended sacrifice of Isaac. As this event constituted the *first grand offering,* commemorated by our ancient brethren, by which the ground-floor of the Apprentice's Lodge was consecrated, it seems to have been very appropriately selected as the passage for this degree. That part of the 28th chapter of Genesis which records the visions of Jacob's ladder was also, with equal appositeness, selected as the passage for the first degree.

The following passage from 1 Kings vi. 8, was, during one part of the last century, used in the second degree:

"The door of the middle chamber was in the right side of the house, and they went up with winding stairs into the middle chamber, and out of the middle into the third."

The appositeness of this passage to the Fellowcraft's degree will hardly be disputed.

At another time the following passage from 2 Chronicles iii. 17, was selected for the second degree; its appropriateness will be equally evident:

"And he reared up the pillars before the temple, one on the right hand, and the other on the left; and he called the name of that on the right Jachin, and the name of that on the left Boaz."

The words of Amos v. 25, 26, were sometimes adopted as the passage for the third degree:

"Have ye offered unto me sacrifice and offerings in the wilderness forty years, O house of Israel? But ye have borne the tabernacle of your Moloch and Chiun your images, the star of your god, which ye made to yourselves."

The allusions in this paragraph are not so evident as the others. They refer to historical matters, which were once embodied in the ancient lectures of Freemasonry. In them the sacrifices of the Israelites to Moloch were fully described, and a tradition, belonging to the third degree, informs us that Hiram Abif did much to extirpate this idolatrous worship from the religious system of Tyre.

The 6th chapter of 2 Chronicles, which contains the prayer of King Solomon at the dedication of the Temple, was also used at one time for the third degree. Perhaps, however, this was with less fitness than any other of the passages quoted, since the events commemorated in the third degree took place at a somewhat earlier period than the dedication. Such a passage might more appropriately be annexed to the ceremonies of the Most Excellent Master as practiced in this country.

At present the usage in England differs in respect to the choice of passages from that adopted in this country.

There the Bible is opened, in the first degree, at Ruth iv. 7:

"Now this was the manner in former time in Israel concerning redeeming and concerning changing, for to confirm all things; a man plucked off his shoe, and gave it to his neighbor: and this was a testimony in Israel."

In the second degree the passage is opened at Judges xii. 6:

"Then said they unto him, Say now Shibboleth: and he said Sibboleth; for he could not frame to pronounce it right. Then they took him, and slew him at the passages of the Jordan. And there fell at that time of the Ephraimites forty and two thousand."

In the third degree the passage is opened at 1 Kings vii. 13, 14:

"And King Solomon sent and fetched Hiram out of Tyre. He was a widow's son of the tribe of Napthali, and his father was a man of Tyre, a worker in brass: and he was filled with wisdom, and understanding, and cunning to work all works in brass. And he came to King Solomon, and wrought all his work."

While from the force of habit, as well as from the extrinsic excellence of the passages themselves, the American Mason will, perhaps, prefer the selections made in our own Lodges, especially for the first and third degrees, he at the same time will not fail to admire the taste and ingenuity of our English brethren in the selections that they have made. In the second degree the passage from Judges is undoubtedly preferable to our own.

In conclusion it may be observed, that to give these passages their due Masonic importance it is essential that they should be covered by the square and compasses. *The Bible, square* and *compasses* are significant symbols of Freemasonry. They are said to allude to the peculiar characteristics of our ancient Grand Masters. The Bible is emblematic of the wisdom of King Solomon; the square of the power of Hiram; and the compasses, of the skill of the Chief Builder. Some Masonic writers have still further spiritualized these symbols by supposing them to symbolize the wisdom, truth, and justice of the Grand Architect of the Universe. In any view they become instructive and inseparably connected portions of the true Masonic ritual, which, to be understood, must be studied together.

847—Of what is the scythe emblematic?

Scythe. The scythe is an emblem of time, which cuts the brittle thread of life, and launches us into eternity. What havoc does the scythe of time make among the human race! If by chance we escape the numerous evils incident to childhood and youth, and arrive in perfect health and strength at the years of vigorous manhood; yet decrepit old age will soon follow, and we must be cut down by the all-devouring scythe of time and be gathered into the land where our fathers have gone before us.

848—What was the legendary virtue of the seal of Solomon?

Seal of Solomon. The double or endless triangle, in one or other of its different forms, constituted the famous seal of Solomon, our ancient Grand Master, which was said to bind the evil genii so fast, that they were unable to release themselves. By virtue of this seal, as the Moslems believed, Solomon compelled the genii to assist him in building the Temple of Jerusalem, and many other magnificent works.

849—To what seat of honor is a Past Master entitled?

Seat in East. Past Masters are entitled to a seat in the East, on the right and left of the Worshipful Master, that he may, on all necessary occasions, avail himself of their counsel and experience in the government of the Lodge; but this is a matter left entirely to his own discretion, for in the deliberations of the Lodge the Master is supreme, and Past Masters possess no other privileges of speaking and voting than belong to all other Master Masons. As a mark of respect, and as a distinction of rank, Past Masters are to be invested with a jewel peculiar to their dignity.

850—What are the teachings of the second degree?

Second Degree. As the darkness of heathenism, or natural religion, preceded the divine revelation vouchsafed to the people of God, so by our initiation into the second degree, we advance still farther into the dawn figured out by the Mosaic dispensation, which preceded the more perfect Christian day. Here the novice is brought to light, to behold and handle tools of a more artificial and ingenious construction, and emblematic of sublimer moral truths. By these he learns to reduce rude matter into due form, and rude manners into the more polished shape of moral and religious rectitude; becoming thereby a more harmonious cornerstone of symmetry in the structure of human society, until he is made a glorious cornerstone in the temple of God.

851—Why do Freemasons enjoin and practice secrecy?

Secrecy. Secrecy is one of the first duties of a Freemason, but those Masons err much who think they do their duty by only exercising it in things concerning the Order of the lodge. It is not for this reason only that secrecy is so often inculcated in the lodge as a Masonic duty, it is that he ought to use secrecy and caution in all his transactions out of the lodge, and especially where his talkativeness might be the means of causing injury or damage to his fellow-men.

Freemasonry, in laying its foundations in secrecy, follows the Divine order of Nature, where all that is grand and beautiful and useful is born of night and mystery. The mighty labors which clothe the earth with fruits and foliage and flowers are "wrought in darkness." The bosom of Nature is a vast laboratory, where the mysterious work of transmutation of substances is perpetually going forward. There is not a point in the universe, the edges of which do not touch the realms of night and silence. God himself is environed with shadows, and "clouds and darkness are around about his throne;" yet his beneficence is felt, and his loving Spirit makes itself visible through all worlds. So Freemasonry works in secrecy, but its benignant fruits are visible in all lands. Besides, this principle of secrecy furnishes a mysterious bond of unity and strength, which can be found nowhere else. The objection often urged against the Order on account of this peculiar feature is too puerile to be considered.

852—What did the ancients teach regarding secrecy and silence?

Secrecy and Silence. These virtues constitute the very essence of all Masonic character; they are the safeguard of the Institution, giving admonitions in all degrees, from the lowest to the highest. The Entered Apprentice begins his Masonic career by learning the duty of secrecy and silence. Hence it is appropriate that in that degree which is the consummation of initiation, in which the whole cycle of Masonic science is completed, the abstruse machinery of symbolism should be employed to impress the same important virtues on the mind of the neophyte.

The same principles of secrecy and silence existed in all the ancient mysteries and systems of worship. When Aristotle was asked what thing appeared to him to be most difficult of performance, he replied, "To be secret and silent."

"If we turn our eyes back to antiquity," says Calcott, "we shall find that the old Egyptians had so great a regard for silence and secrecy in the mysteries of their religion, that they set up the god Harpocrates, to whom they paid peculiar honor and veneration, who was represented with the right hand placed near the heart, and the left down by his side, covered with a skin before, full of eyes."

Apuleius, who was an initiate in the mysteries of Isis, says: "By no peril will I ever be compelled to disclose to the uninitiated the things that I have had intrusted to me on condition of silence."

Lobeck, in his Alaophamus, has collected several examples of the reluctance with which the ancients approached a mystical subject, and the manner in which they shrank from divulging any explanation or fable which had been related to them at the mysteries, under the seal of secrecy and silence.

And, lastly, in the school of Pythagoras, these lessons were taught by the sage to his disciples. A novitiate of five years was imposed upon each pupil, which period was to be passed in total silence, and in religious and philosophical contemplation. And at length, when he was admitted to full fellowship in the society, an oath of secrecy was administered to him on the sacred tetractys, which was equivalent to the Jewish Tetragrammaton.

Silence and secrecy are called "the cardinal virtues of a Select Master," in the ninth or Select Master's degree of the American Rite.

Among the Egyptians the sign of silence was made by pressing the index finger of the right hand on the lips. It was thus that they represented Harpocrates, the god of silence, whose statue was placed at the entrance of all temples of Isis and Serapis, to indicate that silence and secrecy were to be preserved as to all that occurred within.

853—Why are candidates for Masonry not elected VIVA VOCE?

Secrecy of Ballot. The secrecy of the ballot is as essential to its perfection as its unanimity or its independence. If the vote were to be given *viva voce*, it is impossible that the improper influences of fear or interest should not sometimes be exerted, and timid members be thus induced to vote contrary to the dictates of their reason and conscience. Hence, to secure this secrecy and protect the purity of choice, it has been wisely established as a usage, that the vote shall in these cases be taken by a ballot.

854—What are the qualifications of a Secretary of a Lodge?

Secretary. An important office in a lodge, for it is necessary that it should be filled by a man who can not only make out the common transactions of the lodge, but who is also capable of comprehending the spirit of a lecture, and introducing it into the transactions, briefly and at the same time correctly. To write a protocol correctly, so that in the event of any dispute it may serve as written evidence, is, as is well-known, a most difficult task, and requires great experience. The Secretary must be a Master Mason, and, when necessary, the brethren must assist him as copyists.

855—Is it lawful to reimburse the Secretary for the performance of his duties?

Secretary, Compensation of. It is customary in many Lodges, on account of the numerous and often severe duties of the Secretary, to exempt him from the payment of annual dues, and sometimes even to give him a stated salary. I see no objection to this, for he does not thereby cease to be a contributor to the support of the institution. His contribution, though not in the form of money, is in that of valuable services.

856—What are the duties of a Secretary?

Secretary, Duties of. The Secretary, like the Treasurer, is only a business officer of the Lodge, having nothing to do in the ritualistic labors. The charge which he receives at his installation into office, as it is given by Preston, Webb, and Cross, notwithstanding they all differ, does not contain a full summary of his duties, which are very extensive. I am inclined to think that the usage of the craft is at fault in making the Treasurer the senior officer, for I think it will be found that the duties and labors of the Secretary are not only more onerous, but far more important to the interests of the institution.

The Secretary acts, in his relation to the Lodge, in a threefold capacity. He is its recording, corresponding, and collecting agent.

857—Can a Master lawfully preside over a Lodge without having received the secrets of the chair?

Secrets of the Chair. It is the prerogative of the Master of a Lodge to receive from his predecessor the Past Master's degree at the time of his installation. It is a very important question whether it is essential that the Master elect should be invested with the degree of Past Master before he can exercise the functions of his office.

In the discussion of this question, it must be borne in mind that the degree of Past Master constitutes a specified part of the ceremony of installation of the elected Master of a Lodge. No Master is deemed to be regularly installed until he has received the degree. This is the ceremony which in England, and sometimes in this country, is called "passing the chair." The earliest written authorities always refer to it. Anderson alludes to it, in all probability, in his description of the Duke of Wharton's method of constituting a Lodge; Preston says distinctly that the new Master is "to be conducted into an adjacent room, here he is regularly installed;" and Oliver, commenting on this passage, adds, that "this part of the ceremony can only be orally communicated, nor can any but installed Masters be present."

This portion of the installing ceremony constitutes the conferring of the Past Master's degree. It is, in fact, the most important and essential part of the installation service; but the law of Masonry prescribes that no one shall exercise the prerogatives of the office to which he has been elected, until he has been regularly installed. Now, if the conferring of the Past Master's degree composes a necessary part of the ceremony of installation—and of this it seems to me that there can be no doubt—then it follows, as a natural deduction, that until the Master elect has received that degree, he has no right to preside over his Lodge. This decision, however, of course does not apply to the Master of a Lodge under dispensation, who, as the special proxy of the Grand Master, and deriving all his powers immediately from that high officer, as well as exercising them only for a specific purpose, is exonerated from the operation of the rule. Nor is it requisite that the degree should be a second time conferred on a Master who has been re-elected, and who at his previous installation had received it, although a number of years may have elapsed. When once conferred, its effects are for life.

Now, as it is the duty of every Mason to oppose the exercise by any person of the functions and prerogatives of an office until he has been legally installed, the question here suggests itself, how shall a Master Mason, not being himself in possession of the degree, know when it has not been conferred upon a Master elect? To this the reply is, that if the elected Master attempts to assume the chair, without having undergone any semblance of an installation, the greater part of which, it will be recollected, is performed before the members of the Lodge, it must follow, that he cannot have received the Past Master's degree, which constitutes a part of the ceremony of installation. But if he has been installed, no matter how carelessly or incorrectly, it is to be presumed that the degree has been conferred and the installation completed, unless positive evidence be furnished that it has not, because in Masonry as in law, the maxim holds good that "all things shall be presumed to have been done legally and according to form until the contrary be proved."

858—Is Masonry a secret society?

Secret Societies. Secret societies may be divided into two classes: First, those whose secrecy consists in nothing more than methods by which the members are enabled to recognize each other; and in certain doctrines, symbols, or instructions which can be obtained only after a process of initiation, and under the promise that they shall be made known to none who have not submitted to the same initiation; but which, with the exception of these particulars, have no reservations from the public. And secondly, of those societies which, in addition to their secret modes of recognition and secret doctrine, add an entire secrecy as to the object of their association, the time and places of their meeting, and even the very names of their members. To the first of these classes belong all those moral or religious secret associations which have existed from the earliest times. Such were the Ancient Mysteries, whose object was, by their initiations, to cultivate a purer worship than the popular one; such, too, the schools of the old philosophers, like Pythagoras and Plato, who in their esoteric instructions taught a higher doctrine than that which they communicated to their exoteric scholars. Such, too, are the modern secret societies which have adopted an exclusive form only that they may restrict the social enjoyment which it is their object to cultivate, or the system of benevolence for which they are organized, to the persons who are united with them by the tie of a common covenant, and the possession of a common knowledge. Such, lastly, is Freemasonry, which is a secret society only as respects its signs, a few of its legends and traditions, and its method of inculcating its mystical philosophy, but which, as to everything else—its design, its object, its moral and religious tenets, and the great doctrine which it teaches—is as open a society as if it met on the highways beneath the sun of day, and not within the well guarded portals of a lodge. To the second class of secret societies belong those which sprang up first in the Middle Ages, like the *Vehm Gericht* of Westphalia, formed for the secret but certain punishment of criminals; and in the eighteenth century those political societies like the Carbonari, which have been organized at revolutionary periods to resist oppression or overthrow the despotism of tyrannical governments. It is evident that these two classes of secret societies are entirely different in character; but it has been the great error of writers like Barruel and Robison, who have attacked Freemasonry on the ground of its being a secret association, that they utterly confounded the two classes.

859—Why should a Mason seek religion?

Seek. He who is desirous of finding wisdom, must diligently seek for it; and if he would know the real design of Masonry, he must study, and observe, and meditate, on what he hears in the lodge, otherwise the bondage of ignorance will never be removed.

860—Why should a Mason practice brotherly love?

Self-Interest. Let me travel from east to west, or between north and south, when I meet a true brother, I shall find a friend, who will do all in his power to serve me, without having the least view of self-interest; and if I am poor and in distress, he will relieve me, to the utmost of his power, interest or capacity. This is the second grand principle; for relief will follow when there is brotherly love.

861—Why should a Mason strive for self-knowledge?

Self-Knowledge. Every Freemason is earnestly exhorted to study himself. He who does not know himself, his moral weaknesses, his desires, his powers of toleration, and his real, not his imaginary, spiritual strength, cannot live as the Order requires that he ought to live, in the bonds of the closest fraternal love with the whole brotherhood; and if an office is intrusted to him in the lodge, he cannot know whether he is capable of filling it with credit to himself and profit to the Craft. It is quite as necessary that a Freemason should be as well acquainted with his moral strength as he is with his moral weakness; for many Masons are inactive in the lodge and in the Craft, merely because they do not know the power which is within themselves. He who has thoroughly studied himself, and is susceptible of all good impressions, will be subject to much less evil than others.

862—Whose duty is it to carry messages and orders for the Master of a Lodge?

Senior Deacon. The Senior Deacon, as I have already remarked, is the especial attendant of the Master. Seated at his right hand, he is ready at all times to carry messages to and convey orders from him to the Senior Warden, and elsewhere about the lodge.

863—What are the duties of the Senior Warden?

Senior Warden. The duties of the Senior Warden are very briefly described in the Installation service. They are, in the absence of the Master, to preside, and govern the Lodge; in his presence, to assist him in the government of it.

In assisting the Master in the government of the Lodge, it is the duty of both officers to see that due silence is observed around their respective stations, and that the orders issued from the east are strictly obeyed. But most of their duties in their peculiar positions are of a ritualistic nature, and are either unnecessary or improper to be discussed in the present work.

In the absence of the Master, the Senior Warden governs the Lodge. This is his inherent right, and has already been fully considered in the preceding section. He may, and often does, as a matter of courtesy, resign the chair to some Past Master present, but such Past Master always acts under the authority of the Warden, who has first to congregate the Lodge, that is, to call the brethren to labor, before he resigns the gavel of his authority into the hands of the Past Master.

864—In what degree are the five senses explained?

Senses. Man is brought into communication with the external world by means of five senses, or organs of perception. Seeing, Hearing and Feeling are often referred to in Masonic instructions. They are explained in the degree of Fellowcraft.

865—What was the usual period of apprenticeship among operative Masons?

Servitude. The stipulated period of an apprentice's servitude in former times was seven years, but less time will suffice, if found worthy of promotion by possessing the qualities of freedom, fervency, and zeal.

866—Of what is the setting-maul an emblem?

Setting-Maul. A wooden hammer used by Operative Masons to "set" the stones in their proper positions. It is in Speculative Masonry a symbol, in the Third Degree, reminding us of the death of the builder of the Temple, which is said to have been effected by this instrument. In some lodges it is very improperly used by the Master as his gavel from which it totally differs in form and in symbolic signification. The gavel is a symbol of order and decorum; the setting-maul, of death by violence.

867—What was the duty of the Senior Warden at the close of day?

Setting Sun. It was the duty of the Senior Warden to pay and dismiss the Craft at the close of day, when the sun sinks in the west; so now the Senior Warden is said in the Lodge to represent the setting sun.

868—Why does Masonry deny admission to women?

Sex. It is an unquestionable Landmark of the Order, and the very first prerequisite to initiation, that the candidate shall be "a man." This of course prohibits the initiation of a woman. This Landmark arises from the peculiar nature of our speculative science as connected with an operative art. Speculative Masonry is but the application of operative Masonry to moral and intellectual purposes. Our predecessors wrought, according to the traditions of the Order, at the construction of a material temple, while we are engaged in the erection of a spiritual edifice—the temple of the mind. They employed their implements for merely mechanical purposes; we use them symbolically, with a more exalted design. Thus it is that in all our emblems, our language, and our rites, there is a beautiful exemplification and application of the rules of operative Masonry to a spiritual purpose. And as it is evident that King Solomon employed in the construction of his temple only hale and hearty men and cunning workmen, so our Lodges, in imitation of that great exemplar, demand as an indispensable requisite to initiation into our mysteries, that the candidate shall be a *man,* capable of performing such work as the Master shall assign him. This is, therefore, the origin of the Landmark which prohibits the initiation of females.

869—How did our ancient brethren make use of the sword?

Sharp Instrument. The emblematic use of a "sharp instrument," as indicated in the ritual of the first degree, is intended to be represented by a warlike weapon (the old rituals call it " a warlike instrument") such as a dagger or sword. The use of the point of a pair of compasses, as is sometimes improperly done, is an erroneous application of the symbol, which should not be tolerated in a properly conducted lodge. The compasses are, besides, a symbol peculiar to the third degree.

870—Of what are sheep emblematic?

Sheep. The people of God are often typified in the Scriptures under the name of sheep, because of their mild, patient, and inoffensive nature. The lambskin, then, is an appropriate emblem of the innocence. The lamb, too, is of a social nature, and is emblematical of brotherly love. It is easily led.

871—What does the word "shibboleth" signify?

Shibboleth. The word signifies an ear of corn and a stream or flood of water. The name given to a test or criterion by which the ancient Jews sought to distinguish true persons or things from false. The term originated thus: After the battle gained by Jephthah over the Ephraimites (Judges xii.), the Gileadites, commanded by the former, secured all the passes of the river; and, on an Ephraimite attempting to cross, they asked him if he was of Ephraim. If he said no, they bade him pronounce the word *Shibboleth,* which Ephraimites, from inability to give the aspirate, gave *Sibboleth.* By this means he was detected as an enemy, and immediately slain. In modern times this word has been adopted into political and other organizations as a pass or watchword.

872—What is the symbolism of the shoe in Masonry?

Shoe. Among the ancient Israelites, the shoe was made use of in several significant ways. To *put off the shoes* imported reverence, and was done in the presence of God, or on entering the dwelling of a superior. *To unloose one's shoe and give it to another* was the way of confirming a contract. Thus we read in the book of Ruth, that Boaz having proposed to the nearest kinsman of Ruth to exercise his legal right by redeeming the land of Naomi, which was offered for sale, and marrying her daughter-in-law, the kinsman, being unable to do so, resigned his right of purchase to Boaz; and the narrative goes on to say (Ruth iv. 7, 8), "Now this was the manner in former time in Israel concerning redeeming and concerning changing, for to confirm all things, a man plucked off his shoe, and gave it to his neighbor; and this was a testimony in Israel. Therefore the kinsman said unto Boaz, Buy it for thee. So he drew off his shoe." The reference to the shoe in the first degree is therefore really as a symbol of a covenant to be entered into. In the third degree the symbolism is altogether different.

873—Of what is the shovel an emblem?

Shovel. The use of the shovel is to clear away rubbish and loose earth; and it morally depicts the mortal state in which the body is laid in the grave; that when the remains of this body shall have been properly disposed of, we, with humble but holy confidence, hope that the spirit may arise to everlasting life.

874—Is the Grand Hailing Sign the same in all jurisdictions?

Sign of Distress. This is probably one of the original modes of recognition adopted at the revival period, if not before. It is to be found in the earliest rituals extant of the last century, and its connection with the legend of the third degree makes it evident that it probably belongs to that degree. The Craft in the last century called it sometimes "the Master's Clap," and sometimes "the Grand Sign," which latter name has been adopted by the Masons of the present century, who call it the "Grand Hailing Sign," to indicate its use in *hailing* or calling a brother whose assistance may be needed. The true form of the sign has unfortunately been changed by carelessness or ignorance from the ancient one, which is still preserved in Great Britain and on the continent of Europe. It is impossible to be explicit; but it may be remarked, that looking to its traditional origin, the sign is a defensive one, first made in an hour of attack, to give protection to the person. This is perfectly represented by the European and English form, but utterly misrepresented by the American. The German Rite of Schroeder attempted some years ago to induce the Craft to transfer this sign from the third to the first degree. As this would have been an evident innovation, and would have contradicted the ritual history of its origin and meaning, the attempt was not successful.

875—Why should a Mason cultivate silence?

Silence. The first thing that Pythagoras taught his scholars was to be silent; for a certain time he kept them without speaking, to the end they might the better learn to preserve the valuable secrets he had to communicate, and never to speak but when required, expressing thereby that secrecy was the rarest virtue. Aristotle was asked what thing appeared to him most difficult; he answered to be secret and silent. To this purpose St. Ambrose, in his offices, placed among the principal foundations of virtue the patient gift silence.

876—Of what is the silver cord an emblem?

Silver Cord. In the beautiful and affecting description of the body of man suffering under the infirmities of old age given in the twelfth chapter of Ecclesiastes, we find the expression "or ever the silver cord be loosed, or the golden bowl be broken, or the pitcher be broken at the fountain, or the wheel broken at the cistern: then shall the dust return to earth as it was, and the spirit shall return to God who gave it." Dr. Clarke thus explains these beautiful metaphors. The silver cord is the spinal marrow; its loosening is the cessation of all nervous sensibility; the golden bowl is the brain, which is rendered unfit to perform its functions by the approach of death; the pitcher means the great vein which carries the blood to the right ventricle of the heart, here called the fountain; by the wheel is meant the great artery which receives the blood from the left ventricle of the heart, here designated as the cistern. This collection of metaphors is a part of the Scripture reading in the third degree, and forms an appropriate introduction to those sublime ceremonies whose object is to teach symbolically the resurrection and life eternal.

877—Why should Masons be sincere?

Sincerity. A search after truth is the peculiar employment of Masons at their periodical meetings, and therefore they describe it as a divine attribute, and the foundation of every virtue. To be good men and true is the first lesson we are taught in Masonry. On this theme we contemplate, and by its dictates endeavor to regulate our conduct; influenced by this principle, hypocrisy and deceit are unknown in the lodge; sincerity and plain dealing distinguish us; while the heart and tongue join in promoting the general welfare, and rejoicing in each other's prosperity.

878—How is the Masonic Lodge situated?

Situation. The lodge is situated due east and west, for various reasons; but the principal inducement of our ancient brethren to adopt this disposition was that it might serve to commemorate the great deliverance of the Israelites from bondage, by imitating the arrangement of the Tabernacle which was erected by Moses in the wilderness, as a place of public worship until the Lord should reveal the situation which he had chosen for his Holy Name amongst the tribes in the promised land.

879—What is the Masonic definition of slander?

Slander. Inwood, in his sermon on "Union Amongst Masons," says: "To defame our brother, or suffer him to be defamed, without interesting ourselves for the preservation of his name and character, there is scarcely the shadow of an excuse to be formed. Defamation is always wicked. Slander and evil speaking are the pests of civil society, are the disgrace of every degree of religious profession, the poisonous bane of all brotherly love."

880—How can a Lodge protect itself against impostors?

Slinking. It is not only possible, but it has often happened, that men have stole into the lodge who were never worthy of being admitted members of the Order, but who have managed to get initiated by hypocrisy, and because the members have not had sufficient opportunities to prove them, and to watch their previous conduct. But it is quite impossible for any one who has not been initiated to find his way into a lodge to indulge his curiosity. Every cultivated and moral man knows that initiation will not be denied him if he applies in a proper manner for it, and we are assured that they will never attempt, either by force or fraud, to gain admittance into a society where they have no right to be. Should any one, destitute of moral feeling, attempt to do so thinking that from printed works he has made himself acquainted with our customs, and can pass himself off for a Mason, he never can get beyond the ante-chamber for he has no certificate, or if he has, it is not his, and this is soon proved; his name is not upon any list, nor does he know anything of how he should answer the questions which will be put to him. An uneducated man has still less chance of stealing into a lodge, for his answer to the first question put to him would discover him at once. If we were as well secured from the first manner of improperly gaining admittance into a lodge as we are from the last, the Order would be in a more flourishing condition than it now is.

881—What are the social duties of a Master of a Lodge?

Social Duties of a Master. Socially, that is, as a member and officer of a peculiar society, exclusive in its character, he must be "true and trusty, and a lover of the whole fraternity." Each of these indicates a particular quality; his truth and fidelity will secure his obedience to all the regulations of the Order—his observance of its Landmarks and ancient usages—his opposition to all unwarrantable innovations. They will not only induce him to declare at his installation, but to support his declaration during his whole term of office, that "it is not in the power of any man or body of men to make innovations in the body of Masonry." They are his guarantee that he will not violate the promises he has made of fidelity and obedience to the constituted authorities of the Order.

His love of the fraternity will be an evidence of his zeal and fervency in the cause—of his disposition to cultivate all the benign principles of the institution, and to extend its blessings in every unobjectionable way. Where there is love, there must be reasonable service, and affection for the brethren will show its results in devotion to the association of which these brethren form a component part.

882—What are the advantages of being a Mason?

Society. Freemasonry forms a happy center of reunion for worthy men, who are desirous of a select society of friends and brothers, who have bound themselves in a voluntary obligation to love each other; to afford aid and assistance in time of need; to animate one another to acts of virtue and benevolence; and to keep inviolably the secrets which form the great characteristic of the Order.

883—What is a Lodge of Sorrow?

Sorrow Lodge. It is the custom among Masons on the continent of Europe to hold special lodges at stated periods, for the purpose of commemorating the virtues and deploring the loss of their departed members, and other distinguished worthies of the Fraternity who have died. These are called Funeral or Sorrow Lodges. In Germany they are held annually; in France at longer intervals. In this country the custom has been introduced by the Ancient and Accepted Rite, whose Sorrow Lodge ritual is peculiarly beautiful and impressive, and the usage has been adopted by many lodges of the American Rite. On these occasions the lodge is clothed in the habiliments of mourning, and decorated with the emblems of death, solemn music is played, funeral dirges are chanted, eulogies on the life, character and Masonic virtues of the dead are delivered.

884—Why is the Junior Warden stationed in the South?

South. The due course of the sun is from east to south and west; and after the Master are placed the Wardens, to extend his commands and instructions to the west and the north. From the east the sun's rays cannot penetrate into the north and the west at the same time.

885—On what is the Masonic system founded?

Speculative. The Masonic system exhibits a stupendous and beautiful fabric, founded on universal piety. To rule and direct our passions, to have faith and hope in God, and charity towards man, I consider as the objects of what is termed Speculative Masonry.

886—What is the symbolism of the square and compass?

Square and Compasses. These two symbols have been so long and so universally combined—to teach us, as says an early ritual, "to square our actions and to keep them within due bounds," they are so seldom seen apart, but are so kept together, either as two great lights, or as a jewel worn once by the Master of the Lodge, now by the Past Master —that they have come at last to be recognized as the proper badge of a Master Mason, just as the triple tau is of a Royal Arch Mason or the passion cross of a Knight Templar.

So universally has this symbol been recognized, even by the profane world, as the peculiar characteristic of Freemasonry, that it has recently been made in the United States the subject of a legal decision. A manufacturer of a flour having made, in 1873, an application to the Patent Office for permission to adopt the square and compasses as a trademark, the Commissioner of Patents refused permission on the ground that the mark was a Masonic symbol.

"If this emblem," said Mr. J. M. Thacher, the Commissioner, "were something other than precisely what is is—either less known, less significant, or fully and universally understood—all this might readily be admitted. But, considering its peculiar character and relation to the public, an anomalous question is presented. There can be no doubt that this device, so commonly worn and employed by Masons, has an established mystic significance, universally recognized as existing; whether comprehended by all or not, is not material to this issue. In view of the magnitude and extent of the Masonic organization, it is impossible to divest its symbols, or at least this particular symbol—perhaps the best known of all—of its ordinary signification, wherever displayed, either as an arbitrary character or otherwise. It will be universally understood, or misunderstood, as having a Masonic significance; and, therefore, as a trademark, must constantly work deception. Nothing could be more mischievous than to create as a monopoly, and uphold by the power of law, anything so calculated, as applied to purposes of trade, to be misinterpreted, to mislead all classes, and to constantly foster suggestions of mystery in affairs of business."

887—What is the duty of a Mason with respect to the laws of Masonry?

Stand to and Abide by. The covenant of Masonry requires every Mason "to stand to and abide by" the laws and regulations of the Order, whether expressed in the edicts of the Grand Lodge, the by-laws of his lodge, or the Landmarks of the Institution. The terms are not precisely synonymous, although generally considered to be so. *To stand to* has a somewhat active meaning, and signifies to maintain and defend the laws; while *to abide by* is more passive in meaning, and signifies to submit to the award made by such laws.

888—What should the By-Laws of a Lodge contain?

Statutes or Duties. Every Lodge has its statutes, with which every brother should be well acquainted, and which ought frequently to be read in open Lodge. They treat upon the duties of a Freemason both in and out of the Lodge, upon the duties of the officers, on the management of the Lodge, the duties and privileges of the brethren towards each other, and of the locality in which the Lodge is placed.

889—In each step in Masonry with what is the candidate presented?

Step. In the system of Masonry, the candidate is presented at each step with three precious jewels. As an Entered Apprentice, he receives "a listening ear, a silent tongue, and a faithful heart." As a Fellow Craft, it is "faith, hope, and charity." And as a Master Mason, he receives "humanity, friendship, and brotherly love."

890—What are the duties of the Stewards?

Stewards, Duties of. The Stewards are two in number, and are appointed by the Junior Warden. They sit on the right and left of that officer, each one having a white rod, as the insignia of his office, and wearing the cornucopia as a jewel.

Preston says that their duties are "to introduce visitors, and see that they are properly accommodated; to collect subscriptions and other fees, and to keep an exact account of the Lodge expenses." Webb adds to these the further duties of seeing "that the tables are properly furnished at refreshment, and that every brother is suitably provided for," and he makes them the assistants generally of the Deacons and other officers in performing their respective duties.

There can be no doubt, from the nature of the office in other institutions, that the duty of the Stewards was originally to arrange and direct the refreshments of the Lodge, and to provide accommodations for the brethren on such occasions. When the office was first established, refreshments constituted an important and necessary part of the proceedings of every Lodge. Although not yet abolished, the Lodge banquets are now fewer, and occur at greater intervals, and the services of the Stewards are therefore now less necessary, so far as respects their original duties as servitors at the table. Hence new duties are beginning to be imposed upon them, and they are, in many jurisdictions, considered as the proper officers to examine visitors and to prepare candidates.

The examination of visitors, and the preparation of candidates for reception into the different degrees, requires an amount of skill and experience which can be obtained only by careful study. It seems, therefore, highly expedient that instead of intrusting these services to committees appointed as occasion may require, they should be made the especial duty of officers designated at their installation for that purpose, and who will therefore, it is to be supposed, diligently prepare themselves for the correct discharge of the functions of their office.

Preston says that at their installation the Master and Wardens are the representatives of the Master Masons who are absent, the Deacons of the Fellow Crafts, and the Stewards of the Entered Apprentices.

The Stewards, like the Deacons, although not elected, but appointed, cannot, after installation, be removed by the officer who appointed them.

I may remark, in conclusion, that the office is one of great antiquity. since we find it alluded to and the duties enumerated in the Old York Constitutions of 926, where the Steward is directed "to provide good cheer against the hour of refreshment," and to render a true and correct account of the expenses.

891—Who were the Masters and Wardens of the lodges of Masons during the building of King Solomon's temple?

Stone Squarers. These were the Dionysiacs, a society of architects who built the Temple of Hercules at Tyre, and many magnificent edifices in Asia Minor, before the Temple of Solomon was projected. They were the Masters and Wardens of the lodges of Mason during the erection of this famous edifice.

892—What is one of the three principal supports of a Lodge?

Strength. This is said to be one of the three principal supports of a Lodge, as the representative of the whole Institution, because it is necessary that there should be Strength to support and maintain every great and important undertaking, not less than there should be Wisdom to contrive it, and Beauty to adorn it. Hence, Strength is symbolized in Masonry by the Doric column, because, of all the orders of architecture, it is the most massive; by the Senior Warden, because it is his duty to strengthen and support the authority of the Master; and by Hiram of Tyre, because of the material assistance that he gave in men and materials for the construction of the Temple.

893—What is the Masonic meaning of the expression "strict trial?"

Strict Trial. The ritualistic Landmark requires that these forms must be conducted in such a manner as to constitute what is technically called a "strict trial." No question must be omitted that should have been asked, and no answer received unless strictly and categorically correct. The rigor and severity of the rules and forms of a Masonic examination must never be weakened by undue partiality or unjustifiable delicacy. The honor and safety of the institution are to be paramount to every other consideration; and the Masonic maxim is never to be forgotten, that "it is better that ninety and nine true men should, by over strictness, be turned away from the door of a Lodge, than that one cowan should, through the carelessness of an examining committee, be admitted."

894—Why is the third called the sublime degree of Masonry?

Sublime. The third degree is called "the Sublime Degree of a Master Mason," in reference to the exalted lessons that it teaches of God and of a future life. The epithet is, however, comparatively modern. It is not to be found in any of the rituals of the last century. Neither Hutchinson, nor Smith, nor Preston use it; and it was not, therefore, I presume, in the original Prestonian lecture. Hutchinson speaks of "the most sacred and solemn Order of the most exalted," but not of the "sublime" degree. Webb, who based his lectures on the Prestonian system, applies no epithet to the Master's degree. In an addition of the Constitutions, published at Dublin in 1769, the Master's degree is spoken of as "the most respectable;" and forty years ago the epithet "high and honorable" was used in some of the rituals of this country. The first book in which we meet with the adjective *"sublime"* applied to the third degree, is the *Masonic Discourses* of Dr. T. M. Harris, published at Boston in 1801. Cole also used it in 1817, in his *Freemasons' Library;* and about the same time Jeremy Cross, the well-known lecturer, introduced it into his teachings, and used it in his *Hieroglyphic Chart,* which was, for many years, a text-book of American lodges. The word is now, however, to be found in the modern English lectures, and is of universal use in the rituals of the United States, where the third degree is always called "the sublime degree of a Master Mason."

895—What are the tests of Masonic obedience?

Submission. Your obedience must be proved by a close conformity to our laws and regulations; by prompt attention to all signs and summonses; by modest and correct demeanor whilst in the lodge; by abstaining from every topic of religious or political discussion; by a ready acquiescence in all votes and resolutions duly passed by the brethren; and by perfect submission to the Master and his Wardens, whilst acting in the discharge of their respective offices.

896—Of what is the substitute word a symbol?

Substitute Word. This is an expression of very significant suggestion to the thoughtful Master Mason. If the *Word,* is, in Masonry, a symbol of Divine Truth; if the search for the Word is a symbol of the search for that Truth; if the *Lost Word* symbolizes the idea that Divine Truth has not been found, then the *Substitute Word* is a symbol of the unsuccessful search after Divine Truth and the attainment in this life, of which the first Temple is a type, of what is only an approximation to it. The idea of a substitute word and its history is to be found in the oldest rituals of the last century; but the phrase itself is of more recent date, being the result of the fuller development of Masonic science and philosophy.

The history of the substitute word has been an unfortunate one. Subjected from a very early period to a mutilation of form, it underwent an entire change in some Rites, after the introduction of the high degrees, most probably through the influence of the Stuart Masons, who sought by an entirely new word to give a reference to the unfortunate representative of that house as the similitude of the stricken builder. And so it has come to pass that there are now two substitutes in use, of entirely different form and meaning; one used on the continent of Europe, and one in England and this country.

It is difficult in this case, where almost all the knowledge that we can have of the subject is so scanty, to determine the exact time when or the way in which the new word was introduced. But there is, I think abundant internal evidence in the words themselves as to their appropriateness and the languages whence they came (the one being pure Hebrew, and the other, I think, Gaelic), as well as from the testimony of old rituals, to show that the word in use in the United States is the true word, and was the one in use before the revival.

Both of these words have, however, unfortunately been translated by persons ignorant of the languages whence they are derived so that the most incorrect and even absurd interpretations of their significations have been given. The word in universal use in this country has been translated as "rottenness in the bone," or "the builder is dead," or by several other phrases equally as far from the true meaning.

The correct word has been mutilated. Properly, it consists of four syllables, for the last syllable, as it is now pronounced, should properly be divided into two. These four syllables compose three Hebrew words, which constitute a perfect and grammatical phrase, appropriate to the occasion of their utterance. But to understand them, the scholar must seek the meaning in each syllable, and combine the whole. In the language of Apuleius, I must forbear to enlarge upon these holy mysteries.

897—What is the order of succession in event of the death or disability of the Grand Master?

Succession in Office of Grand Master. There never has been any doubt that in case of the death or absence from the jurisdiction of the Grand Master, the Deputy succeeds to the office, for this seems to have been the only object of his appointment. The only mooted point is as to the successor, in the absence of both.

The Fourteenth Regulation of 1721 had prescribed, that if the Grand Master and his Deputy should both be absent from the Grand Lodge, the functions of Grand Master shall be vested in "the present Master of a Lodge that has been the longest a. Freemason," unless there be a Past Grand Master or Past Deputy present. But this was found to be an infringement on the prerogatives of the Grand Wardens, and accordingly a new Regulation appeared in the second edition of the Book of Constitutions, which prescribed that the order of succession should be as follows: the Deputy, a Past Grand Master, a Past Deputy Grand Master, the Senior, and then the Junior Grand Warden, the oldest former Grand Warden present, and lastly, the oldest Freemason who is the Master of a Lodge.

But this order of succession does not appear to be strictly in accordance with the representative character of the Grand Lodge, since

Past Grand officers, who are not by inherent right members of the Grand Lodge, should not be permitted to take precedence of the actual members and representatives. Accordingly, in this country, the Regulation has in general been modified, and here the Deputy succeeds the Grand Master, and after him the Wardens, in order of their rank, and then the Master of the oldest Lodge present, Grand officers being entirely excluded.

898—Who takes the place of the Grand Master or Grand Warden in the event of his absence from a session of the Grand Lodge?

Succession of Grand Lodge Officers. As in a subordinate Lodge, so in the Grand Lodge, the Junior Grand Warden does not occupy the west in the absence of the Senior Grand Warden. The two offices are entirely distinct; and the Junior Grand Warden having been elected and installed to preside in the south, can leave that station only for the east, in the absence of all his superiors. A vacancy in the west must be supplied by temporary appointment.

On the same principle, the Senior Grand Warden cannot supply the place of the absent Deputy Grand Master. In fact, in the absence from the Grand Lodge of the Deputy, it is scarcely necessary that his office should be filled by the temporary appointment of any person; for, in the presence of the Grand Master, the Deputy has no duties to perform.

899—Who succeeds to the chair in the absence or disability of the Master?

Succession to the Chair. Two principles seem now to be very generally admitted by the authorities on Masonic law, in connection with this subject.

1. That in the temporary or permanent absence of the Master, the Senior Warden, or, in his absence, the Junior, succeeds to the chair.

2. That on the permanent removal of the Master by death or expulsion, there can be no election for a successor until the constitutional night of election.

Let us inquire into the foundation of each of these principles.

1. The second of the Regulations of 1721 is in these words:

"In case of death or sickness, or necessary absence of the Master, the Senior Warden shall act as Master *pro tempore,* if no brother is present who has been Master of that Lodge before. For the absent Master's authority reverts to the last Master present, *though he cannot act till the Senior Warden has congregated the Lodge.*"

The lines which I have placed in italics indicate that even at that time the power of calling the brethren together and "setting them to work," which is technically called "congregating the Lodge," was supposed to be vested in the Senior Warden alone during the absence of the Master, although perhaps, from a supposition that he had greater experience, the difficult duty of presiding over the communication was entrusted to a Past Master. The regulation is, however, contradictory in its provisions; for, if the "last Master present" could not act, that is, could not exercise the authority of the Master, until the Senior Warden had congregated the Lodge, then it is evident that the authority of the Master did not revert to him in an unqualified sense, for that officer required no such concert nor consent on the part of the Warden, but could congregate the Lodge himself.

This evident contradiction in the language of the regulation probably caused, in a brief period, a further examination of the ancient usage, and accordingly, on the 25th of November, 1723, a very little more than three years after, the following regulation was adopted:

"If a Master of a particular Lodge is deposed or demits, the Senior Warden shall forthwith fill the Master's chair till the next time of choosing; and ever since, in the Master's absence, he fills the chair, even though a former Master be present."

The present Constitution of the Grand Lodge of England appears to have been formed rather in reference to the Regulation of 1721 than to that of 1723. It prescribes that on the death, removal, or incapacity of the Master, the Senior Warden, or in his absence, the Junior Warden, or in his absence, the immediate Past Master, or in his absence, the Senior Past Master, "shall act as Master in summoning the Lodge, until the next election of officers." But the English Constitution goes on to direct that "in the Master's absence, the immediate Past Master, or if he be absent, the Senior Past Master of the Lodge present shall take the chair. And if no Past Master of the Lodge be present, then the Senior Warden, or in his absence, the Junior Warden shall rule the Lodge."

Here again we find ourselves involved in the intricacies of a divided authority. The Senior Warden congregates the Lodge, but a Past Master rules it; and if the Warden refuses to perform his part of the duty, then the Past Master will have no Lodge to rule. So that after all, it appears that of the two, the authority of the Senior Warden is the greater.

But in this country the usage has always conformed to the Regulation of 1723, as is apparent from a glance at our rituals and monitorial works.

Webb, in his "Freemason's Monitor" (edition of 1808), lays down the rule that "in the absence of the Master, the Senior Warden is to govern the Lodge;" and that officer receives annually, in every Lodge in the United States, on the night of his installation, a charge to that effect. It must be remembered, too, that we are not indebted to Webb himself for this charge, but that he borrowed it, word for word, from Preston, who wrote long before, and who, in his turn, extracted it from the rituals which were in force at the time of his writing.

In the United States, accordingly, it has been held, that on the death or removal of the Master, his authority descends to the Senior Warden, who may, however, by courtesy, offer the chair to some Past Master who is present, after the Lodge has been congregated.

900—What is the prerogative of a Past Master with reference to his successor?

Successor, Installation of. Past Masters are invested with the right of installing their successors. There is, it is true, no Ancient Regulation which expressly confers upon them this prerogative, but it seems always to have been the usage of the fraternity to restrict the installing power to one who had himself been installed, so that there might be an uninterrupted succession in the chair. Thus, in the "Ancient Installation Charges," which date at least as far back as the seventeenth century, in describing the way in which the charges at an installation were given, it is said, "then one of the elders holds the book (of the law), and they place their hand upon it;" where *senioribus* may be very well interpreted as meaning the elder Master, those who have presided over a Lodge: *seniores* being originally a term descriptive of age which was applied to those in authority.

In 1717, the first Grand Master, under the new organization, was installed, as we learn from the book of Constitutions, by the oldest Master of a Lodge. Preston also informs us, in his ritual of installation, that when the Grand Master does not act, any Master of a Lodge may perform the ceremony. Accordingly, Past Masters have been universally considered as alone possessing the right of installation. In this and all similar expressions, it must be understood that Past Masters and installed Masters, although not having been twelve months in the chair, are in Masonic law identical. A Master of a Lodge becomes a Past Master, for all legal purposes, as soon as he is installed.

901—What are the prerogatives of a Deputy Grand Master or a Grand Warden when acting pro tempore as Grand Master?

Successor to Grand Master. The duties and prerogatives to which a Deputy Grand Master or Grand Warden succeeds, in case of the absence of the Grand Master from any communication, are simply those of a presiding officer, although of course they are for the time invested with all the rights which are exercised by the Grand Master in that capacity. But if the Grand Master be within the limits of the jurisdiction, although absent from the Grand Lodge, all their temporary functions cease as soon as the Grand Lodge is closed.

If, however, the Grand Master is absent from the jurisdiction, or has demised, then these officers, in the order already stated, succeed to the Grand Mastership, and exercise all the prerogatives of the office until his return, or, in the case of his death, until the next communication of the Grand Lodge.

902—What should a summons contain?

Summons. The brethren must be invited by summons from the Secretary on every lodge night; which summons must contain the place where, and the time when, the lodge is to be held, as well as what degrees will be wrought.

903—Why does the Worshipful Master sit in the East?

Sun. The sun rises in the east, and in the east is the place for the Worshipful Master. As the sun is the source of all life and warmth, so should the Worshipful Master enliven and warm the brethren to their work. Among the ancient Egyptians, the sun was the symbol of divine providence. Schiller says, "the sun darts his beams equally into every part of infinity."

904—Has the Lodge power to surrender its warrant without the consent of the Master?

Surrender of Warrant. A Lodge may be dissolved by a voluntary surrender of its warrant. This must be by the act of a majority of the members, and at a communication especially called for that purpose. But it has been held that the Master must concur in this surrender; for, if he does not, being the custodian of the instrument, it cannot be taken from him, except upon trial and conviction of a competent offence before the Grand Lodge.

As the warrant of constitution is so important an instrument, being the evidence of the legality of the Lodge, it is essentially necessary that it should be present and open to the inspection of all the members and visitors at each communication of the Lodge. The ritual requires that the three great lights of Masonry should always be present in the Lodge, as necessary to its organization as a just Lodge. Equally necessary is the warrant of constitution to its organization as a legal Lodge; and therefore if the warrant is mislaid or out of the room at the time of opening, it is held by Masonic jurists that the Lodge cannot be opened until that instrument is brought in and deposited in a conspicuous place, the most usual, and perhaps the most proper, being the pedestal of the Master.

905—By what process does a newly organized Grand Lodge issue authority over its constituent Lodges?

Surrender of Warrant. As soon as a new Grand Lodge is organized, it will grant warrants to the Lodges which formed it, to take effect upon their surrendering the warrants under which they originally acted to the Grand Lodges, from which they had derived them. There is no regulation prescribing the precise time at which these warrants are to be surrendered; but it seems reasonable to suppose that they could not surrender them before the new Grand Lodge is organized, because the surrender of a warrant is the extinction of a Lodge, and the Lodges must preserve their vitality to give them power to organize the new authority.

906—What is the Masonic meaning of the word "suspension?"

Suspension. Suspension may be defined to be a temporary privation of the rights and privileges of Masonry. This privation may be for a fixed or indeterminate period, whence results the division of this class of punishments into two kinds—definite and indefinite. The effect of the penalty is, for the time that it lasts, the same in both kinds, but there are some differences in the mode in which restoration to rights is to be effected in each.

907—May a Lodge lawfully suspend its by-laws?

Suspension of By-Laws. From the fact that the by-laws of a Lodge must be submitted to the Grand Lodge for its approval and confirmation arises the doctrine that a subordinate Lodge cannot, even by unanimous consent, suspend a by-law. As there is no error more commonly committed than this by unthinking Masons, who suppose that in a Lodge, as in any other society, a by-law may be suspended by unanimous consent, it will not be amiss to consider the question with some degree of care and attention.

An ordinary society makes its own rules and regulations, independent of any other body, subject to no revision, and requiring no approbation outside of itself. Its own members are the sole and supreme judges of what it may or may not enact for its own government. Consequently, as the members themselves have enacted the rule, the members themselves may unanimously agree to suspend, to amend, or to abolish it.

But a Masonic Lodge presents a different organization. It is not self-created or independent. It derives its power, and indeed its very existence, from a higher body, called a Grand Lodge which constitutes the supreme tribunal to adjudicate for it. A Masonic Lodge has no power to make by-laws without the consent of the Grand Lodge, in whose jurisdiction it is situated. The by-laws of a subordinate Lodge may be said only to be proposed by the Lodge, as they are not operative until they have been submitted to the Grand Lodge, and approved by that body. Nor can any subsequent alteration of any of them take place unless it passes through the same ordeal of revision and approbation by the Grand Lodge.

Hence it is evident that the control of the by-laws, rules and regulations of the Lodge is taken entirely out of its hands. A certain law has been agreed on, we will say, by the members. It is submitted to the Grand Lodge and approved. From that moment it becomes a law for the government of that Lodge, and cannot be repealed without the consent of the Grand Lodge. So far, these statements will be admitted to be correct. But if a Lodge cannot alter, annul or repeal such law, without the consent of the Grand Lodge, it must necessarily follow that it cannot suspend it, which is, for all practical purposes, a repeal for a temporary period.

I will suppose, by way of example, that it is proposed to suspend the by-law which requires that at the annual election all the officers shall be elected by ballot, so as to enable the Lodge, on a particular occasion, to vote *viva voce.* Now, this law must, of course, have been originally submitted to the Grand Lodge, and approved by that body. Such approbation made it the enactment of the Grand Lodge. It had thus declared that in that particular Lodge all elections for officers should be determined by ballot. The regulation became imperative on the Lodge. If it determined, even by unanimous consent, to suspend the rule, and on a certain occasion to proceed to the election of a particular officer by acclamation or *viva voce,* then the Lodge was abrogating for the time a law that the Grand Lodge had declared was binding on it, and establishing in its place a new one, which had not received the approbation of the supreme tribunal. Such a rule would therefore, for want of this confirmation, be inoperative. It would, in fact, be no rule at all, or worse, it would be a rule enacted in opposition to the will of the Grand Lodge. This principle applies, of course, to every other by-law, whether trivial or important, local or general in its character. The Lodge can touch no regulation after the decree of the Grand Lodge for its confirmation has been passed. The regulation has gone out of the control of the Lodge, and its only duty then is implicit obedience. Hence it follows that it is not competent for a subordinate Lodge, even by unanimous consent, to suspend any of its by-laws.

908—In whom does the power of suspending a Master of a Lodge reside?

Suspension of Master. It will sometimes happen that the offences of the Master are of such a nature as to require immediate action, to protect the character of the institution and to preserve the harmony of the Lodge. The Grand Lodge may not be in session, and will not be for some months, and in the meantime the Order is to be protected from the evil effects that would arise from the continuance of a bad Master in office. The remedy provided by the usages of the institution for such an evil are of a summary nature. The Grand Master is, in an extraordinary case like this, invested with extraordinary powers, and may suspend the Master from office until the next communication of the Grand Lodge, when he will be subjected to a trial. In the meantime the Senior Warden will assume the office and discharge the functions of the Master. In New York, the Grand Master immediately appoints in such a case a commission of seven, who must be not lower in rank than Wardens, and who try the question and make up their decision, which is final, unless an appeal is taken from it, within six months, to the Grand Lodge. This, however, is a local regulation, and where it, or some other satisfactory mode of action is not prescribed by the Constitution of a Grand Lodge, the Grand Master may exert his prerogative of suspension under the general usage or common law of Masonry.

909—Who was Emanuel Swedenborg? What was the rite of Swedenborg?

Swedenborg, Rite of. This rite was established by Emanuel Swedenborg, the eminent philosopher, who was born at Stockholm, January 29, 1688, died at London, March 29, 1772. His rite was composed of eight degrees, divided into two Temples. The first Temple contained the degrees of Apprentice, Fellowcraft, Master and Elect. The doctrines of these degrees related to the creation of man, his obedience and punishment, and the penalties inflicted on the body and soul; all of which is represented in the initiation. The second Temple comprises the degrees of Companion Cohen, Master Cohen, Grand Architect and Knight Commander, and Kadosh. The enlightened Mason will find much of the elements of Freemasonry in the writings of Swedenborg, who, for forty-eight years of his life, devoted himself to the cultivation of science, and produced a great number of works, in which he broached many novel and ingenious theories in theology, which obtained for him a remarkable celebrity in several parts of the world. The Marquis de Thome, in 1783, taking up the system that had been adopted in the Lodge of Avignon, in 1760, modified it to suit his own views, and instituted what afterward became known as the Rite of Swedenborg.

Swedenborg was well versed in the ancient languages; philosophy, metaphysics, mineralogy and astronomy were equally familiar to him. He devoted himself to profound researches in regard to the mysteries of Freemasonry, wherein he had been initiated; and in what he wrote respecting it, he established that the doctrines of the institution came from those of the Egyptians, Persians, Jews and Greeks. He endeavored to reform the Roman Catholic religion, and his doctrines were adopted by a great number of persons in Sweden, England, Holland, Russia, Germany, and lastly, in the United States. His religious system is expounded in the book entitled *The Celestial Jerusalem, or the Spiritual World.* If we are to believe him, he wrote it from the dictation of angels, who, for that purpose, appeared to him at fixed periods. Swedenborg divided the Spiritual World, or the Heavenly Jerusalem, into three Heavens; the upper, or third Heaven; the Spiritual, or second, which is in the middle, and the lower or first, relatively to our world. The dwellers in the third Heaven are the most perfect among the angels; they receive the chief portion of the divine influences immediately from God, whom they see face to face. God is the sun of the invisible world. From him flow Love and Truth, of which heat and light are but emblems. The angels of the second Heaven enjoy, through the upper Heaven, the divine influence. They see God distinctly, but not in all his splendor; he is to them a star without rays, such as the moon appears to us, which gives more light than heat. The dwellers in the lower Heaven receive the divine influence mediately through the other two Heavens. The attributes of the two latter classes are Love and Intelligence. Each of these celestial kingdoms is inhabited by innumerable societies; the angels which compose them are male and female. They contract marriages that are eternal, because it is similarity of inclinations and sympathy that attract them to each other. Each pair dwell in a splendid palace, surrounded by delicious gardens. Below the celestial regions is the realm of spirits. Thither all mankind go immediately upon their death. The divine influence, which their material envelope had prevented them from feeling, is revealed to them by degrees, and effects their transformation into angels, if they are predestined to that. The remembrance of the world which they have left is insensibly effaced from their memory; their proper instincts are unrestrainedly developed, and prepare them for heaven or hell. So full as heaven is of splendor, love and delight, so full is hell of darkness and misery, despair and hate. Such were the reveries on which Pernetti and Gabrianca founded their Illuminism.

910—Of what are the sword and naked heart emblematic?

Sword Pointing to the Naked Heart. Webb says that "the sword pointing to the naked heart demonstrates that justice will, sooner or later, overtake us." The symbol is I think, a modern one; but its adoption was probably suggested by the old ceremony, both in English and in continental Lodges, and which is still preserved in some places, in which the candidate found himself surrounded by swords pointing at his heart, to indicate that punishment would duly follow his violation of his obligations.

911—Of what is the sword emblematic?

Swords. In ancient times, every brother was obliged to be armed in the lodge to protect himself, in case the lodge was assaulted, and as a symbol of manly strength. At present, swords are not necessary in many lodges, and in others, they are only used as symbols of obedience, in case that one should be necessary, and to be regarded as the sword of justice. For the protection of his fatherland, every faithful brother ought to draw the sword of defence cheerfully, but he ought never to stain it with a brother's blood, even though that brother is a foe.

912—What should be the shape of the Tiler's sword?

Sword, Tiler's. In modern times the implement used by the Tiler is a sword of the ordinary form. This is incorrect. Formerly, and indeed up to a comparatively recent period, the Tiler's sword was wavy in shape, and so made in allusion to the "flaming sword which was placed at the east of the garden of Eden which turned every way to keep the way of the tree of life." It was, of course, without a scabbard, because the Tiler's sword should ever be drawn and ready for the defense of his post.

913—What is the nature of symbolism?

Symbol. Latin, *Symbolum.* A word derived from the Greek *sumbolon* from *sumballein,* to suspect, divine, compare; a word of various meaning, even with the ancients, who used it to denote a sign, a mark, watchword, signal, token, sealring, etc. Its meaning is still more various in modern times.

Symbol is generally used as synonymous with emblem. It is not confined, however, to visible figures, but embraces every representation of an idea by an image, whether the latter is presented immediately to the senses, or merely brought before the mind by words. Men, in the infancy of society, were incapable of abstract thought, and could convey truths only by means of sensible images. In fact, man, at all times, has a strong propensity to clothe thoughts and feelings in images, to make them more striking and living; and in the early periods of our race, when man lived in intimate communion with nature, he readily found, in natural objects, forms and images for the expression of moral truths; and even his conceptions of the Deity were derived directly from natural objects.

Freemasonry is a complete system of symbolic teaching, and can be known, understood or appreciated only by those who study its symbolism, and make themselves thoroughly acquainted with its occult meaning. To such, Freemasonry has a grand and sublime significance. Its symbols are moral, philosophical and religious, and all these are pregnant with great thoughts, and reveal to the intelligent Mason the awful mystery of life, and the still more awful mystery of death.

914—What is the symbolism of the Jewish tabernacle?

Tabernacle. The Hebrew word properly signifies handsome tent. There were three public tabernacles among the Jews previous to the building of Solomon's Temple. The first, which Moses erected, was called "the Tabernacle of the Congregation." In this he gave audience, heard causes, and inquired of God. The second was that which Moses built for God, by his express command. The third public tabernacle was that which David erected in Jerusalem for the reception of the ark when he received it from the house of Obed-edom.

It is the *second* of these, called *the* Tabernacle, by way of distinction, that we have more particularly to notice. This tabernacle was of an oblong, rectangular form, 30 cubits long, 10 broad, and 16 in height, which is equivalent to 55 feet long, 18 broad, and 18 high. The two sides and the western end were formed of boards of shittim wood, overlaid with thin plates of gold, and fixed in solid sockets or vases of silver. It was so contrived as to be taken to pieces and put together again at pleasure.

The Tabernacle was covered with four different kinds of curtains. The first and inner curtain was composed of fine linen, magnificently embroidered with figures of cherubim, in shades of blue, purple and scarlet; this formed the beautiful ceiling. The next covering was made of goat's hair; the third of rams' skins dyed red; and the fourth, and outward covering, was made of other animals' skins, colored red.

The east end of the Tabernacle was ornamented with five pillars, from which richly-embroidered curtains were suspended. The inside was divided, by a richly-embroidered veil of linen, into two parts, the holy place and the holy of holies; in the first of which were placed the altar of incense, the table with the shew-bread, and the seven-branched candlestick; in the latter place were the ark, the mercy-seat, and the cherubim. Besides this veil of fine linen which separated the most holy place, the tabernacle was furnished with other veils of divers colors, viz: of blue, purple, scarlet, and fine-twined linen (white), from which are derived the emblematic colors of the several degrees of Masonry. Within the chamber of a Royal Arch chapter, a temporary structure, after the plan of the one built by Moses, may be erected, as a representation of the tabernacle constructed by Zerubbabel, near the ruins of the first temple, after the return of the captives from Babylon, while the people were building the second temple.

915—Why should Masons set a guard upon their lips?

Taciturnity. Taciturnity is a proof of wisdom, and an art of inestimable value, which is proved to be an attribute of the Deity, by the glorious example which he gives in concealing from mankind the secret mysteries of his providence. The wisest of men cannot penetrate into the arcana of heaven, nor can they divine to-day what to-morrow may bring forth.

916—What is the Talmud and what is its relation to Freemasonry?

Talmud. A word derived from the Hebrew verb *lamad*, he has learned. It means *doctrine*. Among the modern Jews, it signifies an immense collection of traditions, illustrative of their laws and usages, forming twelve folio volumes. It consists of two parts—the Mishua and the Gemara. The Mishua is a collection of Rabbinical rules and precepts, made in the second century of the Christian era.

917—Of what do the four tassels pendant to the corners of the Lodge remind us?

Tassels. Pendant to the corners of the lodge are four tassels, meant to remind us of the four cardinal virtues; namely, temperance, fortitude, prudence and justice; the whole of which, tradition informs us, were constantly practised by a great majority of our ancient brethren. The distinguishing characters of a good Freemason are virtue, honor, and mercy; and should those be banished from all other societies, may they ever be found in a Mason's breast.

918—Is an unaffiliated Mason liable to Masonic taxation?

Taxation of Unaffiliated Masons. The levying of a tax upon unaffiliated Masons is contrary to the spirit of the institution, the principles of justice, and the dictates of expediency. It is contrary to the spirit of our institution: Masonry is a voluntary association, and no man should be compelled to remain in it a moment longer than he feels the wish to do so. It is contrary to the principles of Justice, for taxation should always be contingent upon representation; but an unaffiliated is not represented in the body which imposes the tax. And lastly, it is contrary to the dictates of expediency, for a tax upon such Masons would be a tacit permission and almost an encouragement of the practice of non-affiliation. It may be said that it is a penalty inflicted for an offence; but in reality it would be considered, like the taxes of the Roman chancery, simply as the cost of a license for the perpetration of a crime. If a Mason refuses, by affiliation and the payment of dues to a Lodge, to support the institution, let him, after due trial, be punished, by deprivation of all his Masonic privileges, by suspension or expulsion; but no Grand Lodge should, by the imposition of a tax, remove from non-affiliation its character of a Masonic offence. The notion would not for a moment be entertained of imposing a tax on all Masons who lived in violation of their obligations; and I can see no difference between the collection of a tax for non-affiliation and that for habitual intemperance, except in the difference of grade between the two offences. The principle is precisely the same.

919—What is the prerogative of the Grand Lodge with respect to levying taxes upon the Fraternity?

Taxing Power of Grand Lodge. The taxing power is a prerogative of a Grand Lodge. Every Grand Lodge has the right to impose a tax on its subordinate Lodges, or on all the affiliated Masons living within its jurisdiction. The tax upon individual Masons is, however, generally indirect. Thus, the Grand Lodge requires a certain contribution or subsidy from each of its subordinates, the amount of which is always in proportion to the number of its members and the extent of its work, and the Lodges make up this contribution by imposing a tax upon their members. It is very rarely that a Grand Lodge resorts to a direct tax upon the Masons of its jurisdiction. At present I recollect but two instances in which such a right has been exercised, namely, by the Grand Lodges of Louisiana and Arkansas. In the former instance, as there appeared to be some opposition to the doctrine, the Grand Lodge in 1855 adopted a resolution, in which it declared that it did not "assert its power to tax unconditionally, or for extraordinary purposes, the constituent Lodges."

I am at some loss to understand the distinct meaning of this proposition; but if it is intended to deny the prerogative of the Grand Lodge to levy any kind or amount of tax that it deems expedient on either the subordinate Lodges or their individual members, I am compelled to refuse my assent to such a proposition. That the power to impose taxes is a prerogative of every sovereignty is a doctrine which it would be an act of supererogation to defend, for no political economist has ever doubted it. The only qualification which it admits is, that the persons taxed should be entitled to a voice, directly or indirectly, in the imposition; for taxation without representation is universally admitted to be one of the most odious forms of tyranny. But as a Grand Lodge, as the supreme Masonic authority in every jurisdiction, is invested with all the attributes of sovereignty, and is besides a representative body, it follows that the unconditional power of taxation must reside in it as one of the prerogatives of its sovereignty. And if the particular species or amount of taxation is deemed oppressive or even inexpedient, it is easy for the subordinate Lodges, by the exercise of the power of instruction which they possess, to amend or altogether to remove the objectionable imposition.

920—What are the symbolic teachings of Freemasonry?

Teachings, Symbolic, of the Degrees. Freemasonry teaches by symbols and symbolical ceremonies, and hence each degree, through these agencies, illustrates and inculcates some particular virtue, or commemorates some important event. The following is an analytical summary of the ideas, which the several degrees of the Order seek to enforce; thus in Ancient Craft Masonry:

1. Dependence; the weak and helpless condition of the human family on their entrance into the world; the ignorance and darkness that surround man until the moral and intellectual light of reason and revelation breaks in upon his mind; obedience, secrecy and humility, and the practice of charity.

2. The struggle for knowledge after the release of the mind from the bondage of darkness and ignorance; its attainment, and the reward due to industry and perseverance.

3. Progress in the great duties of aiding humanity from the thraldom of vice and error; man's regeneration; higher sphere of happiness; integrity; morality of the body, and the immortality of the soul.

4. Order, regularity, and a proper system of discrimination between the worthy and the unworthy; the just reward to the industrious and faithful.

5. Virtue and talent the only proper distinctions of position. All

associations of men must, for the sake of harmony and order, be governed by well regulated laws.

6. The completion and dedication of the temple; the spiritual edifice which man must erect in his soul—that "house not made with hands, eternal in the heavens;" and *acknowledgment* that the labors of man's earthly toil are over, and he is *received* into the abode of the just and perfect.

7. The revelation of the divine law; an exhibition of the toils and vicissitudes of man's pilgrimage through life; a realization of the sublime truths promised, when the veils which obscure the mental vision are drawn aside, and man, raised and regenerated, shall enjoy the blessings of peace and joy in the heavenly temple.

8. The mysteries revealed; man rewarded according to his work; the Alpha and Omega—the first and the last.

9. Skill and ingenuity appreciated; justice and mercy accorded to the faithful and worthy.

921—Why should Masons be temperate?

Temperance. By temperance, we are instructed to govern the passions, and check unruly desires. The health of the body and the dignity of the species are equally concerned in a faithful observance of it.

922—What is the origin and history of the custom of building Temples?

Temple. An edifice erected for religious purposes. As the grand symbols of Freemasonry are a temple and its ornaments, and to construct temples was the business of the original Masons, some remarks upon these structures cannot but be instructive. The word temple is derived from the Latin *Templum,* and this word templum seems to have been derived from the old Latin verb, *Templari,* to contemplate. The ancient augurs undoubtedly applied the name *templa* to those parts of the heavens which were marked out for observance of the flight of birds. Temples, originally, were all open; and hence most likely came their name. These structures are among the most ancient monuments. They were the first built, and the most noticeable of public edifices. As soon as a nation had acquired any degree of civilization the people consecrated particular spots to the worship of their deities. In the earliest instances they contented themselves with erecting altars of earth or ashes in the open air, and sometimes resorted, for the purposes of worship, to the depths of solitary woods. At length they acquired the practice of building cells or chapels within the enclosure of which they placed the image of their divinities, and assembled to offer up their supplications, thanksgiving, and sacrifices. These were chiefly formed like their own dwellings. The Troglodytes adorned their gods in grottoes; the people who lived in cabins erected temples like cabins in shape. Clemens, Alexandrinus, and Eusebius refer the origin of temples to sepulchers; and this notion has been illustrated and confirmed from a variety of testimonies. At the time when the Greeks surpassed all other people in the arts introduced among them from Phoenicia, Syria, and Egypt, they devoted much time, care and expense to the building of temples. No country has surpassed, or perhaps equaled, them in this respect; the Romans alone successfully rivaled them, and they took the Greek structures for models. According to Vitruvius, the situations of the temples were regulated chiefly by the nature and characteristics of the various divinities. Thus the temples of Jupiter, Juno, and Minerva, who were considered by the inhabitants of many cities as their protecting deities, were erected on spots sufficiently elevated to enable them to overlook the whole town, or, at least the principal part of it. Minerva, the tutelary deity of Athens, had her seat on the Acropolis. In like manner the temple of Solomon was built on Mount Moriah.

923—What relation had the Temple of Herod to Freemasonry?

Temple of Herod the Great. This temple far exceeded both of its predecessors in magnificence and perfection. It was surrounded with four courts, rising above each other like terraces. The lower court was 500 cubits square, on three sides surrounded by a double, and on the fourth by a triple row of columns, and was called the "Court of the Gentiles," because individuals of all nations were admitted into it indiscriminately. A high wall separated the court of the women, 135 cubits square, in which the Jewish females assembled to perform their devotions, from the court of the Gentiles. From the court of the women fifteen steps led to the court of the temple, which was enclosed by a colonnade, and divided by trellis-work, into the court of Jewish men and the court of the priests. In the middle of this enclosure stood the temple, of white marble, richly gilt, 100 cubits long and wide, and 60 cubits high, with a porch 100 cubits wide, and three galleries, like the first temple, which it resembled in the interior, except that the most holy place was empty, and the height of Herod's Temple was double the height of Solomon's. The fame of this magnificent temple, which was destroyed by the Romans, and its religious significance with Jews and Christians, render it more interesting to us than any other building of antiquity. Each of these temples holds an important place in the symbolism and instructions of Freemasonry, and furnishes the traditions for a large number of degrees.

924—What was the design of Solomon's Temple?

Temple of Solomon. When Solomon had matured his design of a temple to be consecrated to the Most High, he found it impossible to carry that design into execution without foreign assistance. The

Hebrew nation, constantly struggling for its material existence, and just rising to the condition of a civilized people, had made little proficiency in science and architecture, and especially the ornamental arts. There were few artificers and no architects in Judea. Solomon, consequently, applied to Hiram, King of Tyre, for assistance, and that monarch sent him a company of Tyrian architects, under the superintendence of Hiram Abif, by whom the temple was erected. It was an oblong stone building, 150 feet in length, and 105 in width. On three sides were corridors, rising above each other to the height of three stories, and containing rooms, in which were preserved the holy utensils and treasures. The fourth, or front side was open, and was ornamented with a portico ten cubits in width, supported by two brazen pillars—Jachin and Boaz.

The interior was divided into the most holy place, or oracle, 20 cubits long, which contained the ark of the covenant, and was separated by a curtain, or veil, from the sanctuary or holy place, in which were the golden candlestick, the table of the shew bread, and the altar of incense. The walls of both apartments, and the roof and ceiling of the most holy place, were overlaid with woodwork, skillfully carved. None but the High-Priest was permitted to enter the latter, and only the priests, devoted to the temple service, the former.

The temple was surrounded by an inner court, which contained the altar of burnt offering, the brazen sea and lavers, and such instruments and utensils as were used in the sacrifices which, as well as the prayers, were offered here. Colonnades, with brazen gates, separated this court of the priests from the outer court, which was likewise surrounded by a wall.

This celebrated temple certainly reflected honor on the builders of that age. It was begun on the 2d day of the month Zif, corresponding with the 21st of April, in the year of the world 2992, or 1012 years before the Christian era, and was completed in little more than seven years, on the 8th day of the month Bul, or the 23rd of October, in the year 2999, during which period no sound of axe, hammer or other metallic tool was heard, everything having been cut and prepared in the quarries or on Mount Lebanon, and brought, properly carved, marked and numbered, to Jerusalem, where they were fitted in by means of wooden mauls. So of Freemasonry, it has always been the boast that its members perfect the work of edification by quiet and orderly methods, "without the hammer of contention, the axe of division, or any tool of mischief."

The excellency of the Craft in the days of our Grand Master Solomon was so great, that, although the materials were prepared so far off, when they were put together at Jerusalem, each piece fitted with such exactness that it appeared more like the work of the Great Architect of the Universe than of human hands. The temple retained its pristine splendor but thirty-three years, when it was plundered by Shishak, King of Egypt. After this period it underwent sundry profanations and pillages, and was at length utterly destroyed by Nebuchadnezzar, King of Babylon, A. M. 3416, B. C. 588, and the inhabitants of Jerusalem carried as captives to Babylon.

925—To the Master Mason of what is King Solomon's Temple a symbol?

Temple, Symbolism of the. To the Master Mason, the Temple of Solomon is truly the symbol of human life; for, like life, it was to have its end. For four centuries it glittered on the hills of Jerusalem in all its gorgeous magnificence; now, under some pious descendant of the wise king of Israel, a spot from whose altars arose the burnt-offerings to a living God, and now polluted by some recreant monarch of Judah to the service of Baal; until at length it received the divine punishment through the mighty king of Babylon, and, having been despoiled of all its treasures, was burnt to the ground, so that nothing was left of all its splendor but a smouldering heap of ashes. Variable in its purposes, evanescent in its existence, now a gorgeous pile of architectural beauty, and anon a ruin over which the resistless power of fire has passed, it becomes a fit symbol of human life occupied in the search after divine truth, which is nowhere to be found; now sinning and now repentant; now vigorous with health and strength, and anon a senseless and decaying corpse.

Such is the symbolism of the first Temple, that of Solomon, as familiar to the class of Master Masons. But there is a second and higher class of the Fraternity, the Masons of the Royal Arch, by whom this temple symbolism is still further developed.

The second class, leaving their early symbolism and looking beyond this Temple of Solomon, find in scriptural history another Temple, which, years after the destruction of the first one, was erected upon its ruins; and they have selected the second Temple, the Temple of Zerubbabel, as their prominent symbol. And as the first class of Masons find in their Temple the symbol of mortal life, limited and perishable, they, on the contrary, see in this second Temple, built upon the foundations of the first, a symbol of life eternal, where the lost truth shall be found, where new incense shall arise from a new altar, and whose perpetuity their great Master had promised when, in the very spirit of symbolism, he exclaimed, "Destroy this temple, and in three days I will raise it up."

926—What is the Masonic meaning of temporary exclusion from a Lodge?

Temporary Exclusion. A violation of the rules of order and decorum, either in a member or visitor, subjects such offender to the penalty of exclusion for that communication from the Lodge. It may be inflicted either by a vote of a majority of the Lodge, or, as is more usually done, by the exercise, on the part of the Master, of his prerogative; for the Master of every Lodge has the inherent privilege to exclude any person from visiting the Lodge, or remaining during the communication, if his presence would be productive of injury to the Order, by impairing its harmony or affecting its peaceful pursuit of Masonic labor. If a Mason, whether he be a member or a visitor, apply for admission, the Master, if he knows or believes that the admission of the applicant would result in the production of discord, may exclude him from entrance; and this prerogative he exercises in virtue of being the superintendent of the work.

If a member or visitor shall behave in an unbecoming and disorderly manner, he may be excluded for that communication, either by the Master or the Lodge. The Master possesses the power of exclusion on such an occasion, under the prerogative to which reference has just been made; and the Lodge possesses the same right, by the especial sanction of the ritual, which, at the very opening of the Lodge, forbids all "immoral or unmasonic conduct whereby the peace and harmony of the Lodge may be impaired, under no less a penalty than the by-laws may impose, or a majority of the brethren present see fit to inflict."

The command of the Master, therefore, or the vote of a majority of the Lodge, is sufficient to inflict the penalty of temporary exclusion. The forms of trial are unnecessary, because the infliction of the penalty does not affect the Masonic standing of the person upon whom it is inflicted. An appeal, however, always lies in such cases to the Grand Lodge, which will, after due investigation, either approve or disapprove of the action of the Lodge or the Master, and the vote of censure or disapprobation will be, of course, from the temporary nature of the penalty, the only redress which a Mason, injured by its wrongful infliction, can obtain.

927—What should be the tenure of office of a Grand Lecturer?

Tenure of Grand Lecturer. The only method by which the ritual can be efficiently supervised and taught, so that a uniformity of work may be preserved, and every Mason in the jurisdiction be made acquainted with the true nature of the science of Masonry, is by the appointment of a competent and permanent Grand Lecturer.

The appointment of this officer should be a permanent one. In this advanced age of Masonic improvement, any attempt to appoint a Grand Lecturer by the year, as we hire domestics or employ laborers, is an insult to the intelligence of the Order. When an able teacher is found, he should hold his office, not for a year, or during the pleasure of the Grand Master or the Grand Lodge, but like the judicial tenure of our Supreme Court, or the English Judges—*dum se bene gesserit*—during good behavior. Let him continue for life, if he is "worthy and well qualified"; for, the longer a good teacher labors in his vocation, the better will he discharge its duties. But any attempt to intrust the duty of instructing Lodges to a temporary Lecturer, changed, like the Wardens or the Deacons, every year, must inevitably result in the utter destruction of all that remains to us of the ancient symmetry of our beautiful temple.

928—Of what is the tesselated pavement emblematic?

Tesselated Pavement. The word tesselated is derived from the word *tessela,* diminutive of *tessera.* The pavement which is thus designated is of rich Mosaic work, made of curious square marbles, bricks or tiles, in shape and disposition resembling dice. Various ancient specimens of these have been, from time to time, exhumed in Italy, and other countries of Europe. The tesselated pavement, in the symbolism of Freemasonry, is significant of the varied experiences and vicissitudes of human life.

929—Is it lawful for a profane to testify in a Masonic trial?

Testimony. The testimony of Master Masons is usually taken on their honor, as such. That of others should be by affidavit, or in such other manner as both the accuser and accused may agree upon.

The testimony of profanes, or of those who are of a lower degree than the accused, is to be taken by a committee and reported to the Lodge, or, if convenient, by the whole Lodge, when closed and sitting as a committee. But both the accused and the accuser have a right to be present on such occasions.

There can be no doubt that profanes are competent witnesses in Masonic trials. If their testimony was rejected, the ends of justice would, in many instances, be defeated; for it frequently happens that the most important evidence of a fact is only to be obtained from such persons. The great object of the trial is to investigate the truth and to administer justice, and no method should be rejected by which those objects can be obtained. Again: there may be cases in which the accused is able to prove his innocence only by the testimony of profanes; and surely no one would be willing to deprive him of that means of defence. But if the evidence of profanes for the accused is to be admitted, on account of its importance and necessity, by a parity of reasoning, it should be admitted when and in behalf of the accuser. The testimony which is good in one case must be good in the other.

930—What powers do the Jews attribute to the lost word?

Tetragrammaton. The Jews are quite aware that the true pronunciation of the Word is lost, and regard it as one of the mysteries to be revealed in the days of the Messiah. They hold, however, that the knowledge of the Name of God does exist on earth, and that he by whom the secret is acquired, has, by virtue of it, the powers of the world at his command. Hence they account for the miracles of Jesus by telling us that he had got possession of the Ineffable Name. Rightly understood, they seem to mean that he who calls upon God rightly, by this His true name, cannot fail to be heard by him. In short, this word forms the famous tetragrammaton or quadrilateral name, of which every one has heard.

931—Why should Masons practice the virtues of Faith, Hope and Charity?

Theological Virtues. Faith, Hope and Charity are thus named, and are said to constitute the chief rounds of the Masonic ladder, by the aid of which the good Mason expects at last to ascend to the perfect Lodge above. These virtues are enforced in various parts of the rituals, and enlarged upon in the first lecture of Craft Masonry. The great duties of man to God, his neighbor and himself, are the precepts most strongly enforced; hence the points to direct the steps of the aspirant to higher honors are Faith, Hope and Charity.

932—What does the theory and practice of Masonry include?

Theory. The theory of Masonry contains something of the whole of science; the operative part of Masonry is the practice of all the virtues, of all the sciences. Therefore, to be initiated only into the theory of Masonry, is at least to be in the way of learning well and if we follow on to exercise the practice of Masonry it will as assuredly lead us into the way of doing well, and both to learn and to do well is the whole of our religion, whether as men, as Christians, or as Masons.

933—Who are called Theosophists?

Theosophists. Those who inquire into the science of divine things. Many eminent Freemasons belonged to this class during the last century. The speculations of the Theosophists, however, were generally of a mystical character. Several Masonic systems were theosophical, as, for example, the rites of Swedenborg, St. Martin, Zinnendorff, etc.

934—What are the teachings of the third degree of Masonry?

Third Degree. In the ceremonial of the Third Degree, the last grand mystery is attempted to be illustrated in a forcible and peculiar manner, showing by striking analogy, that the Master Mason cannot be deemed perfect in the glorious science, till by the cultivation of his intellectual powers, he has gained such moral government of his passions, such serenity of mind, that in synonymous apposition with Mastership in operative art, his thoughts, like his actions, have become as useful as human intelligence will permit; and that having passed through the trials of life with fortitude and faith, he is fitted for that grand, solemn, and mysterious consummation, by which alone he can become acquainted with the great secret of eternity.

THE SAINTS JOHN

935—What rights does a Master Mason acquire on the reception of the third degree?

Third Degree, Rights Conferred by. The first right which a Mason acquires, after the reception of the third degree, is that of claiming membership in the Lodge in which he has been initiated. The very fact of his having received that degree makes him at once an inchoate member of the Lodge—that is to say, no further application is necessary, and no new ballot is required; but the candidate, having now become a Master Mason, upon signifying his submission to the regulations of the Society, by affixing his signature to the book of by-laws, is constituted, by virtue of that act, a full member of the Lodge, and entitled to all the rights and prerogatives accruing to that position.

The ancient Constitutions do not, it is true, express this doctrine in so many words; but it is distinctly implied by their whole tenor and spirit, as well as sustained by the uniform usage of the craft, in all countries. There is one passage in the Regulations of 1721 which clearly seems to intimate that there were two methods of obtaining membership in a Lodge, either by initiation, when the candidate is said to be "entered a Brother," or by what is now called "affiliation," when the applicant is said to be "admitted to be a member." But the whole phraseology of the Regulation shows that the rights acquired by each method were the same, and that membership by initiation and membership by affiliation effected the same results. The modern Constitutions of the Grand Lodge of England are explicit on the subject, and declare that "every Lodge must receive as a member, without further proposition or ballot, any Brother initiated therein, provided such Brother express his wish to that effect on the day of his initiation."

The Constitution of the Grand Lodge of New York announces a similar doctrine; and, in fact, I have not met with the by-laws of any particular Lodge in which it is not laid down as a principle, that every initiate is entitled, by his reception in the third degree, to claim the privilege of membership in the Lodge in which he has been initiated.

The reason of this universal Regulation (so universal that were it not for that fact that membership itself, as a permanent characteristic, is of modern origin, it might almost claim to be a Landmark) is at once evident. He who has been deemed worthy, after three ordeals, to receive all the mysteries that it is in the power of a Lodge to communicate, cannot, with any show of reason or consistency, be withheld from admission into that household, whose most important privileges he has just been permitted to share. If properly qualified for the reception of the third degree, he must be equally qualified for the rights of membership, which, in fact, it is the object of the third degree to bestow; and it would be needless to subject that candidate to a fourth ballot, whom the Lodge has already, by the most solemn ceremonies, three times declared worthy "to be taken by the hand as a Brother." And hence the Grand Lodge of England has wisely assigned this as a reason for the law already quoted, namely, that "no Lodge should introduce into Masonry a person whom the Brethren might consider unfit to be a member of their own Lodge."

936—Why is the figure 3 considered a sacred number in Freemasonry?

Three. A sacred number in Freemasonry, with which all labor is commenced and finished. This number reminds us of the three great lights, the three kingdoms of nature, the Holy Trinity, or of the words of Christ: "Where two or three are assembled in my name, there will I be in the midst of you." We may also consider ourselves as the third party in unity and love, whose duty it is to exercise those two cardinal virtues. The Christian can also take the number three as the grand distinguishing doctrine of his faith. There are three principal parts in a man: body, soul, and spirit. Faith, love, and hope support and adorn life.

937—What were the three grand offerings of Masonry?

Three Grand Offerings. These were all performed on the sacred mountain of Moriah. First, the offering of Isaac, when it pleased the Lord to substitute a more agreeable victim in his stead. The second consisted of the many pious prayers and ejaculations of King David, which appeased the wrath of God, and put a stop to the pestilence which raged among his people, owing to his inadvertently having had them numbered. And the third, of the many thanksgivings, oblations, burnt sacrifices, and costly offerings, which King Solomon made at the dedication and consecration of the Temple.

938—What three senses are essential to becoming a Mason?

Three Senses. The three senses, hearing, seeing and feeling, are deemed peculiarly essential amongst Masons, and held in great estimation. Their nature and uses form a part of the instruction in the Fellowcraft's degree.

939—Of what are the three steps emblematic?

Three Steps. The three steps delineated upon a Master's carpet are emblematical of the three principal stages of human life, youth, manhood, and old age.

940—What is the symbolism of the threshing floor?

Threshing Floor. Among the Hebrews, circular spots of hard ground were used, as now, for the purpose of threshing corn. After they were properly prepared for the purpose, they became permanent possessions. One of these, the property of Ornan the Jebusite, was on Mount Moriah. It was purchased by David, for a place of sacrifice, for six hundred shekels of gold, and on it the Temple was afterwards built. Hence it is sometimes used as a symbolic name for the Temple of Solomon or for a Master's Lodge. Thus it is said in the ritual that the Mason comes "from the lofty tower of Babel, where language was confounded and Masonry lost," and that he is traveling "to the threshing floor of Ornan the Jebusite, where language was restored and Masonry found." The interpretation of this rather abstruse symbolic expression is that on his initiation the Mason comes out of the profane world, where there is ignorance and darkness and confusion as there was at Babel, and that he is approaching the Masonic world, where, as at the Temple built on Ornan's threshing floor, there is knowledge and light and order.

941—What is the meaning of the word "tile?"

Tile. A lodge is said to be tiled when the necessary precautions have been taken to prevent the approach of unauthorized persons; and it is said to be the first duty of every Mason to see that this is done before the Lodge is opened. The word to tile is sometimes used in the same sense as to examine, as when it is said that a visitor has been tiled, that is, has been examined. But the expression is not in general use, nor do I think it is a correct employment of the term.

942—What are the qualifications of the Tiler?

Tiler. An officer of a symbolic lodge, whose duty is to guard the door of the lodge, and to permit no one to pass in who is not duly qualified, and who has not the permission of the Master.

A necessary qualification of a Tiler is, therefore, that he should be a Master Mason. Although the lodge may be opened in an inferior degree, no one who has not advanced to the third degree can legally discharge the functions of Tiler.

The Tiler need not be a member of the lodge which he tiles; and in fact, in large cities, one brother very often performs the duties of Tiler of several lodges.

This is a very important office, and, like that of the Master and Wardens, owes its existence, not to any conventional regulations, but to the very landmarks of the Order; for, from the peculiar nature of our Institution, it is evident that there never could have been a meeting of Masons for Masonic purposes, unless a Tiler had been present to guard the lodge from intrusion.

The title is derived from the operative art; for as in Operative Masonry the Tiler, when the edifice is erected, finishes and covers it with the roof (of tiles), so in Speculative Masonry, when the lodge is duly organized, the Tiler closes the door, and covers the sacred precincts from all intrusion.

943—What are the duties of a Tiler?

Tiler, Duties of. As the Tiler is always compensated for his services, he is considered, in some sense, as the servant of the Lodge. It is therefore his duty to prepare the Lodge for its meetings, to arrange the furniture in its proper place, and during the communication to keep a supply of aprons, so as to furnish each brother with one preparatory to his entrance. He is also the messenger of the Lodge, and it is his duty to deliver to the members the summonses which have been written by the Secretary.

944—What rights of membership may a Tiler exercise?

Tiler, Privileges of. The office of Tiler, in a subordinate Lodge, does not, like that of Grand Tiler, disqualify him for membership; and if the Tiler is a member, he is entitled to all the rights of membership, except that of sitting in the communications, which right he has voluntarily relinquished by his acceptance of office.

It is usual, in balloting for candidates, to call the Tiler (if he be a member) in, and request him to vote. On such occasions the Junior Deacon takes his place on the outside, while he is depositing his ballot.

945—What is the Tiler's oath or obligation?

Tiler's Oath. The examination of visitors is accompanied by several forms, which, as they are used in the presence of a person not known to be a Mason, and who, after having participated in them, is often rejected, because he cannot give sufficient proof of his Masonic character, necessarily form no part of the secret portions of our ritual, and can therefore be as safely committed to paper and openly published, as any of the other ordinary business of a Lodge. To assert to the contrary—to say, for instance, that the "Tiler's obligation," so called because it is administered to the visitor in the Tiler's room, and usually in the presence of that officer, is a Masonic secret—is to assert, that that which is secret, and a portion of our mysteries, may be openly presented to a person whom we do not know to be a Mason, and who therefore receives this instruction before he has proved his right to it by "strict trial and due examination." The very fact that the "Tiler's obligation" is to be administered to such an unknown person, is the very best argument that can be adduced that it no more constitutes a part of our secret instructions than do the public ceremonies of laying corner stones, or burying our dead. I do not consequently hesitate to present it to the reader in the form which I have seen usually adopted.

The visitor, therefore, who desires admission into a Lodge, and who presents himself for preparatory examination, is required to take the following oath in the presence of the examining committee, each of whom he may likewise require to take the same oath with him:

"I, A. B., do hereby and hereon solemnly and sincerely swear, that I have been regularly initiated, passed and raised, to the sublime degree of a Master Mason, in a just and legally constituted Lodge of such; that I do not now stand suspended or expelled; and know of no reason why I should not hold Masonic communication with my brethren."

This declaration having been confirmed in the most solemn manner, the examination is then commenced with the necessary forms.

946—What power has a Lodge with respect to fixing and changing its time of meeting?

Time of Meeting. A Lodge has the right to designate and change its time and place of meeting. As the regulation designating the time of meeting is always inserted in the by-laws, it is evident that no change can be made with respect to it, except with the approbation of the Grand Lodge. But there is also another restriction on this subject which is derived from the constant usage of the Order, that a Lodge shall statedly meet once a month at least. There is no specific regulation on this subject; but the general custom of the fraternity, from the beginning of the last century, has made it obligatory on the Lodges not to extend the interval of their regular communications beyond that period. Besides, the regulations in respect to the applications of candidates for initiation or membership, which require "a previous notice of one month," seem to infer that that was the length of time which intervened between two stated meetings of the Lodge. In some jurisdictions it is frequently the case that some of the Lodges meet semi-monthly; and indeed instances are on record where Lodges meet weekly. This is permissible, but in such cases the regulation in relation to the petitions of candidates must be strictly interpreted as meaning that they are required to lie over for one month, and not from one regular meeting to the other, which in such Lodges would only amount to one or two weeks.

947—Who has the prerogative of determining the time of opening and closing a communication of a Lodge?

Time of Opening and Closing the Lodge. Even at the regular communications of the Lodge if the Master be present, the time of opening is left to his discretion, for no one can take from the Master his prerogative of opening the Lodge. But if he be absent when the hour of opening which is specified in the by-laws has arrived, the Senior Warden, if present, and if not, then the Junior may open the Lodge, and the business transacted will be regular and legal, even without the Master's sanction; for it was his duty to be present, and he cannot take advantage of his own remissness of duty to interfere with the business of the Lodge.

The selection of the time of closing is also vested in the Master. He is the sole judge of the proper period at which the labors of the Lodge should be terminated, and may suspend business, even in the middle of a debate, if he supposes that it is expedient to close the Lodge. Hence, no motion for adjournment, or to close, or to call off from labor to refreshment, can ever be admitted in a Masonic Lodge. Such a motion would be an interference with the prerogative of the Master, and could not therefore be entertained.

948—What part do words, signs and tokens play in Masonry?

Tokens. Signs, tokens, and words do not constitute Freemasonry, but are local marks whereby Masons know each other, and may be altered, or entirely done away, without the least injury to scientific Freemasonry. It is with many Freemasons too absurd a belief, and a still more absurd practice, to build our science upon so shallow a foundation as signs, tokens, and words, which I fear constitute with some the only attainment they look for in Freemasonry. That certain signals may be necessary, I do readily allow; but deny that such a mechanism shall constitute a principal part of our institution.

949—What does it mean to be "under the tongue of good report?"

Tongue of Good Report. Being "under the tongue of good report" is equivalent, in Masonic technical language, to being of good character or reputation. It is required that the candidate for initiation should be one out of whom no tongue speaks evil. The phrase is an old one, and is found in the earliest rituals of the last century.

950—Can a word or grip betray the secrets of Freemasonry?

Traitor. Ancient Freemasonry inflicted very severe punishment for the least treason to the order; nevertheless, we have accounts of men who have proved traitors, even as we find accounts of such traitors to the mysteries of the ancients. With the increase of enlightenment and rational reflection, it is admitted that a brother may both speak and write much upon the Order without becoming a traitor to its secrets. How an initiation is conducted, how a word or grip is given, gives no key to the true secret of the Order; but we nevertheless disapprove of such disclosures, for this reason, that the uninitiated could only form a useless chimera from them.

951—Who are called tramping Masons?

Tramping Masons. Unworthy members of the Order, who, using their privileges for interested purposes, traveling from city to city, and from lodge to lodge, that they may seek relief by tales of fictitious distress, have been called "tramping Masons." The true brother should ever obtain assistance; the tramper should be driven from the door of every lodge or the house of every Mason where he seeks to intrude his imposture.

952—If a Lodge be dissolved what becomes of its charter?

Transferring. If a lodge be dissolved, the constitution shall be delivered up to the Grand Master, and shall not, on any account, be transferred without his consent.

953—Who are called transient brethren?

Transient Brethren. Masons who do not reside in a particular place, but only temporarily visit it, are called "transient brethren" or sojourners. They are, if worthy, to be cordially welcomed, but are never to be admitted into a Lodge until, after the proper precautions, they have been provèd to be "true and trusty." This usage of hospitality has the authority of all the Old Constitutions, which are careful to inculcate it. Thus the Lansdowne MS. charges, "that every Mason receive or cherish Strange Fellows when they come over the country, and set them on worke if they will worke, as the manner is (that is to say), if the Mason have any moulde stone in his place, on worke; and if he have none, the Mason shall refresh him with money unto the next Lodge."

Although Speculative Masons no longer visit lodges for the sake of work or wages, the usage of our Operative predecessors has been spiritualized in our symbolic system. Hence visitors are often invited to take part in the labors of the lodge and receive their portion of the light and truth which constitute the symbolic pay of a Speculative Mason.

No stranger should be admitted to the Lodge until he has proved himself a Freemason. When he has done this he should be received with cordiality and fraternal courtesy. A traveling brother, away from his home and friends, naturally longs for companionship, and expects to find it around the altars of Freemasonry. Hospitality to strangers is, always and everywhere, a sacred duty, but it is doubly so to Freemasons. The brother from abroad should be greeted with such warmth and brotherly kindness and interest as will make him feel at home, and that he is surrounded with friends, upon whose sympathy he can rely. Lodges are sometimes too remiss in regard to this duty, and many a warm-hearted brother, when visiting a strange lodge, has been chilled and grieved by the iciness of his reception.

954—In what sense is the word "travel" used in the symbolical language of Masonry?

Travel. In the symbolic language of Masonry, a Mason always travels from west to east in search of light—he travels from the lofty tower of Babel, where language was confounded and Masonry lost, to the threshing floor of Ornan the Jebusite, where language was restored and Masonry found. The Master Mason also travels into foreign countries in search of wages. All this is pure symbolism, unintelligible in any other sense.

Our ancient brethren are masonically said to have traveled from west to east, in search of instruction; and it is an undeniable fact that all knowledge, all religion, all arts and sciences, have traveled, according to the course of the sun, from east to west. From that quarter the Divine glory first came, and thence the rays of divine light continue to diffuse themselves over the face of the earth. From thence came the Bible, and through that the new covenant. From thence came the prophets, the apostles, and the first missionaries that brought the knowledge of God to Europe, to the isles of the sea, and to the west.

955—Who were the traveling Freemasons of the Middle Ages?

Traveling Freemasons. There is no portion of the history of the Order so interesting to the Masonic scholar as that which is embraced by the Middle Ages of Christendom, beginning with about the tenth century, when the whole of civilized Europe was perambulated by those associations of workmen, who passed from country to country and from city to city under the name of "Traveling Freemasons," for the purpose of erecting religious edifices. There is not a country of Europe which does not at this day contain honorable evidences of the skill and industry of our Masonic ancestors. I therefore propose, in the present article, to give a brief sketch of the origin, the progress and the character of these traveling architects.

Mr. George Godwin, in a lecture published in the *Builder,* says: "There are few points in the Middle Ages more pleasing to look back upon than the existence of the Associated Masons; they are the bright spot in the general darkness of that period, the patch of verdure when all around is barren."

Clavel, in his *Histoire Pittoresque de la Franc-Maconnerie,* has traced the organization of these associations to the "collegia artificum," or colleges of artisans, which were instituted at Rome, by Numa, in the year B. C. 714, and whose members were originally Greeks, imported by this lawgiver for the purpose of embellishing the city over which he reigned. They continued to exist as well-established corporations throughout all the succeeding years of the kingdom, the republic and the empire.

These "sodalities," or fraternities, began, upon the invasion of the barbarians, to decline in numbers, in respectability, and in power. But on the conversion of the whole empire, they, or others of a similar character, began again to flourish. The priests of the Christian church became their patrons, and under their guidance they devoted themselves to the building of churches and monasteries. In the tenth century, they were established as a free gild or corporation in Lombardy. For when, after the decline and fall of the empire, the city of Rome was abandoned by its sovereigns for other secondary cities of Italy, such as Milan and Ravenna, and new courts and new capitals were formed, the kingdom of Lombardy sprang into existence as the great centre of all energy in trade and industry, and of refinement in art and literature. It was there, and as a consequence of the great centre of life from Rome, and the development not only of commercial business, but of all sorts of trades and handicrafts, that the corporations known as gilds were first organized.

Among the arts practiced by the Lombards, that of building held a pre-eminent rank. And Muratori tells us that the inhabitants of Como, a principal city of Lombardy, Italy, had become so superior as masons, that the appellation of Magistri Comacini, or Masters from Como, had become generic to all of the profession.

Mr. Hope, in his *Historical Essay on Architecture,* has treated this subject almost exhaustively. He says:

"We cannot then wonder that, at a period when artificers and artists of every class, from those of the most mechanical, to those of the most intellectual nature, formed themselves into exclusive corporations, architects—whose art may be said to offer the most exact medium between those of the most urgent necessity, and those of mere ornament, or indeed, in its wide span to embrace both—should above all others, have associated themselves into similar bodies, which, in conformity to the general style of such corporations, assumed that of Free and Accepted Masons, and was composed of those members who, after a regular passage through the different fixed stages of apprenticeship, were received as masters, and entitled to exercise the profession on their own account.

"In an age, however, in which lay individuals, from the lowest subject to the sovereign himself, seldom built except for mere shelter and safety—seldom sought, nay, rather avoided, in their dwellings an elegance which might lessen their security; in which even the community collectively, in its public and general capacity, divided into component parts less numerous and less varied, required not those numerous public edifices which we possess either for business or pleasure; thus, when neither domestic nor civic architecture of any sort demanded great ability or afforded great employment, churches and monasteries were the only buildings required to combine extent and elegance, and sacred architecture alone could furnish an extensive field for the exercise of great skill, Lombardy itself, opulent and thriving as it was, compared to other countries, soon became nearly saturated with the requisite edifices, and unable to give these companies of Free and Accepted Masons a longer continuance of sufficient custom, or to render the further maintenance of their exclusive privileges of great benefit to them at home. But if, to the south of the Alps, an earlier civilization had at last caused the number of architects to exceed that of new buildings wanted, it fared otherwise in the north of Europe, where a gradually spreading Christianity began on every side to produce a want of sacred edifices, of church and monasteries, to design which architects existed not on the spot.

"Those Italian corporations of builders, therefore, whose services ceased to be necessary in the countries where they had arisen, now began to look abroad towards those northern climes for that employment which they no longer found at home; and a certain number united and formed themselves into a single greater association, or fraternity, which proposed to seek for occupation beyond its native land; and in any ruder foreign region, however remote, where new religious edifices and skillful artists to erect them were wanted to offer their services, and bend their steps to undertake the work."

From Lombardy they passed beyond the Alps into all the countries where Christianity, but recently established, required the erection of churches. The popes encouraged their designs, and more than one bull was dispatched, conferring on them privileges of the most extensive character. A monopoly was granted to them for the erection of all religious edifices; they were declared independent of the sovereigns in whose dominions they might be temporarily residing, and subject only to their own private laws; they were permitted to regulate the amount of their wages; were exempted from all kinds of taxation; and no Mason, not belonging to their association, was permitted to compete with or oppose them in the pursuit of employment. And in one of the papal decrees on the subject of these artisans, the supreme pontiff declares that these regulations have been made "after the example of Hiram, king of Tyre, when he sent artisans to King Solomon, for the purpose of building the Temple of Jerusalem."

After filling the continent with cathedrals, parochial churches, and monasteries, and increasing their own numbers by accessions of new members from all the countries in which they had been laboring, they passed over into England, and there introduced their peculiar style of building. Then they traveled to Scotland, and there have rendered their existence ever memorable by establishing, in the parish of Kilwinning, where they were erecting an abbey, the germ of Scottish Freemasonry, which has regularly descended through the Grand Lodge of Scotland to the present day.

Mr. Hope accounts for the introduction of non-working or unprofessional members into these associations by a theory which is confirmed by contemporary history. He says:

"Often obliged, from religions the most distant, singly to seek the common place of rendezvous and departure of the troop, or singly to follow its earlier detachments to places of employment equally distant; and that, at an era when travelers met on the road every obstruction, and no convenience, when no inns existed at which to purchase hospitality, but lords dwelt everywhere, who only prohibited their tenants from waylaying the traveler because they considered this, like killing game, one of their own exclusive privileges; the members of these communities contrived to render their journeys more easy and safe, by engaging with each other, and perhaps even, in many places, with individuals not directly participating in their profession, in compacts of mutual assistance, hospitality and good services, most valuable to men so circumstanced. They endeavored to compensate for the perils which attended their expeditions, by institutions for their needy or disabled brothers; but lest such as belonged not to their communities should benefit surreptitiously by these arrangements for its advantage, they framed signs of mutual recognition, as carefully concealed from the knowledge of the uninitiated, as the mysteries of their art themselves. Thus supplied with whatever could facilitate such distant journeys and labors as they contemplated, the members of these corporations were ready to obey any summons with the utmost alacrity, and they soon received the encouragement they anticipated. The militia of the church of Rome, which diffused itself all over Europe in the shape of missionaries, to instruct nations, and to establish their allegiance to the Pope, took care not only to make them feel the want of churches and monasteries, but likewise to learn the manner in which the want might be supplied. Indeed, they themselves generally undertook the supply; and it may be asserted, that a new apostle of the Gospel no sooner arrived in the remotest corner of Europe, either to convert the inhabitants to Christianity, or to introduce among them a new religious order, than speedily followed a tribe of itinerant Freemasons to back him, and to provide the inhabitants with the necessary places of worship or reception.

"Thus ushered in, by their interior arrangements assured of assistance and of safety on the road, and, by the bulls of the Pope and the support of his ministers abroad, of every species of immunity and preference at the place of their destination, bodies of Freemasons dispersed themselves in every direction, every day began to advance further, and to proceed from country to country, to the utmost verge of the faithful, in order to answer the increasing demand for them, or to seek more distant custom."

The government of these fraternities, wherever they might be for the time located, was very regular and uniform. When about to commence the erection of a religious edifice, they first built huts, or, as they were termed, lodges, in the vicinity, in which they resided for the sake of economy as well as convenience. It is from these that the present name of our places of meeting is derived. Over every ten men was placed a warden, who paid them wages, and took care that there should be no needless expenditure of materials and no careless loss of implements. Over the whole, a surveyor or master, called in their old documents "magister," presided and directed the general labor.

The Abbie Grandidier, in a letter at the end of the Marquis Luchet's *Essai sur les Illumines,* has quoted from the ancient register of the Masons at Strasburg the regulations of the association which built the splendid cathedral of that city. Its great rarity renders it difficult to obtain a sight of the original work, but the *Histoiree Pittoresque* of Clavel supplies the most prominent details of all that Grandidier has preserved. The cathedral of Strasburg was commenced in the year 1277, under the direction of Erwin of Steinbach. The Masons who, under his directions, were engaged in the construction of this noblest specimen of the Gothic style of architecture, were divided into the separate ranks of Masters, Craftsmen and Apprentices. The place where they assembled was called a "hutte," a German word equivalent to our English term lodge. They employed the implements of masonry as emblems, and received their new members with peculiar and secret ceremonies, admitting, as has already been said, many eminent persons, and especially ecclesiastics, who were not Operative Masons, but who gave to them their patronage and protection.

The fraternity of Strasburg became celebrated throughout Germany, their superiority was acknowledged by the kindred associations, and they in time received the appellation of the "haupt hutte," or Grand Lodge, and exercised supremacy over the *hutten* of Suabia, Hesse, Bavaria, Franconia, Saxony, Thuringia, and the countries bordering on the river Moselle. The Masters of these several lodges assembled at Ratisbon in 1459, and on the 25th of April contracted an act of union, declaring the chief of the Strasburg Cathedral the only and perpetual Grand Master of the General Fraternity of Freemasons of Germany. This act of union was definitely adopted and promulgated at a meeting held soon afterwards at Strasburg.

Similar institutions existed in France and in Switzerland, for wherever Christianity had penetrated, there churches and cathedrals were to be built, and the Traveling Freemasons hastened to undertake the labor.

They entered England and Scotland at an early period. Whatever may be thought of the authenticity of the York and Kilwinning legends, there is ample evidence of the existence of organized associations, gilds, or corporations of Operative Masons at an epoch not long after their departure from Lombardy. From that period, the fraternity, with various intermissions, continued to pursue their labors, and constructed many edifices which still remain as monuments of their skill as workmen and their taste as architects. Kings, in many instances, became their patrons, and their labors were superintended by powerful noblemen and eminent prelates, who, for this purpose, were admitted as members of the fraternity. Many of the old Charges for the better government of their Lodges have been preserved, and are still to be found in our Books of Constitutions, every line of which indicates that there were originally drawn up for associations strictly and exclusively operative in their character.

In glancing over the history of this singular body of architects, we are struck with several important peculiarities.

In the first place, they were strictly ecclesiastical in their constitution. The Pope, the supreme pontiff of the church, was their patron and protector. They were supported and encouraged by bishops and abbots, and hence their chief employment appears to have been in the construction of religious edifices. Like their ancestors, who were engaged in the erection of the magnificent Temple of Jerusalem, they devoted themselves to labor for the "House of the Lord." Masonry was then, as it had been before, and has ever been since, intimately connected with religion.

They were originally all operatives. But the artisans of that period were not educated men, and they were compelled to seek among the clergy, the only men of learning, for those whose wisdom might contrive, and whose cultivated taste might adorn, the plans which they, by their practical skill, were to carry into effect. Hence the germ of that Speculative Masonry which, once dividing the character of the fraternity with the Operative, now completely occupies it to the entire exclusion of the latter.

But lastly, from the circumstances of their union and concert arose a uniformity of design in all the public buildings of that period—a uniformity so remarkable as to find its explanation only in the fact that their construction was committed throughout the whole of Europe, if not always to the same individuals, at least to members of the same association. The remarks of Mr. Hope on this subject are well worthy of perusal. "The architects of all the sacred edifices of the Latin church, wherever such arose—north, south, east or west—thus derived their science from the same central school; obeyed in their designs the same hierarchy; were directed in their constructions by the same principles of propriety and taste; kept up with each other, in the most distant parts to which they might be sent, the most constant correspondence; and rendered every minute improvement the property of the whole body, and a new conquest of the art. The result of this unanimity was, that at each successive period of the monastic dynasty, on whatever point a new church or new monastery might be erected, it resembled all those raised at the same period in every other place, however distant from it, as if both had been built in the same place by the same artist. For instance, we find, at particular epochs, churches as far distant from each other as the north of Scotland and the south of Italy, to be minutely similar in all the essential characteristics."

In conclusion, we may remark, that the world is indebted to this association for the introduction of Gothic, or, as it has lately been denominated, the pointed style of architecture. This style—so different from the Greek or Roman orders—whose pointed arches and minute tracery distinguishes the solemn temples of the olden time, and whose ruins arrest the attention and claim the admiration of the spectator, has been universally acknowledged to be the invention of the Traveling Freemasons of the Middle Ages.

And it is to this association of Operative artists that, by gradual changes into a speculative system, we are to trace the Freemasons of the present day.

956—Can Masonic charges be founded on acts of treason and rebellion?

Treason and Rebellion. Treason and rebellion also, because they are altogether political offences, cannot be inquired into by a Lodge; and although a Mason may be convicted of either of these acts in the courts of his country he cannot be masonically punished; and notwithstanding his treason or rebellion, his relation to the Lodge, to use the language of the old Charges, remains indefeasible.

957—What are the duties of the Treasurer?

Treasurer, Duties of. Although this officer takes no part in the ritual or ceremonial labors of the Lodge, yet the due administration of his duties is closely connected with its welfare. He is the financial officer or banker of the Lodge; and to prevent the possibility of any collusion between himself and the presiding officer, the Constitutions of England, while they give the appointment of all the other officers to the Master, have prudently provided that the Treasurer shall be elected by the Lodge.

The duties of the Treasurer, as detailed in the Installation service, and sanctioned by universal usage, are threefold:

1. He is to receive all moneys due the Lodge from the Secretary.
2. He is to make due entries of the same.
3. He is to pay them out at the order of the Master, and with the consent of the Lodge.

As the banker simply of the Lodge, he has nothing to do with the collections which should be made by the Secretary, and handed over to him. These funds he retains in his hands, and disburses them by the order of the Lodge, which must be certified to him by the Master. His accounts, so far as the receipts of money are concerned, are only with the Secretary. Of his disbursements, of course, he keeps a special account. His accounts should be neatly and accurately kept, and be always ready for the inspection of the Lodge or of the Master.

As his office, as custodian of the funds of the Lodge, is a responsible one, it has been usual to require of him a bond for the faithful discharge of his duties; so that, in case of failure or defalcation, the Lodge may not become the loser of its property.

For all the funds he receives from the Secretary he should give a receipt to that officer, and should take receipts from all persons to whom he pays money. These last receipts become his vouchers, and his books should be examined, and the entries compared with the vouchers, at least once a year, by a committee of the Lodge.

The Treasurer, like every other officer in a Masonic Lodge, cannot resign, nor can his office be vacated by a removal, or any other cause, except death or expulsion. But whenever either of these events occurs, and the office becomes vacant, it is competent for the Lodge, of course, under the authority of a dispensation from the Grand Master, to hold a new election. The objections to such a course, in the case of the Master or Wardens, do not apply to the Treasurer.

958—What is the Masonic trestle-board?

Trestle-Board. The trestle-board is defined to be the board upon which the Master inscribes the designs by which the Craft are to be directed in their labors. The French and German Masons have confounded the *trestle-board* with the tracing-board; and Dr. Oliver has not avoided the error. The two things are entirely different. The trestle is a framework for a stable—in Scotch, *trest;* the *trestle-board* is the board placed for convenience of drawing on that frame. It contains nothing but a few diagrams, usually geometrical figures. The *tracing-board* is a picture formerly drawn on the floor of the Lodge, whence it was called a floor-cloth or carpet. It contains a delineation of the symbols of the degree to which it belongs. The *trestle-board* is to be found only in the Entered Apprentice's degree. There is a *tracing-board* in every degree, from the first to the highest. And, lastly, the *trestle-board* is a symbol; the *tracing-board* is a piece of furniture or picture containing the representation of many symbols.

It is probable that the trestle-board, from its necessary use in Operative Masonry, was one of the earliest symbols introduced into the Speculative system. It is not, however, mentioned in the *Grand Mystery,* published in 1724. But Pritchard, who wrote only six years afterwards, describes it, under the corrupted name of *trasel-board,* as one of the immovable jewels of an Apprentice's Lodge. Browne, in 1800, following Preston, fell into the error of calling it a *tracing-board,* and gives from the Prestonian lecture what he terms "a beautiful degree of comparison," in which the Bible is compared to a tracing-board. But the Bible is not a collection of symbols, which a tracing-board is, but a trestle-board that contains the plan for the construction of a spiritual temple. Webb, however, when he arranged his system of lectures, took the proper view, and restored the true word, trestle-board.

Notwithstanding these changes in the name, trestle-board, trasel-board, tracing-board, and trestle-board again, the definition has continued from the earliest part of the last century to the present day the same. It has always been enumerated among the jewels of the Lodge, although the English system says that it is immovable and the American movable; and it has always been defined as "a board for the master workman to draw his designs upon."

In Operative Masonry, the trestle-board is of vast importance. It was on such an implement that the genius of the ancient masters worked out those problems of architecture that have reflected an unfading lustre on their skill. The trestle-board was the cradle that nursed the infancy of such mighty monuments as the cathedrals of Strasbourg and Cologne; and as they advanced in stature, the trestle-board became the guardian spirit that directed their growth. Often have those old builders pondered by the midnight lamp upon their trestle-board, working out its designs with consummate taste and knowledge—here springing an arch, and turning an angle there, until the embryo edifice stood forth in all the wisdom, strength, and beauty of the Master's art.

What, then, is its true symbolism in Speculative Masonry?

To construct his earthly temple, the Operative Mason followed the architectural designs laid down on the *trestle-board,* or book of plans of the architect. By these he hewed and squared his materials; by these he raised his walls; by these he constructed his arches; and by these strength and durability, combined with grace and beauty, were bestowed upon the edifice which he was constructing.

In the Masonic ritual, the Speculative Mason is reminded that, as the Operative artist erects his temporal building in accordance with the rules and designs laid down on the trestle-board of the master workman, so should he erect that spiritual building, of which the material is a type, in obedience to the rules and desires, the precepts and commands, laid down by the Grand Architect of the Universe in those great books of nature and revelation which constitute the spiritual trestle-board of every Freemason.

The trestle-board is then the symbol of the natural and moral law. Like every other symbol of the Order, it is universal and tolerant in its application; and while, as Christian Masons, we cling with unfaltering integrity to the explanation which makes the Scriptures of both dispensations our trestle-board, we permit our Jewish and Mohammedan brethren to content themselves with the books of the Old Testament or Koran. Masonry does not interfere with the peculiar form or development of any one's religious faith. All that it asks is that the interpretation of the symbol shall be according to what each one supposes to be the revealed will of his Creator. But so rigidly exacting is it that the symbol shall be preserved and, in some rational way, interpreted, that it peremptorily excludes the atheist from its communion, because, believing in no Supreme Being—no Divine Architect—he must necessarily be without a spiritual trestle-board on which the designs of that Being may be inscribed for his direction.

959—Of what is the triad emblematic?

Triad. Three in one. An important symbol in Freemasonry. The number three was thought holy in the earliest antiquity. Numbers, **xix.** 12, furnishes an instance. This must have its reason in the nature of the number. It represents to us unity and opposition, the principle and its development or opposition, and the connecting unity—synthesis. It is the first uneven number in which the first even one is found: herein lie its peculiar signification and perfection. Even in antiquity it could not escape attention, that this number is to be found wherever variety is developed. Hence we have beginning, middle, end, represented in the heavenly rise, point of culmination and setting; morning, noon, evening, and evening, midnight, morning; and in general, in the great divisions of time, the past, the present, and the future. In space, also, this number three occurs, as in above, midst and below; right midst, and left; and in general, in the dimensions of space, as length, breadth, and thickness, or depth. To the eye, the number is represented in the regular figure of the triangle, which has been applied to numberless symbolical representations; the ear perceives it most perfectly in the harmonic triad. As the triple is also the basis of symmetry, that three-figured form is found in architecture, and in simple utensils, without any particular reference to symbolical or other significations. Of this kind are the triglyphs in architecture, the tripod, trident, the three thunderbolts of Jupiter, the ancient three-stringed-lyre, though the number has in these objects, as well as in the three-headed Cerberus, other more symbolical relations. The Triad, represented by the *delta,* is a significant emblem in a large number of Masonic degrees.

960—How are Masonic trials conducted?

Trials, Masonic. As the only object of a trial should be to seek the truth and fairly to administer justice, in a Masonic trial, especially, no recourse should ever be had to legal technicalities, whose use in ordinary courts appears simply to be to afford a means of escape for the guilty.

Masonic trials are, therefore, to be conducted in the simplest and least technical method, that will preserve at once the rights of the Order and of the accused, and which will enable the lodge to obtain a thorough knowledge of all the facts in the case. The rules to be observed in conducting such trials have been already laid down and I shall refer to them in the present article. They are as follows:

1. The preliminary step in every trial is the accusation or charge. The charge should always be made in writing, signed by the accuser,

delivered to the Secretary, and read by that officer at the next regular communication of the Lodge. The accused should then be furnished with an attested copy of the charge, and be at the same time informed of the time and place appointed by the lodge for the trial.

Any Master Mason may be the accuser of another, but a profane cannot be permitted to prefer charges against a Mason. Yet, if circumstances are known to a profane upon which charges ought to be predicated, a Master Mason may avail himself of that information, and out of it frame an accusation, to be presented to the lodge. And such accusation will be received and investigated, although remotely derived from one who is not a member of the Order.

It is not necessary that the accuser should be a member of the same lodge. It is sufficient if he is an affiliated Mason. I say an affiliated Mason; for it is generally held, and I believe correctly, that an unaffiliated Mason is no more competent to prefer charges than a profane.

2. If the accused is living beyond the geographical jurisdiction of the lodge, the charges should be communicated to him by means of a letter through the post-office, and a reasonable time should be allowed for his answer, before the lodge proceeds to trial. But if his residence be unknown, or if it be impossible to hold communication with him, the lodge may then proceed to trial—care being had that no undue advantage be taken of his absence, and that the investigation be as full and impartial as the nature of the circumstances will permit.

3. The trial must commence at a regular communication, for reasons which have already been stated; but having commenced, it may be continued at special communications, called for that purpose; for, if it was allowed only to be continued at regular meetings, which take place but once a month, the long duration of time occupied would materially tend to defeat the ends of justice.

4. The lodge must be opened in the highest degree to which the accuser has attained, and the examinations of all witnesses must take place in the presence of the accused and the accuser, if they desire it. It is competent for the accused to employ counsel for the better protection of his interests, provided such counsel is a Master Mason. But if the counsel be a member of the lodge, he forfeits, by his professional advocacy of the accused, the right to vote at the final decision of the question.

The final decision of the charge, and the rendering of the verdict, whatever be the rank of the accused, must always be made in a lodge opened on the third degree; and at the time of such decision, both the accuser and the accused, as well as his counsel, if he have any, should withdraw from the lodge.

6. It is a general and an excellent rule, that no visitors shall be permitted to be present during a trial.

7. The testimony of Master Masons is usually taken on their honor,

as such. That of others should be by affidavit, or in such other manner as both the accuser and accused may agree upon.

8. The testimony of profanes, or of those who are of a lower degree than the accused, is to be taken by a committee and reported to the lodge, or, if convenient, by the whole lodge, when closed and sitting as a committee. But both the accused and the accuser have a right to be present on such occasions.

9. When the trial is concluded, the accuser and the accused must retire, and the Master will then put the question of guilty, or not guilty, to the lodge.

Not less than two-thirds of the votes should be required to declare the accused guilty. A bare majority is hardly sufficient to divest a brother of his good character, and render him subject to what may perhaps be an ignominious punishment. But on this subject the authorities differ.

10. If the verdict is guilty, the Master must then put the question as to the nature and extent of the punishment to be inflicted, beginning with expulsion and proceeding, if necessary, to indefinite suspension and public and private reprimand. To inflict expulsion or suspension, a vote of two-thirds of those present is required, but for a mere reprimand, a majority will be sufficient. The votes on the nature of the punishment should be *viva voce,* or, rather, according to Masonic usage, by a show of hands.

Trials in a Grand Lodge are to be conducted on the same general principles; but here, in consequence of the largeness of the body, and the inconvenience which would result from holding the examinations in open lodge, and in the presence of all the members, it is more usual to appoint a committee, before whom the case is tried, and upon whose full report of the testimony the Grand Lodge bases its action. And the forms of trial in such committees must conform, in all respects, to the general usage already detailed.

961—What is the symbolism of the Lion of Judah?

Tribe of Judah, Lion of the. The connection of Solomon, as the chief of the tribe of Judah, with the lion, which was the achievement of the tribe, has caused this expression to be referred, in the third degree, to him who brought light and immortality to light. The old Christian interpretation of the Masonic symbols here prevails; and in Ancient Craft Masonry all allusions to the lion, as the *lion's paw,* the *lion's grip,* etc., refer to the doctrine of the resurrection taught by him who is known as "the lion of the tribe of Judah." The expression is borrowed from the Apocalypse, "Behold, the lion which is of the tribe of Judah, the Root of David, hath prevailed to open the book, and to loose the seven seals thereof." The lion was also a mediaeval symbol of the resurrection, the idea being founded on a legend. The poets of that age were fond of referring to this legendary symbol in connection with scriptural idea of the "tribe of Judah." Thus Adam de St. Victor says:

> Thus the strong lion of Judah,
> The gates of cruel death being broken,
> Arose on the third day
> At the loud-sounding voice of the Father.

The lion was the symbol of strength and sovereignty, in the human-headed figures of the Nimrod gateway, and in other Babylonish remains. In Egypt, it was worshiped at the city of Leontoplis as typical of Dom, the Egyptian Hercules. Plutarch says that the Egyptians ornamented their temples with gaping lions' mouths, because the Nile began to rise when the sun was in the constellation Leo. Among the Talmudists there was a tradition of the lion, which has been introduced into the higher degrees of Masonry.

But in the symbolism of Ancient Craft Masonry, where the lion is introduced, as in the third degree, in connection with the "lion of the tribe of Judah," he becomes simply a symbol of the resurrection; thus restoring the symbology of the mediaeval ages, which was founded on a legend that the lion's whelp was born dead, and only brought to life by the roaring of its sire. Philip de Thaun, in his *Bestiary,* written in the twelfth century, gives the legend, which has thus been translated by Mr. Wright from the original old Norman French:

"Know that the lioness, if she bring forth a dead cub, she holds her cub and the lion arrives; he goes about and cries, till it revives on the third day. . . . Know that the lioness signifies St. Mary, and the lion Christ, who gave himself to death for the people; three days he lay in the earth to gain our souls. . . . By the cry of the lion they understand the power of God, by which Christ was restored to life and robbed hell."

The phrase, "Lion of the tribe of Judah," therefore, when used in the Masonic ritual, referred in its original interpretation to Christ, him who "brought life and immortality to light."

962—Of what is the trowel emblematic?

Trowel. The trowel is appropriated to the Master's degree, because, as the lectures say, it is as Master Masons only we are recognized as members of the Masonic family. Again this implement is considered as the appropriate working tool of the Master Mason, because, in operative Masonry, while the Entered Apprentice prepares the materials, and the Fellowcraft places them in their proper situation, the Master Mason spreads the cement with a trowel, which binds them together. In speculative Masonry the Master of the lodge is the cement which unites the brethren, and binds them together in peace, harmony, and brotherly love.

963—What is the symbolism of the trowel and sword?

Trowel and Sword. Emblems in the degree of Knights of the East. They are borrowed evidently from a religious and mechanical society, called the *Brethren of the Bridge,* which was founded at an early period in France, when a state of anarchy existed, and there was little security for travelers, particularly in passing rivers, on which they were subject to the rapacity of banditti. The object of this society was to put a stop to these outrages by forming fraternities for the purpose of building bridges and establishing ferries and caravansaries on their banks. Always prepared for an attack from the marauders, they carried a sword in one hand and a trowel or hammer in the other. Ramsay says that they adopted this custom in imitation of the Jews at the building of the second temple; and he endeavors to establish some connection between them and the Knights of the Temple, and of St. John of Jerusalem.

964—Why should a Mason be truthful?

True. The Mason should not only be true to the brotherhood and the Order, but to all mankind. Every Mason ought to act in such a manner as to render it unnecessary to doubt his truth. Flattering words, which are only calculated to entrap the weak and the unwary, do not strengthen that truth which is expected amongst brethren. We must be able to depend with as much confidence upon the word of a Mason as if he had given us a written undertaking.

965—In whom do Masons put their trust?

Trust in God. Every candidate on his initiation is required to declare that his trust is in God. And so he who denies the existence of a Supreme Being is debarred the privilege of initiation, for atheism is a disqualification for Masonry. This pious principle has distinguished the Fraternity from the earliest period; and it is a happy coincidence that the company of Operative Freemasons instituted in 1477 should have adopted as their motto, the truly Masonic sentiment, "The Lord is all our Trust."

966—What is the real end and aim of all Masonic labors and ceremonies?

Truth. The real object of Freemasonry, in a philosophical and religious sense, is the search for truth. This truth is, therefore, symbolized by the Word. From the first entrance of the Apprentice into the lodge, until his reception of the highest degree, this search is continued. It is not always found, and a substitute must sometimes be provided. Yet whatever be the labors he may perform, whatever the ceremonies through which he may pass, whatever the symbols in which he may be instructed, whatever the reward he may obtain, the true end of all is the attainment of truth. This idea of truth is not the same as that expressed in the lecture of the first degree, where Brotherly Love, Relief, and Truth are there said to be the "three great tenets of a Mason's profession." In that connection, truth, which is called a "divine attribute, the foundation of every virtue," is synonymous with sincerity, honesty of expression, and plain dealing. The higher idea of truth which pervades the whole Masonic system, and which is symbolized by the Word, is that which is properly expressed as a knowledge of God.

Truth is one of the great tenets of a Freemason's profession. It is the foundation of all Masonic virtues; it is one of our grand principles; for to be good men and true is a part of the first lesson we are taught; and at the commencement of our freedom we are exhorted to be fervent and zealous in the pursuit of truth and goodness. It is not sufficient that we walk in the light, unless we do so in the truth also. All hypocrisy and deceit must be banished from among us. Sincerity and plain dealing complete the harmony of a lodge, and render us acceptable in the sight of him unto whom all hearts are open, all desires known, and from whom no secrets are hid. There is a charm in truth, which draws and attracts the mind continually toward it. The more we discover, the more we desire; and the great reward is wisdom, virtue, and happiness. This is an edifice founded on a rock, which malice cannot shake or time destroy. In the ancient mythology of Rome, Truth was called the mother of Virtue, and was depicted with white and flowing garments. Her looks were cheerful and pleasant, though modest and serene. She was the protectress of honor and honesty, and the light and joy of human society.

967—What four children founded the beginning of all the sciences in the world?

Tubal Cain. Of Tubal Cain, the sacred writings, as well as the Masonic legends, give us but scanty information. All that we hear of him in the book of Genesis is that he was the son of Lamech and Zillah, and was an instructor of every artificer in brass and iron. The Hebrew original does not justify the common version, for *lotesh* does not mean "an instructor," but "a sharpener,"—one who whets or sharpens instruments. Hence Dr. Raphall translates the passage as one "who sharpened various tools in copper and iron." The authorized version has, however, almost indelibly impressed the character of Tubal Cain as the father of artificers; and it is in this sense that he has been introduced from a very early period into the legendary history of Masonry.

The first Masonic reference to Tubal Cain is found in the "Legend of the Craft," where he is called "the founder of smithcraft." I cite this part of the legend from the Dowland MS. simply because of its more modern orthography; but the story is substantially the same in all the old manuscript Constitutions. In that Manuscript we find the following account of Tubal Cain:

"Before Noah's flood, there was a man called Lamech, as it is written in the Bible, in the fourth chapter of Genesis; and this Lamech had two wives, the one named Ada and the other named Zillah; by his first wife, Ada, he got two sons, the one Jabel, and the other Jubal; and by the other wife he got a son and a daughter. And these four children founded the beginning of all the sciences in the world. The elder son, Jabel, founded the science of geometry, and he carried flocks of sheep and lambs into the fields, and first built houses of stone and wood, as it is noted in the chapter above named. And his brother Jubal founded the science of music and songs of the tongue, the harp and organ. And the third brother, Tubal Cain, founded smithcraft, of gold, silver, copper, iron, and steel, and the daughter founded the art of weaving. And these children knew well that God would take vengeance for sin, either by fire or water, wherefore they wrote the sciences that they had found, on two pillars that they might be found after Noah's flood. The one pillar was marble, for that would not burn with fire; and the other was of brass, for that would not drown in water."

Similar to this is an old Rabbinical tradition, which asserts that Jubal, who was the inventor of writing as well as of music, having heard Adam say that the universe would be twice destroyed, once by fire and once by water, inquired which catastrophe would first occur; but Adam refusing to inform him, he inscribed the system of music which he had invented upon two pillars of stone and brick. A more modern Masonic tradition ascribes the construction of these pillars to Enoch.

To this account of Tubal Cain must be added the additional particulars, recorded by Josephus, that he exceeded all men in strength, and was renowned for his warlike achievements.

The only other account of the protometallurgist that we meet with in any ancient author is that which is contained in the celebrated fragment of Sanconiatho, who refers to him under the name Chrysor, which is evidently, as Bochart affirms, a corruption of the Hebrew *chores ur,* a worker in fire, that is, a smith. Sanconiatho was a Phoenician author, who is supposed to have flourished before the Trojan war, probably, as Sir William Drummond suggests, about the time when Gideon was Judge of Israel, and who collected the different accounts and traditions of the origin of the world which were extant at the period in which he lived. A fragment only of this work has been preserved, which, translated into Greek by Philo Byblius, was inserted by Eusebius in his *Proeparatio Evangelica,* and has thus been handed down to the present day. That portion of the history by Sanconiatho, which refers to Tubal Cain, is contained in the following words:

"A long time after the generation of Hypsoaranois, the inventors of hunting and fishing, Agreas and Alieas, were born; after whom the people were called hunters and fishers, and from whom sprang two brothers, who discovered iron, and the manner of working it. One of these two, called Chrysor, was skilled in eloquence, and composed verses and prophecies. He was the same with Hephaistos, and invented fishing-hooks, bait for taking fish, cordage and rafts, and was the first of all mankind who had navigated. He was therefore worshipped as a god after his death, and was called Diamichios. It is said that these brothers were the first who contrived partition walls of brick."

Hephaistos, it will be observed, is the Greek of the god who was called by the Romans Vulcan. Hence the remark of Sanconiatho, and the apparent similarity of names as well as occupations, have led some writers of the last, and even of the present century, to derive Vulcan from Tubal Cain by a process not very devious, and therefore familiar to etymologists. By the omission in Tubal Cain of the initial T, which is the Phoenician article, and its valueless vowel, we get *Balcan,* which, by the interchangeable nature of B and V, is easily transformed to *Vulcan.*

"That Tubal Cain," says Bishop Stillingfleet, "gave first occasion to the name and worship of Vulcan, hath been very probably conceived, both from the very great affinity of the names, and that Tubal Cain is expressly mentioned to be an instructor of every artificer in brass and iron, and as near relation as Apollo had to Vulcan, Jubal had to Tubal Cain, who was the inventor of music, or the father of all such as handle the harp and organ, which the Greeks attribute to Apollo."

Vossius, in his treatise *de Idolatria,* makes this derivation of Vulcan from Tubal Cain. But Bryant, in his *Analysis of Ancient Mythology,* denies the etymology, and says that among the Egyptians and Babylonians, Vulcan was equivalent to Arus or Osiris, symbols of the sun. He traces the name to the words *Ball Cahen,* Holy Bel, or sacred Lord. Bryant's etymology may be adopted, however, without any interference with the identity of Vulcan and Tubal Cain. He who discovered the uses of fire may well, in the corruptions of idolatry, have typified the solar orb, the source of all heat. It might seem that Tubal is an attribute compounded of the definite particle T and the word Baal, signifying Lord. Tubal Cain would then signify "the Lord Cain." Again, *dhu* or *du,* in Arabic, signifies Lord; and we trace the same signification of this affix, in its various interchangeable forms of *Du, Tu,* and *Di,* in many Semitic words. But the question of the identical origin of Tubal Cain and Vulcan has at length been settled by the researches of comparative philologists. Tubal Cain is Semitic in origin and Vulcan is Aryan. The latter may be traced to the Sanscrit *ulka,* a firebrand, from which we get also the Latin *fulgur* and *fulmen,* names of the lightning.

From the mention made of Tubal Cain in the "Legend of the Craft," the word was long ago adopted as significant in the primary degrees, and various attempts have been made to give it an interpretation.

Hutchinson, in an article in his *Spirit of Masonry* devoted to the consideration of the third degree, has the following reference to the word:

"The Mason advancing to this state of Masonry, pronounces his own sentence, as confessional of the imperfection of the second stage of his profession, and as probationary of the exalted degree to which he aspires, in the Greek distich, Struo tumulum: 'I prepare my sepulchre; I make my grave in the pollutions of the earth; I am under the shadow of death.' This distich has been vulgarly corrupted among us, and an expression takes place scarcely similar in sound, and entirely inconsistent with Masonry, and unmeaning in itself."

But however ingenious this interpretation of Hutchinson may be, it is generally admitted that it is incorrect.

The modern English Masons, and through them the French, have derived Tubal Cain from the Hebrew *tabel,* earth, and *hanah,* to acquire possession, and, with little respect for the grammatical rules of the Hebrew language, interpret it as meaning *worldly possessions.*

In the Hemming lectures, now the authorized English system, we find the answer to the question, "What does Tubal Cain denote?" is "Worldly possessions." And Delaunay, in his *Thuilleur,* denies the reference to the proto-smith, and says: "If we reflect on the meaning of the two Hebrew words we will easily recognize in their connection the secret wish of the hierophant of the Templar, of the Freemason, and of every mystical sect to govern the world in accordance with its own principles and its own laws." It is fortunate I think, that the true meaning of the words will authorize no such interpretation. The fact is that even if Tubal Cain were derived from *tebel* and *kanah,* the precise rules of Hebrew construction would forbid affixing to their union any such meaning as "worldly possessions." Such an interpretation of it in the French and English system, is therefore, a very forced and inaccurate one.

The use of Tubal Cain as a significant word in the Masonic ritual is derived from the "Legend of the Craft," by which the name was made familiar to the Operative and then to the Speculative Masons; and it refers not symbolically, but historically to his scriptural and traditional reputation as an artificer. If he symbolized anything, it would be labor; and a Mason's labor is to acquire *truth,* and not worldly possessions. The English and French interpretations have fortunately never been introduced into this country.

968—What is the first and simplest form of architecture?

Tuscan. The Tuscan, being the first, is the most simple and solid of the five orders. It was invented in Tuscany, whence it derives its name. The simplicity of the construction of this column renders it eligible where solidity is the chief object, and where ornament would be superfluous.

969—Of what is the twenty-four inch rule emblematic?

Twenty-Four Inch Rule. An instrument made use of by operative Masons to measure and lay out their work; but we, as Free and Accepted Masons, are taught to make use of it for the more noble and glorious purpose of dividing our time. It being divided into twenty-four equal parts, is emblematical of the twenty-four hours of the day, which we are taught to divide into three parts, whereby we find a portion for the service of God, and the relief of a worthy distressed brother; a portion for our usual avocations; and a portion for refreshment and sleep.

970—What are the status and rights of unaffiliated Masons?

Unaffiliated Masons. To entitle him to the right of visit, a Master Mason must be affiliated with some Lodge. Of this doctrine there is no question. All Masonic authorities concur in confirming it. But as a Mason may take his demit from a particular Lodge, with the design of uniting again with some other, it is proper that he should be allowed the opportunity of visiting various Lodges, for the purpose—where there are more than one in the same place—of making his selection. But that no encouragement may be given to him to protract the period of his withdrawal of Lodge membership, this privilege of visiting must be restricted within the narrowest limits. Accordingly, the Grand Lodge of England has laid down the doctrine in its Constitutions in the following words:

"A Brother, who is not a subscribing member to some Lodge, shall not be permitted to visit any one Lodge in the town or place in which he resides, more than once during his secession from the craft."

A similar usage appears very generally, indeed universally, to prevail; so that it may be laid down as a law, fixed by custom and confirmed in most jurisdictions by statutory enactment, that an unaffiliated Mason cannot visit any Lodge more than once. By ceasing to be affiliated, he loses his general right of visit.

971—What, in brief, is the status of an unaffiliated Mason?

Unaffiliated Masons, Status of. The following principles are supported by the law on the subject of unaffiliated Masons:

1. An unaffiliated Mason is still bound by all those Masonic duties and obligations which refer to the Order in general, but not by those which relate to Lodge organization.

2. He possesses, reciprocally, all those rights which are derived from membership in the Order, but none of those which result from membership in a Lodge.

3. He has a right to assistance when in imminent peril, if he asks for that assistance in the conventional way.

4. He has no right to pecuniary aid from a Lodge.

5. He has no right to visit Lodges, or to walk in Masonic processions.

6. He has no right to Masonic burial.

7. He still remains subject to the government of the Order, and may be tried and punished for any offence, by the Lodge within whose geographical jurisdiction he resides.

8. And, lastly, as non-affiliation is a violation of Masonic law, he may, if he refuses to abandon that condition, be tried and punished for it, even by expulsion if deemed necessary or expedient, by any Grand Lodge within whose jurisdiction he lives.

972—Does an unaffiliated Mason enjoy the privilege of Masonic visitation?

Unaffiliates. There is no precept more explicitly expressed in the ancient Constitutions than that every Mason should belong to a Lodge. The foundation of the law which imposes this duty is to be traced as far back as the Gothic Constitutions of 926, which tell us that "the workman shall labor diligently on work-days, that he may deserve his holidays." The obligation that every Mason should thus labor is implied in all the subsequent Constitutions, which always speak of Masons as *working members* of the fraternity, until we come to the Charges approved in 1722, which explicitly state that "every Brother ought to belong to a Lodge, and to be subject to its By-Laws and the General Regulations."

Explicitly, however, as the law has been announced, it has not, in modern times, been observed with that fidelity which should have been expected, perhaps, because no precise penalty was annexed to its violation. The word "ought" has given to the regulation a simply declaratory form; and although we are still compelled to conclude that its violation is a neglect of Masonic duty, and therefore punishable by a Masonic tribunal, Masonic jurists have been at a loss to agree upon the nature and extent of the punishment that should be inflicted.

In short, while the penalty inflicted for non-affiliation has varied in different jurisdictions, I know of no Grand Lodge that has not concurred in the view that it is a Masonic offence, to be visited by some penalty, or the deprivation of some rights.

And certainly, as it is an undoubted precept of our Order, that every Mason should belong to a Lodge, and contribute, as far as his means will allow, to the support of the institution; and as, by his continuance in a state of non-affiliation, he violates this precept, and disobeys the law which he had promised to support, it necessarily follows that an unaffiliated Mason is placed in a very different position, morally and legally, from that occupied by an affiliated one.

973—Why is the ballot required to be unanimous?

Unanimity of Ballot. Unanimity in the ballot is necessary to secure the harmony of the Lodge, which may be as seriously impaired by the admission of a candidate contrary to the wishes of one member as of three or more; for every man has his friends and his influence. Besides, it is unjust to any member, however humble he may be, to introduce among his associates one whose presence might be unpleasant to him, and whose admission would probably compel him to withdraw from the meetings, or even altogether from the Lodge. Neither would any advantage really accrue to a Lodge by such a forced admission; for while receiving a new and untried member into its fold, it would be losing an old one. For these reasons, in this country, except in a few jurisdictions, the unanimity of the ballot has always been insisted on; and it is evident, from what has been here said, that any less stringent Regulation is a violation of the ancient law and usage.

974—Why must a ballot be unanimous?

Unanimous. A ballot is unanimous when there are no black balls. This unanimity must be founded upon the proper exercise of the rules and regulations laid down for our guidance in this important part of our duty, and a perfect unanimity in the opinions of the brethren on the moral character of the candidate.

In order to secure and perpetuate the peace and harmony of the Craft, it has long been the settled policy of the Masonic Fraternity to receive no person to membership, only by the consent of all the brethren who may be present at the time the ballot is taken. Among the regulations of the Grand Lodge of England we find the following in regard to this subject: "No man can be entered a brother in any particular lodge, or admitted a member thereof, without the unanimous consent of all the members of the lodge then present, when the candidate is proposed, and when their consent is formally asked by the Master. They are to give their consent in their own prudent way, either virtually or in form, but with unanimity. Nor is this inherent privilege subject to a dispensation; because the members of a particular lodge are the best judges of it; and because, if a turbulent member should be imposed upon them, it might spoil their harmony, or hinder the freedom of their communications, or even break up and disperse the lodges, which ought to be avoided by all true and faithful brothers."

975—What is called the bulwark of Masonry?

Unanimous Consent. In the beginning of the last century, when Masonry was reviving from the condition of decay into which it had fallen, and when the experiment was tried of transforming it from a partly operative to a purely speculative system, the great object was to maintain a membership which, by the virtuous character of those who composed it, should secure the harmony and prosperity of the infant Institution. A safeguard was therefore to be sought in the care with which Masons should be selected from those who were likely to apply for admission. It was the quality, and not the quantity, that was desired. This safeguard could only be found in the unanimity of the ballot. Hence, in the sixth of the General Regulations, adopted in 1721, it is declared that "no man can be entered a Brother in any particular Lodge, or admitted to be a member thereof, without the *unanimous consent* of all the members of that Lodge then present when the candidate is proposed, and their consent is formally asked by the Master." And to prevent the exercise of any undue influence of a higher power in forcing an unworthy person upon the Order, it is further said in the same article: "Nor is this inherent privilege subject to a dispensation; because the members of a particular Lodge are the best judges of it; and if a fractious member should be imposed on them, it might spoil their harmony, or hinder their freedom; or even break and disperse the Lodge." But a few years after, the Order being now on a firm footing, this prudent fear of "spoiling harmony," or "dispersing the Lodge," seems to have been lost sight of, and the brethren began in many Lodges to desire a release from the restrictions laid upon them by the necessity for unanimous consent. Hence Anderson says in his second edition: "But it was found inconvenient to insist upon unanimity in several cases. And, therefore, the Grand Masters have allowed the Lodges to admit a member if not above three ballots are against him; though some Lodges desire no such allowance." This rule still prevails in England; and its modern Constitution still permits the admission of a Mason where there are not more than three ballots against him, though many of the Lodges still demand unanimity.

In the United States, where Masonry is more popular than in any other country, it was soon seen that the danger of the Institution lay not in the paucity, but in the multitude of its members, and that the only provision for guarding its portals was the most stringent regulation of the ballot. Hence, in every jurisdiction of the United States, I think, without an exception, unanimous consent is required. And this rule has been found to work with such advantage to the Order, that the phrase, "the black ball is the bulwark of Masonry," has become a proverb.

976—Should a ballot be taken on an unfavorable report?

Unfavorable Report. Should the committee of investigation on the character of a petitioner for initiation make an unfavorable report, the general usage is (although some Grand Lodges have decided otherwise) to consider the candidate rejected by such report, without proceeding to the formality of a ballot, which is therefore dispensed with. This usage is founded on the principles of common sense; for, as by the ancient Constitutions one black ball is sufficient to reject an application, the unfavorable report of a committee must necessarily, and by consequence, include two unfavorable votes at least. It is therefore unnecessary to go into a ballot after such a report, as it is to be taken for granted that the brethren who reported unfavorably would, on a resort to the ballot, cast their negative votes. Their report is indeed virtually considered as the casting of such votes, and the applicant is therefore at once rejected without a further and unnecessary ballot.

977—Why should Masons observe the same usages and customs?

Uniformity. All lodges are particularly bound to observe the same usages and customs; every deviation, therefore, from the established mode of working is highly improper, and cannot be justified or countenanced. In order to preserve this uniformity, and to cultivate a good understanding among Freemasons, some members of every lodge should be deputed to visit other lodges as often as may be convenient. If any lodge shall give its sanction for a lodge of instruction being held under its warrant, such lodge shall be responsible that the proceedings in the lodge of instruction are correct and regular, and that the mode of working there adopted has received the sanction of the Grand Lodge.

978—How may the Masonic system be extended to unoccupied territory?

Unoccupied Territory. It only remains to consider the proper mode of organizing a Grand Lodge in a territory where no such body has previously existed. Perfectly to understand this subject, it will be necessary to commence with the first development of Masonry in any country.

Let us suppose, then, that there is a territory of country within whose political bounds Freemasonry has never yet been introduced in an organized form. There may be, and indeed for the execution of the law which is about to be explained, there must be an adequate number of Master Masons, but there is no Lodge. Now, the first principle of Masonic law to which attention is to be directed, in this condition of things, is, that any territory into which Masonry has not been introduced in the organized form of Lodges, is ground common to all the Masonic authorities of the world; and therefore that it is competent for any Grand Lodge to grant a warrant of constitution, and establish a Lodge in such unoccupied territory, on the petition, of course, of a requisite number of Masons. And this right of granting warrants insures to every Grand Lodge in the world, and may be exercised by as many as choose to do so, as long as no Grand Lodge is organized in the territory. So that there may be ten or a dozen Lodges working at the same time in the same territory, and each one of them deriving its legal existence from a different Grand Lodge.

In such a case, neither of the Grand Lodges who have granted warrants acquires, by any such act, exclusive jurisdiction over the territory, which is still open for the admission of any other Grand Lodge, with a similar power of granting warrants. The jurisdiction exercised in this condition of Masonry by the different Grand Lodges is not over the territory, but over the Lodge or Lodges which each of them has established.

But afterwards these subordinate Lodges may desire to organize a Grand Lodge, and they are competent to do so, under certain restrictions.

979—What should be the attitude of the Craft toward unworthy brethren?

Unworthy Members. That there are men in our Order whose lives and characters reflect no credit on the Institution, whose ears turn coldly from its beautiful lessons of morality, whose hearts are untouched by its soothing influences of brotherly kindness, whose hands are not opened to aid in its deeds of charity, is a fact which we cannot deny, although we may be permitted to express our grief while we acknowledge its truth. But these men, though in the Temple, are not of the Temple; they are among us, but are not with us; they belong to our household, but they are not of our faith; they are of Israel, but they are not Israel. We have sought to teach them, but they would not be instructed; seeing, they have not perceived; and hearing, they have not understood the symbolic language in which our lessons of wisdom are communicated. The fault is not with us, that we have not given, but with them that they have not received. And, indeed, hard and unjust would it be to censure the Masonic institution, because, partaking of the infirmity and weakness of human wisdom and human means it has been unable to give strength and perfection to all who come within its pale. The denial of a Peter, the doubtings of a Thomas, or even the betrayal of a Judas, could cast no reproach on that holy band of Apostles of which each formed a constituent part.

"Is Freemasonry answerable," says Dr. Oliver, "for the misdeeds of an individual Brother? By no means. He has had the advantage of Masonic instruction, and has failed to profit by it. He has enjoyed Masonic privileges, but has not possessed Masonic virtue." Such a man it is our duty to reform, or to dismiss; but the world should not condemn us, if we fail in our attempt at reformation. God alone can change the heart. Masonry furnishes precepts and obligations of duty which, if obeyed, must make its members wiser, better, happier men; but it claims no power of regeneration. Condemn when our instruction is evil, but not when our pupils are dull, and deaf to our lessons; for, in so doing, you condemn the holy religion which you profess. Masonry prescribes no principles that are opposed to the sacred teachings of the Divine Lawgiver, and sanctions no acts that are not consistent with the sternest morality and the most faithful obedience to government and the laws; and while this continues to be its character, it cannot, without the most atrocious injustice, be made responsible for the acts of its unworthy members.

Of all human societies, Freemasonry is undoubtedly, under all circumstances, the fittest to form the truly good man. But however well conceived may be its laws, they cannot completely change the natural disposition of those who ought to observe them. In truth, they serve as lights and guides; but as they can only direct men by restraining the impetuosity of their passions, these last too often become dominant, and the Institution is forgotten.

980—Why are Lodges held in upper chambers?

Upper Chamber. Our lodges are formed in upper chambers, and carefully guarded by tiled doors and drawn swords. The highest of hills and the lowest of valleys are situations least exposed to unauthorized intrusion. Thus Masons are said to meet in these situations, to commemorate a remarkable custom of the ancient Jews in the building of their temples, schools, and synagogues; and as by the Jewish law, whenever ten of them assembled together for that purpose, they proceeded to work, so it was with our ancient brethren, who formed themselves into a lodge, whenever ten operative Masons were assembled, consisting of the Master, two Wardens, and seven Fellowcrafts.

981—What is the symbolism of the upright posture?

Upright Posture. The upright posture of the Apprentice in the northeast corner, as a symbol of upright conduct, was introduced into the ritual by Preston, who taught in his lectures that the candidate then represented "a just and upright man and Mason." The same symbolism is referred to by Hutchinson, who says that "as the builder raises his column by the plane and perpendicular, so should the Mason carry himself towards the world." Indeed, the application of the cornerstone, or the square stone, as a symbol of uprightness of conduct, which is precisely the Masonic symbolism of the candidate in the northeast, was familiar to the ancients; for Plato says that he who valiantly sustains the shocks of adverse fortune, demeaning himself uprightly, is truly good and of a square posture.

Every Freemason remembers the instructions given him in the lodge at the time of his reception, in regard to the "upright posture." "God created man to be *upright,*" i. e., to stand erect. This is the peculiar prerogative of man. All the outward forms and features of the sentient world, whether human or brutal, are created by the nature, disposition or spirit of each race and each individual. The nature of beasts and reptiles is earthly. Prone to the earth, they move horizontally, with downward gaze, or crawl in the dust. To them the ideal world is closed. The glory of the heavens, the grandeur of nature, the beauty of flowers, the wonderful harmonies of sight and sound, which so inspire and elevate man, are unknown to them. Their gaze is downward, and their life is extinguished in the dust. Man, on the contrary, stands erect, and his eyes sweep through the immense regions of space which stretch above his head. His mind, endowed with a divine energy, reaches to the most distant star, and measures it, in weight and size, as accurately as one measures the apple that is held in the palm of the hand. The "upright posture" also has an important moral significance for the intelligent Mason. As it reminds him of his relationship to the celestial powers, and that he is endowed with some of the attributes of the Divinity, and with a life which will endure forever, he is admonished thereby that he should live in a manner worthy of so illustrious an origin, and so glorious a destiny.

982—To what do the usages and customs of Masons correspond?

Usages. The usages and customs of Masons have ever corresponded with those of the ancient Egyptians, to which they bear a near affinity. Their philosophers, unwilling to expose their mysteries to vulgar eyes, concealed their particular tenets, and principles of polity and philosophy, under hieroglyphical figures, and expressed their notions of government by signs and symbols, which they communicated to their priests alone, who were bound by oath not to reveal them.

983—Can the office of Master be filled by an election in the event of his death or disability?

Vacancy in the Office of Master. Whether the Senior Warden or a Past Master is to succeed, the Regulations of 1721 makes no provision for an election, but implies that the vacancy shall be temporarily supplied during the official term, while that of 1723 expressly states that such temporary succession shall continue "till the next time of choosing," or, in the words of the present English Constitution, "until the next election of officers."

But, in addition to the authority of the Ancient Regulation and general and uniform usage, reason and justice seem to require that the vacancy shall not be supplied permanently until the regular time of election. By holding the election at an earlier period, the Senior Warden is deprived of his right as a member, to become a candidate for the vacant office, for the Senior Warden having been regularly installed, has of course been duly obligated to serve in the office to which he had been elected during the full term. If, then, an election takes place before the expiration of that term, he must be excluded from the list of candidates, because if elected, he could not vacate his present office without a violation of his obligation. The same disability would affect the Junior Warden, who, by a similar obligation, is bound to the faithful discharge of his duties in the south. So that by anticipating the election, the two most prominent officers of the Lodge, and the two most likely to succeed the Master in due course of rotation, would be excluded from the chance of promotion. A grievous wrong would thus be done to these officers, which it could never have been the intention of the law to inflict.

But even if the Wardens were not ambitious of office, or were not likely, under any circumstances, to be elected to the vacant office, another objection arises to the anticipation of an election for Master, which is worthy of consideration.

The Wardens, having been installed under the solemnity of an obligation to discharge the duties of their respective offices to the best of their ability, and the Senior Warden having been expressly charged that "in the absence of the Master he is to rule the Lodge," a conscientious Senior Warden might very naturally feel that he was neglecting these duties and violating this obligation, by permitting the office which he has sworn to temporarily occupy in the absence of his Master, to be permanently filled by any other person.

On the whole, then, the Old Regulations, as well as ancient, uninterrupted and uniform usage, and the principles of reason and justice, seem imperatively to require that on the death or removal of the Master, there shall be no election to supply the vacancy; but that the authority of the absent Master shall be vested in the Senior Warden, and in his absence, in the Junior.

984—May an officer of a Lodge, duly elected and installed, lawfully resign his office?

Vacation of Lodge Officers. An office terminates in Masonry only in three ways—by the expiration of the term, by death, or by expulsion. Suspension does not vacate an office, but simply suspends the office bearer from the privilege of discharging the duties of the office, and restoration immediately restores him to the enjoyment of all the prerogatives of his office.

It is now held by a large majority of authorities that an officer, after having once accepted of installation, cannot resign the office to which he has been elected. And this seems to be in accordance with reason; for, by the installation, the officer promises to discharge the functions of the office for the constitutional period, and a resignation would be a violation of his oath of office, which no Lodge should be willing to sanction. So, too, when an officer has removed from the jurisdiction, although it may be at the time with an intention never to return, it is impossible, in the uncertainty of human events, to say how far that intention will be fulfilled, and the office must remain vacant until the next regular period of election. In the meantime the duties are to be discharged by the temporary appointment, by the Master, of a substitute; for, should the regularly elected and installed officer change his intention and return, it would at once become not only his privilege but his duty to resume the discharge of the functions of his office.

985—How may a Tiler be removed from office?

Vacation of Office of Tiler. The Tiler is sometimes appointed by the Master, but is more usually elected by the Lodge. After installation, he holds his office, by the same tenure as the other officers, and can only be removed by death or expulsion. Of course the Tiler, like every other officer, may, on charges preferred and trial had, be suspended from discharging the functions of his office, during which suspension a temporary Tiler shall be appointed by the Master. But as I have already said, such suspension does not vacate the office, nor authorize a new election.

986—When and where must the verdict in a Lodge trial be rendered?

Verdict, Announcement of. The final decision upon charges, and the rendering of the verdict, whatever be the rank of the accused, must always be made in a Lodge opened on the third degree; and at the time of such decision, both the accuser and the accused, as well as his counsel, if he have any, should withdraw from the Lodge.

987—How is the verdict at a Masonic trial arrived at?

Verdict, How Arrived at. When the trial is concluded, the accuser and the accused must retire, and the Master will then put the question of guilty, or not guilty, to the Lodge. Masonic authorities differ as to the mode in which the vote is taken. In England, it is done by a show of hands. The Grand Lodges of Ohio and South Carolina require it to be by ballot, and that of California by each brother, as his name is called, rising and giving his answer "in a distinct and audible manner." I confess, that in this diversity of authorities, I am inclined to be in favor of the vote by ballot, as the independence of opinion is thus better secured; for many a man who conscientiously believed in the guilt of the accused, might be too timid to express that opinion openly. Not less, I think, than two-thirds of the votes should be required to declare the accused guilty. A bare majority is hardly sufficient to divest a brother of his good character, and render him subject to what may perhaps be an ignominous punishment. But on this subject the authorities differ.

988—What forms may the verdict of a Grand Lodge on appeal take in the settlement of an appeal?

Verdict of a Grand Lodge on Appeal. A Grand Lodge may restore in part, and not in whole. It may mitigate the amount of punishment, as being too severe or disproportioned to the offence. It may reduce expulsion to suspension, and indefinite to definite suspension, or it may abridge the period of the last. But all these are matters of justice and expediency, to be judged of by the Grand Lodge, according to the particular circumstances of each case.

989—What violation of Masonic Landmarks and Regulations may subject a Mason to Masonic discipline?

Violations of Masonic Landmarks and Regulations. A class of crimes which are cognizable by a Masonic tribunal are violations of the Landmarks and Regulations of the Order. These are so numerous that space cannot be afforded for even a bare catalogue. Reference must be made only to a few of the most important character.

A disclosure of any of the secrets which a Mason "has promised to conceal and never reveal" is a heinous crime, and one which the monitorial lecture of the first degree expressly says, "would subject him to the contempt and detestation of all good Masons."

Disobedience and want of respect to Masonic superiors is an offence for which the transgressor subjects himself to punishment.

The bringing of "private piques or quarrels" into the Lodge is strictly forbidden by the old Charges, and the violation of this precept is justly considered as a Masonic offence.

A want of courtesy and kindness to the brethren, speaking calumniously of one behind his back, or in any other way attempting to injure him, is each a violation of the precepts of Masonry, and should be made the subject of investigation.

Striking a Mason, except in self-defence, is a heinous transgression of the law of brotherly love, which is the foundation of Masonry. It is not, therefore, surprising that the more serious offence of duelling among Masons has been specifically condemned, under the severest penalties, by several Grand Lodges.

The ancient Installation Charges in the time of James II. expressly prohibit a Mason from doing any dishonor to the wife or daughter of his brother; but it is scarcely necessary to remark that still higher authority for this prohibition may be found in the ritualistic Landmarks of the Order.

Gambling is also declared to be a Masonic offence in the old Charges.

As I have already said, it would be possible, but hardly necessary, to extend this list of Masonic offences against the Constitutions and Regulations of the Order. They must be learned from a diligent perusal of these documents, and the study of the Landmarks and ritualistic observances. It is sufficient to say that whatever is a violation of fidelity to solemn engagements, a neglect of prescribed duties, or a transgression of the cardinal principles of friendship, morality and brotherly love, is a Masonic crime, and renders the offender liable to Masonic punishment.

990—What virtues does Masonry inculcate?

Virtues. In all ages it has been the object of Freemasonry, not only to inform the minds of its members, by instructing them in the sciences and useful arts, but to better their hearts, by enforcing the precepts of religion and morality. In the course of the ceremonies of initiation, brotherly love, loyalty, and other virtues are inculcated in hieroglyphic symbols, and the candidate is often reminded that there is an eye above, which observeth the workings of his heart, and is ever fixed upon the thoughts and actions of men.

991—What rights has a Grand Master or his representative in a subordinate Lodge?

Visitation. Masonic usage requires that the Grand Master and other officers of the Grand Lodge should periodically visit the subordinate lodges, to examine their books and work, and make a general inspection of their affairs. This formal visit is called a visitation. When such an event occurs, the Grand Officers, after being received with the usual honors, take charge of the lodge. According to the English Constitutions, "the Grand Master has full authority to preside in any lodge, and to order his Grand Officers to attend him; his Deputy is to be placed on his right hand, and the Master of the lodge on his left hand. His Wardens are also to act as Wardens of that particular lodge during his presence. The Deputy Grand Master has full authority, unless the Grand Master or Pro-Grand Master be present, to preside, with the Master of the lodge on his right hand. The Grand Wardens, if present, are to act as Wardens."

992—What is the prerogative of a Grand Master with respect to a Masonic visitation?

Visitation, Grand Master's Prerogative of. Concomitant with the Grand Master's prerogative of presiding in any Lodge, is that of visitation. This is not simply the right of visit, which every Master Mason in good standing possesses, but it is a prerogative of a more important nature, and which has received the distinctive appellation of the *right of visitation*. It is the right to enter any Lodge, to inspect its proceedings, to take a part in its business transactions, and to correct its errors. The right is specifically recognized in the Regulations of 1721, but it is also an inherent prerogative; for the Grand Master is, *virtute officii,* the head of the whole fraternity, and is not only entitled, but bound, in the faithful discharge of his duty, to superintend the transactions of the craft, and to interfere in all congregations of Masons to prevent the commission of wrong, and to see that the Landmarks and usages of antiquity, and the Constitutions and laws of the Grand Lodge, and of every Lodge in the jurisdiction, are preserved and obeyed. The Regulations of 1721 prescribe that when the Grand Master makes such a visitation, the Grand Wardens are to attend him, and act as Wardens of the Lodge while he presides. This Regulation, however, rather refers to the rights of the Grand Wardens than to the prerogative of the Grand Master, whose right to make an official visitation to any Lodge is an inherent one, not to be limited or directed by any comparatively modern Regulation.

993—Has a Mason the right to visit any Lodge where he may happen to be?

Visit, Right of. While the right of a Mason to visit any lodge, where he may happen to be, is generally conceded, various regulations, limiting this right, have been made at different times, and in divers jurisdictions, concerning the propriety and necessity of which intelligent Masons entertain quite different opinions. By the most ancient charges it is ordered, "That every Mason receive and cherish strange fellowes when they come over the countrie, and sett them on worke if they will worke, as the manner is; that is to say, if the Mason have any mould-stone in his place, he shall give him a mould-stone, and sett him on worke; and if he have none, the Mason shall refresh him with money unto the next lodge." This regulation recognizes the right of a *traveling* brother as absolute. But, as early as 1663, it was ordered by a General Assembly held on the 27th of December of that year, "That no person hereafter, who shall be accepted a Freemason, shall be admitted into any lodge or assembly, until he has brought a certificate of the time and place of his acceptation, from the lodge that accepted him, unto the Master of that limit or division where such a lodge is kept." In 1772, the Grand Lodge of England renewed this statute, and some Grand Lodges in this country have adopted it. Of course, no stranger can be admitted to a lodge without "due trial and examination," or unless he is vouched for by a known brother present. The Grand Lodge of England also has the following regulation, which has been adopted in many other jurisdictions: "A brother who is not a subscribing member to some lodge shall not be permitted to visit any one lodge in the town or place where he resides, more than once during his secession from the Craft." The object of the above rule is to exclude all drones from the hive of Masonry. Whoever partakes of the advantages of Freemasonry should contribute something to its support.

994—Does the Master of a Lodge have the right to cast more than one vote?

Vote of Master. The Master has one vote in all questions, as every other member, and, in addition, a casting vote, if there be a tie. This usage, which is very general, owes its existence, in all probability, to the fact that a similar privilege is, by the Regulations of 1721, enjoyed by the Grand Master in the Grand Lodge. I cannot, however, find a written sanction for the usage in any of the Ancient Constitutions, and am not prepared to say that the Master possesses it by inherent right. The local regulations of some jurisdictions explicitly recognize the prerogative, while others are silent on the subject. I know of none that denies it in express words. I am disposed to believe that it has the authority of ancient usage, and confess that I am partial to it, on mere grounds of expediency, while the analogy of the Grand Master's similar prerogative gives it a show of authority.

995—Why is every member present required to vote when the ballot is taken?

Voting on a Ballot. From the fact that the vote which is given on the ballot for a candidate must be one in which the unanimous consent of all present is to be given, it follows that all the members then present are under an obligation to vote. From the discharge of this duty no one can be permitted to shrink. And, therefore, in balloting on a petition, every member, as his name is called, is bound to come forward and deposit either a white or a black ball. No one can be exempted from the performance of this responsible act, except by the unanimous consent of the Lodge; for, if a single member were allowed to decline voting, it is evident that the candidate, being then admitted by the affirmative votes of the others, such admission would, nevertheless, not be in compliance with the words and spirit of the law. The "unanimous consent of all the members of the Lodge then present" would not have been given—one, at least, having withheld that consent by the non-user of his prerogative.

996—Under what circumstances is a voucher demanded?

Vouch. The term vouch means to bear witness, or give testimony, and a voucher accordingly is a witness. When a person applies for admission to the Masonic society, his application should bear the signatures of two brethren, one of whom is called the voucher, because he thus testifies that the petitioner possesses the required qualifications. So a stranger can visit a lodge without trial or examination, if a brother present *knows* him to be a Mason and vouches for him.

997—Has an Entered Apprentice or Fellowcraft the right of vouching for a visitor?

Vouching for Strangers. An examination may sometimes be dispensed with, when a Brother who is present, and acquainted with the visitor, is able and willing to vouch for him as a Master Mason in good standing. This prerogative, of vouching for a stranger, is strictly one of the rights of a Master Mason, because neither Entered Apprentices nor Fellowcrafts are permitted to exercise it, in reference to those who have attained to their respective degrees. But the right is one of so important a nature—its imprudent exercise would be attended with such evil consequences to the institution—that Grand Lodges have found it necessary to restrict it by the most rigid rules. The Grand Lodges of Iowa and Mississippi, for instance, have declared that no visitor can be permitted to take his seat in a Lodge, on the strength of being vouched for by a Brother, unless that Brother has sat in a Lodge with him.

998—What are the wages of a Mason?

Wages of a Mason. The operative Mason, in ancient times, received, as compensation for his labor, corn, wine and oil—the products of the earth—or whatever would contribute to his physical comfort and support. His labor being material, his wages were outward and material. The Free and Accepted Mason, on the other hand, performs a moral work, and hence his reward is interior and spiritual. The enlightened brother finds his reward in the grand and gratifying results of his studies, and in the joyful fruits of his Masonic deeds. He sees the glory of the Divinity permeating all worlds, and all parts of the universe reveal to his soul celestial meanings. All nature overflows with beauty, love, melody and song, and unspeakably rich are the delights he derives from communion with her spirit. If he be a child of fortune, and raised above the necessity of labor, he finds the purest pleasure in practice of charity and the exercise of benevolence; for charity, like mercy, brings its own recompense.

"It droppeth, as the gentle rain from heaven,
Upon the place beneath: it is twice bless'd;
It blesseth him that gives, and him that takes."

If, like our ancient brethren, he is a laborer, his wages are still ample and enduring. Thus, while the ignorant man toils on, drearily cheered by no bright and living thoughts, his mind destitute of all ideas, and his heart moved by no glad inspiration, the Masonic laborer welcomes his toil with joy, because Freemasonry has taught him that labor is a divine vocation, *"Labourare est orare."* He goes forth in the morning, and the world on which he looks, swimming in sunbeams, and glittering with dewy diamonds, is less bright and fair than the world that lays in his heart, and which science has illuminated with her everlasting light. The mountains, barren, rocky and storm-blackened, or crowned with sylvan splendors; the valleys, flower-robed and ribboned with meandering streams; the rivers, hastening to the sea, and making music as they go; the trees, and rocks, and flowers; all the activities of nature, and the great enterprises of man, speak with eloquence to his soul, and reveal to his enlightened spirit the glad secrets of Nature and of Nature's God. These noble, ample and enduring enjoyments are the wages of the true Mason.

999—What is the origin of the office of Wardens?

Wardens. Every Lodge has two officers, who are distinguished as the Senior and Junior Wardens. The word is derived from the Saxon *weardian,* "to guard or watch," and signifies therefore a guardian or watchman. The French and German titles for the same officers, which are *surveillant* in the former language, and *aufseher* in the latter, are equally significant, as they denote an *overseer.* The title is derived from the fact that in the old rituals these officers were supposed to sit at the two columns of the porch, and *oversee* or *watch* the Fellow Crafts and Apprentices—the Senior Warden overlooking the former, and the Junior

Warden the latter. This ritual is still observed in the Lodges of the French rite, where the two Wardens sit in the west, at what is supposed to be the pedestals of the two columns of the porch of the temple; and in the York rite, although the allusion is somewhat impaired by the removal of the Junior Warden to the south, they still retain on their pedestals miniature columns, the representatives of the temple pillars, and which in all processions they carry as the insignia of their office.

1000—What was the origin of Masonic warrants?

Warrant. In former times a lodge formed itself without any ceremony, wherever a sufficient number of brethren dwelt to form a lodge, or one of the neighboring lodges formed it for them. But in 1722 the Grand Lodge in London determined that every new lodge in England should have a patent, and since that time all those brethren who wish to form a new lodge, strive to obtain a warrant from the Grand Lodge. The new lodge then joins the Grand Lodge as a daughter lodge, binds itself to work according to its system, and to keep within the ancient landmarks. Then is such a lodge called just, perfect, and regular.

1001—What is the distinction between a dispensation and a warrant?

Warrant of Constitution, Granting of. The most important prerogative that a Grand Lodge can exercise in its legislative capacity is that of granting warrants of constitution for the establishment of subordinate Lodges. Important, however, as is this prerogative, it is not an inherent one, possessed by the Grand Lodge from time immemorial, but is the result of a concession granted by the Lodges in the year 1717; for formerly, as I have already shown, all Masons enjoyed the right of meeting in Lodges without the necessity of a warrant, and it was not until the re-organization of the Grand Lodge, in the beginning of the last century, that this right was surrendered. Preston gives the important Regulations which was adopted in 1717, in which it is declared that warrants must be granted by the Grand Master, "with the consent and approbation of the Grand Lodge in communication." Anderson does not give this Regulation, nor will anything be found in the Regulations which were approved in 1721, respecting the necessity of the consent and approbation of the Grand Lodge. On the contrary, the whole tenor of those Regulations appears to vest the right of granting warrants in the Grand Lodge exclusively, and the modern Constitutions of the Grand Lodge of England are to the same effect. But in this country it has been the universal usage to restrict the power of the Grand Master to the granting of temporary dispensations, while the prerogative of granting permanent warrants is exclusively vested in the Grand Lodge.

1002—What rights has a Lodge with respect to its warrant of constitution?

Warrant of Constitution, Nature of. A Lodge under dispensation can be cancelled by the revocation of the dispensation by either the

Grand Master or the Grand Lodge, in which event the Lodge would cease to exist; but a Lodge under dispensation may terminate its existence in a more favorable way, by being changed into a Lodge working under a warrant of constitution.

At the communication of the Grand Lodge, which takes place next after the granting of the dispensation by the Grand Master, that officer states the fact to the Grand Lodge, of his having granted such an authority, when a vote being taken on the question whether the dispensation shall or shall not be confirmed, if a majority are in favor of the confirmation, the Grand Secretary is directed to issue a warrant of constitution.

This instrument differs from a dispensation in many important particulars. A dispensation emanates from a Grand Master; a warrant from a Grand Lodge. The one is temporary and definite in its duration; the other permanent and indefinite. The one is revocable at pleasure by the Grand Master; the other, only upon cause shown by the Grand Lodge. The one confers only a name; the other, a number upon the Lodge. The one restricts the authority it bestows to the making of Masons; the other extends that authority to the installation of officers and the succession in office. The one contains within itself no power of self-perpetuation; the other does. From these differences in the two documents arise important peculiarities in the prerogatives of the two bodies which are respectively organized under their authority.

1003—What is the prerogative of Grand Lodges with respect to issuing warrants of constitution?

Warrant of Constitution, Right to. A Lodge has the right to retain possession of its warrant of constitution. In this respect we see at once a manifest difference between a warranted Lodge and one working under dispensation. The latter derives its authority from the Grand Master, and the dispensation, which is the instrument by which that authority is delegated, may at any time be revoked by the officer from whom it emanated. In such an event there is no mode of redress provided by law. The dispensation is the voluntary act of the Grand Master, is granted *ex gratia,* and may be withdrawn by the same act of will which first prompted the grant. There can be no appeal from such an act of revocation, nor can any Masonic tribunal require that the Grand Master should show cause for this exertion of his prerogative.

But the warrant having been granted by the Grand Lodge, the body of Masons thus constituted form at once a constituent part of the Grand Lodge. They acquire permanent rights which cannot be violated by any assumption of authority, nor abrogated except in due course of Masonic law. The Grand Master may, in the conscientious discharge of his duty, suspend the work of a chartered Lodge, when he believes that that suspension is necessary for the good of the Order; but he cannot recall or revoke the warrant. From that suspension of work there is of course an appeal to the Grand Lodge, and that body alone can, on cause shown, and after due and legal investigation, withdraw or revoke the warrant.

1004—Of what is the weeping virgin emblematic?

Weeping Virgin. The weeping virgin with dishevelled hair, in the monument of the third degree, used in the American Rite, is interpreted as a symbol of grief for the unfinished state of the Temple. Jeremy Cross, who is said to have fabricated the monumental symbol, was not, we are satisfied, acquainted with hermetic science. Yet a woman thus portrayed, standing near a tomb, was a very appropriate symbol for the third degree, whose dogma is the resurrection. In hermetic science, according to Nicholas Flammel, a woman having her hair dishevelled and standing near a tomb is a symbol of the soul.

1005—What formula is used by the Grand Master at the laying of a cornerstone?

Well Formed, True and Trusty. A formula used by the Grand Master at the laying of a cornerstone. Having applied the square, level and plumb to its different surfaces and angles, he declares it to be "well formed, true and trusty." Borrowing from the technical language of Operative Masonry, it is symbolically applied in reference to the character which the Entered Apprentice should sustain when, in the course of his initiation, he assumes the place of a typical cornerstone in the Lodge.

1006—What is the symbolism of the West?

West. Where the sun closes its daily race, there the thanks of the inhabitants of the world follow it, and with the ensuing morning it again commences its benevolent course. Every brother draws near to the evening of his days; and well will it be with him if at the close of his labors he can look forward with hope for a good reward for his work.

1007—Of what is the color white emblematic?

White. This color has even been regarded as emblematic of purity and innocence. In the York rite the apron is always of this color, though the trimming varies in the symbolic and chapitral degrees. "Let thy garments be always WHITE," etc.

1008—What rules apply to the relief of Masonic widows and orphans?

Widows and Orphans. The wives and children of Masons, while claiming relief through the right of their husbands and fathers, are subject to the same principles and restrictions as those which govern the application of Masons themselves. The destitute widow or orphans of a deceased Mason have a claim for relief upon the whole fraternity, which is to be measured by the same standard that would be applied if the Brother himself were alive, and asking for assistance.

1009—Under what circumstances does the widow of a Mason forfeit her claim to Masonic relief?

Widows of Masons. The Committee on Foreign Correspondence of the Grand Lodge of New York, in 1851, announced the doctrine that the widow of a Mason does not forfeit her right to claim relief, although she may have married a second time. I regret that I cannot concur in this too liberal view. It appears to me that the widow of a Mason derives her claim to Masonic relief from the fact of her widowhood only, and therefore, that when she abandons that widowhood, she forfeits her claim. On her second marriage, her relations to the Order are obliterated as completely as are her relations to him whose name she has abandoned for that of another. If her new husband is not a Mason, I cannot see upon what ground she could rest her claim to Masonic protection; not as the wife of her second husband, for that would give no foundation for such a claim—not certainly as the widow of the first, for she is no longer a widow.

1010—Who was called the widow's son, and why?

Widow's Son. Hiram, the architect, is described in two places of Scripture; in the first he is called a widow's son, of the tribe of Naphtali, and in the other is called the son of a woman of the daughters of Dan; but in both that his father was a man of Tyre; that is, she was of the daughters of the city of Dan, in the tribe of Naphtali, and is called a widow of Naphtali, as her husband was a Naphtalite; for he is not called a Tyrian by descent, but a man of Tyre by habitation.

1011—Of what is the winding staircase emblematic?

Winding Staircase. When the Fellowcrafts went to receive their wages, they ascended a winding staircase, the steps of which, like all the Masonic symbols, are illustrative of discipline and doctrine, as well as of natural, mathematical, and metaphysical science, and open to us an extensive range of moral and speculative inquiry. In their delineation, the steps, which count odd numbers, should be more particularly marked as one, three, five, seven, eleven; and in ascending them the Fellowcraft should pause on each alternate step, and consider the several stages of his progress, as well as the important lessons which are there inculcated.

1012—What is the legend of the winding stairs?

Winding Stairs, Legend of the. In an investigation of the symbolism of the winding stairs, we shall be directed to the true explanation by a reference to their origin, their number, the objects which they recall, and their termination, but above all by a consideration of the great design which an ascent upon them was intended to accomplish.

The steps of this winding staircase commenced, we are informed, at the porch of the Temple; that is to say, at its very entrance. But nothing is more undoubted in the science of Masonic symbolism than that the Temple was the representative of the world purified by the Shekinah, or Divine Presence. The world of the profane is without the Temple, the world of the initiated is within its sacred walls. Hence to enter the Temple, to pass within the porch, to be made a Mason, and to be born into the world of Masonic light, are all synonymous and convertible terms. Here, then, the symbolism of the winding stairs. begins.

The Apprentice, having entered within the porch of the Temple, has begun his Masonic life. But the first degree in Masonry, like the lesser mysteries of the ancient systems of initiation, is only a preparation and purification for something higher. The Entered Apprentice is the child in Masonry. The lessons which he receives are simply intended to cleanse the heart and prepare the recipient for that mental illumination which is to be given in the succeeding degrees.

As a Fellowcraft, he has advanced another step, and as the degree is emblematic of youth, so it is here that the intellectual education of the candidate begins. And therefore, here, at the very spot which separates the porch from the sanctuary, where childhood ends and manhood begins, he finds stretching out before him a winding stair which invites him as it were, to ascend, and which, as the symbol of discipline and instruction, teaches him that here must commence his Masonic labor—here he must enter upon those glorious though difficult researches the end of which is to be the possession of divine truth. The winding stairs begin after the candidate has passed within the porch and between the pillars of strength and establishment, as a significant symbol to teach him that as soon as he has passed beyond the years of irrational childhood, and commenced his entrance upon manly life, the laborious task of self-improvement is the first duty that is placed before him. He cannot stand still, if he would be worthy of his vocation; his destiny as an immortal being requires him to ascend, step by step, until he has reached the summit, where the treasures of knowledge await him.

The number of these steps in all the systems has been odd. Vitruvious remarks—and the coincidence is at least curious—that the ancient temples were always ascended by an odd number of steps; and he assigns as the reason, that, commencing with the right foot at the bottom, the worshipper would find the same foot foremost when he entered the temple, which was considered as a fortunate omen. But the fact is, that the symbolism of numbers was borrowed by the Masons from Pythagoras, in whose system of philosophy it plays an important part, and in which odd numbers were considered as more perfect than even ones. Hence, throughout the Masonic system we find a predominance of odd numbers; and while three, five, seven, nine, fifteen, and twenty-seven are all-important symbols, we seldom find a reference to two, four, six, eight or ten. The odd number of the stairs was therefore intended to symbolize the idea of perfection, to which it was the object of the aspirant to attain.

As to the particular number of the stairs, this has varied at different periods. Tracing-boards of the last century have been found, in which only *five* steps are delineated, and others in which they amount to *seven*. The Prestonian lectures, used in England in the beginning of this century, gave the whole number as thirty-eight, dividing them into series of one, three, five, seven, nine and eleven. The error of making an even number, which was a violation of the Pythagorean principle of odd numbers as the symbol of perfection, was corrected in the Hemming lectures, adopted at the union of the two Grand Lodges of England, by striking out the eleven, which was also objectionable as receiving a sectarian explanation. In this country the number was still further reduced to *fifteen*, divided into three series of *three, five*, and *seven*. I shall adopt this American division in explaining the symbolism; although, after all, the particular number of the steps, of the peculiar method of their division into series, will not in any way affect the general symbolism of the whole legend.

The candidate, then, in the second degree of Masonry, represents a man starting forth on the journey of life, with the great task before him of self-improvement. For the faithful performance of this task, a reward is promised, which reward consists in the development of all his intellectual faculties, the moral and spiritual elevation of his character, and the acquisition of truth and knowledge. Now, the attainment of this moral and intellectual condition supposes an elevation of character, an ascent from a lower to a higher life, and a passage of toil and difficulty, through rudimentary instruction, to the full fruition of wisdom. This is therefore beautifully symbolized by the winding stairs, at whose foot the aspirant stands ready to climb the toilsome steep, while at its top is placed "that hieroglyphic bright which none but Craftsmen ever saw," as the emblem of divine truth. And hence a distinguished writer has said that "these steps, like all the Masonic symbols, are illustrative of discipline and doctrine, as well as of natural, mathematical and metaphysical science, and open to us an extensive range of moral and speculative inquiry."

The candidate, incited by the love of virtue and the desire of knowledge, and withal eager for the reward of truth which is set before him, begins at once the toilsome ascent. At each division he pauses to gather instruction from the symbolism which these divisions present to his attention.

At the first pause which he makes he is instructed in the peculiar organization of the order of which he has become a disciple. But the information here given, if taken in its naked, literal sense, is barren, and unworthy of his labor. The rank of the officers who govern, and the names of the degrees which constitute the Institution, can give him no knowledge which he has not before possessed. We must look therefore to the symbolic meaning of these allusions for any value which may be attached to this part of the ceremony.

The reference to the organization of the Masonic institution is intended to remind the aspirant of the union of men in society, and the development of the social state out of the state of nature. He is thus reminded, in the very outset of his journey, of the blessings which arise from civilization and of the fruits of virtue and knowledge which are derived from that condition. Masonry itself is the result of civilization; while, in grateful return, it has been one of the most important means of extending that condition of mankind.

All the monuments of antiquity that the ravages of time have left combine to prove that man had no sooner emerged from the savage into the social state, than he commenced the organization of religious mysteries, and the separation, by a sort of divine instinct, of the sacred from the profane. Then came the invention of architecture as a means of providing convenient dwellings and necessary shelter from the inclemencies and vicissitudes of the seasons, with all the mechanical arts connected with it; and lastly, geometry, as a necessary science to enable the cultivators of land to measure and designate the limits of their possessions. All these are claimed as peculiar characteristics of Speculative Masonry, which may be considered as the type of civilization, the former bearing the same relation to the profane world as the latter does to the savage state. Hence we at once see the fitness of the symbolism which commences the aspirant's upward progress in the cultivation of knowledge and the search after truth, by recalling to his mind the condition of civilization and the social union of mankind as necessary preparations for the attainment of these objects. In the allusions to the officers of a lodge, and the degrees of Masonry as explanatory of the organization of our own society, we clothe in our symbolic language the history of the organization of society.

Advancing in his progress, the candidate is invited to contemplate another series of instructions. The human senses, as the appropriate channels through which we receive all our ideas of perception, and which, therefore, constitute the most important sources of our knowledge, are here referred to as a symbol of intellectual cultivation. Architecture, as the most important of the arts which conduce to the comfort of mankind, is also alluded to here, not simply because it is so closely connected with the operative institution of Masonry, but also as the type of all the other useful arts. In his second pause, in the ascent of the winding stairs, the aspirant is therefore reminded of the necessity of cultivating practical knowledge.

So far, then, the instructions he has received relate to his own condition in society as a member of the great social compact, and to his means of becoming, by a knowledge of the arts of practical life, a necessary and useful member of that society.

But his motto will be, "Excelsior." Still must he go onward and forward. The stair is still before him; its summit is not yet reached, and still further treasures of wisdom are to be sought for, or the reward will not be gained, nor the *middle chamber,* the abiding-place of truth, be reached.

In his third pause, he therefore arrives at that point in which the whole circle of human science is to be explained. Symbols, we know, are in themselves arbitrary and of conventional signification, and the complete circle of human science might have been as well symbolized by any other sign or series of doctrines as by the seven liberal arts and sciences. But Masonry is an institution of the olden time; and this selection of the liberal arts and sciences as a symbol of the completion of human learning is one of the most pregnant evidences that we have of its antiquity.

In the seventh century, and for a long time afterwards, the circle of instruction to which all the learning of the most eminent schools and most distinguished philosophers was confined, was limited to what were then called the liberal arts and sciences, and consisted of two branches, the *trivium* and the *quadrivium.* The *trivium* included grammar, rhetoric and logic; the *quadrivium* comprehended arithmetic, geometry, music and astronomy.

"These seven heads," says Enfield, "were supposed to include universal knowledge. He who was master of these was thought to have no need of a preceptor to explain any books or to solve any questions which lay within the compass of human reason, the knowledge of *trivium* having furnished him with the key to all language, and that of the *quadrivium* having opened to him the secret laws of nature."

At a period, says the same writer, when few were instructed in the *trivium,* and very few studied the *quadrivium,* to be master of both was sufficient to complete the character of a philosopher. The propriety, therefore, of adopting the seven liberal arts and sciences as a symbol of the completion of human learning is apparent. The candidate, having reached this point, is now supposed to have accomplished the task upon which he had entered—he has reached the last step, and is now ready to receive the full fruition of human learning.

So far, then, we are able to comprehend the true symbolism of the winding stairs. They represent the progress of an inquiring mind, with the toils and labors, of intellectual cultivation and study, and the preparatory acquisition of all human science, as a preliminary step to the attainment of divine truth, which, it must be remembered, is always symbolized in Masonry by the WORD.

Here let me again allude to the symbolism of numbers, which is for the first time presented to the consideration of the Masonic student in the legend of the winding stairs. The theory of numbers as the symbols of certain qualities was originally borrowed by the Masons from the school of Pythagoras. It will be impossible, however, to develop this doctrine, in its entire extent, in the present article, for the numeral symbolism of Masonry would itself constitute materials for an ample essay. It will be sufficient to advert to the fact that the total number of the steps, amounting in all to *fifteen* in the American system, is a significant symbol. For *fifteen* was a sacred number among the Orientals, because the letters of the holy name JAH, were, in their numerical value, equivalent to fifteen; and hence a figure in which the nine digits were so disposed as to make fifteen either way when added together perpendicularly, horizontally, or diagonally, constituted one of their most sacred talismans. The fifteen steps in the winding stairs are therefore symbolic of the name of God.

But we are not yet done. It will be remembered that a reward was promised for all this toilsome ascent of the winding stairs. Now, what are the wages of a Speculative Mason? Not money, nor corn, nor wine, nor oil. All these are but symbols. His wages are Truth, or that approximation to it which will be most appropriate to the degree into which he has been initiated. It is one of the most beautiful, but at the same time abstruse, doctrines of the science of Masonic symbolism that the Mason is ever to be in search of truth, but is never to find it. This divine truth, the object of all his labors, is symbolized by the Word, for which we all know he can only obtain a *substitute;* and this is intended to teach the humiliating but necessary lesson that the knowledge of the nature of God and of man's relation to him, which knowledge constitutes divine truth, can never be acquired in this life. It is only when the portals of the grave open to us, and give us an entrance into a more perfect life, that this knowledge is to be attained. "Happy is the man," says the father of lyric poetry, "who descends beneath the hollow earth, having beheld these mysteries; he knows the end, he knows the origin of life."

The middle chamber is therefore symbolic of this life, where the symbol only of the Word can be given, where the truth is to be reached by approximation only, and yet where we are to learn that that truth will consist in a perfect knowledge of the G. A. O. T. U. This is the reward of the inquiring Mason; in this consist the wages of a Fellowcraft; he is directed to the truth, but must travel farther and ascend still higher to attain it.

It is, then, as a symbol, and a symbol only, that we must study this beautiful legend of the winding stairs. If we attempt to adopt it as a historical fact, the absurdity of its details stares us in the face, and wise men wonder at our credulity. Its inventors had no desire thus to impose upon our folly; but offering it to us as a great philosophical myth, they did not for a moment suppose that we would pass over its sublime moral teachings to accept the allegory as a historical narrative without meaning, and wholly irreconciliable with the records of Scripture, and opposed by all the principles of probability. To suppose that eighty thousand craftsmen were weekly paid in the narrow precincts of the Temple chambers, is simply to suppose an absurdity. But to believe that all this pictorial representation of an ascent by a winding staircase to the place where the wages of labor were to be received was an allegory to teach us the ascent of the mind from ignorance, through all the toils of study and the difficulties of obtaining knowledge, receiving here a little and there a little, adding something to the stock of our ideas at each step, until in the middle chamber of life—in the full fruition of manhood—the reward is attained, and the purified and elevated intellect is invested with the reward in the direction how to seek God and God's truth; to believe this, is to believe and to know the true design of Speculative Masonry, the only design which makes it worthy of a good or a wise man's study.

Its historical details are barren, but its symbols and allegories are fertile with instruction.

1013—How can a Mason acquire wisdom?

Wisdom. Those alone are wise who exercise the powers of the mind in secrecy, and who, without any selfish object, endeavor to promote the universal happiness of mankind, neither fortune nor misfortune are able to drive from a calm and steady progress through life. To possess Masonic wisdom it is not necessary to be very learned, or to have a most penetrating genius; the man of good plain common sense may be more Masonically wise than the most learned man in existence. It is not the act of a wise man to make a great profession of wisdom; and the secrets of our lodges ought to teach us how to exercise our Masonic wisdom.

1014—Is it lawful for a member to demit without making application for membership in another Lodge?

Withdrawal from Membership. The only question of Masonic jurisprudence on this subject which has given rise to any discussion is, whether a member can demit from a Lodge for the distinct purpose of severing all active connection with the Order, and becoming an unaffiliated Mason. And it may be observed, that it is only within a few years that the right to do even this has been denied.

The Grand Lodge of Connecticut, in 1853, decided "that no Lodge should grant a demit to any of its members, except for the purpose of joining some other Lodge; and that no member shall be considered as having withdrawn from one Lodge until he has actually become a member of another."

The Grand Lodge of Texas, governed by a similar view of the subject, has declared that it does not recognize the right of a Mason to demit or separate himself from the Lodge in which he was made or may afterwards be admitted, except for the purpose of joining another Lodge, or when he may be about to remove without the jurisdiction of the Lodge of which he is a member.

I regret that I cannot concur in the correctness, in point of law, of these decisions and others of a similar import that have been made by some other Grand Lodges. Of course it is admitted that there is no Masonic duty more explicitly taught in the ancient Constitutions than that which requires every Mason to be a member of some Lodge. But I cannot deny to any man the right of withdrawing, whenever he pleases, from a voluntary association. The laws of the land would not sustain the Masonic authorities in the enforcement of such a regulation, and our own self-respect, if there were no other motive, should prevent us from attempting it.

Freemasonry is, in all respects, a voluntary association, and as no one is expected or permitted to enter within its folds unless it be of his "own free will and accord," so should his continuance in it be through an exercise of the same voluntary disposition. These are the views which were entertained by a committee whose report was adopted in 1854 by the Grand Lodge of Ohio, and which they have expressed in the following language:

"We recognize fully the doctrine laid down in the ancient Constitutions, 'that it is the duty of every Mason to belong to some regular Lodge.' But as his entrance into the fraternity is of his own free will and accord, so should be the performance of this and every other Masonic duty. When, from whatever cause, he desires to withdraw his membership from the Lodge, it is his undoubted right to ask, and the duty of the Lodge, if there be no objection to his moral standing, to grant him an honorable discharge."

This, then, appears to me to be the state of the law on this subject; a Mason, being in good standing, has a right to claim a demit from his Lodge, and the Lodge cannot withhold it. But a demit from a Lodge, as it severs the relation of the demitting member to his Lodge, and releases him from the obligation to pay dues, deprives him also of certain privileges with which his membership had invested him. These, however, will become the subject of consideration when we treat of unaffiliated Masons, in which class a demit necessarily places the individual who receives it.

Although, as I have already said, there is no law in any of the ancient Constitutions which forbids the granting of demits to individual Masons, yet the whole spirit of the institution is opposed to such a system. To ask for a demit, without the intention to unite with another Lodge, is an act which no Mason can commit without violating the obligations which he owes to the Order. It is an abandonment of his colors, and although we have no power to prevent his desertion, yet we can visit his unfaithfulness with moral condemnation.

1015—Under what circumstances is it lawful for a number of members to withdraw at the same time from a Lodge?

Withdrawal of Members to Form a New Lodge. When several brethren at one time apply for demits, the regulation prescribes that these demits shall be granted only where the Lodge is already too numerous, and the intention of the demitting brethren is to form a new Lodge, they have a dispensation for that purpose from the Grand Master, or at once to unite themselves with another Lodge. The withdrawal of many members at one time from a small Lodge would manifestly tend to its injury, and perhaps cause its dissolution; and when this is done without the intention of those who have withdrawn to unite with any other Lodge, it is to be presumed that the act has been the result of pique or anger, and should not, therefore, be encouraged by the law.

Still, however, we are again met with the difficulty which opposes us in the consideration of an application for a single demit. How is the law to be enforced? The Regulation of 1721 simply declares that "no set or number of brethren shall withdraw or separate themselves from the Lodge," but it affixes no penalty for the violation of the regulation, and if a number of brethren should desire to withdraw I know of no power in the Masonic institution which can prevent them from exercising that right. It is true, that if an unmasonic feeling of anger or pique is plainly exhibited, so that a charge can be predicated on it, the demits may be withheld until the charge is disproved. But unless such charge is made, the demits must be granted.

1016—Is it permissable to withdraw a petition after it has been read?

Withdrawal of Petition. A petition having been once read cannot be withdrawn. It must go through the ordeal of investigation and ballot. This, too, is a regulation derived from constant and universal usage, rather than from an expressed statutory provision. The Ancient Constitutions say nothing on the subject; but so general has been the custom that it may now be considered as having the force of an unwritten law. Many Grand Lodges have, in fact, adopted it as a specific regulation, and in others, the practice is pursued, as it were, by tacit consent. Besides, the analogy of our speculative institution to an operative art gives sanction to the usage. The candidate for Masonry has always been considered, symbolically, as material brought up for the building of the temple. This material must be rejected or accepted. It cannot be carried elsewhere for further inspection. The Lodge to which it is first brought must decide upon its fitness. To withdraw the petition would be to prevent the Lodge from making that decision, and therefore no petition for initiation, having been once read, can be withdrawn; it must go through the necessary forms.

1017—What regulations govern the right of a Lodge to do the work of Ancient Craft Masonry?

Work of Ancient Craft Masonry. A Lodge has the right to do all the work of ancient craft Masonry. This is the principal object for which the Lodge was constituted. Formerly, Lodges were empowered to exalt their candidates to the Royal Arch degree, but since the beginning of this century this power has been transferred in this country to Chapters, and a Lodge is now only authorized to confer the three degrees of symbolic Masonry, and also, at the time of installation, to invest its Master with the degree or order of Past Master. But this power to do the work of Masonry is restricted and controlled by certain very important regulations.

The candidate upon whom the Lodge is about to confer any of the degrees of ancient craft Masonry must apply by petition, duly recommended; for no Lodge has the right to intrude the secrets of the institution upon any person who has expressed no anxiety to receive them.

The candidate must be possessed of the proper qualifications.

His application must undergo a ballot, and he must be unanimously elected.

The Regulations of 1721 prescribe that a Lodge cannot confer the degrees on more than five candidates at one time, which last words have been interpreted to mean at the same communication. In the second and all subsequent editions of the Constitution, this law was modified by the qualification "without an urgent necessity;" and this seems to be the view now taken of it by the authorities of the Order, for it is held that it may be set aside by the dispensation of the Grand Master.

It seems also to be a very general regulation that no Lodge shall confer more than one degree on the same candidate at one communication, unless it be on urgent necessity, by the dispensation of the Grand Master. We find no such rule in the General Regulations of 1721, because there was no necessity at that time for it, as subordinate Lodges conferred only one degree, that of Entered Apprentice. But subsequently, when the usage was adopted of conferring all the degrees in the subordinate Lodges, it was found necessary, in this way, to restrain the too rapid advancement of candidates; and accordingly, in 1753, it was ordered that no Lodge shall "be permitted to make and raise the same brother at one and the same meeting, without a dispensation from the Grand Master." But as no such regulation is to be found in any of the written or unwritten laws previous to 1717, it can only have such authority as is derived from the local enactment of a Grand Lodge, or the usage in a particular jurisdiction. But the usage in this country always has been opposed to conferring more than one degree at the same communication, without a dispensation.

1018—Who may knock at the doors of Masonry?

Worldly Wealth. Masonry regards no man on account of his worldly wealth and honor. The poor as well as the rich may knock at the door of our temple, and gain admission. All are welcome if found worthy to receive light. This is strictly spiritual: "Seek, and ye shall find; ask, and ye shall receive; knock, and the door shall be opened unto you."

1019—What is the supreme duty of a Mason?

Worship of God. The highest duty of a Freemason is expressed by these words. The expression of veneration for the Supreme Being, of submission to his will, and of thankfulness for his goodness, though it may be offered in the secret stillness of the heart, will often be conveyed by external visible signs, through which the feelings of awe and love endeavor to manifest themselves in the most favorable and lively manner. These acts of homage to a superior power will be characterized by more or less of rudeness or elevation, as the conceptions of the object of worship are more or less gross or spiritual. Prayer or sacrifice, accompanied with various ceremonies, are the most general external acts by which the feelings of religious veneration are expressed; and while some nations and sects are eager to surround these acts with all the splendor of earthly pomp, others think to render them more worthy of the Being to whom they are addressed by reducing them to the simplest form. Freemasonry, through all its degrees, and in every part of its ritual, earnestly inculcates this duty of worship.

1020—What is the proper title of a Master of a Lodge, and why?

Worshipful Master. He who has attained the third degree in Freemasonry is a Master; and where they do not work in the so-called high degrees, has attained the summit of his profession. None but Fellowcrafts who have been found worthy can obtain this degree. As a Master Mason he has a voice in all the consultations of the officers of the lodge, and he may, if possessed of sufficient Masonic skill, be appointed to any office in the lodge, even that of Worshipful Master. This is the highest preferment a Mason can obtain in St. John's Masonry, through the three degrees of which every candidate for the Past Master's degree must have passed. If there are members in the lodge who have the higher degrees, they are generally elected Worshipful Master, but although it is by no means necessary to possess those degrees to enable a brother to be elected to the chair, it is absolutely necessary that he should be a man of good moral character, and extensive Masonic information; he is then elected by his brother Master Masons for one year. The greatest care and caution ought to be used by the brethren at this election to prevent the lodge being injured by the election of an improper person. He must also be well acquainted with the Order, its doctrines, its secrets, its history, and constitution, and must possess the power of communicating his own reflection upon all these subjects, in a clear, comprehensive form, to the brethren.

1021—What is the Masonic meaning of the word "worthy?"

Worthy. The applicant must be worthy. In the language of the Charge already quoted, he must be "a true and genuine Brother." The word *true* is here significant. It is the pure old Saxon *treawe,* which means faithful, and implies that he must be one who have been faithful to his duties, faithful to his trusts, faithful to his obligations. The bad man, and especially the bad Mason, is unfaithful to all these, and is not true. There is no obligation either in the written law, or the ritualistic observances of the Order, that requires a Mason to relieve such an unworthy applicant. By his infidelity to his promises, he brings discredit on the institution, and forfeits all his rights to relief. A suspended or expelled Mason, or one who, though neither, is yet of bad character and immoral conduct, cannot rightfully claim the assistance of a Mason, or a Lodge of Masons.

1022—Is it lawful to accept a letter of introduction as an avouchment?

Written Avouchment. No written avouchment, however distinguished may be the Mason who sends it, or however apparently respectable may be the person who brings it, is of any value in Masonry. Letters of introduction, in which light only such an avouchment can be considered, are liable to be forged or stolen; and it is not permitted to trust the valuable secrets of Masonry to contingencies of so probable a nature. Hence, whatever confidence we may be disposed to place in the statements of an epistle from a friend, so far as they respect the social position of the bearer, we are never to go further; but any declarations of Masonic character or standing are to be considered as valueless, unless confirmed by an examination.

1023—What is the basis of Masonic chronology?

Year of Masonry. The birth of Christ is commonly given to the autumn of the year 5 before Christ, which is an apparent anomaly, which may require a few words of explanation. The era of the birth of Christ was not in use until about 532 A.D., in the time of Justinian, when it was introduced by Dionysius Exiguus, a Scythian by birth, and a Roman abbot; and it only began to prevail in the West about the time of Charles Martel and Pope Gregory II., A.D. 730. It has long been agreed by all chronologers that Dionysius made a mistake in placing the birth of Christ some years too late; but the amount of the difference has been variously estimated at two, three, four, five, and even eight years. The general conclusion is that which is adopted in our Bibles, and which places the birth of Christ four years before the common era, or more probably a few months more. In Masonry we add 4000 up to the birth of Christ, and that sum constitutes the reputed year of Masonry.

1024—Upon what legend is based the old York Constitution of 926?

York Constitution of 926. The "Old York Constitutions" were so called from the city of York, where they were enacted, and sometimes the "Gothic Constitutions," from the fact that they were written in the old Gothic character. Of these constitutions, which are the oldest now extant, the history is given in a record written in the reign of Edward IV., the substance of which is copied by Anderson. According to this record, we learn that Prince Edwin, having been taught Masonry, obtained from his brother, King Athelstan, a free charter, "for the Masons having a correction among themselves (as it was anciently expressed), or a freedom and power to regulate themselves, to amend what might happen amiss, and to hold a yearly communication and general assembly.

"Accordingly, Prince Edwin summoned all the Masons in the realm to meet him in a congregation at York, who came and composed a General Lodge, of which he was Grand Master; and having brought with them all the writings and records extant, some in Greek, some in Latin, some in French and other languages, from the contents thereof that assembly did frame the Constitution and Charges of an English Lodge, made a law to preserve and observe the same in all time coming, and ordained good pay for the working Masons," &c.

The Constitutions thus framed at the city of York, in the year 926, were seen, approved and confirmed, as we are informed by Anderson, in the reign of Henry I., and were then recognized as the fundamental law of Masonry. The document containing them was lost for a long time, although, according to Oliver, copies are known to have been taken during the reign of Richard II.; at the revival of Masonry, however, in 1717, not a transcript was to be found. A copy was, however, discovered in 1838, by Mr. James Orchard Halliwell, in the British Museum, and published.

1025—Who was the builder of the second Temple?

Zerubbabel. The son of Salathiel, of the royal race of David. Cyrus committed to his care the sacred vessels of the temple, with which he returned to Jerusalem. He is always named first, as being the chief of the Jews that returned to their own country, where he laid the foundations of the second temple. When the Samaritans offered to assist in rebuilding the temple, Zerubbabel and the principal men of Judah refused them this honor, since Cyrus had granted his commission to the Jews only.

Form of Petition Used by Operative Masons, with Charges and Obligations

It will be of great interest to the craft to learn the ceremonies of conferring the degrees in the Operative Lodges, and to note their similarity to the ceremonies of the Speculative Lodges.

This information has been gathered from many sources but we are indebted to Bro. Geo. Thornburgh, Past Grand Master of Arkansas, for the complete forms of petitions, charges, etc.

The form of the petition to an Operative Lodge for apprenticeship was as follows:

"I, ..., being the son of a Free Man and ...... years of age, humbly crave to be made an apprentice to the Ancient and Honorable Craft. I am prompted by a favorable opinion preconceived of the fraternity, and I desire full knowledge to enable me to work at the trade. I promise that I will conform to all the ancient usages and established customs of the Order."

The candidate had to be proposed by one Mason, seconded by another and supported by five more. The application for apprenticeship was posted at the entrance of the quarry or workshop for fourteen days. On three occasions he must stand by his application, when the men are going to and from work, so that all may see him; and if anyone knows anything against him, it must be reported at the head office, and the matter investigated. If accepted, he had to appear on the appointed day—the sixth of the week—at high twelve, at the quarry or workshop. He applies at the door, and is admitted on giving the proper password, which had been given him. He is admitted within the entrance of the Lodge, usually a porch with double doors, and takes an oath not to reveal any part of the proceedings. This is sealed by his kissing the book. The candidate puts his fee on the lower ledge of a foot stone.

It may be interesting just at this point to describe briefly the Lodge room of the Operatives, as they are about to confer the first degree. There are three Masters. They sit in the west so that they face and can see the rising sun. The Junior Warden sits in the north so that he can see the sun at its meridian height, and the Senior Warden sits in the east so that he can see the setting sun. The altar is in the center of the Lodge; over it is suspended the letter G, and the Rough Ashlar stone is on its east side. There are three Deacons present, one for the Masters and one for each Warden.

Inside the porch the candidate is divested of all money and hoodwinked. Then three men come out of the Lodge, divest him of all his clothes, and dirty him with mud. The doctor then arrives and removes the hoodwink. He is told to "Wash and be clean." The bath is ready and the candidate bathes. Seven times does he dip. The doctor then examines him to see that he is sound in wind and limb and reports him "perfect in all his parts." Then he is elected by the "cleanhand" sign. He is clothed in a white cloak, whence the original symbol of white, signifying a candidate, is obtained, the word candidate meaning literally "I am white." The candidate is again hoodwinked, still clothed in the white cloak. He has also a blue cord looped around his neck, held by a man in front and a man behind, and a second blue cord around his center, held by a man on each side. The neck cord being longer than the center cord, the four men make a diamond, with the candidate in the center. This diamond had a reference to Operative Masonry, and the candidate and his four attendants make "five points," which has another reference to Operative methods.

The candidate now makes application at the inner door. The sword is held to his n. l. b. so as to draw blood. He is then admitted and led to the N. E. corner. Here he is questioned. What age are you? What is your character? What is your knowledge? Where have you been working? Have you been a member of any Guild or Company before? Do you swear you have never been expelled, discharged or "run away" from any work? In all cases of D. and D. I. W. D. you put y. t.? In El Shaddai is all my t. Right. Rise. The brothers in E., S., W., and N. will take notice that ——— is about to pass before them. He is asked if he sees anything. He replies No, and the hoodwink is slightly raised, so that by bending his head a little forward he is able to see his own feet and two or three feet in front of them. He is then cautioned to keep strictly to the rack or tesselated border, and is led once around it. He has put one foot in front of the other, toe to heel, and so on; it is called "end on work," or "work in line." The candidate has to make this perambulation once correctly without failure. From the N. E. corner he goes to the S. E., then to S. W., then to N. W. Then he comes to the Junior Warden, who bars his progress. On due report the bar is raised and the candidate proceeds. Then back to the N. E. corner and to Senior Warden, who bars progress again. On due report the bar is removed and then a strip of scarlet is laid down leading to the Rough Ashlar stone on the east side of the altar, so that the candidate shall not step on the squares of the Mosaic Pavement as he is led to the Ashlar stone. Here he kneels with both knees bare on the rough Ashlar stone, with the left hand S. T. H. B. T. R. R. T.

It is interesting to note that this is still preserved as a sign in the

Lodges under the Scotch Grand Lodge, as well as among the Operative Freemasons.

He then takes the following obligation:

"I, ..., do in the presence of El Shaddai and of this worshipful assembly of Freemasons, Rough Masons, Wallers, Slaters, Paviors, Plasterers and Bricklayers, promise and declare that I will not at any time hereafter, by any act or circumstance whatsoever, directly or indirectly, write, print, cut, mark, publish, discover, reveal or make known any part or parts of the trade secrets, privileges or councils of the Worshipful Fraternity or Fellowship of Freemasonry, which I may have known at any time, or at any time hereafter shall be made known unto me.

"The penalty for breaking this great oath shall be the loss of my life.

"That I shall be branded with the mark of the traitor and slain according to ancient customs by being throatalled. * * * SO THAT MY SOUL HAVE NO REST BY NIGHT OR DAY.

"Given under my hand and sealed with my lips.

"So help me El Shaddai and the holy contents of this book.

The form of these oaths explains the archaic form of the obligation in the Speculative Ritual. People of the Middle Ages believed the soul could not rest unless the body was properly buried, hence the craving was for Christian burial. It is really the remnant of a Pagan idea transmitted to Christian times. The ancient Romans believed that the soul of an unburied body could not pass the Styx for at least a hundred years.

There is no doubt that in ancient times it was contemplated that these penalties should be actually inflicted; indeed, at a time when physical mutilation such as amputation of a hand, and hanging, drawing and quartering were still in our statute books, there was nothing incongruous in such an oath. Papworth and Gould record that in 1099 a Bishop of Utrecht was slain for extracting the grand secret from the son of a Master Mason.

After taking the obligation the candidate is requested to seal it with his lips. As his lips are brought to the book, a large seal of soft wax is placed underneath them; his head is forcibly pushed downward so that an actual impression of his lips is taken by the wax, and his obligation is "sealed with his lips" actually and literally. When the obligation is finished the Master says to the Deacons, "Give light that he may place his hand to the bond." A pen is put in his hand, and he signs the bond, "Given under my hand and sealed with my lips."

The candidate is then assisted to rise with the words, "Rise, apprentice to the Craft of Freemasons."

He is then given the grip, which is the same as that of the Speculatives, only it must be "covered;" and the word is "Jabal." Then the charge is given as follows:

CHARGE TO THE APPRENTICE TO THE CRAFT OF FREEMASONS

1. You shall truly honor El Shaddai, and his holy church, the King, your Master, and Warden; you shall not absent yourself, but with the license of one or both of them from their service, by day or by night.

2. You shall not purloin or steal, or be privy or accessory to the purloining or stealing of the value of six pence from them or either of them.

3. You shall not commit adultery or fornication in the house of your Master, with his wife, daughter or maid.

4. You shall not disclose your Master's or Wardens' secrets or councils, which they have reported unto you, or what is to be concealed, spoken or done within the privities of their house, by them or either of them, or by any Freemason.

5. You shall not maintain any disobedient argument with your Master, Warden, or any Freemason.

6. You shall reverently behave yourself toward all Freemasons, using neither cards, dice or any other unlawful games, Christmas time excepted.

7. You shall not haunt or frequent any taverns or alehouses, or so much as to go inside any of them, except it be your Master's or your Wardens', with their or the one of their consents.

8. You shall not commit adultery or fornication in any man's house where you shall be at table or work.

9. You shall not marry, or contract yourself to any woman during your apprenticeship.

10. You shall not steal any man's goods, but especially your Master's or any of his fellow-Masons, nor suffer any to steal their goods, but shall hinder the felon if you can; and if you cannot, then you shall acquaint the Master and his fellows presently.

11. All these articles and charges, which I have now recited unto you, you shall well and truly observe, perform and keep to the best of your power and knowledge.

So help you El Shaddai and the true and holy contents of this book.

From this charge you will see that the Operative Freemasons require their apprentices to respect chastity of the womenkind of Freemasons. It is also noteworthy that the dame of the house where they hold a Lodge is protected, and she is also sworn not to lead any member of the Craft into sin.

The candidate is then actually presented with his working tools, which are the chisel, the small maul and the straight edge, and is invested with the apprentice's apron.

He is next taken to the N. E. cornerstone. Here he is asked by the foreman how he is going to live until he draws his first week's money. If he says he is poor, then his foreman takes him before the Masters in the chair and reports that he has no means of living. The Masters crave charity for him and a collection is taken on his behalf. (This is, doubtless, the origin of the deposit Speculative Freemasons ask of their candidate.) If, however, he says he has money or will live with his father, no collection is made. For seven years he remains an apprentice, being taught his trade. During this time he wears his blue neck cord as a sign that he is still bound as an apprentice.

This wearing a collar as a sign of bondage is a very old custom. In Anglo-Saxon and Norman days, serfs and bondsmen were accustomed to wear collars of metal securely riveted around their necks. (In many jurisdictions the blue collar is now worn and in some Lodges in Arkansas they are found. They are worn by the officers and the jewels are suspended from the lower end of them.)

At the end of the seven years the apprentice applies to be made free of his bond. The following application has to be posted up at the entrance of the stoneyard quarry or works.

"Application to the Superintendent of the Works of the Worshipful Society of Freemasons, Rough Masons, Wallers, Slaters, Plaisterers and Bricklayers.

"I, ..., having well and truly served an entered apprentice to the Craft of Freemasons for seven years, and being to the full age of twenty-one years, humbly crave to be made free of that bond, to enable me to be passed to the honorable degree of Fellow of the Craft of Freemason. I further promise and swear that if once admitted to the fellowship I will forever conform to the ancient charges, usages, and established customs of the Fraternity, as Fellows have done in all ages."

The applicant has to go and kneel on the same Ashlar he was bound seven years before. The bond is torn up, the blue cord is removed from his neck.

"Rise, free brother; you are now superior to an apprentice, but inferior to a Fellow of the Craft of Freemasons."

He is then given the pass grip and pass word leading from the first to the second degree. Both are the same as the Speculatives. * * * There again the grip must be "covered." He then takes a formal farewell of the apprentices, and for the future he must associate with the Fellows.

Before the candidate can be accepted as suitable to be passed to the second degree he has to prepare a rough dressed Ashlar stone as a specimen of his work. A rough dressed Ashlar stone is the Ashlar as it is prepared in the first degree or apprentice yard for the more expert workman. It is dressed one-sixteenth of an inch too large all over; and this stone has to be prepared by the candidate and passed by the Inspector of Material before the free brother can be passed as a Fellow of the Craft.

When the candidate goes into the second degree Lodge to be made a Fellow of the Craft, he must have this specimen of his work with him. He must swear it is all his own work. "No man hath used a tool upon it." (Here is a hint at the Mark degree.)

At the appointed time, again at 12 noon on a Friday, he goes to the door of the second degree yard and knocks. On giving the pass grip and pass word he is admitted. The Master gives notice, "The Fellows in the E., S., W., and N., will take notice that Brother .... is about to pass in view before them to show that he is a candidate properly prepared to be made a Fellow of the Craft of Freemasons." He is then led around the candidate's track twice. This time his right foot is put transversely across the axis of the Lodge and then his left foot parallel to the axis of the Lodge. This is "header and stretcher" work, or "one and one," the Operatives call it. He is then led to the altar, where, kneeling on a rough dressed Ashlar stone, on both knees bare, he takes the obligation, as follows:

"I, ..., do in the presence of El Shaddai and of this worshipful assembly of Fellows of the Craft of Free Masons, Rough Masons, Wallers, Paviors, Plaisterers and Bricklayers here present, promise and declare that I will not at any time hereafter, by any act or circumstance, whatsoever, directly or indirectly, publish, discover, reveal or make known any of the secrets, privities or councils of the Fellows of the Craft of Freemasons which at this time, or any time hereafter, shall be made known unto me. That I will not permit or suffer any laborer to be employed in the proper work of Freemasonry; that I will not work with those that are not free, and that I will not teach laborers and unaccepted Masons, as I would teach apprentices or Fellows of the Craft of Freemasons.

"I further promise and declare that I will strictly preserve the honor of all Freemasons of whatever degree; that I will not commit adultry or fornication with the wife, daughter or maid of any Freemason.

"The penalty for breaking this great oath shall be the loss of my life. That I shall be branded with the mark of the traitor and slain according to the ancient custom.

"Given under my hand and sealed with my lips twice. So help me El Shaddai and the holy contents of this book."

After the obligation it is said to him, "Rise, accepted Fellow of the Craft of Freemasons." Then the signs of a Fellow are given. They are the same as the Speculative, the word is "Bonai." This word proves he is a Fellow of the Craft, and means builder. The traditional history is now recited to him by the first Master Mason.

THE TRADITIONAL HISTORY

"Good Fellow of the Craft of Freemasons, you have been passed as a Fellow of this ancient and worshipful Fraternity. It is our purpose to tell you how and in what manner this worthy Craft of Masonry was begun, and afterward how it was kept by worthy Kings and Princes and by many other worshipful men.

"Before Noah's flood there was a man that was called Lamech, and this Lamech had two wives, the one called Adah, and the other Zillah. By his first wife, Adah, he gat two sons, the one called Jabal and the other Jubal. And by the other wife, Zillah, he gat a son, Tubal Cain, and a daughter, Nazmah, and these four children founded the beginning of all the crafts in the world. The eldest son, Jabal, founded the craft of geometry; he had sheep and lambs in the field, and was the first Mason who wrought houses and walls of stone. And his brother, Jubal, founded the craft of music, song of mouth, harp, organ and trumpet. And the third son, Tubal Cain, found out the smith's craft of working in gold, silver, copper, iron and steel and all manner of forging. And the daughter, Nazmah, founded the craft of weaving. These four children knew well that God would do vengeance for sin, either by fire or water, wherefore they wrote the sciences that they had founded on two pillars of stone that they might be found after either fire or flood. The one pillar was made of marble, for that it cannot burn with fire, and the other pillar was made of stone called laternes, for that it cannot drown in any water. Our intent is to tell you truly in what manner these stones were found, on which were written these sciences.

"After the destruction of the world by Noah's flood, the great Hermarives, that was Cubies' son, afterwards called Hermes, the father of wisdom, found one of the seven sciences written thereon, and he taught it to other men. The first of the seven sciences is *Grammar,* and that teacheth a man to speak truly and write truly. The second is *Rhetoric,* and that teacheth a man to speak fair and in subtle terms. The third is *Logic,* and teacheth a man to discern or know the truth from falsehood. The fourth is *Arithmetic,* and teacheth a man to reckon and to count all manner of numbers. The fifth is *Geometry,* and that teacheth a man to mete and measure the earth, and all other things on which science is founded, Masonry and architecture. The sixth is called *Music,* and that teacheth a man of the craft of song, and voice of tongue, organ, harp and trumpet. And the seventh science is called *Astronomy,* and that teacheth a man to know the course of the sun, of the moon, and of the stars of heaven.

"These be the seven liberal sciences of the which all be founded by one; that is geometry, for geometry teacheth a man measure, ponderation and weight of all things on earth; for there is no man that worketh in any craft, but he worketh by some measure; and every man that buyeth or selleth, buy or sell by some measure or weight, and all this is geometry. And the merchants, craftsmen and all other sciences, and especially the plowmen, and tillers of all manner of grain and seeds, vines and plants, and the setters of all manner of fruit, cannot find mete and measure without geometry; wherefore the said science of geometry is the most worthy, as all the others are founded upon it.

"At the making of the Tower of Babylon was Masons first made much of, and the great king of Babylon called Nimrod was himself a Master Mason. He loved well the Craft and made the Masons free men and Freemasons in his kingdom. And when the city of Nineveh and other cities of the East were built, Nimrod, the King of Babylon, sent thither sixty Lodges of his Freemasons to Ashur, the King of Nineveh, his cousin, and when he sent them forth he gave them a charter and a charge after his manner."

(The second Master gives "The Charge.")

CHARGES OF NIMROD—SECOND DEGREE

"That the Freemasons shall be true to El Shaddai, their King, their Lord and their Masters.

"That they shall truly serve their Masters for their pay, so that their Masters have worship, and all that belongeth to them.

"That they shall ordain the most wise and cunning men to be Masters of the work, and neither for love, riches nor favor set another that hath little cunning to be master of any work whereby the Lords should be ill served and the science shamed.

"That they shall be true one to another, and that they shall live truly together.

"That they shall assemble together once every year, to see how they might best serve the King and the Master for their profit and their own worship.

"That they shall correct within themselves, those that have trespassed against the Craft, so the worthy science be not dishonored.

"To all these charges he made them swear a great oath that men used at that time, and he ordained for them reasonable pay whereby they might live honestly.

"Long after, when the children of Israel were come into the land of Beerhest, that is now called mongst us the country of Jerusalem, King David began to prepare the ground and the stone for the Temple of Jerusalem. And the same King David loved well the Freemasons, and cherished them much and gave them good pay—and the charges right nigh as they be now.

"And after the decease of King David, Solomon, that was King David's son, performed out the temple that his father had begun, and he sent for Freemasons into diverse countries and lands and gathered them together so that he had four score thousand workmen that were workers of stone, and were all Freemasons, and he chose of them three thousand, three hundred that were ordained to be Masters and Governors of his works.

"And this same Solomon confirmed both the charges and manners that his father had given to the Masons, and thus was that worthy Craft confirmed in the country of Jerusalem and in many other kingdoms."

ANCIENT CHARGE
TO THE FELLOW OF THE CRAFT OF FREEMASONS.

"1. I am to admonish you to honor El Shaddai in his holy church; that you use no heresy, schism, and error in your undertakings, or discredit man's teachings.

"2. To be true to our Sovereign Lord, the King, his heirs and lawful successors; committing no treason, misprison or felony; and if any man shall commit treason that you know of, you shall forthwith give notice thereof to his Majesty, his privy councilors, or some other person that hath commission to inquire thereof.

"3. You shall be true to your Fellows and brethren of the science of Masonry, and do unto them as you would be done unto.

"4. You shall keep secret the obscure and intricate parts of the science, not disclosing them to any but such as study and use the same.

"5. You shall do your work truly and faithfully, endeavoring the profit and advantage of him that is owner of the said work.

"6. You shall call Masons your Fellows and Brethren without addition of knaves and other bad language.

"7. You shall not take your neighbor's wife villainously, nor his daughter, nor his maid or his servant, to use ungodly.

"8. You shall not carnally lie with any woman that is belonging to the house where you are at table.

"9. You shall truly pay for your meat and drink where you are at table.

"10. You shall not undertake any man's work, knowing yourself unable or unexpert to perform and effect the science, or the Lord or owner of the said work be any way prejudiced.

"11. You shall not take any work to do at excessive or unreasonable rates, to deceive the owner thereof, but so as he may be truly and faithfully served with his own goods.

"12. You shall so take your work that thereby you may live honestly and pay your Fellow the wages as the science doth require.

"13. You shall not supplant any of your Fellows of their work, if he or any of them hath or have taken any work upon him or them, or he or they stand Master or Masters of any Lord of owner's work, that you shall not put him or them out from the said work, although you perceive him or them unable to finish the same.

"14. You shall not take any apprentice to serve you in the said science of Masonry, under the terms of seven years, nor any but such as are descended of good and honest parentage; that no scandal may be imputed to the said science of Masonry.

"15. You shall not take upon you to make any Mason, without the privity or consent of six, or five at least, of your Fellows, and not but such as is free born, and whose parents live in good fame and name, and that hath his right and perfect limbs, and able body to attend the said science.

"16. You shall not pay any of your Fellows more money than he or they have deserved, that you be not deceived by slight or false working and the owner thereof much wronged.

"17. You shall not slander any of your Fellows behind their backs to impair their temporal estate or good name.

"18. You shall not, without any urgent cause, answer your Fellow doggedly or ungodly, but as becomes a loving brother in the said science.

"19. You shall duly reverence your Fellows, that the bond of charity and mutual love may continue steadfast and stable among you.

"20. You shall not (except in Christmas time) use any lawless games as dice, cards or such like.

"21. You shall not frequent any houses of bawdery or be a pander to any of your Fellows or others, which will be a great scandal to the science.

"22. You shall not go out to drink by night, or if occasion happen that you must go, you shall not stay past eight of the clock, having some of your Fellows, or one at the least, to bear you witness of the honest places you were in, and your good behavior to avoid scandal.

"23. You shall come to the yearly assembly, if you know where it is kept, being within ten miles of the place of your abode, submitting yourself to the censure of your Fellows, wherein you have to make satisfaction or else to defend by order of the King's laws.

"24. You shall not make any mould, square or rule to mould stones withal, but such as are allowed by the Fraternity.

"25. You shall set strangers at work, having employment for them, at least a fortnight, and pay them their wages truly; and if you want work for them, then you shall relieve them with money to defray their reasonable charges to the next Lodge.

"26. You shall truly attend your work, and truly end the same, whether it be task or journey work, if you have the payment and wages according to your agreement made with the Master or owner thereof.

"All these articles and charges, which I have now recited unto you,

you shall well and truly observe, perform and keep to the best of your power and knowledge. So help you El Shaddai and the true and holy contents of this book."

Then the third Master, addressing the candidate, says: "The traditional history and the charges which have just been so ably delivered to you are the foundation stone, the commencement of the Worshipful Society of Freemasons, in all parts of the world, and in all ages." The new "Fellow of the Craft of Freemasons" is now invested with the Fellow's apron and is presented with his actual working tools, which are the plumb, the level and the square, another straight edge, and the perfect Ashlar square, which is a wooden frame with the ends overlapping like an Oxford frame, being the exact size of a royal cubit, or 21⅞ inches inside. He is now a free man and a Freemason, and in olden days became a free man of the city or town in which he had been apprenticed.

When he begins to work in the Fellow's or second degree yard, he is told to commence in the N. E. corner with the new Fellows and there he is taught to make his rough dressed Ashlar stone true and polished. Then his perfect work has to be submitted for inspection and to be tried. If the work is satisfactory, he is given the word "Giblim," which means perfect stone squarer or expert Mason.

With this additional or superior word, Giblim, he also has an additional sign given to him of which there is no trace in the Speculative Ritual.

The sign is given by placing his left arm and hand, with thumb extended, in a perpendicular position, pointing upward, and his right arm and hand, with thumb extended, in a horizontal position. Thus he represents all three of his new tools, the "square" by the angle of 90 degrees formed by his two arms, the upright of "plumb rule" by his left arm, and the "level" by his right arm.

Having made his test piece which has been passed by the Inspector of Material, and having served for a year as a Fellow, he is now eligible to apply to be advanced to the third degree, that of a Super Fellow. The following form has to be filled up and posted at the yard or quarry entrance:

"Application to the Superintendent of the Works of the Worshipful Society of Freemasons, Rough Masons, Wallers, Slaters, Paviors, Plaisterers and Bricklayers.

I, ..., having well and truly served as a Fellow of the Craft of Freemasons for one year, and being of the age of twenty-two years, humbly crave to be advanced to the honorable degree of Super Fellow of the Craft of Freemasons.

"I further promise and swear that if once advanced to the third degree of the fellowship, I will forever conform to all the ancient charges, usages and established customs of the Fraternity, as Super Fellows have done in all ages."

THE SUPER FELLOW'S THIRD AND FOURTH DEGREES

The word "Giblim" and the sign described in the last chapter, left arm perpendicular and right arm horizontal, are the pass word and pass sign leading from the second to the third degree; and the perfect Ashlar stone the candidate has himself made is the proof for advancement to the Super Fellows or third degree.

The Operative third degree and the first part of the modern Mark degree corresponding to the old Mark Mason of the Speculatives are so very similar that a Speculative Mark Mason would find himself quite at home in the Operative work. The word and sign of the Operative and Super Fellow or third degree is the same as the Speculative Mark degree.

It is obvious that this precludes a Speculative Mark Mason from describing the ceremony fully in print. The Super Fellow is alloted his Mark, and as a Super Fellow he is charged to produce "fare work and square."

In this degree the candidate is led around the Lodge three times and he takes his obligation on the polished Ashlar stone with both knees bare.

"Application to the Superintendent of the Works of the Worshipful Society of Freemasons, Rough Masons, Wallers, Slaters, Paviors, Plaisterers and Bricklayers.

"I, ..., having well and truly served as a Super Fellow of the Craft of Freemasons for one year, and being of the age of twenty-three, humbly crave to be further advanced to the honorable degree of Super Fellow Erector of the Craft of Freemasons.

"I further promise and swear that if once advanced to the fourth degree of fellowship, I will forever conform to all the ancient charges, usages, and established customs of the Fraternity, as Super Fellow Erectors have done in all ages."

The next degree for the Operative Free Mason is that of an Erector, still Super Fellow, but one who is qualified and entitled to erect and put in position on the site the stones prepared in the first, second and third yards and marked in the third stone yard. This is the Operative's fourth degree. The Super Fellow Erector ascertains from the marks the exact position in which each stone is intended to be placed.

This is very similar to the second part of the modern Speculative

Mark Mason's degree, corresponding to the old Speculative Mark Master's degree; which again precludes a Mark Mason from describing the ceremony fully in print.

In the square division it is the chief N. E. corner headstone that is missing, and in the arch division it is the keystone of the arch that has been lost. The moral is the same in both cases. "The stone which the builders refused is become the headstone of the corner." The Arch Masons reject the corner stone, and the Square Masons reject the keystone.

In the Operative account it is the negligent mark man who neglected to mark well who are "hove over" with a thirty-cubit drop, and form the completion sacrifice; which is certainly in accordance with the spirit of the times of the building of King Solomon's temple.

In this fourth degree the candidate takes his obligation on a perfect polished Ashlar stone, both knees bare as before, and he is led around the Lodge four times. The work and sign are the same as in the Speculative Mark degree.

All Operative Freemasons have these two Mark degrees, although the Mark was struck out by those who formulated Modern Speculative Freemasonry in 1717.

The majority of Operative Freemasons do not proceed beyond this, the fourth degree; as to take the fifth degree, that of Superintendent, requires considerable technical knowledge.

"Application to the Superintendent of the Works of the Worshipful Society of Freemasons, Rough Masons, Wallers, Slaters, Paviors, Plaisterers and Bricklayers.

"I, ..., having well and truly served as a Super Fellow Erector of the Craft of Freemasons for one year, and being of the age of twenty-four years, humbly crave to be raised to the honorable degree of Intendant of the Craft of Freemasons.

"I further promise and swear that if once raised to the fifth degree of fellowship, I will forever conform to all the ancient charges, usages, and established customs of the Fraternity, as Intendants have done in all ages."

THE OVERSEER—FIFTH AND SIXTH DEGREES

There is no degree in Speculative Freemasonry exactly corresponding to the fifth degree of Superintendent in Operative Freemasonry, although Overseers are used in the Speculative Mark Master.

The ceremony is, however, somewhat similar to the appointment and investiture of officers at a Speculative installation meeting. Every officer is examined as to his knowledge—actual technical knowledge—and has to take the officer's oath and be installed in his chair.

"Application to the Masters of the Worshipful Society of Freemasons, Rough Masons, Wallers, Slaters, Paviors, Plaisterers, and Bricklayers.

"I, ..., having well and truly served as Intendant and Superintendent of the Craft of Freemasons for one year, and being of the age of twenty-five years, humbly crave to be exalted to the honorable degree of Passed Master of the Craft of Freemasons.

"I further promise and swear that if once exalted to the sixth degree of the fellowship, I will forever conform to all the ancient charges, usages, and established customs of the Fraternity, as Harodim have done in all ages."

The next Operative degree, that of a Passed Master, sixth degree, requires still more knowledge than the fifth degree. A man who takes it—and the number in a Lodge is limited to fifteen—must be able to conduct building operations and generally understand his profession thoroughly, consequently requiring much more technical knowledge than does a craftsman. He has to be able to lay schemes, draw plans and take complete charge of a department. The Senior Passed Master is really the Deputy Master. His Masonic title is Adoniram. He is practically general manager and works manager and is responsible to the three Masters. The word of this degree is "Harod," plural "Harodim." The fifth degree Mason is led around the Lodge five times and the sixth degree Mason six times.

THE THREE MASTERS—SEVENTH DEGREE

The last and final, or seventh, degree is that of a Grand Master, of which there are three. These correspond in some measure to the Speculative Grand Master, Pro Grand Master and Deputy Grand Master in England, and to the Grand Master and Grand Wardens in this country. They represent Solomon, King of Israel; Hiram, King of Tyre, and Hiram Abif. On being admitted to this degree each Master is led around the Lodge seven times.

The first and second Grand Masters hold office for life, or until superannuated. The third Grand Master is ritually slain on the 2nd of October, and a fresh one is appointed every year.

"Application to the Masters of the Worshipful Society of Freemasons, Rough Masons, Wallers, Slaters, Paviors, Plaisterers and Bricklayers.

"I, ..., having well and truly served as Passed Master and Deputy Master Mason for five years, and being at the age of thirty-five years, humbly crave to be enthroned in the honorable and exalted degree of Master Mason of the Craft of Freemasons.

"I further promise and swear that if once enthroned in the seventh degree of the fellowship, I will forever conform to all the ancient charges, usages and established customs of the Fraternity, as Enthroned Master Masons have done in all ages."

In filling the "Certificates of Character and Skill" for the foregoing, the only acceptable character is that found in II Chronicles, chapter 2, verses 13 and 14.

"A cunning man, endued with understanding."

"Skillful to work in gold, and in silver, in brass, in iron, in stone, and in timber, in purple, in blue and in fine linen, and in crimson; also to grave any manner of graving, and to find out every device which shall be put to him."

Attention is called to the plan of the sixth and seventh degree lodges. The Masters' chairs are in the west, on a raised dais with seven steps, each step representing one of the Masonic sciences—Grammar, Rhetoric, Logic, Arithmetic, Geometry, Music and Astronomy. Adoniram, the Deputy Master, is just within the sixth degree Lodge room, and there are three pillars, hexagonal in shape, in the Lodge room, one in front of King Solomon in the west, another in the northeast, and the third in the southeast. The one in the west represents Mount Moriah, the one in the northeast represents Mount Tabor, and the one in the southeast represents Mount Sinai.

On ordinary occasions the seventh degree of Grand Master's Lodge is opened by the three in private, and the sixth degree or Passed Master's Lodge is opened by them in the same manner; then the door or screen or curtain between these two Lodge rooms is opened and work goes on. But when the annual assembly or one of the three great commemorations is to be celebrated, then the Sanhedrim must be opened by these two degrees together and conjointly.

At the Sanhedrim there is no Warden present as such; King Solomon occupies the central seat of the Master's chairs, with Hiram, King of Tyre, on his right, and Hiram Abif on his left hand. The first Master asks the second and third Masters if they agree that the Sanhedrim be opened; on their acquiescence all members of the sixth degree must prove themselves members by forming in three and make the word Sanhedrim by each giving a syllable in turn.

It is in this Sanhedrim that at the foundation commemoration in April the first Master says, quoting I Kings, chapter 5, verses 3, 4 and 5, "Thou knowest how that David, my father, could not build an house unto the name of the Lord his God for the wars which were about him on every side, until the Lord put them under the soles of his feet. But now the Lord my God hath given me rest on every side so that there is neither adversary nor evil occurrent. And behold, I purpose to build an house unto the name of the Lord my God, as the Lord spake unto David, my father, saying, Thy son whom I will set upon thy throne in thy room, he shall build an house unto my name."

He then commands a levy of men, verse 13, "A levy out of all Israel; and the levy was thirty thousand men." And according to I Kings 6:7, that "neither hammer nor axe nor any tool of iron shall be 'heard in the house while building.' This necessitates the marking of the different parts."

Next the sixth degree Masons have to get out plans and specifications and make all arrangements.

Then follows the ceremony of the founding and construction of the temple.

At the dedication commemoration the same process of opening the Sanhedrim has to be gone through. In this ceremony the occupant of the chair in the southeast acts as chaplain, and represents Jachin, and is regarded as being placed on Mount Sinai. The occupant of the chair in the northeast represents Boaz, and is regarded as being placed on Mount Tabor. The hexagonal pillars in front of them as they face the west bear the same names as the occupants of the chairs, and the Operatives point out that the Scriptural narrative in I Kings 7–21 confirms their arrangement as King Solomon stands in the west and faces east, "And he set up the pillars in the porch of the temple; and he set up the right pillar and called the name thereof Jachin; and he set up the left pillar, and called the name thereof Boaz."

The Grand Deputy Master, whose chair is at the feet of the three Grand Masters, hands a blue cord up to King Solomon, who fixes it to the pillar in front of him by passing it around it, and commands that it be carried to Boaz, who fixes it to the pillar in front of him, then it is carried from Boaz to Jachin, who fixes it to the pillar in front of him and sends it back to King Solomon. Three separate persons take the three angles, and these, when handed to the first Master, acting as King Solomon, must add up to 180; if they do not, the ceremony must be repeated. This blue cord is regarded as the great line of communication between the three great mountains or high places, Moriah, Tabor and Sinai.

The Operatives further explain that the first Master represents the King, and that as Jachin was High Priest at the time of the dedication, so he represents the Church, and Boaz, the founder of the Royal House of David, represents the State, so that King and Church and State are all represented and are all united by the symbolical blue cord.

At the end of the ceremony of dedication the first Master goes in state to the pillars at the east end; as he stands facing them he points with his right hand and says, "This on my right hand I name Jachin," and pointing with his left hand, "This on my left hand I name Boaz." The Goldsmith's Guild, which is represented, then fixes a gold plate on each pillar bearing its name, and the first Master, representing King Solomon himself, fixes the last gold bolt. These plates are fixed on the bases of the pillars and on their east side, so that all entering see the name as they approach. The first Master then raises his hands and his eyes to heaven, and addressing El Shaddai, says, "I have completed the work that my Father commanded me to perform." The grand sevenfold salute of the Grand Masters is then given to El Shaddai twenty-one times, thus: Seven times, then a pause and seven times again, and then a pause, and seven times again. Then first Master blesses the congregation, who all stand up according to I Kings 8:14, "And the King turned his face about and blessed all the congregation of Israel; (and all the congregation of Israel stood)."

Then the special sign of the triangle is given. This is done by putting the tips of the thumbs together, the thumbs being held in the same horizontal line, then join the tips of the forefingers together and you get as nearly as possible an equilateral triangle; bring the hands in front of the face so that the two eyes look through the triangle thus formed. The word J. A. H. is uttered and the sign of dispersal, You can go, is given.

"The work is finished." Then the Sanhedrim is closed, and after that the seventh degree and sixth degree Lodges. This ends the ceremony.

The fifteen articles in the old charges for the Master are as follows:

1. He must be steadfast, trusty and true; pay his fellows truly, take no bribe; and as a judge stand upright.

2. Every Master (that is a Mason) must be at the general congregation, provided he be told where the assembly shall be held; except to have reasonable excuse; is disobedient to the Craft; is with falsehood overtaken; or sickness disable him from attendance.

3. The Master must take no apprentice, without good assurance he will dwell seven years with him in order to learn his Craft, as with less period his services might be unprofitable.

4. The Master must be careful not to make a bondman his apprentice, or take him out of covetousness, as the Lord he is bound to may fetch him wheresoever he goes, and if captured in the Lodge much inconvenience might result, since all Masons that were there would stand together as companions. For more ease, then, the apprentice should be taken of higher degree, and it was in older time written that he should be of gentle birth.

5. The apprentice must be of lawful blood, and the Master shall for no advantage make one that is not perfect, which means that he must have his limbs whole.

6. The Master shall do the Lord no prejudice, to take for his apprentice, as much as for the Fellows, who in their Craft are quite

perfect, which he is not. But the apprentice shall be informed that his pay shall soon increase.

7. No Master, out of fear or favor, shall either clothe or feed a thief, neither shall he harbor thieves, nor him that hath killed a man.

8. The Master may change any man of Craft, who is not so perfect as he ought to be, and take in his place a more perfect, that is skilled man, as the former, through recklessness, might do the Craft little honor.

9. The Master ought to be wise and discreet, and should undertake no work that he cannot both perform and complete. Also, it should be equally to the profit of the Lord and Craft, while the ground ought to be well taken, so that it may neither "Fle" nor crack.

10. No Master shall supplant another, or any man that hath taken a work upon him, under penalty of not less than ten pounds (on being found guilty) to him who first took the work in hand. For no man in Masonry shall supplant another, except the execution be such that it turn the work to naught; for the man who begins a work, if "he be Mason good and sound," had the right to bring it to an end.

11. The Master shall be both fair and liberal, and must prohibit any Mason from working at night, unless in the pursuit of knowledge, which shall be sufficient excuse.

12. No Mason shall deprave his Fellow's work, but recommend it with honest words and assist him in improving it.

13. If the Master have an apprentice, he must instruct him fully in the points, so that he may have fully learned his Craft, withersoever he may go.

14. A Master shall take no apprentice, without making proper provision that he shall learn of him within his terms of servitude "diverse points."

15. The Master shall take upon himself no false maintenance, nor for any reward maintain his Fellows in their sin. Neither must he suffer them to swear any false oaths.

The fifteen points for the Craftsman accompanying the Master's articles are as follows:

1. The worthy Craftsman must love well God and the holy church, the Master he is with and his Fellows also.

2. The Mason must work truly on the work day, so as to deserve his pay for holy day.

3. The apprentice must keep his Master's counsel, and also that of his Fellows, closely. The privities of the chamber he must not lay bare, nor tell to any man whatsoever he hears or sees done in the Lodge. The counsel of hall and likewise of bower he must also keep inviolable.

4. No man shall be false to his Craft, or maintain an error against it, neither shall he do any act to the prejudice of his Master or Fellows. The same injunctions apply to the apprentice, though "under awe."

5. The Mason must take the pay ordered him weekly, but the Master, before the ninth hour, i. e., 3 p. m., must warn those for whom he hath no further employment, and to this direction they must submit without strife.

6. Love day shall only be celebrated on a holiday, or when the work has come to an end.

7. No man shall lie with his Master's wife, or with the wife or concubine of his Fellows.

8. The Mason must be faithful to his Master; a true mediator between his Master and his Fellows; and to act fairly by both parties.

9. The Stewards of the hall are lovingly to serve one another, to see that every man is charged alike; to pay for all victuals consumed, and to keep full and good accounts.

10. If a Mason lead a bad life, and slander his Fellows without cause, he shall be cited to appear at the next assembly, and unless he attend must forswear the Craft, and shall be punished according to the law established in the old days.

11. A Mason who is well skilled in the Craft, and sees his Fellow hewing a stone, which he is in a fair way to spoil, should help him without loss of time, if able to do so, and also instruct him how to do better, so that the whole work may not be ruined.

12. At the assembly there shall be, besides the Masters and Fellows, many great Lords, the Sheriff of the county, the Mayor of the city, Knights, Squires and Aldermen. The ordinances then made shall be put into effect by them against any man belonging to the Craft, who if he dispute the laws so enacted, will be taken into their keeping.

13. Each Mason shall swear not to be a thief, nor to succor anyone in his false Craft.

14. Each Mason must swear a good true oath to his Master and Fellows present at the assembly. He must also be steadfast and true to all the ordinances; to his liege Lord and King; and to all the points heretofore cited all shall swear the same oath of the Masons, be they willing or unwilling, to these points that have been ordained by good authority; and if any man be found guilty in either one of them he is to be sought for and brought before the assembly.

15. Should those that shall be sworn to observe the ordinances made at the assembly, before the great Lords and Masters, before named, be obedient to the resolutions there passed, and the same be proven openly at the assembly—except they be willing to make amends for their faults—then they must forsake the Craft, refuse to

work in it, and swear never more to use it. Not unless they subsequently make amends will they be allowed to resume their Craft; and if they will not do so, the Sheriffs shall arrest them and put their bodies into prison, and take their goods and chattels, holding themselves and property at the King's will.

APPENDIX

Aaron. Hebrew Aharon, a word of doubtful etymology, but generally supposed to signify *a mountaineer*. He was the brother of Moses, and the first high priest under the Mosaic dispensation, whence the priesthood established by that lawgiver is known as the "Aaronic." He is alluded to in the English lectures of the second degree, in reference to a certain sign which is said to have taken its origin from the fact that Aaron and Hur were present on the hill from which Moses surveyed the battle which Joshua was waging with the Amalekites, when these two supported the weary arms of Moses in an upright posture, because upon his uplifted hands the fate of the battle depended. See Exodus xvii. 10–12. Aaron is also referred to in the latter section of the Royal Arch degree in connection with the memorials that were deposited in the ark of the covenant. In the degree of "Chief of the Tabernacle," which is the 23d of the Ancient and Accepted Rite, the presiding officer represents Aaron, and is styled "Most Excellent High Priest."

Aaron's Rod. The method by which Moses caused a miraculous judgment as to which tribe should be invested with the priesthood, is detailed in the Book of Numbers (ch. xvii.). He directed that twelve rods should be laid up in the Holy of Holies of the Tabernacle, one for each tribe; that of Aaron, of course, represented the tribe of Levi. On the next day these rods were brought out and exhibited to the people, and while all the rest remained dry and withered, that of Aaron alone budded and blossomed and yielded fruit. There is no mention in the Pentateuch of this rod having been placed in the ark, but only that it was put before it. But as St. Paul, or the author of the Epistle to the Hebrews (Hebrews ix. 4), asserts that the rod and the pot of manna were both within the ark, Royal Arch Masons have followed this later authority. Hence the rod of Aaron is found in the ark; but its import is only historical, as if to identify the substitute ark as a true copy of the original, which had been lost. No symbolical instruction accompanies its discovery.

Ablution. A ceremonial purification by washing, much used in the Ancient Mysteries and under the Mosaic dispensation. It is also employed in some of the high degrees of Masonry. The better technical term for this ceremony is *lustration,* which see.

Adam. The Entered Apprentice degree symbolizes the creation of man and his first perception of light. In the Elohist form of the Creation we read, "Elohim said, 'Let us make man in our image, according to our likeness, and let him have dominion over the fishes of the sea, over the fowls of the air, over the cattle, and over all the earth, and over every reptile that creeps upon the earth!' And Elohim created man in his image; in the image of Elohim he created him; male and female he created them. . . . And Yahveh Elohim formed man of the dust of the ground, and breathed in his nostrils the breath of life, and man was made a living being." Without giving more than a passing reference to the speculative origin and production of man and to his spontaneous generation as set forth by the Egyptians, when we are told that "the fertilizing mud left by the Nile, and exposed to the vivifying action of heat induced by the sun's rays, brought forth germs which spring up as the bodies of men," accepted cosmogonies only will be hereinafter mentioned; thus in that of Peru, the first man, created by the Divine Omnipotence, is called *Alpa Camasca*, "Animated earth." The Mandans, one of the North American tribes, relate that the Great Spirit molded two figures of clay, which he dried and animated with the breath of his mouth, one receiving the name of First Man, and the other that of Companion. Taeroa, the god of Tahiti, formed man of the red earth, say the inhabitants; and so we might continue. But as François Lenormant remarks in the *Beginnings of History,* let us confine ourselves to the cosmogony offered by the sacred traditions of the great civilized nations of antiquity. "The Chaldeans call Adam the man whom the earth produced. And he lay without movement, without life, and without breath, just like an image of the heavenly Adam, until his soul had been given him by the latter." The cosmogonic account peculiar to Babylon, as given by Berossus, says: "Belos, seeing that the earth was uninhabited, though fertile, cut off his own head, and the other gods, after kneading with earth the blood that flowed from it, formed men, who therefore are endowed with intelligence, and share in the divine thought," etc. The term employed to designate "man," in his connection with his Creator, is *admu,* the Assyrian counterpart of the Hebrew Adam.

Admiration, Sign of. A mode of recognition alluded to in the Most Excellent Master's Degree, or the Sixth of the American Rite. Its introduction in that place is referred to a Masonic legend in connection with the visit of the Queen of Sheba to King Solomon, which states that, moved by the wide-spread reputation of the Israelitish monarch, she had repaired to Jerusalem to inspect the magnificent works of which she had heard so many encomiums. Upon arriving there, and beholding for the first time the Temple, which glittered with gold, and which was so accurately adjusted in all its parts as to seem to be composed of but a single piece of marble, she raised her hands and eyes to heaven in an attitude of admiration, and at the same time exclaimed, "Rabboni!" equivalent to saying, "A most excellent master hath done this!" This action has since been perpetuated in the ceremonies of the degree of Most Excellent Master. The legend is, however, no doubt apocryphal, and is really to be considered only as allegorical, like so many other of the legends of Masonry.

Admonition. According to the ethics of Freemasonry, it is made a duty obligatory upon every member of the Order to conceal the faults of a brother, that is, not to blazon forth his errors and infirmities, to let them be learned by the world from some other tongue than his, and to admonish him of them in private. So there is another but a like duty or obligation, which instructs him to whisper good counsel in his brother's ear and to warn him of approaching danger. And this refers not more to the danger that is without and around him than to that which is within him; not more to the peril that springs from the concealed foe who would waylay him and covertly injure him, than to that deeper peril of those faults and infirmities which lie within his own heart, and which, if not timely crushed by good and earnest resolution of amendment, will, like the ungrateful serpent in the fable, become warm with life only to sting the bosom that has nourished them.

Admonition of a brother's fault is, then, the duty of every Mason, and no true one will, for either fear or favor, neglect its performance. But as the duty is Masonic, so is there a Masonic way in which that duty should be discharged. We must admonish not with self-sufficient pride in our own reputed goodness—not in imperious tones, as though we looked down in scorn upon the degraded offender—not in language that, by its harshness, will wound rather than win, will irritate more than it will reform; but with that persuasive gentleness that gains the heart—with the all-subduing influences of "mercy unrestrained"—with the magic might of love—with the language and the accents of affection, which mingle grave displeasure for the offense with grief and pity for the offender.

This, and this alone, is Masonic admonition. I am not to rebuke my brother in anger, for I, too, have my faults, and I dare not draw around me the folds of my garment lest they should be polluted by my neighbor's touch; but I am to admonish in private, not before the world, for that would degrade him; and I am to warn him, perhaps from my own example, how vice ever should be followed by sorrow, for that goodly sorrow leads to repentance, and repentance to amendment, and amendment to joy.

Adonai. In Hebrew, being the plural of excellence for *Adon,* and signifying *the Lord.* The Jews, who reverently avoided the pronunciation of the sacred name JEHOVAH, were accustomed, whenever that name occurred, to substitute for it the word *Adonai* in reading. As to the use of the plural form instead of the singular, the Rabbis say, "Every word indicative of dominion, though singular in meaning, is made plural in form." This is called the "pluralis excellentiæ." The Talmudists also say (Buxtroff, *Lex. Talm.*) that the tetragrammaton is called *Shem* *hamphorash,* the name that is explained, because it is explained, uttered, and set forth by the word *Adonai.* Adonai is used as a significant word in several of the high degrees of Masonry, and may almost always be considered as allusive to or symbolic of the True Word.

Adonhiram. This has been adopted by the disciples of Adonhiramite Masonry as the spelling of the name of the person known in Scripture and in other Masonic systems as *Adoniram* (which see). They correctly derive the word from the Hebrew *Adon* and *hiram,* signifying the *master who is exalted,* which is the true meaning of Adoniram, the ה or *h* being omitted in the Hebrew by the coalescence of the two words. Hiram Abif has also sometimes been called Adonhiram, the Adon having been bestowed on him by Solomon, it is said, as a title of honor.

Adonhiramite Masonry. Of the numerous controversies which arose from the middle to near the end of the eighteenth century on the Continent of Europe, and especially in France, among the students of Masonic philosophy, and which so frequently resulted in the invention of new degrees and the establishment of new rites, not the least prominent was that which related to the person and character of the Temple Builder. The question, Who was the architect of King Solomon's Temple? was answered differently by different theorists, and each answer gave rise to a new system, a fact by no means surprising in those times, so fertile in the production of new Masonic systems. The general theory was then, as it is now, that this architect was Hiram Abif, the widow's son, who had been sent to King Solomon by Hiram, King of Tyre, as a precious gift, and "a curious and cunning workman." This theory was sustained by the statements of the Jewish Scriptures, so far as they threw any light on the Masonic legend. It was the theory of the English Masons from the earliest times; was enunciated as historically correct in the first edition of the *Book of Constitutions,* published in 1723 (p. 11); has continued ever since to be the opinion of all English and American Masons; and is, at this day, the only theory entertained by any Mason in the two countries who has a theory at all on the subject. This, therefore, is the orthodox faith of Masonry.

But such was not the case in the last century on the Continent of Europe. At first the controversy arose not as to the man himself, but as to his proper appellation. All parties agreed that the architect of the Temple was that Hiram, the widow's son, who is described in the 1st Book of Kings, chapter vii., verses 13 and 14, and in the 2d Book of Chronicles, chapter ii., verses 13 and 14, as having come out of Tyre with the other workmen of the Temple who had been sent by King Hiram to Solomon. But one party called him *Hiram Abif,* and the other, admitting that his original name was Hiram, supposed that, in consequence of the skill he had displayed in the construction of the Temple, he had received the honorable affix of *Adon,* signifying *Lord* or *Master,* whence his name became *Adonhiram.*

There was, however, at the Temple another Adoniram, of whom it will be necessary in passing to say a few words, for the better understanding of the present subject.

The first notice that we have of this Adoniram in Scripture is in the 2d Book of Samuel, chapter xx., verse 24, where, in the abbreviated form of his name, *Adoram,* he is said to have been "over the tribute" in the house of David; or, as Gesenius translates it, "prefect over the tribute service," or, as we might say in modern phrase, principal collector of the taxes. Seven years afterward, we find him exercising the same office in the household of Solomon; for it is said in 1 Kings iv. 6 that Adoniram, "the son of Abda, was over the tribute." And lastly, we hear of him still occupying the same station in the household of King Rehoboam, the successor of Solomon. Forty-seven years after he is first mentioned in the Book of Samuel, he is stated under the name of Adoram (1 Kings xii. 18), or Hadoram (2 Chron. x. 18), to have been stoned to death, while in the discharge of his duty, by the people, who were justly indignant at the oppressions of his master.

The legends and traditions of Masonry which connect this Adoniram with the Temple at Jerusalem derive their support from a single passage in the 1st Book of Kings (v. 14), where it is said that Solomon made a levy of thirty thousand workmen from among the Israelites; that he sent these in courses of ten thousand a month to labor on Mount Lebanon, and that he placed Adoniram over these as their superintendent.

The ritual-makers of France, who were not all Hebrew scholars, nor well versed in Biblical history, seem, at times, to have confounded two important personages, and to have lost all distinction between Hiram the Builder, who had been sent from the court of the King of Tyre, and Adoniram, who had always been an officer in the court of King Solomon. And this error was extended and facilitated when they had prefixed the title *Adon,* that is to say, lord or master, to the name of the former, making him *Adon Hiram,* or the Lord Hiram.

Adoptive Masonry. An organization which bears a very imperfect resemblance to Freemasonry in its forms and ceremonies, which was established in France for the initiation of women, called by the French Adoptive Masonry, meeting places called Adoptive Lodges.

As to the exact date of its introduction, there are several theories, some of which are wholly untenable, being founded on an unwarrantable mixture of facts and fictions of positive statements and problematic conjectures.

These Lodges of Adoption seem to owe their existence to those secret associations of men and women which sprang up in France before the middle of the 18th century. About that time they spread from France into Germany, Poland and even Russia. England, being more conservative, refused to recognize them.

Adoptive Masonry never gained recognition in America and is unknown here.

Adoptive Masonry, American. The Rite of Adoption as practised on the continent of Europe, and especially in France, has never been introduced into America. The system does not accord with the manners or habits of the people, and undoubtedly never would become popular. But Rob. Morris attempted, in 1855, to introduce an imitation of it, which he had invented, under the name of the "American Adoptive Rite." It consisted of a ceremony of initiation, which was intended as a preliminary trial of the candidate, and of five degrees, named as follows: 1. Jephthah's Daughter, or the daughter's degree. 2. Ruth, or the widow's degree. 3. Esther, or the wife's degree. 4. Martha, or the sister's degree. 5. Electa, or the Christian Martyr's degree. The whole assemblage of the five degrees was called the Eastern Star.

The objects of this Rite, as expressed by the framer, were "to associate in one common bond the worthy wives, widows, daughters, and sisters of Freemasons, so as to make their adoptive privileges available for all the purposes contemplated in Masonry; to secure to them the advantages of their claim in a moral, social, and charitable point of view, and from them the performance of corresponding duties." Hence, no females but those holding the above recited relations to Freemasons were eligible for admission. The male members were called "Protectors"; the female, "Stellæ"; the reunions of these members were styled "Constellations"; and the Rite was presided over and governed by a "Supreme Constellation." There is some ingenuity and even beauty in many of the ceremonies, although it is by no means equal in this respect to the French Adoptive system. Much dissatisfaction was, however, expressed by the leading Masons of the country at the time of its attempted organization; and therefore, notwithstanding very strenuous efforts were made by its founder and his friends to establish it in some of the Western States, it was slow in winning popularity. It has, however, within a few years past, gained much growth under the name of "The Eastern Star." Bro. Albert Pike has also recently printed, for the use of Scottish Rite Masons, *The Masonry of Adoption.* It is in seven degrees, and is a translation from the French system, but greatly enlarged, and is far superior to the original.

The last phase of this female Masonry to which our attention is directed is the system of androgynous degrees which are practised to some extent in the United States. This term "androgynous" is derived from two Greek words, ἀνήρ (ἄνδρος), a man, and γυνή, a woman, and it is equivalent to the English compound, *masculo-feminine.* It is applied to those "side degrees" which are conferred on both males and females. The essential regulation prevailing in these degrees, is that they can be conferred only on Master Masons (and in some instances only on Royal

Arch Masons) and on their female relatives, the peculiar relationship differing in the different degrees.

Thus there is a degree generally called the "Mason's Wife," which can be conferred only on Master Masons, their wives, unmarried daughters and sisters, and their widowed mothers. Another degree, called the "Heroine of Jericho," is conferred only on the wives and daughters of Royal Arch Masons; and the third, the only one that has much pretension of ceremony or ritual, is the "Good Samaritan," whose privileges are confined to Royal Arch Masons and their wives.

In some parts of the United States these degrees are very popular, while in other places they are never practised, and are strongly condemned as modern innovations. The fact is, that by their friends as well as their enemies these so-called degrees have been greatly misrepresented. When females are told that in receiving these degrees they are admitted into the Masonic Order, and are obtaining Masonic information, under the name of "Ladies' Masonry," they are simply deceived. When a woman is informed that, by passing through the brief and unimpressive ceremony of any one of these degrees, she has become a Mason, the deception is still more gross and inexcusable. But it is true that every woman who is related by ties of consanguinity to a Master Mason is at all times and under all circumstances peculiarly entitled to Masonic protection and assistance. Now, if the recipient of an androgynous degree is candidly instructed that, by the use of these degrees, the female relatives of Masons are put in possession of the means of making their claims known by what may be called a sort of oral testimony, which, unlike a written certificate, can be neither lost nor destroyed; but that, by her initiation as a "Mason's Wife" or as a "Heroine of Jericho," she is brought no nearer to the inner portal of Masonry than she was before—if she is honestly told all this, then there can hardly be any harm, and there may be some good in these forms if prudently bestowed. But all attempts to make Masonry of them, and especially that anomalous thing called "Female Masonry," are reprehensible, and are well calculated to produce opposition among the well-informed and cautious members of the Fraternity.

Adoration. The act of paying divine worship. The Latin word *adorare* is derived from *ad*, "to," and *os, oris*, "the mouth," and we thus etymologically learn that the primitive and most general method of adoration was by the application of the fingers to the mouth. Hence we read in Job (xxxi. 26): "If I beheld the sun when it shined, or the moon walking in brightness, and my heart hath been secretly enticed, or *my mouth hath kissed my hand*, this also were an iniquity to be punished by the judges; for I should have denied the God that is above." Here the mouth kissing the hand is an equipollent expression to adoration, as if he had said, "If I have adored the sun or the moon." This mode of adoration is said to have originated among the Persians, who, as worshipers of the sun, always turned their faces to the east and kissed their hands to that luminary. The gesture was first used as a token of respect to their monarchs, and was easily transferred to objects of worship. Other additional forms of adoration were used in various countries, but in almost all of them this reference to kissing was in some degree preserved. It is yet a practice of quite common usage for Orientals to kiss what they deem sacred or that which they wish to adore—example, Wailing Place of the Jews at Jerusalem. The marble toes of the statue of St. Peter in the Cathedral of St. Peter's at Rome have been worn away by the kissings of Catholics and have been replaced by bronze. Among the ancient Romans the act of adoration was thus performed: The worshiper, having his head covered, applied his right hand to his lips, thumb erect, and the forefinger resting on it, and then, bowing his head, he turned round from right to left. And hence Apuleius (*Apolog.*) uses the expression "to apply the hand to the lips," *manum labris admovere,* to express the act of adoration. The Grecian mode of adoration differed from the Roman in having the head uncovered, which practise was adopted by the Christians. The Oriental nations cover the head, but uncover the feet. They also express the act of adoration by prostrating themselves on their faces and applying their foreheads to the ground. The ancient Jews adored by kneeling, sometimes by prostration of the whole body, and by kissing the hand. This act, therefore, of kissing the hand was an early and a very general symbol of adoration. But we must not be led into the error of supposing that a somewhat similar gesture used in some of the high degrees of Freemasonry has any allusion to an act of worship. It refers to that symbol of silence and secrecy which is figured in the statues of Harpocrates, the god of silence. The Masonic idea of adoration has been well depicted by the medieval Christian painters, who represented the act by angels *prostrated before a luminous triangle.*

Advancement Hurried. Nothing can be more certain than that the proper qualifications of a candidate for admission into the mysteries of Freemasonry, and the necessary proficiency of a Mason who seeks advancement to a higher degree, are the two great bulwarks which are to protect the purity and integrity of our Institution. Indeed, we know not which is the more hurtful—to admit an applicant who is unworthy, or to promote a candidate who is ignorant of his first lessons. The one affects the external, the other the internal character of the Institution. The one brings discredit upon the Order among the profane, who already regard us, too often, with suspicion and dislike; the other introduces ignorance and incapacity into our ranks, and dishonors the science of Masonry in our own eyes. The one covers our walls with imperfect and worthless stones, which mar the outward beauty and impair the strength of our temple; the other fills our interior apartments with confusion and disorder, and leaves the edifice, though externally strong, both inefficient and inappropriate for its destined uses.

But, to the candidate himself, a too hurried advancement is often attended with the most disastrous effects. As in geometry, so in Masonry, there is no "royal road" to perfection. A knowledge of its principles and its science, and consequently an acquaintance with its beauties, can only be acquired by long and diligent study. To the careless observer it seldom offers, at a hasty glance, much to attract his attention or secure his interest. The gold must be deprived, by careful manipulation, of the dark and worthless ore which surrounds and envelops it, before its metallic luster and value can be seen and appreciated.

Hence, the candidate who hurriedly passes through his degrees without a due examination of the moral and intellectual purposes of each, arrives at the summit of our edifice without a due and necessary appreciation of the general symmetry and connection that pervade the whole system. The candidate, thus hurried through the elements of our science, and unprepared, by a knowledge of its fundamental principles, for the reception and comprehension of the corollaries which are to be deduced from them, is apt to view the whole system as "a rude and indigested mass" of frivolous ceremonies and puerile conceits, whose intrinsic value will not adequately pay him for the time, the trouble, and expense that he has incurred in his forced initiation. To him, Masonry is as incomprehensible as was the veiled statue of Isis to its blind worshipers, and he becomes, in consequence, either a useless drone in our hive, or speedily retires in disgust from all participation in our labors.

But the candidate who by slow and painful steps has proceeded through each apartment of our mystic Temple, from its porch to its sanctuary, pausing in his progress to admire the beauties and to study the uses of each, learning, as he advances, "line upon line, and precept upon precept," is gradually and almost imperceptibly imbued with so much admiration of the Institution, so much love for its principles, so much just appreciation of its design as a conservator of divine truth, and an agent of human civilization, that he is inclined, on beholding, at last, the whole beauty of the finished building, to exclaim, as did the wondering Queen of Sheba: "A Most Excellent Master must have done all this!"

The usage in many jurisdictions of the United States, when the question is asked in the ritual whether the candidate has made suitable proficiency in his preceding degree, is to reply, "Such as time and circumstances would permit." We have no doubt that this was an innovation originally invented to evade the law, which has always required a due proficiency. To such a question no other answer ought to be given than the positive and unequivocal one that "he has." Neither "time nor circumstances" should be permitted to interfere with his attainment of the necessary knowledge, nor excuse its absence. This, with the wholesome rule, very generally existing, which requires an interval between the conferring of the degrees, would go far to remedy the evil of too hurried and unqualified advancement, of which all intelligent Masons are now complaining.

After these views of the necessity of a careful examination of the claims of a candidate for advancement in Masonry, and the necessity, for his own good as well as that of the Order, that each one should fully prepare himself for this promotion.

American Rite. It has been proposed, and I think with propriety, to give this name to the series of degrees conferred in the United States. The York Rite, which is the name by which they are usually designated, is certainly a misnomer, for the York Rite properly consists of only the degrees of Entered Apprentice, Fellow-Craft, and Master Mason, including in the last degree the Holy Royal Arch. This was the Masonry that existed in England at the time of the revival of the Grand Lodge in 1717. The abstraction of the Royal Arch from the Master's Degree, and its location as a separate degree, produced that modification of the York Rite which now exists in England, and which should properly be called the Modern York Rite, to distinguish it from the Ancient York Rite, which consisted of only three degrees. But in the United States still greater additions have been made to the Rite, through the labors of Webb and other lecturers, and the influence insensibly exerted on the Order by the introduction of the Ancient and Accepted Scottish Rite into this country. The American modification of the York Rite, or the American Rite, consists of nine degrees, viz.:

Degrees	
1. Entered Apprentice. 2. Fellow-Craft. 3. Master Mason.	Given in Symbolic Lodges, and under the control of Grand Lodges.
4. Mark Master. 5. Past Master. 6. Most Excellent Master. 7. Holy Royal Arch.	Given in Chapters, and under the control of Grand Chapters.
8. Royal Master. 9. Select Master.	Given in Councils, and under the control of Grand Councils.

A tenth degree, called Super-Excellent Master, is conferred in some Councils as an honorary rather than as a regular degree; but even as such it is repudiated by many Grand Councils. To these, perhaps, should be added three more degrees, namely, Knight of the Red Cross, Knight Templar, and Knight of Malta, which are given in Commanderies, and are under the control of Grand Commanderies, or, as they are sometimes called, Grand Encampments. But the degrees of the Commandery, which are also known as the degrees of Chivalry, can hardly be called a part of the American Rite. The possession of the Eighth and Ninth Degrees is not considered a necessary qualification for receiving them.

The true American Rite consists only of the nine degrees above enumerated.

There is, or may be, a Grand Lodge, Grand Chapter, Grand Council, and Grand Commandery in each State, whose jurisdiction is distinct and sovereign within its own territory. There is no General Grand Lodge, or Grand Lodge of the United States, though several efforts have been made to form one (see *General Grand Lodge*); there is a General Grand Chapter, but all Grand Chapters are not subject to it, and a Grand Encampment to which all Grand Commanderies of the States are subject.

Androgynous Degrees. (From ἀνής, *a man,* and γυνή, *a woman.*) Those degrees of Masonry which are conferred on both men and women. Besides the degrees of the Adoptive Rite, which are practised in France, there are several of these degrees which are, as "side degrees," conferred in America. Such are the "Mason's Wife," conferred on the wives, daughters, sisters, and mothers of Master Masons, and the "Knight and Heroine of Jericho," conferred on the wives and daughters of Royal Arch Masons. A few years ago, Rob. Morris invented, and very generally promulgated through the Western States of this country, a series of androgynous degrees, which he called "The Star of the East." There is another androgynous degree, sometimes conferred on the wives of Royal Arch Masons, known as the "Good Samaritan."

In some parts of the United States these degrees are very popular, while in other places they are never practised, and are strongly condemned as improper innovations. The fact is, that by their friends as well as by their enemies, these so-called degrees have been greatly misrepresented. When females are told that in receiving these degrees they are admitted into the Masonic Order, and are obtaining Masonic information under the name of "Ladies' Masonry," they are simply deceived. Every woman connected by ties of consanguinity to a Master Mason is peculiarly entitled to Masonic assistance and protection. If she is told this, and also told that by these androgynous degrees she is to be put in possession of the means of making her claims known by a sort of what may be called oral testimony, but that she is by their possession no nearer to the portals of Masonry than she was before, if she is honestly told this, then there is no harm, but the possibility of some good, in these forms if carefully bestowed and prudently preserved. But all attempts to make Masonry of them, and especially that anomalous thing called *Co-Masonry,* are wrong, imprudent, and calculated to produce opposition among the well-informed and cautious members of the Fraternity.

Ark. In the ritual of the American Royal Arch Degree three arks are referred to: 1. The Ark of Safety, or of Noah; 2. The Ark of the Covenant, or of Moses; 3. The Substitute Ark, or the Ark of Zerubbabel. In what is technically called "the passing of the veils," each of these arks has its commemorative illustration, and in the order in which they have been named. The first was constructed by Shem, Ham, and Japheth, the sons of Noah; the second by Moses, Aholiab, and Bezaleel; and the third was discovered by Joshua, Haggai, and Zerubbabel.

Ark, Noah's, or the Ark of Safety, constructed by Shem, Ham, and Japheth, under the superintendence of Noah, and in it, as a chosen tabernacle of refuge, the patriarch's family took refuge. It has been called by many commentators a tabernacle of Jehovah; and Dr. Jarvis, speaking of the word צהר, ZoHaR, which has been translated *window,* says that, in all other passages of Scripture where this word occurs, it signifies the meridian light, the brightest effulgence of day, and therefore it could not have been an aperture, but a source of light itself. He supposes it therefore to have been the Divine Shekinah, or Glory of Jehovah, which afterward dwelt between the cherubim over the Ark of the Covenant in the tabernacle and the Temple. (*Church of the Redeemed,* i., 20.)

Ark of the Covenant. The Ark of the Covenant or of the Testimony was a chest originally constructed by Moses at God's command (Exod. xxv. 10), in which were kept the two tables of stone, on which were engraved the Ten Commandments. It contained, likewise, a golden pot filled with manna, Aaron's rod, and the tables of the covenant. It was at first deposited in the most sacred place of the tabernacle and afterward placed by Solomon in the Sanctum Sanctorum of the Temple, and was lost upon the destruction of that building by the Chaldeans. The later history of this ark is buried in obscurity. It is supposed that, upon the destruction of the first Temple by the Chaldeans, it was carried to Babylon among the other sacred utensils which became the spoil of the conquerors. But of its subsequent fate all traces have been lost. It is, however, certain that it was not brought back to Jerusalem by Zerubbabel. The Talmudists say that there were five things which were the glory of the first Temple that were wanting in the second; namely, the Ark of the Covenant, the Shekinah or Divine Presence, the Urim and Thummim, the holy fire upon the altar, and the spirit of prophecy. The Rev. Salem Towne, it is true, has endeavored to prove, by a very ingenious argument, that the original Ark of the Covenant was concealed by Josiah, or by others, at some time previous to the destruction of Jerusalem, and that it was afterward, at the building of the second Temple, discovered and brought to light. But such a theory is entirely at variance with all the legends of the degree of Select Master and of Royal Arch Masonry. To admit it would lead to endless confusion and contradictions in the traditions of the Order. It is, besides, in conflict with the opinions of the Rabbinical writers and every Hebrew scholar. Josephus and the Rabbis allege that in the second Temple the Holy of Holies was empty, or contained only the Stone of Foundation which marked the place which the ark should have occupied.

The ark was made of shittim wood, overlaid, within and without, with pure gold. It was about three feet nine inches long, two feet three inches wide, and of the same extent in depth. It had on the side two rings of gold, through which were placed staves of shittim wood, by which, when necessary, it was borne by the Levites. Its covering was of pure gold, over which was placed two figures called cherubim, with expanded wings. The covering of the ark was called *kaphiret,* from *kaphar,* "to forgive sin," and hence its English name of "mercy-seat," as being the place where the intercession for sin was made.

The researches of archeologists in the last few years have thrown much light on the Egyptian mysteries. Among the ceremonies of that ancient people was one called the Procession of Shrines, which is mentioned in the Rosetta stone, and depicted on the Temple walls. One of these shrines was an ark, which was carried in procession by the priests, who supported it on their shoulders by staves passing through metal rings. It was thus brought into the Temple and deposited on a stand or altar, that the ceremonies prescribed in the ritual might be performed before it. The contents of these arks were various, but always of a mystical character. Sometimes the ark would contain symbols of Life and Stability; sometimes the sacred beetle, the symbol of the Sun; and there was always a representation of two figures of the goddess Theme or Truth and Justice, which overshadowed the ark with their wings. These coincidences of the Egyptian and Hebrew arks must have been more than accidental.

Ark, Substitute. The chest or coffer which constitutes a part of the furniture, and is used in the ceremonies of a Chapter of Royal Arch Masons, and in a Council of Select Masters according to the American system, is called by Masons the Substitute Ark, to distinguish it from the other ark, that which was constructed in the wilderness under the direction of Moses, and which is known as the Ark of the Covenant. This the Substitute Ark was made to represent under circumstances that are recorded in the Masonic traditions, and especially in those of the Select Degree.

The ark used in Royal Arch and Cryptic Masonry in this country is generally of this form:

Prideaux, on the authority of Lightfoot, contends that, as an ark was indispensable to the Israelitish worship, there was in the second Temple an ark which had been expressly made for the purpose of supplying the place of the first or original ark, and which, without possessing any of its prerogatives or honors, was of precisely the same shape and dimensions, and was deposited in the same place. The Masonic legend, whether authentic or not, is simple and connected. It teaches that there was an ark in the second Temple, but that it was neither the Ark of the Covenant, which had been in the Holy of Holies of the first Temple, nor one that had been constructed as a substitute for it after the building of the second Temple. It was that ark which was presented to us in the

Select Master's Degree, and which being an exact copy of the Mosaical ark, and intended to replace it in case of its loss, which is best known to Freemasons as the *Substitute Ark.*

Lightfoot gives these Talmudic legends, in his *Prospect of the Temple,* in the following language: "It is fancied by the Jews, that Solomon, when he built the Temple, foreseeing that the Temple should be destroyed, caused very obscure and intricate vaults under ground to be made, wherein to hide the ark when any such danger came; that howsoever it went with the Temple, yet the ark, which was the very life of the Temple, might be saved. And they understand that passage in 2 Chron. xxxv. 3, 'Josiah said unto the Levites, Put the holy ark into the house which Solomon, the son of David, did build,' etc., as if Josiah, having heard by the reading of Moses' manuscript, and by Huldah's prophecy of the danger that hung over Jerusalem, commanded to convey the ark into this vault, that it might be secured; and with it, say they, they laid up Aaron's rod, the pot of manna, and the anointing oil. For while the ark stood in its place upon the stone mentioned—they hold that Aaron's rod and the pot of manna stood before it; but, now, were all conveyed into obscurity—and the stone upon which the ark stood lay over the mouth of the vault. But Rabbi Solomon, which useth not, ordinarily, to forsake such traditions, hath given a more serious gloss upon the place; namely, that whereas Manasseh and Amon had removed the ark out of its habitation, and set up images and abominations there of their own—Joshua speaketh to the priests to restore it to its place again. What became of the ark, at the burning of the temple by Nebuchadnezzar, we read not; it is most likely it went to the fire also. However it sped, it was not in the second Temple; and is one of the five choice things that the Jews reckon wanting there. Yet they had an ark there also of their own making, as they had a breastplate of judgment; which, though they both wanted the glory of the former, which was giving of oracles, yet did they stand current as to the other matters of their worship, as the former breastplate and ark had done."

The idea of the concealment of an ark and its accompanying treasures always prevailed in the Jewish church. The account given by the Talmudists is undoubtedly mythical; but there must, as certainly, have been some foundation for the myth, for every myth has a substratum of truth. The Masonic tradition differs from the Rabbinical, but is in every way more reconcilable with truth, or at least with probability. The ark constructed by Moses, Aholiab, and Bezaleel was burned at the destruction of the first Temple; but there was an exact representation of it in the second.

Assassins of the Third Degree. There is in Freemasonry a legend of certain unworthy Craftsmen who entered into a conspiracy to extort from a distinguished brother a secret of which he was the possessor. The legend is altogether symbolic, and when its symbolism is truly comprehended, becomes surpassingly beautiful. By those who look at it as having the pretension of an historical fact, it is sometimes treated with indifference, and sometimes considered an absurdity. But it is not thus that the legends and symbols of Masonry must be read, if we would learn their true spirit. To behold the goddess in all her glorious beauty, the veil that conceals her statue must be withdrawn. Masonic writers who have sought to interpret the symbolism of the legend of the conspiracy of the three assassins, have not agreed always in the interpretation, although they have finally arrived at the same result, namely, that it has a spiritual signification. Those who trace Speculative Masonry to the ancient solar worship, of whom Ragon may be considered as the exponent, find in this legend a symbol of the conspiracy of the three winter months to destroy the life-giving heat of the sun. Those who, like the disciples of the Rite of Strict Observance, trace Masonry to a Templar origin, explain the legend as referring to the conspiracy of the three renegade knights who falsely accused the Order, and thus aided King Philip and Pope Clement to abolish Templarism, and to slay its Grand Master. Hutchinson and Oliver, who labored to give a Christian interpretation to all the symbols of Masonry, referred the legend to the crucifixion of the Messiah, the type of which is, of course, the slaying of Abel by his brother Cain. Others, of whom the Chevalier Ramsay was the leader, sought to give it a political significance; and, making Charles I. the type of the Builder, symbolized Cromwell and his adherents as the conspirators. The Masonic scholars whose aim has been to identify the modern system of Freemasonry with the Ancient Mysteries, and especially with the Egyptian, which they supposed to be the germ of all the others, interpret the conspirators as the symbol of the Evil Principle, or Typhon, slaying the Good Principle, or Osiris; or, when they refer to the Zoroastic Mysteries of Persia, as Ahriman contending against Ormuzd. And lastly, in the Philosophic degrees, the myth is interpreted as signifying the war of Falsehood, Ignorance, and Superstition against Truth. Of the supposed names of the three Assassins, there is hardly any end of variations, for they materially differ in all the principal rites. Thus, we have Jubela, Jubelo, and Jubelum in in the York and American Rites. In the Adonhiramite system we have Romvel, Gravelot, and Abiram. In the Scottish Rite we find the names given in the old rituals as Jubelum Akirop, sometimes Abiram, Jubelo Romvel, and Jubela Gravelot. Schterke and Oterfüt are in some of the German rituals, while other Scottish rituals have Abiram, Romvel, and Hobhen. In all these names there is manifest corruption, and the patience of many Masonic scholars has been well-nigh exhausted in seeking for some plausible and satisfactory derivation.

Aum. A mystic syllable among the Hindus, signifying the Supreme God of Gods, which the Brahmans, from its awful and sacred meaning, hesitate to pronounce aloud, and in doing so place one of their hands before the mouth so as to deaden the sound. This triliteral name of God, which is as sacred among the Hindus as the Tetragrammatam is among the Jews, is composed of three Sanskrit letters, sounding AUM. The first letter, A, stands for the Creator; the second, U, for the Preserver; and the third, M, for the Destroyer, or Brahma, Vishnu, and Siva. Benfey, in his *Sanskrit-English Dictionary,* defines the word as "a particle of reminiscence"; and this may explain the Brahmanical saying, that a Brahman beginning or ending the reading of a part of the Veda or Sacred Books, must always pronounce, *to himself,* the syllable AUM; for unless that syllable precede, his learning will slip away from him, and unless it follow, nothing will be long retained. An old passage in the Parana says, "All the rites ordained in the Vedas, the sacrifices to fire, and all sacred purifications, shall pass away, but the word AUM shall never pass away, for it is the symbol of the Lord of all things." The word has been indifferently spelled, O'M, AOM, and AUM; but the last is evidently the most proper, as the second letter is OO = U in the Sanskrit alphabet.

Babylon. The ancient capital of Chaldea, situated on both sides of the Euphrates, and once the most magnificent city of the ancient world. It was here that, upon the destruction of Solomon's Temple by Nebuchadnezzar in the year of the world 3394, the Jews of the tribes of Judah and Benjamin, who were the inhabitants of Jerusalem, were conveyed and detained in captivity for seventy-two years, until Cyrus, King of Persia, issued a decree for restoring them, and permitting them to rebuild their temple, under the superintendence of Zerubbabel, the Prince of the Captivity, and with the assistance of Joshua the High Priest and Haggai the Scribe.

Babylon the Great, as the prophet Daniel calls it, was situated four hundred and seventy-five miles in a nearly due east direction from Jerusalem. It stood in the midst of a large and fertile plain on each side of the river Euphrates, which ran through it from north to south. It was surrounded with walls which were eighty-seven feet thick, three hundred and fifty in height, and sixty miles in compass. These were all built of large bricks cemented together with bitumen. Exterior to the walls was a wide and deep trench lined with the same material. Twenty-five gates on each side, made of solid brass, gave admission to the city. From each of these gates proceeded a wide street fifteen miles in length, and the whole was separated by means of other smaller divisions, and contained six hundred and seventy-six squares, each of which was two miles and a quarter in circumference. Two hundred and fifty towers placed upon the walls afforded the means of additional strength and protection. Within this immense circuit were to be found palaces and temples and other edifices of the utmost magnificence, which have caused the wealth, the luxury, and splendor of Babylon to become the favorite theme of the historians of antiquity, and which compelled the prophet Isaiah, even while denouncing its downfall, to speak of it as "the glory of kingdoms, the beauty of the Chaldees' excellency."

Babylon, which, at the time of the destruction of the Temple of Jerusalem, constituted a part of the Chaldean empire, was subsequently taken, B.C. 538, after a siege of two years, by Cyrus, King of Persia.

Banners, Royal Arch. Much difficulty has been experienced by ritualists in reference to the true colors and proper arrangements of the banners used in an American Chapter of Royal Arch Masons. It is admitted that they are four in number, and that their colors are blue, purple, scarlet, and white; and it is known too, that the devices on these banners are a lion, an ox, a man, and an eagle; but the doubt is constantly arising as to the relation between these devices and these colors, and as to which of the former is to be appropriated to each of the latter. The question, it is true, is one of mere ritualism, but it is important that the ritual should be always uniform, and hence the object of the present article is to attempt the solution of this question.

The banners used in a Royal Arch Chapter are derived from those which are supposed to have been borne by the twelve tribes of Israel during their encampment in the wilderness, to which reference is made in the second chapter of the Book of Numbers, and the second verse: "Every man of the children of Israel shall pitch by his own standard." But as to what were the devices on the banners, or what were their various colors, the Bible is absolutely silent. To the inventive genius of the Talmudists are we indebted for all that we know or profess to know on this subject. These mystical philosophers have given to us with wonderful precision the various devices which they have borrowed from the death-bed prophecy of Jacob, and have sought, probably in their own fertile imaginations, for the appropriate colors.

The English Royal Arch Masons, whose system differs very much from that of their American Companions, display in their Chapters the twelve banners of the tribes in accordance with the Talmudic devices and colors. These have been very elaborately described by Dr. Oliver in his *Historical Landmarks* (ii., 583–97), and beautifully exemplified by Companion Harris in his *Royal Arch Tracing Boards.*

But our American Royal Arch Masons, as we have seen, use only four banners, being those attributed by the Talmudists to the four principal tribes—Judah, Ephraim, Reuben, and Dan. The devices on these banners are respectively a lion, an ox, a man, and an eagle. As to this there is no question, all authorities, such as they are, agreeing on this point. But, as has been before said, there is some diversity of opinion as to the colors of each, and necessarily as to the officers by whom they should be borne.

Some of the Targumists, or Jewish biblical commentators, say that the color of the banner of each tribe was analogous to that of the stone which represented that tribe in the breastplate of the High Priest. If this were correct, then the colors of the banners of the four leading tribes would be red and green, namely, red for Judah, Ephraim, and Reuben, and green for Dan; these being the colors of the precious stones sardonyx, ligure, carbuncle, and chrysolite, by which these tribes were represented in the High Priest's breastplate. Such an arrangement would not, of course, at all suit the symbolism of the American Royal Arch banners.

Equally unsatisfactory is the disposition of the colors derived from the arms of Speculative Masonry, as first displayed by Dermott in his *Ahiman Rezon,* which is familiar to all American Masons, from the copy published by Cross, in his *Hieroglyphic Chart.* In this piece of blazonry, the two fields occupied by Judah and Dan are *azure,* or blue, and those of Ephraim and Reuben are *or,* or golden yellow; an appropriation of colors altogether uncongenial with Royal Arch symbolism.

We must, then, depend on the Talmudic writers solely for the disposition and arrangement of the colors and devices of these banners. From their works we learn that the color of the banner of Judah was white; that of Ephraim, scarlet; that of Reuben, purple; and that of Dan, blue; and that the devices of the same tribes were respectively the lion, the ox, the man, and the eagle.

Hence, under this arrangement—and it is the only one upon which we can depend—the four banners in a Chapter of Royal Arch Masons, working in the American Rite, must be distributed as follows among the banner-bearing officers:

1st. An eagle, on a blue banner. This represents the tribe of Dan, and is borne by the Grand Master of the first veil.

2d. A man, on a purple banner. This represents the tribe of Reuben, and is borne by the Grand Master of the second veil.

3d. An ox, on a scarlet banner. This represents the tribe of Ephraim, and is borne by the Grand Master of the third veil.

4th. A lion, on a white banner. This represents the tribe of Judah, and is borne by the Royal Arch Captain.

Battery. A given number of blows by the gavels of the officers, or by the hands of the Brethren, as a mark of approbation, admiration, or reverence, and at times accompanied by the acclamation.

Beauceant, Social Order of the. The S.O.O.B., known as the Social Order of the Beauceant, is an organization of women whose membership is limited to the wives and widows of Knights Templar. It was founded in the city of Denver, Colorado, February 20th, 1890. The first suggestion for uniting the wives and widows of Knights Templar, into a society or order was given by several Sir Knights in 1889, after the Grand Encampment of Knights Templar decided to hold its twenty-fifth Triennial Conclave in Denver August, 1892. On February 20th, 1890, the first meeting was held at the home of Mrs. William H. H.

Cranmer, 925 Seventeenth Avenue, Denver. There were twenty three charter members present;—Mesdames Richard W. Moseley, Charles P. Wickes, Frank E. Edbrook, Nelson Franklin, James H. Crandell, William H. Cranmer, Silas W. Chaney, William R. Harp, John G. Hoffer, Jessie E. Kinport, Lawrence N. Greenleaf, William G. Parkhurst, Thomas Nicholl, Alonzo G. Rhoads, Leonard K. Watkins, Smith M. Shattuc, Thomas J. Morrison, William Toovey, Ben J. Bowen, Herbert S. DeSollar, William D. Peirce, Frank J. Hard, Harry L. Wadsworth. By July 1938 the membership was 6210, with 85 chartered Assemblies.

The governing body is called an Assembly. The principal officers are;—President, First, Second and Third Vice Presidents, Secretary and Treasurer. The appointive officers are;—Chaplin, Guard and Marshall.

The S.O.O.B. Society was the name adopted. Its slogan;—"Some Of Our Business to make this Society an attractive center from which shall radiate bright, joyous and happy influences. . . . It is Some Of Our Business to be helpful, hopeful and inspiring, . . . to make life purer, better and sweeter."

Its purposes are social and benevolent, helping its own members and others in need or distress.

Its Supreme Assembly meets annually. It has a very beautiful Ritual, which is secret.

Beauseant. The vexillum belli, or war-banner of the ancient Templars, which is also used by the modern Masonic Order. The upper half of the banner was black, and the lower half white: black, to typify terror to foes, and white, fairness to friends. It bore the pious inscription, *Non nobis, Domine non nobis, sed nomini.* With regard to the double signification of the white and black banner, the Orientalists have a legend of Alexander the Great, which may be appropriately quoted on the present occasion,

Alexander was the lord of light and darkness: when he went out with his army the light was before him, and behind him was the darkness, so that he was secure against all ambuscades; and by means of a miraculous white and black standard he had also the power to transform the clearest day into midnight and darkness, or black night into noonday, just as he unfurled the one or the other. Thus he was unconquerable, since he rendered his troops invisible at his pleasure, and came down suddenly upon his foes. Might there not have been some connection between the mythical white and black standard of Alexander and the Beauseant of the Templars? We know that the latter were familiar with Oriental symbolism.

Beauseant was also the war-cry of the Ancient Templars.

Beauty. Said to be symbolically one of the three supports of a Lodge. It is represented by the Corinthian column, because the Corinthian is the most beautiful of the ancient orders of Architecture;

and by the Junior Warden, because he symbolizes the meridian sun—the most beautiful object in the heavens. Hiram Abif is also said to be represented by the Column of Beauty, because the Temple was indebted to his skill for its splendid decorations. The idea of Beauty as one of the supports of the Lodge is found in the earliest rituals of the eighteenth century, as well as the symbolism which refers it to the Corinthian column and the Junior Warden. Preston first introduced the reference to the Corinthian column and to Hiram Abif.

Bone. This word, which is now corruptly pronounced in one syllable, is the Hebrew word *boneh*, בונה, "builder," from the verb *banah*, בנה, "to build." It was peculiarly applied, as an epithet, to Hiram Abif, who superintended the construction of the Temple as its chief builder. Master Masons will recognize it as the terminal portion of a significant word. Its true pronunciation would be, in English letters, *bonay;* but the corruption into one syllable as *bone* has become too universal ever to be corrected.

Burning Bush. In the third chapter of Exodus it is recorded that, while Moses was keeping the flock of Jethro on Mount Horeb, "the angel of the Lord appeared unto him in a flame of fire out of the midst of a bush," and there communicated to him for the first time his Ineffable Name. This occurrence is commemorated in the "Burning Bush" of the Royal Arch Degree. In all the systems of antiquity, fire is adopted as a symbol of Deity; and the "Burning Bush," or the bush filled with fire which did not consume, whence came forth the Tetragrammaton, the symbol of Divine Light and Truth, is considered, in the higher degrees of Masonry, like the "Orient" in the lower, as the great source of true Masonic light; wherefore Supreme Councils of the Thirty-third Degree date their balustres, or official documents, "near the B.'. B.'.," or "Burning Bush," to intimate that they are, in their own rite, the exclusive source of all Masonic instruction.

It is recorded in the third chapter of Exodus, that when Moses was tending the flocks of Jethro, the priest of Midian, who was the father-in-law of Moses, he came to the mountain of God—even to Horeb. And an angel of the Lord appeared unto him in a flame of fire out of the midst of the bush, and the bush was not consumed. And Moses said "I will turn aside and see this great sight—why the bush is not consumed." And God called to him commanding that he should make the necessary preparation to bring the children of Israel out of the land of Egypt—the land of materiality—where they had been for years in bondage to Pharaoh.

Now while this lonely sheep herder was quietly tending his flocks, undisturbed by the sights and sounds of civilization, he had much time for observation, and realized what an enormous task had been placed upon him by the Lord God Jehovah. When, therefore, the phenomenon of the burning bush appeared, naturally he desired to see and study it.

In this experience there dawned upon him the great part he should play in leading his fellow men out of the bondage of materiality into the promised land of spirituality. It is narrated that God commanded him to "take off thine shoes, for the place whereon thou standest is holy ground."

Now, as then, in Egypt and in the Holy Land, the burning bush is a natural sight—not a phenomenon—and Moses was so spiritually minded that he realized he was in God's presence always, that "the angels of the Lord" were God's good thoughts coming to him, as they come to you and to me today. Only as we are spiritually minded do we recognize them.

The experience of the burning bush let Moses to recognize more clearly his own true sonship and to help the children of Israel to discover theirs. As a noted poet has so beautifully written;—"The earth is crammed with Heaven—God in every burning bush—but only those who see—take off their shoes."

As we come more fully to realize the truth of what a noted metaphysician has so wonderfully written;—"Heaven is a state of bliss where no inharmony prevails—a present possibility here and now."—may the scales fall from our eyes and may we come seeing, with bared heads and feet—in token of our sincerity—realizing that we, too, are on holy ground, letting no inharmony prevail, cleansing our thoughts and minds of the vices and superfluities of material life, thereby fitting ourselves as living stones in that "house eternal—that house not made with hands."

Canada. Upon the advent of Confederation, July 1, 1867, local control in each Province for the government of the Masonic Fraternity of the Dominion took a strong hold as a predominant idea, and prevailed. Each Province has now a Grand Lodge, and in order of their organization are as follows: Canada, having jurisdiction only in Ontario, 1855; Nova Scotia, 1866; New Brunswick, 1867; Quebec, 1869; British Columbia, 1871; Manitoba, 1875; Prince Edward Island, 1875; Alberta, 1905; Saskatchewan, 1906. The first marks of the Ancient Craftsman have been found in Nova Scotia. A mineralogical survey in 1827 found on the shore of Goat Island in the Annapolis Basin, partly covered with sand, a slab of rock 2½ × 2 feet, bearing on it those well-known Masonic emblems, "the Square and Compasses," and the date 1606. Who were the Craftsmen and how the stone came there, must be left to conjecture. [Will H. Whyte, P. G. M. : : K. T. of Canada.]

Candlestick, Golden. The golden candlestick of seven branches, which is a part of the furniture of a Royal Arch Chapter, is derived from "the holy candlestick" which Moses was instructed to construct of beaten gold for the use of the tabernacle. Smith (*Dict. of the Bible*) thus abbreviates Lightfoot's explanation of the description given in Exodus: "The foot of it was gold, from which went up a shaft straight, which was the middle light. Near the foot was a golden dish wrought almondwise; and a little above that a golden knop, and above that a golden flower. Then two branches one on each side bowed,—and coming up as high as the middle shaft. On each of them were three golden cups placed almondwise, in sharp, scallop-shell fashion; above which was a golden knop, a golden flower, and the socket. Above the branches on the middle shaft was a golden boss, above which rose two shafts more; above the coming out of these was another boss and two more shafts, and then on the shaft upwards were three golden scallop-cups, a knop, and a flower; so that the heads of the branches stood an equal height.'' In the tabernacle, the candlestick was placed opposite the table of shew-bread, which it was intended to illumine, in an oblique position, so that the lamps looked to the east and south. What became of the candlestick between the time of Moses and that of Solomon is unknown; but it does not appear to have been present in the first Temple, which was lighted by ten golden candlesticks similarly embossed, which were connected by golden chains and formed a sort of railing before the veil.

These ten candlesticks became the spoil of the Chaldean conqueror at the time of the destruction of the Temple, and could not have been among the articles afterward restored by Cyrus; for in the second Temple, built by Zerubbabel, we find only a single candlestick of seven branches, like that of the tabernacle. Its form has been perpetuated on the Arch of Titus, on which it was sculptured with other articles taken by that monarch, and carried to Rome as *spolia opima,* after he had destroyed the Herodian Temple. This is the candlestick which is represented as a decoration in a Royal Arch Chapter.

In Jewish symbolism, the seven branches were supposed by some to refer to the seven planets, and by others to the seventh day or Sabbath. The primitive Christians made it allusive to Christ as the ''light of the world,'' and in this sense it is a favorite symbol in early Christian art. In Masonry it seems to have no symbolic meaning, unless it be the general one of light; but is used in a Royal Arch Chapter simply to indicate that the room is a representation of the tabernacle erected near the ruins of the first Temple, for the purpose of temporary worship during the building of the second, and in which tabernacle this candlestick is supposed to have been present.

Capitular Degrees. The degrees conferred under the charter of an American Royal Arch Chapter, which are Mark Master, Past Master, Most Excellent Master, and Royal Arch Mason. The capitular degrees are almost altogether founded on and composed of a series of events in Masonic history. Each of them has attached to it some tradition or legend which it is the design of the degree to illustrate, and the memory of which is preserved in its ceremonies and instructions. Most of these legends are of symbolic signification. But this is their interior sense. In their outward and ostensible meaning, they appear before us simply as legends. To retain these legends in the memory of Masons appears to have been the primary design in the establishment of the higher degrees; and as the information intended to be communicated in these degrees is of an historical character, there can of course be but little room for symbols or for symbolic instruction; the profuse use of which would rather tend to an injury than to a benefit, by complicating the purposes of the ritual and confusing the mind of the aspirant. These remarks refer exclusively to the Mark and Most Excellent Master's Degree of the American Rite, but are not so applicable to the Royal Arch, which is eminently symbolic. The legends of the second Temple, and the lost word, the peculiar legends of that degree, are among the most prominent symbols of the Masonic system.

Capitular Masonry. The Masonry conferred in a Royal Arch Chapter of the York and American Rites. There are Chapters in the Ancient and Accepted, Scottish, and in the French and other Rites; but the Masonry therein conferred is not called capitular.

Captivity. The Jews reckoned their national captivities as four:—the Babylonian, Medean, Grecian, and Roman. The present article will refer only to the first, when there was a forcible deportation of the inhabitants of Jerusalem by Nebuzaradan, the general of King Nebuchadnezzar, and their detention at Babylon until the reign of Cyrus, which alone is connected with the history of Masonry, and is commemorated in the Royal Arch Degree.

Between that portion of the ritual of the Royal Arch which refers to the destruction of the first Temple, and that subsequent part which symbolizes the building of the second, there is an interregnum (if we may be allowed the term) in the ceremonial of the degree, which must be considered as a long interval in history, the filling up of which, like the interval between the acts of a play, must be left to the imagination of the spectator. This interval represents the time passed in the captivity of the Jews at Babylon. That captivity lasted for seventy years—from the reign of Nebuchadnezzar until that of Cyrus—although but fifty-two of these years are commemorated in the Royal Arch Degree. This event took place in the year 588 B.C. It was not, however, the beginning of the "seventy years' captivity," which had been foretold by the prophet Jeremiah, which commenced eighteen years before. The captives were conducted to Babylon. What was the exact number removed we have no means of ascertaining. We are led to believe, from certain passages of Scripture, that the deportation was not complete. Calmet says that Nebuchadnezzar carried away only the principal inhabitants, the warriors and artisans of every kind, and that he left the husbandmen, the laborers, and, in general, the poorer classes, that constituted the great body of the people. Among the prisoners of distinction, Josephus mentions the high priest, Seraiah, and Zephaniah, the priest that was next to him, with the three rulers that guarded the Temple, the eunuch who was over the armed men, seven friends of Zedekiah, his scribe, and sixty other rulers.

Zedekiah, the king, had attempted to escape previous to the termination of the siege, but being pursued, was captured and carried to Riblah, the headquarters of Nebuchadnezzar, where, having first been compelled to behold the slaughter of his children, his eyes were then put out, and he was conducted in chains to Babylon.

A Masonic tradition informs us that the captive Jews were bound by their conquerors with triangular chains, and that this was done by the Chaldeans as an additional insult, because the Jewish Masons were known to esteem the triangle as an emblem of the sacred name of God, and must have considered its appropriation to the form of their fetters as a desecration of the Tetragrammaton.

Notwithstanding the ignominious mode of their conveyance from Jerusalem and the vindictiveness displayed by their conqueror in the destruction of their city and Temple, they do not appear, on their arrival at Babylon, to have been subjected to any of the extreme rigors of slavery. They were distributed into various parts of the empire, some remaining in the city, while others were sent into the provinces. The latter probably devoted themselves to agricultural pursuits, while the former were engaged in commerce or in the labors of architecture. Smith says that the captives were treated not as slaves but as colonists. They were permitted to retain their personal property, and even to purchase lands and erect houses. Their civil and religious government was not utterly destroyed, for they kept up a regular succession of kings and high priests, one of each of whom returned with them, as will be seen hereafter, on their restoration. Some of the principal captives were advanced to offices of dignity and power in the royal palace, and were permitted to share in the councils of state. Their prophets, Daniel and Ezekiel, with their associates, preserved among their countrymen the pure doctrines of their religion. Although they had neither place nor time of national gathering, nor temple, and therefore offered no sacrifices, yet they observed the Mosaic laws with respect to the rite of circumcision. They preserved their tables of genealogy and the true succession to the throne of David. The rightful heir being called the Head of the Captivity, Jehoiachin, who was the first king of Judea carried captive to Babylon, was succeeded by his son Shealtiel, and he by his son Zerubbabel, who was the Head of the Captivity, or nominal prince of Judea at the close of the captivity. The due succession of the high-priesthood was also preserved, for Jehosadek, who was the high priest carried by Nebuchadnezzar to Babylon, where he died during the captivity, was succeeded by his eldest son, Joshua. The Jewish captivity terminated in the first year of the reign of Cyrus, B.C. 536. Cyrus, from his conversations with Daniel and the other Jewish captives of learning and piety, as well as from his perusal of their sacred books, more especially the prophecies of Isaiah, had become imbued with a knowledge of true religion, and hence had even publicly annouuced to his subjects his belief in the God "which the nation of the Israelites worshipped." He was consequently impressed with an earnest desire to fulfil the prophetic declarations of which he was the subject, and to rebuild the Temple of Jerusalem. Cyrus therefore issued a decree by which the Jews were permitted to return to their country. According to Milman, 42,360 besides servants availed themselves of this permission, and returned to Jerusalem under Zerubbabel their prince and Joshua their high priest, and thus ended the first or Babylonian captivity, the only one which has any connection with the legends of Freemasonry as commemorated in the Royal Arch Degree.

Chamber of Reflection. In the French and Scottish Rites, a small room adjoining the Lodge, in which, preparatory to initiation, the candidate is enclosed for the purpose of indulging in those serious meditations which its somber appearance and the gloomy emblems with which it is furnished are calculated to produce. It is also used in some of the high degrees for a similar purpose. Its employment is very appropriate, for, "It is only in solitude that we can deeply reflect upon our present or future undertakings, and blackness, darkness, or solitariness, is ever a symbol of death. A man who has undertaken a thing after mature reflection seldom turns back."

Charleston. A city in the United States of America, and the metropolis of the State of South Carolina. It was there that the first Supreme Council of the Ancient and Accepted Scottish Rite was established in 1801, whence all other Supreme Councils have emanated, directly or indirectly. Hence, it has assumed the title of "Mother Council of the world." Its seat was removed in 1870 to the city of Washington.

Commander. 1. The presiding officer in a Commandery of Knights Templar. His style is "Eminent," and the jewel of his office is a cross, from which issue rays of light. In England and Canada he is now styled "Preceptor." 2. The Superintendent of a Commandery, as a house or residence of the Ancient Knights of Malta, was so called.

Commandery. 1. In the United States all regular assemblies of Knights Templar are called Commanderies, and must consist of the following officers: Eminent Commander, Generalissimo, Captain-General, Prelate, Senior Warden, Junior Warden, Treasurer, Recorder, Warder, Standard-Bearer, Sword-Bearer, and Sentinel. These Commanderies derive their warrants of Constitution from a Grand Commandery, or, if there is no such body in the State in which they are organized, from the Grand Encampment of the United States. They confer the degrees of Companion of the Red Cross, Knight Templar, and Knight of Malta.

In a Commandery of Knights Templars, the throne is situated in the East. Above it are suspended three banners: the center one bearing a cross, surmounted by a glory; the left one having inscribed on it the emblems of the Order, and the right one, a paschal lamb. The Eminent Commander is seated on the throne; the Generalissimo, Prelate, and Past Commanders on his right; the Captain-General on his left; the Treasurer and Recorder, as in a Symbolic Lodge; the Senior Warden at the southwest angle of the triangle, and upon the right of the first division; the Junior Warden at the northwest angle of the triangle, and on the left of the third division; the Standard-Bearer in the West, between the Sword-Bearer on his right, and the Warder on his left; and in front of him is a stall for the initiate. The Knights are arranged in equal numbers on each side, and in front of the throne. In England and Canada a body of Knights Templars is called a "Preceptory."

2. The houses or residences of the Knights of Malta were called Commanderies, and the aggregation of them in a nation was called a Priory or Grand Priory.

Commandery, Grand. When three or more Commanderies are instituted in a State, they may unite and form a Grand Commandery under the regulations prescribed by the Grand Encampment of the United States. They have the superintendence of all Commanderies of Knights Templars that are holden in their respective jurisdictions.

A Grand Commandery meets at least annually, and its officers consist of a Grand Commander, Deputy Grand Commander, Grand Generalissimo, Grand Captain-General, Grand Prelate, Grand Senior and Junior Warden, Grand Treasurer, Grand Recorder, Grand Warder, Grand Standard-Bearer, and Grand Sword-Bearer.

Conclave. Commanderies of Knights Templars in England and Canada were called Conclaves, and the Grand Encampment, the Grand Conclave, but the terms now in use are "Preceptory" and "Great Priory" respectively. The word is also applied to the meetings in some other of the high degrees. The word is derived from the Latin *con*, "with," and *clavis*, "a key," to denote the idea of being locked up in seclusion, and in this sense was first applied to the apartment in which the cardinals are literally locked up when met to elect a Pope.

Consistory. The meetings of members of the Thirty-second Degree, or Sublime Princes of the Royal Secret in the Ancient and Accepted Scottish Rite, are called Consistories. The elective officers are, according to the ritual of the Southern Jurisdiction of the United States, a Commander-in-Chief, Seneschal, Preceptor, Chancellor, Minister of State, Almoner, Registrar, and Treasurer. In the Northern Jurisdiction it is slightly different, the second and third officers being called Lieutenant-Commanders. A Consistory confers the Thirty-first and Thirty-second degrees of the Rite.

Contumacy. In civil law, it is the refusal or neglect of a party accused to appear and answer to a charge preferred against him in a court of justice. In Masonic jurisprudence, it is disobedience of or rebellion against superior authority, as when a Mason refuses to obey the edict of his Lodge, or a Lodge refuses to obey that of the Grand Master or the Grand Lodge. The punishment, in the former case, is generally suspension or expulsion; in the latter, arrest of charter or forfeiture of warrant.

Corn, Wine, and Oil. Corn, wine, and oil are the Masonic elements of consecration. The adoption of these symbols is supported by the highest antiquity. Corn, wine, and oil were the most important productions of Eastern countries; they constituted the wealth of the people, and were esteemed as the supports of life and the means of refreshment. David enumerates them among the greatest blessings that we enjoy, and speaks of them as "*wine* that maketh glad the heart of man, and *oil* to make his face to shine, and *bread* which strengtheneth man's heart." (Ps. civ. 15.) In devoting anything to religious purposes, the anointing with oil was considered as a necessary part of the ceremony, a rite which has descended to Christian nations. The tabernacle in the wilderness, and all its holy vessels, were, by God's express command, anointed with oil; Aaron and his two sons were set apart for the priesthood with the same ceremony; and the prophets and kings of Israel were consecrated to their offices by the same rite. Hence, Freemasons' Lodges, which are but temples to the Most High, are consecrated to the sacred purposes for which they were built by strewing corn, wine, and oil upon the "*Lodge*," the emblem of the Holy Ark. Thus does this mystic ceremony instruct us to be nourished with the hidden manna of righteousness, to be refreshed with the Word of the Lord, and to rejoice with *joy* unspeakable in the riches of divine grace. "Wherefore, my brethren," says the venerable Harris (*Disc.*, iv., 81), "wherefore do you carry *corn, wine,* and *oil* in your processions, but to remind you that in the pilgrimage of human life you are to impart a portion of your *bread* to feed the hungry, to send a cup of your *wine* to cheer the sorrowful, and to pour the healing *oil* of your consolation into the wounds which sickness hath made in the bodies, or affliction rent in the hearts, of your fellow-travellers?"

In processions, the corn alone is carried in a golden pitcher, the wine and oil are placed in silver vessels, and this is to remind us that the first, as a necessity and the "staff of life," is of more importance and more worthy of honor than the others, which are but comforts.

Cresset. An open lamp formerly having a cross-piece filled with combustible material, such as naphtha, and recognized as the symbol of Light and Truth.

Christianization of Freemasonry. The interpretation of the symbols of Freemasonry from a Christian point of view is a theory adopted by some of the most distinguished Masonic writers of England and this country, but one which I think does not belong to the ancient system. Hutchinson, and after him Oliver—profoundly philosophical as are the Masonic speculations of both—have, I am constrained to believe, fallen into a great error in calling the Master Mason's Degree a Christian institution. It is true that it embraces within its scheme the great truths of Christianity upon the subject of the immortality of the soul and the resurrection of the body; but this was to be presumed, because Freemasonry is truth, and all truth must be identical. But the origin of each is different; their histories are dissimilar. The principles of Freemasonry preceded the advent of Christianity. Its symbols and its legends are derived from the Solomonic Temple and from the people even anterior to that. Its religion comes from the ancient priesthood; its faith was that primitive one of Noah and his immediate descendants. If Masonry were simply a Christian institution, the Jew and the Moslem, the Brahman and the Buddhist, could not conscientiously partake of its illumination. But its universality is its boast. In its language citizens of every nation may converse; at its altar men of all religions may kneel; to its creed disciples of every faith may subscribe.

Yet it cannot be denied that since the advent of Christianity a Christian element has been almost imperceptibly infused into the Masonic system, at least among Christian Masons. This has been a necessity; for it is the tendency of every predominant religion to pervade with its influence all that surrounds it or is about it, whether religious, political, or social. This arises from a need of the human heart. To the man deeply imbued with the spirit of his religion, there is an almost unconscious desire to accommodate and adapt all the business and the amusements of life—the labors and the employments of his everyday existence—to the indwelling faith of his soul.

The Christian Mason, therefore, while acknowledging and appreciating the great doctrines taught in Masonry, and also while grateful that these doctrines were preserved in the bosom of his ancient Order at a time when they were unknown to the multitudes of the surrounding nations, is still anxious to give to them a Christian character; to invest them, in some measure, with the peculiarities of his own creed, and to bring the interpretation of their symbolism more nearly home to his own religious sentiments.

The feeling is an instinctive one, belonging to the noblest aspirations of our human nature; and hence we find Christian Masonic writers indulging in it to an almost unwarrantable excess, and, by the extent of their sectarian interpretations, materially affecting the cosmopolitan character of the Institution.

This tendency to Christianization has, in some instances, been so universal, and has prevailed for so long a period, that certain symbols and myths have been, in this way, so deeply and thoroughly imbued with the Christian element as to leave those who have not penetrated into the cause of this peculiarity, in doubt whether they should attribute to the symbol an ancient or a modern and Christian origin.

Cross. We can find no symbolism of the cross in the primitive degrees of Ancient Craft Masonry. It does not appear among the symbols of the Apprentice, the Fellow-Craft, the Master, or the Royal Arch. This is undoubtedly to be attributed to the fact that the cross was considered, by those who invented those degrees, only in reference to its character as a Christian sign. The subsequent archeological investigations that have given to the cross a more universal place in iconography were unknown to the rituals. It is true, that it is referred to, under the name of the *rode* or *rood,* in the manuscript of the fourteenth century, published by Halliwell; this was, however, one of the Constitutions of the Operative Freemasons, who were fond of the symbol, and were indebted for it to their ecclesiastical origin, and to their connection with the Gnostics, among whom the cross was a much used symbol. But on the revival in 1717, when the ritual was remodified, and differed very greatly from that meager one in practise among the medieval Masons, all allusion to the cross was left out, because the revivalists laid down the principle that the religion of Speculative Masonry was not sectarian but universal. And although this principle was in some points, as in the "lines parallel," neglected, the reticence as to the Christian sign of salvation has continued to the present day; so that the cross cannot be considered as a symbol in the primary and original degrees of Masonry.

But in the high degrees the cross has been introduced as an important symbol. In some of them—those which are to be traced to the Temple system of Ramsay—it is to be viewed with reference to its Christian origin and meaning. Thus, in the original Rose Croix and Kadosh—no matter what may be the modern interpretation given to it—it was simply a representation of the cross of Christ. In others of a philosophical character, such as the Ineffable degrees, the symbolism of the cross was in all probability borrowed from the usages of antiquity, for from the earliest times and in almost all countries the cross has been a sacred symbol. It is depicted on the oldest monuments of Egypt, Assyria, Persia, and Hindustan. It was, says Faber (*Cabir.*, ii., 390), a symbol throughout the Pagan world long previous to its becoming an object of veneration to Christians. In ancient symbology it was a symbol of eternal life. M. de Mortillet, who, in 1866, published a work entitled *Le Signe de la Croix avant le Christianisme,* found in the very earliest epochs three principal symbols of universal occurrence: viz., the *circle,* the *pyramid,* and the *cross.* Leslie (*Man's Origin and Destiny,* p. 312), quoting from him in reference to the ancient worship of the cross, says: "It seems to have been a worship of such a peculiar nature as to exclude the worship of idols." This sacredness of the crucial symbol may be one reason why its form was often adopted, especially by the Celts, in the construction of their temples.

"The symbol that beyond all others has fascinated the human mind, THE CROSS, finds here its source and meaning. Scholars have pointed out its sacredness in many natural religions, and have reverently accepted it as a mystery, or offered scores of conflicting, and often debasing, interpretations. *It is but another symbol of the four cardinal points, the four winds of heaven.* This will luminously appear by a study of its use and meaning in America." (P. 95.) And Mr. Brinton gives many instances of the religious use of the cross by several of the aboriginal tribes of this continent, where the allusion, it must be confessed, seems evidently to be to the four cardinal points, or the four winds, or four spirits of the earth. If this be so, and if it is probable that a similar reference was adopted by the Celtic and other ancient peoples, then we would have in the cruciform temple as much a symbolism of the world, of which the four cardinal points constitute the boundaries, as we have in the square, the cubical, and the circular.

Crucifix. A cross with the image of the Savior suspended on it. A part of the furniture of a Commandery of Knights Templar and of a Chapter of Princes of Rose Croix.

Crusades. There was between Freemasonry and the Crusades a much more intimate relation than has generally been supposed. In the first place, the communications frequently established by the Crusaders, and especially the Knights Templar, with the Saracens, led to the acquisition, by the former, of many of the dogmas of the secret societies of the East, such as the Essenes, the Assassins, and the Druses. These were brought by the knights to Europe, and subsequently, on the establishment by Ramsay and his contemporaries and immediate successors of Templar Masonry, were incorporated into the high degrees, and still exhibit their influence. Indeed, it is scarcely to be doubted that many of these degrees were invented with a special reference to the events which occurred in Syria and Palestine. Thus, for instance, the Scottish degree of Knights of the East and West must have originally alluded, as its name imports, to the legend which teaches a division of the Masons after the Temple was finished, when the Craft dispersed—a part remaining in Palestine, as the Assideans, whom Lawrie, citing Scaliger, calls the "Knights of the Temple of Jerusalem," and another part passing over into Europe, whence they returned on the breaking out of the Crusades. This, of course, is but a legend, yet the influence is felt in the invention of the higher rituals.

But the influence of the Crusades on the Freemasons and the architecture of the Middle Ages is of a more historical character. In 1836, Mr. Westmacott, in a course of lectures on art before the Royal Academy, remarked that the two principal causes which materially tended to assist the restoration of literature and the arts in Europe were Freemasonry and the Crusades. The adventurers, he said, who returned from the Holy Land brought back some ideas of various improvements, particularly in architecture, and, along with these, a strong desire to erect castellated, ecclesiastical, and palatial edifices, to display the taste they had acquired; and in less than a century from the first Crusade above six hundred buildings of the above description had been erected in Southern and Western Europe. This taste was spread into almost all countries by the establishment of the Fraternity of Freemasons, who, it appears, had, under some peculiar form of brotherhood, existed for an immemorial period in Syria and other parts of the East, from whence some bands of them migrated to Europe, and after a time a great efflux of these ingenious men—Italian, German, French, Spanish, etc.—had spread themselves in communities through all civilized Europe; and in all countries where they settled we find the same style of architecture from that period, but differing in some points of treatment, as suited the climate.

Cubit. A measure of length, originally denoting the distance from the elbow to the extremity of the middle finger, or the fourth part of a well-proportioned man's stature. The Hebrew cubit, according to Bishop Cumberland, was twenty-one inches; but only eighteen according to other authorities. There were two kinds of cubits, the sacred and profane—the former equal to thirty-six, and the latter to eighteen inches. It is by the common cubit that the dimensions of the various parts of the Temple are to be computed.

Declaration of the Master. Every Master of a Lodge, after his election and before his installation, is required to give, in the presence of the brethren, his assent to the following fifteen charges and regulations:

1. Do you promise to be a good man and true, and strictly to obey the moral law? 2. Do you promise to be a peaceable citizen, and cheerfully to conform to the laws of the country in which you reside? 3. Do you promise not to be concerned in plots and conspiracies against the government of the country in which you live, but patiently to submit to the decisions of the law and the constituted authorities? 4. Do you promise to pay proper respect to the civil magistrates, to work diligently, live creditably, and act honorably by all men? 5. Do you promise to hold in veneration the original rulers and patrons of the Order of Freemasonry, and their regular successors, supreme and subordinate, according to their stations; and to submit to the awards and resolutions of your brethren in Lodge convened, in every case consistent with the constitutions of the Order? 6. Do you promise, as much as in you lies, to avoid private piques and quarrels, and to guard against intemperance and excess? 7. Do you promise to be cautious in your behavior, courteous to your brethren, and faithful to your Lodge? 8. Do you promise to respect genuine and true brethren, and to discountenance impostors and all dissenters from the Ancient Landmarks and Constitutions of Masonry? 9. Do you promise, according to the best of your abilities, to promote the general good of society, to cultivate the social virtues, and to propagate the knowledge of the mystic art, according to our statutes? 10. Do you promise to pay homage to the Grand Master for the time being, and to his officers when duly installed; and strictly to conform to every edict of the Grand Lodge or General Assembly of Masons that is not subversive of the principles and groundwork of Masonry? 11. Do you admit that it is not in the power of any man, or body of men, to make innovations in the body of Masonry? 12. Do you promise a regular at-

tendance on the committees and communications of the Grand Lodge, on receiving proper notice, and to pay attention to all the duties of Masonry, on convenient occasions? 13. Do you admit that no new Lodge can be formed without permission of the Grand Lodge; and that no countenance ought to be given to any irregular Lodge, or to any person clandestinely initiated therein, as being contrary to the ancient charges of the Order? 14. Do you admit that no person can be regularly made a Freemason in, or admitted a member of, any regular Lodge, without previous notice, and due inquiry into his character? 15. Do you agree that no visitors shall be received into your Lodge without due examination, and producing proper vouchers of their having been initiated in a regular Lodge?

Dedication of the Temple. There are five dedications of the Temple of Jerusalem which are recorded in Jewish history: 1. The dedication of the Solomonic Temple, B.C. 1004. 2. The dedication in the time of Hezekiah, when it was purified from the abominations of Ahaz, B.C. 726. 3. The dedication of Zerubbabel's Temple, B.C. 513. 4. The dedication of the Temple when it was purified after Judas Maccabæus had driven out the Syrians, B.C. 164. 5. The dedication of Herod's Temple, B.C. 22. The fourth of these is still celebrated by the Jews in their "Feast of the Dedication." The first only is connected with the Masonic ritual, and is commemorated in the Most Excellent Master's Degree of the American Rite as the "Celebration of the Cape-Stone." This dedication was made by King Solomon in the year of the world 3000, and lasted eight days, commencing in the month of Tisri, 15th day, during the Feast of Tabernacles. The dedication of the Temple is called, in the English system of Lectures, "the third grand offering which consecrates the floor of a Mason's Lodge." The same Lectures contain a tradition that on that occasion King Solomon assembled the nine Deputy Grand Masters in the holy place, from which all natural light had been carefully excluded, and which only received the artificial light which emanated from the east, west, and south, and there made the necessary arrangements. The legend must be considered as a myth; but the inimitable prayer and invocation which were offered up by King Solomon on the occasion are recorded in the eighth chapter of the 1st Book of Kings, which contains the Scriptural account of the dedication.

Degrees of Chivalry. The religious and military orders of knighthood which existed in the Middle Ages, such as the Knights Templar and Knights of Malta, which were incorporated into the Masonic system and conferred as Masonic degrees, have been called Degrees of Chivalry. They are Christian in character, and seek to perpetuate in a symbolic form the idea on which the original Orders were founded. The Companion of the Red Cross, although conferred, in this country, in a Commandery of Knights Templar, and as preliminary to that degree, is not properly a degree of chivalry.

Deus Meumque Jus. *God and my right.* The motto of the Thirty-third Degree of the Ancient and Accepted Scottish Rite, and hence adopted as that also of the Supreme Council of the Rite. It is a Latin translation of the motto of the royal arms of England, which is "Dieu et mon droit," and concerning which we have the following tradition. Richard Cœur de Leon, besieging Gisors, in Normandy, in 1198, gave, as a parole, "Dieu et mon droit," because Philip Augustus, King of France, had, without *right,* taken that city, which then belonged to England. Richard, having been victorious with that righteous parole, hence adopted it as his motto; and it was afterward marshaled in the arms of England.

Eagle, Double-Headed. The *eagle displayed,* that is, with extended wings, as if in the act of flying, has always, from the majestic character of the bird, been deemed an emblem of imperial power. Marius, the consul, first consecrated the eagle, about eight years B.C., to be the sole Roman standard at the head of every legion, and hence it became the standard of the Roman Empire ever afterward. As the single-headed eagle was thus adopted as the symbol of imperial power, the double-headed eagle naturally became the representative of a double empire; and on the division of the Roman dominions into the eastern and western empire, which were afterward consolidated by the Carlovingian race into what was ever after called the Holy Roman Empire, the double-headed eagle was assumed as the emblem of this double empire; one head looking, as it were, to the West, or Rome, and the other to the East, or Byzantium. Hence the escutcheons of many persons now living, the descendants of the princes and counts of the Holy Roman Empire, are placed upon the breast of a double-headed eagle. Upon the dissolution of that empire, the emperors of Germany, who claimed their empire to be the representative of ancient Rome, assumed the double-headed eagle as their symbol, and placed it in their arms, which were blazoned thus: *Or,* an eagle displayed *sable,* having two heads, each enclosed within an amulet, *or* beaked and armed *gules,* holding in his right claw a sword and scepter *or,* and in his left the imperial mound. Russia also bears the double-headed eagle, having added, says Brewer, that of Poland to her own, and thus denoting a double empire. It is, however, probable that the double-headed eagle of Russia is to be traced to some assumed representation of the Holy Roman Empire based upon the claim of Russia to Byzantium; for Constantine, the Byzantine emperor, is said to have been the first who assumed this device to intimate the division of the empire into East and West.

The statement of Millington (*Heraldry in History, Poetry, and Romance,* p. 290) is doubtful that "the double-headed eagle of the Austrian and Russian empires was first assumed during the Second Crusade and typified the great alliance formed by the Christian sovereigns of Greece and Germany against the enemy of their common faith, and it is retained by Russia and Austria as representations of those empires."

The theory is more probable as well as more generally accepted which connects the symbol with the eastern and western empires of Rome. It is, however, agreed by all that while the single-headed eagle denotes imperial dignity, the extension and multiplication of that dignity is symbolized by the two heads.

The double-headed eagle was probably first introduced as a symbol into Masonry in the year 1758. In that year the body calling itself the Council of Emperors of the East and West was established in Paris. The double-headed eagle was likely to have been assumed by this Council in reference to the double jurisdiction which it claimed, and which is represented so distinctly in its title. Its ritual, which consisted of twenty-five degrees, all of which are now contained in the Ancient and Accepted Scottish Rite, was subsequently established in the city of Berlin, and adopted by the Grand Lodge of the Three Globes.

The jewel of the Thirty-third Degree, or Sovereign Grand Inspector-General of the Ancient and Accepted Scottish Rite, is a double-headed eagle (which was originally black, but is now generally of silver), a golden crown resting on both heads, wings displayed, beak and claws of gold, his talons grasping a wavy sword, the emblem of cherubic fire, the hilt held by one talon, the blade by the other. The banner of the Order is also a double-headed eagle crowned.

Eastern Star, Order of the. Degrees for women, under the title of the "Masonry of Adoption," were as long ago as 1765 in vogue on the continent of Europe. These were administered under the patronage of the ruling Masonic body and especially flourished in the palmy days of the Empire in France, the Empress Josephine being at the head of the Order and many women of the highest standing were active members.

The term "Adoption," so it is said, was given to the organization because the Freemasons formally adopted the ladies to whom the mysteries of the several degrees were imparted.

Albert Pike, who took great interest in this "Masonry of Adoption" and made a translation of the ritual into English with some elaboration dictated by his profound knowledge of symbolism and philosophy, points out the reason that in his judgment existed for the conferring of degrees upon the women of a Mason's family. He says in the preface to his ritual of the Masonry of Adoption, "Our mothers, sisters, wives and daughters cannot, it is true, be admitted to share with us the grand mysteries of Freemasonry, but there is no reason why there should not be also a Masonry for them, which may not merely enable them to make themselves known to Masons, and so to obtain assistance and protection; but by means of which, acting in concert through the tie of association and mutual obligation, they may cooperate in the great labors of Masonry by assisting in and, in some respects, directing their charities, and toiling in the cause of human progress. The object of 'la Maçonnerie des Dames' is, therefore, very inadequately expressed, when it is said to be the improvement and purification of the sentiments.''

The Order of the Eastern Star has become just such an organization, strong enough to take an active and powerful cooperative concern in the beneficent labors of Masons for the care of the indigent and the afflicted. While entirely different and distinct from the Masonry of Adoption, being indeed of American and not French development, all the expectations so ably expressed by Brother Pike have in no other fraternal association been so admirably fulfilled as in the Order of the Eastern Star.

Some mystery involves the origin of the Order. In this respect the Order of the Eastern Star is closely akin to the various branches of the Masonic brotherhood. To unravel the truth from the entanglement of myth is, with many of these knotty problems, a troublesome and perhaps a never wholly satisfactory task. Evidence having few and incomplete records, dependent rather upon memory than in documents of authority is the usual subject-matter of discussion when laboring at the historic past of human institutions.

First of all let us take the testimony of Brother Rob Morris, than whom no one person has, it is conceded, given more freely of his service in the early development of the Order. None ought to know of the Eastern Star's inception story more than he, the acknowledged pioneer propagandist during its tender infancy and struggling youth.

During the latter part of 1884 Brother Rob Morris gave an account of the origination of the Eastern Star, which is in part as follows:

''In the winter of 1850 I was a resident of Jackson, Mississippi. For some time previous I had contemplated, as hinted above, the preparation of a Ritual of Adoptive Masonry, the degrees then in vogue appearing to me poorly conceived, weakly wrought out, unimpressive and particularly defective in point of motive. I allude especially to those degrees styled the Mason's Daughter, and the Heroines of Jericho. But I do expressly except from this criticism, the Good Samaritan, which in my judgment possesses dramatic elements and machinery equal to those that are in the Templar's Orders, the High Priesthood, the Cryptic Rite, and other organizations of Thomas Smith Webb. I have always recommended the Good Samaritan, and a thousand times conferred it in various parts of the world.

''About the first of February, 1850, I was laid up for two weeks with a sharp attack of rheumatism, and it was this period which I gave to the work in hand. By the aid of my papers and the memory of Mrs. Morris, I recall even the trivial occurrences connected with the work, how I hesitated for a theme, how I dallied over a name, how I wrought face to face with the clock that I might keep my drama within due limits of time, etc. The name was first settled upon—The Eastern Star. Next the number of points, five, to correspond with the emblem on the Master's carpet. This is the pentagon, 'The signet of King Solomon,' and eminently proper to Adoptive Masonry.

"From the Holy Writings I culled four biographical sketches to correspond with my first four points, viz., Jephthah's Daughter (named 'Adah' for want of a better), Ruth, Esther, and Martha. These were illustrations of four great congeries of womanly virtues, and their selection has proved highly popular. The fifth point introduced me to the early history of the Christian Church, where, amidst a noble army of martyrs, I found many whose lives and death overflowed the cup of martyrdom with a glory not surpassed by any of those named in Holy Writ. This gave me Electa, the 'Elect Lady,' friend of St. John the Christian woman whose venerable years were crowned with the utmost splendor of the crucifixion.

"The colors, the emblems, the floral wreaths, the esotery proper to these five heroines, were easy of invention. They seemed to fall ready-made into my hands. The only piece of mechanism difficult to fit into the construction was the cabalistic motto, but this occurred to me in ample time for use.

"The compositions of the lectures was but a recreation. Familiar from childhood as I had been with the Holy Scriptures, I scarcely needed to look up my proof texts, so tamely did they come to my call. A number of odes were also composed at that time, but the greater part of the three-score odes and poems of the Eastern Star that I have written were the work of subsequent years. The first Ode of the series of 1850 was one commencing 'Light from the East, 'tis gilded with hope.'

"The theory of the whole subject is succinctly stated in my 'Rosary of the Eastern Star,' published in 1865: To take from the ancient writings five prominent female characters, illustrating as many Masonic virtues, and to adopt them into the fold of Masonry. The selections were: I. Jephthah's Daughter, as illustrating respect to the binding force of a vow; II. Ruth, as illustrating devotion to religious principles; III. Esther, as illustrating fidelity to kindred and friends; IV. Martha, as illustrating undeviating faith in the hour of trial; and V. Electa, as illustrating patience and submission under wrong. These are all Masonic virtues, and they have nowhere in history more brilliant exemplars than in the five characters presented in the lectures of the Eastern Star. It is a fitting comment upon these statements that in all the changes that the Eastern Star has experienced at so many hands for thirty-four years, no change in the names, histories or essential lessons has been proposed.

"So my Ritual was complete, and after touching and retouching the manuscript, as professional authors love to do, I invited a neighboring Mason and his wife to join with my own, and to them, in my own parlor, communicated the Degrees. They were the first recipients—the first of twice fifty thousand who have seen the signs, heard the words, exchanged the touch, and joined in the music of the Eastern Star. When I take a retrospect of that evening—but thirty-four years ago—and consider the abounding four hundred Eastern Star Chapters at work today, my heart swells with gratitude to God, who guided my hand during that period of convalescence to prepare a work, of all the work of my life the most successful.

"Being at that time, and until a very recent period, an active traveler, visiting all countries where lodges exist—a nervous, wiry, elastic man, unwearying in work—caring little for refreshments or sleep, I spread abroad the knowledge of the Eastern Star wherever I went. Equally in border communities, where ladies came in homespun, as in cities, where ladies came in satins, the new degree was received with ardor, and eulogized in strongest terms, so that every induction led to the call for more. Ladies and gentlemen are yet living who met that immense assemblage at Newark, New Jersey, in 1853 and the still greater one in Spring Street Hall, New York City, a little earlier, where I stood up for two hours or three, before a breathless and gratified audience, and brought to bear all that I could draw from the Holy Scriptures, the Talmud, and the writings of Josephus, concerning the five 'Heroines of the Eastern Star.'

"Not that my work met no opposition. Quite the reverse. It was not long until editors, report writers, newspaper critics and my own private correspondents, began to see the evil of it. The cry of 'Innovation' went up to heaven. Ridicule lent its aid to a grand assault upon my poor little figment. Ingenious changes were rung upon the idea of 'petticoat Masonry.' More than one writer in Masonic journals (men of an evil class—we had them; men who knew the secrets, but have never applied the principles of Masonry), more than one such expressed in language indecent and shocking, his opposition to the Eastern Star and to me. Letters were written me, some signed, some anonymous, warning me that I was periling my own Masonic connections in the advocacy of this scheme. In New York City the opponents of the Eastern Star even started a rival project to break it down. They employed a literary person, a poet of eminence, a gentleman of social merit, to prepare rituals under an ingenious form, and much time and money were spent in the effort to popularize it, but it survived only a short year and is already forgotten.

"But the Eastern Star glittered steadily in the ascendant. In 1855 I arranged the system of 'Constellations of the Eastern Star,' of which the 'Mosaic Book' was the index, and established more than one hundred of these bodies. Looking over that book, one of the most original and brilliant works to which I ever put my hand, I have wondered that the system did not succeed. It must be because the times were not ripe for it. The opposition to 'Ladies' Masonry' was too bitter. The advocates of the plan were not sufficiently influential. At any rate it fell through.

"Four years later I prepared an easier plan, styled 'Families of the

Eastern Star,' intended, in its simplicity and the readiness by which it could be worked, to avoid the complexity of the 'Constellations.' This ran well enough until the war broke out, when all Masonic systems fell together with a crash.

"This ended my work in systematizing the Eastern Star, and I should never have done more with it, save confer it in an informal manner as at first, but for Brother Robert Macoy of New York, who in 1868, when I had publicly announced my intentions of confining my labors during the remainder of my life to Holy Land investigations, proposed the plan of Eastern Star Chapters now in vogue. He had my full consent and endorsement, and thus became the instigator of a third and more successful system. The history of this organization, which is now disseminated in more than four hundred chapters, extending to thirty-three states and territories, I need not detail. The annual proceedings of Grand Chapters, the indefatigable labors of the Rev. Willis D. Engle, Grand Secretary of the General Grand Chapter, the liberal manner in which the Masonic journals have opened their columns to the proceedings of the Adoptive Order, the annual festivals, the sociables, concerts, picnics, etc., which keep the name of the Society before the public, make a history of their own better than I can write."

In another statement under date of 1884, Brother Morris further informs us: "Some writers have fallen into the error of placing the introduction of the Eastern Star as far back as 1775, and this they gather from my work, 'Lights and Shadows of Freemasonry,' published in 1852. What I intended to say in that book was that the French officers introduced Adoptive Masonry into the Colonies in 1775, but nothing like the degree called the Eastern Star, which is strictly my own origination."

The statements of Brother Morris are deserving of the utmost consideration and confidence. His devotion to Masonic service was long and honorable, freely acknowledged by his brethren with promotions to places of the highest prominence within their gift. We can thus approach his assertions confident of their accuracy so far as the intent of Brother Morris is concerned. Candor, nevertheless, compels the conclusion that our excellent brother did not in his various and valuable contributions to the history of the Eastern Star, and the related bodies, always clearly define his positions, and the studious reader is therefore somewhat in doubt whether on all occasions the meaning is unmistakable. For example, the foregoing references are in themselves very clear that Brother Morris was the originator of the Eastern Star. It is substantially shown in detail how the several items of consequence were actually put into practice by him.

Let us now briefly mention what may be set forth on the other side. The "Mosaic Book," by Brother Rob Morris, and published in 1857, says in Chapter II, Section 2: "In selecting some Androgynous Degree, extensively known, ancient in date, and ample in scope, for the basis of this

Rite, the choice falls, without controversy, upon the 'Eastern Star.' For this is a degree familiar to thousands of the most enlightened York Masons and their female relations—established in this country at least before 1778—and one which popularly bears the palm in point of doctrine and elegance over all others. In scope, by the addition of a ceremonial and a few links in the chain of recognition, was broad enough to constitute a graceful and consistent system, worthy, it is believed, of the best intellect of either sex."

Brother Willis D. Engle, the first R. W. Grand Secretary of the General Grand Chapter of the Order, says on page 12 of his History that "The fact is that Brother Morris received the Eastern Star degree at the hands of Giles M. Hillyer, of Vicksburg, Mississippi, about 1849."

Puzzling as is this mixture of statements, there is the one possible explanation that in speaking of the Order, Brother Morris had two quite different things in mind and that he may have inadvertently caused some to understand him to be speaking of the one when he referred to the other, or to both, as the case might be. We know that he had received Adoptive degrees and we are well aware that he had prepared more than one arrangement of Eastern Star degrees or of allied ceremonies. What more likely that in speaking of the one his thoughts should dwell upon the other; the one, Adoptive Masonry, being as we might say the subject in general; the other, the Eastern Star, being the particular topic. He could very properly think of the degree as an old idea, the Masonry of Adoption, and he could also consider it as being of novelty in the form of the Eastern Star; in the one case thinking of it as given him, and in the second instance thinking of it as it left his hands.

In any event, the well-known sincerity and high repute of Brother Morris absolve him from any stigma of wilful misrepresentation.

Certainly it is due his memory that the various conflicting assertions be given a sympathetic study and as friendly and harmonious a construction as is made at all possible by their terms.

Another curious angle of the situation develops in "The Thesauros of the Ancient and Honorable Order of the Eastern Star as collected and arranged by the committee, and adopted by the Supreme Council in convocation, assembled May, 1793." A copy of this eighteen-page pamphlet is in possession of Brother Alonzo J. Burton, Past Grand Lecturer, New York. This book of monitorial instruction has been reprinted and does afford a most interesting claim for the existence of an Eastern Star organization as early as the eighteenth century.

A Supreme Constellation was organized by Brother Rob Morris in 1855 with the following principal officers: Most Enlightened Grand Luminary, Rob Morris; Right Enlightened Deputy Grand Luminary and Grand Lecturer, Joel M. Spiller, Delphi, Ind.; Very Enlightened Grand Treasurer, Jonathan R. Neill, New York, and Very Enlightened Grand Secretary, John W. Leonard, New York. Deputies were appointed for several States and by the end of 1855 seventy-five charters for subordinate Constellations had been granted. These Constellations were made up of five or more persons of each sex, with a limit of no more than twenty-five of the one sex, and several Constellations might be associated with a single lodge.

There subsequently arose a second governing body of which James B. Taylor of New York became Grand Secretary. This organization was known as the "Supreme Council of the Ancient Rite of Adoptive Masonry for North America." How much of a real existence was lived by this body is now difficult of determination because of the secrecy with which its operations were conducted. Early in the seventies it expired after a discouraging struggle for life.

Brother Morris was not a partner in the above enterprise and had in 1860 begun the organizing of "Families" of the Eastern Star. To use his own expression, "The two systems of 'Constellations' and 'Families' are identical in spirit, the latter having taken the place of the former." A further statement by Brother Morris was to the effect that the ladies who were introduced to the advantages of Adoptive Masonry under the former system retained their privileges under the latter. During the next eight years more than a hundred "Families" were organized.

Brother Robert Macoy of New York had in 1866 prepared a manual of the Eastern Star. In this work he mentions himself as "National Grand Secretary." He also maintained the semblance of a Supreme Grand Chapter of the Adoptive Rite. Brother Morris decided in 1868 to devote his life to Masonic exploration in Palestine. His Eastern Star powers were transferred to Brother Macoy, as has been claimed. The latter in later years described himself as "Supreme Grand Patron."

Still another attempt at the formal organization of a governing body occurred in 1873 at New York, when the following provisional officers of a "Supreme Grand Council of the World, Adoptive Rite," were selected: Supreme Grand Patron, Robert Macoy, of New York; Supreme Grand Matron, Frances E. Johnson, of New York; Associate Supreme Grand Patron, Andres Cassard, of New York; Deputy Supreme Grand Patron, John L. Power, of Mississippi; Deputy Supreme Grand Matron, Laura L. Burton, of Mississippi; Supreme Treasurer, W. A. Prall, of Missouri; Supreme Recorder, Rob Morris, of Kentucky; Supreme Inspector, P. M. Savery, of Mississippi. But nothing further came of this organization except that when later on measures were taken to make a really effective controlling body, the old organization had claimants in the field urging its prior rights, though to all intents and purposes its never more than feeble breath of life had then utterly failed.

The various bodies of the Order under this fugitive guidance became ill-assorted of method. Laws were curiously conflicting. A constitution governing a State Grand Chapter had in one section the requirement that "Every member present must vote" on petitions; which another section of the same constitution forbade Master Masons "when admitted to membership" from balloting for candidates or on membership. There was equal or even greater inconsistency between the laws of one State and another. Serious defects had been discovered in the ritual. Some resentment had been aroused over the methods employed in the propaganda of the Order. The time was ripe for a radical change.

Rev. Willis D. Engle, in 1874, publicly proposed a Supreme Grand Chapter of Representatives from the several Grand Chapters and "a revision and general boiling down and finishing up of the ritual which is now defective both in style and language."

Not content with saying this was a proper thing to do, Brother Engle vigorously started to work to bring about the conditions he believed to be most desirable. Delegates from the Grand Chapters of California, Illinois, Indiana, Missouri, and New Jersey, met in Indianapolis, November 15–16, 1876, on the invitation of the Grand Chapter of Indiana.

Grand Patron, James S. Nutt, of Indiana, welcomed the visitors and opened the meeting. Brother John M. Mayhew, of New Jersey, was elected President, and Brother John R. Parson, of Missouri, Secretary. A Constitution was adopted, a committee appointed on revision of the ritual, and a General Grand Chapter duly organized.

The second session of the General Grand Chapter was held in Chicago, May 8–10, 1878, and the name of the organization became officially "the General Grand Chapter of the Order of the Eastern Star." The Most Worthy Grand Patron was then the executive head, though in later years this was decided to be the proper province of the Most Worthy Grand Matron. In 1880 Mrs. Lorraine J. Pitkin, of Chicago, became the Most Worthy Grand Matron, and afterwards the Grand Secretary, being elected in 1883. She joined the Order in 1866.

The Grand Chapters with their dates of organization are as follows:

Alabama	March 6, 1901
Alberta	July 20, 1912
Arizona	November 15, 1900
Arkansas	October 2, 1876
British Columbia	July 21, 1912
California	May 8, 1873
Colorado	June 6, 1892
Connecticut	August 11, 1874
District of Columbia	April 30, 1896
Florida	June 7, 1904
Georgia	February 21, 1901
Idaho	April 17, 1902
Illinois	November 6, 1875
Indiana	May 6, 1874
Iowa	July 30, 1878

Kansas	October 18, 1878
Kentucky	June 10, 1903
Louisiana	October 4, 1900
Maine	August 24, 1892
Maryland	December 23, 1898
Massachusetts	December 11, 1876
Michigan	October 31, 1867
Minnesota	October 18, 1878
Mississippi	May 29, 1906
Montana	September 25, 1890
Missouri	October 13, 1875
Nebraska	June 22, 1875
Nevada	September 19, 1905
New Hampshire	May 12, 1891
New Jersey	July 18, 1870
New York	November 31, 1870
New Mexico	April 11, 1902
North Carolina	May 20, 1905
North Dakota	June 14, 1894
Ohio	July 28, 1889
Oklahoma	February 14, 1902
Ontario	April 27, 1915
Oregon	October 3, 1889
Pennsylvania	November 21, 1894
Porto Rico	February 17, 1914
Rhode Island	August 22, 1895
Saskatchewan	May 16, 1916
Scotland	August 20, 1904
South Carolina	June 1, 1907
South Dakota	July 10, 1889
Tennessee	October 18, 1900
Texas	May 5, 1884
Utah	September 20, 1905
Vermont	November 12, 1873
Virginia	June 22, 1904
Washington	June 12, 1889
West Virginia	June 28, 1904
Wisconsin	February 19, 1891
Wyoming	September 14, 1908

Of the above Grand Chapters there are three not constituent members of the General Grand Chapter. These independent bodies are New Jersey, New York, and Scotland.

Chapters of the Eastern Star are also to be found in Alaska, the Canal Zone at Panama, the Hawaiian Islands, the Philippine Islands,

Manitoba, New Brunswick, Quebec, Cuba, Delaware, India, Mexico, and in the Yukon.

A Concordat or treaty agreement adopted by the General Chapter on September 20, 1904, and by a convention of Scottish Chapters of the Eastern Star held at Glasgow on August 20, 1904, was to the following effect:

"The Grand Chapter of Scotland shall have supreme and exclusive jurisdiction over Great Britain, Ireland, and the whole British dominions (excepting only those upon the Continent of America), and that a Supreme or General Grand Chapter of the British Empire shall be formed as soon as Chapters are instituted therein and it seems expedient to do so."

According to the terms of this agreement the territory in the East Indies wherein Chapters were already instituted, as at Benares and Calcutta, was ceded to the Grand Chapter of Scotland, which retains control. The other Chapters not so released are still under the jurisdiction of the General Grand Chapter.

* * * * * * *

Fraternalism is not confined to men only, but has been taken up by the mothers, sisters, wives, daughters and widows of Master Masons, and bids fair to be an important factor in developing and promoting the Masonic ideal.

The Eastern Star is pre-eminent along this line of endeavor. It stands for good work, square work, and true work, and only those who are worthy are permitted to enter its sacred portals. It is the exemplification of charity, the promulgation of the doctrine of the lowly Nazarene. It brings hope to the despondent and ministers to the widows and orphans. It stands for individual righteousness, elevating society by elevating its units. It is educational, for in its confines, its members are taught to be better men and women, and that purity of mind and purpose, thru the individual saveth the Nation.

The objective of all effort is toward perfection, hence all its efforts are directed toward that goal. It has become an important factor among Masons and deserves the very best we can give it. Surely it has a right to be proud of its past achievements, and Masonry should glory in its future. Its sweet ministrations fall as the gentle rain from the heavens, upon the just and the unjust, soothing the fevered brow and comforting the widows and orphans. It is the charity that suffers long, is kind and envieth not, casting its bread upon the waters, not that it may return again, but with a spirit of love, and not from a sense of duty. It is a living, vitalizing force today, and its influence and activities are greater now than ever before. Its past record is only an earnest of its future, and so long as grief, sorrow, sin, and want exist among us, just so long will there be absolute necessity for this glorious Order.

International Eastern Star Temple. In the year 1926 a movement was begun for the ultimate erection of an International Eastern Star Temple, to be located in the City of Washington, District of Columbia, by the General Grand Chapter, Order of the Eastern Star. This hope was realized in 1927. The historic Belmont Mansion, Washington City, was purchased for the Temple, which was dedicated in 1936.

Edict of Cyrus. Five hundred and thirty-six years before the Christian era, Cyrus issued his edict permitting the Jews to return from the captivity at Babylon to Jerusalem, and to rebuild the House of the Lord. At the same time he restored to them all the sacred vessels and precious ornaments of the first Temple, which had been carried away by Nebuchadnezzar, and which were still in existence. This is commemorated in the Royal Arch Degree of the York and American Rites. It is also referred to in the Fifteenth Degree, or Knight of the East of the Scottish Rite.

Edicts. The decrees of a Grand Master or of a Grand Lodge are called Edicts, and obedience to them is obligatory on all the Craft.

Eheyeh asher Eheyeh. The pronunciation which means, *I am that I am,* and is one of the pentateuchal names of God. It is related in the third chapter of Exodus, that when God appeared to Moses in the burning bush, and directed him to go to Pharaoh and to the children of Israel in Egypt, Moses required that, as preliminary to his mission, he should be instructed in the name of God, so that, when he was asked by the Israelites, he might be able to prove his mission by announcing what that name was; and God said to him, (Eheyeh), *I am that I am;* and he directed him to say, "*I am* hath sent you." *Eheyeh asher eheyeh* is, therefore, the name of God, in which Moses was instructed at the burning bush.

Maimonides thinks that when the Lord ordered Moses to tell the people that (Eheyeh) sent him, he did not mean that he should only mention his name; for if they were already acquainted with it, he told them nothing new, and if they were not, it was not likely that they would be satisfied by saying such a name sent me, for the proof would still be wanting that this was really the name of God; therefore, he not only told them the name, but also *taught* them its signification. In those times, Sabaism being the predominant religion, almost all men were idolaters, and occupied themselves in the contemplation of the heavens and the sun and the stars, without any idea of a personal God in the world. Now, the Lord, to deliver his people from such an error, said to Moses, "Go and tell them I AM THAT I AM hath sent me unto you," which name (Eheyeh), signifying Being, is derived from (heyeh), the verb of existence, and which, being repeated so that the second is the predicate of the first, contains the mystery. This is as if he had said, "Explain to them that *I am what I am:* that is, that my Being is within myself, independent of every other, different from all other beings, who *are* so alone by virtue of my distributing it to them, and might not have *been,* nor could actually *be* such without it." So that denotes the Divine Being Himself, by which he taught Moses not only the name, but the infallible demonstration of the Fountain of Existence, as the name itself denotes. The Kabbalists say that Eheyeh is the *crown* or highest of the Sephiroth, and that it is the name that was hidden in the most secret place of the tabernacle.

Essenes. Lawrie, in his *History of Freemasonry,* in replying to the objection, that if the Fraternity of Freemasons had flourished during the reign of Solomon, it would have existed in Judea in after ages, attempts to meet the argument by showing that there did exist, after the building of the Temple, an association of men resembling Freemasons in the nature, ceremonies, and object of their institution. The association to which he here alludes is that of the Essenes, whom he subsequently describes as an ancient Fraternity originating from an association of architects who were connected with the building of Solomon's Temple.

Lawrie evidently seeks to connect historically the Essenes with the Freemasons, and to impress his readers with the identity of the two Institutions. I am not prepared to go so far; but there is such a similarity between the two, and such remarkable coincidences in many of their usages, as to render this Jewish sect an interesting study to every Freemason, to whom therefore some account of the usages and doctrines of this holy brotherhood will not, perhaps, be unacceptable.

At the time of the advent of Jesus Christ, there were three religious sects in Judea—the Pharisees, the Sadducees, and the Essenes; and to one of these sects every Jew was compelled to unite himself. The Savior has been supposed by many writers to have been an Essene, because, while repeatedly denouncing the errors of the two other sects, he has nowhere uttered a word of censure against the Essenes; and because, also, many of the precepts of the New Testament are to be found among the laws of this sect.

In ancient authors, such as Josephus, Philo, Porphyry, Eusebius, and Pliny, who have had occasion to refer to the subject, the notices of this singular sect have been so brief and unsatisfactory, that modern writers have found great difficulty in properly understanding the true character of Essenism.

Flaming Sword. A sword whose blade is of a spiral or twisted form is called by the heralds a flaming sword, from its resemblance to the ascending curvature of a flame of fire. Until very recently, this was the form of the Tiler's sword. Carelessness or ignorance has now in many Lodges substituted for it a common sword of any form. The flaming sword of the Tiler refers to the flaming sword which guarded the entrance to Paradise, as described in Genesis (iii., 24): "So he drove out the man; and he placed at the east of the garden of Eden cherubims and a *flaming sword* which turned every way, to keep the way of the tree of life"; or, as Raphall has translated it, "the *flaming sword* which revolveth, to guard the way to the tree of life." In former times, when symbols and ceremonies were more respected than they are now; when collars were worn, and not ribbons in the buttonhole; and when the standing column of the Senior Warden, and the recumbent one of the Junior during labor, to be reversed during refreshment, were deemed necessary for the complete furniture of the Lodge, the cavalry sword was unknown as a Masonic implement, and the Tiler always bore a flaming sword. It were better if we could get back to the old customs.

Forty. The multiple of two perfect numbers—four and ten. This was deemed a sacred number, as commemorating many events of religious signification, some of which are as follows: The alleged period of probation of our first parents in Eden: the continuous deluge of forty days and nights, and the same number of days in which the waters remained upon the face of the earth; the Lenten season of forty days' fast observed by Christians with reference to the fast of Jesus in the Wilderness, and by the Hebrews to the earlier desert fast for a similar period; of the forty years spent in the Desert by Moses and Elijah and the Israelites, which succeeded the concealment of Moses the same number of years in the land of Midian. Moses was forty days and nights on the Mount. The days for embalming the dead were forty. The forty years of the reign of Saul, of David, and of Solomon; the forty days of grace allotted to Nineveh for repentance; the forty days' fast before Christmas in the Greek Church; as well as its being the number of days of mourning in Assyria, Phenicia, and Egypt, to commemorate the death and burial of their Sun God; and as well the period in the festivals of the resurrection of Adonis and Osiris; the period of forty days thus being a bond by which the whole world, ancient and modern, Pagan, Jewish, and Christian, is united in religious sympathy. Hence, it was determined as the period of mourning by the Supreme Council of the A. A. Scottish Rite of the Northern Jurisdiction U. S.

Furniture of a Lodge. The Bible, square, and compasses are technically said to constitute the furniture of a Lodge. They are respectfully dedicated to God, the Master of the Lodge, and the Craft. Our English brethren differ from us in their explanation of the furniture. Oliver gives their illustration, from the English lectures, as follows:

"The Bible is said to derive from God to man in general; because the Almighty has been pleased to reveal more of His divine will by that holy book than by any other means. The Compasses being the chief implement used in the construction of all architectural plans and designs, are assigned to the Grand Master in particular as emblems of his dignity, he being the chief head and ruler of the Craft. The square is given to the whole Masonic body, because we are all obligated within it, and are consequently bound to act thereon." (*Landmarks*, i., 169.) But the lecture of the early part of the last century made the furniture consist of the Mosaic Pavement, Blazing Star, and the Indented Tarsel, while the Bible, square, and compass were considered as additional furniture.

General Grand Lodge. Ever since the Grand Lodges of this country began, at the commencement of the Revolutionary War, to abandon their dependence on the Grand Lodges of England and Scotland—that is to say, as soon as they emerged from the subordinate position of Provincial Grand Lodges, and were compelled to assume a sovereign and independent character—attempts have, from time to time, been made by members of the Craft to destroy this sovereignty of the State Grand Lodges, and to institute in its place a superintending power, to be constituted either as a Grand Master of North America or as a General Grand Lodge of the United States. Led, perhaps, by the analogy of the united Colonies under one federal head, or, in the very commencement of the Revolutionary struggle, controlled by long habits of dependence on the mother Grand Lodges of Europe, the contest had no sooner begun, and a disseverance of political relations between England and America taken place, than the attempt was made to institute the office of Grand Master of the United States, the object being—of which there can hardly be a doubt—to invest Washington with the distinguished dignity.

The effort emanated, it appears, with the military Lodges in the army.

The proposition was again made in 1803, by the Grand Lodge of North Carolina, and with a like want of success.

In 1806, the subject of a General Grand Lodge was again presented to the consideration of the Grand Lodges of the Union, and propositions were made for conventions to be held in Philadelphia in 1807, and in Washington city in 1808, neither of which was convened.

An unsuccessful attempt was again made to hold a convention at Washington in January, 1811, "for the purpose of forming a Superintending Grand Lodge of America."

But the friends of a General Grand Lodge did not abandon the hope of effecting their object, and in 1857 the Grand Lodge of Maine issued a circular, urging the formation of a General Grand Lodge at a convention to be held at Chicago in September, 1859, during the session of the General Grand Chapter and General Grand Encampment at that city. This call was generally and courteously responded to; the convention was held, but it resulted in a failure. Other attempts have been made by its friends to carry this measure, but with no results.

Grand Orient. Most of the Grand Lodges established by the Latin races, such as those of France, Spain, Italy, and the South American States, are called Grand Orients. The word is thus, in one sense, synonymous with Grand Lodge; but these Grand Orients have often a more extensive obedience than Grand Lodges, frequently exercising jurisdiction over the highest degrees, from which English and American Grand Lodges refrain. The Grand Orient of France exercises jurisdiction over the seven degrees of its own Rite, over the thirty-three of the Ancient and Accepted, and over all the other Rites which are practised in France.

Grand Orient is also used in English, and especially in American, Masonry to indicate the seat of the Grand Lodge of highest Masonic power, and is thus equivalent to *Grand East.*

Grotto. The complete name of this organization is Mystic Order Veiled Prophets of the Enchanted Realm. The origin and development of the Order is explained at length in Mackey's revised History of Freemasonry.

The Grotto was born of an effort for stronger sociability among the members of Hamilton Lodge No. 120, Free and Accepted Masons, Hamilton, New York, in 1889. It was at first intended only as a local affair. The requirements for membership are that a man must be a Master Mason, in good standing.

The Supreme Council was organized and set in operation June 13th, 1890. The principal officers are;—Grand Monarch, Deputy Grand Monarch, Grand Chief Justice, Grand Master Meremonies, Grand Treasurer, Grand Secretary, Grand Keeper of Archives, Grand Orator, and three trustees.

Hah. The Hebrew definite article "the."

In Hoc Signo Vinces. On the Grand Standard of a Commandery of Knights Templar these words are inscribed over "a blood-red Passion Cross," and they constitute in part the motto of the American branch of the Order. Their meaning, "by this sign thou shalt conquer," is a substantial, but not literal, translation of the original Greek, ἐν τουτω νίκα. For the origin of the motto, we must go back to a well-known legend of the Church, which has, however, found more doubters than believers among the learned. Eusebius, who wrote a life of Constantine, says that while the emperor was in Gaul, in the year 312, preparing for war with his rival, Maxentius, about the middle hours of the day, as the sun began to verge toward its setting, he saw in the heavens, with his own eyes, the sun surmounted with the trophy of the cross, which was composed of light, and a legend annexed, which said *"by this conquer."* This account Eusebius affirms to be in the words of Constantine. Lactantius, who places the occurrence at a later date and on the eve of a battle with Maxentius, in which the latter was defeated, relates it not as an actual occurrence, but as a dream or vision; and this is now the generally received opinion of those who do not deem the whole legend a fabrication. On the next day Constantine had an image of this cross made into a banner, called the *labarum,* which he ever afterward used as the imperial standard. Eusebius describes it very fully. It was not a Passion Cross, such as is now used on the modern Templar standard, but the monogram of Christ. The shaft was a very long spear. On the top was a crown composed of gold and precious stones, and containing the sacred symbol, namely, the Greek letter *rho* or P, intersected by the *chi* or X, which two letters are the first and second of the name CHRIST. If, then, the Templars retain the motto on their banner, they should, for the sake of historical accuracy, discard the Passion Cross, and replace it with the Constantinian Chronogram, or Cross of the Labarum. But the truth is, that the ancient Templars used neither the Passion Cross, nor that of Constantine, nor yet the motto *in hoc signo vinces* on their standard. Their only banner was the black and white Beauseant, and at the bottom of it was inscribed their motto, "Non nobis Domine, non nobis, sed nomini tuo da gloriam"—*not unto us, O Lord, not unto us, but unto thee give the glory.* This was the song or shout of victory sung by the Templars when triumphant in battle.

I.·.N.·.R.·.I.·. The initials of the Latin sentence which was placed upon the cross: *Jesus Nazarenus Rex Judæorum.* The Rosicrucians used them as the initials of one of their Hermetic secrets: *Igne Natura Renovatur Integra,* "By fire, nature is perfectly renewed." They also adopted them to express the names of their three elementary principles —salt, sulphur, and mercury—by making them the initials of the sentence, *Igne Nitrum Roris Invenitur.* Ragon finds in the equivalent Hebrew letters ינרי the initials of the Hebrew names of the ancient elements: *Iaminim,* water; *Nour,* fire; *Ruach,* air; and *Iebschah,* earth.

Jewels, Official. Jewels are the names applied to the emblems worn by the officers of Masonic bodies as distinctive badges of their offices. For the purpose of reference, the jewels worn in Symbolic Lodges, in Chapters, Councils, and Encampments are here appended.

1. *In Symbolic Lodges.*

W.·. Master wears a square.
Senior Warden wears a level.
Junior Warden wears a plumb.
Treasurer wears cross keys.
Secretary wears cross pens.
Senior Deacon wears square and compass, sun in the center.
Junior Deacon wears square and compass, moon in the center.
Steward wears a cornucopia.
Tiler wears cross swords.

The jewels are of silver in a subordinate Lodge, and of gold in a Grand Lodge. In English Lodges, the jewel of the Deacon is a dove and olive branch.

2. *In Royal Arch Chapters.*

High Priest wears a miter.
King wears a level surmounted by a crown.
Scribe wears a plumb-rule surmounted by a turban.
Captain of the Host wears a triangular plate inscribed with a soldier.
Principal Sojourner wears a triangular plate inscribed with a pilgrim.
Royal Arch Captain wears a sword.

Grand Master of the Veils wears a sword.

The other officers as in a Symbolic Lodge. All the jewels are of gold, and suspended within an equilateral triangle.

3. *In Royal and Select Councils.*

T. I. Grand Master wears a trowel and square.

I. Hiram of Tyre wears a trowel and level.

Principal Conductor of the Works wears a trowel and plumb.

Treasurer wears a trowel and cross keys.

Recorder wears a trowel and cross pens.

Captain of the Guards wears a trowel and sword.

Steward wears a trowel and cross swords.

Marshal wears a trowel and baton.

If a Conductor of the Council is used, he wears a trowel and baton, and then a scroll is added to the Marshal's baton to distinguish the two officers.

All jewels are of silver, and are enclosed within an equilateral triangle.

4. *In Commanderies of Knights Templars.*

Eminent Commander wears a cross surmounted by rays of light.

Generalissimo wears a square surmounted by a paschal lamb.

Captain-General wears a level surmounted by a cock.

Prelate wears a triple triangle.

Senior Warden wears a hollow square and sword of justice.

Junior Warden wears eagle and flaming sword.

Treasurer wears cross keys.

Recorder wears cross pens.

Standard-Bearer wears a plumb surmounted by a banner.

Warder wears a square plate inscribed with a trumpet and cross swords.

Three Guards wears a square plate inscribed with a battle-ax.

The jewels are of silver.

Kadosh. The name of a very important degree in many of the Masonic Rites. The word is Hebrew, and signifies *holy* or *consecrated,* and is thus intended to denote the elevated character of the degree and the sublimity of the truths which distinguish it and its possessors from the other degrees. Pluche says that in the East, a person preferred to honors bore a scepter, and sometimes a plate of gold on the forehead, called a *Kadosh,* to apprise the people that the bearer of this mark or rod was a public person, who possessed the privilege of entering into hostile camps without the fear of losing his personal liberty.

The degree of Kadosh, though found in many of the Rites and in various countries, seems, in all of them, to have been more or less connected with the Knights Templar. In some of the Rites it was placed at the head of the list, and was then dignified as the *ne plus ultra* of Masonry.

It was sometimes given as a separate order or Rite within itself, and then it was divided into the three degrees of Illustrious Knight of the Temple, Knight of the Black Eagle, and Grand Elect.

Oliver enumerates five degrees of Kadosh: the Knight Kadosh; Kadosh of the Chapter of Clermont; Philosophical Kadosh; Kadosh Prince of Death; and Kadosh of the Ancient and Accepted Scottish Rite.

The French rituals speak of seven: Kadosh of the Hebrews; Kadosh of the first Christians; Kadosh of the Crusades; Kadosh of the Templars; Kadosh of Cromwell or the Puritans; Kadosh of the Jesuits; and the True Kadosh. But the correctness of this enumeration is doubtful, for it cannot be sustained by documentary evidence. In all of these Kadoshes the doctrine and the modes of recognition are substantially the same, though in most of them the ceremonies of initiation differ.

Ragon mentions a Kadosh which is said to have been established at Jerusalem in 1118; but here he undoubtedly refers to the Order of Knights Templar. He gives also in his *Tuileur Général* the nomenclature of no less than fourteen Kadosh degrees.

The doctrine of the Kadosh system is that the persecutions of the Knights Templar by Philip the Fair of France, and Pope Clement V., however cruel and sanguinary in its results, did not extinguish the Order, but it continued to exist under the forms of Freemasonry. That the ancient Templars are the modern Kadoshes, and that the builder at the Temple of Solomon is now replaced by James de Molay, the martyred Grand Master of the Templars, the assassins being represented by the King of France, the Pope, and Naffodei the informer against the Order; or, it is sometimes said, by the three informers, Squin de Florian, Naffodei, and the Prior of Montfauçon.

As to the history of the Kadosh degree, it is said to have been first invented at Lyons, in France, in 1743, where it appeared under the name of the *Petit Elu.* This degree, which is said to have been based upon the Templar doctrine heretofore referred to, was afterward developed into the Kadosh, which we find in 1758 incorporated as the *Grand Elect Kadosh* into the system of the Council of Emperors of the East and West, which was that year formed at Paris, whence it descended to the Scottish Rite Masons.

Of all the Kadoshes, two only are now important, viz.: the Philosophic Kadosh, which has been adopted by the Grand Orient of France, and the Knight Kadosh, which constitutes the Thirtieth Degree of the Ancient and Accepted Scottish Rite, this latter being the most generally diffused of the Kadoshes.

Knight of the Red Cross. This degree, whose legend dates it far anterior to the Christian era, and in the reign of Darius, has no analogy with the chivalric orders of knighthood. It is purely Masonic, and intimately connected with the Royal Arch Degree, of which, in fact, it ought rightly to be considered as an appendage. It is, however, now always conferred in a Commandery of Knights Templar in this country, and is given as a preliminary to reception in that degree. Formerly, the degree was sometimes conferred in an independent council, which Webb (edit. 1812, p. 123) defines to be "a council that derives its authority immediately from the Grand Encampment unconnected with an Encampment of Knights Templars." The embassy of Zerubbabel and four other Jewish chiefs to the court of Darius to obtain the protection of that monarch from the encroachments of the Samaritans, who interrupted the labors in the reconstruction of the Temple, constitutes the legend of the Red Cross Degree. The history of this embassy is found in the eleventh book of the *Antiquities* of Josephus, whence the Masonic ritualists have undoubtedly taken it. The only authority of Josephus is the apocryphal record of Esdras, and the authenticity of the whole transaction is doubted or denied by modern historians. The legend is as follows: After the death of Cyrus, the Jews, who had been released by him from their captivity, and permitted to return to Jerusalem, for the purpose of rebuilding the Temple, found themselves obstructed in the undertaking by the neighboring nations, and especially by the Samaritans. Hereupon they sent an embassy, at the head of which was their prince, Zerubbabel, to Darius, the successor of Cyrus, to crave his interposition and protection. Zerubbabel, awaiting a favorable opportunity, succeeded not only in obtaining his request, but also in renewing the friendship which formerly existed between the king and himself. In commemoration of these events, Darius is said to have instituted a new order, and called it the Knights of the East. They afterward assumed their present name from the red cross borne in their banners. Webb, or whoever else introduced it into the American Templar system, undoubtedly took it from the Sixteenth Degree, or Prince of Jerusalem of the Ancient and Accepted Rite. It has, within a few years, been carried into England, under the title of the "Red Cross of Babylon." In New Brunswick, it has been connected with Cryptic Masonry. It is there as much out of place as it is in a Commandery of Knights Templar. Its only true connection is with the Royal Arch Degree.

Knights Templar. The piety or the superstition of the age had induced multitudes of pilgrims in the eleventh and twelfth centuries to visit Jerusalem for the purpose of offering their devotions at the sepulcher of the Lord and the other holy place in that city. Many of these religious wanderers were weak or aged, almost all of them unarmed, and thousands of them were subjected to insult, to pillage, and often to death, inflicted by the hordes of Arabs who, even after the capture of Jerusalem by the Christians, continued to infest the sea coast of Palestine and the roads to the capital.

To protect the pious pilgrims thus exposed to plunder and bodily outrage, nine French knights, the followers of Baldwyn, united, in the year 1118, in a military confraternity or brotherhood in arms, and entered into a solemn compact to aid each other in clearing the roads, and in defending the pilgrims in their passage to the holy city.

The Templars soon became preeminently distinguished as warriors of the cross. St. Bernard, who visited them in their Temple retreat, speaks in the warmest terms of their self-denial, their frugality, their modesty, their piety, and their bravery. "Their arms," he says, "are their only finery, and they use them with courage, without dreading either the number or the strength of the barbarians. All their confidence is in the Lord of Hosts, and in fighting for his cause they seek a sure victory or a Christian and honorable death."

Their banner was the Beauseant, of divided white and black, indicative of peace to their friends, but destruction to their foes. At their reception each Templar swore never to turn his back on three enemies, but should he be alone, to fight them if they were infidels. It was their wont to say that a Templar ought either to vanquish or die, since he had nothing to give for his ransom but his girdle and his knife.

The Order of the Temple, at first exceedingly simple in its organization, became in a short time very complicated. In the twelfth century it was divided into three classes, which were Knights, Chaplains, and Serving Brethren.

Commanderies are under the control of Grand Commanderies in States in which those bodies exist. Where they do not, the Warrants are derived directly from the Grand Encampment.

The supreme authority of the Order is exercised by the Grand Encampment of the United States, which meets triennially. The presiding officer is a Grand Master.

Light. Light is an important word in the Masonic system. It conveys a far more recondite meaning than it is believed to possess by the generality of readers. It is in fact the first of all the symbols presented to the neophyte, and continues to be presented to him in various modifications throughout all his future progress in his Masonic career. It does not simply mean, as might be supposed, *truth* or *wisdom,* but it contains within itself a far more abstruse allusion to the very essence of Speculative Masonry, and embraces within its capacious signification all the other symbols of the Order. Freemasons are emphatically called the "sons of light," because they are, or at least are entitled to be, in possession of the true meaning of the symbol; while the profane or uninitiated who have not received this knowledge are, by a parity of expression, said to be in darkness.

The connection of material light with this emblematic and mental illumination, was prominently exhibited in all the ancient systems of religion and esoteric mysteries.

Among the Egyptians, the hare was the hieroglyphic of eyes that are open, because that animal was supposed to have his eyes always open. The priests afterward adopted the hare as the symbol of the moral illumination revealed to the neophytes in the contemplation of the Divine truth, and hence, according to Champollion, it was also the symbol of Osiris, their principal divinity, and the chief object of their mystic rites —thus showing the intimate connection that they maintained in their symbolic language between the process of initiation and the contemplation of divinity. On this subject a remarkable coincidence has been pointed out by M. Portal, in the Hebrew language. There the word for "hare" is *arnebet,* which seems to be compounded of *aur,* "light," and *nabat,* "to see"; so that the word which among the Egyptians was used to designate an initiation, among the Hebrews meant to see the light.

If we proceed to an examination of the other systems of religion which were practised by the nations of antiquity, we shall find that light always constituted a principal object of adoration, as the primordial source of knowledge and goodness, and that darkness was with them synonymous with ignorance and evil. Dr. Beard attributes this view of the Divine origin of light among the Eastern nations, to the fact that "light in the East has a clearness and brilliancy, is accompanied by an intensity of heat, and is followed in its influence by a largeness of good, of which the inhabitants of less genial climates have no conception. Light easily and naturally became, in consequence, with Orientals, a representative of the highest human good. All the more joyous emotions of the mind, all the pleasing sensations of the frame, all the happy hours of domestic intercourse, were described under imagery derived from light. The transition was natural—from earthly to heavenly, from corporeal to spiritual things; and so light came to typify true religion and the felicity which it imparts. But as light not only came from God, but also makes man's way clear before him, so it was employed to signify moral truth, and preeminently that divine system of truth which is set forth in the Bible, from its earliest gleamings onward to the perfect day of the Great Sun of Righteousness."

As light was thus adored as the source of goodness, darkness, which is the negation of light, was abhorred as the cause of evil, and hence arose that doctrine which prevailed among the ancients, that there were two antagonistic principles continually contending for the government of the world.

"Light is a source of positive happiness: without it man could barely exist. And since all religious opinion is based on the ideas of pleasure and pain, and the corresponding sensations of hope and fear, it is not to be wondered if the heathen reverenced light. Darkness, on the contrary, by replunging nature, as it were, into a state of nothingness, and depriving man of the pleasurable emotions conveyed through the organ of sight, was ever held in abhorrence, as a source of misery and fear. The two opposite conditions in which man thus found himself placed, occasioned by the enjoyment or the banishment of light, induced him to imagine the existence of two antagonistic principles in nature, to whose dominion he was alternately subjected."

Such was the dogma of Zoroaster, the great Persian philosopher, who, under the names of Ormuzd and Ahriman, symbolized these two principles of light and darkness.

Such was also the doctrine, though somewhat modified, of Manes, the founder of the sect of Manichees, who describes God the Father as ruling over the kingdom of light and contending with the powers of darkness.

Pythagoras also maintained this doctrine of two antagonistic principles. He called the one, unity, *light,* the right hand, equality, stability, and a straight line; the other he named binary, *darkness,* the left hand, inequality, instability, and a curved line. Of the colors, he attributed white to the good principle, and black to the evil one.

The Jewish Kabbalists believed that, before the creation of the world, all space was filled with the Infinite Intellectual Light, which afterward withdrew itself to an equal distance from a central point in space, and afterward by its emanation produced future worlds. The first emanation of this surrounding light into the abyss of darkness produced what they called the "Adam Kadmon," the first man, or the first production of the Divine energy.

In the Bhagvat Geeta (one of the religious books of the Brahmans), it is said: "Light and darkness are esteemed the world's eternal ways; he who walketh in the former path returneth not—that is, he goeth immediately to bliss; whilst he who walketh in the latter cometh back again upon the earth."

In fact, in all the ancient systems, this reverence for light, as an emblematic representation of the Eternal Principle of Good, is predominant. In the mysteries, the candidate passed, during his initiation, through scenes of utter darkness, and at length terminated his trials by an admission to the splendidly illuminated sacellum, where he was said to have attained pure and perfect light, and where he received the necessary instructions which were to invest him with that knowledge of the Divine truth which had been the object of all his labors.

Mah. The Hebrew interrogative pronoun signifying *what?* It is a component part of a significant word in Masonry. The combination *mahhah,* literally "what! the," is equivalent, according to the Hebrew method of ellipsis, to the question, "What! is this the——?"

Mark Master. The Fourth Degree of the American Rite. The traditions of the degree make it of great historical importance, since by them we are informed that by its influence each Operative Mason at the building of the Temple was known and distinguished, and the disorder and confusion which might otherwise have attended so immense an undertaking was completely prevented. Not less useful is it in its symbolic signification. As illustrative of the Fellow-Craft, the Fourth Degree is particularly directed to the inculcation of order, regularity, and discipline. It teaches us that we should discharge all the duties of our several stations with precision and punctuality; that the work of our hands and the thoughts of our hearts should be good and true—not unfinished and imperfect, not sinful and defective—but such as the Great Overseer and Judge of heaven and earth will see fit to approve as a worthy oblation from his creatures. If the Fellow-Craft's Degree is devoted to the inculcation of learning, that of the Mark Master is intended to instruct us how that learning can most usefully and judiciously be employed for our own honor and the profit of others. And it holds forth to the desponding the encouraging thought that although our motives may sometimes be misinterpreted by our erring fellow mortals, our attainments be underrated, and our reputations be traduced by the envious and malicious, there is one, at least, who sees not with the eyes of man, but may yet make that stone which the builders rejected, the head of the corner. The intimate connection then, between the Second and Fourth degrees of Masonry, is this, that while one inculcates the necessary exercise of all the duties of life, the other teaches the importance of performing them with systematic regularity. The true Mark Master is a type of that man mentioned in the sacred parable, who received from his master this approving language—"Well done, good and faithful servant; thou hast been faithful over a few things, I will make thee ruler over many things: enter thou into the joys of thy Lord."

Mason's Wife and Daughter. A degree frequently conferred in the United States on the wives, daughters, sisters, and mothers of Masons, to secure to them, by investing them with a peculiar mode of recognition, the aid and assistance of the Fraternity. It may be conferred by any Master Mason, and the requirement is that the recipient shall be the wife, unmarried daughter, unmarried sister, or widowed mother of a Master Mason. It is sometimes called the Holy Virgin, and has been by some deemed of so much importance that a Manual of it, with the title of *The Ladies' Masonry, or Hieroglyphic Monitor,* was published at Louisville, Kentucky, in 1851, by Past Grand Master William Leigh, of Alabama.

Mexico. Masonry was introduced into Mexico, in the Scottish Rite, some time prior to 1810, by the civil and military officers of Spain, but the exact period of its introduction is unknown. The first Work Charters were granted for a Lodge at Vera Cruz in 1816, and one at Campeche in 1817, by the Grand Lodge of Louisiana, followed by a Charter for a Lodge at Vera Cruz in 1823 by the "City" Grand Lodge of New York, and one in the same city in 1824 from the Grand Lodge of Pennsylvania. February 10, 1826, five Charters were granted for Lodges in the City of Mexico by the "Country" Grand Lodge of New York, on the recommendation of Joel R. Poinsett, Past Deputy Grand Master of South Carolina, at that time United States Minister to Mexico, who constituted the Lodges and organized them into a Grand Lodge with Jose Ignacio Esteva as Grand Master.

The Masonic bodies, both York and Scottish Rite, however, soon degenerated into rival political clubs, and the bitter fractionalism became so strong that in 1833 the authorities issued an edict suppressing all secret societies. The bodies met, however, secretly, and about 1834 the National Mexican Rite was organized with nine degrees copied after the Scottish Rite. In 1843 a Lodge was chartered at Vera Cruz, and in 1845 at Mexico by the Grand Orient of France. In 1859 a Supreme Council 33°, with jurisdiction over the Symbolic degrees, was organized by authority of Albert Pike, and for a time the Supreme Council dominated all the bodies. In 1865 the Grand Lodge Valle de Mexico was organized as a York Rite Grand Lodge, and worked as such until 1911, when a number of the Lodges, under the leadership of Past Grand Masters Levi and Pro, left the Grand Lodge and organized a rival body, under the obedience of the Supreme Council.

Molay, James de. The twenty-second and last Grand Master of the Templars at the destruction of the Order in the fourteenth century. He was born about the year 1240, at Besançon, in Burgundy, being descended from a noble family. He was received into the Order of Knights Templar in 1265, by Imbert de Peraudo, Preceptor of France, in the Chapel of the Temple at Beaune. He immediately proceeded to Palestine, and greatly distinguished himself in the wars against the infidels, under the Grand Mastership of William de Beaujeu. In 1298, while absent from the Holy Land, he was unanimously elected Grand Master upon the death of Theobald Gaudinius. In 1305, he was summoned to France by Pope Clement V., upon the pretense of a desire, on the part of the Pontiff, to effect a coalition between the Templars and the Hospitalers. He was received by Philip the Fair, the treacherous King of France, with the most distinguished honors, and even selected by him as the godfather of one of his children. In April, 1307, he repaired, accompanied by three of his knights, to Poitiers, where the Pope was then residing, and as he supposed satisfactorily exculpated the Order from the charges which had been preferred against it. But both Pope and King were guilty of the most infamous deceit.

On the 12th of September, 1307, the order was issued for the arrest of the Templars, and De Molay endured an imprisonment for five years and a half, during which period he was subjected to the utmost indignities and sufferings for the purpose of extorting from him a confession of the guilt of his Order. But he was firm and loyal, and on the 11th of March, 1314, he was publicly burnt in front of the Cathedral of Nôtre Dame, in Paris. When about to die, he solemnly affirmed the innocence of the Order, and, it is said, summoned Pope Clement to appear before the judgment-seat of God in forty days and the King of France within a year, and both, it is well known, died within the periods specified.

Order of Business. In every Masonic body, the by-laws should prescribe an "Order of Business," and in proportion as that order is rigorously observed will be the harmony and celerity with which the business of the Lodge will be despatched.

In Lodges whose by-laws have prescribed no settled order, the arrangement of business is left to the discretion of the presiding officer, who, however, must be governed, to some extent, by certain general rules founded on the principles of parliamentary law, or on the suggestions of common sense.

The order of business may, for convenience of reference, be placed in the following tabular form:

1. Opening of the Lodge.
2. Reading and confirmation of the minutes.
3. Reports on petitions.
4. Balloting for candidates.
5. Reports of special committees.
6. Reports of standing committees.
7. Consideration of motions made at a former meeting, if called up by a member.
8. New business.
9. Initiations.
10. Reading of the minutes for information and correction.
11. Closing of the Lodge.

Order, Rules of. Every permanent deliberative body adopts a code of rules of order to suit itself; but there are certain rules derived from what may be called the common law of Parliament, the wisdom of which having been proven by long experience, that have been deemed of force at all times and places, and are, with a few necessary exceptions, as applicable to Lodges as to other societies.

The rules of order, sanctioned by uninterrupted usage and approved by all authorities, may be enumerated under the following distinct heads, as applied to a Masonic body:

1. Two independent original propositions cannot be presented at the same time to the meeting.
2. A subsidiary motion cannot be offered out of its rank of precedence.
3. When a brother intends to speak, he is required to stand up in his place, and to address himself always to the presiding officer.
4. When two or more brethren rise nearly at the same time, the presiding officer will indicate, by mentioning his name, the one who, in his opinion, is entitled to the floor.
5. A brother is not to be interrupted by any other member, except for the purpose of calling him to order.

6. No brother can speak oftener than the rules permit; but this rule may be dispensed with by the Master.

7. No one is to disturb the speaker by hissing, unnecessary coughing, loud whispering, or other unseemly noise, nor should he pass between the speaker and the presiding officer.

8. No personality, abusive remarks, or other improper language should be used by any brother in debate.

9. If the presiding officer rises to speak while a brother is on the floor, that brother should immediately sit down, that the presiding officer may be heard.

10. Everyone who speaks should speak to the question.

11. As a sequence to this, it follows that there can be no speaking unless there be a question before the Lodge. There must always be a motion of some kind to authorize a debate.

Origin of Freemasonry. The origin and source whence first sprang the institution of Freemasonry, such as we now have it, has given rise to more difference of opinion and discussion among Masonic scholars than any other topic in the literature of the Institution. Writers on the history of Freemasonry have, at different times, attributed its origin to the following sources. 1. To the Patriarchal religion. 2. To the Ancient Pagan Mysteries. 3. To the Temple of King Solomon. 4. To the Crusaders. 5. To the Knights Templar. 6. To the Roman Colleges of Artificers. 7. To the Operative Masons of the Middle Ages. 8. To the Rosicrucians of the sixteenth century. 9. To Oliver Cromwell, for the advancement of his political schemes. 10. To the Pretender, for the restoration of the House of Stuart to the British throne. 11. To Sir Christopher Wren at the building of St. Paul's Cathedral. 12. To Dr. Desaguliers and his associates in the year 1717. Each of these twelve theories has been from time to time, and the twelfth within a recent period, sustained with much zeal, if not always with much judgment, by their advocates. A few of them, however, have long since been abandoned, but the others still attract attention and find defenders. Dr. Mackey has his own views of the subject in his book *History of Freemasonry,* to which the reader is referred.

Perfection, Lodge of. The Lodge in which the Fourteenth Degree of the Ancient and Accepted Scottish Rite is conferred. In England and America this degree is called Grand Elect Perfect and Sublime Mason, but the French designate it Grand Scottish Mason of the Sacred Vault of James VI., or *Grand écossais de la Voûte Sacrée du Jacques VI.* This is one of the evidences—and a very pregnant one—of the influence exercised by the exiled Stuarts and their adherents on the Masonry of that time in making it an instrument for the restoration of James II., and then of his son, to the throne of England.

This degree, as concluding all reference to the first Temple, has been called the ultimate degree of ancient Masonry. It is the last of what is technically styled the Ineffable degrees, because their instructions relate to the Ineffable word.

Its place of meeting is called the Sacred Vault. Its principal officers are a Thrice Puissant Grand Master, two Grand Wardens, a Grand Treasurer, and Grand Secretary. In the first organization of the Rite in this country, the Lodges of Perfection were called "Sublime Grand Lodges," and, hence, the word "Grand" is still affixed to the title of the officers.

The following mythical history is connected with and related in this degree.

When the Temple was finished, the Masons who had been employed in constructing it acquired immortal honor. Their Order became more uniformly established and regulated than it had been before. Their caution and reserve in admitting new members produced respect, and merit alone was required of the candidate. With these principles instilled into their minds, many of the Grand Elect left the Temple after its dedication, and, dispersing themselves among the neighboring nations, instructed all who applied and were found worthy in the sublime degrees of Ancient Craft Masonry.

The Temple was completed in the year of the world 3000. Thus far, the wise King of Israel had behaved worthy of himself, and gained universal admiration; but in process of time, when he had advanced in years, his understanding became impaired; he grew deaf to the voice of the Lord, and was strangely irregular in his conduct. Proud of having erected an edifice to his Maker, and intoxicated with his great power, he plunged into all manner of licentiousness and debauchery, and profaned the Temple, by offering to the idol Moloch that incense which should have been offered only to the living God.

The Grand Elect and Perfect Masons saw this, and were sorely grieved, afraid that his apostasy would end in some dreadful consequences, and bring upon them those enemies whom Solomon had vaingloriously and wantonly defied. The people, copying the vices and follies of their King, became proud and idolatrous, and neglected the worship of the true God for that of idols.

As an adequate punishment for this defection, God inspired the heart of Nebuchadnezzar, King of Babylon, to take vengeance on the kingdom of Israel. This prince sent an army with Nebuzaradan, Captain of the Guards, who entered Judah with fire and sword, took and sacked the city of Jerusalem, razed its walls, and destroyed the Temple. The people were carried captive to Babylon, and the conquerors took with them all the vessels of silver and gold. This happened four hundred and seventy years, six months, and ten days after its dedication.

When, in after times, the princes of Christendom entered into a league to free the Holy Land from the oppression of the infidels, the good and virtuous Masons, anxious for the success of so pious an undertaking, voluntarily offered their services to the confederates, on condition that they should be permitted a chief of their own election, which was granted; they accordingly rallied under their standard and departed.

The valor and fortitude of these elected knights was such that they were admired by, and took the lead of, all the princes of Jerusalem, who, believing that their mysteries inspired them with courage and fidelity in the cause of virtue and religion, became desirous of being initiated. Upon being found worthy, their desires were complied with; and thus the royal art, meeting the approbation of great and good men, became popular and honorable, was diffused through their various dominions, and has continued to spread through a succession of ages to the present day.

The symbolic color of this degree is red—emblematic of fervor, constancy, and assiduity. Hence, the Masonry of this degree was formerly called Red Masonry on the Continent of Europe.

The jewel of the degree is a pair of compasses extended on an arc of ninety degrees, surmounted by a crown, and with a sun in the center. In the Southern Jurisdiction the sun is on one side and a five-pointed star on the other.

The apron is white with red flames, bordered with blue, and having the jewel painted on the center and the stone of foundation on the flap.

Prentice Pillar. In the southeast part of the Chapel of Roslyn Castle, in Scotland, is the celebrated column which goes by this name, and with which a Masonic legend is connected. The pillar is a plain fluted shaft, having a floral garland twined around it, all carved out of the solid stone. The legend is, that when the plans of the chapel were sent from Rome, the master builder did not clearly understand about this pillar, or, as another account states, had lost this particular portion of his plans, and, in consequence, had to go to Rome for further instructions or to procure a fresh copy. During his absence, a clever apprentice, the only son of a widow, either from memory or from his own invention, carved and completed the beautiful pillar. When the master returned and found the work completed, furious with jealous rage, he killed the apprentice, by striking him a frightful blow on the forehead with a heavy setting maul. In testimony of the truth of the legend, the visitor is shown three heads in the west part of the chapel—the master's, the apprentice's, with the gash on his forehead, and the widow's. There can be but little doubt that this legend referred to that of the Third Degree, which is thus shown to have existed, at least substantially, at that early period.

Rainbow for Girls, Order of. An organization planned to sow the seeds of love, law, religion, patriotism, and service in the hearts and minds of the girlhood of America for harvest in the coming years. The organization was prompted and founded by Rev. William Mark Sexson, McAllister Oklahoma, then Grand Chaplain for Oklahoma. The Order was formed in 1922, under the name of the Order of the Rainbow for

Girls. The following four years the Order was extended to thirty one states of the Union and quickly grew to a membership of forty thousand. The Order of the Rainbow is not Freemasonry, nor is it Eastern Star, but it is very dear to each of these organizations. Local Lodges or Bodies are called Assemblies. Before an Assembly can be instituted it must be sponsored by a Masonic or an Eastern Star organization, that will promise to look after its welfare. Its membership is made up of girls between the ages of thirteen and eighteen, must be children of Masonic or Eastern Star families, or the friends and chums of such children. This is the only relationship to Freemasonry, tho it has no secrets from Freemasons nor members of the Eastern Star, who are eligible to attend any Assembly. The Order is designed to teach the girls to serve. It offers a channel thru which it will be of real service to the City, County, State and Nation. The three virtues taught are;—Faith, Hope and Charity. They are taught that the Bible contains the rule of right living for all and that its heroines are those who have in the past stood for the Trinity of Home, Church and Nation.

The seven lessons represented by the seven colors of the rainbow are the lessons of Love, Religion, Nature, Immortality, Fidelity, Patriotism and Service.

Red Cross of Constantine. A degree founded on the circumstance of the vision of a cross, with the inscription EN TOYTΩ NIKA, which appeared in the heavens to the Emperor Constantine. It formed originally a part of the Rosaic Rite, and is now practised in England, Ireland, Scotland, and some of the English colonies, as a distinct Order; the meetings being called "Conclaves," and the presiding officer of the Grand Imperial Council of the whole Order, "Grand Sovereign." Its existence in England as a Masonic degree has been traced, according to Bro. R. W. Little (*Freemas. Mag.*), to the year 1780, when it was given by Bro. Charles Shirreff. It was reorganized in 1804 by Walter Rodwell Wright, who supplied its present ritual. The ritual of the Order contains the following legend:

"After the memorable battle fought at Saxa Rubra, on the 28th October, A.D. 312, the emperor sent for the chiefs of the Christian legion, and—we now quote the words of an old ritual—'in presence of his other officers constituted them into an Order of Knighthood, and appointed them to wear the form of the Cross he had seen in the heavens upon their shields, with the motto *In hoc signo vinces* round it, surrounded with clouds; and peace being soon after made, he became the Sovereign Patron of the Christian Order of the Red Cross.' It is also said that this Cross, together with a device called the *Labarum,* was ordered to be embroidered upon all the imperial standards. The Christian warriors were selected to compose the body-guard of Constantine, and the command of these privileged soldiers was confided to Eusebius, Bishop of Nicomedia, who was thus considered the second officer of the Order."

Revelation. The following is an extract from Mackenzie's *Royal Masonic Cyclopædia* upon this subject: "With infinite learning and patience the author of *The Book of God,* who preserves strict anonymity, has endeavoured to show that the work (Apocalypse) was originally revealed to a primæval John, otherwise Oannes, and identical with the first messenger of God to man. This theory is sufficiently remarkable to be mentioned here. The messengers, twelve in number, are supposed by the author to appear at intervals of 600 years. Thus: 1, Adam, A.M. 3000; 2, Enoch, A.M. 3600; 3, Fohi, A.M. 4200; 4, Brigoo, A.M. 4800; 5, Zaratusht, A.M. 5400; 6, Thoth, A.M. 6000; 7, Amosis or Moses, A.M. 6600; 8, Laotseu, A.M. 7200; 9, Jesus, A.M. 7800; 10, Mohammed, A.M. 8400; 11, Chengiz-Khan, A.M. 9000; and, 12, the twelfth messenger yet to be revealed, A.M. 9600. With the aid of this theory, the whole history of the world, down to our own days, is shown to be foretold in the Apocalypse, and although it is difficult to agree with the accomplished writer's conclusions, supported by him with an array of learning and a sincere belief in what is stated, no one with any taste for these studies should be without this wonderful series of books. The same author has published, in two volumes, a revised edition of the *Book of Enoch,* with a commentary, and he promises to continue, and, if possible, complete his design."

Rose Croix, Prince of. French, *Souverain Rosenkruz.* This important degree is, of all the high grades, the most widely diffused, being found in numerous Rites. It is the Eighteenth of the Ancient and Accepted Scottish Rite. It was also given, formerly, in some Encampments of Knights Templars, and was the Sixth of the degrees conferred by the Encampment of Baldwyn at Bristol, in England. It must not, however, be confounded with the Rosicrucians, who, however, similar in name. were only a Hermetic and mystical Order.

The degree is known by various names: sometimes its possessors are called "Sovereign Princes of Rose Croix," sometimes "Princes of Rose Croix de Heroden," and sometimes "Knights of the Eagle and Pelican." In relation to its origin, Masonic writers have made many conflicting statements, some giving it a much higher antiquity than others; but all agreeing in supposing it to be one of the earliest of the higher degrees. The name has, undoubtedly, been the cause of much of this confusion in relation to its history; and the Masonic Degree of Rose Croix has, perhaps, often been confounded with the Kabbalistical and alchemical sect of "Rosicrucians," or "Brothers of the Rosy Cross," among whose adepts the names of such men as Roger Bacon, Paracelsus, and Elias Ashmole, the celebrated antiquary, are to be found. Notwithstanding the invidious attempts of Barruel and other foes of Masonry to confound the two Orders, there is a great distinction between them. Even their names, although somewhat similar in sound, are totally different in signification. The Rosicrucians, who were alchemists, did not derive their name, like the Rose Croix Masons, from the emblems of the rose and cross—for they had nothing to do with the rose—but from the Latin *ros*, signifying *dew*, which was supposed to be of all natural bodies the most powerful solvent of gold, and *crux*, the cross, a chemical hieroglyphic of light.

Baron de Westerode, who wrote in 1784, in the *Acta Latomorum* (i., 336), gives the earliest origin of any Masonic writer to the degree of Rose Croix. He supposes that it was instituted among the Knights Templars in Palestine, in the year 1188, and he adds that Prince Edward, the son of Henry III. of England, was admitted into the Order by Raymond Lully in 1196. De Westerode names Ormesius, an Egyptian priest, who had been converted to Christianity, as its founder.

Some have sought to find its origin in the labors of Valentine Andreä, the reputed founder of the Rosicrucian fraternity. But the Rose Croix of Masonry and the Hermetic Rosicrucianism of Andreä were two entirely different things; and it would be difficult to trace any connection between them, at least any such connection as would make one the legitimate successor of the other.

The Baron de Gleichen, who was, in 1785, the German secretary of the Philalethan Congress at Paris, says that the Rose Croix and the Masons were united in England under King Arthur. (*Acta Lat.*, i., 336.) But he has, undoubtedly, mixed up Rosicrucianism with the Masonic legends of the Knights of the Round Table, and his assertions must go for nothing.

Clavel, with his usual boldness of assertion, which is too often independent of facts, declares that the degree was invented by the Jesuits for the purpose of countermining the insidious attacks of the freethinkers upon the Roman Catholic religion, but that the philosophers parried the attempt by seizing upon the degree and giving to all its symbols an astronomical signification. Clavel's opinion is probably derived from one of those sweeping charges of Professor Robison, in which that systematic enemy of our Institution declares that, about the beginning of the eighteenth century, the Jesuits interfered considerably with Masonry, "insinuating themselves into the Lodges, and contributing to increase that religious mysticism that is to be observed in all the ceremonies of the Order." But there is no better evidence than these mere vague assertions of the connection of the Jesuits with the Rose Croix Degree.

Oliver (*Landm.*, ii., 81) says that the earliest notice that he finds of this degree is in a publication of 1613. But he adds, that "it was known much sooner, although not probably as a degree in Masonry; for it existed as a cabalistic science from the earliest times in Egypt, Greece, and Rome, as well as amongst the Jews and Moors in times more recent."

Oliver, however, undoubtedly, in the latter part of this paragraph, confounds the Masonic Rose Croix with the alchemical Rosicrucians; and the former is singularly inconsistent with the details that he gives in reference to the Rosy Cross of the Royal Order of Scotland.

The subject, however, is in a state of inextricable confusion, and I confess that, after all my researches, I am still unable distinctly to point to the period when, and to the place where, the present degree of Rose Croix received its organization as a Masonic grade.

It was, indeed, on its first inception, an attempt to Christianize Freemasonry; to apply the rites, and symbols, and traditions of Ancient Craft Masonry to the last and greatest dispensation; to add to the first Temple of Solomon and the second of Zerubbabel a third, that to which Christ alluded when he said, "Destroy this temple, and in three days will I raise it up." The great discovery which was made in the Royal Arch ceases to be of value in this degree; for it another is substituted of more Christian application; the Wisdom, Strength, and Beauty which supported the ancient Temple are replaced by the Christian pillars of Faith, Hope and Charity; the great lights, of course, remain, because they are of the very essence of Masonry; but the three lesser give way to the thirty-three, which allude to the years of the Messiah's sojourning on earth. Everything, in short, about the degree, is Christian; but, as I have already said, the Christian teachings of the degree have been applied to the sublime principles of a universal system, and an interpretation and illustration of the doctrines of the "Master of Nazareth," so adapted to the Masonic dogma of tolerance, that men of every faith may embrace and respect them. It thus performs a noble mission. It obliterates, alike, the intolerance of those Christians who sought to erect an impassable barrier around the sheepfold, and the equal intolerance of those of other religions who would be ready to exclaim, "Can any good thing come out of Nazareth?"

In the Ancient and Accepted Scottish Rite, whence the Rose Croix Masons of the United States have received the degree, it is placed as the eighteenth on the list. It is conferred in a body called a "Chapter," which derives its authority immediately from the Supreme Council of the Thirty-third, and which confers with it only one other and inferior degree, that of "Knights of the East and West." Its principal officers are a Most Wise Master and two Wardens. Maundy Thursday and Easter Sunday are two obligatory days of meeting.

The aspirant for the degree makes the usual application duly recommended; and if accepted, is required, before initiation, to make certain declarations which shall show his competency for the honor which he seeks, and at the same time prove the high estimation entertained of the degree by those who already possess it.

The jewel of the Rose Croix is a golden compass, extended on an arc to the sixteenth part of a circle, or twenty-two and a half degrees. The head of the compass is surmounted by a triple crown, consisting of three series of points arranged by three, five, and seven. Between the legs of the compass is a cross resting on the arc; its center is occupied by a full-blown rose, whose stem twines around the lower limb of the cross; at the foot of the cross, on the same side on which the rose is exhibited, is the figure of a pelican wounding its breast to feed its young which are in a nest surrounding it, while on the other side of the jewel is the figure of an eagle with wings displayed. On the arc of the circle, the P.·.W.·. of the degree is engraved in the cipher of the Order.

In this jewel are included the most important symbols of the degree. The *Cross,* the *Rose,* the *Pelican,* and the *Eagle* are all important symbols, the explanations of which will go far to a comprehension of what is the true design of the Rose Croix Order. They may be seen in this work under their respective titles.

Rosicrucianism. Many writers have sought to discover a close connection between the Rosicrucians and the Freemasons, and some, indeed, have advanced the theory that the latter are only the successors of the former. Whether this opinion be correct or not, there are sufficient coincidences of character between the two to render the history of Rosicrucianism highly interesting to the Masonic student.

The Rosicrucians had a large number of symbols, some of which were in common with those of the Freemasons, and some peculiar to themselves. The principal of these were the globe, the circle, the compasses, the square (both the working-tool and the geometrical figure), the triangle, the level, and the plummet. These are, however, interpreted, not like the Masonic, as symbols of the moral virtues, but of the properties of the philosopher's stone.

Royal Arch Badge. The triple tau, consisting of three tau crosses conjoined at their feet, constitutes the Royal Arch badge. The English Masons call it the "emblem of all emblems," and the "grand emblem of Royal Arch Masonry." The English Royal Arch lecture thus defines it: "The triple tau forms two right angles on each of the exterior lines, and another at the centre, by their union; for the three angles of each triangle are equal to two right angles. This, being triplified, illustrates the jewel worn by the companions of the Royal Arch, which, by its intersection, forms a given number of angles that may be taken in five several combinations." It is used in the Royal Arch Masonry of Scotland, and has, for the last ten or fifteen years, been adopted officially in the United States.

Royal Arch Robes. In the working of a Royal Arch Chapter in the United States, great attention is paid to the robes of the several officers. The High Priest wears, in imitation of the high priest of the Jews, a robe of blue, purple, scarlet, and white linen, and is decorated with the breastplate and miter. The King wears a scarlet robe, and has a crown and scepter. The Scribe wears a purple robe and turban. The Captain of the Host wears a white robe and cap, and is armed with a sword. The

Principal Sojourner wears a dark robe, with tessellated border, a slouched hat, and pilgrim's staff. The Royal Arch Captain wears a white robe and cap, and is armed with a sword. The three Grand Masters of the Veils wear, respectively, the Grand Master of the third veil a scarlet robe and cap, of the second veil a purple robe and cap; of the first veil a blue robe and cap. Each is armed with a sword. The Treasurer, Secretary, and Sentinel wear no robes nor peculiar dress. All of these robes have either an historical or symbolical allusion.

Schools. None of the charities of Freemasonry have been more important or more worthy of approbation than those which have been directed to the establishment of schools for the education of the orphan children of Masons; and it is a very proud feature of the Order, that institutions of this kind are to be found in every country where Freemasonry has made a lodgment as an organized society. In England, the Royal Freemasons' Girls' School was established in 1788. In 1798, a similar one for boys was founded. At a very early period charity schools were erected by the Lodges in Germany, Denmark, and Sweden. The Masons of Holland instituted a school for the blind in 1808. In the United States much attention has been paid to this subject. In 1842, the Grand Lodge of Missouri instituted a Masonic college, and the example was followed by several other Grand Lodges. But colleges have been found too unwieldly and complicated in their management for a successful experiment, and the scheme has generally been abandoned. But there are numerous schools in the United States which are supported in whole or in part by Masonic Lodges.

Scottish Rite. French writers call this the "Ancient and Accepted Rite," but as the Latin Constitutions of the Order designate it as the "Antiquus Scoticus Ritus Acceptus," or the "Ancient and Accepted Scottish Rite," that title has now been very generally adopted as the correct name of the Rite. Although one of the youngest of the Masonic Rites, having been established not earlier than the year 1801, it is at this day the most popular and the most extensively diffused. Supreme Councils or governing bodies of the Rite are to be found in almost every civilized country of the world, and in many of them it is the only Masonic obedience. The history of its organization is briefly this: In 1758, a body was organized at Paris called the "Council of Emperors of the East and West." This Council organized a Rite called the "Rite of Perfection," which consisted of twenty-five degrees, the highest of which was "Sublime Prince of the Royal Secret." In 1761, this Council granted a Patent or Deputation to Stephen Morin, authorizing him to propagate the Rite in the Western continent, whither he was about to repair. In the same year, Morin arrived at the city of St. Domingo, where he commenced the dissemination of the Rite, and appointed many Inspectors, both for the West Indies and for the United States. Among others, he conferred the degrees on M. Hayes, with a power of appointing others when necessary.

Hayes accordingly appointed Isaac Da Costa Deputy Inspector-General for South Carolina, who in 1783 introduced the Rite into that State by the establishment of a Grand Lodge of Perfection in Charleston. Other Inspectors were subsequently appointed, and in 1801 a Supreme Council was opened in Charleston by John Mitchell and Frederick Dalcho. There is abundant evidence in the Archives of the Supreme Council that up to that time the twenty-five degrees of the Rite of Perfection were alone recognized. But suddenly, with the organization of the Supreme Council, there arose a new Rite, fabricated by the adoption of eight more of the continental high degrees, so as to make the Thirty-third and not the Twenty-fifth Degree the summit of the Rite.

The Rite consists of thirty-three degrees, which are divided into seven sections, each section being under an appropriate jurisdiction.

Seven. In every system of antiquity there is a frequent reference to this number, showing that the veneration for it proceeded from some common cause. It is equally a sacred number in the Gentile as in the Christian religion. Oliver says that this can scarcely be ascribed to any event, except it be the institution of the Sabbath. Higgins thinks that the peculiar circumstance, perhaps accidental, of the number of the days of the week coinciding exactly with the number of the planetary bodies probably procured for it its character of sanctity. The Pythagoreans called it a perfect number, because it was made up of 3 and 4, the triangle and the square, which are the two perfect figures. They called it also a virgin number, and without mother, comparing it to Minerva, who was a motherless virgin, because it cannot by multiplication produce any number within ten, as twice two does four, and three times three does nine; nor can any two numbers, by their multiplication, produce it.

Seven is a sacred number in Masonic symbolism. It has always been so. In the earliest rituals of the last century it was said that a Lodge required seven to make it perfect; but the only explanation to be found in any of those rituals of the sacredness of the number is the seven liberal arts and sciences, which, according to the old "Legend of the Craft," were the foundation of Masonry. In modern ritualism the symbolism of seven has been transferred from the First to the Second Degree, and there it is made to refer only to the seven steps of the Winding Stairs; but the symbolic seven is to be found diffused in a hundred ways over the whole Masonic system.

Shrine. The Shrine, the familiar name applied to the Ancient Arabic Order, Nobles of the Mystic Shrine, has an origin about which the various writers upon the subject have not agreed. The point on which there is general agreement is that the real work of preparing a Ritual and organizing a Temple in the City of New York and four years later organized what was first known as the "Imperial Grand Council of the Ancient Order of Nobles of the Mystic Shrine for the United States of America," was done by Dr. Walter M. Fleming, Charles T. McClenachan, and others. The Ritual is presented in an alluring Oriental style. So much of this is in evidence that even those active in the Shrine from the earlier years found difficulty in saying with precision how much or how little confidence should be placed in any claims made for an exclusively foreign origin of the institution.

In 1870 the first Temple in America was instituted at New York City and was called "Gotham," which was changed to the name "Mecca" when it was decided that all Temples should have an Arabic or an Egyptian title. Noble Dr. Walter M. Fleming was the first Grand Imperial Potentate and Noble William S. Patterson was first Recorder. The word "Grand" in the titles was discarded by the Imperial Council in 1887.

The Order of the Nobles of the Mystic Shrine in America does not advocate Mohammedanism as a sect, but inculcates the same respect to Deity here as elsewhere, and hence the secret of its profound grasp on the intellect and heart of all cultured people.

The Imperial Council of the Ancient Arabic Order of Nobles of the Mystic Shrine for the United States of America was organized June 6th, 1876. At the meeting of the Imperial Council at Indianapolis in 1919 it was proposed to establish a home for friendless, orphaned and crippled children, to be supported by the Nobles of the Mystic Shrine of North America. The matter was laid over until the meeting at Portland, Oregon in 1920. At this time a resolution was adopted authorizing the establishment of a hospital to be supported on an annual per capita basis and to be known as the Shrine Hospital for Crippled Children. An assessment of Two Dollars per capita was levied upon the entire membership. A Committee of Seven was appointed to select a site and secure plans and specifications. Provision made for an annual levy to support the institution. Since that time a number of hospitals have been built also mobile units supported in other hospitals to carry on the work of rehabilitating crippled children thru the channel of orthopedic surgery. The first child admitted for surgical treatment by a Shriner's surgeon was a patient at Shreveport, Louisiana in September 1922.

The Shriners' hospitals and mobile units are open to every crippled child, without restriction as to race or religion, subject to the following requirements; The parents or guardians must be financially unable to pay for its treatment. The child must not be over fourteen years of age, of normal mentality, and there must be reasonable hope of materially improving the child's condition thru orthopedic surgery.

The other activities of the Shrine are largely social and fraternal.

To be eligible to membership a man must be a Knight Templar or a member of the Ancient Accepted Scottish Rite of the Thirty Second Degree.

The governing body is called a Divan. The officers are; Potentate, Chief Rabban, Assistant Rabban, High Priest and Prophet, Oriental Guide, Recorder and Treasurer. The elective officers are; First Ceremonial Master, Second Ceremonial Master, Marshall, Captain of Guard, Lieutenant of Guard, Outer Guard, Class Director, Director of Work, Physician, Orator, Band Manager. A Band and a Patrol complete the active workers.

Side Degrees. There are certain Masonic degrees, which, not being placed in the regular routine of the acknowledged degrees, are not recognized as a part of Ancient Masonry, but receive the name of "Honorary or Side Degrees." They constitute no part of the regular ritual, and are not under the control of either Grand Lodges, Grand Chapters, or any other of the legal, administrative bodies of the Institution. Although a few of them are very old, the greater number are of a comparatively modern origin, and are generally supposed to have been indebted for their invention to the ingenuity of either Grand Lecturers, or other distinguished Masons. Their history and ceremonies are often interesting, and so far as we have been made acquainted with them, their tendency, when they are properly conferred, is always moral. They are not given in Lodges or Chapters, but at private meetings of the brethren or companions possessing them, informally and temporarily called for the sole purpose of conferring them. These temporary assemblies owe no allegiance to any supreme, controlling body, except so far as they are composed of Master or Royal Arch Masons, and when the business of conferring the degrees is accomplished, they are dissolved at once, not to meet again, except under similar circumstances and for a similar purpose.

Some of them are conferred on Master Masons, some on Royal Arch Masons, and some only on Knights Templar. There is another class which females, connected by certain ties of relationship with the Fraternity, are permitted to receive; and this fact, in some measure, assimilates these degrees to the Masonry of Adoption, or Female Masonry, which is practised in France and some other European countries, although there are important points of difference between them. These female side degrees have received the name of "androgynous degrees," from two Greek words signifying *man* and *woman*, and are thus called to indicate the participation in them by both sexes.

The principal side degrees practised in America are as follows:

1. Secret Monitor.
2. Knight of the Three Kings.
3. Knight of Constantinople.
4. Mason's Wife and Daughter.
5. Ark and Dove.
6. Mediterranean Pass.
7. Knight and Heroine of Jericho.
8. Good Samaritan.
9. Knight of the Mediterranean Pass.

Solomon. In writing the life of King Solomon from a Masonic point of view, it is impossible to omit a reference to the legends which have been preserved in the Masonic system. But the writer, who, with this preliminary notice, embodies them in his sketch of the career of the wise King of Israel, is by no means to be held responsible for a belief in their authenticity. It is the business of the Masonic biographer to relate all that has been handed down by tradition in connection with the life of Solomon; it will be the duty of the severer critic to seek to separate out of all these materials that which is historical from that which is merely mythical, and to assign to the former all that is valuable as fact, and to the latter all that is equally valuable as symbolism.

Solomon, the King of Israel, the son of David and Bathsheba, ascended the throne of his kingdom 2989 years after the creation of the world, and 1015 years before the Christian era. He was then only twenty years of age, but the youthful monarch is said to have commenced his reign with the decision of a legal question of some difficulty, in which he exhibited the first promise of that wise judgment for which he was ever afterward distinguished.

One of the great objects of Solomon's life, and the one which most intimately connects him with the history of the Masonic institution, was the erection of a temple to Jehovah. This, too, had been a favorite design of his father David. For this purpose, that monarch, long before his death, had numbered the workmen whom he found in his kingdom; had appointed the overseers of the work, the hewers of stones, and the bearers of burdens; had prepared a great quantity of brass, iron, and cedar; and had amassed an immense treasure with which to support the enterprise. But on consulting with the prophet Nathan, he learned from that holy man, that although the pious intention was pleasing to God, yet that he would not be permitted to carry it into execution, and the Divine prohibition was proclaimed in these emphatic words: "Thou hast shed blood abundantly, and hast made great wars; thou shalt not build a house unto my name, because thou hast shed much blood upon the earth in my sight." The task was, therefore, reserved for the more peaceful Solomon, his son and successor.

Hence, when David was about to die, he charged Solomon to build the Temple of God as soon as he should have received the kingdom. He also gave him directions in relation to the construction of the edifice, and put into his possession the money, amounting to ten thousand talents of gold and ten times that amount of silver, which he had collected and laid aside for defraying the expense.

Solomon had scarcely ascended the throne of Israel, when he prepared to carry into execution the pious designs of his predecessor. For this purpose, however, he found it necessary to seek the assistance of Hiram, King of Tyre, the ancient friend and ally of his father. The Tyrians and Sidonians, the subjects of Hiram, had long been distinguished for their great architectural skill; and, in fact, many of them, as the members of a mystic operative society, the fraternity of Dionysian artificers, had long monopolized the profession of building in Asia Minor. The Jews, on the contrary, were rather more eminent for their military valor than for their knowledge of the arts of peace, and hence King Solomon at once conceived the necessity of invoking the aid of these foreign architects, if he expected to complete the edifice he was about to erect, either in a reasonable time or with the splendor and magnificence appropriate to the sacred object for which it was intended. For this purpose he addressed the following letter to King Hiram:

"Know thou that my father would have built a temple to God, but was hindered by wars and continual expeditions, for he did not leave off to overthrow his enemies till he made them all subject to tribute. But I give thanks to God for the peace I, at present, enjoy, and on that account I am at leisure, and design to build a house to God, for God foretold to my father, that such a house should be built by me; wherefore I desire thee to send some of thy subjects with mine to Mount Lebanon, to cut down timber, for the Sidonians are more skilful than our people in cutting of wood. As for wages to the hewers of wood, I will pay whatever price thou shalt determine."

Hiram, mindful of the former amity and alliance that had existed between himself and David, was disposed to extend the friendship he had felt for the father to the son, and replied, therefore, to the letter of Solomon in the following epistle:

"It is fit to bless God that he hath committed thy father's government to thee, who art a wise man endowed with all virtues. As for myself, I rejoice at the condition thou art in, and will be subservient to thee in all that thou sendest to me about; for when, by my subjects, I have cut down many and large trees of cedar and cypress wood, I will send them to sea, and will order my subjects to make floats of them, and to sail to what places soever of thy country thou shalt desire, and leave them there, after which thy subjects may carry them to Jerusalem. But do thou take care to procure us corn for this timber, which we stand in need of, because we inhabit in an island."

Hiram lost no time in fulfilling the promise of assistance which he had thus given; and accordingly we are informed that Solomon received thirty-three thousand six hundred workmen from Tyre, besides a sufficient quantity of timber and stone to construct the edifice which he was about to erect. Hiram sent him, also, a far more important gift than either men or materials, in the person of an able architect, "a curious and cunning workman," whose skill and experience were to be exercised in superintending the labors of the craft, and in adorning and beautifying the building. Of this personage, whose name was also Hiram, and who plays so important a part in the history of Freemasonry, an account will be found in the article *Hiram Abif,* to which the reader is referred.

King Solomon commenced the erection of the Temple on Monday, the second day of the Hebrew month Zif, which answers to the twenty-first of April, in the year of the world 2992, and 1012 years before the Christian era. Advised in all the details, as Masonic tradition informs us, by the wise and prudent counsels of Hiram, King of Tyre, and Hiram Abif, who, with himself, constituted at that time the three Grand Masters of the Craft, Solomon made every arrangement in the disposition and government of the workmen, in the payment of their wages, and in the maintenance of concord and harmony which should insure despatch in the execution and success in the result.

To Hiram Abif was entrusted the general superintendence of the building, while subordinate stations were assigned to other eminent artists, whose names and offices have been handed down in the traditions of the Order.

In short, the utmost perfection of human wisdom was displayed by this enlightened monarch in the disposition of everything that related to the construction of the stupendous edifice. Men of the most comprehensive minds, imbued with the greatest share of zeal and fervency, and inspired with the strongest fidelity to his interests, were employed as masters to instruct and superintend the workmen; while those who labored in inferior stations were excited to enthusiasm by the promise of promotion and reward.

The Temple was at length finished in the month Bul, answering to our November, in the year of the world 3000, being a little more than seven years from its commencement.

As soon as the magnificent edifice was completed, and fit for the sacred purposes for which it was intended, King Solomon determined to celebrate the consummation of his labors in the most solemn manner. For this purpose he directed the ark to be brought from the king's house, where it had been placed by King David, and to be deposited with impressive ceremonies in the holy of holies, beneath the expanded wings of the cherubim. This important event is commemorated in the beautiful ritual of the Most Excellent Master's Degree.

Our traditions inform us, that when the Temple was completed, Solomon assembled all the heads of the tribes, the elders and chiefs of Israel to bring the ark up out of Zion, where King David had deposited it in a tabernacle until a more fitting place should have been built for its reception. This duty, therefore, the Levites now performed, and delivered the ark of the covenant into the hands of the priests, who fixed it in its place in the center of the holy of holies.

Here the immediate and personal connection of King Solomon with the Craft begins to draw to a conclusion. It is true, that he subsequently employed those worthy Masons, whom the traditions say, at the completion and dedication of the Temple, he had received and acknowledged as Most Excellent Masters, in the erection of a magnificent palace and other edifices, but in process of time he fell into the most grievous errors; abandoned the path of truth; encouraged the idolatrous rites of Spurious Masonry; and, induced by the persuasions of those foreign wives and concubines whom he had espoused in his later days, he erected a fane for the celebration of these heathen mysteries, on one of the hills that overlooked the very spot where, in his youth, he had consecrated a temple to the one true God. It is however believed that before his death he deeply repented of this temporary aberration from virtue, and in the emphatic expression, "Vanity of vanities! all is vanity," he is supposed to have acknowledged that in his own experience he had discovered that falsehood and sensuality, however they may give pleasure for a season, will, in the end, produce the bitter fruits of remorse and sorrow.

That King Solomon was the wisest monarch that swayed the scepter of Israel, has been the unanimous opinion of posterity. So much was he beyond the age in which he flourished, in the attainments of science, that the Jewish and Arabic writers have attributed to him a thorough knowledge of the secrets of magic, by whose incantations they suppose him to have been capable of calling spirits and demons to his assistance; and the Talmudists and Mohammedan doctors record many fanciful legends of his exploits in controlling these ministers of darkness. As a naturalist, he is said to have written a work on animals of no ordinary character, which has however perished; while his qualifications as a poet were demonstrated by more than a thousand poems which he composed, of which his epithalamium on his marriage with an Egyptian princess and the Book of Ecclesiastes alone remain. He has given us in his Proverbs an opportunity of forming a favorable opinion of his pretensions to the character of a deep and right-thinking philosopher; while the long peace and prosperous condition of his empire for the greater portion of his reign, the increase of his kingdom in wealth and refinement, and the encouragement which he gave to architecture, the mechanic arts, and commerce, testify his profound abilities as a sovereign and statesman.

After a reign of forty years he died, and with him expired forever the glory and the power of the Hebrew empire.

Sovereign Grand Inspector-General. The Thirty-third and last degree of the Ancient and Accepted Scottish Rite. The Latin Constitutions of 1786 call it "Tertius et trigesimus et sublimissimus gradus," i. e., "the Thirty-third and Most Sublime Degree"; and it is styled "the Protector and Conservator of the Order." The same Constitutions, in Articles I. and II., say:

"The thirty-third degree confers on those Masons who are legitimately invested with it, the quality, title, privilege, and authority of Sovereign [Supremorum] Grand Inspectors-General of the Order.

"The peculiar duty of their mission is to teach and enlighten the brethren; to preserve charity, union, and fraternal love among them; to maintain regularity in the works of each degree, and to take care that it is preserved by others; to cause the dogmas, doctrines, institutes, constitutions, statutes, and regulations of the Order to be reverently regarded, and to preserve and defend them on every occasion; and, finally, everywhere to occupy themselves in works of peace and mercy."

The body in which the members of this degree assemble is called a Supreme Council.

The symbolic color of the degree is white, denoting purity.

The distinctive insignia are a sash, collar, jewel, Teutonic cross, decoration, and ring.

The sash is a broad, white watered ribbon, bordered with gold, bearing on the front a triangle of gold glittering with rays of gold, which has in the center the numerals 33, with a sword of silver, directed from above, on each side of the triangle, pointing to its center. The sash, worn from the right shoulder to the left hip, ends in a point, and is fringed with gold, having at the junction a circular band of scarlet and green containing the jewel of the Order.

The collar is of white watered ribbon fringed with gold, having the rayed triangle at its point and the swords at the sides. By a regulation of the Southern Supreme Council of the United States, the collar is worn by the active, and the sash by the honorary, members of the Council.

The jewel is a black double-headed eagle, with golden beaks and talons, holding in the latter a sword of gold, and crowned with the golden crown of Prussia.

The red Teutonic cross is affixed to the left side of the breast.

The decoration rests upon a Teutonic cross. It is a nine-pointed star, namely, one formed by three triangles of gold one upon the other, and interlaced from the lower part of the left side to the upper part of the right a sword extends, and in the opposite direction is a hand of (as it is called) *Justice*. In the center is the shield of THE ORDER, *azure* charged with an eagle like that on the banner, having on the dexter side a Balance *or*, and on the sinister side a Compass of the second, united with a Square of the second. Around the whole shield runs a band of the first, with the Latin inscription, of the second, ORDO AB CHAO, which band is enclosed by two circles, formed by two Serpents of the second, each biting his own tail. Of the smaller triangles that are formed by the intersection of the greater ones, those nine that are nearest the band are of crimson color, and each of them has one of the letters that compose the word S. A. P. I. E. N. T. I. A.

The ring is a triple one, like three small rings, each one-eighth of an inch wide, side by side, and having on the inside a delta surrounding the figures 33, and inscribed with the wearer's name, the letters

S.·. G.·. I.·. G.·., and the motto of the Order, "Deus meumque Jus." It is worn on the fourth finger of the left hand in the Southern Jurisdiction and on the third in the Northern Jurisdiction of America.

Until the year 1801, the Thirty-third Degree was unknown. Until then the highest degree of the Rite, introduced into America by Stephen Morin, was the Sublime Prince of the Royal Secret, or the Twenty-fifth of the Rite established by the Emperors of the East and West. The administrative heads of the Order were styled Grand Inspectors-General and Deputy Inspectors-General; but these were titles of official rank and not of degree. Even as late as May 24, 1801, John Mitchell signs himself as "Kadosh, Prince of the Royal Secret and Deputy Inspector-General." The document thus signed is a Patent which certifies that Frederick Dalcho is a Kadosh, and Prince of the Royal Secret, and which creates him a Deputy Inspector-General. But on May 31, 1801, the Supreme Council was created at Charleston, and from that time we hear of a Rite of thirty-three degrees, eight having been added to the twenty-five introduced by Morin, and the last being called Sovereign Grand Inspector-General. The degree being thus legitimately established by a body which, in creating a Rite, possessed the prerogative of establishing its classes, its degrees and its nomenclature were accepted unhesitatingly by all subsequently created Supreme Councils; and it continues to be recognized as the administrative head of the Ancient and Accepted Scottish Rite.

Square. This is one of the most important and significant symbols in Freemasonry. As such, it is proper that its true form should be preserved. The French Masons have almost universally given it with one leg longer than the other, thus making it a carpenter's square. The American Masons, following the incorrect delineations of Jeremy L. Cross, have, while generally preserving the equality of length in the legs, unnecessarily marked its surface with inches; thus making it an instrument for measuring length and breadth, which it is not. It is simply the *trying square* of a stone-mason, and has a plain surface; the sides or legs embracing an angle of ninety degrees, and is intended only to test the accuracy of the sides of a stone, and to see that its edges subtend the same angle.

In Freemasonry, it is a symbol of morality. This is its general signification, and is applied in various ways: 1. It presents itself to the neophyte as one of the three great lights; 2. To the Fellow-Craft as one of his working-tools; 3. To the Master Mason as the official emblem of the Master of the Lodge. Everywhere, however, it inculcates the same lesson of morality, of truthfulness, of honesty. So universally accepted is this symbolism, that it has gone outside of the Order, and has been found in colloquial language communicating the same idea. Square, says Halliwell (*Dict. Archaisms*), means honest, equitable, as in "square dealing." To *play upon the square* is proverbial for *to play honestly.* In this sense the word is found in the old writers.

As a Masonic symbol, it is of very ancient date, and was familiar to the Operative Masons. In the year 1830, the architect, in rebuilding a very ancient bridge called Baal Bridge, near Limerick, in Ireland, found under the foundation-stone an old brass square, much eaten away, containing on its two surfaces the following inscription: I. WILL. STRIUE. TO. LIUE.—WITH. LOUE. & CARE.—UPON. THE. LEUL. —BY. THE. SQUARE., and the date 1517. The modern Speculative Mason will recognize the idea of *living on the level and by the square.* This discovery proves, if proof were necessary, that the familiar idea was borrowed from our Operative brethren of former days.

The square, as a symbol in Speculative Masonry, has therefore presented itself from the very beginning of the revival period. In the very earliest catechism of the last century, of the date of 1725, we find the answer to the question, "How many make a Lodge?" is "God and the Square, with five or seven right or perfect Masons." God and the Square, religion and morality, must be present in every Lodge as governing principles. Signs at that early period were to be made by squares, and the furniture of the Lodge was declared to be the Bible, Compasses, and Square.

In all rites and in all languages where Masonry has penetrated, the square has preserved its primitive signification as a symbol of morality.

Square and Compasses. These two symbols have been so long and so universally combined—to teach us, as says an early ritual, "to square our actions and to keep them within due bounds," they are so seldom seen apart, but are so kept together, either as two great lights, or as a jewel worn once by the Master of the Lodge, now by the Past Master—that they have come at last to be recognized as the proper badge of a Master Mason, just as the triple tau is of a Royal Arch Mason or the passion cross of a Knights Templar.

So universally has this symbol been recognized, even by the profane world, as the peculiar characteristic of Freemasonry, that it has recently been made in the United States the subject of a legal decision. A manufacturer of flour having made, in 1873, an application to the Patent Office for permission to adopt the square and compasses as a trade-mark, the Commissioner of Patents refused the permission on the ground that the mark was a Masonic symbol.

"If this emblem," said Mr. J. M. Thacher, the Commissioner, "were something other than precisely what it is—either less known, less significant, or fully and universally understood—all this might readily be admitted. But, considering its peculiar character and relation to the public, an anomalous question is presented. There can be no doubt that this device, so commonly worn and employed by Masons, has an established mystic significance, universally recognized as existing; whether comprehended by all or not, is not material to this issue. In view of the magnitude and extent of the Masonic organization, it is impossible to divest its symbols, or at least this particular symbol—perhaps the best known of all—of its ordinary signification, wherever displayed, either as an arbitrary character or otherwise. It will be universally understood, or misunderstood, as having a Masonic significance; and, therefore, as a trade-mark, must constantly work deception. Nothing could be more mischievous than to create as a monopoly, and uphold by the power of law, anything so calculated, as applied to purposes of trade, to be misinterpreted, to mislead all classes, and to constantly foster suggestions of mystery in affairs of business."

In a religious work by John Davies, entitled *Summa Totalis*, or *All in All and the Same Forever,* printed in 1607, we find an allusion to the square and compasses by a profane in a really Masonic sense. The author, who proposes to describe mystically the form of the Deity, says in his dedication:

"Yet I this forme of formelesse DEITY,
Drewe by the Squire and Compasse of our Creed."

In Masonic symbolism the Square and Compasses refer to the Mason's duty to the Craft and to himself; hence it is properly a symbol of brotherhood, and there significantly adopted as the badge or token of the Fraternity.

Berage, in his work on the high degrees (*Les plus secrets Mystères des Hauts Grades*), gives a new interpretation to the symbol. He says: "The square and the compasses represent the union of the Old and New Testaments. None of the high degrees recognize this interpretation, although their symbolism of the two implements differs somewhat from that of symbolic Masonry. The square is with them peculiarly appropriated to the lower degrees, as founded on the operative art; while the compasses, as an implement of higher character and uses, is attributed to the degrees, which claim to have a more elevated and philosophical foundation. Thus they speak of the initiate, when he passes from the blue Lodge to the Lodge of Perfection, as 'passing from the square to the compasses,' to indicate a progressive elevation in his studies. Yet even in the high degrees, the square and compasses combined retain their primitive signification as a symbol of brotherhood and as a badge of the Order."

Sublime Prince of the Royal Secret. This is the Thirty-second Degree of the Ancient and Accepted Rite. There is abundant internal evidence, derived from the ritual and from some historical facts, that the degree of Sublime Prince of the Royal Secret was instituted by the founders of the Council of Emperors of the East and West, which body was established in the year 1758. It is certain that before that period we hear nothing of such a degree in any of the Rites. The Rite of

Heredom or of Perfection, which was that instituted by the Council of Emperors, consisted of twenty-five degrees. Of these the Twenty-fifth, and highest, was the Prince of the Royal Secret. It was brought to America by Morin, as the summit of the High Masonry which he introduced, and for the propagation of which he had received his Patent. In the subsequent extension of the Scottish Rite about the beginning of the present century, by the addition of eight new degrees to the original twenty-five, the Sublime Prince of the Royal Secret became the Thirty-second.

Bodies of the Thirty-second Degree are called Consistories, and where there is a superintending body erected by the Supreme Council for the government of the inferior degrees in a State or Province, it is called a Grand Consistory.

Syllable. To pronounce the syllables, or only one of the syllables, of a Sacred Word, such as a name of God, was among the Orientalists considered far more reverent than to give to it in all its syllables a full and continuous utterance. Thus the Hebrews reduced the holy name JEHOVAH to the syllable JAH; and the Brahmans, taking the initial letters of the three words which expressed the three attributes of the Supreme Brahma, as Creator, Preserver, and Destroyer, made of it the syllable AUM, which, on account of its awful and sacred meaning, they hesitated to pronounce aloud. To divide a word into syllables, and thus to interrupt the sound, either by pausing or by the alternate pronunciation by two persons, was deemed a mark of reverence.

Temple, Order of. The Order of the Temple was instituted by the Crusaders during their attempts to wrest control over the Holy Land from the infidels, having as its chief objects to provide for the helpless and destitute, and the care of the sick and wounded.

The first Grand Master of the Order was Hugh de Payens, who was the Head of the Order from A.D. 1118 to 1138. The organization remained active until A.D. 1314, the last Grand Master of the Order being Jacques de Molay (1298–1314) who gave up his life in defense of the Christian principles of the Order.

The American Order of the Temple came into existence in 1816, with DeWitt Clinton as its first Grand Master. The Grand Encampment of Knights Templar of the United States has Jurisdiction over all Grand Commanderies in the United States and Dependencies thereof. In turn, each Commandery of Knights Templar is obedient to the Grand Commandery of the State in which it is located, and is designated "constituent." Some Commanderies are obedient directly to the Grand Encampment, and are designated as "subordinate."

Veils, Symbolism of the. Neither the construction nor the symbolism of the veils in the Royal Arch tabernacle is derived from that of the Sinaitic. In the Sinaitic tabernacle there were no veils of separation between the different parts, except the one white one that hung before the most holy place. The decorations of the tabernacle were curtains, like modern tapestry, interwoven with many colors; no curtain being wholly of one color, and not running across the apartment, but covering its sides and roof. The exterior form of the Royal Arch tabernacle was taken from that of Moses, but the interior decoration from a passage of Josephus not properly understood.

Josephus has been greatly used by the fabricators of high degrees of Masonry, not only for their ideas of symbolism, but for the suggestion of their legends. In the Second Book of Chronicles (iii. 14) it is said that Solomon "made the veil of blue, and purple, and crimson, and fine linen, and wrought cherubims thereon." This description evidently alludes to the single veil, which, like that of the Sinaitic tabernacle, was placed before the entrance of the holy of holies. It by no means resembles the four separate and equidistant veils of the Masonic tabernacle.

But Josephus had said (*Antiq.*, l. viii., c. iii., § 3) that the king "also had veils of blue, and purple, and scarlet, and the brightest and softest linen, with the most curious flowers wrought upon them, which were to be drawn before these doors." To this description—which is a very inaccurate one, which refers, too, to the interior of the first Temple, and not to the supposed tabernacle subsequently erected near its ruins, and which, besides, has no Biblical authority for its support—we must trace the ideas, even as to the order of the veils, which the inventors of the Masonic tabernacle adopted in their construction of it. That tabernacle cannot be recognized as historically correct, but must be considered, like the three doors of the Temple in the Symbolic degrees, simply as a symbol. But this does not at all diminish its value.

The symbolism of the veils must be considered in two aspects: first, in reference to the symbolism of the veils as a whole, and next, as to the symbolism of each veil separately.

As a whole, the four veils, constituting four divisions of the tabernacle, present obstacles to the neophyte in his advance to the most holy place where the Grand Council sits. Now he is seeking to advance to that sacred spot that he may there receive his spiritual illumination, and be invested with a knowledge of the true Divine name. But Masonically, this Divine name is itself but a symbol of Truth, the object, as has been often said, of all a Mason's search and labor. The passage through the veils is, therefore, a symbol of the trials and difficulties that are encountered and must be overcome in the search for and the acquisition of Truth.

This is the general symbolism; but we lose sight of it, in a great degree, when we come to the interpretation of the symbolism of each veil independently of the others, for this principally symbolizes the various virtues and affections that should characterize the Mason. Yet the two symbolisms are really connected, for the virtues symbolized are those which should distinguish everyone engaged in the Divine search.

The symbolism, according to the system adopted in the American

Rite, refers to the colors of the veils and to the miraculous signs of Moses, which are described in Exodus as having been shown by him to prove his mission as the messenger of Jehovah.

Blue is a symbol of universal friendship and benevolence. It is the appropriate color of the Symbolic degrees, the possession of which is the first step in the progress of the search for truth to be now instituted. The Mosaic sign of the serpent was the symbol among the ancients of resurrection to life, because the serpent, by casting his skin, is supposed continually to renew his youth. It is the symbol here of the loss and the recovery of the Word.

Purple is a symbol here of union, and refers to the intimate connection of Ancient Craft and Royal Arch Masonry. Hence it is the appropriate color of the intermediate degrees, which must be passed through in the prosecution of the search. The Mosaic sign refers to the restoration of the leprous hand to health. Here again, in this representation of a diseased limb restored to health, we have a repetition of the allusion to the loss and the recovery of the Word; the Word itself being but a symbol of Divine truth, the search for which constitutes the whole science of Freemasonry, and the symbolism of which pervades the whole system of initiation from the first to the last degree.

Scarlet is a symbol of fervency and zeal, and is appropriated to the Royal Arch Degree because it is by these qualities that the neophyte, now so far advanced in his progress, must expect to be successful in his search. The Mosaic sign of changing water into blood bears the same symbolic reference to a change for the better—from a lower to a higher state—from the elemental water in which there is no life to the blood which is the life itself—from darkness to light. The progress is still onward to the recovery of that which had been lost, but which is yet to be found.

White is a symbol of purity, and is peculiarly appropriate to remind the neophyte, who is now almost at the close of his search, that it is only by purity of life that he can expect to be found worthy of the reception of Divine truth. "Blessed," says the Great Teacher, "are the pure in heart, for they shall see God." The Mosaic signs now cease, for they have taught their lesson; and the aspirant is invested with the Signet of Truth, to assure him that, having endured all trials and overcome all obstacles, he is at length entitled to receive the reward for which he has been seeking; for the Signet of Zerubbabel is a royal signet, which confers power and authority on him who possesses it.

And so we now see that the Symbolism of the Veils, however viewed, whether collectively or separately, represents the laborious, but at last successful, search for Divine truth.

Wages of the Workmen at the Temple. Neither the Scriptures, nor Josephus, give us any definite statement of the amount of wages paid, nor the manner in which they were paid, to the workmen who were engaged in the erection of King Solomon's Temple. The cost of its construction, however, must have been immense, since it has been estimated that the edifice alone consumed more gold and silver than at present exists upon the whole earth; so that Josephus very justly says that "Solomon made all these things for the honor of God, with great variety and magnificence, sparing no cost, but using all possible liberality in adorning the Temple." We learn, as one instance of this liberality, from the 2d Book of Chronicles, that Solomon paid annually to the Tyrian Masons, the servants of Hiram, "twenty thousand measures of beaten wheat, and twenty thousand measures of barley, and twenty thousand baths of wine, and twenty thousand baths of oil." The *bath* was a measure equal to seven and a half gallons wine measure; and the *cor* or *chomer,* which we translate by the indefinite word *measure,* contained ten baths; so that the corn, wine, and oil furnished by King Solomon, as wages to the servants of Hiram of Tyre, amounted to one hundred and ninety thousand bushels of the first, and one hundred and fifty thousand gallons each of the second and third. The sacred records do not inform us what further wages they received, but we elsewhere learn that King Solomon gave them as a free gift a sum equal to more than thirty-two millions of dollars. The whole amount of wages paid to the craft is stated to have been about six hundred and seventy-two millions of dollars; but we have no means of knowing how that amount was distributed; though it is natural to suppose that those of the most skill and experience received the highest wages. The Harodim, or chiefs of the workmen, must have been better paid than the Ish Sabal, or mere laborers.

The legend-makers of Masonry have not been idle in their invention of facts and circumstances in relation to this subject, the whole of which have little more for a foundation than the imaginations of the inventors. They form, however, a part of the legendary history of Masonry, and are interesting for their ingenuity, and sometimes even for their absurdity.

Weary Sojourners. Spoken of in the American legend of the Royal Arch as three of the captives who had been restored to liberty by Cyrus, and, after sojourning or remaining longer in Babylon than the main body of their brethren, had at length repaired to Jerusalem to assist in rebuilding the Temple.

It was while the workmen were engaged in making the necessary excavations for laying the foundation, and while numbers continued to arrive at Jerusalem from Babylon, that these three worn and weary sojourners, after plodding on foot over the rough and devious roads between the two cities, offered themselves to the Grand Council as willing participants in the labor of erection. Who these sojourners were, we have no historical means of discovering; but there is a Masonic tradition (entitled, perhaps, to but little weight) that they were Hananiah, Mishael, and Azariah, three holy men, who are better known to general readers by their Chaldaic names of Shadrach, Meshech, and Abed-nego, as having been miraculously preserved from the fiery furnace of Nebuchadnezzar.

Their services were accepted, and from their diligent labors resulted that important discovery, the perpetuation and preservation of which constitutes the great end and design of the Royal Arch Degree.

Such is the legend of the American Royal Arch. It has no known foundation in history, and is therefore altogether mythical. But it presents, as a myth, the symbolic idea of arduous and unfaltering search after truth, and the final reward that such devotion receives.

White Shrine of Jerusalem, Order of. Founded by Charles D. Magee, at Chicago, Illinois, U.S.A., in 1894. The Order comprises both men and women, who must be members in good standing of the Order of the Eastern Star. The White Shrine was not recognized, however, as a branch of the Order of the Eastern Star. During the term of office as Most Worthy Grand Matron of the Order of the Eastern Star, 1892 to 1895, Mrs. Mary G. Snedden refused her approval and this position was concurred in by the General Grand Chapter in 1895. It was ruled by the General Grand Chapter that there were no degrees connected in any way or manner with the Order of the Eastern Star, other than those provided for and taught in their Ritual. Any member wilfully representing to any one that there are side degrees, or higher degrees, or any degrees other than those taught and provided for by their Ritual, shall be guilty of conduct unbecoming a member of the Order, and upon conviction thereof, shall be suspended or expelled from the Order. Therefore be it thoroughly understood that the White Shrine of Jerusalem is no part of the Order of the Eastern Star.

During the first years of its existence, its growth was slow, but in recent years the growth has been more marked. It now has 445 chartered Shrines with a membership of 85,635 operating in 35 states. Several Canadian Provinces and in Scotland. The requirements for membership are;—membership in the Order of the Eastern Star, in good standing and thoroughly loyal to that organization; and a believer in the Christian religion. Male members must be Master Masons in good standing and Christians. The Ritual of the White Shrine of Jerusalem is based upon the story of the travels of the Three Wise Men to the birthplace of the Christian Savior, dealing in a beautiful and impressive manner with the various incidents as described in the Gospelsin connection with the birth of Jesus the Christ. The story of the life of Jesus the Christ is the most inspiring one known to the Christian world, and the Ritual of the White Shrine being illustrative of His life and teachings, affords a wonderful opportunity for beautiful work, and to make a lasting impression upon its members.

The work is usually rendered by officers clothed in regalia representative of the time in which Jesus lived.

The governing body is called The Supreme White Shrine of Jerusalem. Its officials are:—Supreme Worthy High Priestess, Supreme Watchman of Shepherds, Supreme Noble Prophetess, Supreme Associate Watchman of Shepherds, Supreme Worthy Scribe, Supreme Worthy Treasurer, Supreme Chaplain, Supreme Shepherdess, Supreme Guide, Supreme Worthy Herold, Supreme First, Second and Third Wise Men, Supreme King, Supreme Queen, Supreme First, Second and Third Hand Maids, Supreme Organist, Supreme Worthy Guardian, Supreme Worthy Guard.

Wisdom. In Ancient Craft Masonry, wisdom is symbolized by the East, the place of light, being represented by the pillar that there supports the Lodge and by the Worshipful Master. It is also referred to King Solomon, the symbolical founder of the Order. In Masonic architecture the Ionic column, distinguished for the skill in its construction, as it combines the beauty of the Corinthian and the strength of the Doric, is adopted as the representative of wisdom.

King Solomon has been adopted in Speculative Masonry as the type or representative of wisdom, in accordance with the character which has been given to him in the 1st Book of Kings (iv. 30–32): "Solomon's wisdom excelled the wisdom of all the children of the east country, and all the wisdom of Egypt. For he was wiser than all men; than Ethan the Ezrahite, and Heman and Chalcol and Darda, the sons of Mahol; and his fame was in all the nations round about."

This idea, so universally diffused throughout the East, is said to have been adopted into the secret doctrine of the Templars, who are supposed to have borrowed much from the Basilideans, the Manicheans, and the Gnostics. From them it easily passed over to the high degrees of Masonry, which were founded on the Templar theory. Hence, in the great decoration of the Thirty-third Degree of the Scottish Rite, the points of the triple triangle are inscribed with the letters S.A.P.I.E.N. T.I.A., or Wisdom.

It is not difficult now to see how this word *Wisdom* came to take so prominent a part in the symbolism of Ancient Masonry, and how it was expressly appropriated to King Solomon. As wisdom, in the philosophy of the East, was the creative energy—the architect, so to speak, of the world, as the emanation of the Supreme Architect—so Solomon was the architect of the Temple, the symbol of the world. He was to the typical world or temple what wisdom was to the great world of the creation. Hence wisdom is appropriately referred to him and to the Master of the Lodge, who is the representative of Solomon. Wisdom is always placed in the east of the Lodge, because thence emanate all light, and knowledge, and truth.

Word, Mason. In the minutes and documents of the Lodges of Scotland during the sixteenth, seventeenth, and eighteenth centuries, the expression "Mason word" is constantly used. This continuous use would indicate that but one word was then known. Nicolai, in his *Essay on the*

Accusations against the Templars, quotes a "small dictionary published at the beginning of the eighteenth century," in which the "Mason's word" is defined.

Word, Sacred. A term applied to the chief or most prominent word of a degree, to indicate its peculiarly sacred character, in contradistinction to a password, which is simply intended as a mode of recognition. It is sometimes ignorantly corrupted into "secret word." All significant words in Masonry are *secret.* Only certain ones are *sacred.*

Word, True. Used in contradistinction to the *Lost Word* and the *Substitute Word.* To find it is the object of all Masonic search and labor. For as the Lost Word is the symbol of death, the True Word is the symbol of life eternal. It indicates the change that is always occurring—truth after error, light after darkness, life after death. Of all the symbolism of Speculative Masonry, that of the True Word is the most philosophic and sublime.

Work. See *Labor.*

Working-Tools. In each of the degrees of Masonry, certain implements of the Operative art are consecrated to the Speculative science, and adopted to teach as symbols lessons of morality. With these the Speculative Mason is taught to erect his spiritual temple, as his Operative predecessors with the same implements constructed their material temples. Hence they are called the working-tools of the degree. They vary but very slightly in the different Rites, but the same symbolism is preserved. The principal working-tools of the Operative art that have been adopted as symbols in the Speculative science, confined, however, to Ancient Craft Masonry, and not used in the higher degrees, are, the twenty-four-inch gage, common gavel, square, level, plumb, skirrit, compasses, pencil, trowel, mallet, pickax, crow, and shovel.

York Rite. This is the oldest of all the Rites, and consisted originally of only three degrees: 1. Entered Apprentice; 2. Fellow-Craft; 3. Master Mason. The last included a part which contained the True Word, but which was disrupted from it by Dunckerley in the latter part of the last century, and has never been restored. The Rite in its purity does not now exist anywhere. The nearest approach to it is the St. John's Masonry of Scotland, but the Master's Degree of the Grand Lodge of Scotland is not the Master's Degree of the York Rite. When Dunckerley dismembered the Third Degree, he destroyed the identity of the Rite. In 1813, it was apparently recognized by the United Grand Lodge of England, when it defined "pure Ancient Masonry to consist of three degrees, and no more: viz., those of the Entered Apprentice, the Fellow Craft, and the Master Mason, including the Supreme Order of the Holy Royal Arch." Had the Grand Lodge abolished the Royal Arch Degree, which was then practised as an independent Order in England, and reincorporated its secrets in the degree of Master Mason, the York Rite would have been revived. But by recognizing the Royal Arch as a separate degree, and retaining the Master's Degree in its mutilated form, they repudiated the Rite. In the United States it has been the almost universal usage to call the Masonry there practised the York Rite. But it has no better claim to this designation than it has to be called the Ancient and Accepted Rite, or the French Rite, or the Rite of Schröder. It has no pretensions to the York Rite. Of its first three degrees, the Master's is the mutilated one which took the Masonry of England out of the York Rite, and it has added to these three degrees six others which were never known to the Ancient York Rite, or that which was practised in England, in the earlier half of the eighteenth century, by the legitimate Grand Lodge. In all my writings for years past, I have ventured to distinguish the Masonry practised in the United States, consisting of nine degrees, as the "American Rite," a title to which it is clearly and justly entitled, as the system is peculiar to America, and is practised in no other country.

Bro. Hughan, speaking of the York Rite says "there is no such Rite, and what it *was* no one *now* knows." I think that this declaration is too sweeping in its language. He is correct in saying that there is at this time no such Rite. I have just described its decadence; but he is wrong in asserting that we are now ignorant of its character. In using the title, there is no reference to the Grand Lodge of all England, which met for some years during the last century, but rather to the York legend, and to the hypothesis that York was the cradle of English Masonry. The York Rite was that Rite which was most probably organized or modified at the revival in 1717, and practised for fifty years by the Constitutional Grand Lodge of England. It consisted of only the three Symbolic degrees, the last one, or the Master's, containing within itself the secrets now transferred to the Royal Arch. This Rite was carried in its purity to France in 1725, and into America at a later period. About the middle of the eighteenth century the continental Masons, and about the end of it the Americans, began to superimpose upon it those high degrees which, with the necessary mutilation of the third, have given rise to numerous other Rites. But the Ancient York Rite, though no longer cultivated, must remain on the records of history as the oldest and purest of all the Rites.

Zeredathah. The name of the place between which and Succoth are the clay grounds where Hiram Abif is said to have cast the brazen utensils for the use of the Temple.

Zerubbabel. In writing the life of Zerubbabel from a Masonic point of view, it is incumbent that reference should be made to the legends as well as to the more strictly historical details of his eventful career. With the traditions of the Royal Arch, and some other of the high degrees, Zerubbabel is not less intimately connected than is Solomon with those of Symbolic or Ancient Craft Masonry. To understand those traditions properly, they must be placed in their appropriate place in the life of him who plays so important a part in them. Some of these legends have the concurrent support of Scripture, some are related by Josephus, and some appear to have no historical foundation. Without, therefore, vouching for their authenticity, they must be recounted, to make the Masonic life of the builder of the second Temple complete.

Zerubbabel, who, in the Book of Ezra, is called "Sheshbazzar, the prince of Judah," was the grandson of that King Jehoiachin, or Jeconiah, who had been deposed by Nebuchadnezzar and carried as a captive to Babylon. In him, therefore, was vested the regal authority, and on him, as such, the command of the returning captives was bestowed by Cyrus, who on that occasion, according to a Masonic tradition, presented to him the sword which Nebuchadnezzar had received from his grandfather, Jehoiachin.

As soon as the decree of the Persian monarch had been promulgated to his Jewish subjects, the tribes of Judah and Benjamin, with the priests and Levites, assembled at Babylon, and prepared to return to Jerusalem, for the purpose of rebuilding the Temple. Some few from the other tribes, whose love of their country and its ancient worship had not been obliterated by the luxuries of the Babylonian court, united with the followers of Zerubbabel, and accompanied him to Jerusalem. The greater number, however, remained; and even of the priests, who were divided into twenty-four courses, only four courses returned, who, however, divided themselves, each class into six, so as again to make up the old number. Cyrus also restored to the Jews the greater part of the sacred vessels of the Temple which had been carried away by Nebuchadnezzar, and five thousand and four hundred were received by Zerubbabel, the remainder being brought back, many years after, by Ezra. Only forty-two thousand three hundred and sixty Israelites, exclusive of servants and slaves, accompanied Zerubbabel, out of whom he selected seven thousand of the most valiant, whom he placed as an advanced guard at the head of the people. Their progress homeward was not altogether unattended with danger; for tradition informs us that at the river Euphrates they were opposed by the Assyrians, who, incited by the temptation of the vast amount of golden vessels which they were carrying, drew up in hostile array, and, notwithstanding the remonstrances of the Jews, and the edict of Cyrus, disputed their passage. Zerubbabel, however, repulsed the enemy with such ardor as to insure a signal victory, most of the Assyrians having been slain in the battle, or drowned in their attempt to cross the river in their retreat. The rest of the journey was uninterrupted, and, after a march of four months, Zerubbabel arrived at Jerusalem, with his weary followers, at seven o'clock in the morning of the 22d of June, five hundred and thirty-five years before Christ.

During their captivity, the Jews had continued, without intermission, to practise the rights of Freemasonry, and had established at various places regular Lodges in Chaldea. Especially, according to the Rabbinical traditions, had they instituted their mystic fraternity at Naharda, on the Euphrates; and, according to the same authority, we are informed that Zerubbabel carried with him to Jerusalem all the secret knowledge which was the property of that Institution, and established a similar fraternity in Judea. This coincides with, and gives additional strength to, the traditions of the Royal Arch Degree.

As soon as the pious pilgrims had arrived at Jerusalem, and taken a needful rest of seven days, a tabernacle for the temporary purposes of Divine worship was erected near the ruins of the ancient Temple, and a Council was called, in which Zerubbabel presided as King, Jeshua as High Priest, and Haggai as Scribe, or principal officer of State. It was there determined to commence the building of the second Temple upon the same holy spot which had been occupied by the first, and the people liberally contributed sixty-one thousand drachms of gold, and five thousand minas of silver, or nearly a quarter of a million of dollars, toward defraying the expenses; a sum which sinks into utter insignificance, when compared with the immense amount appropriated by David and Solomon to the construction of their Temple.

The site having been thus determined upon, it was found necessary to begin by removing the rubbish of the old Temple, which still encumbered the earth, and prevented the workmen from making the necessary arrangements for laying the foundation. It was during this operation that an important discovery was made by three sojourners, who had not originally accompanied Zerubbabel, but who, sojourning some time longer at Babylon, followed their countrymen at a later period, and had arrived at Jerusalem just in time to assist in the removal of the rubbish. These three sojourners, whose fortune it was to discover that stone of foundation, so intimately connected with the history of Freemasonry, and to which we have before had repeated occasion to allude, are supposed by a Masonic tradition to have been Esdras, Zachariah, and Nehemiah, the three holy men, who, for refusing to worship the golden image, had been thrown by Nebuchadnezzar into a fiery furnace, from which they emerged uninjured. In the Chaldee language, they were known by the names of Shadrach, Meshach, and Abed-nego. It was in penetrating into some of the subterranean vaults, that the Masonic stone of foundation, with other important mysteries connected with it, were discovered by the three fortunate sojourners, and presented by them to Zerubbabel and his companions Jeshua and Haggai, whose traditionary knowledge of Masonry, which they had received in a direct line from the builders of the first Temple, enabled them at once to appreciate the great importance of these treasures.

As soon as that wonderful discovery was made, on which depends not only the existence of the Royal Arch Degree, but the most important mystery of Freemasonry, the Jews proceeded on a certain day, before the rising of the sun, to lay the foundation-stone of the second Temple; and for that purpose, we are told, Zerubbabel selected that stone of foundation which had been discovered by the three sojourners. On this occasion, we learn that the young rejoiced with shouts and acclamations, but that the ancient people disturbed them with their groans and lamentations, when they reflected on the superb magnificence of the first Temple, and compared it with the expected inferiority of the present structure. As in the building of the first Temple, so in this, the Tyrians and Sidonians were engaged to furnish the timber from the forests of Lebanon, and to conduct it in the same manner on floats by sea to Joppa.

Scarcely had the workmen well commenced their labors, when they were interrupted by the Samaritans, who made application to be permitted to unite with them in the construction of the Temple. But the Jews, who looked upon them as idolaters, refused to accept of their services. The Samaritans in consequence became their bitter enemies, and so prevailed, by misrepresentations, with the ministers of Cyrus, as to cause them to put such obstructions in the way of the construction of the edifice as seriously to impede its progress for several years. With such difficulty and danger were the works conducted during this period, that the workmen were compelled to labor with the trowel in one hand and the sword in the other. To commemorate these worthy craftsmen, who were thus ready, either to fight or to labor in the cause of God, as circumstances might require, the sword and trowel crosswise, or, as the heralds would say, *en saltire,* have been placed upon the Royal Arch Tracing-Board or Carpet of our English brethren. In the American ritual this expressive symbol of valor and piety has been unfortunately omitted.

In the seventh year after the restoration of the Jews, Cyrus, their friend and benefactor, died, and his son Cambyses, in Scripture called Ahasuerus, ascended the throne. The Samaritans and the other enemies of the Jews, now becoming bolder in their designs, succeeded in obtaining from Cambyses a peremptory order for the stoppage of all the works at Jerusalem, and the Temple consequently remained in an unfinished state until the second year of the reign of Darius, the successor of Cambyses.

Darius appears to have had, like Cyrus, a great friendship for the Israelites, and especially for Zerubbabel, with whom he was well acquainted in his youth. We are informed, as an evidence of this, that, when a private man, he made a vow, that if he should ever ascend the throne, he would restore all the vessels of the Temple that had been retained by Cyrus. Zerubbabel, being well aware of the friendly disposition of the king, determined, immediately after his accession to power, to make a personal application to him for his assistance and protection in rebuilding the Temple. Accordingly he departed from Jerusalem, and after a journey full of peril, in which he was continually attacked by parties of his enemies, he was arrested as a spy by the Persian guards in the vicinity of Babylon, and carried in chains before Darius, who, however immediately recognized him as the friend and companion of his youth, and ordering him instantly to be released from his bonds, invited him to be present at a magnificent feast which he was about to give to the Court. It is said that on this occasion, Zerubbabel, having explained to Darius the occasion of his visit, implored the interposition of his authority for the protection of the Israelites engaged in the restoration of the Temple. The king promised to grant all his requests, provided he would reveal to him the secrets of Freemasonry. But this the faithful prince at once refused to do. He declined the favor of the monarch at the price of his infamy, and expressed his willingness rather to meet death or exile, than to violate his sacred obligations as a Mason. This firmness and fidelity only raised his character still higher in the estimation of Darius, who seems, indeed, to have been endowed with many noble qualities both of heart and mind.

It was on this occasion, at the feast given by King Darius, that, agreeably to the custom of Eastern monarchs, he proposed to his courtiers the question whether the power of wine, women, or the king, was the strongest. Answers were made by different persons, assigning to each of these the precedency in power; but when Zerubbabel was called on to assert his opinion, he declared that though the power of wine and of the king might be great, that of women was still greater, but that above all things truth bore the victory. Josephus says that the sentiments of Zerubbabel having been deemed to contain the most wisdom, the king commanded him to ask something over and above what he had promised as the prize of the victor in the philosophic discussion. Zerubbabel then called upon the monarch to fulfil the vow that he had made in his youth, to rebuild the Temple, and restore the vessels that had been taken away by Nebuchadnezzar. The king forthwith granted his request, promised him the most ample protection in the future prosecution of the works, and sent him home to Jerusalem laden with honors, and under the conduct of an escort.

Henceforth, although from time to time annoyed by their adversaries, the builders met with no serious obstruction, and finally, twenty years after its commencement, in the sixth year of the reign of Darius, and on the third day of the month Adar, 515 years B.C., the Temple was completed, the cope-stone celebrated, and the house solemnly dedicated to Jehovah with the greatest joy.

After this we hear nothing further of Zerubbabel, nor is the time or manner of his death either recorded in Scripture or preserved by Masonic tradition. We have, however, reason for believing that he lived to a good old age, since we find no successor of him mentioned until Artaxerxes appointed Ezra as the Governor of Judea, fifty-seven years after the completion of the Temple.

A WORD TO YOU

In presenting "MASONRY DEFINED" to the Craft, we had but one thought in mind, and that was to furnish the Masonic student, and more especially the newly made Mason, with the information he should have at a price he could afford to pay.

We also felt that if we could be instrumental in getting the newly made Mason started right, and enable him to learn the real purpose of Masonry, that a better and more intelligent body of Masons would be developed and our Lodges be the meeting ground of thoughtful, earnest members.

A man's interest in Masonry is in exact ratio to what he knows about it. If he has learned something of its history, traditions, legends and symbolism his interest never wanes, but grows stronger with the passing years. If a Mason has merely taken his degrees and considers himself a Mason in all that the term implies, and makes no effort to inform himself, he cannot be other than an indifferent Mason, of no benefit whatever to the great Fraternity, and to such a man the Fraternity can be of little benefit.

What a wonderful organization we would be if every Mason would catch the vision of Masonry; the vision of service and usefulness. What a wonderful thing it would be if we could all carry into our Lodges and homes a higher conception of a just and upright Mason.

Reference has been made that a man is expected to be a good man when he enters into Masonry, but he should realize that he must and can be better. We have in effect declared that we have found something better than the average man. We have come into a state calculated to lift us above the average man, and so we have a great profession to live up to, and we have a great claim to make good before the world. Upon every Mason, in the eyes of a critical world, depend the honor, the truth and the efficacy of Masonry. The only real way to build an institution of men firm and strong is in the character of the men who compose it.

One of the lamentable weaknesses of Masonry today lies in the fact that the newly made Mason is not instructed in the things he should know concerning Masonry.

The fundamentals of Masonry may be impressed upon the mind of the candidate with each obligation he takes, but real study and research are necessary to acquire the real philosophy of Masonry.

We do not claim anything new in "MASONRY DEFINED." Everything in it can be found in any well equipped Masonic Library if you know where to look for and have time to dig it out.

A prominent man once remarked that "There is nothing new in anything except the manner in which it is presented." We do claim that our system of pertinent questions is something of an innovation, and from the great number of opinions given us by prominent Masons, we believe that we have accomplished something that the Craft has long wished for.

The reception given "MASONRY DEFINED" has far exceeded our expectations. Men prominent in Masonic affairs who have their finger on the pulse of Masonic thought, have been quick to realize that "MASONRY DEFINED" brought to the newly made Mason the information he should have in such shape that he could easily get at it.

The young Mason, after taking his degrees, has been left to shift for himself, to find out as he could, the meaning of the ritual and the real purpose of the institution. It was too much to ask him to start in and devote a lot of time to reading ponderous volumes in the hope that he could find what he wanted to know. "MASONRY DEFINED" has done for him what he could not do for himself, and has laid before him in concrete form priceless information that it would take him years to secure through the ordinary channels.

The price of the average histories has been beyond him and too much to ask him to pay.

It has been said of "MASONRY DEFINED" that "it gives the Mason the information he should have at a price he could afford to pay."

THE PUBLISHERS.

Abiram. One of the traitorous craftsmen, whose act of perfidy forms so important a part of the Third Degree, receives in some of the high degrees the name of *Abiram Akirop.* These words certainly have a Hebrew look; but the significant words of Masonry have, in the lapse of time and in their transmission through ignorant teachers, become so corrupted in form that it is almost impossible to trace them to any intelligent root. They may be Hebrew or they may be anagrammatized (see *Anagram*); but it is only chance that can give us the true meaning which they undoubtedly have. The word "Abiram" means "father of loftiness," and may have been chosen as the name of the traitorous craftsman with allusion to the Biblical story of Korah, Dathan and Abiram who conspired against Moses and Aaron. (Numbers xvi.) In the French ritual of the Second Elu it is said to mean *murderer* or *assassin,* but this would not seem to be correct etymologically.

Agnus Dei. The Agnus Dei, Lamb of God, also called the Paschal Lamb, or the Lamb offered in the paschal sacrifice, is one of the jewels of a Commandery of Knights Templar in America, and is worn by the Generalissimo.

The lamb is one of the earliest symbols of Christ in the iconography of the Church, and as such was a representation of the Savior, derived from that expression of St. John the Baptist (John i. 29), who, on beholding Christ, exclaimed, "Behold the Lamb of God." "Christ," says Didron (*Christ. Iconog.,* i., 318), "shedding his blood for our redemption, is the Lamb slain by the children of Israel, and with the blood of which the houses to be preserved from the wrath of God were marked with the celestial tau. The Paschal Lamb eaten by the Israelites on the night preceding their departure from Egypt is the type of that other divine Lamb of whom Christians are to partake at Easter, in order thereby to free themselves from the bondage in which they are held by vice."

The earliest representation that is found in Didron of the Agnus Dei is of the sixth century, and consists of a lamb supporting in his right foot a cross. In the eleventh century we find a banneret attached to this cross, and the lamb is then said to support "the banner of the resurrection." This is the modern form in which the Agnus Dei is represented.

Aholiab. A skilful artificer of the tribe of Dan, who was appointed, together with Bezaleel, to construct the tabernacle in the wilderness and the ark of the covenant. (Exodus xxxi. 6.) He is referred to in the Royal Arch degree of the English and American systems.

Alexandria, School of. When Alexander built the city of Alexandria in Egypt, with the intention of making it the seat of his empire, he invited thither learned men from all nations, who brought with them their peculiar notions. The Alexandria School of Philosophy which was thus established, by the commingling of Orientalists, Jews, Egyptians, and Greeks, became eclectic in character, and exhibited a heterogeneous mixture of the opinions of the Egyptian priests, of the Jewish Rabbis, of

Arabic teachers, and of the disciples of Plato and Pythagoras. From this school we derive Gnosticism and the Kabbala, and, above all, the system of symbolism and allegory which lay at the foundation of the Masonic philosophy. To no ancient sect, indeed, except perhaps the Pythagoreans, have the Masonic teachers been so much indebted for the substance of their doctrines, as well as the esoteric method of communicating them, as to that of the School of Alexandria. Both Aristobulus and Philo, the two most celebrated chiefs of this school, taught, although a century intervened between their births, the same theory, that the sacred writings of the Hebrews were, by their system of allegories, the true source of all religious and philosophic doctrine, the literal meaning of which alone was for the common people, the esoteric or hidden meaning being kept for the initiated. Freemasonry still carries into practise the same theory.

Allegiance. Every Mason owes allegiance to the Lodge, Chapter, or other body of which he is a member, and also to the Grand Lodge, Grand Chapter or other supreme authority from which that body has received its charter. But this is not a divided allegiance. If, for instance, the edicts of a Grand and a Subordinate Lodge conflict, there is no question which is to be obeyed. Supreme or governing bodies in Masonry claim and must receive a paramount allegiance.

Allegory. A discourse or narrative in which there is a literal and a figurative sense, a patent and a concealed meaning; the literal or patent sense being intended, by analogy or comparison, to indicate the figurative or concealed one. Its derivation from the Greek, ἄλλος and ἀγορεύειν, *to say something different,* that is, to say something where the language is one thing and the true meaning another, exactly expresses the character of an allegory. It has been said that there is no essential difference between an allegory and a symbol. There is not in design, but there is in their character. An allegory may be interpreted without any previous conventional agreement, but a symbol cannot. Thus, the legend of the Third Degree is an allegory, evidently to be interpreted as teaching a restoration to life; and this we learn from the legend itself, without any previous understanding. The sprig of acacia is a symbol of the immortality of the soul. But this we know only because such meaning had been conventionally determined when the symbol was first established. It is evident, then, that an allegory whose meaning is obscure is imperfect. The enigmatical meaning should be easy of interpretation.

Allocution. The address of the presiding officer of a Supreme Council of the Ancient and Accepted Scottish Rite is sometimes so called. It was first used by the Council for the Southern Jurisdiction of the United States, and is derived from the usage of the Roman Church, where certain addresses of the Pope to the Cardinals are called allocutions, and this is to be traced to the customs of Pagan Rome, where the harangues of the Generals to their soldiers were called *allocutions.*

Almoner. An officer elected or appointed in the continental Lodges of Europe to take charge of the contents of the alms-box, to carry into effect the charitable resolutions of the Lodge, and to visit sick and needy brethren. A physician is usually selected in preference to any other member for this office. An almoner may also be appointed among the officers of an English Lodge. In the United States the officer does not exist, his duties being performed by a committee of charity. It is an important office in all bodies of the Scottish Rite.

Almsgiving. Although almsgiving, or the pecuniary relief of the destitute, was not one of the original objects for which the Institution of Freemasonry was established, yet, as in every society of men bound together by a common tie, it becomes incidentally, yet necessarily, a duty to be practised by all its members in their individual as well as in their corporate capacity. In fact, this virtue is intimately interwoven with the whole superstructure of the Institution, and its practise is a necessary corollary from all its principles. At an early period in his initiation the candidate is instructed in the beauty of charity by the most impressive ceremonies, which are not easily to be forgotten, and which, with the same benevolent design, are repeated from time to time during his advancement to higher degrees, in various forms and under different circumstances. "The true Mason," says Bro. Pike, "must be, and must have a right to be, content with himself; and he can be so only when he lives not for himself alone, but for others who need his assistance and have a claim upon his sympathy." And the same eloquent writer lays down this rule for a Mason's almsgiving: "Give, looking for nothing again, without consideration of future advantages; give to children, to old men, to the unthankful, and the dying, and to those you shall never see again; for else your alms or courtesy is not charity, but traffic and merchandise. And omit not to relieve the needs of your enemy and him who does you injury." (See *Exclusiveness of Masonry.*)

Alms-Box. A box which, toward the close of the Lodge, is handed around by an appropriate officer for the reception of such donations for general objects of charity as the brethren may feel disposed to bestow. This laudable custom is very generally practised in the Lodges of England, Scotland, and Ireland, and universally in those of the Continent. The newly initiated candidate is expected to contribute more liberally than the other members. Bro. Hyde Clarke says (*Lon. Freem. Mag.*, 1859, p. 1166) that "some brethren are in the habit, on an occasion of thanksgiving with them, to contribute to the box of the Lodge more than on other occasions." This custom has not been adopted in the Lodges of America, except in those of French origin and in those of the Ancient and Accepted Scottish Rite.

Amar-jas. Hebrew אמריה, *God spake;* a significant word in the high degrees of the Ancient and Accepted Scottish Rite.

Anno Inventionis. *In the Year of the Discovery;* abbreviated A.·. I.·. or A.·. Inv.·. The date used by Royal Arch Masons. Found by adding 530 to the Vulgar Era; thus, 1911 + 530 = 2441.

Anno Lucis. *In the Year of Light;* abbreviated A.·. L.·. The date used in ancient Craft Masonry; found by adding 4000 to the Vulgar Era; thus, 1911 + 4000 = 5911.

Anno Mundi. *In the Year of the World.* The date used in the Ancient and Accepted Rite; found by adding 3760 to the Vulgar Era until September. After September, add one year more; this is because the year used is the Hebrew one, which begins in September. Thus, July, 1911 + 3760 = 5671, and October, 1911 + 3760 + 1 = 5672.

Anno Ordinis. *In the Year of the Order;* abbreviated A.·.O.·. The date used by Knights Templars; found by subtracting 1118 from the Vulgar Era; thus, 1911 − 1118 = 793.

Annual Communication. All the Grand Lodges of the United States, except those of Massachusetts, Maryland, the District of Columbia, and Pennsylvania, hold only one annual meeting; thus reviving the ancient custom of a yearly Grand Assembly. The Grand Lodge of Massachusetts, like that of England, holds Quarterly Communications. At these annual communications it is usual to pay the representatives of the subordinate Lodges a per diem allowance, which varies in different Grand Lodges from one to three dollars, and also their mileage or traveling expenses.

Annual Proceedings. Every Grand Lodge in the United States publishes a full account of its proceedings at its Annual Communication, to which is also almost always added a list of the subordinate Lodges and their members. Some of these Annual Proceedings extend to a considerable size, and they are all valuable as giving an accurate and official account of the condition of Masonry in each State for the past year. They also frequently contain valuable reports of committees on questions of Masonic law. The reports of the Committees of Foreign Correspondence are especially valuable in these pamphlets. (See *Committee on Foreign Correspondence.*)

Ancient of Days. A title applied, in the visions of Daniel, to Jehovah, to signify that his days are beyond reckoning. Used by Webb in the Most Excellent Master's song.

"Fulfilled is the promise
By the Ancient of Days,
To bring forth the cape-stone
With shouting and praise."

Ask, Seek, Knock. In referring to the passage of Matthew vii. 7, "Ask, and it shall be given you; seek, and ye shall find; knock, and it shall be opened unto you," Dr. Clarke says: "These three words—*ask, seek,* *knock*—include the ideas of *want, loss,* and *earnestness.*" The application made to the passage theologically is equally appropriate to it in a Masonic Lodge. You *ask* for *acceptance,* you *seek* for *light,* you *knock* for *initiation,* which includes the other two.

Antiquity Manuscript. This celebrated MS. is now, and has long been, in the possession of the Lodge of Antiquity, at London. It is stated in the subscription to have been written, in 1686, by "Robert Padgett, Clearke to the Worshipful Society of the Freemasons of the city of London." The whole manuscript was first published by W. J. Hughan in his *Old Charges of British Freemasons* (p. 64), but a part had been previously inserted by Preston in his *Illustrations* (b. ii., sect. vi.). And here we have evidence of a criminal inaccuracy of the Masonic writers of the last century, who never hesitated to alter or interpolate passages in old documents whenever it was required to confirm a preconceived theory. Thus, Preston had intimated that there was before 1717 an Installation ceremony for newly elected Masters of Lodges (which is not true), and inserts what he calls "the ancient Charges that were used on this occasion," taken from the MS. of the Lodge of Antiquity. To confirm the statement, that they were used for this purpose, he cites the conclusion of the MS. in the following words: "These be all the charges and covenants that ought to be read at the *installment of Master,* or making of a Freemason or Freemasons." The words in italics are not to be found in the original MS., but were inserted by Preston. Bro. E. Jackson Barron had an exact transcript made of this MS., which he carefully collated, and which was published by Bro. Hughan. Bro. Barron gives the following description of the document:

"The MS. copy of the Charges of Freemasons is on a roll of parchment nine feet long by eleven inches wide, the roll being formed of four pieces of parchment glued together; and some few years ago it was partially mounted (but not very skilfully) on a backing of parchment for its better preservation.

"The Rolls are headed by an engraving of the Royal Arms, after the fashion usual in deeds of the period; the date of the engraving in this case being fixed by the initials at the top, I. 2. R.

"Under this engraving are emblazoned in separate shields the Arms of the city of London, which are too well known to require description, and the Arms of the Masons Company of London, *Sable on a chevron between three castles argent, a pair of compasses of the first surrounded by appropriate mantling.*

"The writing is a good specimen of the ordinary law writing of the times, interspersed with words in text. There is a margin of about an inch on the left side, which is marked by a continuous double red ink line throughout, and there are similar double lines down both edges of the parchment. The letter U is used throughout the MS. for V, with but two or three exceptions." (Hughan's *Old Charges,* 1872, p. 14.)

Apron Lectures. The following monitorial presentation lectures ιs used by various Grand Jurisdictions.

The coming years may bring you success,
The victory laurel wreath may deck your brow,
And you may feel Love's hallowed caress,
And have withal domestic tenderness,
And fortune's god may smile on you as now,
And jewels fit for Eastern potentate
Hang over your ambitious heart, and Fate

May call thee "Prince of Men" or "King of Hearts,"
While Cupid strives to pierce you with his darts.
Nay, even more than these, with coming light
Your feet may press fame's loftiest dazzling height,
And looking down upon the world below
You may exclaim, "I cannot greater grow!"
But, nevermore, O worthy Brother mine,
Can innocence and purity combine
With all that's sweet and tender here below
As in this emblem which I now bestow.
'Tis yours to wear thruout a life of Love,
And when your spirit wings to realms above
'Twill with your cold clay rest beneath the sod,
While breeze kissed flowers whisper of your God.
O, may its stainless, spotless surface be
An emblem of that perfect purity
Distinguished far above all else on earth
And sacred as the virtue of the hearth,
And when at last your naked soul shall stand
Before the throne in yon great Temple grand,
O, may it be your portion there to hear
"Well done," and find a host of Brothers near
To join the angel choir in glad refrain
Till Northeast corner echoes come again.
Then while the hosts in silent grandeur stand
The Supreme Builder smiling in command
Shall say to you to whom this emblem's given,
"Welcome art thou to all the joys of heaven."
And then shall dawn within your 'lightened soul
The purpose divine that held control—
The full fruition of the Builder's plan—
The Fatherhood of God—The Brotherhood of man.

• • •

"— Lambskin or white leathern apron. It is an emblem of innocence and the badge of a Mason: more ancient than the Golden Fleece or Roman Eagle, and when worthily worn, more honorable than the Star and Garter, or any other Order that can be conferred upon you at this or any future period by king, prince, potentate, or any other person, except he be a Mason and within the Body of a just and legally constituted Lodge of such.

"It may be that, in the years to come, upon your head shall rest the laurel wreaths of victory; pendant from your breast may hang jewels fit to grace the diadem of an Eastern potentate; yea, more than these; for with the coming Light your ambitious feet may tread round after round the ladder that leads to fame in our mystic circle, and even the purple of our Fraternity may rest upon your honored shoulders; but never again by mortal hands, never again until your enfranchised spirit shall have passed upward and inward thru the gates of pearl, shall any honor so distinguished, so emblematic of purity and all perfection, be bestowed upon you as this, which I now confer. It is yours; yours to wear thru an honorable life, and at your death to be placed upon the coffin which contains your earthly remains, and with them hid beneath the silent clods of the valley.

"Let its pure and spotless surface be to you an ever-present reminder of 'purity of life and rectitude of conduct, 'a never-ending argument for higher thoughts, for nobler deeds, for greater achievements; and when at last your weary feet shall have reached the end of their toilsome journey, and from your nerveless grasp forever drop the working tools of a busy life, may the record of your life and conduct be as pure and spotless as this fair emblem which I place within your hands tonight; and when your trembling soul shall stand naked and alone before the great white throne, there to receive judgment for the deeds done while here in the body, may it be your portion to hear from Him who sitteth as Judge Supreme these welcome words; 'Well done, thou good and faithful servant, enter thou into the joy of thy Lord.' "I charge you—take it, wear it with pleasure to yourself and an honor to the Fraternity."

• • •

"This emblem is now yours; to wear, we hope, with equal pleasure to yourself, and honor to the Fraternity. If you disgrace it, the disgrace will be augmented by the consciousness that you have been taught in this Lodge, the principles of a correct and manly life. It is yours to wear as a Mason so long as the vital spark shall animate your mortal frame, and at last, whether in youth, manhood or age, your spirit having winged its flight to that 'House not made with hands' when amid the tears and sorrows of surviving relatives and friends, and by the hands of sympathizing Brother Masons, your body shall be lowered to the confines of that narrow house appointed for all living it will still be yours, yours to be placed with the evergreen upon the coffin that shall enclose your remains, and to be buried with them.

"My Brother, may you so wear this emblem of spotless white that no act of yours shall ever stain its purity, or cast a reflection upon this ancient and honorable institution that has outlived the fortunes of Kings and the mutations of Empires. May you so wear it and:

"So live, that when thy summons comes to join
The innumerable caravan that moves
To pale realms of shade, where each shall take
His chamber in the silent halls of death,
Thou go not, like the quarry slaves at night,
Scourged to his dungeon, but, sustained and soothed
By an unfaltering trust, approach thy grave
Like one who wraps the drapery of his couch
About him, and lies down to pleasant dreams."

Aspirant. One who eagerly seeks to know or to attain something. Thus, Warburton speaks of "the aspirant to the Mysteries." It is applied also to one about to be initiated into Masonry. There seems, however, to be a shade of difference in meaning between the words *candidate* and *aspirant*. The candidate is one who asks for admission; so called from the Lat. *candidatus* "clothed in white," because candidates for office at Rome wore a white dress. The aspirant is one already elected and in process of initiation, and coming from *aspiro,* to seek eagerly, refers to the earnestness with which he prosecutes his search for light and truth.

Babel. In Hebrew, בבל; which the writer of Genesis connects with בלל, *balal,* "to confound," in reference to the confusion of tongues; but the true derivation is probably from BAB-EL, the "gate of El" or the "gate of God," because perhaps a temple was the first building raised by the primitive nomads. It is the name of that celebrated tower attempted to be built on the plains of Shinar, A.M. 1775, about one hundred and forty years after the deluge, which tower, Scripture informs us, was destroyed by a special interposition of the Almighty. The Noachite Masons date the commencement of their Order from this destruction, and much traditionary information on this subject is preserved in the degree of "Patriarch Noachite." At Babel, Oliver says that what has been called Spurious Freemasonry took its origin. That is to say, the people there abandoned the worship of the true God, and by their dispersion lost all knowledge of his existence, and of the principles of truth upon which Masonry is founded. Hence it is that the rituals speak of the lofty tower of Babel as the place *where language was confounded and Masonry lost.*

This is the theory first advanced by Anderson in his *Constitutions,* and subsequently developed more extensively by Dr. Oliver in all his works, but especially in his *Landmarks.* As history, the doctrine is of no value, for it wants the element of authenticity. But in a symbolic point of view it is highly suggestive. If the tower of Babel represents the profane world of ignorance and darkness, and the threshing-floor of Ornan the Jebusite is the symbol of Freemasonry, because the Solomonic Temple, of which it was the site, is the prototype of the spiritual temple which Masons are erecting, then we can readily understand how Masonry and the true use of language is lost in one and recovered in the other, and how the progress of the candidate in his initiation may properly be compared to the progress of truth from the confusion and ignorance of the Babel builders to the perfection and illumination of the temple builders, which temple builders all Freemasons are. And so, when in the ritual the neophyte, being asked "whence he comes and whither is he traveling," replies, "from the lofty tower of Babel, where language was confounded and Masonry lost, to the threshing-floor of Ornan the Jebusite, where language was restored and Masonry found," the questions and answers become intelligible from this symbolic point of view.

Baldrick. A portion of military dress, being a scarf passing from the shoulder over the breast to the hip. In the dress regulations of the Grand Encampment of Knights Templar of the United States, adopted in 1862, it is called a "scarf," and is thus described: "Five inches wide in the whole, of white bordered with black, one inch on either side, a strip of navy lace one-fourth of an inch wide at the inner edge of the black. On the front centre of the scarf, a metal star of nine points, in allusion to the nine founders of the Temple Order, inclosing the Passion Cross, surrounded by the Latin motto, *In hoc signo vinces;* the star to be three and three-quarter inches in diameter. The scarf to be worn from the right shoulder to the left hip, with the ends extending six inches below the point of intersection."

Baphomet. The imaginary idol, or, rather, symbol, which the Knights Templars were accused of employing in their mystic rights. The forty-second of the charges preferred against them by Pope Clement is in these words: *Item quod ipsi per singulas provincias habeant idola: videlicet captita quorum aliqua habebant tres facies, et alia unum: et aliqua cranium humanum habebant.* Also, that in all of the provinces they have idols, namely, heads, of which some had three faces, some one, and some had a human skull. Von Hammer, a bitter enemy of the Templars, in his book entitled *The Mystery of Baphomet Revealed,* revived this old accusation, and attached to the Baphomet an impious signification. He derived the name from the Greek words, βαφή, *baptism,* and μῆτις, *wisdom,* and thence supposed that it represented the admission of the initiated into the secret mysteries of the Order. From this gratuitous assumption he deduces his theory, set forth even in the very title of his work, that the Templars were convicted, by their own monuments, of being guilty as Gnostics and Ophites, of apostasy, idolatry, and impurity. Of this statement he offers no other historical testimony than the Articles of Accusation, themselves devoid of proof, but through which the Templars were made the victims of the jealousy of the Pope and the avarice of the King of France.

Others again have thought that they could find in *Baphomet* a corruption of *Mahomet,* and hence they have asserted that the Templars had been perverted from their religious faith by the Saracens, with whom they had so much intercourse, sometimes as foes and sometimes as friends. Nicolai, who wrote an *Essay on the Accusations brought against the Templars,* published at Berlin, in 1782, supposes, but doubtingly, that the figure of the Baphomet, *figura Baffometi,* which was depicted on a bust representing the Creator, was nothing else but the Pythagorean pentagon, the symbol of health and prosperity, borrowed by the Templars from the Gnostics, who in turn had obtained it from the School of Pythagoras.

King, in his learned work on the Gnostics, thinks that the Baphomet may have been a symbol of the Manicheans, with whose widespreading heresy in the Middle Ages he does not doubt that a large portion of the inquiring spirits of the Temple had been intoxicated.

Amid these conflicting views, all merely speculative, it will not be uncharitable or unreasonable to suggest that the Baphomet, or skull of the ancient Templars, was, like the *relic* of their modern Masonic representatives, simply an impressive symbol teaching the lesson of mortality, and that the latter has really been derived from the former.

Baptism, Masonic. The term "Masonic Baptism" has been recently applied in this country by some authorities to that ceremony which is used in certain of the high degrees, and which, more properly, should be called "Lustration." It has been objected that the use of the term is calculated to give needless offense to scrupulous persons who might suppose it to be an imitation of a Christian sacrament. But, in fact, the Masonic baptism has no allusion whatsoever, either in form or design, to the sacrament of the Church. It is simply a lustration or purification by water, a ceremony which was common to all the ancient initiations. (See *Lustration.*)

Bastard. The question of the ineligibility of bastards to be made Freemasons was first brought to the attention of the Craft by Brother Chalmers I. Paton, who, in several articles in *The London Freemason,* in 1869, contended that they were excluded from initiation by the Ancient Regulations. Subsequently, in his compilation entitled *Freemasonry and its Jurisprudence,* published in 1872, he cites several of the *Old Constitutions* as explicitly declaring that the men made Masons shall be "no bastards." This is a most unwarrantable interpolation not to be justified in any writer on jurisprudence; for on a careful examination of all the old manuscript copies which have been published, no such words are to be found in any one of them. As an instance of this literary disingenuousness (to use no harsher term), I quote the following from his work (p. 60): "The charge in this second edition [of Anderson's *Constitu-*

tions] is in the following unmistakable words: 'The men made Masons must be freeborn, no bastard, (or no bondmen,) of mature age and of good report, hale and sound, not deformed or dismembered at the time of their making.' "

Now, with a copy of this second edition lying open before me, I find the passage thus printed: "The men made Masons must be freeborn, (or no bondmen,) of mature age and of good report, hale and sound, not deformed or dismembered at the time of their making." The words "no bastard" are Paton's interpolation.

Again, Paton quotes from Preston the Ancient Charges at makings, in these words: "That he that be made be able in all degrees; that is, freeborn, of a good kindred, true, and no bondsman or bastard, and that he have his right limbs as a man ought to have."

But on referring to Preston (edition of 1775, and all subsequent editions) we find the passage to be correctly thus: "That he that be made be able in all degrees; that is, freeborn, of a good kindred, true, and no bondsman, and that he have his limbs as a man ought to have."

Positive law authorities should not be thus cited, not merely carelessly, but with designed inaccuracy to support a theory.

But although there is no regulation in the *Old Constitutions* which *explicitly* prohibits the initiation of bastards, it may be implied from their language that such prohibition did exist. Thus, in all the old manuscripts, we find such expressions as these: he that shall be made a Mason "must be freeborn and *of good kindred*" (Sloane MS., No. 3323), or "come of good kindred" (Edinburgh Kilwinning MS.), or, as the Roberts Print more definitely has it, "of honest parentage."

It is not, I therefore think, to be doubted.

Bay-Tree. An evergreen plant, and a symbol in Freemasonry of the immortal nature of Truth. By the bay-tree thus referred to in the ritual of the Companion of the Red Cross, is meant the laurel, which, as an evergreen, was among the ancients a symbol of immortality. It is, therefore, properly compared with truth, which Josephus makes Zerubbabel say is "immortal and eternal."

Benakar. The name of a cavern to which certain assassins fled for concealment.

Bendekar. A significant word in the high degrees. One of the Princes or Intendants of Solomon, in whose quarry some of the traitors spoken of in the Third Degree were found. He is mentioned in the catalogue of Solomon's princes, given in 1 Kings iv. 9. The Hebrew word is בןדקר, *the son of him who divides or pierces.* In some old rituals we find a corrupt form, *Bendaca.*

Benedict XIV. A Roman pontiff whose family name was Prosper Lambertini. He was born at Bologna in 1675, succeeded Clement XII. as Pope in 1740, and died in 1758. He was distinguished for his learning and was a great encourager of the Arts and Sciences. He was, however, an implacable enemy of secret societies, and issued on the 18th of May, 1751, his celebrated bull, renewing and perpetuating that of his predecessor which excommunicated the Freemasons. (See *Bull.*)

Benediction. The solemn invocation of a blessing in the ceremony of closing a Lodge is called the benediction. The usual formula is as follows:

"May the blessing of Heaven rest upon us, and all regular Masons; may brotherly love prevail, and every moral and social virtue cement us." The response is, "So mote it be. Amen"; which should always be audibly pronounced by all the Brethren.

Beneficiary. One who receives the support or charitable donations of a Lodge. Those who are entitled to these benefits are affiliated Masons, their wives or widows, their widowed mothers, and their minor sons and unmarried daughters. Unaffiliated Masons cannot become the beneficiaries of a Lodge, but affiliated Masons cannot be deprived of its benefits on account of non-payment of dues. Indeed, as this non-payment often arises from poverty, it thus furnishes a stronger claim for fraternal charity.

Behold Your Master. When, in the installation services, the formula is used, "Brethren, behold your master," the expression is not simply exclamatory, but is intended, as the original use of the word *behold* implies, to invite the members of the Lodge to fix their attention upon the new relations which have sprung up between them and him who has just been elevated to the Oriental Chair, and to impress upon their minds the duties which they owe to him and which he owes to them. In like manner, when the formula is continued, "Master, behold your brethren," the Master's attention is impressively directed to the same change of relations and duties. These are not mere idle words, but convey an important lesson, and should never be omitted in the ceremony of installation.

Bel. בל, *Bel,* is the contracted form of בעל, *Baal,* and was worshiped by the Babylonians as their chief deity. The Greeks and Romans so considered and translated the word by Zeus and Jupiter. It has, with *Jah* and *On,* been introduced into the Royal Arch system as a representative of the Tetragrammaton, which it and the accompanying words have sometimes ignorantly been made to displace. At the session of the General Grand Chapter of the United States, in 1871, this error was corrected; and while the Tetragrammaton was declared to be the true omnific word, the other three were permitted to be retained as merely explanatory.

Blazing Star. The Blazing Star, which is not, however, to be confounded with the Five-Pointed Star, is one of the most important symbols of Freemasonry, and makes its appearance in several of the degrees. "It is," says Hutchinson, "the first and most exalted object that demands our attention in the Lodge." It undoubtedly derives this importance, first, from the repeated use that is made of it as a Masonic emblem; and secondly, from its great antiquity as a symbol derived from other and older systems.

Extensive as has been the application of this symbol in the Masonic ritual, it is not surprising that there has been a great difference of opinion in relation to its true signification. But this difference of opinion has been almost entirely confined to its use in the First Degree. In the higher degrees, where there has been less opportunity of innovation, the uniformity of meaning attached to the star has been carefully preserved.

In the Twenty-eighth Degree of the Ancient and Accepted Scottish Rite, the explanation given of the Blazing Star, is, that it is symbolic of a true Mason, who, by perfecting himself in the way of truth, that is to say, by advancing in knowledge, becomes like a blazing star, shining with brilliancy in the midst of darkness. The star is, therefore, in this degree, a symbol of truth.

In the Fourth Degree of the same Rite, the star is again said to be a symbol of the light of Divine Providence pointing out the way of truth.

In the Ninth Degree, this symbol is called "the star of direction"; and while it primitively alludes to an especial guidance given for a particular purpose expressed in the degree, it still retains, in a remoter sense, its usual signification as an emblem of Divine Providence guiding and directing the pilgrim in his journey through life.

When, however, we descend to Ancient Craft Masonry, we shall find a considerable diversity in the application of this symbol.

In the earliest rituals, immediately after the revival of 1717, the Blazing Star is not mentioned, but it was not long before it was introduced. In the ritual of 1735 it is detailed as a part of the furniture of a Lodge, with the explanation that the "Mosaic Pavement is the Ground Floor of the Lodge, the Blazing Star, the Centre, and the Indented Tarsel, the Border round about it!" In a primitive Tracing Board of the Entered Apprentice, copied by Oliver, in his *Historical Landmarks* (i., 133), without other date than that it was "published early in the last century," the Blazing Star occupies a prominent position in the center of the Tracing Board. Oliver says that it represented BEAUTY, and was called "the glory in the centre."

In the lectures subsequently prepared by Dunckerley, and adopted by the Grand Lodge, the Blazing Star was said to represent "the star which led the wise men to Bethlehem, proclaiming to mankind the nativity of the Son of God, and here conducting our spiritual progress to the Author of our redemption."

In the Prestonian lecture, the Blazing Star, with the Mosaic Pavement and the Tesselated Border, are called the Ornaments of the Lodge, and the Blazing Star is thus explained:

"The Blazing Star, or glory in the centre, reminds us of that awful period when the Almighty delivered the two tables of stone, containing the ten commandments, to His faithful servant Moses on Mount Sinai, when the rays of His divine glory shone so bright that none could behold it without fear and trembling. It also reminds us of the omnipresence of the Almighty, overshadowing us with His divine love, and dispensing His blessings amongst us; and by its being placed in the centre, it further reminds us, that wherever we may be assembled together, God is in the midst of us, seeing our actions, and observing the secret intents and movements of our hearts."

In the lectures taught by Webb, and very generally adopted in this country, the Blazing Star is said to be "commemorative of the star which appeared to guide the wise men of the East to the place of our Saviour's nativity," and it is subsequently explained as hieroglyphically representing Divine Providence. But the commemorative allusion to the Star of Bethlehem seeming to some to be objectionable, from its peculiar application to the Christian religion, at the revision of the lectures made in 1843 by the Baltimore Convention, this explanation was omitted, and the allusion to Divine Providence alone retained.

Blow. The three blows given to the Builder, according to the legend of the Third Degree, have been differently interpreted as symbols in the different systems of Masonry, but always with some reference to adverse or malignant influences exercised on humanity, of whom Hiram is considered as the type. Thus, in the symbolic degrees of Ancient Craft Masonry, the three blows are said to be typical of the trials and temptations to which man is subjected in youth and manhood, and to death, whose victim he becomes in old age. Hence the three Assassins are the three stages of human life. In the high degrees, such as the Kadoshes, which are founded on the Templar system of Ramsay, the reference is naturally made to the destruction of the Order, which was effected by the combined influences of Tyranny, Superstition, and Ignorance, which are therefore symbolized by the three blows; while the three Assassins are also said sometimes to be represented by Squire de Floreau, Naffodei, and the Prior of Montfaucon, the three perjurers who swore away the lives of De Molay and his Knights. In the astronomical theory of Freemasonry, which makes it a modern modification of the ancient sun-worship, a theory advanced by Ragon, the three blows are symbolic of the destructive influences of the three winter months, by which Hiram, or the Sun, is shorn of his vivifying power. Des Etangs has generalized the Templar theory, and, supposing Hiram to be the symbol of eternal reason, interprets the blows as the attacks of those vices which deprave and finally destroy humanity. However interpreted for a special theory, Hiram the Builder always represents, in the science of Masonic symbolism, the principle of good; and then the three blows are the contending principles of evil.

Blue. This is emphatically the color of Masonry. It is the appropriate tincture of the Ancient Craft degrees. It is to the Mason a symbol of universal friendship and benevolence, because, as it is the color of the vault of heaven, which embraces and covers the whole globe, we are thus reminded that in the breast of every brother these virtues should be equally as extensive. It is therefore the only color, except white, which should be used in a Master's Lodge. Decorations of any other color would be highly inappropriate.

Among the religious institutions of the Jews, blue was an important color. The robe of the high priest's ephod, the ribbon for his breastplate, and for the plate of the miter, were to be blue. The people were directed to wear a ribbon of this color above the fringe of their garments; and it was the color of one of the veils of the tabernacle, where, Josephus says, it represented the element of air. The Hebrew word used on these occasions to designate the color blue is תבלת *'tekelet;* and this word seems to have a singular reference to the symbolic character of the color, for it is derived from a root signifying *perfection;* now it is well known that, among the ancients, initiation into the mysteries and perfection were synonymous terms; and hence the appropriate color of the greatest of all the systems of initiation may well be designated by a word which also signifies perfection.

This color also held a prominent position in the symbolism of the Gentile nations of antiquity. Among the Druids, blue was the symbol of *truth,* and the candidate, in the initiation into the sacred rites of Druidism, was invested with a robe composed of the three colors, white, blue, and green.

The Egyptians esteemed blue as a sacred color, and the body of Amun, the principal god of their theogony, was painted light blue, to imitate, as Wilkinson remarks, "his peculiarly exalted and heavenly nature."

The ancient Babylonians clothed their idols in blue, as we learn from the prophet Jeremiah. The Chinese, in their mystical philosophy, represented blue as the symbol of the Deity, because, being, as they say, compounded of black and red, this color is a fit representation of the obscure and brilliant, the male and female, or active and passive principles.

The Hindus assert that their god, Vishnu, was represented of a celestial blue, thus indicating that wisdom emanating from God was to be symbolized by this color.

Among the medieval Christians blue was sometimes considered as an emblem of immortality, as red was of the Divine love. Portal says that blue was the symbol of perfection, hope, and constancy. "The color of the celebrated dome, azure," says Weale, in his treatise on *Symbolic Colors,* "was in divine language the symbol of eternal truth; in consecrated language, of immortality; and in profane language, of fidelity."

Besides the three degrees of Ancient Craft Masonry, of which blue is the appropriate color, this tincture is also to be found in several other degrees, especially of the Scottish Rite, where it bears various symbolic significations; all, however, more or less related to its original character as representing universal friendship and benevolence.

In the degree of Grand Pontiff, the Nineteenth of the Scottish Rite, it is the predominating color, and is there said to be symbolic of the mildness, fidelity, and gentleness which ought to be the characteristics of every true and faithful brother.

In the degree of Grand Master of all Symbolic Lodges, the blue and yellow, which are its appropriate colors, are said to refer to the appearance of Jehovah to Moses on Mount Sinai in clouds of azure and gold, and hence in this degree the color is rather an historical than a moral symbol.

The blue color of the tunic and apron, which constitutes a part of the investiture of a Prince of the Tabernacle, or Twenty-fourth Degree in the Scottish Rite, alludes to the whole symbolic character of the degree, whose teachings refer to our removal from this tabernacle of clay to "that house not made with hands, eternal in the heavens." The blue in this degree is, therefore, a symbol of heaven, the seat of our celestial tabernacle.

Blue Degrees. The first three degrees of Freemasonry are so called from the blue color which is peculiar to them.

Blue Lodge. A Symbolic Lodge, in which the first three degrees of Masonry are conferred, is so called from the color of its decorations.

Box of Fraternal Assistance. A book of convenient shape and size under the charge of the Hospitaler or Almoner, in the Modern French and A. A. Scottish Rites, wherein is collected the obligatory contributions of the duly assembled Brethren at every convocation, which collections can only be used for secret charitable purposes, first among the members, but if not there required, among worthy profane; the Master and the Hospitaler being the only ones cognizant of the name of the beneficiary, together with the brother who suggests an individual in need of the assistance.

Bread, Consecrated. Consecrated bread and wine, that is to say, bread and wine used not simply for food, but made sacred by the purpose of symbolizing a bond of brotherhood, and the eating and drinking of which are sometimes called the "Communion of the Brethren," is found in some of the higher degrees, such as the Order of High Priesthood in the American Rite, and the Rose Croix of the French and Scottish Rites.

It was in ancient times a custom religiously observed, that those who sacrificed to the gods should unite in partaking of a part of the food that had been offered. And in the Jewish church it was strictly commanded that the sacrificers should "eat before the Lord," and unite in a feast of joy on the occasion of their offerings. By this common partaking of that which had been consecrated to a sacred purpose, those who partook of the feast seemed to give an evidence and attestation of the sincerity with which they made the offering; while the feast itself was, as it were, the renewal of the covenant of friendship between the parties.

Breast, The Faithful. One of the three precious jewels of a Fellow-Craft. It symbolically teaches the initiate that the lessons which he has received from the instructive tongue of the Master are not to be listened to and lost, but carefully treasured in his heart, and that the precepts of the Order constitute a covenant which he is faithfully to observe.

Breast to Breast. See *Points of Fellowship*.

Brethren. This word, being the plural of Brother in the solemn style, is more generally used in Masonic language, instead of the common plural, *Brothers*. Thus Masons always speak of "The Brethren of the Lodge," and not of "The Brothers of the Lodge."

Chalice. A cup used in religious rites. It forms a part of the furniture of a Commandery of Knights Templar, and of some of the higher degrees of the French and Scottish Rites. It should be made either of silver or of gilt metal. The stem of the chalice should be about four inches high and the diameter from three to six.

Chalk, Charcoal, and Clay. By these three substances are beautifully symbolized the three qualifications for the servitude of an Entered Apprentice—freedom, fervency, and zeal. Chalk is the freest of all substances, because the slightest touch leaves a trace behind. Charcoal, the most fervent, because to it, when ignited, the most obdurate metals yield; and clay, the most zealous, because it is constantly employed in man's service, and is as constantly reminding us that from it we all came, and to it we must all return. In the earlier lectures of the last century, the symbols, with the same interpretation, were given as "Chalk, Charcoal, and Earthen Pan."

Charity. "Though I speak with the tongues of men and of angels, and have not charity, I am become as sounding brass, or a tinkling cymbal. And though I have the gift of prophecy, and understand all mysteries and all knowledge; and though I have all faith, so that I could remove mountains, and have not charity, I am nothing." (1 Corinth. xiii. 1, 2.) Such was the language of an eminent apostle of the Christian church, and such is the sentiment that constitutes the cementing bond of Freemasonry. The apostle, in comparing it with faith and hope, calls it the greatest of the three, and hence in Masonry it is made the topmost round of its mystic ladder. We must not fall into the too common error that charity is only that sentiment of commiseration which leads us to assist the poor with pecuniary donations. Its Masonic, as well as its Christian application is more noble and more extensive. The word used by the apostle is, in the original, ἀγάπη, or *love*, a word denoting that kindly state of mind which renders a person full of good-will and affectionate regard toward others. John Wesley expressed his regret that the Greek had not been correctly translated as *love* instead of *charity*, so that the apostolic triad of virtues would have been, not "faith, hope, and charity," but "faith, hope, and love." Then would we have understood the comparison made by St. Paul, when he said, "Though I bestow all my goods to feed the *poor,* and though I give my body to be burned, and have not *love,* it profiteth me nothing." Guided by this sentiment, the true Mason will "suffer long and be kind." He will be slow to anger and easy to forgive. He will stay his falling brother by gentle admonition, and warn him with kindness of approaching danger. He will not open his ear to his slanderers, and will close his lips against all reproach. His faults and his follies will be locked in his breast, and the prayer for mercy will ascend to Jehovah for his brother's sins. Nor will these sentiments of benevolence be confined to those who are bound to him by ties of kindred or worldly friendship alone; but, extending them throughout the globe, he will love and cherish all who sit beneath the broad canopy of our universal Lodge. For it is the boast of our Institution, that a Mason, destitute and worthy, may find in every clime a brother, and in every land a home.

Chaos. A confused and shapeless mass, such as is supposed to have existed before God reduced creation into order. It is a Masonic symbol of the ignorance and intellectual darkness from which man is rescued by the light and truth of Masonry. Hence, *ordo ab chao,* or, "order out of chaos," is one of the mottoes of the Institution.

Chapter, Royal Arch. A convocation of Royal Arch Masons is called a Chapter. In Great Britain, Royal Arch Masonry is connected with and practically under the same government as the Grand Lodge; but in America the jurisdictions are separate. In America a Chapter of Royal Arch Masons is empowered to give the preparatory degrees of Mark, Past, and Most Excellent Master; although, of course, the Chapter, when meeting in either of these degrees, is called a Lodge. In some Chapters the degrees of Royal and Select Master are also given as preparatory degrees; but in most of the States, the control of these is conferred upon separate bodies, called "Councils of Royal and Select Masters."

The presiding officers of a Chapter are the High Priest, King, and Scribe, who are, respectively, representatives of Joshua, Zerubbabel, Haggai, and son of Josedech. In the English Chapters, these officers are generally styled either by the founders' names, as above, or as First, Second, and Third Principals. In the Chapters of Ireland the order of the officers is King, High Priest, and Chief Scribe. Chapters of Royal Arch Masons in America are primarily under the jurisdiction of State Grand Chapters, as Lodges are under Grand Lodges; and secondly, under the General Grand Chapter of the United States, whose meetings are held triennially, and which exercises a general supervision over this branch of the Order throughout the Union.

Chisel. In the American Rite the chisel is one of the working tools of a Mark Master, and symbolizes the effects of education on the human mind. For as the artist, by the aid of this instrument, gives form and regularity to the shapeless mass of stone, so education, by cultivating the ideas and by polishing the rude thoughts, transforms the ignorant savage into the civilized being.

In the English ritual, the chisel is one of the working tools of the Entered Apprentice. With the same reference to the advantages of education. Preston (B. II., Sect. vi.) thus elaborates its symbolism as one of the implements of Masonry: "The chisel demonstrates the advantages of discipline and education. The mind, like the diamond in its original state, is unpolished; but as the effects of the chisel on the external coat soon present to view the latent beauties of the diamond, so education discovers the latent virtues of the mind and draws them forth to range the large field of matter and space, in order to display the summit of human knowledge, our duty to God and to man." (*Illustrations*, ed. 1812, p. 86, footnote.) But the idea is not original with Preston. It is found in Hutchinson, who, however, does not claim it as his own. It formed, most probably, a portion of the lectures of the period. In the French system, the chisel is placed on the tracing board of the Fellow-Craft as an implement with which to work upon and polish the Rough Ashlar. It has, therefore, there the same symbolic signification.

Civilization and Freemasonry. Those who investigate in the proper spirit the history of Speculative Masonry will be strongly impressed with the peculiar relations that exist between the history of Masonry and that of civilization. They will find these facts to be patent: that Freemasonry has ever been the result of civilization; that in the most ancient times the spirit of Masonry and the spirit of civilization have always gone together; that the progress of both has been with equal strides; that where there has been no appearance of civilization there has been no trace of Masonry; and, finally, that wherever Masonry has existed in any of its forms, there it has been surrounded and sustained by civilization, which social condition it in turn elevated and purified.

Speculative Masonry, therefore, seems to have been a necessary result of civilization. It is, even in its primitive and most simple forms, to be found among no barbarous or savage people. Such a state of society has never been capable of introducing or maintaining its abstract principles of Divine truth.

But while Speculative Masonry is the result of civilization, existing only in its bosom and never found among barbarous or savage races, it has, by a reactionary law of sociology, proved the means of extending and elevating the civilization to which it originally owed its birth. Civilization has always been progressive. That of Pelasgic Greece was far behind that which distinguished the Hellenic period of the same country. The civilization of the ancient world was inferior to that of the modern, and every century shows an advancement in the moral, intellectual, and social condition of mankind. But in this progress from imperfection to perfection the influence of those speculative systems that are identical with Freemasonry has always been seen and felt. Let us, for an example, look at the ancient heathen world and its impure religions. While the people of Paganism bowed, in their ignorance, to a many-headed god, or, rather, worshiped at the shrines of many gods, whose mythological history and character must have exercised a pernicious effect on the moral purity of their worshipers, Speculative Philosophy, in the form of the "Ancient Mysteries," was exercising its influence upon a large class of neophytes and disciples, by giving this true symbolic interpretation of the old religious myths. In the adyta of their temples in Greece and Rome and Egypt, in the sacred caves of India, and in the consecrated groves of Scandinavia and Gaul and Britain, these ancient sages were secretly divesting the Pagan faith of its polytheism and of its anthropomorphic deities, and were establishing a pure monotheism in its place, and illustrating, by a peculiar symbolism, the great dogmas—since taught in Freemasonry—of the unity of God and the immortality of the soul. And in modern times, when the religious thought of mankind, under a better dispensation, has not required this purification, Masonry still, in other ways, exerts its influence in elevating the tone of civilization; for through its working the social feelings have been strengthened, the amenities and charities of life been refined and extended, and, as we have had recent reason to know and see, the very bitterness of strife and the blood-guiltiness of war have been softened and oftentimes obliterated.

We then arrive at these conclusions, namely, that Speculative Masonry is a result of civilization, for it exists in no savage or barbarous state of society, but has always appeared with the advent in any country of a condition of civilization, "grown with its growth and strengthened with its strength"; and, in return, has proved, by a reactionary influence, a potent instrument in extending, elevating, and refining the civilization which gave it birth, by advancing its moral, intellectual, and religious character.

Clandestine. The ordinary meaning of this word is secret, hidden. The French word *clandestin,* from which it is derived, is defined by Boiste to be something "fait en cachette et contre les lois," done in a hiding-place and against the laws, which better suits the Masonic signification, which is *illegal, not authorized. Irregular* is often used for small departures from custom.

Clandestine Lodge. A body of Masons uniting in a Lodge without the consent of a Grand Lodge, or, although originally legally constituted, continuing to work after its charter has been revoked, is styled a "Clandestine Lodge." Neither Anderson nor Entick employ the word. It was first used in the *Book of Constitutions* in a note by Noorthouck, on page 239 of his edition. (*Constitutions,* 1784.) Irregular Lodge would be the better term.

Clandestine Mason. One made in or affiliated with a clandestine Lodge. With clandestine Lodges or Masons, regular Masons are forbidden to associate or converse on Masonic subjects.

Communication. The meeting of a Lodge is so called. There is a peculiar significance in this term. "To communicate," which, in the Old

English form, was "to common," originally meant to share in common with others. The great sacrament of the Christian church, which denotes a participation in the mysteries of the religion and a fellowship in the church, is called a "communion," which is fundamentally the same as a "communication," for he who partakes of the communion is said "to communicate." Hence, the meetings of Masonic Lodges are called *communications,* to signify that it is not simply the ordinary meeting of a society for the transaction of business, but that such meeting is the fellowship of men engaged in a common pursuit, and governed by a common principle, and that there is therein a communication or participation of those feelings and sentiments that constitute a true brotherhood.

The communications of Lodges are regular or stated and special or emergent. Regular communications are held under the provision of the by-laws, but special communications are called by order of the Master. It is a regulation that no special communication can alter, amend, or rescind the proceedings of a regular communication.

Communication, Grand. The meeting of a Grand Lodge.

Communication of Degrees. When the peculiar mysteries of a degree are bestowed upon a candidate by mere verbal description of the bestower, without his being made to pass through the constituted ceremonies, the degree is technically said to be *communicated.* This mode is, however, entirely confined in America to the Ancient and Accepted Scottish Rite. The degrees may in that Rite be thus conferred in any place where secrecy is secured; but the prerogative of communicating is restricted to the presiding officers of bodies of the Rite, who may communicate certain of the degrees upon candidates who have been previously duly elected, and to Inspectors and Deputy Inspectors-General of the Thirty-third Degree, who may communicate all the degrees of the Rite, except the last, to any persons whom they may deem qualified to receive them.

Compasses. As in Operative Masonry, the compasses are used for the admeasurement of the architect's plans, and to enable him to give those just proportions which will ensure beauty as well as stability to his work; so, in Speculative Masonry, is this important implement symbolic of that even tenor of deportment, that true standard of rectitude which alone can bestow happiness here and felicity hereafter. Hence are the compasses the most prominent emblem of virtue, the true and only measure of a Mason's life and conduct. As the *Bible* gives us *light* on our duties to God, and the *square* illustrates our duties to our neighborhood and brother, so the *compasses* give that additional *light* which is to instruct us in the duty we owe to ourselves—the great, imperative duty of circumscribing our passions, and keeping our desires within due bounds. "It is ordained," says the philosophic Burke, "in the eternal constitution of things, that men of intemperate passions cannot be free; their passions forge their fetters." Those brethren who delight to trace our emblems to an astronomical origin, find in the compasses a symbol of the sun, the circular pivot representing the body of the luminary, and the diverging legs his rays.

In the earliest rituals of the last century, the compasses are described as a part of the furniture of the Lodge, and are said to belong to the Master. Some change will be found in this respect in the ritual of the present day.

Conversation. Conversation among the brethren during Lodge hours is forbidden by the *Charges of 1722* in these words: "You are not to hold private committees or separate conversation without leave from the Master." (*Constitutions,* 1723, p. 53.)

Convocation. The meetings of Chapters of Royal Arch Masons are so called from the Latin *convocatio,* a calling together. It seems very properly to refer to the convoking of the dispersed Masons at Jerusalem to rebuild the second Temple, of which every Chapter is a representation.

Convocation, Grand. The meeting of a Grand Chapter is so styled.

Courtesy. Politeness of manners, as the result of kindness of disposition, was one of the peculiar characteristics of the knights of old. "No other human laws enforced," says M. de St. Palaye, "as chivalry did, sweetness and modesty of temper, and that politeness which the word *courtesy* was meant perfectly to express." We find, therefore, in the ritual of Templarism, the phrase "a true and courteous knight"; and Knights Templars are in the habit of closing their letters to each other with the expression, *Yours in all knightly courtesy.* Courtesy is also a Masonic virtue, because it is the product of a feeling of kindness; but it is not so specifically spoken of in the symbolic degrees, where *brotherly love* assumes its place, as it is in the orders of knighthood.

Coustos, John. The sufferings inflicted, in 1743, by the Inquisition at Lisbon, on John Coustos, a Freemason, and the Master of a Lodge in that city; and the fortitude with which he endured the severest tortures, rather than betray his trusts and reveal the secrets that had been confided to him, constitute an interesting episode in the history of Freemasonry. Coustos, after returning to England, published, in 1746, a book, detailing his sufferings, from which the reader is presented with the following abridged narrative.

John Coustos was born at Berne, in Switzerland, but emigrated, in 1716, with his father to England, where he became a naturalized subject. In 1743 he removed to Lisbon, in Portugal, and began the practise of his profession, which was that of a lapidary, or dealer in precious stones.

In consequence of the bull or edict of Pope Clement XII. denouncing the Masonic institution, the Lodges at Lisbon were not held at public houses, as was the custom in England and other Protestant countries, but privately, at the residences of the members. Of one of these Lodges, Coustos, who was a zealous Mason, was elected the Master. A female, who was cognizant of the existence of the Lodge over which Coustos presided, revealed the circumstance to her confessor, declaring that, in her opinion, the members were "monsters in nature, who perpetrated the most shocking crimes." In consequence of this information, it was resolved, by the Inquisition, that Coustos should be arrested and subjected to the tender mercies of the "Holy Office." He was accordingly seized, a few nights afterward, in a coffee-house—the public pretense of the arrest being that he was privy to the stealing of a diamond, of which they had falsely accused another jeweler, the friend and Warden of Coustos, whom also they had a short time previously arrested.

Coustos was then carried to the prison of the Inquisition, and after having been searched and deprived of all his money, papers, and other things that he had about him, he was led to a lonely dungeon, in which he was immured, being expressly forbidden to speak aloud or knock against the walls, but if he required anything, to beat with a padlock that hung on the outward door, and which he could reach by thrusting his arm through the iron grate. "It was there," says he, "that, struck with the horrors of a place of which I had heard and read such baleful descriptions, I plunged at once into the blackest melancholy; especially when I reflected on the dire consequences with which my confinement might very possibly be attended."

On the next day he was led, bareheaded, before the President and four Inquisitors, who, after having made him reply on oath to several questions respecting his name, his parentage, his place of birth, his religion, and the time he had resided in Lisbon, exhorted him to make a full confession of all the crimes he had ever committed in the whole course of his life; but, as he refused to make any such confession, declaring that, from his infancy, he had been taught to confess not to man but to God, he was again remanded to his dungeon.

Three days after, he was again brought before the Inquisitors, and the examination was renewed. This was the first occasion on which the subject of Freemasonry was introduced, and there Coustos for the first time learned that he had been arrested and imprisoned solely on account of his connection with the forbidden Institution.

The result of this conference was that Coustos was conveyed to a deeper dungeon, and kept there in close confinement for several weeks, during which period he was taken three times before the Inquisitors. In the first of these examinations they again introduced the subject of Freemasonry, and declared that if the Institution was as virtuous as their prisoner contended that it was, there was no occasion for concealing so industriously the secrets of it. Coustos did not reply to this objection to the Inquisitorial satisfaction, and he was remanded back to his dungeon, where a few days after he fell sick.

After his recovery, he was again taken before the Inquisitors, who asked him several new questions with regard to the tenets of Freemasonry—among others, whether he, since his abode in Lisbon, had received any Portuguese into the society? He replied that he had not.

When he was next brought before them, "they insisted," he says, "upon my letting them into the secrets of Freemasonry; threatening me, in case I did not comply." But Coustos firmly and fearlessly refused to violate his obligations.

After several other interviews, in which the effort was unavailingly made to extort from him a renunciation of Masonry, he was subjected to the torture, of which he gives the following account:

"I was instantly conveyed to the torture-room, built in form of a square tower, where no light appeared but what two candles gave; and to prevent the dreadful cries and shocking groans of the unhappy victims from reaching the ears of the other prisoners, the doors are lined with a sort of quilt.

"The reader will naturally suppose that I must be seized with horror, when, at my entering this infernal place, I saw myself, on a sudden, surrounded by six wretches, who, after preparing the tortures, stripped me naked, (all to linen drawers,) when, laying me on my back, they began to lay hold of every part of my body. First, they put round my neck an iron collar, which was fastened to the scaffold; they then fixed a ring to each foot; and this being done, they stretched my limbs with all their might. They next wound two ropes round each arm, and two round each thigh, which ropes passed under the scaffold, through holes made for that purpose, and were all drawn tight at the same time, by four men, upon a signal made for this purpose.

"The reader will believe that my pains must be intolerable, when I solemnly declare that these ropes, which were of the size of one's little finger, pierced through my flesh quite to the bone, making the blood gush out at eight different places that were thus bound. As I persisted in refusing to discover any more than what has been seen in the interrogatories above, the ropes were thus drawn together four different times. At my side stood a physician and a surgeon, who often felt my temples, to judge of the danger I might be in—by which means my tortures were suspended, at intervals, that I might have an opportunity of recovering myself a little.

"Whilst I was thus suffering, they were so barbarously unjust as to declare, that, were I to die under the torture, I should be guilty, by my obstinacy, of self-murder. In fine, the last time the ropes were drawn tight, I grew so exceedingly weak, occasioned by the blood's circulation being stopped, and the pains I endured, that I fainted quite away; insomuch that I was carried back to my dungeon, without perceiving it.

"These barbarians, finding that the tortures above described could not extort any further discovery from me; but that, the more they made me suffer, the more fervently I addressed my supplications, for patience, to heaven; they were so inhuman, six weeks after, as to expose me to another kind of torture, more grievous, if possible, than the former. They made me stretch my arms in such a manner that the palms of my hands were turned outward; when, by the help of a rope that fastened them together at the wrist, and which they turned by an engine, they drew them gently nearer to one another behind, in such a manner that the back of each hand touched, and stood exactly parallel one to another; whereby both my shoulders were dislocated, and a considerable quantity of blood issued from my mouth. This torture was repeated thrice; after which I was again taken to my dungeon, and put into the hands of physicians and surgeons, who, in setting my bones, put me to exquisite pain.

"Two months after, being a little recovered, I was again conveyed to the torture-room, and there made to undergo another kind of punishment twice. The reader may judge of its horror, from the following description thereof.

"The torturers turned twice around my body a thick iron chain, which, crossing upon my stomach, terminated afterwards at my wrists. They next set my back against a thick board, at each extremity whereof was a pulley, through which there ran a rope, that catched the ends of the chains at my wrists. The tormentors then stretched these ropes, by means of a roller, pressed or bruised my stomach, in proportion as the means were drawn tighter. They tortured me on this occasion to such a degree, that my wrists and shoulders were put out of joint.

"The surgeons, however, set them presently after; but the barbarians not yet having satiated their cruelty, made me undergo this torture a second time, which I did with fresh pains, though with equal constancy and resolution. I was then remanded back to my dungeon, attended by the surgeons, who dressed my bruises; and here I continued until their *auto-da-fé*, or gaol delivery."

On that occasion, he was sentenced to work at the galleys for four years. Soon, however, after he had commenced the degrading occupation of a galley slave, the injuries which he had received during his inquisitorial tortures having so much impaired his health, that he was unable to undergo the toils to which he had been condemned, he was sent to the infirmary, where he remained until October, 1744, when he was released upon the demand of the British minister, as a subject to the King of England. He was, however, ordered to leave the country. This, it may be supposed, he gladly did, and repaired to London, where he published the account of his sufferings in a book entitled *The Sufferings of John Coustos for Freemasonry, and for refusing to turn Roman Catholic, in the Inquisition at Lisbon, etc., etc.* London, 1746; 8vo, 400 pages. (Reprinted at Birmingham, 1790.) Such a narrative is well worthy of being read. John Coustos has not, by his literary researches, added anything to the learning or science of our Order; yet, by his fortitude and fidelity under the severest sufferings, inflicted to extort from him a knowledge he was bound to conceal, he has shown that Freemasonry makes no idle boast in declaring that its secrets "are locked up in the depository of faithful breasts."

Council. In several of the high degrees of Masonry the meetings are styled Councils; as, a Council of Royal and Select Masters, or Princes of Jerusalem, or Companions of the Red Cross.

Council Chamber. A part of the room in which the ceremonies of the Companions of the Red Cross are performed.

Council of Companions of the Red Cross. A body in which the First Degree of the Templar system in this country is conferred. It is held under the Charter of a Commandery of Knights Templar, which, when meeting as a council, is composed of the following officers: A Sovereign Master, Chancellor, Master of the Palace, Prelate, Master of Despatches, Master of Cavalry, Master of Infantry, Standard-Bearer, Sword-Bearer, Warder, and Sentinel.

Council of Royal and Select Masters. The united body in which the Royal and Select degrees are conferred. In some jurisdictions this Council confers also the degree of Super-Excellent Master.

Council of Royal Masters. The body in which the degree of Royal Master, the eighth in the American Rite, is conferred. It receives its Charter from a Grand Council of Royal and Select Masters, and has the following officers: Thrice Illustrious Grand Master, Illustrious Hiram of Tyre, Principal Conductor of the Works, Master of the Exchequer, Master of Finances, Captain of the Guards, Conductor of the Council, and Steward.

Council of Select Masters. The body in which the degree of Select Masters, the ninth in the American Rite, is conferred. It receives its Charter from a Grand Council of Royal and Select Masters. Its officers are: Thrice Illustrious Grand Master, Illustrious Hiram of Tyre, Principal Conductor of the Works, Treasurer, Recorder, Captain of the Guards, Conductor of the Council, and Steward.

Crux Ansata. This signifies, in Latin, the *cross with a handle.* It is formed by a Tau cross surmounted by a circle or, more properly, an oval. It was one of the most significant of the symbols of the ancient Egyptians, and is depicted repeatedly on their monuments borne in the hands of their deities, and especially Phtha. Among them it was the symbol of life, and with that meaning it has been introduced into some of the higher degrees of Masonry. The Crux Ansata, surrounded by a serpent in a circle, is the symbol of immortality, because the cross was the symbol of life, and the serpent of eternity.

Crypt. From the Greek κρύπτω (to hide). A concealed place, or subterranean vault. The caves, or cells underground, in which the primitive Christians celebrated their secret worship, were called cryptæ; and the vaults beneath our modern churches receive the names of crypts. The existence of crypts or vaults under the Temple of Solomon is testified to by the earliest as well as by the most recent topographers of Jerusalem. Their connection with the legendary history of Masonry is more fully noticed under the head of *Vault Secret.*

Cryptic Degrees. The degrees of Royal and Select Masters. Some modern ritualists have added to the list the degree of Super-excellent Master; but this, although now often conferred in a Cryptic Council, is not really a Cryptic degree, since its legend has no connection with the crypt or secret vault.

Cryptic Masonry. That division of the Masonic system which is directed to the investigation and cultivation of the Cryptic degrees. It is, literally, the Masonry of the secret vault.

Cubical Stone. This symbol is called by the French Masons, *pierre cubique,* and by the German, *cubik stein.* It is the Perfect Ashlar of the English and American systems. (See *Ashlar.*)

Discovery, Year of the. "Anno Inventionis," or "in the Year of the Discovery," is the style assumed by the Royal Arch Masons, in commemoration of an event which took place soon after the commencement of the rebuilding of the Temple by Zerubbabel.

Dispersion of Mankind. The dispersion of mankind at the tower of Babel and on the plain of Shinar, which is recorded in the Book of Genesis, has given rise to a Masonic tradition of the following purport. The knowledge of the great truths of God and immortality were known to Noah, and by him communicated to his immediate descendants, the Noachidæ or Noachites, by whom the true worship continued to be cultivated for some time after the subsidence of the deluge; but when the human race were dispersed, a portion lost sight of the Divine truths which had been communicated to them from their common ancestor, and fell into the most grievous theological errors, corrupting the purity of the worship and the orthodoxy of the religious faith which they had primarily received.

These truths were preserved in their integrity by but a very few in the patriarchal line, while still fewer were enabled to retain only dim and glimmering portions of the true light.

The first class was confined to the direct descendants of Noah, and the second was to be found among the priests and philosophers, and, perhaps, still later, among the poets of the heathen nations, and among those whom they initiated into the secrets of these truths.

The system of doctrine of the former class has been called by Masonic writers the "Pure or Primitive Freemasonry" of antiquity, and that of the latter class the "Spurious Freemasonry" of the same period. These terms were first used by Dr. Oliver, and are intended to refer—the word *pure* to the doctrines taught by the descendants of Noah in the Jewish line, and the word *spurious* to those taught by his descendants in the heathen or Gentile line.

DeMolay, Order of. Founded March 24th, 1919, at Kansas City Missouri, where the International DeMolay Headquarters are maintained. Its founder was Frank S. Land, whose purpose was to promote and maintain a social and fraternal club for boys between the ages of ——— and twenty-one years. Upon attaining the age of twenty-one, a DeMolay automatically ceases to be an active member. The order became popular from its beginning, and in a few years became International in scope.

To become a member of DeMolay, the applicant must be endowed with those finer qualifications of character. He need not be the son of a Freemason. Membership in The Order of DeMolay is by no means a stepping stone into Freemasonry.

The basic principles of the DeMolay ritual, in its initiatory degree, are built on the Seven Cardinal Virtues. These virtues represent the basis of every DeMolay's life.

The DeMolay Degree is historical and spectacular, being presented in dramatic form. Its portrayal of the trials, the tortures and the final martyrdom of Jacques DeMolay, who was Grand Master of the powerful Order of Knights Templar, during the latter part of the Thirteenth Century, in France. This order had been formed during the Twelfth Century, to protect the Christian church, and the Christians on their pilgrimages to Jerusalem. The original need for such an order having passed, but it continued in effect to protect the church, and for the charitable distribution of alms, made it a powerful and influential factor in Europe. DeMolay, on account of his position and activities, was imprisoned by Phillip The Fair, King of France, and with the aid of Clement 12th, Pope of Rome, underwent various, tortures and finally put to death by being burned at the stage, on The Isle de Cite, in the River Seine, in Paris, March 18th, 1314. Any Master Mason in good standing is privileged to attend all DeMolay meetings and witness the degrees.

The entire international organization of the Order of DeMolay is unified and governed by a group of outstanding Masons known as the Grand Council of the Order of DeMolay. The purpose of this body is not only to establish regulations which are for the protection, advancement and benefit of the organization, but to see that the rulings are carried out and the Order benefited and expanded. A Member or a duly appointed Deputy of The Grand Council has direct supervision in each state, province or division thereof established by the Grand Council. To obtain a Charter, the proposed Chapter must be sponsored by representative Masons, locally, who must become responsible for the Chapter activities generally. One representative from each Blue Lodge in town in which the Chapter is located, or other body sponsoring the Chapter, must be appointed. The Chapter is directly under the control of the Chapter "Dad."

The Chapter officers are: Master, Senior and Junior Councilor; Treasurer; Senior and Junior Deacon; Senior and Junior Steward; Chaplain; Almoner; Marshal; Standard Bearer; Orator; First, Second, Third, Fourth, Fifth, Sixth, Seventh Preceptors; Sentinel.

Dormant Lodge. A Lodge whose Charter has not been revoked, but which has ceased to meet and work for a long time, is said to be dormant.

It can be restored to activity only by the authority of the Grand Master or the Grand Lodge on the petition of some of its members, one of whom, at least, ought to be a Past Master.

Dotage. The regulations of Masonry forbid the initiation of an old man in his dotage; and very properly, because the imbecility of his mind would prevent his comprehension of the truths presented to him.

Double Cube. A cubical figure, whose length is equal to twice its breadth and height. Solomon's Temple is said to have been of this figure, and hence it has sometimes been adopted as the symbol of a Masonic Lodge.

Exalted. A candidate is said to be exalted, when he receives the Degree of Holy Royal Arch, the seventh in American Masonry. Exalted means *elevated* or *lifted up,* and is applicable both to a peculiar ceremony of the degree, and to the fact that this degree, in the Rite in which it is practised, constitutes the summit of ancient Masonry.

The rising of the sun of spring from his wintry sleep into the glory of the vernal equinox was called by the old sun-worshipers his "exaltation"; and the Fathers of the Church afterward applied the same term to the resurrection of Christ. St. Athanasius says that by the expression, "God hath exalted him," St. Paul meant the resurrection. Exaltation, therefore, technically means a rising from a lower to a higher sphere, and in Royal Arch Masonry may be supposed to refer to the being lifted up out of the first temple of this life into the second temple of the future life. The candidate is *raised* in the Master's Degree, he is *exalted* in the Royal Arch. In both the symbolic idea is the same.

Elus. The French word *elu* means *elected;* and the degrees, whose object is to detail the detection and punishment of the actors in the crime traditionally related in the Third Degree, are called Elus, or the degrees of the Elected, because they referred to those of the Craft who were chosen or elected to make the discovery, and to inflict the punishment. They form a particular system of Masonry, and are to be found in every Rite, if not in all in name, at least in principle. In the York and American Rites, the Elu is incorporated in the Master's Degree; in the French Rite it constitutes an independent degree; and in the Scottish Rite it consists of three degrees, the Ninth, Tenth, and Eleventh. Ragon counts the five preceding degrees among the Elus, but they more properly belong to the Order of Masters. The symbolism of these Elu degrees has been greatly mistaken and perverted by anti-Masonic writers, who have thus attributed to Masonry a spirit of vengeance which is not its characteristic. They must be looked upon as conveying only a symbolic meaning. Those higher degrees, in which the object of the election is changed and connected with Templarism, are more properly called *Kadoshes.* Thory says that all the Elus are derived from the degree of Kadosh, which preceded them. The reverse, we think, is the truth. The Elu system sprang naturally from the Master's Degree, and was only applied to Templarism when De Molay was substituted for Hiram the Builder.

Emanation. Literally, "a flowing forth." The doctrine of emanations was a theory predominant in many of the Oriental religions, such, especially, as Brahmanism and Parseeism, and subsequently adopted by the Kabbalists and the Gnostics, and taught by Philo and Plato. It assumed that all things emanated, flowed forth (which is the literal meaning of the word), or were developed and descended by degrees from the Supreme Being. Thus, in the ancient religion of India, the *anima mundi*, or soul of the word, the mysterious source of all life, was identified with Brahma, the Supreme God. The doctrine of Gnosticism was that all beings emanated from the Deity; that there was a progressive degeneration of these beings from the highest to the lowest emanation, and a final redemption and return of all to the purity of the Creator. Philo taught that the Supreme Being was the Primitive Light or the Archetype of Light, whose rays illuminate, as from a common source, all souls. The theory of emanations is interesting to the Mason, because of the reference in many of the higher degrees to the doctrines of Philo, the Gnostics, and the Kabbalists.

Emanuel. A sacred word in some of the high degrees, being one of the names applied in Scripture to the Lord Jesus Christ. It is a Greek form from the Hebrew, Immanual, עמנואל, and signifies "God is with us."

Emeritus. Latin; plural, *emeriti*. The Romans applied this word —which comes from the verb *emerere*, to gain by service—to a soldier who had served out his time; hence, in the Supreme Councils of the Ancient and Accepted Scottish Rite of this country, an active member, who resigns his seat by reason of age, infirmity, or for other cause deemed good by the Council, may be elected an Emeritus member, and will possess the privilege of proposing measures and being heard in debate, but not of voting.

Emeth. Hebrew. One of the words in the high degrees. It signifies *integrity, fidelity, firmness*, and constancy in keeping a promise, and especially TRUTH, as opposed to falsehood. In the Scottish Rite, the Sublime Knights Elect of Twelve of the Eleventh Degree are called "Princes Emeth," which mean simply men of exalted character who are devoted to truth.

Eminent. The title given to the Commander or presiding officer of a Commandery of Knights Templar, and to all officers below the Grand Commander in a Grand Commandery. The Grand Commander is styled "Right Eminent," and the Grand Master of the Grand Encampment of the United States, "Most Eminent." The word is from the Latin *eminens*, "standing above," and literally signifies "exalted in rank." Hence, it is a title given to the cardinals in the Roman Church.

Emounah. (*Fidelity, Truth.*) The name of the Fourth Step of the mystic ladder of the Kadosh of the A. A. Scottish Rite.

Emunah. **אמונה.** Sometimes spelled *Amunah,* but not in accordance with the Masoretic points. A significant word in the high degrees signifying fidelity, especially in fulfilling one's promises.

Encampment. All regular assemblies of Knights Templar were formerly called Encampments. They are now styled Commanderies in America, and Grand Encampments of the States are called Grand Commanderies. In England they are now called "Preceptories." (See *Commandery* and *Commandery, Grand.*)

Encampment, General Grand. The title, before the adoption of the Constitution of 1856, of the Grand Encampment of the United States.

Encampment, Grand. The Grand Encampment of the United States was instituted on the 22d of June, 1816, in the city of New York. It consists of a Grand Master, Deputy Grand Master, and other Grand Officers who are similar to those of a Grand Commandery, with Past Grand Officers and the representatives of the various Grand Commanderies, and of the subordinate Commanderies deriving their warrants immediately from it. It exercises jurisdiction over all the Templars of the United States, and meets triennially. The term Encampment is borrowed from military usage, and is very properly applied to the temporary congregation at stated periods of the army of Templars, who may be said to be, for the time being, in camp.

Encyclical. Circular; sent to many places or persons. Encyclical letters, containing information, advice, or admonition, are sometimes issued by Grand Lodges or Grand Masters to the Lodges and Masons of a jurisdiction. The word is not in very common use; but in 1848 the Grand Lodge of South Carolina issued "an encyclical letter of advice, of admonition, and of direction," to the subordinate Lodges under her jurisdiction; and a similar letter was issued in 1865 by the Grand Master of Iowa.

Extended Wings of the Cherubim. An expression used in the ceremonies of Royal Master, the Tenth Degree of the American Rite, and intended to teach symbolically that he who comes to ask and to seek Divine Truth symbolized by the True Word, should begin by placing himself under the protection of that Divine Power who alone is Truth, and from whom alone Truth can be obtained. Of him the cherubim with extended wings in the Holy of Holies were a type.

The candidate in the degree of Royal Master of the American Rite is said to be received "beneath the extended wings of the cherubim." The expression is derived from the passage in the 1st Book of Kings (vi. 27), which describes the setting of "the cherubim within the inner house." Practically, there is an anachronism in the reference to the cherubim in this degree. In the older and purer ritual, the ceremonies are supposed to take place in the council-chamber or private apartment of King Solomon, where, of course, there were no cherubim. And even in some more modern rituals, where a part of the ceremony referred to in the tradition is said to have occurred in the Holy of Holies, that part of the Temple was at that time unfinished, and the cherubim had not yet been placed there. But symbolically the reference to the cherubim in this degree, which represents a searcher for truth, is not objectionable. For although there is a great diversity of opinion as to their exact signification, yet there is a very general agreement that, under some one manifestation or another, they allude to and symbolize the protecting and overshadowing power of the Deity. When, therefore, the initiate is received *beneath the extended wings of the cherubim,* we are taught by this symbolism how appropriate it is, that he who comes to ask and to seek Truth, symbolized by the True Word, should begin by placing himself under the protection of that Divine Power who alone is Truth, and from whom alone truth can be obtained.

Faith. In the theological ladder, the explanation of which forms a part of the ritual of the First Degree of Masonry, *faith,* is said to typify the lowest round. Faith, here, is synonymous with *confidence* or *trust,* and hence we find merely a repetition of the lesson which had been previously taught that the first, the essential qualification of a candidate for initiation, is that he should *trust in God.*

In the lecture of the same degree, it is said that "Faith may be lost in sight; Hope ends in fruition; but Charity extends beyond the grave, through the boundless realms of eternity." And this is said, because as faith is "the evidence of things not seen," when we see we no longer believe by faith but through demonstration; and as hope lives only in the expectation of possession, it ceases to exist when the object once hoped for is at length enjoyed, but charity, exercised on earth in acts of mutual kindness and forbearance, is still found in the world to come.

Field Lodge, or Army Lodge. A lodge duly instituted under proper authority from a grand body of competent jurisdiction, and authorized to exercise during its peripatetic existence all the powers and privileges that it might possess if permanently located. Charters of this nature, as the name implies, are intended for the tented field, and have been of the greatest service to humanity in its trying hours, when the worst of passions are appealed to.

Fifteen. A sacred number symbolic of the name of God, because the letters of the holy name, JAH, are equal, in the Hebrew mode of numeration by the letters of the alphabet, to fifteen; for י is equal to ten, and ה is equal to five. Hence, from veneration for this sacred name, the Hebrews do not, in ordinary computations, when they wish to express the number fifteen, make use of these two letters, but of two others, which are equivalent to nine and six.

Five. Among the Pythagoreans *five* was a mystical number, because it was formed by the union of the first even number and the first odd, rejecting unity; and hence it symbolized the mixed conditions of order and disorder, happiness and misfortune, life and death. The same union of the odd and even, or male and female, numbers made it the symbol of marriage. Among the Greeks it was a symbol of the world, because, says Diodorus, it represented ether and the four elements. It was a sacred round number among the Hebrews. In Egypt, India, and other Oriental nations, says Gesenius, the five minor planets and the five elements and elementary powers were accounted sacred. It was the pentas of the Gnostics and the Hermetic Philosophers; it was the symbol of their quintessence, the fifth or highest essence of power in a natural body. In Masonry, five is a sacred number, inferior only in importance to three and seven. It is especially significant in the Fellow-Craft's Degree, where five are required to hold a Lodge, and where, in the winding stairs, the five steps are referred to the orders of architecture and the human senses. In the Third Degree, we find the reference to the five points of fellowship and their symbol, the five-pointed star. Geometry, too, which is deemed synonymous with Masonry, is called the fifth science; and, in fact, throughout nearly all the degrees of Masonry, we find abundant allusions to five as a sacred and mystical number.

Five-Pointed Star. The five-pointed star, which is not to be confounded with the blazing star, is not found among the old symbols of Masonry; indeed, some writers have denied that it is a Masonic emblem at all. It is undoubtedly of recent origin, and was probably introduced by Jeremy Cross, who placed it among the plates in the emblems of the Third Degree prefixed to his *Hieroglyphic Chart.* It is not mentioned in the ritual or the lecture of the Third Degree, but the Masons of this country have, by tacit consent, referred to it as a symbol of the Five Points of Fellowship. The outlines of the five-pointed star are the same as those of the pentalpha of Pythagoras, which was the symbol of health. M. Jomard, in his *Description de l'Egypte* (tom. viii., p. 423), says that the star engraved on the Egyptian monuments, where it is a very common hieroglyphic, has constantly five points, never more nor less.

Formula. A prescribed mode or form of doing or saying anything. The word is derived from the technical language of the Roman law, where, after the old legal actions had been abolished, suits were practised according to certain prescribed forms called *formulæ.*

Formulas in Freemasonry are very frequent. They are either oral or monitorial. Oral formulas are those that are employed in various parts of the ritual, such as the opening and closing of a Lodge, the investiture of a candidate, etc. From the fact of their oral transmission they are frequently corrupted or altered, which is one of the most prolific sources of non-conformity so often complained of by Masonic teachers. Monitorial formulas are those that are committed to writing, and are to be found in the various monitors and manuals. They are such as relate to public installations, to laying foundation-stones, to dedications of halls, to funerals, etc. Their monitorial character ought to preserve them from change; but uniformity is not even here always attained, owing to the whims of the compilers of manuals or of monitors, who have often unnecessarily changed the form of words from the original standard.

Forty-Seventh Problem. The forty-seventh problem of Euclid's first book, which has been adopted as a symbol in the Master's Degree, is thus enunciated: "In any right-angled triangle, the square which is described upon the side subtending the right angle is equal to the squares described upon the sides which contain the right angle." Thus, in a triangle whose perpendicular is 3 feet, the square of which is 9, and whose base is 4 feet, the square of which is 16, the hypothenuse, or subtending side, will be 5 feet, the square of which will be 25, which is the sum of 9 and 16. This interesting problem, on account of its great utility in making calculations and drawing plans for buildings, is sometimes called the "Carpenter's Theorem."

For the demonstration of this problem the world is indebted to Pythagoras, who, it is said, was so elated after making the discovery, that he made an offering of a hecatomb, or a sacrifice of a hundred oxen, to the gods. The devotion to learning which this religious act indicated in the mind of the ancient philosopher has induced Masons to adopt the problem as a memento, instructing them to be lovers of the arts and sciences.

The triangle, whose base is 4 parts, whose perpendicular is 3, and whose hypothenuse is 5, and which would exactly serve for a demonstration of this problem, was, according to Plutarch, a symbol frequently employed by the Egyptian priests, and hence it is called by M. Jomard, in his *Exposition du Système Métrique des Anciens Egyptiens,* the Egyptian triangle. It was, with the Egyptians, the symbol of universal nature, the base representing Osiris, or the male principle; the perpendicular, Isis, or the female principle; and the hypothenuse, Horus, their son, or the product of the two principles. They added that 3 was the first perfect odd number, that 4 was the square of 2, the first even number, and that 5 was the result of 3 and 2.

But the Egyptians made a still more important use of this triangle. It was the standard of all their measures of extent, and was applied by them to the building of the pyramids. The researches of M. Jomard, on the Egyptian system of measures, published in the magnificent work of the French savants on Egypt, has placed us completely in possession of the uses made by the Egyptians of this forty-seventh problem of Euclid, and of the triangle which formed the diagram by which it was demonstrated.

If we inscribe within a circle a triangle, whose perpendicular shall be 300 parts, whose base shall be 400 parts, and whose hypothenuse shall be 500 parts, which, of course, bear the same proportion to each other as 3, 4, and 5; then if we let a perpendicular fall from the angle of the perpendicular and base to the hypothenuse, and extend it through the hypothenuse to the circumference of the circle, this cord or line will be equal to 480 parts, and the two segments of the hypothenuse, on each side of it, will be found equal, respectively, to 180 and 320. From the point where this chord intersects the hypothenuse let another line fall perpendicularly to the shortest side of the triangle, and this line will be equal to 144 parts, while the shorter segment, formed by its junction with the perpendicular side of the triangle, will be equal to 108 parts. Hence, we may derive the following measures from the diagram: 500, 480, 400, 320, 180, 144, and 108, and all these without the slightest fraction. Supposing, then, the 500 to be cubits, we have the measure of the base of the great pyramid of Memphis. In the 400 cubits of the base of the triangle we have the exact length of the Egyptian stadium. The 320 gives us the exact number of Egyptian cubits contained in the Hebrew and Babylonian stadium. The stadium of Ptolemy is represented by the 480 cubits, or length of the line falling from the right angle to the circumference of the circle, through the hypothenuse. The number 180, which expresses the smaller segment of the hypothenuse being doubled, will give 360 cubits, which will be the stadium of Cleomedes. By doubling the 144, the result will be 288 cubits, or the length of the stadium of Archimedes; and by doubling the 108, we produce 216 cubits, or the precise value of the lesser Egyptian stadium. In this manner, we obtain from this triangle all the measures of length that were in use among the Egyptians; and since this triangle, whose sides are equal to 3, 4, and 5, was the very one that most naturally would be used in demonstrating the forty-seventh problem of Euclid; and since by these three sides the Egyptians symbolized Osiris, Isis, and Horus, or the two producers and the product, the very principle, expressed in symbolic language, which constitutes the terms of the problem as enunciated by Pythagoras, that the sum of the squares of the two sides will produce the square of the third, we have no reason to doubt that the forty-seventh problem was well known to the Egyptian priests, and by them communicated to Pythagoras.

Dr. Lardner, in his edition of Euclid, says: "Whether we consider the forty-seventh proposition with reference to the peculiar and beautiful relation established in it, or to its innumerable uses in every department of mathematical science, or to its fertility in the consequences derivable from it, it must certainly be esteemed the most celebrated and important in the whole of the elements, if not in the whole range, of mathematical science. It is by the influence of this proposition, and that which establishes the similitude of equiangular triangles (in the sixth book), that geometry has been brought under the dominion of algebra; and it is upon the same principles that the whole science of trigonometry is founded.

"The XXXIId and XLVIIth propositions are said to have been discovered by Pythagoras, and extraordinary accounts are given of his exultation upon his first perception of their truth. It is, however, supposed by some that Pythagoras acquired a knowledge of them in Egypt, and was the first to make them known in Greece."

Fourfold Cord. In the ritual of the Past Master's Degree in America we find the following expression: "A twofold cord is strong, a threefold cord is stronger, but a fourfold cord is not easily broken." The expression is taken from a Hebrew proverb which is to be found in the Book of Ecclesiastes (iv. 12): "And if one prevail against him, two shall withstand him; and a threefold cord is not quickly broken." The form of the Hebrew proverb has been necessarily changed to suit the symbolism of the degree.

Gabaon. A significant word in the high degrees. Oliver says (*Landm.*, i., 335), "in philosophical Masonry, heaven, or, more correctly speaking, *the third heaven,* is denominated Mount Gabaon, which is feigned to be accessible only by the seven degrees that compose the winding staircase. These are the degrees terminating in the Royal Arch." *Gabaon* is defined to signify "a high place." It is the Septuagint and Vulgate form of גבעון, *Gibeon,* which was the city in which the tabernacle was stationed during the reigns of David and Solomon. The word means *a city built on a hill,* and is referred to in 2 Chron. i. 3. "So Solomon, and all the congregation with him, went to the high place that was at Gibeon; for there was the tabernacle of the congregation of God."

In a ritual of the middle of the last century, it is said that Gabanon is the name of a Master Mason. This word is a striking evidence of the changes which Hebrew words have undergone in their transmission to Masonic rituals, and of the almost impossibility of tracing them to their proper root. It would seem difficult to find a connection between *Gabanon* and any known Hebrew word. But if we refer to Guillemain's *Ritual of Adonhiramite Masonry,* we will find the following passage:

"*Q.* How is a Master called?

"*A.* Gabaon, which is the name of the place where the Israelites deposited the ark in the time of trouble.

"*Q.* What does this signify?

"*A.* That the heart of a Mason ought to be pure enough to be a temple suitable for God." (P. 95.)

There is abundant internal evidence that these two rituals came from a common source, and that *Gabaon* is a French distortion, as *Gabanon* is an English one, of some unknown word—connected, however, with the Ark of the Covenant as the place where that article was deposited.

Now, we learn from the Jewish records that the Philistines, who had captured the ark, deposited it "in the house of Abinadad that was in Gibeah"; and that David, subsequently recapturing it, carried it to Jerusalem, but left the tabernacle at Gibeon. The ritualist did not remember that the tabernacle at Gibeon was without the ark, but supposed that it was still in that sacred shrine. Hence, *Gabaon* or *Gabanon* must have been corrupted from either *Gibeah* or *Gibeon*, because the ark was considered to be at some time in both places. But Gibeon had already been corrupted by the Septuagint and the Vulgate versions into *Gabaon;* and this undoubtedly is the word from which *Gabanon* is derived, through either the Septuagint or the Vulgate, or perhaps from Josephus, who calls it *Gabao.*

Gabaonne. In French Masonic language, the widow of a Master Mason. Derived from *Gabaon.*

Gabor. Heb., גבר, *strong.* A significant word in the high degrees.

Gabriel. Heb., גבריאל, *a man of God.* The name of one of the archangels, referred to in some of the high degrees. He interpreted to Daniel the vision of the ram and the he-goat, and made the prophecy of the "seventy weeks" (Dan. viii. and ix.); he announced the future appearance of the Messiah (Dan. ix. 21, 27). In the New Testament he foretold to Zacharias the birth of John the Baptist (Luke i. 19), and to Mary the birth of Christ (Luke i. 26). Among the Rabbis Gabriel is entrusted with the care of the souls of the dead, and is represented as having taught Joseph the seventy languages spoken at Babel. In addition, he was the only angel who could speak Chaldee and Syriac. The *Talmud* speaks of him as the Prince of Fire, the Spirit presiding over thunder. The Mohammedans term him the Spirit of Truth, and believe that he dictated the *Koran* to Mohammed.

The Garden of Eden. There was a tradition of the Garden of Eden long before the time of Jesus, and they used to try to find an actual location that would fit the allegorical description of one fruitful river flowing into the Garden, and four rivers flowing out. A philosopher and scholar named Philo (the Jew), who lived in Jesus' time (20 B.C. to 40 A.D.) was perhaps the first to consider the tradition to be an allegory. He maintained, 1700 years before the founding of the administrative structure of modern Masonry, that Eden was a soul, delighting in virtue, and the four rivers were the four specific virtues of prudence, temperance, courage and justice. Any Mason will instantly recognize these allegorical references.

Genesis ii. 15. And the Lord God (Jehovah) took the man, and put him into the Garden of Eden, to dress it and to keep it. The name Eden, means pleasure, delight.

G. O. D. The initials of Gomer, Oz, Dabar. It is a singular coincidence, and worthy of thought, that the letters composing the English name of Deity should be the initials of the Hebrew words wisdom, strength, and beauty; the three great pillars, or metaphorical supports, of Masonry. They seem to present almost the only reason that can reconcile a Mason to the use of the initial "G" in its conspicuous suspension in the East of the Lodge in place of the Delta. The incident seems to be more than an accident.

דבר	Dabar,	Wisdom, D.
עז	Oz,	Strength, O.
גמר	Gomer,	Beauty, G.

Thus the initials conceal the true meaning.

Golden Candlestick. The golden candlestick which was made by Moses for the service of the tabernacle, and was afterward deposited in the holy place of the temple to throw light upon the altar of incense, and the table of shewbread, was made wholly of pure gold, and had seven branches; that is, three on each side, and one in the center. These branches were at equal distances, and each one was adorned with flowers like lilies, gold knobs after the form of an apple, and similar ones resembling an almond. Upon the extremities of the branches were seven golden lamps, which were fed with pure olive-oil, and lighted every evening by the priests on duty. Its seven branches are explained in the Ineffable degrees as symbolizing the seven planets. It is also used as a decoration in Chapters of the Royal Arch, but apparently without any positive symbolic signification.

Giblim. Heb., גבלם. A significant word in Masonry. It is the plural of the Gentile noun Gibli (the *g* pronounced hard), and means, according to the idiom of the Hebrew, *Giblites,* or inhabitants of the city of Gebal. The Giblim, or Giblites, are mentioned in Scripture as assisting Solomon's and Hiram's builders to prepare the trees and the stones for building the Temple, and from this passage it is evident that they were clever artificers. The passage is in 1 Kings v. 18, and, in our common version, is as follows: "And Solomon's builders and Hiram's builders did hew them, and the stone-squarers; so they prepared timber and stones to build the house," where the word translated in the authorized version by *stone-squarers* is, in the original, *Giblim.* It is so also in that translation known as the *Bishop's Bible.* The Geneva version has *masons.* The French version of Martin has *tailleurs de pierres,* following the English; but Luther, in his German version, retains the original word *Giblim.*

It is probable that the English translation followed the Jewish Targum, which has a word of similar import in this passage. The error has, however, assumed importance in the Masonic ritual, where *Giblim* is supposed to be synonymous with a Mason. And Sir Wm. Drummond confirms this by saying in his *Origines* (vol. iii., b. v., ch. iv., p. 129) that "the Gibalim were Master Masons who put the finishing hand to King Solomon's Temple."

Green. Green, as a Masonic color, is almost confined to the four degrees of Perfect Master, Knight of the East, Knight of the Red Cross, and Prince of Mercy. In the degree of Perfect Master it is a symbol of the moral resurrection of the candidate, teaching him that being dead to vice he should hope to revive in virtue.

In the degree of Knight of the Red Cross, this color is employed as a symbol of the immutable nature of truth, which, like the bay tree, will ever flourish in immortal green.

This idea of the unchanging immortality of that which is divine and true, was always connected by the ancients with the color of green. Among the Egyptians, the god Phtha, the active spirit, the creator and regenerator of the world, the goddess Pascht, the Divine preserver, and Thoth, the instructor of men in the sacred doctrines of truth, were all painted in the hieroglyphic system with green flesh.

Portal says, in his essay on *Symbolic Colors,* that "green was the symbol of victory"; and this reminds us of the motto of the Red Cross Knights, "magna est veritas et prævalebit"—*great is truth and mighty above all things;* and hence green is the symbolic color of that degree.

In the degree of Prince of Mercy, or the Twenty-sixth Degree of the Scottish Rite, green is also symbolic of truth, and is the appropriate color of the degree, because truth is there said to be the palladium of the Order.

In the degree of Knight of the East, in the Ancient and Accepted Scottish Rite, green is also the symbolic color. We may very readily suppose, from the close connection of this degree in its ritual with that of the Companion of the Red Cross, that the same symbolic explanation of the color would apply to both, and I think that such an explanation might very properly be made; but it is generally supposed by its possessors that the green of the Knights of the East alludes to the waters of the river Euphrates, and hence its symbolism is not moral but historical.

The *evergreen* of the Third Degree is to the Master Mason an emblem of immortality. Green was with the Druids a symbol of hope, and the virtue of hope with a Mason illustrates the hope of immortality. In all the Ancient Mysteries, this idea was carried out, and green symbolized the birth of the world, and the moral creation or resurrection of the initiate. If we apply this to the evergreen of the Master Mason we shall again find a resemblance, for the acacia is emblematic of a new creation of the body, and a moral and physical resurrection.

Greeting. This word means salutation, and, under the form of "Thrice Greeting," it is very common at the head of Masonic documents. In the beginning of the last century it was usual at the meeting of Masons to say, "God's good *greeting* be to this our happy meeting." Browne gives the formula as practised in 1800: "The recommendation I bring is from the right worthy and worshipful brothers and fellows of the Holy Lodge of St. John, who *greet* your worship well." This formula is obsolete, but the word *greeting* is still in use among Freemasons. In Masonic documents it is sometimes found in the form of S.˙. S.˙. S.˙., which three letters are the initials of the Latin word *salutem* or *health,* three times repeated, and therefore equivalent to "Thrice Greeting."

High Priest. The presiding officer of a Chapter of Royal Arch Masons according to the American system. His title is "Most Excellent," and he represents Joshua, or Jeshua, who was the son of Josedech, and the High Priest of the Jews when they returned from the Babylonian exile. He is seated in the east, and clothed in the apparel of the ancient High Priest of the Jews. He wears a robe of blue, purple, scarlet, and white linen, and is decorated with a breastplate and miter. On the front of the miter is inscribed the words, "HOLINESS TO THE LORD." His jewel is a miter.

High Priesthood, Order of. This order is an honorarium, to be bestowed upon the High Priest of a Royal Arch Chapter in the United States, and consequently no one is legally entitled to receive it until he has been duly elected to preside as High Priest in a regular Chapter of Royal Arch Masons. It should not be conferred when a less number than three duly qualified High Priests are present. Whenever the ceremony is performed in ample form, the assistance of at least nine High Priests, who have received it, is requisite. The General Grand Chapter of the United States has the Hebrew letters ם and ק inserted upon them. Each side of each triangle should be one inch in length, and may be ornamented at the fancy of the wearer. The breastplate may be plainly engraved or set with stones. It was adopted in 1856, on the suggestion of the author of this work, at a very general but informal meeting of Grand and Past Grand High Priests during the session of the General Grand Chapter held at Hartford, Conn. It is now in general use.

It is impossible, from the want of authentic documents, to throw much light upon the historical origin of this degree. No allusion to it can be found in any ritual works out of America, nor even here anterior to about the end of the last and beginning of this century.

Honorary Degrees. The Supreme Council of the Southern Jurisdiction, U. S. A., has three specific honors that it confers upon meritorious brethren of its Jurisdiction. The first is that of Knight Commander of the Court of Honour, which is officially known as the rank and decoration of Knight Commander of the Court of Honour. When a brother, for meritorious service, has been elected to receive this rank and decoration, immediately he has that title. There is a ceremony of investiture which is optional, but it is usually performed upon those who have been elected to the honor. Let it be distinctly understood that this is not a degree or a part of a degree, nor is the investiture ceremony the conferring of a degree. Two years must elapse after a Mason receives the Thirty Second Degree before he is eligible to be nominated for the rank and decoration of Knight Commander of the Court of Honour, but it is rare that anyone does receive this honor in that short a time.

The next honor is a degree and is designated as the rank and dignity of the Thirty Third Degree Inspector General Honorary. Four years is the minimum that must elapse before a Knight Commander of the

Court of Honour may be nominated to receive the Thirty Third Degree. This degree is conferred as the last feature of the biennial session of the Supreme Council. Those who are unable to come to Washington to receive this degree have it conferred upon them at a later date in their respective jurisdictions. There are more than twice the number of Knights Commander of the Court of Honour elected at each session of the Supreme Council than there are Thirty Third Degree elections, so it is evident that not half of the Knights Commander of the Court of Honour will ever receive the Thirty Third Degree; nevertheless it is a distinctive honor. Not every man who becomes a Master Mason becomes Master of his Lodge, so not every Knight Commander of the Court of Honour receives the Thirty Third Degree. The third honor is that of Grand Cross of the Court of Honour and one must be a Thirty Third Degree Honorary Member of the Supreme Council before he can be nominated for this honor. No more than three can be elected at one session and it is very rare that this is done. This honor is given for extraordinary meritorious service. These honors are given by the Supreme Council for meritorious service and labor. They should not be applied for and, if they are applied or asked for, they must be denied.

All the Active Members of the Supreme Council possess all three honors.

Honorary Degrees. 1. The Mark Master's Degree in the American system is called the "Honorary Degree of Mark Master," because it is traditionally supposed to have been conferred in the Temple upon a portion of the Fellow-Crafts as a mark of honor and of trust. The degrees of Past Master and of High Priesthood are also styled honorary, because each is conferred as an honorarium or reward attendant upon certain offices; that of Past Master upon the elected Master of a Symbolic Lodge, and that of High Priesthood upon the elected High Priest of a Chapter of Royal Arch Masons.

2. Those degrees which are outside of the regular series, and which are more commonly known by the epithet "side degrees," are also sometimes called honorary degrees, because no fee is usually exacted for them.

Honorary Thirty-Thirds. The Supreme Councils of the Ancient and Accepted Scottish Rite in this country have, within a few years past, adopted the custom of electing honorary members, who are sometimes called "Honorary Thirty-Thirds." They possess none of the rights of Inspectors-General or Active Members, except that of being present at the meetings of the Council, taking part to a limited extent in its deliberations, except when it holds an executive session.

Horn of Plenty. The jewel of the Steward of a Lodge. (See *Cornucopia.*)

Horns of the Altar. In the Jewish Temple, the altars of burnt-offering and of incense had each at the four corners four horns of shittim wood. Among the Jews, as well as all other ancient peoples, the altar was considered peculiarly holy and privileged; and hence, when a criminal, fleeing, took hold of these horns, he found an asylum and safety. As the Masonic altar is a representation of the altar of the Solomonic member, it should be constructed with these horns; and Cross has very properly so represented it in his *Hieroglyphic Chart*.

Humility. The Divine Master has said, "He that humbleth himself shall be exalted" (Luke xiv. 2), and the lesson is emphatically taught by a portion of the ritual of the Royal Arch Degree. Indeed, the first step toward the acquisition of truth is a humility of mind which teaches us our own ignorance and our necessity for knowledge, so that thus we may be prepared for its reception. Dr. Oliver has greatly erred in saying (*Landmarks*, ii., 471) that bare feet are a Masonic symbol of humility. They are properly a symbol of reverence. The true Masonic symbol of humility is bodily prostration, and it is so exemplified in the Royal Arch Degree.

Immanuel. A Hebrew word signifying "God with us," from *immanu*, "with us," and *el*, "God." It was the symbolical name given by the prophet Isaiah to the child who was announced to Ahaz and the people of Judah as the sign which God would give of their deliverance from their enemies, and afterward applied by the Apostle Matthew to the Messiah born of the Virgin. As one of the appellations of Christ, it has been adopted as a significant word in modern Templarism, where, however, the form of *Emanuel* is most usually employed.

Internal Qualifications. Those qualifications of a candidate which refer to a condition known only to himself, and which are not patent to the world, are called internal qualifications. They are: 1st. That he comes forward of his own free-will and accord, and unbiased by the solicitations of others. 2d. That he is not influenced by mercenary motives; and, 3rd, That he has a disposition to conform to the usages of the Order. The knowledge of these can only be obtained from his own statements, and hence they are included in the preliminary questions which are proposed before initiation.

Jah. In Hebrew, יה. Maimonides calls it the "two-lettered name," and derives it from the Tetragrammaton, of which he says it is an abbreviation. Others have denied this, and assert that *Jah* is a name independent of Jehovah, but expressing the same idea of the Divine Essence. It is uniformly translated in the authorized version of the Bible by the word LORD, being thus considered as synonymous with Jehovah, except in Psalm lxviii. 4, where the original word is preserved: "Extol him that rideth upon the heavens by his name JAH," upon which the Targum comment is: "Extol him who sitteth on the throne of glory in the ninth heaven; YAH is his name." It seems, also, to have been well known to the Gentile nations as the triliteral name of God; for, although biliteral among the Hebrews, it assumed among the Greeks the triliteral form, as ΙΑΩ. Macrobius, in his *Saturnalia*, says that this was the sacred name of the Supreme Deity; and the Clarian Oracle being asked which of the gods was Jao, replied, "The initiated are bound to conceal the mysterious secrets. Learn thou that ΙΑΩ is the Great God Supreme who ruleth over all." (See *Jehovah.*)

Jesus, Description of the Person of. The following was taken from a manuscript in the possession of Lord Kelly—and in his library—and was from an original letter of Publius Lentullus at Rome. It being the custom of Roman governors to advise the Senate and people of such material things as happened in their province in the days of Liberius Ceasar. Publius Lentullus, president of Judea, wrote the following epistle to the Senate concerning our Savior;

"There appeared in these days a man of great virtue, named Jusus Christ, who is yet living among us, and of the Gentiles is accepted for a prophet of truth, but his own disciples call him the Son of God.

"He raiseth the dead and cures all manner of diseases. A man of stature somewhat tall and comely, with very reverend countenance such as the beholders may love and fear.

"His hair, the color of chestnuts full ripe, plain to the ears whence downward it was more orient, and curling and wavering about his shoulders. In the midst of his head is a seam or partition after the manner of the Nazerites. His forehead, plain and very delicate. His face without a spot or wrinkle—beautiful with a lovely red. His nose and mouth so formed as nothing can be reprehended. His beard thickish—in color like his hair—not very long, but forked.

"His look innocent and mature. His eyes grey—clear and quick.

"In reproving he is terrible—in admonishing courteous. Plain spoken—pleasant in conversation—modest with gravity. It can not be remembered that any have seen him laugh, but many have seen him weep.

"In proportion of body most excellent. His hands and arms most delicate to behold.

"In speaking, very temperate, modest and wise. A man for his singular beauty, surpassing the children of men."

Jerusalem, New. The symbolic name of the Christian church (Rev. xxi. 2–21; iii. 12). The Apostle John (Rev. xxi.), from the summit of a high mountain, beheld, in a pictorial symbol or scenic representation, a city resplendent with celestial brightness, which seemed to descend from the heavens to the earth. It was stated to be a square of about 400 miles, or 12,000 stadia, equal to about 16,000 miles in circumference—of course, a mystical number, denoting that the city was capable of holding almost countless myriads of inhabitants. The New Jerusalem was beheld, like Jacob's ladder, extending from earth to heaven. It plays an important part in the ritual of the Nineteenth Degree, or Grand Pontiff of the Ancient and Accepted Scottish Rite, where the descent of the New Jerusalem is a symbol of the descent of the empire of Light and Truth upon the earth.

Jesuits. In the last century the Jesuits were charged with having an intimate connection with Freemasonry, and the invention of the degree of Kadosh was even attributed to those members of the Society who constituted the College of Clermont. This theory of a Jesuitical Masonry seems to have originated with the Illuminati, who were probably governed in its promulgation by a desire to depreciate the character of all other Masonic systems in comparison with their own, where no such priestly interference was permitted. Barruel scoffs at the idea of such a connection, and calls it (*Hist. de Ja.*, iv., 287) "la fable de la Franc-Maçonnerie Jésuitique." For once he is right. Like oil and water, the tolerance of Freemasonry and the intolerance of the "Society of Jesus" cannot commingle.

Yet it cannot be denied that, while the Jesuits have had no part in the construction of pure Freemasonry, there are reasons for believing that they took an interest in the invention of some degrees and systems which were intended to advance their own interests. But wherever they touched the Institution they left the trail of the serpent. They sought to convert its pure philanthropy and toleration into political intrigue and religious bigotry. Hence it is believed that they had something to do with the invention of those degrees, which were intended to aid the exiled house of Stuart in its efforts to regain the English throne, because they believed that would secure the restoration in England of the Roman Catholic religion. Almost a library of books has been written on both sides of this subject in Germany and in France.

Jews, Disqualification of. The great principles of religious and political toleration which peculiarly characterize Freemasonry would legitimately make no religious faith which recognized a Supreme Being a disqualification for initiation. But, unfortunately, these principles have not always been regarded, and from an early period the German Lodges, and especially the Prussian, were reluctant to accord admission to Jews. This action has given great offense to the Grand Lodges of other countries which were more liberal in their views, and were more in accord with the Masonic spirit, and was productive of dissensions among the Masons of Germany, many of whom were opposed to this intolerant policy. But a better spirit now prevails; and very recently the Grand Lodge of the Three Globes at Berlin, the leading Masonic body of Prussia, has removed the interdict, and Judaism is there no longer a disqualification for initiation.

Jerusalem. The capital of Judea, and memorable in Masonic history as the place where was erected the Temple of Solomon. It is early mentioned in Scripture, and is supposed to be the Salem of which Melchizedek was king. At the time that the Israelites entered the Promised Land, the city was in possession of the Jebusites, from whom, after the death of Joshua, it was conquered, and afterward inhabited by the tribes of Judah and Benjamin. The Jebusites were not, however, driven out;

and we learn that David purchased Mount Moriah from Ornan or Araunah the Jebusite as a site for the Temple. It is only in reference to this Temple that Jerusalem is connected with the legends of Ancient Craft Masonry. In the degrees of chivalry it is also important, because it was the city where the holy places were situated, and for the possession of which the Crusaders so long and so bravely contested. It was there, too, that the Templars and the Hospitalers were established as Orders of religious and military knighthood.

Modern Speculative Masonry was introduced into Jerusalem by the establishment of a Lodge in 1872, the warrant for which, on the application of Robert Morris and others, was granted by the Grand Lodge of Canada. Recently a Lodge has been warranted in England to meet at Chester, but to be in due course removed to Jerusalem, named "King Solomon's Temple," No. 3464.

Jewish Rites and Ceremonies. A period of excitement in favor of the rites of Judaism centered upon and pervaded the people of various nations during the early portion of the fourteenth century. The ceremonies grew and took fast hold upon the minds of the Romans, and, combining with their forms, spread to Constantinople and northwest to Germany and France. The Jewish rites, traditions, and legends thus entered the mystic schools. It was during this period that the legend of Hiram first became known (Bro. G. H. Fort), and Jehovah's name, and mystic forms were transmitted from Byzantine workmen to Teutonic sodalities and German gilds. Thus, also, when the Christian enthusiasm pervaded the North, Paganism gave way, and the formal toasts at the ceremonial banquets were drunk in the name of the saints in lieu of those of the Pagan gods.

Josephus, Flavius. A Jewish author who lived in the first century, and wrote in Greek, among other works, a *History of the Jews,* to which recourse has been had in some of the high degrees, such as the Prince of Jerusalem, and Knight of the Red Cross, or Red Cross of Babylon, for details in framing their rituals.

Joshua. The high priest who, with Zerubbabel the Prince of Judah, superintended the rebuilding of the Temple after the Babylonian captivity. He was the high priest by lineal descent from the pontifical family, for he was the son of Josadek, who was the son of Seraiah, who was the high priest when the Temple was destroyed by the Chaldeans. He was distinguished for the zeal with which he prosecuted the work of rebuilding, and opposed the interference of the Samaritans. He is represented by the High Priest in the Royal Arch Degree according to the York and American Rites.

Knight Commander of the Court of Honor. The Court of Honor is an honorary body between the Thirty Second and the Thirty Third Degrees of the Southern Jurisdiction of the United States of America, Ancient and Accepted Scottish Rite. It was established to confer honor on certain Brethren whose zeal and work for the Scottish Rite Freemasonry entitled them to recognition. This Court of Honor is composed of all Thirty Third Degree Masons, whether active or honorary, and also such Thirty Second Degree Masons as the Supreme Council may select. In the Court of Honor there are two ranks, that of Knight Commander and that of Grand Cross. Only three Grand Crosses can be selected at each regular session of the Supreme Council. Each active Thirty Third Degree member may nominate one Thirty Second Degree member for the honor and decoration of Knight Commander. In addition, he is entitled to nominate for this honor one Thirty Second Degree member for every forty Fourteenth Degree Masons made in his Jurisdiction since the preceding regular session of the Supreme Council. The rank of Knight Commander or Grand Cross cannot be applied for, and if applied for, must be refused. The Court of Honor assembles as a body when called together by the Grand Commander, and is presided over by the Grand Cross named by the Grand Commander.

Knight of the Brazen Serpent. The Twenty Fifth Degree of the Ancient and Accepted Scottish Rite. The history of this Degree is founded upon the circumstances related in Numbers xxl 6–9, which see.

Knight of the East and West. The Seventeenth Degree of the Ancient and Accepted Scottish Rite. The oldest instructions of the Degree were very imperfect, and did not connect it with Freemasonry. Its legend would most probably indicate that the Degree originated with the Templar system of Ramsay.

Knight Kadosh, formerly called Grand Èlect Knight Kadosh. (*Grand Elu du Chevalier Kadosch.*) The Knight Kadosh is the Thirtieth Degree of the Ancient and Accepted Scottish Rite, called also Knight of the White and Black Eagle. While retaining the general Templar doctrine of the Kadosh system, it symbolizes and humanizes the old lesson of vengeance. It is the most popular of all the Kadoshes.

In the Knight Kadosh of the Ancient and Accepted Scottish Rite, the meetings are called Councils. The principal officers are, according to the recent rituals, a Commander, two Lieutenant Commanders, called also Prior and Preceptor; a Chancellor, Orator, Almoner, Recorder, and Treasurer. The jewel, as described in the ritual of the Southern Supreme Council, is a double-headed eagle, displayed resting on a teutonic cross, the eagle silver, the cross gold enameled red. The Northern Council uses instead of the eagle the letters J. B. M. The Kadoshes, as representatives of the Templars, adopt the Beauseant as their standard. In this degree, as in all the other Kadoshes, we find the mystical ladder of seven steps.

Knight of Malta, Masonic. The degree of Knight of Malta is conferred in the United States as "an appendant Order" in a Commandery of Knights Templar. There is a ritual attached to the degree, but very few are in possession of it, and it is generally communicated after the candidate has been created a Knights Templar; the ceremony consisting generally only in the reading of the passage of Scripture prescribed in the Monitors, and the communication of the modes of recognition.

How anything so anomalous in history as the commingling in one body of Knights Templar and Knights of Malta, and making the same person a representative of both Orders, first arose, it is now difficult to determine. It was, most probably, a device of Thomas S. Webb, and was, it may be supposed, one of the results of a too great fondness for the accumulation of degrees. Mitchell, in his *History of Freemasonry* (ii., 83), says: "The degree, so called, of Malta, or St. John of Jerusalem, crept in, we suppose, by means of a bungler, who, not knowing enough of the ritual to confer it properly, satisfied himself by simply adding a few words in the ceremony of dubbing; and thus, by the addition of a few signs and words but imperfectly understood, constituted a Knights Templar also a Knight of Malta, and so the matter stands to this day." I am not generally inclined to place much confidence in Mitchell as an historian; yet I cannot help thinking that in this instance his guess is not very far from the truth, although, as usual with him, there is a tinge of exaggeration in his statement.

There is evidence that the degree was introduced at a very early period into the Masonry of this country. In the Constitution of the "United States Grand Encampment," adopted in 1805, one section enumerates "Encampments of Knights of Malta, Knights Templars, and Councils of Knights of the Red Cross," now Companions of the Red Cross. It will be observed that the Knight of Malta precedes the Knights Templar; whereas, in the present system, the former is made the ultimate degree of the series. Yet, in this Constitution, no further notice is taken of the degree; for while the fees for the Red Cross and the Templar degrees are prescribed, there is no reference to any to be paid for that of Malta. In the revised Constitution of 1816, the order of the series was changed to Red Cross, Templar, and Malta, which arrangement has ever since been maintained. The Knights of Malta are designated as one of the "Appendant Orders," a title and a subordinate position which the pride of the old Knights of Malta would hardly have permitted them to accept.

In 1856, the Knights Templar of the United States had become convinced that the incorporation of the Order of Malta with the Knights Templar, and making the same person the possessor of both Orders, was so absurd a violation of all historic truth, that at the session of the General Grand Encampment in that year, at Hartford, Connecticut, on the suggestion of the author, the degree was unanimously stricken from the Constitution; but at the session of 1862, in Columbus, Ohio, it was, I think, without due consideration, restored, and is now communicated in the Commanderies of Knights Templar.

There is no fact in history better known than that there existed from their very birth a rivalry between the two Orders of the Temple and of

St. John of Jerusalem, which sometimes burst forth into open hostility. Porter says (*Hist. K. of Malta,* i., 107), speaking of the dissensions of the two Orders, "instead of confining their rivalry to a friendly emulation, whilst combating against their common foe, they appeared more intent upon thwarting and frustrating each other, than in opposing the Saracens."

To such an extent had the quarrels of the two Orders proceeded, that Pope Alexander III. found it necessary to interfere; and in 1179 a hollow truce was signed by the rival houses of the Temple and the Hospital; the terms of which were, however, never strictly observed by either side. On the dissolution of the Templars so much of their possessions as were not confiscated to public use were given by the sovereigns of Europe to the Knights of Malta, who accepted the gift without compunction. And there is a tradition that the surviving Templars, indignant at the spoliation and at the mercenary act of their old rivals in willingly becoming a party to the robbery, solemnly registered a vow never thereafter to recognize them as friends.

The attempt at this day to make a modern Knights Templar accept initiation into a hated and antagonistic Order is to display a lamentable ignorance of the facts of history.

Another reason why the degree of Knight of Malta should be rejected from the Masonic system is that the ancient Order never was a secret association. Its rites of reception were open and public, wholly unlike anything in Masonry. In fact, historians have believed that the favor shown to the Hospitalers, and the persecutions waged against the Templars, are to be attributed to the fact that the latter Order had a secret system of initiation which did not exist in the former. The ritual of reception, the signs and words as modes of recognition now practised in the modern Masonic ceremonial, are all a mere invention of a very recent date. The old Knights knew nothing of such a system.

A third, and perhaps the best, reason for rejecting the Knights of Malta as a Masonic degree is to be found in the fact that the Order still exists, although in a somewhat decayed condition; and that its members, claiming an uninterrupted descent from the Knights who, with Hompesch, left the island of Malta in 1797, and threw themselves under the protection of Paul of Russia, utterly disclaim any connection with the Freemasons, and almost contemptuously repudiate the so-called Masonic branch of the Order. In 1858, a manifesto was issued by the supreme authority of the Order, dated from "the Magisterial Palace of the Sacred Order" at Rome, which, after stating that the Order, as it then existed, consisted only of the Grand Priories in the Langues of Italy and Germany, the knights in Prussia, who trace descent from the Grand Bailiwick of Brandenburg, and a few other knights who had been legally received by the Mastership and Council, declares that:

"Beyond and out of the above-mentioned Langues and Priories, and excepting the knights created and constituted as aforesaid, all those who may so call or entitle themselves *are legally ignored* by our Sacred Order."

There is no room there provided for the so-called Masonic Knights of Malta. But a writer in *Notes and Queries* (3d Ser., iii., 413), who professes to be in possession of the degree, says, in reply to an inquiry, that the Masonic degree "has nothing whatever to do with the Knights Hospitalers of St. John of Jerusalem." This is most undoubtedly true in reference to the American degree. Neither in its form, its ritual, the objects it professes, its tradition, nor its historical relations, is it in the slightest degree assimilated to the ancient Order of Hospitalers, afterward called Knights of Rhodes, and, finally, Knights of Malta. To claim, therefore, to be the modern representatives of that Order, to wear its dress, to adopt its insignia, to flaunt its banners, and to leave the world to believe that the one is but the uninterrupted continuation of the other, are acts which must be regarded as a very ridiculous assumption, if not actually entitled to a less courteous appellation.

For all these reasons, I think that it is much to be regretted that the action of the Grand Encampment in repudiating the degree in 1856 was reversed in 1862. The degree has no historical or traditional connection with Masonry; holds no proper place in a Commandery of Templars, and ought to be wiped out of the catalogue of Masonic degrees.*

Knight of St. Andrew, Grand Scottish. (*Grand Ecossais de Saint André.*) Sometimes called "Patriarch of the Crusades." The Twenty-ninth Degree of the Ancient and Accepted Scottish Rite. Its ritual is founded on a legend, first promulgated by the Chevalier Ramsay, to this effect: that the Freemasons were originally a society of knights founded in Palestine for the purpose of building Christian churches; that the Saracens, to prevent the execution of this design, sent emissaries among them, who disguised themselves as Christians, and were continually throwing obstacles in their way; that on discovering the existence of these spies, the knights instituted certain modes of recognition to serve as the means of detection; that they also adopted symbolic ceremonies for the purpose of instructing the proselytes who had entered the society in the forms and principles of their new religion; and finally, that the Saracens, having become too powerful for the knights any longer to con-

* A different view is now generally held by Templars regarding the Knights of Malta, and a modified ritual has been adopted from the Canadian work where the Malta is the principal degree of their Priories. The adoption of this ritual among the Commanderies of America is optional, but when once adopted must be conformed to in their work. This change was brought about by the visiting influence from Canada and also the reasons for the Malta being a degree of chivalry. For a similar reason the Knights of the Red Cross has been justly changed to Companion of the Red Cross, and properly never deserved a place in the degrees of chivalry, as the ritual plainly shows. [E. E. C.]

tend with them, they had accepted the invitation of a king of England, and had removed into his dominions, where they thenceforth devoted themselves to the cultivation of architecture and the fine arts. On this mythical legend, which in reality was only an application of Ramsay's theory of the origin of Freemasonry, the Baron de Tschoudy is said, about the middle of the last century, to have formed this degree, which Ragon says (*Orthod. Maçon.*, p. 138) at his death, in 1769, he bequeathed in manuscript to the Council of Emperors of the East and West. On the subsequent extension of the twenty-five degrees of the Rite of Perfection, instituted by that body, to the thirty-three degrees of the Ancient and Accepted Rite, this degree was adopted as the twenty-ninth, and as an appropriate introduction to the Knights of Kadosh, which it immediately precedes. Hence the jewel, a St. Andrew's cross, is said, by Ragon, to be only a concealed form of the Templar Cross. In allusion to the time of its supposed invention, it has been called "Patriarch of the Crusades." On account of the Masonic instruction which it contains, it also sometimes receives the title of "Grand Master of Light."

The Lodge is decorated with red hangings supported by white columns. There are eighty-one lights, arranged as follows: four in each corner before a St. Andrew's cross, two before the altar, and sixty-three arranged by nines in seven different parts of the room. There are three officers, a Venerable Grand Master and two Wardens. The jewel is a St. Andrew's cross, appropriately decorated, and suspended from a green collar bordered with red.

In the ritual of the Southern Jurisdiction, the leading idea of a communication between the Christian knights and the Saracens has been preserved; but the ceremonies and the legend have been altered. The lesson intended to be taught is toleration of religion.

This degree also constitutes the sixty-third of the collection of the Metropolitan Chapter of France; the fifth of the Rite of Clerks of Strict Observance; and the twenty-first of the Rite of Mizraim. It is also to be found in many other systems.

Knight of the Brazen Serpent. (*Chevalier du Serpent d'Airain.*) The Twenty-fifth Degree of the Ancient and Accepted Scottish Rite. The history of this degree is founded upon the circumstances related in Numbers ch. xxi. ver. 6–9: "And the Lord sent fiery serpents among the people, and they bit the people; and much people of Israel died. Therefore the people came to Moses, and said, We have sinned; for we have spoken against the Lord, and against thee: pray unto the Lord that he take away the serpents from us. And Moses prayed for the people. And the Lord said unto Moses, Make thee a fiery serpent, and set it upon a pole: and it shall come to pass, that every one that is bitten, when he looketh upon it shall live. And Moses made a serpent of brass, and put it upon a pole; and it came to pass, that if a serpent had bitten any man, when he beheld the serpent of brass, he lived." In the old rituals the

Lodge was called the Court of Sinai; the presiding officer was styled Most Puissant Grand Master, and represented Moses; while the two Wardens, or Ministers, represented Aaron and Joshua. The Orator was called Pontiff; the Secretary, Grand Graver; and the candidate, a Traveler. In the modern ritual adopted in this country, the Council represents the camp of the Israelites. The first three officers represent Moses, Joshua, and Caleb, and are respectively styled Most Puissant Leader, Valiant Captain of the Host, and Illustrious Chief of the Ten Tribes. The Orator represents Eleazar; the Secretary, Ithamar; the Treasurer, Phinehas; and the candidate an intercessor for the people. The jewel is a crux ansata, with a serpent entwined around it. On the upright of the cross is engraved חלתי, khalati, *I have suffered,* and on the arms נחושתן, nakhushtan, *a serpent.* The French ritualists would have done better to have substituted for the first word חטאתי, khatati, *I have sinned;* the original in Numbers being חטאנו, Kathanu, *we have sinned.* The apron is white, lined with black, and symbolically decorated.

There is an old legend which says that this degree was founded in the time of the Crusades, by John Ralph, who established the Order in the Holy Land as a military and monastic society, and gave it the name of the Brazen Serpent, because it was a part of their obligation to receive and gratuitously nurse sick travelers, to protect them against the attacks of the Saracens, and escort them safely to Palestine; thus alluding to the healing and saving virtues of the Brazen Serpent among the Israelites in the wilderness.

Knight of the East. (*Chevalier d'Orient.*) This is a degree which has been extensively diffused through the most important Rites, and it owes its popularity to the fact that it commemorates in its legend and its ceremonies the labors of the Masons in the construction of the second Temple.

1. It is the Fifteenth Degree of the Ancient and Accepted Scottish Rite, the description of which will apply with slight modifications to the same degree in all the other Rites. It is founded upon the history of the assistance rendered by Cyrus to the Jews, who permitted them to return to Jerusalem, and to commence the rebuilding of the house of the Lord. Zerubbabel, therefore, as the Prince of the Jews, and Cyrus the King of Persia, as his patron, are important personages in the drama of reception; which is conducted with great impressiveness even in the old and somewhat imperfect ritual of the last century, but which has been greatly improved in the modern rituals adopted by the Supreme Councils of the United States.

The cordon of a Knight of the East is a broad green watered ribbon, worn as a baldric from left to right. The sash or girdle is of white watered silk, edged above, and fringed below with gold. On it is embroidered a bridge, with the letters L. D. P. on the arch, and also on other parts of the girdle human heads, and mutilated limbs, and crowns, and swords. The apron is crimson, edged with green, a bleeding head and two swords crossed on the flap, and on the apron three triangles interlaced formed of triangular links of chains. The jewel is three triangles interlaced enclosing two naked swords.

Knight of the East and West. (*Chevalier d'Orient et d'Occident.*) 1. The Seventeenth Degree of the Ancient and Accepted Scottish Rite. The oldest rituals of the degree were very imperfect, and did not connect it with Freemasonry. They contained a legend that upon the return of the knights from the Holy Land, in the time of the Crusaders, they organized the Order, and that in the year 1118 the first knights, to the number of eleven, took their vows between the hands of Garinus, patriarch. The allusion, here, is evidently to the Knights Templar; and this legend would most probably indicate that the degree originated with the Templar system of Ramsay. This theory is further strengthened by the other legend, that the Knights of the East represented the Masons who remained in the East after the building of the first Temple, while the Knights of the East and West represented those who traveled West and disseminated the Order over Europe, but who returned during the Crusades and reunited with their ancient brethren, whence we get the name.

The modern ritual as used in the United States has been greatly enlarged. It still retains the apocalyptic character of the degree which always attached to it, as is evident from the old tracing-board, which is the figure described in the first chapter of the Revelation of St. John. The jewel is a heptagon inscribed with symbols derived from the Apocalypse, among which are the lamb and the book with seven seals. The apron is yellow, lined and edged with crimson. In the old ritual its device was a two-edged sword. In the new one it is a tetractys of ten dots. This is the first of the philosophical degrees of the Scottish Rite. 2. The Seventeenth Degree of the Chapter of Emperors of the East and West.

Knights Templar, Masonic. The connection of the Knights Templar with the Freemasons may much more plausibly be traced than that of the Knights of Malta. Yet, unfortunately, the sources from which information is to be derived are for the most part traditionary; authentic dates and documents are wanting. Tradition has always been inclined to trace the connection to an early period, and to give to the Templar system of secret reception a Masonic character, derived from their association during the Crusades with the mystical Society of the Assassins in Syria. Lawrie (*Hist.*, p. 87), or Sir David Brewster, the real author of the work which bears Lawrie's name, embodies the tradition in this form:

"Almost all the secret associations of the ancients either flourished or originated in Syria and the adjacent countries. It was here that the Dionysian artists, the Essenes and the Kasideans arose. From this country also came several members of that trading association of Masons which appeared in Europe during the dark ages; and we are assured, that, notwithstanding the unfavorable condition of that province, there exists at this day, on Mount Libanus, one of these Syriac fraternities. As the Order of the Templars, therefore, was originally formed in Syria, and existed there for a considerable time, it would be no improbable supposition that they received their Masonic knowledge from the Lodges in that quarter. But we are fortunately, in this case, not left to conjecture, for we are expressly informed by a foreign author [Adler, *de Drusis*], who was well acquainted with the history and customs of Syria, that the Knights Templar were actually members of the Syriac fraternities."

Even if this hypothesis were true, although it might probably suggest the origin of the secret reception of the Templars, it would not explain the connection of the modern Templars with the Freemasons, because there is no evidence that these Syriac fraternities were Masonic.

There are four sources from which the Masonic Templars are said to have derived their existence; making, therefore, as many different divisions of the Order.

1. The Templars who claim John Mark Larmenius as the successor of James de Molay.

2. Those who recognize Peter d'Aumont as the successor of De Molay.

3. Those who derive their Templarism from the Count Beaujeu, the nephew of Molay.

4. Those who claim an independent origin, and repudiate alike the authority of Larmenius, of Aumont, and of Beaujeu.

From the first class spring the Templars of France, who professed to have continued the Order by authority of a charter given by De Molay to Larmenius. This body of Templars designate themselves as the "Order of the Temple." Its seat is in Paris. The Duke of Sussex received from it the degree and the authority to establish a Grand Conclave in England. He did so; and convened that body once, but only once. During the remaining years of his life, Templarism had no activity in England, as he discountenanced all Christian and chivalric Masonry. (See *Temple, Order of the.*)

The second division of Templars is that which is founded on the theory that Peter d'Aumont fled with several knights into Scotland, and there united with the Freemasons. This legend is intimately connected with Ramsay's tradition—that Freemasonry sprang from Templarism, and that all Freemasons are Knights Templar. The Chapter of Clermont adopted this theory; and in establishing their high degrees asserted that they were derived from these Templars of Scotland. The Baron Hund carried the theory into Germany, and on it established his Rite of Strict Observance, which was a Templar system. Hence the Templars of Germany must be classed under the head of the followers of Aumont. (See *Strict Observance.*)

The third division is that which asserts that the Count Beaujeu, a nephew of the last Grand Master, De Molay, and a member of the Order of Knights of Christ—the name assumed by the Templars of Portugal—had received authority from that Order to disseminate the degree. He is said to have carried the degree and its ritual into Sweden, where he incorporated it with Freemasonry. The story is, too, that Beaujeu collected his uncle's ashes and interred them in Stockholm, where a monument was erected to his memory. Hence the Swedish Templar Masons claim their descent from Beaujeu, and the Swedish Rite is through this source a Templar system.

Of the last class, or the Templars who recognized the authority of neither of the leaders who have been mentioned, there were two subdivisions, the Scotch and the English; for it is only in Scotland and England that this independent Templarism found a foothold.

It was only in Scotland that the Templars endured no persecution. Long after the dissolution of the Order in every other country of Europe, the Scottish Preceptories continued to exist, and the knights lived undisturbed. One portion of the Scottish Templars entered the army of Robert Bruce, and, after the battle of Bannockburn, were merged in the "Royal Order of Scotland," then established by him. (See *Royal Order of Scotland.*)

Another portion of the Scottish Templars united with the Knights Hospitalers of St. John. They lived amicably in the same houses, and continued to do so until the Reformation. At this time many of them embraced Protestantism. Some of them united with the Freemasons, and established "the Ancient Lodge" at Stirling, where they conferred the degrees of Knight of the Sepulcher, Knight of Malta, and Knights Templar. It is to this division that we are to trace the Masonic Templars of Scotland.

Knight of the Royal Ax. (*Chevalier de la royale Hache.*) The Twenty-second Degree of the Ancient and Accepted Scottish Rite, called also Prince of Libanus, or Lebanon. It was instituted to record the memorable services rendered to Masonry by the "mighty cedars of Lebanon." The legend of the degree informs us that the Sidonians were employed in cutting cedars on Mount Libanus or Lebanon for the construction of Noah's ark. Their descendants subsequently cut cedars from the same place for the ark of the covenant; and the descendants of these were again employed in the same offices, and in the same place, in obtaining materials for building Solomon's Temple. Lastly, Zerubbabel employed them in cutting the cedars of Lebanon for the use of the second Temple. This celebrated nation formed colleges on Mount Lebanon, and in their labors always adored the Great Architect of the Universe. No doubt this last sentence refers to the Druses, that secret sect of Theists who still reside upon Mount Lebanon and in the adjacent parts of Syria and Palestine, and whose mysterious ceremonies have attracted so much of the curiosity of Eastern travelers.

The apron of the Knights of the Royal Ax is white, lined and bordered with purple.

Knight of the Sun. (*Chevalier du Soleil.*) The Twenty-eighth Degree of the Ancient and Accepted Scottish Rite, called also Prince of the Sun, Prince Adept, and Key of Masonry, or Chaos Disentangled. It is a Kabbalistic and Hermetic degree, and its instructions and symbols are full of the Kabbala and Alchemy. Thus, one of its favorite words is Stibium, which, with the Hermetic Philosophers, meant the primal matter of all things. The principal officers are Father Adam and Brother Truth, allegorizing in the old rituals the search of Man after Truth. The other officers are named after the seven chief angels, and the brethren are called Sylphs, or, in the American ritual, Aralim or Heroes. The jewel is a golden sun, having on its reverse a hemisphere with the six northern signs of the zodiac. There is but one light in the Lodge, which shines through a globe of glass.

This degree is not confined to the Scottish Rite, but is found sometimes with a different name, but with the same Hermetic design, more or less developed in other Rites. Ragon, with whom Delaunay and Chemin-Dupontès concur, says that it is not, like many of the high degrees, a mere modern invention, but that it is of the highest antiquity; and was, in fact, the last degree of the ancient initiations teaching, under an Hermetic appearance, the doctrines of natural religion, which formed an essential part of the Mysteries. But Ragon must here evidently refer to the general, philosophic design rather than to the particular organization of the degree. Thory (*Acta Lat.*, i., 339), with more plausibility, ascribes its invention as a Masonic degree to Pernetty, the founder of the Hermetic Rite. Of all the high degrees, it is, perhaps, the most important and the most interesting to the scholar who desires to investigate the true secret of the Order. Its old catechisms, now unfortunately too much neglected, are full of suggestive thoughts, and in its modern ritual, for which we are indebted to the inventive genius of Bro. Albert Pike, it is by far the most learned and philosophical of the Scottish degrees.

Koran. The sacred book of the Mohammedans, and believed by them to contain a record of the revelations made by God to Mohammed, and afterward dictated by him to an amanuensis, since the prophet could neither read nor write. In a Lodge consisting wholly of Mohammedans, the Koran would be esteemed as the Book of the Law, and take the place on the altar which is occupied in Christian Lodges by the Bible. It would thus become the symbol to them of the Tracing-Board of the Divine Architect. But, unlike the Old and New Testaments, the Koran has no connection with, and gives no support to, any of the Masonic legends or symbols, except in those parts which were plagiarized by the prophet from the Jewish and Christian Scriptures. Finch, however, in one of his apocryphal works, produced a system of Mohammedan Masonry, consisting of twelve degrees, founded on the teachings of the Koran, and the

Hadeeses or traditions of the prophet. This system was a pure invention of Finch.

Krishna or **Christna.** One of the Trimurti in the Hindu religious system. The myth proceeds to state that Devanaguy, upon the appearance of Vishnu, fell in a profound ecstasy, and having been *overshadowed* (Sanskrit), the spirit was incarnated, and upon the birth of a child, the Virgin and Son were conducted to a sheepfold belonging to Nanda, on the confines of the territory of Madura. The newly born was named Krishna (in Sanskrit, sacred). The Rajah of Madura had been informed in a dream that this son of Devanaguy should dethrone and chastise him for all his crimes; he therefore sought the certain destruction of the child, and ordained the massacre, in all his states, of all the children of the male sex born during the night of the birth of Krishna. A troop of soldiers reached the sheepfold of Nanda, the lord of a small village on the banks of the Ganges, and celebrated for his virtues. The servants were about to arm in defense, when the child, who was at his mother's breast, suddenly grew to the appearance and size of a child ten years of age, and running, amused himself amidst the flock of sheep. The exploits of this wonder child, his preaching the new or reformed doctrine of India, his disciples and loved companion Ardjouna, the parables, philosophic teaching, the myth of his transfiguration, his ablutions in the Ganges before his death, and tragic end, together with the story of his revival after three days, and ascension, are graphically told by many authors, perhaps more brilliantly in *La Bible dans l'Inde,* as translated into English by Louis Jacolliot.

Lamb, Paschal. The paschal lamb, sometimes called the Holy Lamb, was the lamb offered up by the Jews at the paschal feast. This has been transferred to Christian symbolism, and naturally to chivalric Masonry; and hence we find it among the symbols of modern Templarism. The paschal lamb, as a Christian and Masonic symbol, called also the *Agnus Dei,* or the Lamb of God, first appeared in Christian art after the sixth century. It is depicted as a lamb standing on the ground, holding by the left forefoot a banner, on which a cross is inscribed. This paschal lamb, or Lamb of God, has been adopted as a symbol by the Knights Templar, being borne in one of the banners of the Order, and constituting, with the square which it surmounts, the jewel of the Generalissimo of a Commandery. The lamb is a symbol of Christ; the cross, of his passion; and the banner, of his victory over death and hell. Mr. Barrington states (*Archæologia,* ix., 134) that in a deed of the English Knights Templar, granting lands in Cambridgeshire, the seal is a Holy Land, and the arms of the Master of the Temple at London were argent, a cross gules, and on the nombril point thereof a Holy Lamb, that is, a paschal or Holy Lamb on the center of a red cross in a white field.

Legend of the Royal Arch Degree. Much of this legend is a myth, having very little foundation, and some of it none, in historical accuracy.

But underneath it all there lies a profound stratum of philosophical symbolism. The destruction and the rebuilding of the Temple by the efforts of Zerubbabel and his compatriots, the captivity and the return of the captives, are matters of sacred history; but many of the details have been invented and introduced for the purpose of giving form to a symbolic idea. And this idea, expressed in the symbolism of the Royal Arch, is the very highest form of that which the ancient Mystagogues called the *euresis*, or the *discovery*. There are some portions of the legend which do not bear directly on the symbolism of the second Temple as a type of the second life, but which still have an indirect bearing on the general idea. Thus the particular legend of the *three weary sojourners* is undoubtedly a mere myth, there being no known historical testimony for its support; but it is evidently the enunciation symbolically of the religious and philosophical idea that Divine truth may be sought and won only by successful perseverance through all the dangers, trials, and tribulations of life, and that it is not in this, but in the next life, that it is fully attained.

The legend of the English and the American systems is identical; that of the Irish is very different as to the time and events; and the legend of the Royal Arch of the Scottish Rite is more usually called the *legend of Enoch.*

Libation. Among the Greeks and Romans the libation was a religious ceremony, consisting of the pouring of wine or other liquid upon the ground, or, in a sacrifice, upon the head of the victim after it had been first tasted by the priest and by those who stood next to him. The libations were usually of unmixed wine, but were sometimes of mingled wine and water. Libations are used in some of the chivalric and the high degrees of Masonry.

Lustration. A religious rite practised by the ancients, and performed before any act of devotion. It consisted in washing the hands, and sometimes the whole body, in lustral or consecrated water. It was intended as a symbol of the internal purification of the heart. It was a ceremony preparatory to initiation in all the Ancient Mysteries. The ceremony is practised with the same symbolic import in some of the high degrees of Masonry. So strong was the idea of a connection between lustration and initiation, that in the low Latin of the Middle Ages *lustrare* meant to initiate. Thus Du Cange (*Glossarium*) cites the expression "lustrare religione Christianorum" as signifying "to initiate into the Christian religion."

Magi. The ancient Greek historians so term the hereditary priests among the Persians and Medians. The word is derived from *mog* or *mag,* signifying priest in the Pehlevi language. The Illuminati first introduced the word into Masonry, and employed it in the nomenclature of their degrees to signify men of superior wisdom.

Magi, The Three. The "Wise Men of the East" who came to Jerusalem, bringing gifts to the infant Jesus. The traditional names of the three are Melchior, an old man, with a long beard, offering gold; Jasper, a beardless youth, who offers frankincense; Balthazar, a black or Moor, with a large spreading beard, who tenders myrrh. The patron saints of travelers. "Tradition fixed their number at three, probably in allusion to the three races springing from the sons of Noah. The Empress Helena caused their corpses to be transported to Milan from Constantinople. Frederick Barbarossa carried them to Cologne, the place of their special glory as the Three Kings of Cologne."—YONGE. The three principal officers ruling the society of the Rosicrucians are styled Magi.

Master Mason. In all the Rites of Masonry, no matter how variant may be their organization in the high degrees, the Master Mason constitutes the Third Degree. In form this degree is also everywhere substantially the same, because its legend is an essential part of it; and, as on that legend the degree must be founded, there can nowhere be any important variation, bcause the tradition has at all times been the same.

The Master Mason's Degree was originally called the summit of Ancient Craft Masonry; and so it must have been before the disseverance from it of the Royal Arch, by which is meant not the ritual, but the symbolism of Arch Masonry. But under its present organization the degree is actually incomplete, because it needs a complement that is only to be supplied in a higher one. Hence its symbolism is necessarily restricted, in its mutilated form, to the first Temple and the present life, although it gives the assurance of a future one.

As the whole system of Craft Masonry is intended to present the symbolic idea of man passing through the pilgrimage of life, each degree is appropriated to a certain portion of that pilgrimage. If, then, the First Degree is a representation of youth, the time to learn, and the Second of manhood or the time to work, the Third is symbolic of old age, with its trials, its sufferings, and its final termination in death. The time for toiling is now over—the opportunity to learn has passed away—the spiritual temple that we all have been striving to erect in our hearts, is now nearly completed, and the wearied workman awaits only the word of the Grand Master of the Universe, to call him from the labors of earth to the eternal refreshments of heaven. Hence, this is, by far, the most solemn and sacred of the degrees of Masonry; and it has, in consequence of the profound truths which it inculcates, been distinguished by the Craft as the sublime degree. As an Entered Apprentice, the Mason was taught those elementary instructions which were to fit him for further advancement in his profession, just as the youth is supplied with that rudimentary education which is to prepare him for entering on the active duties of life; as a Fellow-Craft, he is directed to continue his investigations in the science of the Institution, and to labor diligently in the tasks it prescribes, just as the man is required to enlarge his mind by the acquisition of new ideas, and to extend his usefulness to his fellow-creatures; but, as a Master Mason, he is taught the last, the most important, and the most necessary of truths, that having been faithful to all his trusts, he is at last to die, and to receive the reward of his fidelity.

It was the single object of all the ancient rites and mysteries practised in the very bosom of Pagan darkness, shining as a solitary beacon in all that surrounding gloom, and cheering the philosopher in his weary pilgrimage of life, to teach the immortality of the soul. This is still the great design of the Third Degree of Masonry. This is the scope and aim of its ritual. The Master Mason represents man, when youth, manhood, old age, and life itself, have passed away as fleeting shadows, yet raised from the grave of iniquity, and quickened into another and a better existence. By its legend and all its ritual, it is implied that we have been redeemed from the death of sin and the sepulcher of pollution. "The ceremonies and the lecture," says Dr. Crucefix, "beautifully illustrate this all-engrossing subject; and the conclusion we arrive at is, that youth, properly directed, leads us to honorable and virtuous maturity, and that the life of man, regulated by morality, faith, and justice, will be rewarded at its closing hour, by the prospect of eternal bliss."

Masonic historians have found much difficulty in settling the question as to the time of the invention and composition of the degree. The theory that at the building of the Temple of Jerusalem the Craft were divided into three or even more degrees, being only a symbolic myth, must be discarded in any historical discussion of the subject. The real question at issue is whether the Master Mason's Degree, as a degree, was in existence among the Operative Freemasons before the eighteenth century, or whether we owe it to the Revivalists of 1717. Bro. Wm. J. Hughan, in a very able article on this subject, published in 1873, in the *Voice of Masonry*, says that "so far the evidence respecting its history goes no farther back than the early part of the last century." The evidence, however, is all of a negative character. There is none that the degree existed in the seventeenth century or earlier, and there is none that it did not. All the old manuscripts speak of Masters and Fellows, but these might have been and probably were only titles of rank. The Sloane MS., No. 3329, speaks, it is true, of modes of recognition peculiar to Masters and Fellows, and also of a Lodge consisting of Masters, Fellows, and Apprentices. But even if we give to this MS. its earliest date, that which is assigned to it by Findel, near the end of the seventeenth century, it will not necessarily follow that these Masters, Fellows, and Apprentices had each a separate and distinct degree. Indeed, it refers only to one Lodge, which was, however, constituted by three different ranks; and it records but one oath, so that it is possible that there was only one common form of initiation.

The first positive historical evidence that we have of the existence of a Master's Degree is to be found in the General Regulations compiled by Payne in 1720. It is there declared that Apprentices must be admitted Masters and Fellow-Crafts only in the Grand Lodge. The degree was then in existence. But this record would not militate against the theory advanced by some that Desaguliers was its author in 1717.

Documentary evidence is yet wanting to settle the precise time of the composition of the Third Degree as we now have it. But it would not be prudent to oppose too positively the theory that it must be traced to the second decade of the eighteenth century. The proofs, as they arise day by day, from the resurrection of old manuscripts, seem to incline that way.

But the legend, perhaps, is of much older date. It may have made a part of the general initiation; but there is no doubt that, like the similar one of the Compagnons de la Tour in France, it existed among the Operative Gilds of the Middle Ages as an esoteric narrative. Such a legend all the histories of the Ancient Mysteries prove to us belongs to the spirit of initiation. There would have been no initiation worth preservation without it.

Mark. The appropriate jewel of a Mark Master. It is made of gold or silver, usually of the former metal, and must be in the form of a keystone. On the obverse or front surface, the device or "mark" selected by the owner must be engraved within a circle composed of the following letters: H. T. W. S. S. T. K. S. On the reverse or posterior surface, the name of the owner, the name of his Chapter, and the date of his advancement, may be inscribed, although this is not absolutely necessary. The "mark" consists of the device and surrounding inscription on the obverse. The Mark jewel, as prescribed by the Supreme Grand Chapter of Scotland, is of mother-of-pearl. The circle on one side is inscribed with the Hebrew letters הצבאשׁאמש, and the circle on the other side with letters containing the same meaning in the vernacular tongue of the country in which the Chapter is situated, and the wearer's mark in the center. The Hebrew letters are the initials of a Hebrew sentence equivalent to the English one familiar to Mark Masons. It is but a translation into Hebrew of the English mystical sentence.

It is not requisite that the device or mark should be of a strictly Masonic character, although Masonic emblems are frequently selected in preference to other subjects. As soon as adopted it should be drawn or described in a book kept by the Chapter for that purpose, and it is then said to be "recorded in the Book of Marks," after which time it can never be changed by the possessor for any other, or altered in the slightest degree, but remains as his "mark" to the day of his death.

This mark is not a mere ornamental appendage of the degree, but is a sacred token of the rites of friendship and brotherly love, and its presentation at any time by the owner to another Mark Master, would claim, from the latter, certain acts of friendship which are of solemn obligation among the Fraternity. A mark thus presented, for the purpose of obtaining a favor, is said to be *pledged;* though remaining in the possession of the owner, it ceases, for any actual purposes of advantage, to be his pro·

erty; nor can it be again used by him until, either by the return of the favor, or with the consent of the benefactor, it has been redeemed; for it is a positive law of the Order, that no Mark Master shall "pledge his mark a second time until he has redeemed it from its previous pledge." By this wise provision, the unworthy are prevented from making an improper use of this valuable token, or from levying contributions on their hospitable brethren. Marks or pledges of this kind were of frequent use among the ancients, under the name of *tessera hospitalis* and "arrhabo." The nature of the *tessera hospitalis,* or, as the Greeks called it, σύμβολον, cannot be better described than in the words of the Scholiast on the *Medea of Euripides,* v. 613, where Jason promises Medea, on her parting from him, to send her the symbols of hospitality which should procure her a kind reception in foreign countries. It was the custom, says the Scholiast, when a guest had been entertained, to break a die in two parts, one of which parts was retained by the guest, so that if, at any future period he required assistance, on exhibiting the broken pieces of the die to each other, the friendship was renewed. Plautus, in one of his comedies gives us an exemplification of the manner in which these *tesseræ* or pledges of friendship were used at Rome, whence it appears that the privileges of this friendship were extended to the descendants of the contracting parties. Pœnulus is introduced, inquiring for Agorastocles, with whose family he had formerly exchanged the *tessera.*

These *tesseræ,* thus used, like the Mark Master's mark, for the purposes of perpetuating friendship and rendering its union more sacred, were constructed in the following manner: they took a small piece of bone, ivory, or stone, generally of a square or cubical form, and dividing it into equal parts, each wrote his own name, or some other inscription, upon one of the pieces; they then made a mutual exchange, and, lest falling into other hands it should give occasion to imposture, the pledge was preserved with the greatest secrecy, and no one knew the name inscribed upon it except the possessor.

The primitive Christians seem to have adopted a similar practise, and the *tessera* was carried by them in their travels, as a means of introduction to their fellow Christians. A favorite inscription with them were the letters Π. Υ. Α. Π., being the initials of Πατηρ, Υιος, Αγιον Πνευμα, or Father, Son, and Holy Ghost. The use of these *tesseræ* in the place of written certificates, continued, says Dr. Harris (*Diss. on the Tess. Hosp.*), until the eleventh century, at which time they are mentioned by Burchardus, Archbishop of Worms, in a visitation charge.

The "arrhabo" was a similar keepsake, formed by breaking a piece of money in two. The etymology of this word shows distinctly that the Romans borrowed the custom of these pledges from the ancient Israelites, for it is derived from the Hebrew *arabon,* a pledge.

With this detail of the customs of the ancients before us, we can easily explain the well-known passage in Revelation ii. 17: "To him that overcometh will I give a white stone, and in it a new name written, which no man knoweth saving he that receiveth it." That is, to borrow the interpretation of Harris, "To him that overcometh will I give a pledge of my affection, which shall constitute him my friend, and entitle him to privileges and honors of which none else can know the value or the extent."

Materials of the Temple. Masonic tradition tells us that the trees out of which the timbers were made for the Temple were felled and prepared in the forest of Lebanon, and that the stones were hewn, cut, and squared in the quarries of Tyre. But both the Book of Kings and Josephus concur in the statement that Hiram of Tyre furnished only cedar and fir trees for the Temple. The stones were most probably (and the explorations of modern travelers confirm the opinion) taken from the quarries which abound in and around Jerusalem. The tradition, therefore, which derives these stones from the quarries of Tyre, is incorrect.

Melchizedek. King of Salem, and a priest of the Most High God, of whom all that we know is to be found in the passages of Scripture read at the conferring of the degree of High Priesthood. Some theologians have supposed him to have been Shem, the son of Noah. The sacrifice of offering bread and wine is first attributed to Melchizedek; and hence, looking to the similar Mithraic sacrifice, Higgins is inclined to believe that he professed the religion of Mithras. He abandoned the sacrifice of slaughtered animals, and, to quote the words of St. Jerome, "offered bread and wine as a type of Christ." Hence, in the New Testament, Christ is represented as a priest after the order of Melchizedek. In Masonry, Melchizedek is connected with the order or degree of High Priesthood, and some of the high degrees.

Morgan, William. Born in Culpeper County, in Virginia, in 1775. He published in 1826 a pretended *Exposition of Masonry,* which attracted at the time more attention than it deserved. Morgan soon after disappeared, and the Masons were charged by some enemies of the Order with having removed him by foul means. What was the real fate of Morgan has never been ascertained. There are various myths of his disappearance, and subsequent residence in other countries. They may or may not be true, but it is certain that there is no evidence of his death that would be admitted in a Court of Probate. He was a man of questionable character and dissolute habits, and his enmity to Masonry is said to have originated from the refusal of the Masons of Le Roy to admit him to membership in their Lodge and Chapter.

Moriah, Mount. An eminence situated in the southeastern part of Jerusalem. In the time of David it must have been cultivated, for it is called "the threshing-floor of Ornan the Jebusite," from whom that monarch purchased it for the purpose of placing there an altar. Solomon subsequently erected there his magnificent Temple. Mount Moriah was always profoundly venerated by the Jews, among whom there is an early tradition that on it Abraham was directed to offer up his son. The truth of this tradition has, it is true, been recently denied by some Biblical writers, but it has been as strenuously maintained by others. The Masons, however, have always accepted it, and to them, as the site of the Temple, it is especially sacred, and, combining with this the Abrahamic legend, they have given to Mount Moriah the appellation of the ground floor of the Lodge, and assign it as the place where what are called "the three grand offerings were made."

North. The north is Masonically called a place of darkness. The sun in his progress through the ecliptic never reaches farther than 23° 28′ north of the equator. A wall being erected on any part of the earth farther north than that, will therefore, at meridian, receive the rays of the sun only on its south side, while the north will be entirely in shadow at the hour of meridian. The use of the north as a symbol of darkness is found, with the present interpretation, in the early rituals of the last century. It is a portion of the old sun worship, of which we find so many relics in Gnosticism, in Hermetic philosophy, and in Freemasonry. The east was the place of the sun's daily birth, and hence highly revered; the north the place of his annual death, to which he approached only to lose his vivific heat, and to clothe the earth in the darkness of long nights and the dreariness of winter.

However, this point of the compass, or place of Masonic darkness, must not be construed as implying that in the Temple of Solomon no light or ventilation was had from this direction. The Talmud, and as well Josephus, allude to an extensive opening toward the North, framed with costly magnificence, and known as the great "Golden Window." There were as many openings in the outer wall on the north as on the south side. There were three entrances through the "Chel" on the north and six on the south. (See *Temple.*)

While once within the walls and Chel of the Temple all advances were made from east to west, yet the north side was mainly used for stabling, slaughtering, cleansing, etc., and contained the chambers of broken knives, defiled stones, of the house of burning, and of sheep. The Masonic symbolism of the entrance of an initiate from the north, or more practically from the northwest, and advancing toward the position occupied by the corner-stone in the northeast, forcibly calls to mind the triplet of Homer:

> "Two marble doors unfold on either side;
> Sacred the South by which the gods descend;
> But mortals enter on the Northern end."

So in the Mysteries of Dionysos, the gate of entrance for the aspirant was from the north; but when purged from his corruptions, he was termed indifferently new-born or immortal, and the sacred south door was thence accessible to his steps.

In the Middle Ages, below and to the right of the judges stood the accuser, facing north; to the left was the defendant, in the north facing south. Bro. George F. Fort, in his *Antiquities of Freemasonry,* says: "In the centre of the court, directly before the judge, stood an altar piece or shrine, upon which an open Bible was displayed. The south, to the right of the justiciaries, was deemed honorable and worthy for a plaintiff; but the north was typical of a frightful and diabolical sombreness." Thus, when a solemn oath of purgation was taken in grievous criminal accusations, the accused turned toward the north. "The judicial headsman, in executing the extreme penalty of outraged justice, turned the convict's face northward, or towards the place whence emanated the earliest dismal shades of night. When Earl Hakon bowed a tremulous knee before the deadly powers of Paganism, and sacrificed his seven-year-old child, he gazed out upon the far-off, gloomy north.

"In Nastrond, or shores of death, stood a revolting hall, whose portals opened toward the north—the regions of night. North, by the Jutes, was denominated black or sombre; the Frisians called it fear corner. The gallows faced the north, and from these hyperborean shores everything base and terrible proceeded. In consequence of this belief, it was ordered that, in the adjudication of a crime, the accused should be on the north side of the court enclosure. And in harmony with the Scandinavian superstition, no Lodge of Masons illumines the darkened north with a symbolic light, whose brightness would be unable to dissipate the gloom of that cardinal point with which was associated all that was sinstrous and direful." (P. 292.)

Nine. If the number three was celebrated among the ancient sages, that of three times three had no less celebrity; because, according to them, each of the three elements which constitute our bodies is ternary: the water containing earth and fire; the earth containing igneous and aqueous particles; and the fire being tempered by globules of water and terrestrial corpuscles which serve to feed it. No one of the three elements being entirely separated from the others, all material beings composed of these three elements, whereof each is triple, may be designated by the figurative number of three times three, which has become the symbol of all formations of bodies. Hence the name of ninth envelop given to matter. Every material extension, every circular line, has for its representative sign the number nine among the Pythagoreans, who had observed the property which this number possesses of reproducing itself incessantly and entire in every multiplication; thus offering to the mind a very striking emblem of matter, which is incessantly composed before our eyes, after having undergone a thousand decompositions.

The number nine was consecrated to the Spheres and the Muses. It is the sign of every circumference; because a circle of 360 degrees is equal to 9, that is to say, $3 + 6 + 0 = 9$. Nevertheless, the ancients regarded this number with a sort of terror; they considered it a bad presage; as the symbol of versatility, of change, and the emblem of the frailty of human affairs. Wherefore they avoided all numbers where nine appears, and chiefly 81, the product of 9 multiplied by itself, and the addition whereof, 8 + 1, again presents the number 9.

As the figure of the number 6 was the symbol of the terrestrial globe, animated by a Divine spirit, the figure of the number 9 symbolized the earth, under the influence of the Evil Principle; and thence the terror it inspired. Nevertheless, according to the Kabbalists, the cipher 9 symbolizes the generative egg, or the image of a little globular being, from whose lower side seems to flow its spirit of life.

The Ennead, signifying an aggregate of nine things or persons, is the first square of unequal numbers.

Everyone is aware of the singular properties of the number 9, which, multiplied by itself or any other number whatever, gives a result whose final sum is always 9, or always divisible by 9.

9, multiplied by each of the ordinary numbers, produces an arithmetical progression, each member whereof, composed of two figures, presents a remarkable fact; for example:

1 . 2 . 3 . 4 . 5 . 6 . 7 . 8 . 9 . 10
9 . 18 . 27 . 36 . 45 . 54 . 63 . 72 . 81 . 90

The first line of figures gives the regular series, from 1 to 10.

The second reproduces this line doubly; first ascending from the first figure of 18, and then returning from the second figure of 81.

In Freemasonry, 9 derives its value from its being the product of 3 multiplied into itself, and consequently in Masonic language the number 9 is always denoted by the expression 3 times 3. For a similar reason, 27, which is 3 times 9, and 81, which is 9 times 9, are esteemed as sacred numbers in the higher degrees.

Nineveh. The capital of the ancient kingdom of Assyria, and built by Nimrod. The traditions of its greatness and the magnificence of its buildings were familiar to the Arabs, the Greeks, and the Romans. The modern discoveries of Rich, of Botta, and other explorers, have thrown much light upon its ancient condition, and have shown that it was the seat of much architectural splendor and of a profoundly symbolical religion, which had something of the characteristics of the Mithraic worship. In the mythical relations of the Old Constitutions, which make up the legend of the Craft, it is spoken of as the ancient birthplace of Masonry, where Nimrod, who was its builder, and "was a Mason and loved well the Craft," employed 60,000 Masons to build it, and gave them a charge "that they should be true," and this, says the Harleian MS., No. 1942, was the first time that any Mason had any charge of Craft.

Nisan. ניסן. The seventh month of the Hebrew civil year, and corresponding to the months of March and April, commencing with the new moon of the former.

Noachidæ. The descendants of Noah. A term applied to Freemasons on the theory, derived from the "legend of the Craft," that Noah was the Father and founder of the Masonic system of theology. And hence the Freemasons claim to be his descendants, because in times past they preserved the pure principles of his religion amid the corruptions of surrounding faiths.

Dr. Anderson first used the word in this sense in the second edition of the *Book of Constitutions*: "A Mason is obliged by his tenure to observe the moral law as a true Noachida." But he was not the inventor of the term, for it occurs in a letter sent by the Grand Lodge of England to the Grand Lodge of Calcutta in 1735, which letter is preserved among the Rawlinson MSS. in the Bodleian Library, Oxford. (See *Ars Quatuor Coronatorum*, xi., 35.)

Noachite, or **Prussian Knight.** (*Noachite ou Chevalier Prussien.*) 1. The Twenty-first Degree of the Ancient and Accepted Scottish Rite. The history as well as the character of this degree is a very singular one. It is totally unconnected with the series of Masonic degrees which are founded upon the Temple of Solomon, and is traced to the tower of Babel. Hence the Prussian Knights call themselves Noachites, or Disciples of Noah, while they designate all other Masons as Hiramites, or Disciples of Hiram. The early French rituals state that the degree was translated in 1757 from the German by M. de Beraye, Knight of Eloquence in the Lodge of the Count St. Gelaire, Inspector-General of Prussian Lodges in France. Lenning gives no credit to this statement, but admits that the origin of the degree must be attributed to the year above named. The destruction of the tower of Babel constitutes the legend of the degree, whose mythical founder is said to have been Peleg, the chief builder of that edifice. A singular regulation is that there shall be no artificial light in the Lodge room, and that the meetings shall be held on the night of the full moon of each month.

The degree was adopted by the Council of Emperors of the East and West, and in that way became subsequently a part of the system of the Scottish Rite. But it is misplaced in any series of degrees supposed to emanate from the Solomonic Temple. It is, as an unfitting link, an unsightly interruption of the chain of legendary symbolism substituting Noah for Solomon, and Peleg for Hiram Abif. The Supreme Council for the Southern Jurisdiction has abandoned the original ritual and made the degree a representation of the Vehmgericht or Westphalian Franc Judges. But this by no means relieves the degree of the objection of Masonic incompatibility. That it was ever adopted into the Masonic system is only to be attributed to the passion for high degrees which prevailed in France in the middle of the last century.

In the modern ritual the meetings are called Grand Chapters. The officers are a Lieutenant Commander, two Wardens, an Orator, Treasurer, Secretary, Master of Ceremonies, Warder, and Standard-Bearer. The apron is yellow, inscribed with an arm holding a sword and the Egyptian figure of silence. The order is black, and the jewel a full moon or a triangle traversed by an arrow. In the original ritual there is a coat of arms belonging to the degree, which is thus emblazoned: Party per fess; in chief, *azure,* semé of stars, *or* a full moon, *argent;* in base, *sable,* an equilateral triangle, having an arrow suspended from its upper point, barb downward, *or.*

The legend of the degree describes the travels of Peleg from Babel to the north of Europe, and ends with the following narrative: "In trenching the rubbish of the salt-mines of Prussia was found in A.D. 553, at a depth of fifteen cubits, the appearance of a triangular building in which was a column of white marble, on which was written in Hebrew the whole history of the Noachites. At the side of this column was a tomb of freestone on which was a piece of agate inscribed with the following epitaph: Here rest the ashes of Peleg, our Grand Architect of the tower of Babel. The Almighty had pity on him because he became humble."

This legend, although wholly untenable on historic grounds, is not absolutely puerile. The dispersion of the human race in the time of Peleg had always been a topic of discussion among the learned. Long dissertations had been written to show that all the nations of the world, even America, had been peopled by the three sons of Noah and their descendants. The object of the legend seems, then, to have been to impress the idea of the thorough dispersion. The fundamental idea of the degree is, under the symbol of Peleg, to teach the crime of assumption and the virtue of humility.

2. The degree was also adopted into the Rite of Mizraim, where it is the Thirty-fifth.

Omnific Word. The Tetragrammaton is so called because of the omnific powers attributed by the Kabbalists to its possession and true pronunciation. (See *Tetragrammaton.*) The term is also applied to the most significant word in the Royal Arch system.

On. This is a significant word in Royal Arch Masonry, and has been generally explained as being the name by which Jehovah was worshiped among the Egyptians. As this has been recently denied, and the word asserted to be only the name of a city in Egypt, it is proper that some inquiry should be made into the authorities on the subject. The first mention of On in the Bible is in the history of Joseph, to whom Pharaoh gave "to wife Asenath, the daughter of Poti-pherah, priest of On." The city of On was in Lower Egypt, between the Nile and the Red Sea, and "adorned," says Philippson, "by a gorgeous temple of the sun, in which a numerous priesthood officiated."

The investigations of modern Egyptologists have shown that this is an error. On was the name of a city where the sun-god was worshiped, but On was not the name of that god.

Champollioin, in his *Dictionnaire Egyptien,* gives the phonetic characters, with the figurative symbols of a serpent and disk, and a seated figure, as the name of the sun-god. Now, of these two characters, the upper one has the power of R, and the lower of A, and hence the name of the god is *Ra.* And this is the concurrent testimony of Bunsen, Lepsius, Gliddon, and all recent authorities.

But although On was really the name of a city, the founders of the Royal Arch had, with the lights then before them, assumed that it was the name of a god, and had so incorporated it with their system. With better light than theirs, we can no longer accept their definition; yet the word may still be retained as a symbol of the Egyptian god. I know not who has power to reject it; and if scholars preserve, outside of the symbolism, the true interpretation, no harm will be done. It is not the only significant word in Masonry whose old and received meaning has been shown to be incorrect, and sometimes even absurd. Higgins (*Celt. Druids,* 171) quotes an Irish commentator as showing that the name AIN or ON was the name of a triad of gods in the Irish language. "All etymologists," Higgins continues, "have supposed the word On to mean the sun; but how the name arose has not before been explained." In another work (*Anacalypsis,* vol. i., p. 109), Higgins makes the following important remarks: "Various definitions are given of the word ON; but they are all unsatisfactory. It is written in the Old Testament in two ways, און, *aun,* and אן, *an.* It is usually rendered in English by the word On. This word is supposed to mean the sun, and the Greeks translated it by the word ἥλιος, or Sol. But I think it only stood for the sun, as the emblem of the procreative power of nature." Bryan says (*Ant. Mythol.,* i., 19), when speaking of this word: "On, Eon or Aon, was another title of the sun among the Amonians. The Seventy, where the word occurs in the Scriptures, interpret it the sun, and call the city of On, Heliopolis; and the Coptic Pentateuch renders the city On by the city of the sun." Plato, in his *Timæus,* says: "Tell me of the god ON, which is, and never knew beginning." And although Plato may have been here thinking of the Greek word ΩN, which means *Being,* it is not improbable that he may have referred to the god worshiped at On, or Heliopolis, as it was thence that the Greeks derived so much of their learning. It would be vain to attempt to make an analogy between the Hindu sacred word AUM and the Egyptian ON. The fact that the M in the former word is the initial of some secret word, renders the conversion of it into N impossible, because it would thereby lose its signification.

The old Masons, misled by the authority of St. Cyril, and by the translation of the name of the city into "City of the Sun" by the Hebrews and the Greeks, very naturally supposed that On was the Egyptian sun-god, their supreme deity, as the sun always was, wherever he was worshiped. Hence, they appropriated that name as a sacred word explanatory of the Jewish Tetragrammaton.

Perfect Master. (*Maître Parfait.*) The Fifth Degree in the Ancient and Accepted Scottish Rite. The ceremonies of this degree were originally established as a grateful tribute of respect to a worthy departed brother. The officers of the Lodge are a Master, who represents Adoniram, the Inspector of the Works at Mount Lebanon, and one Warden. The symbolic color of the degree is green, to remind the Perfect Master that, being dead in vice, he must hope to revive in virtue. His jewel is a compass extended sixty degrees, to teach him that he should act within measure, and ever pay due regard to justice and equity.

The apron is white, with a green flap; and in the middle of the apron must be embroidered or painted, within three circles, a cubical stone, in the center of which the letter J is inscribed, according to the old rituals; but the Samaritan *yod* and *he,* according to the ritual of the Southern Jurisdiction.

Delaunay, in his *Thuileur de l'Ecossisme,* gives the Tetragrammaton in this degree, and says the degree should more properly be called Past Master, *Ancien Maître,* because the Tetragrammaton makes it in some sort the complement of the Master's Degree. But the Tetragrammaton is not found in any of the approved rituals, and Delaunay's theory falls therefore to the ground. But besides, to complete the Master's with this degree would be to confuse all the symbolism of the Ineffable degrees, which really conclude with the Fourteenth.

Perfect Stone. A name frequently given to the cubic stone discovered in the Thirteenth Degree of Perfection, the tenth of the Ineffable Series. It denotes justice and firmness, with all the moral lessons and duties in which the mystic cube is calculated to instruct us.

Points of Entrance, Perfect. In the earliest lectures of the last century these were called "Principal Points." The designation of them as "Perfect Points of Entrance" was of a later date. They are described both in the English and the American systems. Their specific names, and their allusion to the four cardinal virtues, are the same in both; but the verbal explanations differ, although not substantially. They are so called because they refer to four important points of the initiation. The Guttural refers to the entrance upon the penal responsibilities; the Pectoral, to the entrance into the Lodge; the Manual, to the entrance on the covenant; and the Pedal, to the entrance on the instructions in the northeast.

Pillars of Cloud and Fire. The pillar of cloud that went before the Israelites by day, and the pillar of fire that preceded them by night, in their journey through the wilderness, are supposed to be alluded to by the pillars of Jachin and Boaz at the porch of Solomon's Temple. We find this symbolism at a very early period in the last century, having been incorporated into the lecture of the Second Degree, where it still remains. "The pillar on the right hand," says Calcott (*Cand. Disq.,* 66), "represented the pillar of the cloud, and that on the left the pillar of fire." If this symbolism be correct, the pillars of the porch, like those of the wilderness, would refer to the superintending and protecting power of Deity.

Pillars of Enoch. Two pillars which were erected by Enoch, for the preservation of the antediluvian inventions, and which are repeatedly referred to in the "Legend of the Craft," contained in the *Old Constitutions,* and in the high degrees of modern times. (See *Enoch.*)

Pillars of the Porch. The pillars most remarkable in Scripture history were the two erected by Solomon at the porch of the Temple, and which Josephus (*Antiq.,* lib. i., cap. ii.) thus describes: "Moreover, this Hiram made two hollow pillars, whose outsides were of brass, and the thickness of the brass was four fingers' breadth, and the height of the pillars was eighteen cubits, (27 feet,) and the circumference twelve cubits, (18 feet;) but there was cast with each of their chapiters lily-work, that stood upon the pillar, and it was elevated five cubits, (7½ feet,) round about which there was net-work interwoven with small palms made of brass, and covered the lily-work. To this also were hung two hundred pomegranates, in two rows. The one of these pillars he set at the entrance of the porch on the right hand, (*or south,*) and called it Jachin, and the other at the left hand, (*or north,*) and called it Boaz."

It has been supposed that Solomon, in erecting these pillars, had reference to the pillar of cloud and the pillar of fire which went before the Israelites in the wilderness, and that the right hand or south pillar represented the pillar of cloud, and the left hand or north pillar represented that of fire. Solomon did not simply erect them as ornaments to the Temple, but as memorials of God's repeated promises of support to his people of Israel. For the pillar יבין (*Jachin*), derived from the words יה (*Jah*), "Jehovah," and הבין (*achin*), "to establish," signifies that "God will establish his house of Israel"; while the pillar בעז (*Boaz*), compounded of ב (*b*), "in" and עז (*oaz*), "strength," signifies that "in strength shall it be established." And thus were the Jews, in passing through the porch to the Temple, daily reminded of the abundant promises of God, and inspired with confidence in his protection and gratitude for his many acts of kindness to his chosen people.

The construction of these pillars.—There is no part of the architecture of the ancient Temple which is so difficult to be understood in its details as the Scriptural account of these memorable pillars. Freemasons, in general, intimately as their symbolical signification is connected with some of the most beautiful portions of their ritual, appear to have but a confused notion of their construction and of the true disposition of the various parts of which they are composed. Mr. Ferguson says (Smith, *Dict. Bib.*) that there are no features connected with the Temple which have given rise to so much controversy, or been so difficult to explain, as the form of these two pillars.

The true description, then, of these memorable pillars, is simply this. Immediately within the porch of the Temple, and on each side of the door, were placed two hollow brazen pillars. The height of each was twenty-seven feet, the diameter about six feet, and the thickness of the brass three inches. Above the pillar, and the covering its upper part to the depth of nine inches, was an oval body or chapiter seven feet and a half in height. Springing out from the pillar, at the junction of the chapiter with it, was a row of lotus petals, which, first spreading around the chapiter, afterward gently curved downward toward the pillar, something like the Acanthus leaves on the capital of a Corinthian column. About two-fifths of the distance from the bottom of the chapiter, or just below its most bulging part, a tissue of network was carved, which extended over its whole upper surface. To the bottom of this network was suspended a series of fringes, and on these again were carved two rows of pomegranates, one hundred being in each row.

This description, it seems to me, is the only one that can be reconciled with the various passages in the Books of Kings, Chronicles, and Josephus, which relate to these pillars, and the only one that can give the Masonic student a correct conception of the architecture of these important symbols.

What was the original or Scriptural symbolism of the pillars has been very well explained by Dudley in his *Naology*. He says (p. 121) that "the pillars represented the sustaining power of the great God."

Philosophic Degrees. All the degrees of the Ancient and Accepted Scottish Rite above the Eighteenth and below the Thirty-third are called philosophic degrees, because, abandoning the symbolism based on the Temple, they seek to develop a system of pure theosophy. Some writers have contended that the Seventeenth and Eighteenth degrees should be classed with the philosophic degrees. But this is not correct, since both of those degrees have preserved the idea of the Temple system. They ought rather to be called apocalyptic degrees, the Seventeenth especially, because they do not teach the ancient philosophies, but are connected in their symbolism with the spiritual temple of the New Jerusalem.

Point within a Circle. This is a symbol of great interest and importance, and brings us into close connection with the early symbolism of the solar orb and the universe, which was predominant in the ancient sun-worship. The lectures of Freemasonry give what modern Monitors have made an exoteric explanation of the symbol, in telling us that the point represents an individual brother, the circle the boundary line of his duty to God and man, and the two perpendicular parallel lines the patron saints of the Order—St. John the Baptist and St. John the Evangelist.

But that this was not always its symbolic signification, we may collect from the true history of its connection with the phallus of the Ancient Mysteries. The phallus, as I have already shown under the word, was among the Egyptians the symbol of fecundity, expressed by the male generative principle. It was communicated from the rites of Osiris to the religious festivals of Greece. Among the Asiatics the same emblem, under the name of lingam, was, in connection with the female principle. worshiped as the symbols of the Great Father and Mother, or producing causes of the human race, after their destruction by the deluge. On this subject, Captain Wilford (*Asiat. Res.*) remarks "that it was believed in India, that, at the general deluge, everything was involved in the common destruction except the male and female principles, or organs of generation, which were destined to produce a new race, and to repeople the earth when the waters had subsided from its surface. The female principle, symbolized by the moon, assumed the form of a lunette or crescent; while the male principle, symbolized by the sun, assuming the form of the lingam, placed himself erect in the center of the lunette, like the mast of a ship. The two principles, in this united form, floated on the surface of the waters during the period of their prevalence on the earth; and thus became the progenitors of a new race of men." Here, then, was the first outline of the point within a circle, representing the principle of fecundity, and doubtless the symbol, connected with a different history, that, namely, of Osiris, was transmitted by the Indian philosophers to Egypt, and to the other nations, who derived, as I have elsewhere shown, all their rites from the East.

It was in deference to this symbolism that, as Higgins remarks (*Anacal.*, ii., 306), circular temples were in the very earliest ages universally erected in cyclar numbers to do honor to the Deity.

In India stone circles, or rather their ruins, are everywhere found; among the oldest of which, according to Moore (*Panth.*, 242), is that of Dipaldiana, and whose execution will compete with that of the Greeks. In the oldest monuments of the Druids we find, as at Stonehenge and Abury, the circle of stones. In fact, all the temples of the Druids were circular, with a single stone erected in the center. A Druidical monument in Pembrokeshire, called Y Cromlech, is described as consisting of several rude stones pitched on end in a circular order, and in the midst of the circle a vast stone placed on several pillars. Near Keswick, in Cumberland, says Oliver (*Signs and Symbols*, 174), is another specimen of this Druidical symbol. On a hill stands a circle of forty stones placed perpendicularly, of about five feet and a half in height, and one stone in the center of greater altitude.

Among the Scandinavians, the hall of Odin contained twelve seats, disposed in the form of a circle, for the principal gods, with an elevated seat in the center for Odin. Scandinavian monuments of this form are still to be found in Scania, Zealand, and Jutland.

But it is useless to multiply examples of the prevalence of this symbol among the ancients. And now let us apply this knowledge to the Masonic symbol.

We have seen that the phallus and the point within a circle come from the same source, and must have been identical in signification. But the phallus was the symbol of fecundity, or the male generative principle, which by the ancients was supposed to be the sun (they looking to the creature and not to the Creator), because by the sun's heat and light the earth is made prolific, and its productions are brought to maturity. The point within the circle was then originally the symbol of the sun; and as the lingam of India stood in the center of the lunette, so it stands within the center of the Universe, typified by the circle, impregnating and vivifying it with its heat. And thus the astronomers have been led to adopt the same figure as their symbol of the sun.

Now it is admitted that the Lodge represents the world or the universe, and the Master and Wardens within it represent the sun in three positions. Thus we arrive at the true interpretation of the Masonic symbolism of the point within the circle. It is the same thing, but under a different form, as the Master and Wardens of a Lodge. The Master and Wardens are symbols of the sun, the Lodge of the universe, or world, just as the point is the symbol of the same sun, and the surrounding circle of the universe.

An addition to the above may be given, by referring to one of the oldest symbols among the Egyptians, and found upon their monuments, which was a circle centered by an A U M, supported by two erect parallel serpents; the circle being expressive of the collective people of the world, protected by the parallel attributes, the Power and Wisdom of the Creator. The Alpha and Omega, or the W.ll representing the Egyptian omnipotent God, surrounded by His creation, having for a boundary no other limit than what may come within his boundless scope, his Wisdom and Power. At times this circle is represented by the Ananta (Sanskrit,) *eternity*), a serpent with its tail in its mouth. The parallel serpents were of the cobra species.

It has been suggestively said that the Masonic symbol refers to the circuits or circumambulation of the initiate about the sacred Altar, which supports the three Great Lights as a central point, while the brethren stand in two parallel lines.

Presidents of the United States of America, Masonic. George Washington, first president, born February 22nd, 1732. Passed on December 14th, 1799. Initiated November 4th, 1752, passed March 3rd, 1753, raised August 4th, 1753, in Fredericksburg, Virginia, Fredericksburg Lodge No. 4.

Andrew Jackson, seventh president, born March 15th, 1767. Passed on June 8th, 1845. It is not clear where he received his degrees. He was Grand Master of Tennessee 1822-23.

James Knox Polk, eleventh president, born November 2nd, 1795. Passed on June 15th, 1849. Initiated June 5th, 1820, passed August 7th, 1820, raised October 2nd, 1820, in Columbia Lodge No. 31, Columbia, Tennessee.

James Buchanan, fifteenth president, born April 23rd, 1791. Passed on June 1st, 1868. Received his Masonic Degrees in Lodge No. 43, in Pennsylvania (name not given), January 24th, 1817.

Andrew Johnson, seventeenth president, born December 29th, 1808. Passed on July 31st, 1875. Received his Masonic Degrees in Greeneville Lodge No. 119, now No. 3, Greeneville, Tennessee, in May, 1851.

James Abram Garfield, twentieth president, born November 19th, 1831. Passed on September 19th, 1881. Initiated November 22nd, 1861, passed December 3rd, 1861, in Magnolia Lodge No. 20, Columbus, Ohio, raised November 22nd, 1864, in Columbus Lodge No. 30, request Magnolia Lodge, Columbus, Ohio.

William McKinley, twenty-fifth president, born January 29th, 1843. Passed on September 14th, 1901. Initiated May 1st, 1865, passed May 2nd and raised May 3rd, in Winchester Hiram Lodge No. 21, Winchester, Virginia.

Theodore Roosevelt, twenty-sixth president, born October 27th, 1858. Passed on January 6th, 1919. Initiated January 2nd, 1901, passed March 27th, 1901, raised April 24th, 1901, in Matinecock Lodge No. 806, Oyster Bay, New York.

William Howard Taft, twenty-seventh president, born September 15th, 1857. He was made a Mason at sight, on February 18th, 1909, by Kilwinning Lodge No. 356, Cincinnati, Ohio.

Warren Gamaliel Harding, twenty-ninth president, born November 2nd, 1865. Passed on August 2nd, 1923. Initiated June 28th, 1901, passed August 13th, 1920, raised August 27th, 1920, in Marion Lodge No. 70, Marion, Ohio.

Franklin Delano Roosevelt, thirty-second president, born January 30th, 1882. Initiated October 10th, 1911, passed November 14th, 1911, raised November 28th, 1911, in Holland Lodge No. 8, New York, N. Y.

Prior. 1. The superiors of the different nations or provinces into which the Order of the Templar was divided, were at first called Priors or Grand Priors, and afterward Preceptors or Grand Preceptors.

2. Each of the languages of the Order of Malta was divided into Grand Priories, of which there were twenty-six, over which a Grand Prior presided. Under him were several Commanderies.

3. The second officer in a Council of Kadosh, under the Supreme Council for the Southern Jurisdiction of the United States.

4. The Grand Prior is the third officer in the Supreme Council of the Ancient and Accepted Scottish Rite for the Southern Jurisdiction of the United States.

Principal Sojourner. The Hebrew word גר, *ger,* which we translate "a sojourner," signifies a man living out of his own country, and is used in this sense throughout the Old Testament. The children of Israel were, therefore, during the captivity, sojourners in Babylon, and the person who is represented by this officer, performed, as the incidents of the degree relate, an important part in the restoration of the Israelites to Jerusalem. He was the spokesman and leader of a party of three sojourners, and is, therefore, emphatically called the chief, or principal sojourner.

In the English Royal Arch system there are three officers called Sojourners. But in the American system the three Historical Sojourners are represented by the candidates, while only the supposed chief of them is represented by an officer called the Principal Sojourner. His duties are those of a conductor, and resemble, in some respects, those of a Senior Deacon in a Symbolic Lodge; which office, indeed, he occupies when the Chapter is open on any of the preliminary degrees.

Prince Mason. A term applied in the old Scottish Rite Constitutions to the possessors of the high degrees above the Fourteenth. It was first assumed by the Council of the Emperors of the East and West. Rose Croix Masons in Ireland are still known by this name.

Prince of Jerusalem. (*Prince de Jerusalem.*) This was the Sixteenth Degree of the Rite of Perfection, whence it was transferred to the Ancient and Accepted Scottish Rite, where it occupies the same numerical position. Its legend is founded on certain incidents which took place during the rebuilding of the second Temple, when the Jews were so much incommoded by the attacks of the Samaritans and other neighboring nations, that an embassy was sent to King Darius to implore his favor and protection, which was accordingly obtained. This legend, as developed in the degree, is contained neither in Ezra nor in the apocryphal books of Esdras. It is found only in the *Antiquities* of Josephus (lib. xi., cap. iv., sec. 9), and thence there is the strongest internal evidence to show that it was derived by the inventor of the degree. Who that inventor was we can only conjecture. But as we have the statements of both Ragon and Kloss that the Baron de Tschoudy composed the degree of Knight of the East, and as that degree is the first section of the system of which the Prince of Jerusalem is the second, we may reasonably suppose that the latter was also composed by him. The degree being one of those adopted by the Emperors of the East and West in their system, which Stephen Morin was authorized to propagate in America, it was introduced into America long before the establishment of the Supreme Council of the Scottish Rite. A Council was established by Henry A. Francken, about 1767, at Albany, in the State of New York, and a Grand Council organized by Myers, in 1788, in Charleston, South Carolina. This body exercised sovereign powers even after the establishment of the Supreme Council, May 31, 1801, for, in 1802, it granted a Warrant for the establishment of a Mark Lodge in Charleston, and another in the same year, for a Lodge of Perfection, in Savannah, Georgia. But under the present regulations of the Ancient and Accepted Scottish Rite, this prerogative has been abolished, and Grand Councils of Princes of Jerusalem no longer exist. The old regulation, that the Master of a Lodge of Perfection must be at least a Prince of Jerusalem, which was contained in the Constitution of the Grand Council, has also been repealed, together with most of the privileges which formerly appertained to the degree. A decision of the Supreme Council, in 1870, has even obliterated Councils of the Princes of Jerusalem as a separate organization, authorized to confer the preliminary degree of Knights of the East, and placed such Councils within the bosom of Rose Croix Chapters, a provision of which, as a manifest innovation on the ancient system, the expediency, or at least the propriety, may be greatly doubted.

Bodies of this degree are called Councils. According to the old rituals, the officers were a Most Equitable, a Senior and Junior Most Enlightened, a Grand Treasurer, and Grand Secretary. The more recent ritual of the Southern Jurisdiction of the United States has substituted for these a Most Illustrious Tarshatha, a Most Venerable High Priest, a Most Excellent Scribe, two Most Enlightened Wardens, and other officers. Yellow is the symbolic color of the degree, and the apron is crimson (formerly white), lined and bordered with yellow. The jewel is a medal of gold, on one side of which is inscribed a hand holding an equally poised balance, and on the other a double-edged, cross-hilted sword erect, between three stars around the point, and the letters D and Z on each side.

The Prince of Jerusalem is also the Fifty-third Degree of the Metropolitan Chapter of France, and the Forty-fifth of the Rite of Mizraim.

Prince of Jerusalem, Jewel of. Should be a gold incrustation on a lozenge-shaped piece of mother-of-pearl. Equipoise scales held by hand, sword, five stars, one larger than the other four, and the letters D and Z in Hebrew, one on either side of the scales. The five-pointed crown, within a triangle of gold, has also been used as a jewel of this Sixteenth Degree.

Prince of Mercy. (*Prince du Merci.*) The Twenty-sixth Degree of the Ancient and Accepted Scottish Rite, called also *Scottish Trinitarian* or *Ecossais Trinitaire*. It is one of the eight degrees which were added on the organization of the Scottish Rite to the original twenty-five of the Rite of Perfection.

It is a Christian degree in its construction, and treats of the triple covenant of mercy which God made with man; first with Abraham by circumcision; next, with the Israelites in the wilderness, by the intermediation of Moses; and lastly, with all mankind, by the death and sufferings of Jesus Christ. It is in allusion to these three acts of mercy, that the degree derives its two names of Scottish Trinitarian and Prince of Mercy, and not, as Ragon supposes, from any reference to the Fathers of Mercy, a religious society formerly engaged in the ransoming of Christian captives at Algiers. Chemin Dupontès (*Mem. Sur l'Ecoss*, p. 373) says that the Scottish rituals of the degree are too full of the Hermetic philosophy, an error from which the French Cahiers are exempt; and he condemns much of its doctrines as "hyperbolique plaisanterie." But the modern rituals as now practised are obnoxious to no such objection. The symbolic development of the number three of course constitutes a large part of its lecture; but the real dogma of the degree is the *importance of Truth,* and to this all its ceremonies are directed.

Bodies of the degree are called Chapters. The presiding officer is called Most Excellent Chief Prince, the Wardens are styled Excellent. In the old rituals these officers represented Moses, Aaron, and Eleazar; but the abandonment of these personations in the modern rituals is, I think, an improvement. The apron is red bordered with white, and the jewel is an equilateral triangle, within which is a heart. This was formerly inscribed with the Hebrew letter *tau,* now with the letters I. H. S.; and, to add to the Christianization which these letters give to the degree, the American Councils have adopted a tessera in the form of a small fish of ivory or mother-of-pearl, in allusion to the well-known usage of the primitive Christians.

Prince of the Tabernacle. (*Prince du Tabernacle.*) The Twenty-fourth Degree of the Ancient and Accepted Scottish Rite. In the old rituals the degree was intended to illustrate the directions given for the building of the tabernacle, the particulars of which are recorded in the twenty-fifth chapter of Exodus. The Lodge is called a Hierarchy, and its officers are a Most Powerful Chief Prince, representing Moses, and three Wardens, whose style is Powerful, and who respectively represent Aaron, Bezaleel, and Aholiab. In the modern rituals of the United States, the three principal officers are called the Leader, the High Priest, and the Priest, and respectively represent Moses, Aaron, and Ithamar, his son. The ritual is greatly enlarged; and while the main idea of the degree is retained, the ceremonies represent the initiation into the mysteries of the Mosaic tabernacle.

The jewel is the letter A, in gold, suspended from a broad crimson ribbon. The apron is white, lined with scarlet and bordered with green. The flap is sky-blue. On the apron is depicted a representation of the tabernacle.

This degree appears to be peculiar to the Scottish Rite and its modifications. I have not met with it in any of the other Rites.

Proclamation. At the installation of the officers of a Lodge, or any other Masonic body, and especially a Grand Lodge or Grand Chapter, proclamation is made in a Lodge or Chapter by the installing officer, and in a Grand Lodge or Grand Chapter by the Grand Marshal. Proclamation is also made on some other occasions, and on such occasions the Grand Marshal performs the duty.

Proclamation of Cyrus. A ceremony in the American Royal Arch. We learn from Scripture that in the first year of Cyrus, the King of Persia, the captivity of the Jews was terminated. Cyrus, from his conversations with Daniel and the other Jewish captives of learning and piety, as well as from his perusal of their sacred books, more especially the prophecies of Isaiah, had become imbued with a knowledge of true religion, and hence had even publicly announced to his subjects his belief in the God "which the nation of the Israelites worshipped." He was consequently impressed with an earnest desire to fulfil the prophetic declarations of which he was the subject, and to rebuild the Temple of Jerusalem. Accordingly, he issued a proclamation, which we find in Ezra, as follows:

"Thus saith Cyrus, King of Persia, The Lord God of heaven hath given me all the kingdoms of the earth; and he hath charged me to build him a house at Jerusalem, which is in Judea. Who is there among you of all his people? his God be with him, and let him go up to Jerusalem, which is in Judea, and build the house of the Lord God of Israel (he is the God) which is in Jerusalem."

With the publication of this proclamation of Cyrus commences what may be called the second part of the Royal Arch Degree.

Progressive Masonry. Freemasonry is undoubtedly a progressive science, and yet the fundamental principles of Freemasonry are the same now as they were at the very beginning of the Institution. Its landmarks are unchangeable. In these there can be no alteration, no diminution, no addition. When, therefore, we say that Freemasonry is progressive in its character, we of course do not mean to allude to this unalterable part of its constitution. But there is a progress which every science must undergo, and which many of them have already undergone, to which the science of Freemasonry is subject. Thus we say of chemistry that it is a progressive science. Two hundred years ago, all its principles, so far as they were known, were directed to such futile inquiries as the philosopher's stone and the elixir of immortality. Now these principles have become more thoroughly understood, and more definitely established, and the object of their application is more noble and philosophic. The writings of the chemists of the former and the present period sufficiently indicate this progress of the science. And yet the elementary principles of chemistry are unchangeable. Its truths were the same then as they are now. Some of them were at that time unknown, because no mind of sufficient research had discovered them; but they existed as truths, from the very creation of matter; and now they have only been developed, not invented.

So it is with Freemasonry. It too has had its progress. Masons are now expected to be more learned than formerly in all that relates to the science of the Order. Its origin, its history, its objects, are now considered worthy of the attentive consideration of its disciples. The rational explanation of its ceremonies and symbols, and their connection with ancient systems of religion and philosophy, are now considered as necessary topics of inquiry for all who desire to distinguish themselves as proficients in Masonic science.

In all these things we see a great difference between the Masons of the present and of former days. In Europe, a century ago, such inquiries were considered as legitimate subjects of Masonic study. Hutchinson published in 1760, in England, his admirable work entitled *The Spirit of Freemasonry,* in which the deep philosophy of the Institution was fairly developed with much learning and ingenuity. Preston's *Illustrations of Masonry,* printed at a not much later period, also exhibits the system treated, in many places, in a philosophical manner. Lawrie's *History of Freemasonry,* published in Scotland in 1804, is a work containing much profound historical and antiquarian research. And in the present century, the works of Oliver alone would be sufficient to demonstrate to the most cursory observer that Freemasonry has a claim to be ranked among the learned institutions of the day. In Germany and France, the press has been borne down with the weight of abstruse works on our Order, written by men of the highest literary pretensions.

In America, notwithstanding the really excellent work of Salem Town on *Speculative Masonry,* published in 1818, and the learned *Discourses* of Dr. T. M. Harris, published in 1801, it is only within a few years that Masonry has begun to assume the exalted position of a literary institution.

Proficiency. The necessity that anyone who devotes himself to the acquisition of a science should become a proficient in its elementary instructions before he can expect to grasp and comprehend its higher branches, is so almost self-evident as to need no argument. But as Speculative Masonry is a science, it is equally necessary that a requisite qualification for admission to a higher degree should be a suitable proficiency in the preceding one. It is true, that we do not find in express words in the Old Constitutions any regulations requiring proficiency as preliminary to advancement, but their whole spirit is evidently to that effect; and hence we find it prescribed in the Old Constitutions, that no Master shall take an apprentice for less than seven years, because it was expected that he should acquire a competent knowledge of the *mystery* before he could be admitted as a Fellow. The modern Constitution of the Grand Lodge of England provides that no Lodge shall confer a higher degree on any brother until he has passed an examination in open Lodge on the preceding degrees (Rule 195), and many, perhaps most, of the Grand Lodges of this country have adopted a similar regulation. The ritual of all the Symbolic degrees, and, indeed, of the higher degrees, and that too in all rites, makes the imperative demand of every candidate whether he has made suitable proficiency in the preceding degree, an affirmative answer to which is required before the rites of initiation can be proceeded with. This answer is, according to the ritual, that "he has"; but some Masons have sought to evade the consequence of an acknowledgment of ignorance and want of proficiency by a change of the language of the ritual into "such as time and circumstances would permit." But this is an innovation, unsanctioned by any authority, and should be repudiated. If the candidate has not made proper proficiency, the ritual, outside of all statutory regulations, refuses him advancement.

Anderson, in the second edition of his *Constitutions* (p. 71), cites what he calls "an old record," which says that in the reign of Edward III. of England it was ordained "that Master Masons, or Masters of work, shall be examined whether they be able of cunning to serve their respective Lords, as well the Highest as the Lowest, to the Honour and Worship of the aforesaid Art, and to the Profit of their Lords."

Here, then, we may see the origin of that usage, which is still practised in every well-governed Lodge, not only of demanding a proper degree of proficiency in the candidate, but also of testing that proficiency by an examination.

This cautious and honest fear of the Fraternity lest any brother should assume the duties of a position which he could not faithfully discharge, and which is, in our time, tantamount to a candidate's advancing to a degree for which he is not prepared, is again exhibited in all the Old Constitutions. Thus in the Lansdowne Manuscript, whose date is referred to the middle of the sixteenth century, it is charged "that no Mason take on him no Lord's work, nor other man's but if [unless] he know himself well able to perform the work, so that the Craft have no slander." The same regulation, and almost in the same language, is to be found in all the subsequent manuscripts.

In the Charges of 1722, it is directed that "a younger brother shall be instructed in working, to prevent spoiling the materials for want of judgment, and for encreasing and continuing of brotherly love." (*Constitutions,* 1723, p. 53.) It was, with the same view, that all of the Old Constitutions made it imperative that no Master should take an apprentice for less than seven years, because it was expected that he should acquire a competent knowledge of the mystery of the Craft before he could be admitted as a Fellow.

Notwithstanding these charges had a more particular reference to the operative part of the art, they clearly show the great stress that was placed by our ancient brethren upon the necessity of skill and proficiency; and they have furnished the precedents upon which are based all the similar regulations that have been subsequently applied to Speculative Masonry.

Provincial Grand Officers. The officers of a Provincial Grand Lodge correspond in title to those of the Grand Lodge. The Provincial Grand Treasurer is elected, but the other officers are nominated by the Provincial Grand Master. They are not by such appointment members of the Grand Lodge, nor do they take any rank out of their province. They must all be residents of the province and subscribing members to some Lodge therein. Provincial Grand Wardens must be Masters or Past Masters of a Lodge, and Provincial Grand Deacons, Wardens, or Past Wardens.

Provincial Master of the Red Cross. The Sixth Degree of the Rite of Clerks of Strict Observance.

Provost and Judge. (*Prévôt et Juge.*) The Seventh Degree of the Ancient and Accepted Scottish Rite. The history of the degree relates that it was founded by Solomon, King of Israel, for the purpose of strengthening his means of preserving order among the vast number of craftsmen engaged in the construction of the Temple. Tito, Prince Harodim, Adoniram, and Abda his father, were first created Provosts and Judges, who were afterward directed by Solomon to initiate his favorite and intimate secretary, Joabert, and to give him the keys of all the building. In the old rituals, the Master of a Lodge of Provosts and Judges represents Tito, Prince Harodim, the first Grand Warden and Inspector of the three hundred architects. The number of lights is six, and the symbolic color is red. In the more recent ritual of the Southern Jurisdiction of the United States there has been a slight change. The legend is substantially preserved, but the presiding officer represents Azarias, the son of Nathan.

The jewel is a golden key, having the letter A within a triangle engraved on the ward. The collar is red. The apron is white, lined with red, and is furnished with a pocket.

This was one of Ramsay's degrees, and was originally called *Maître Irlandais,* or Irish Master.

Proxy Installation. The Regulations of 1721 provide that, if the new Grand Master be absent from the Grand Feast, he may be proclaimed if proper assurance be given that he will serve, in which case the old Grand Master shall act as his proxy and receive the usual homage. This has led to a custom, once very common in America, but now getting into disuse, of installing an absent officer by proxy. Such installations are called proxy installations. Their propriety is very questionable.

Proxy Master. In the Grand Lodge of Scotland, a Lodge is permitted to elect any Master Mason who holds a diploma of the Grand Lodge, although he may not be a member of the Lodge, as its Proxy Master. He nominates two Proxy Wardens, and the three then become members of the Grand Lodge and representatives of the Lodge. Great opposition has recently been made to remind us of the classic method of representing her statutes with a rule or measure in her hand.

Prussia. Frederick William I. of Prussia was so great an enemy of the Masonic Institution, that until his death it was scarcely known in his dominions, and the initiation, in 1738, of his son, the Crown Prince, was necessarily kept a secret from his father. But in 1740 Frederick II. ascended the throne, and Masonry soon felt the advantages of a royal patron. The Baron de Bielefeld says (*Lettres,* i., 157) that in that year the king himself opened a Lodge at Charlottenburg, and initiated his brother, Prince William, the Margrave of Brandenburg, and the Duke of Holstein-Beck. Bielefeld and the Counselor Jordan, in 1740, established the Lodge of the Three Globes at Berlin, which soon afterward assumed the rank of a Grand Lodge. There are now in Prussia three Grand Lodges, the seats of all of them being at Berlin. These are the Grand Lodge of the Three Globes, established in 1740, the Grand Lodge Royal York of Friendship, established in 1760, and the National Grand Lodge of Germany, established in 1770. There is no country in the world where Freemasonry is more profoundly studied as a science than in Prussia, and much of the abstruse learning of the Order, for which Germany has been distinguished, is to be found among the members of the Prussian Lodges. Unfortunately, they have, for a long time, been marked with an intolerant spirit toward the Jews, whose initiation was strictly forbidden until very recently, when that stain was removed, and the tolerant principles of the Order were recognized by the abrogation of the offensive laws.

Prussian Knight. See *Noachite.*

Publications, Masonic. The fact that, within the past few years, Freemasonry has taken its place—and an imposing one, too—in the literature of the times; that men of genius and learning have devoted themselves to its investigation; that its principles and its system have become matters of study and research; and that the results of this labor of inquiry have been given, and still continue to be given, to the world at large, in the form of treatises on Masonic science, have at length introduced the new question among the Fraternity, whether Masonic books are of good or of evil tendency to the Institution. Many well-meaning but timid members of the Fraternity object to the freedom with which Masonic topics are discussed in printed works. They think that the veil is too much withdrawn by modern Masonic writers, and that all doctrine and instruction should be confined to oral teaching, within the limits of the Lodge room. Hence, to them, the art of printing becomes useless for the diffusion of Masonic knowledge; and thus, whatever may be the attainments of a Masonic scholar, the fruits of his study and experience would be confined to the narrow limits of his personal presence. Such objectors draw no distinction between the ritual and the philosophy of Masonry. Like the old priests of Egypt, they would have everything concealed under hieroglyphics, and would as soon think of opening a Lodge in public as they would of discussing, in a printed book, the principles and design of the Institution.

The Grand Lodge of England, some years ago, adopted a regulation which declared it penal to print or publish any part of the proceedings of a Lodge, or the names of the persons present as such a Lodge, without the permission of the Grand Master. The rule, however, evidently referred to local proceedings only, and had no relation whatever to the publication of Masonic authors and editors; for the English Masonic press, since the days of Hutchinson, in the Middle of the last century, has been distinguished for the freedom, as well as learning, with which the most abstruse principles of our Order have been discussed.

Fourteen years ago the Committee of Foreign Correspondence of a prominent Grand Lodge affirmed that Masonic literature was doing more "harm than good to the Institution." About the same time the committee of another equally prominent Grand Lodge were not ashamed to express their regret that so much prominence of notice is, "in several Grand Lodge proceedings, given to Masonic publications. Masonry existed and flourished, was harmonious and happy, in their absence."

When one reads such diatribes against Masonic literature and Masonic progress—such blind efforts to hide under the bushel the light that should be on the hill-top—he is incontinently reminded of a similar iconoclast, who, more than four centuries ago, made a like onslaught on the pernicious effects of learning.

The immortal Jack Cade, in condemning Lord Say to death as a patron of learning, gave vent to words of which the language of these enemies of Masonic literature seems to be but the echo:

"Thou hast most traitoriously corrupted the youth of the realm, in erecting a grammar-school; and whereas, before, our forefathers had no other books but the score and the tally, thou hast caused printing to be used; and contrary to the king, his crown, and dignity, thou hast built a paper-mill. It will be proved to thy face that thou hast men about thee that usually talk of a noun and a verb, and such abominable words as no Christian ear can endure to hear."

I belong to no such school. On the contrary, I believe that too much cannot be written and printed and read about the philosophy and history, the science and symbolism of Freemasonry; provided always the writing is confided to those who rightly understand their art. In Masonry, as in astronomy, in geology, or in any other of the arts and sciences, a new book by an expert must always be esteemed a valuable contribution. The production of silly and untutored minds will fall of themselves into oblivion without the aid of official persecution; but that which is really valuable—which presents new facts, or furnishes suggestive thoughts—will, in spite of the denunciations of the Jack Cades of Masonry, live to instruct the brethren, and to elevate the tone and standing of the Institution.

Dr. Oliver, who has written more on Masonry than any other author, says on this subject: "I conceive it to be an error in judgment to discountenance the publication of philosophical disquisitions on the subject of Freemasonry, because such a proceeding would not only induce the world to think that our pretensions are incapable of enduring the test of inquiry, but would also have a tendency to restore the dark ages of superstition, when even the sacred writings were prohibited, under an apprehension that their contents might be misunderstood or perverted to the propagation of unsound doctrines and pernicious practices; and thus would ignorance be transmitted, as a legacy, from one generation to another."

Still further pursuing this theme, and passing from the unfavorable influence which must be exerted upon the world by our silence, to the injury that must accrue to the Craft, the same learned writer goes on to say, that "no hypotheses can be more untenable than that which forebodes evil to the Masonic Institution from the publication of Masonic treatises illustrative of its philosophical and moral tendency." And in view of the meager and unsatisfactory nature of the lectures, in the form in which they are delivered in the Lodges, he wisely suggests that "if strictures on the science and philosophy of the Order were placed within every brother's reach, a system of examination and research would soon be substituted for the dull and uninteresting routine which, in so many instances, characterizes our private meetings. The brethren would become excited by the inquiry, and a rich series of new beauties and excellences would be their reward."

Of such a result I have no doubt. In consequence of the increase of Masonic publications in this country within a few years, Masonry has already been elevated to a high position. If there be any who still deem it a merely social institution, without a philosophy or literature; if there be any who speak of it with less admiration than it justly deserves, we may be assured that such men have read as little as they have thought on the subject of its science and its history. A few moments of conversation with a Mason will show whether he is one of those contracted craftsmen who suppose that Masonic *"brightness"* consists merely in a knowledge of the correct mode of working one's way into a Lodge, or whether he is one who has read and properly appreciated the various treatises on the "royal art," in which men of genius and learning have developed the true spirit and design of the Order.

Such is the effect of Masonic publications upon the Fraternity; and the result of all my experience is, that *enough has not been published.* Cheap books on all Masonic subjects, easily accessible to the masses of the Order, are necessaries essential to the elevation and extension of the Institution. Too many of them confine their acquirements to a knowledge of the signs and the ceremonies of initiation. There they cease their researches. They make no study of the philosophy and the antiquities of the Order. They do not seem to know that the modes of recognition are simply intended as means of security against imposition, and that the ceremonial rites are worth nothing without the symbolism of which they are only the external exponents. Masonry for them is nerveless—senseless—lifeless; it is an empty voice without meaning—a tree of splendid foliage, but without a single fruit.

The monitorial instructions of the Order, as they are technically called, contain many things which probably, at one time, it would have been deemed improper to print; and there are some Masons, even at this day, who think that Webb and Cross were too free in their publications. And yet we have never heard of any evil effects arising from the reading of our Monitors, even upon those who have not been initiated. On the contrary, meager as are the explanations given in those works, and unsatisfactory as they must be to one seeking for the full light of Masonry, they have been the means, in many instances, of inducing the profane, who have read them, to admire our Institution, and to knock at the "door of Masonry" for admission—while we regret to say that they sometimes comprise the whole instruction that a candidate gets from an ignorant Master. Without these published Monitors, even that little beam of light would be wanting to illuminate his path.

But if the publication and general diffusion of our elementary text-books have been of acknowledged advantage to the character of the Institution, and have, by the information, little as it is, which they communicate, been of essential benefit to the Fraternity, we cannot see why a more extensive system of instruction on the legends, traditions, and symbols of the Order should not be productive of still greater good.

Years ago, we uttered on this subject sentiments which we now take occasion to repeat.

Without an adequate course of reading, no Mason can now take a position of any distinction in the ranks of the Fraternity. Without extending his studies beyond what is taught in the brief lectures of the Lodge, he can never properly appreciate the end and nature of Freemasonry as a speculative science. The lectures constitute but the skeleton of Masonic science. The muscles and nerves and blood-vessels, which are to give vitality, and beauty, and health, and vigor to that lifeless skeleton, must be found in the commentaries on them which the learning and research of Masonic writers have given to the Masonic student.

The objections to treatises and disquistions on Masonic subjects, that there is danger, through them, of giving too much light to the world without, has not the slightest support from experience. In England, in France, and in Germany, scarcely any restriction has been observed by Masonic writers, except as to what is emphatically esoteric; and yet we do not believe that the profane world is wiser in those countries than in our own in respect to the secrets of Freemasonry. In the face of these publications, the world without has remained as ignorant of the aporrheta of our art, as if no work had ever been written on the subject; while the world within—the Craft themselves—have been enlightened and instructed, and their views of Masonry (not as a social or charitable society, but as a philosophy, a science, a religion) have been elevated and enlarged.

The truth is, that men who are not Masons never read authentic Masonic works. They have no interest in the topics discussed, and could not understand them, from a want of the preparatory education which the

Lodge alone can supply. Therefore, were a writer even to trench a little on what may be considered as being really the *arcana* of Masonry, there is no danger of his thus making an improper revelation to improper persons.

Public Ceremonies. Most of the ceremonies of Masonry are strictly private, and can be conducted only in the presence of the initiated. But some of them, from their nature, are necessarily performed in public. Such are the burials of deceased brethren, the laying of corner-stones of public edifices, and the dedications of Masonic halls. The installation of the officers of a Lodge, or Grand Lodge, are also sometimes conducted in public in America. But the ceremonies in this case differ slightly from those of a private installation in the Lodge room, portions of the ceremony having to be omitted. The reputation of the Order requires that these ceremonies should be conducted with the utmost propriety, and the Manuals and Monitors furnish the fullest details of the order of exercises. Preston, in his *illustrations,* was the first writer who gave a printed account of the mode of conducting these public ceremonies, and to him we are most probably indebted for their ritual. Anderson, however, gave in the first edition of the *Constitutions* the prescribed form for constituting new Lodges, and installing their officers, which is the model upon which Preston, and other writers, have subsequently framed their more enlarged formulæ.

Puerility of Freemasonry. "The absurdities and puerilities of Freemasonry are fit only for children, and are unworthy of the time or attention of wise men." Such is the language of its adversaries, and the apothegm is delivered with all that self-sufficiency which shows that the speaker is well satisfied with his own wisdom, and is very ready to place himself in the category of those wise men whose opinion he invokes. This charge of a puerility of design and object of Freemasonry is worth examination.

Is it then possible, that those scholars of unquestioned strength of intellect and depth of science, who have devoted themselves to the study of Masonry, and who have in thousands of volumes given the result of their researches, have been altogether mistaken in the direction of their labors, and have been seeking to develop, not the principles of a philosophy, but the mechanism of a toy, Or is the assertion that such is the fact a mere sophism, such as ignorance is every day uttering, and a conclusion to which men are most likely to arrive when they talk of that of which they know nothing, like the critic who reviews a book that he has never read, or the skeptic who attacks a creed that he does not comprehend? Such claims to an inspired infallibility are not uncommon among men of unsound judgment. Thus, when Gall and Spurzheim first gave to the world their wonderful discoveries in reference to the organization and the functions of the brain—discoveries which have since wrought a marked revolution in the sciences of anatomy, physiology, and ethics—the Edinburgh reviewers attempted to demolish these philosophers and their new system, but succeeded only in exposing their own ignorance of the science they were discussing. Time, which is continually evolving truth out of every intellectual conflict, has long since shown that the German philosophers were right and that their Scottish critics were wrong. How common is it, even at this day, to hear men deriding Alchemy as a system of folly and imposture, cultivated only by madmen and knaves, when the researches of those who have investigated the subject without prejudice, but with patient learning, have shown, without any possibility of doubt, that these old alchemists, so long the objects of derision to the ignorant, were religious philosophers, and that their science had really nothing to do with the discovery of an elixir of life or the transmutation of the baser metals into gold, but that they, like the Freemasons, with whom they have a strong affinity, concealed under profound symbols, intelligible only to themselves, the search after Divine Truth and the doctrine of immortal life. Truth was the gold which they eliminated from all mundane things, and the immortality of the soul was the elixir of everlasting life which perpetually renewed youth, and took away the power of death.

So it is with Freemasonry. Those who abuse it know nothing of its inner spirit, of its profound philosophy, of the pure religious life that it inculcates.

To one who is at all acquainted with its organization, Freemasonry presents itself under two different aspects:

First, as a secret society distinguished by a peculiar ritual;

And secondly, as a society having a philosophy on which it is founded, and which it proposes to teach to its disciples.

These by way of distinction may be called the *ritualistic* and the *philosophical* elements of Freemasonry.

The *ritualistic* element of Freemasonry is that which relates to the due performance of the rites and ceremonies of the Order. Like the rubrics of the church, which indicate when the priest and congregation shall kneel and when they shall stand, it refers to questions such as these: What words shall be used in such a place, and what ceremony shall be observed on such an occasion? It belongs entirely to the inner organization of the Institution, or to the manner in which its services shall be conducted, and is interesting or important only to its own members. The language of its ritual or the form of its ceremonies has nothing more to do with the philosophic designs of Freemasonry than the rubrics of a church have to do with the religious creed professed by that church. It might at any time be changed in its most material points, without in the slightest degree affecting the essential character of the Institution.

Of course, this ritualistic element is in one sense important to the members of the society, because, by a due observance of the ritual, a general uniformity is preserved. But beyond this, the Masonic ritual makes no claim to the consideration of scholars, and never has been made, and, indeed, from the very nature of its secret character, never can be made, a topic of discussion with those who are outside of the Fraternity.

But the other, the *philosophical* element of Freemasonry, is one of much importance. For it, and through it, I do make the plea that the Institution is entitled to the respect, and even veneration, of all good men, and is well worth the careful consideration of scholars.

A great many theories have been advanced by Masonic writers as to the real origin of the Institution, as to the time when and the place where it first had its birth. It has been traced to the mysteries of the ancient Pagan world, to the Temple of King Solomon, to the Roman Colleges of Artificers, to the Crusades for the recovery of the Holy Land, to the Gilds of the Middle Ages, to the Stone-Masons of Strasburg and Cologne and even to the revolutionary struggle in England in the time of the commonwealth, and to the secret efforts of the adherents of the house of Stuart to recover the throne. But whatever theory may be selected, and wheresoever and whensoever it may be supposed to have received its birth, one thing is certain, namely, that for generations past, and yet within the records of history, it has, unlike other mundane things, presented to the world an unchanged organization. Take, for instance, the theory which traces it back to one of the most recent periods, that, namely, which places the organization of the Order of Freemasons at the building of the Cathedral of Strasburg, in the year 1275. During all the time that has since elapsed, full six hundred years, how has Freemasonry presented itself? Why, as a brotherhood organized and controlled by a secret discipline, engaged in important architectural labors, and combining with its operative tasks speculations of great religious import. If we see any change, it is simply this, that when the necessity no longer existed, the operative element was laid aside, and the speculative only was retained, but with a scrupulous preservation (as if it were for purposes of identification) of the technical language, the rules and regulations, the working-tools, and the discipline of the operative art. The material only on which they wrought was changed. The disciples and followers of Erwin of Steinbach, the Master Builder of Strasburg, were engaged, under the influence of a profoundly religious sentiment, in the construction of a material edifice to the glory of God. The more modern workers in Freemasonry are under the same religious influence, engaged in the construction of a spiritual temple. Does not this long continuance of a brotherhood employed in the same pursuit, or changing it only from a material to a spiritual character, but retaining its identity of organization, demand for itself some respect, and, if for nothing else, at least for its antiquity, some share of veneration?

But this is not all. This society or brotherhood, or confraternity as it might more appropriately be called, is distinguished from all other associations by the possession of certain symbols, myths, and, above all else, a *Golden Legend,* all of which are directed to the purification of the heart, to the elevation of the mind, to the development of the great doctrine of immortality.

Now the question where and when these symbols, myths, and legends arose is one that is well worth the investigation of scholars, because it is intimately connected with the history of the human intellect. Did the Stone-Masons and building corporations of the Middle Ages invent them? Certainly not, for they are found in organizations that existed ages previously. The Greeks at Eleusis taught the same dogma of immortal life in the same symbolic mode, and their legend, if it differed from the Masonic in its accidents, was precisely identical in its substance. For Hiram there was Dionysus, for the acacia the myrtle, but there were the same mourning, the same discovery, the same rejoicing, because what had been lost was found, and then the same ineffable light, and the same sacred teaching of the name of God and the soul's immortality. And so an ancient orator, who had passed through one of these old Greek Lodges—for such, without much violence of language, they may well be called—declared that those who have endured the initiation into the mysteries entertain better hopes both of the end of life and of the eternal future. Is not this the very object and design of the legend of the Master's Degree? And this same peculiar form of symbolic initiation is to be found among the old Egyptians and in the island of Samothracia, thousands of years before the light of Christianity dawned upon the world to give the seal of its Master and Founder to the Divine truth of the resurrection.

This will not, it is true, prove the descent of Freemasonry, as now organized, from the religious mysteries of antiquity; although this is one of the theories of its origin entertained and defended by scholars of no mean pretension. But it will prove an identity of design in the moral and intellectual organization of all these institutions, and it will give the Masonic student subjects for profound study when he asks the interesting questions—Whence came these symbols, myths, and legends? Who invented them? How and why have they been preserved? Looking back into the remotest days of recorded history, we find a priesthood in an island of Greece and another on the banks of the Nile, teaching the existence of a future life by symbols and legends, which convey the lesson in a peculiar mode. And now, after thousands of years have elapsed, we find the same symbolic and legendary method of instruction, for the same purpose, preserved in the depository of what is comparatively a modern institution. And between these two extremes of the long past and the present now, we find the intervening period occupied by similar associations, succeeding each other from time to time, and spreading over different countries, but all engaged in the same symbolic instruction, with substantially the same symbols and the same mythical history.

Does not all this present a problem in moral and intellectual philosophy, and in the archeology of ethics, which is well worthy of an attempted solution? How unutterably puerile seem the objections and the objurgations of a few contracted minds, guided only by prejudice, when we consider the vast questions of deep interest that are connected with Freemasonry as a part of those great brotherhoods that have filled the world for so many ages, so far back, indeed, that some philosophic historians have supposed that they must have derived their knowledge of the doctrines which they taught in their mystic assemblies from direct revelation through an ancient priesthood that gives no other evidence of its former existence but the results which it produced.

Man needs something more than the gratification of his animal wants. The mind requires food as well as the body, and nothing can better give that mental nutriment than the investigation of subjects which relate to the progress of the intellect and the growth of the religious sentiment.

Again, man was not made for himself alone. The old Stoic lived only for and within himself. But modern philosophy and modern religion teach no such selfish doctrine. Man is but part of the great brotherhood of man, and each one must be ready to exclaim with the old poet, "Homo sum; humani nihil à me alienum puto," *I am a man, and I deem nothing relating to mankind to be foreign to my feelings.* Men study ancient history simply that they may learn what their brother men have done in former times, and they read the philosophers and poets of Greece and Rome that they may know what were the speculations of those old thinkers, and they strive to measure the intellect of man as it was then and as it is now, because the study of the growth of intellectual philosophy and the investigation of the mental and moral powers come home to us all as subjects of common interest.

Looking, then, upon Freemasonry as one of those associations which furnish the evidence and the example of the progress of man in intellectual, moral, and religious development, it may be well claimed for it that its design, its history, and its philosophy, so far from being puerile, are well entitled to the respect of the world, and are worth the careful research of scholars.

Purity. In the Ancient Mysteries purity of heart and life was an essential prerequisite to initiation, because by initiation the aspirant was brought to a knowledge of God, to know whom was not permitted to the impure. For, says Origen (*Cont. Cel.*, vi.), "a defiled heart cannot see God, but he must be pure who desires to obtain a proper view of a pure Being." And in the same spirit the Divine Master says: "Blessed are the pure in heart, for they shall see God." But "to see God" is a Hebraism, signifying to possess him, to be spiritually in communion with him, to know his true character. Now to acquire this knowledge of God, symbolized by the knowledge of his Name, is the great object of Masonic, as it was of all ancient initiation; and hence the candidate in Masonry is required to be pure, for "he only can stand in the holy place who hath clean hands and a pure heart."

Quatuor Coronati Lodge. This Lodge, No. 2076 on the roll of the Grand Lodge of England, was established in 1886, for the purpose of studying the History, Symbols, and Legends of Freemasonry, and it is in fact a Masonic Literary and Archeological Society, meeting as a tiled Lodge. Attached to the Lodge proper, which is limited to 40 full members, is a Correspondence Circle established in 1887, and now numbering over 3,000 members drawn from all parts of the world. The transactions of the Lodge are published under the title of *Ars Quatuor Coronatorum.* The Lodge is named after the "Four Crowned Martyrs" (*q.v.*). All Master Masons in good standing are eligible to membership in the Correspondence Circle. The dues are $2.50 a year, for which the valuable Transactions of the Lodge are sent to each member.

Rabboni. רבוני. Literally, *my Master,* equivalent to the pure Hebrew, *Adoni.* As a significant word in the higher degrees, it has been translated *"a most excellent Master,"* and its usage by the later Jews will justify that interpretation. Buxtorf (*Lex. Talmud.*) tells us that about the time of Christ this title arose in the school of Hillel, and was given to only seven of their wise men who were preeminent for their learning. Jahn (*Arch. Bib.,* § 106) says that Gamaliel, the preceptor of St. Paul, was one of these. They styled themselves the children of wisdom, which is an expression very nearly corresponding to the Greek φιλοσοφοι. The word occurs once, as applied to Christ, in the New Testament (John xx. 16), "Jesus said unto her, Mary. She turned herself, and saith unto him, Rabboni, which is to say, Master." The Masonic myth in the "Most Excellent Master's Degree," that it was the title addressed by the Queen of Sheba to King Solomon on beholding the magnificence and splendor of the Temple, wants the element of plausibility, inasmuch as the word was not in use in the time of Solomon.

Recusant. A term applied in English history to one who refused to acknowledge the supremacy of the king as head of the church. In Masonic law, the word is sometimes used to designate a Lodge or a Mason that refuses to obey an edict of the Grand Lodge. The arrest of the Charter, or the suspension or expulsion of the offender, would be the necessary punishment of such an offense.

Red. Red, scarlet, or crimson, for it is indifferently called by each of these names, is the appropriate color of the Royal Arch Degree, and is said symbolically to represent the ardor and zeal which should actuate all who are in possession of that sublime portion of Masonry. Portal (*Couleurs Symb.,* p. 116) refers the color red to fire, which was the symbol of the regeneration and purification of souls. Hence there seems to be a congruity in adopting it as the color of the Royal Arch, which refers historically to the regeneration or rebuilding of the Temple, and symbolically to the regeneration of life.

In the religious services of the Hebrews, red, or scarlet, was used as one of the colors of the veils of the tabernacle, in which, according to

Josephus, it was an emblem of the element of fire; it was also used in the ephod of the high priest, in the girdle, and in the breastplate. Red was, among the Jews, a color of dignity, appropriated to the most opulent or honorable, and hence the prophet Jeremiah, in describing the rich men of his country, speaks of them as those who "were brought up in scarlet."

In the Middle Ages, those knights who engaged in the wars of the Crusades, and especially the Templars, wore a red cross, as a symbol of their willingness to undergo martyrdom for the sake of religion; and the priests of the Roman Church still wear red vestments when they officiate on the festivals of those saints who were martyred.

Red is in the higher degrees of Masonry as predominating a color as blue is in the lower. Its symbolic significations differ, but they may generally be considered as alluding either to the virtue of fervency when the symbolism is moral, or to the shedding of blood when it is historical. Thus in the degree of Provost and Judge, it is historically emblematic of the violent death of one of the founders of the Institution; while in the degree of Perfection it is said to be a moral symbol of zeal for the glory of God, and for our own advancement toward perfection in Masonry and virtue.

In the degree of Rose Croix, red is the predominating color, and symbolizes the ardent zeal which should inspire all who are in search of that which is lost.

Where red is not used historically, and adopted as a memento of certain tragical circumstances in the history of Masonry, it is always, under some modification, a symbol of zeal and fervency.

These three colors, blue, purple, and red, were called in the former English lectures "the old colors of Masonry," and were said to have been selected "because they are royal, and such as the ancient kings and princes used to wear; and sacred history informs us that the veil of the Temple was composed of these colors."

Regeneration. In the Ancient Mysteries the doctrine of regeneration was taught by symbols: not the theological dogma of regeneration peculiar to the Christian church, but the philosophical dogma as a change from death to life—a new birth to immortal existence. Hence the last day of the Eleusinian mysteries, when the initiation was completed, was called, says Court de Gebelin (*M. P.*, iv., 322), *the day of regeneration.* This is the doctrine in the Masonic mysteries, and more especially in the symbolism of the Third Degree. We must not say that the Mason is regenerated when he is initiated, but that he has been indoctrinated into the philosophy of the regeneration, or the new birth of all things—of light out of darkness, or life out of death, of eternal life out of temporal death.

Refreshment. In Masonic language, *refreshment* is opposed in a peculiar sense to *labor.* While a Lodge is in activity it must be either at labor or at refreshment. If a Lodge is permanently closed until its next communication, the intervening period is one of abeyance, its activity for

Masonic duty having for the time been suspended; although its powers and privileges as a Lodge still exist, and may be at any time resumed. But where it is only temporarily closed, with the intention of soon again resuming labor, the intermediate period is called a time of refreshment, and the Lodge is said not to be closed, but to be called from labor to refreshment. The phrase is an old one, and is found in the earliest rituals of the last century. *Calling from labor to refreshment* differs from closing in this, that the ceremony is a very brief one, and that the Junior Warden then assumes the control of the Craft, in token of which he erects his column on his stand or pedestal, while the Senior Warden lays his down. This is reversed in *calling on,* in which the ceremony is equally brief.

The word *refreshment* no longer bears the meaning among Masons that it formerly did. It signifies not necessarily eating and drinking, but simply cessation from labor. A Lodge at refreshment may thus be compared to any other society when in a recess.

At the present day, the banquets of Lodges, when they take place, are always held after the Lodge is closed; although they are still supposed to be under the charge of the Junior Warden. When modern Lodges are called to refreshment, it is either as a part of the ceremony of the Third Degree, or for a brief period; sometimes extending to more than a day, when labor, which had not been finished, is to be resumed and concluded.

The mythical history of Masonry tells us that high twelve or noon was the hour at Solomon's Temple when the Craft were permitted to suspend their labor, which was resumed an hour after. In reference to this myth, a Lodge is at all times supposed to be called from labor to refreshment at "high twelve," and to be called on again "one hour after high twelve."

Regalia. Strictly speaking, the word regalia, from the Latin, *regalia,* royal things, signifies the ornaments of a king or queen, and is applied to the apparatus used at a coronation, such as the crown, scepter, cross, mound, etc. But it has in modern times been loosely employed to signify almost any kind of ornaments. Hence the collar and jewel, and sometimes even the apron, are called by many Masons the regalia. The word has the early authority of Preston. In the second edition of his *Illustrations* (1775), when on the subject of funerals, he uses the expression, "the body, with the regalia placed thereon, and two swords crossed." And at the end of the service he directs that "the *regalia* and ornaments of the deceased, if an officer of a Lodge, are returned to the Master in due form, and with the usual ceremonies." *Regalia* cannot here mean the Bible and *Book of Constitutions,* for there is a place in another part of the procession appropriated to them. It might have been supposed that by regalia, Preston referred to some particular decorations of the Lodge, had not his subsequent editors, Jones and Oliver, both interpolated the word "other" before ornaments, so as to make the sentence read "regalia and *other* ornaments," thus clearly indicating that they deemed the regalia a part of the ornaments of the deceased. The word is thus used in one of the headings of the modern Constitutions of the Grand Lodge of England. But in the text the more correct words "clothing and insignia" (Rule 282) are employed. There is, however, so great an error in the use of the word *regalia* to denote Masonic clothing, that it would be better to avoid it.

Rising Sun. The rising sun is represented by the Master, because as the sun by his rising opens and governs the day, so the Master is taught to open and govern his Lodge with equal regularity and precision.

Rite. The Latin word *ritus,* whence we get the English *rite,* signifies an approved usage or custom, or an external observance. Vossius derives it by metathesis from the Greek τρίβειν, whence literally it signifies a trodden path, and, metaphorically, a long-followed custom. As a Masonic term its application is therefore apparent. It signifies a method of conferring Masonic light by a collection and distribution of degrees. It is, in other words, the method and order observed in the government of a Masonic system.

The original system of Speculative Masonry consisted of only the three Symbolic degrees, called, therefore, Ancient Craft Masonry. Such was the condition of Freemasonry at the time of what is called the revival in 1717. Hence, this was the original Rite or approved usage, and so it continued in England until the year 1813, when at the union of the two Grand Lodges the "Holy Royal Arch" was declared to be a part of the system; and thus the English Rite was made legitimately to consist of four degrees.

But on the Continent of Europe, the organization of new systems began at a much earlier period, and by the invention of what are known as the high degrees a multitude of Rites was established. All of these agreed in one important essential. They were built upon the three Symbolic degrees, which, in every instance, constituted the fundamental basis upon which they were erected. They were intended as an expansion and development of the Masonic ideas contained in these degrees. The Apprentice, Fellow-Craft, and Master's degrees were the porch through which every initiate was required to pass before he could gain entrance into the inner temple which had been erected by the founders of the Rite. They were the text, and the high degrees the commentary.

Hence arises the law, that whatever may be the constitution and teachings of any Rite as to the higher degrees peculiar to it, the three Symbolic degrees being common to all the Rites, a Master Mason, in any one of the Rites, may visit and labor in a Master's Lodge of every other Rite. It is only after that degree is passed that the exclusiveness of each Rite begins to operate.

There has been a multitude of these Rites. Some of them have lived only with their authors, and died when their parental energy in fostering them ceased to exert itself. Others have had a more permanent existence, and still continue to divide the Masonic family, furnishing, however, only diverse methods of attaining to the same great end, the acquisition of Divine Truth by Masonic light.

Royal Arch Apron. At the triennial meeting of the General Grand Chapter of the United States at Chicago, in 1859, a Royal Arch apron was prescribed, consisting of a lambskin (silk or satin being strictly prohibited), to be lined and bound with scarlet, on the flap of which should be placed a triple tau cross within a triangle, and all within a circle.

Royal Arch Badge. The triple tau, consisting of three tau crosses conjoined at their feet, constitutes the Royal Arch badge. The English Masons call it the "emblem of all emblems," and the "grand emblem of Royal Arch Masonry." The English Royal Arch lecture thus defines it: "The triple tau forms two right angles on each of the exterior lines, and another at the centre, by their union; for the three angles of each triangle are equal to two right angles. This, being triplified, illustrates the jewel worn by the companions of the Royal Arch, which, by its intersection, forms a given number of angles that may be taken in five several combinations." It is used in the Royal Arch Masonry of Scotland, and has, for the last ten or fifteen years, been adopted officially in the United States.

Royal Arch Captain. The sixth officer in a Royal Arch Chapter according to the American system. He represents the *sar hatabahim,* or Captain of the King's Guards. He sits in front of the Council and at the entrance to the fourth veil, to guard the approaches to which is his duty. He wears a white robe and cap, is armed with a sword, and bears a white banner on which is inscribed a lion, the emblem of the tribe of Judah. His jewel is a triangular plate of gold inscribed with a sword. In the preliminary Lodges of the Chapter he acts as Junior Deacon.

Royal Arch Clothing. The clothing or regalia of a Royal Arch Mason in the American system consists of an apron (already described), a scarf of scarlet velvet or silk, on which is embroidered or painted, on a blue ground, the words, "Holiness to the Lord"; and if an officer, a scarlet collar, to which is attached the jewel of his office. The scarf, once universally used, has, within a few years past, been very much abandoned. Every Royal Arch Mason should also wear at his buttonhole, attached by a scarlet ribbon, the jewel of the Order.

Royal Arch Colors. The peculiar color of the Royal Arch Degree is red or scarlet, which is symbolic of fervency and zeal, the characteristics of the degree. The colors also used symbolically in the decorations of a Chapter are blue, purple, scarlet, and white, each of which has a symbolic meaning. (See *Veils, Symbolism of the.*)

Royal Arch Degree. The early history of this degree is involved in obscurity, but in the opinion of the late Bro. W. J. Hughan its origin may be ascribed to the fourth decade of the eighteenth century. The earliest known mention of it occurs in a contemporary account of the meeting of a Lodge (No. 21) at Youghal, in Ireland, in 1743, when the members walked in procession and the Master was preceded by "the Royal Arch carried by two Excellent Masons."

This passage makes it plain that the Royal Arch Degree was conferred in London before 1744 (say about 1740), and would suggest that York was considered to be its place of origin. Also as Laurence Dermott became a Royal Arch Mason in 1746 it is clear that he could not have been, as is sometimes asserted, the inventor of the Rite.

The next mention of the degree occurs in the minutes of the "Ancients" Grand Lodge for March 4, 1752, when "A formal complaint was made by several brethren against Thos. Phealon and John Macky, better known as 'leg of mutton Masons' for clandestinely making Masons for the mean consideration of a leg of mutton for dinner of supper. Upon examining some brothers whom they pretended to have made Royal Arch men, the parties had not the least idea of that secret. The Grand Secretary had examined Macky, and stated that he had not the least idea or knowledge of Royal Arch Masonry, but instead thereof he had told the people he had deceived, a long story about twelve white marble stones, &c., &c., and that the rainbow was the Royal Arch, with many other absurdities equally foreign and ridiculous."

The earliest known record of the degree being actually conferred is a minute of the Fredericksburg Lodge, Virginia, U. S. A., stating that on December 22, 1753, three brethren were raised to the degree of Royal Arch Mason (for a facsimile of this entry see *Ars Quatuor Coronatorum*, iv., p. 222); while the earliest records traced in England are of the year 1758, during which year several brethren were "raised to the degree of Royal Arch" in a Lodge meeting at The Crown at Bristol.

This Lodge was a "Modern" one and its records therefore make it abundantly clear that the Royal Arch Degree was not by any means confined to the "Ancients," though it was not officially recognized by the Grand Lodge of the "Moderns," whose Secretary wrote in 1759, "Our Society is neither Arch, Royal Arch or Ancient."

However, at the Union of "Ancients" and "Moderns," in 1813, it was declared that "pure Ancient Masonry consists of three degrees, and no more, *viz.*, those of the Entered Apprentice, the Fellow Craft, and the Master Mason, including the Supreme Order of the Holy Royal Arch."

And this lends color to the idea that at some time or other the Royal Arch had formed part of the Master Mason's Degree, though when and by whom it was separated from it no one has yet discovered, for we may dismiss as utterly uncorroborated by any proof the assertion that Ramsay was the fabricator of the Royal Arch Degree, and equally unsupported is the often made assertion that Dunckerley invented it, though he undoubtedly played a very active part in extending it.

The late Bro. W. J. Hughan, in his *Origin of the English Rite of Free Masonry* (ed. 1909, p. 90), favors "the theory that a *word* was placed in the Royal Arch *prominently* which was previously given in the *sections* of the Third Degree and known 'as the ancient word of a Master Mason,' " and considers that "according to this idea, that *which was once lost, and then found,* in the Third Degree (in one of the sections), was subsequently under the new regime discovered in the 'Royal Arch,' only *much extended, and under most exalted and dignified surroundings.*"

In England, Scotland, and the United States, the legend of the degree is the same, though varying in some of the details, but the ceremony in Ireland differs much, for it has nothing to do with the rebuilding of the Temple as narrated by Ezra, but with the repairing of the Temple by Josiah, the three chief Officers, or Principals, being the King (Josiah), the Priest (Hilkiah), and the Scribe (Shaphan), not as in England Zerubbabel, Haggai, and Jeshua, or as in America, High Priest, King, and Scribe.

At one time in England only Past Masters were eligible for the degree, and this led to a system called "passing the chair," by which a sort of degree of Past Master was conferred upon brethren who had never really served in the chair of a Lodge; now a Master Mason who has been so for four weeks is eligible for exaltation.

Royal Arch Jewel. The jewel which every Royal Arch Mason is permitted to wear as a token of his connection with the Order. In America it is usually suspended by a scarlet ribbon to the button. In England it is to be worn pendant from a narrow ribbon on the left breast, the color of the ribbon varying with the rank of the wearer. It is of gold, and consists of a triple tau cross within a triangle, the whole circumscribed by a circle. This jewel is eminently symbolic, the *tau* being the mark mentioned by Ezekiel (ix. 4), by which those were distinguished who were to be saved from the wicked who were to be slain; the *triple tau* is symbolic of the peculiar and more eminent separation of Royal Arch Masons from the profane; the *triangle* or *delta,* is a symbol of the sacred name of God, known only to those who are thus separated; and the *circle* is a symbol of the eternal life, which is the great dogma taught by Royal Arch Masonry. Hence, by this jewel, the Royal Arch Mason makes the profession of his separation from the unholy and profane, his reverence for God, and his belief in the future and eternal life.

In America, the emblem worn by Royal Arch Masons without the Chapter is a Keystone, on which are the letters H. T. W. S. S. T. K. S. arranged in a circle and within the circle may or should be his mark.

Royal Arch Masonry. That division of Speculative Masonry which is engaged in the investigation of the mysteries connected with the Royal Arch, no matter under what name or in what Rite. Thus the mysteries of the Knight of the Ninth Arch constitute the Royal Arch Masonry of so for four weeks is eligible for exaltation.

the Ancient and Accepted Scottish Rite just as much as those of the Royal Arch of Zerubbabel do the Royal Arch of the American Rite.

Royal Master. The Eighth Degree of the American Rite, and the first of the degrees conferred in a Council of Royal and Select Masters. Its officers are a Thrice Illustrious Grand Master, representing King Solomon; Illustrious Hiram of Tyre, Principal Conductor of the Works, representing Hiram Abif; Master of the Exchequer, Master of Finances, Captain of the Guards, Conductor of the Council and Steward. The place of meeting is called the "Council Chamber," and represents the private apartment of King Solomon, in which he is said to have met for consultation with his two colleagues during the construction of the Temple. Candidates who receive this degree are said to be "honored with the degree of Royal Master." Its symbolic colors are black and red—the former significant of grief, and the latter of martyrdom, and both referring to the chief builder of the Temple.

The events recorded in this degree, looking at them in a legendary point of view, must have occurred at the building of the first Temple, and during that brief period of time after the death of the builder which is embraced between the discovery of his body and its "Masonic interment." In all the initiations into the mysteries of the ancient world, there was, as it is well known to scholars, a legend of the violent death of some distinguished personage, to whose memory the particular mystery was consecrated, of the concealment of the body, and of its subsequent discovery. That part of the initiation which referred to the concealment of the body was called the *Aphanism,* from a Greek verb which signifies "to conceal," and that part which referred to the subsequent finding was called the *euresis,* from another Greek verb which signifies "to discover." It is impossible to avoid seeing the coincidences between the system of initiation and that practised in the Masonry of the Third Degree. But the ancient initiation was not terminated by the *euresis* or discovery. Up to that point, the ceremonies had been funereal and lugubrious in their character. But now they were changed from wailing to rejoicing. Other ceremonies were performed by which the restoration of the personage to life, or his apotheosis or change to immortality, was represented, and then came the autopsy or illumination of the neophyte, when he was invested with a full knowledge of all the religious doctrines which it was the object of the ancient mysteries to teach—when, in a word, he was instructed in Divine truth.

Now, a similar course is pursued in Masonry. Here also there is an illumination, a symbolic teaching, or, as we call it, an *investiture* with that which is the representative of Divine truth. The communication to the candidate, in the Master's Degree, of that which is admitted to be merely a representation of or a substitution for that symbol of Divine truth (the search for which, under the name of the *true word,* makes so important a part of the degree), how imperfect it may be in comparison with that more thorough knowledge which only future researches can enable the Master Mason to attain, constitutes the *autopsy* of the Third Degree. Now, the principal event recorded in the legend of the Royal Master, the interview between Adoniram and his two Royal Masters, is to be placed precisely at that juncture of time which is between the *euresis* or discovery in the Master Mason's Degree and the autopsy, or investiture with the great secret. It occurred between the discovery by means of the sprig of acacia and the final interment. It was at the time when Solomon and his colleague, Hiram of Tyre, were in profound consultation as to the mode of repairing the loss which they then supposed had befallen them.

We must come to this conclusion, because there is abundant reference, both in the organized form of the Council and in the ritual of the degree, to the death as an event that had already occurred; and, on the other hand, while it is evident that Solomon had been made acquainted with the failure to recover, on the person of the builder, that which had been lost, there is no reference whatever to the well-known *substitution* which was made at the time of the interment.

If, therefore, as is admitted by all Masonic ritualists, the *substitution* was precedent and preliminary to the establishment of the Master Mason's Degree, it is evident that at the time that the degree of Royal Master is said to have been founded in the ancient Temple, by our "first Most Excellent Grand Master," all persons present, except the first and second officers, must have been merely Fellow-Craft Masons. In compliance with this tradition, therefore, a Royal Master is, at this day, supposed to represent a Fellow-Craft in the search, and making his demand for that reward which was to elevate him to the rank of a Master Mason.

If from the legendary history we proceed to the symbolism of the degree, we shall find that, brief and simple as are the ceremonies, they present the great Masonic idea of the laborer seeking for his reward. Throughout all the symbolism of Masonry, from the first to the last degree, the search for the WORD has been considered but as a symbolic expression for the search after TRUTH. The attainment of this truth has always been acknowledged to be the great object and design of all Masonic labor. Divine truth—the knowledge of God—concealed in the old Kabbalistic doctrine, under the symbol of his ineffable name—and typified in the Masonic system under the mystical expression of the True Word, is the reward proposed to every Mason who has faithfully wrought his task. It is, in short, the "Master's wages."

Now, all this is beautifully symbolized in the degree of Royal Master. The reward has been promised, and the time had now come, as Adoniram thought, when the promise was to be redeemed, and the true word—Divine truth—was to be imparted. Hence, in the person of Adoniram, or the Royal Master, we see symbolized the Speculative Mason, who, having labored to complete his spiritual temple, comes to the Divine Master that he may receive his reward, and that his labor may be consummated by the acquisition of truth. But the temple that he had been building is the temple of this life; that first temple which must be destroyed by death that the second temple of the future life may be built on its foundations. And in this first temple the truth cannot be found. We must be contented with its substitute.

Rubric. In the Ancient and Accepted Scottish Rite, edicts, summonses or other documents, written or printed in red letters, are supposed to be of more binding obligation, and to require more implicit obedience, than any others. Hence, in the same Rite, to publish the name of one who has been expelled in red letters is considered an especial mark of disgrace. It is derived from the custom of the Middle Ages, when, as Muratori shows (*Antiq. Ital. Med.*), red letters were used to give greater weight to documents; and he quotes an old Charter of 1020, which is said to be confirmed "per literas rubeas," or by red letters.

Salaam. The name of the Arabic form of salutation, which is by bowing the head and bringing the extended arms from the sides until the thumbs touch, the palms being down.

Scales, Pair of. "Let me be weighed in an even balance," said Job, "that God may know mine integrity"; and Solomon says that "a false balance *is* abomination to the Lord, but a just weight is his delight." So we find that among the ancients a balance, or pair of scales, was a well-known recognized symbol of a strict observation of justice and fair dealing. This symbolism is also recognized in Masonry, and hence in the degree of Princes of Jerusalem, the duty of which is to administer justice in the inferior degrees, a pair of scales is the most important symbol.

Scallop-Shell. The scallop-shell, the staff, and sandals form a part of the costume of a Masonic Knights Templar in his character as a Pilgrim Penitent. Shakespeare makes Ophelia sing—

"And how shall I my true love know
From any other one?
O, by his scallop-shell and staff,
And by his sandal shoon!"

The scallop-shell was in the Middle Ages the recognized badge of a pilgrim; so much so, that Dr. Clarke (*Travels*, ii., 538) has been led to say: "It is not easy to account for the origin of the shell as a badge worn by the pilgrims, but it decidedly refers to much earlier Oriental customs than the journeys of Christians to the Holy Land, and its history will probably be found in the mythology of eastern nations." He is right as to the question of antiquity, for the shell was an ancient symbol of the Syrian goddess Astarte, Venus Pelagia, or Venus rising from the sea. But it is doubtful whether its use by pilgrims is to be traced to so old or so Pagan an authority. Strictly, the scallop-shell was the badge of pilgrims visiting the shrine of St. James of Compostella, and hence it is called by naturalists the *pecten Jacobæus*—the comb shell of St. James. Fuller (*Ch. Hist.*, ii., 228) says: "All pilgrims that visit St. James of Compostella in Spain returned thence *obsiti conchis*, 'all beshelled about' on their clothes, as a religious donative there bestowed upon them." Pilgrims were, in fact, in Medieval times distinguished by the peculiar badge which they wore, as designating the shrine which they had visited. Thus pilgrims from Rome wore the keys, those from St. James the scallop-shell, and those from the Holy Land palm branches, whence such a pilgrim was sometimes called a *palmer*. But this distinction was not always rigidly adhered to, and pilgrims from Palestine frequently wore the shell. At first the shell was sewn on the cloak, but afterward transferred to the hat; and while, in the beginning, the badge was not assumed until the pilgrimage was accomplished, eventually pilgrims began to wear it as soon as they had taken their vow of pilgrimage, and before they had commenced their journey.

Both of these changes have been adopted in the Templar ritual. The pilgrim, although symbolically making his pilgrimage to the Holy Sepulcher in Palestine, adopts the shell more properly belonging to the pilgrimage to Compostella; and adopts it, too, not after his visit to the shrine, but as soon as he has assumed the character of a pilgrim, which, it will be seen from what has been said, is historically correct, and in accordance with the later practise of Medieval pilgrims.

Scenic Representations. In the Ancient Mysteries scenic representations were employed to illustrate the doctrines of the resurrection, which it was their object to inculcate. Thus the allegory of the initiation was more deeply impressed, by being brought vividly to the sight as well as to the mind of the aspirant. Thus, too, in the religious mysteries of the Middle Ages, the moral lessons of Scripture were dramatized for the benefit of the people who beheld them. The Christian virtues and graces often assumed the form of personages in these religious plays, and fortitude, prudence, temperance, and justice appeared before the spectators as living and acting beings, inculcating by their actions and by the plot of the drama those lessons which would not have been so well received or so thoroughly understood, if given merely in a didactic form. The advantage of these scenic representations, consecrated by antiquity and tested by long experience, is well exemplified in the ritual of the Third Degree of Masonry, where the dramatization of the great legend gives to the initiation a singular force and beauty. It is surprising, therefore, that the English system never adopted, or, if adopted, speedily discarded, the drama of the Third Degree, but gives only in the form of a narrative what the American system more wisely and more usefully presents by living action. Throughout America, in every State excepting Pennsylvania, the initiation into the Third Degree constitutes a scenic representation. The latter State alone preserves the less impressive didactic method of the English system. The rituals of the Continent of Europe pursue the same scenic form of initiation, and it is therefore most probable that this was the ancient usage, and that the present English ritual is of comparatively recent date.

Scepter. An ensign of sovereign authority, and hence carried in several of the high degrees by officers who represent kings.

Secret Master. The Fourth Degree in the Ancient and Accepted Scottish Rite, and the first of what are called the "Ineffable Degrees." It refers to those circumstances which occurred at the Temple when Solomon repaired to the building for the purpose of supplying the loss of its illustrious builder by the appointment of seven experts, among whom were to be divided the labors which heretofore had been entrusted to one gigantic mind. The lecture elaborately explains the mystic meaning of the sacred things which were contained in the Sanctum Sanctorum, or Holy of Holies.

The Lodge is hung with black curtains strewed with tears, symbolic of grief. There should be eighty-one lights, distributed by nine times nine; but this number is often dispensed with, and three times three substituted. Later rituals reduce them to eight.

There are but two presiding officers—a Master, styled "Puissant," and representing King Solomon, and an Inspector, representing Adoniram, the son of Abda, who had the inspection of the workmen on Mount Lebanon, and who is said to have been the first Secret Master.

Solomon is seated in the east, clothed in mourning robes lined with ermine, holding a scepter in his hand, and decorated with a blue sash from the right shoulder to the left hip, from which is suspended a triangle of gold. Before him is placed a triangular altar, on which is deposited a wreath of laurel and olive leaves.

Adoniram, called "Venerable Inspector," is seated in the west, but without any implement of office, in commemoration of the fact that the works were suspended at the time of the institution of this degree. He is decorated with a triangular white collar, bordered with black, from which is suspended an ivory key, with the letter Z engraved thereon, which constitute the collar, and jewel of the degree. These decorations are worn by all the brethren.

The apron is white edged with black and with black strings; the flap blue, with an open eye thereon embroidered in gold. The modern ritual prescribes that two branches of olive and laurel crossing each other shall be on the middle of the apron.

Selamu Aleikum, Es. The Arabic salutation of "Peace be with you"; which meets with the response *"Aleikum es Selaam."* These expressions are prominently in use by ancient Arabic associations.

Select Master. The Ninth Degree in the American Rite, and the last of the two conferred in a Council of Royal and Select Masters. Its officers are a Thrice Illustrious Grand Master, Illustrious Hiram of Tyre, Principal Conductor of the Works, Treasurer, Recorder, Captain of the Guards, Conductor of the Council, and Steward. The first three represent the three Grand Masters at the building of Solomon's Temple. The symbolic colors are black and red, the former significant of secrecy, silence, and darkness; the latter of fervency and zeal. A Council is supposed to consist of neither more nor less than twenty-seven; but a smaller number, if not less than nine, is competent to proceed to work or business. The candidate, when initiated, is said to be "chosen as a Select Master." The historical object of the degree is to commemorate the deposit of an important secret or treasure which, after the preliminary preparations, is said to have been made by Hiram Abif. The place of meeting represents a secret vault beneath the Temple.

A controversy has sometimes arisen among ritualists as to whether the degree of Select Master should precede or follow that of Royal Master in the order of conferring. But the arrangement now existing, by which the Royal Master is made the First and the Select Master the Second Degree of Cryptic Masonry, has been very generally accepted, and this for the best of reasons. It is true that the circumstances referred to in the degree of Royal Master occurred during a period of time which lies between the death of the Chief Builder of the Temple and the completion of the edifice, while those referred to in the degree of Select Master occurred anterior to the builder's death. Hence, in the order of time, the events commemorated in the Select Master's Degree took place anterior to those which are related in the degree of Royal Master; although in Masonic sequence the latter degree is conferred before the former. This apparent anachronism is, however, reconciled by the explanation that the secrets of the Select Master's Degree were not brought to light until long after the existence of the Royal Master's Degree had been known and recognized.

In other words, to speak only from the traditional point of view, Select Masters had been designated, had performed the task for which they had been selected, and had closed their labors, without ever being openly recognized as a class in the Temple of Solomon. The business in which they were engaged was a secret one. Their occupation and their very existence, according to the legend, were unknown to the great body of the Craft in the first Temple. The Royal Master's Degree, on the contrary, as there was no reason for concealment, was publicly conferred and acknowledged during the latter part of the construction of the Temple of Solomon; whereas the degree of Select Master, and the important incidents on which it was founded, are not supposed to have been revealed to the Craft until the building of the temple of Zerubbabel. Hence the Royal Master's Degree should always be conferred anterior to that of the Select Master.

The proper jurisdiction under which these degrees should be placed, whether under Chapters and to be conferred preparatory to the Royal

Arch Degree or under Councils and to be conferred after it, has excited discussion. The former usage prevails in Maryland and Virginia, but the latter in all the other States. There is no doubt that these degrees belonged originally to the Ancient and Accepted Rite, and were conferred as honorary degrees by the Inspectors of that Rite. This authority and jurisdiction the Supreme Council for the Southern Jurisdiction of the Rite continued to claim until the year 1870; although, through negligence, the Councils of Royal and Select Masters in some of the States had been placed under the control of independent jurisdictions called Grand Councils. Like all usurped authority, however, this claim of the State Grand Councils does not seem to have ever been universally admitted or to have been very firmly established. Repeated attempts have been made to take the degrees out of the hands of the Councils and to place them in the Chapters, there to be conferred as preparatory to the Royal Arch. The General Grand Chapter, in the triennial session of 1847, adopted a resolution granting this permission to all Chapters in States where no Grand Councils exist. But, seeing the manifest injustice and inexpediency of such a measure, at the following session of 1850 it refused to take any action on the subject of these degrees. In 1853 it disclaimed all control over them, and forbade the Chapters under its jurisdiction to confer them. As far as regards the interference of the Ancient and Accepted Scottish Rite, that question was set at rest in 1870 by the Mother Council, which, at its session at Baltimore, formally relinquished all further control over them.

Senatorial Chamber. When the Supreme Council of the Ancient and Accepted Scottish Rite meets in the Thirty Third Degree, it is said to meet in its senatorial chember.

Sentinel. An officer in a Royal Arch Chapter, in a council of Knights of the Red Cross, and in a Commandery of Knights Templar, whose duties are similar to those of a Tiler in a Symbolic Lodge. In some bodies the word *Janitor* has been substituted for *Sentinel,* but the change is hardly a good one. Janitor has been more generally appropriated to the porter of a collegiate institution, and has no old Masonic authority for its use.

Sepulcher. The spirit of gratitude has from the earliest period led men to venerate the tombs in which have been deposited the remains of their benefactors. In all of the ancient religions there were sacred tombs to which worship was paid. The tombs of the prophets, preserved by the Israelites, gave testimony to their reverence for the memory of these holy personages. After the advent of Christianity, the same sentiment of devotion led the pilgrims to visit the Holy Land, that they might kneel at what was believed to be the sepulcher of their Lord. In many of the churches of the Middle Ages there was a particular place near the altar called the sepulcher, which was used at Easter for the performance of solemn rites commemorative of the Savior's resurrection. This custom still prevails in some of the churches on the Continent. In Templar Masonry, which is professedly a Christian system, the sepulcher forms a part of the arrangements of a Commandery. In England, the sepulcher is within the Asylum, and in front of the Eminent Commander. In America it is placed without; and the scenic representation observed in every well-regulated and properly arranged Commandery furnishes a most impressive and pathetic ceremony.

Seven. In every system of antiquity there is a frequent reference to this number, showing that the veneration for it proceeded from some common cause. It is equally a sacred number in the Gentile as in the Christian religion. Oliver says that this can scarcely be ascribed to any event, except it be the institution of the Sabbath. Higgins thinks that the peculiar circumstance, perhaps accidental, of the number of the days of the week coinciding exactly with the number of the planetary bodies probably procured for it its character of sanctity. The Pythagoreans called it a perfect number, because it was made up of 3 and 4, the triangle and the square, which are the two perfect figures. They called it also a virgin number, and without mother, comparing it to Minerva, who was a motherless virgin, because it cannot by multiplication produce any number within ten, as twice two does four, and three times three does nine; nor can any two numbers, by their multiplication, produce it.

It is singular to observe the important part occupied by the number seven in all the ancient systems. There were, for instance, *seven* ancient planets, *seven* Pleiades, and *seven* Hyades; *seven* altars burned continually before the god Mithras; the Arabians had *seven* holy temples; the Hindus supposed the world to be enclosed within the compass of *seven* peninsulas; the Goths had *seven* deities, viz., the Sun, the Moon, Tuisco, Woden, Thor, Friga, and Seatur, from whose names are derived our days of the week; in the Persian mysteries were *seven* spacious caverns, through which the aspirant had to pass; in the Gothic mysteries, the candidate met with *seven* obstructions, which were called the "road of the seven stages"; and, finally, sacrifices were always considered as most efficacious when the victims were *seven* in number.

Much of the Jewish ritual was governed by this number, and the etymology of the word shows its sacred import, for the radical meaning of שבע, *shabang,* is, says Parkhurst, *sufficiency* or *fulness.* The Hebrew idea, therefore, like the Pythagorean, is that of *perfection.* To both the seven was a perfect number. Again: שבע, means *to swear,* because oaths were confirmed either by seven witnesses, or by seven victims offered in sacrifice, as we read in the covenant of Abraham and Abimelech. (Gen. xxi. 28.) Hence, there is a frequent recurrence to this number in the Scriptural history. The Sabbath was the *seventh* day; Noah received *seven* days' notice of the commencement of the deluge, and was commanded to select clean beasts and fowls by *sevens; seven* persons accompanied him into the ark; the ark rested on Mount Ararat in the *seventh* month; the intervals between despatching the dove were, each time, *seven* days; the walls of Jericho were encompassed *seven* days by *seven* priests, bearing *seven* rams' horns; Solomon was *seven* years building the Temple, which was dedicated in the *seventh* month, and the festival lasted *seven* days; the candlestick in the tabernacle consisted of *seven* branches; and, finally, the tower of Babel was said to have been elevated *seven* stories before the dispersion.

Seven is a sacred number in Masonic symbolism. It has always been so. In the earliest rituals of the last century it was said that a Lodge required seven to make it perfect; but the only explanation to be found in any of those rituals of the sacredness of the number is the seven liberal arts and sciences, which, according to the old "Legend of the Craft," were the foundation of Masonry. In modern ritualism the symbolism of seven has been transferred from the First to the Second Degree, and there it is made to refer only to the seven steps of the Winding Stairs; but the symbolic seven is to be found diffused in a hundred ways over the whole Masonic system.

*The sun was naturally the great central planet of the ancient seven, and is ever represented as the central light of the seven in the branched candlestick. Of the days of the week one was known as Sol's day, or Sunday, and as the Sun was the son of Saturn, he was ushered in by his father Saturn or Saturday), whom he superseded. The Jews got their Sabbath from the Babylonians about 700 B.C. (*Anc. Faiths,* p. 863; also see *Philo Judæus, Josephus,* and *Clement of Alexandria*), while Sol's day dates from time immemorial, and was always a sacred one. In a phallic sense, when the sun has been in conjunction with the moon, he only leaves Luna after impregnation, and as Forlong, in his *Rivers of Life,* expresses it, "the young sun is that faint globe we so often see in the arms of the new moon," which is in gestation with the sun. The occult meaning of the word Mi-mi perhaps is here revealed, as mentioned in 2 Kings xviii. 27, being defined *Firewater. Mi* is the name of the sun, and as well signifies gold. It is designated in the musical scale, and is also the name of *fire* in Burmese, Siamese, and cognate tongues, as mentioned by Forlong in treating of the *Early Faiths of Western Asia* (vol. ii., p. 65).

Next to the sun in beauty and splendor the moon leads all the hosts of heaven. And the Occidental, as well as the Oriental, nations were strongly moved in their imaginations by the awful majesty, the solemn silence, and the grandeur of that brilliant body progressing nightly through the starry vault: from the distant plains of India to ancient Egypt, and even those far-off lands where the Incas ruled, altars were erected to the worship of the Moon. On every seventh day the moon assumed a new phase, which gave rise to festivals to Luna being correspondingly celebrated; the day so set apart was known as *Moon*-day, or the second day of the week, that following *Sun*-day. "The Moon, whose phases marked and appointed their holy days." (Cicero, *Tusculan Disputations,* Book I., ch. 28.) In the Hebrew, Syrian, Persian, Phœnician, Chaldean, and Saxon, the word Seven signifies *full* or *complete,* and every seventh day after the first quarter the moon is complete in its change. In all countries the moon is best known under the beautiful figure of the *unveiling Queen of Heaven.*

The relative values of Seven in the musical scale and in the ancient planetary formula are as follows:

Si	Moon . . .	Silver.
Ut	Mercury . .	Quicksilver.
Re	Venus . . .	Copper.
Mi	Sun . . .	Gold.
Fa	Mars . . .	Iron.
Sol	Jupiter . .	Tin.
La	Saturn . .	Lead.

The eminent professor of music, Carl Bergstein, in connection herewith, furnishes the information that Guido Aretinus, Monk, in the eleventh century, the great reformer of music, invented the staff, several keys, and the names *ut, re, mi, fa, sol, la, si;* they being taken from a prayer to St. John to protect the voice, running thus:

Ut queant laxis *Re*sonare fibris
*Mi*ra gestorum *Fa*muli tuorum
*Sol*ve polluti *La*bii reatum, Sancte Johannes.

The literal translation of which would be rendered:

"For that (or to enable) with expanded breast
Thy servants are able to sing the praise of Thy
Deeds, forgive the polluted lips the sins uttered."

The syllable *ut* has since been changed for the more satisfactory *do.*

In the year 1562 there was printed at Leipzig a work entitled *Heptalogium Virgilii Salsburgensis,* in honor of the number Seven. It consists of seven parts, each embracing seven divisions. In 1624 appeared in London a curious work on the subject of numbers, bearing the following title: "*The Secret of Numbers according to Theological, Arithmetical, Geometrical, and Harmonical Computation; drawn, for the better part, out of those Ancients, as well as Neoteriques.* Pleasing to read, profitable to understand, opening themselves to the capacities of both learned and unlearned; being no other than a key to lead men to any doctrinal knowledge whatsoever." In the ninth chapter the author has given many notable opinions from learned men, to prove the excellency of the number

Seven. "First, it neither begets nor is begotten, according to the saying of Philo. Some numbers, indeed, within the compass of ten, beget, but are not begotten; and that is the unarie. Others are begotten, but beget not, as the octonarie. Only the septenaries have a prerogative above them all, they neither beget nor are begotten. This is its first divinity or perfection. Secondly, this is a harmonical number, and the well and fountain of that fair and lovely Sigamma, because it includeth within itself all manner of harmony. Thirdly, it is a theological number, consisting of perfection. Fourthly, because of its compositure; for it is compounded of the first two perfect numbers equal and unequal, three and four; for the number two, consisting of repeated unity, which is no number, is not perfect. Now every one of these being excellent of themselves (as hath been demonstrated), how can this number be but far more excellent, consisting of them all, and participating, as it were, of all their excellent virtues?"

Hippocrates says that the septenary number, by its occult virtue, tends to the accomplishment of all things, is the dispenser of life and fountain of all its changes; and, like Shakespeare, he divides the life of man into seven ages. In seven months a child may be born and live, and not before. Anciently a child was not named before seven days, not being accounted fully to have life before that periodical day. The teeth spring out in the seventh month, and are renewed in the seventh year, when infancy is changed into childhood. At thrice seven years the faculties are developed, manhood commences, and we become legally competent to all civil acts; at four times seven man is in full possession of his strength; at five times seven he is fit for the business of the world; at six times seven he becomes grave and wise, or never; at seven times seven he is in his apogee, and from that time he decays; at eight times seven he is in his first climacteric; at nine times seven, or sixty-three, he is in his grand climacteric, or years of danger; and ten times seven, or threescore years and ten, has, by the Royal Prophet, been pronounced the natural period of human life.

Seven Synonyms for God:—Spirit; Soul; Mind; Principle; Life; Truth; Love.

Seven Synonyms for Man:—Idea; image; likeness; witness; representative; expression; manifestation.

Seven years in building Solomon's Temple; Seven days of Creation; Seven days of the week, Seven ages in the life of man; Seven openings in the head of a man; Jesus was on the cross Seven hours; Jesus spoke Seven times while on the cross; Jesus appeared Seven times after the crucifixion; Seven heavens; Seven notes of music; Seven primary colors; Seven wonders of the world; Seven seas, and many other sevens.

Seven Stars. In the Tracing-Board of the Seventeenth Degree, or Knight of the East and West, is the representation of a man clothed in a white robe, with a golden girdle round his waist, his right hand extended, and surrounded with seven stars. The Seventeenth is an apocalyptic degree, and this symbol is taken from the passage in Revelation i. 16, "and he had in his right hand seven stars." It is a symbol of the seven churches of Asia.

Serpent. As a symbol, the serpent obtained a prominent place in all the ancient with the password, is given to the Tiler on entering the Temple.

Signet of Truth. The signet of Zerubbabel, used in the ritual of the Royal Arch Degree, is also there called the *Signet of Truth,* to indicate that the neophyte who brings it to the Grand Council is in search of Divine Truth, and to give to him the promise that he will by its power speedily obtain his reward in the possession of that for which he is seeking. The Signet of Truth is presented to the aspirant to assure him that he is advancing in his progress to the attainment of truth, and that he is thus invested with the power to pursue the search.

Signet of Zerubbabel. This is used in the American ritual of the Royal Arch Degree. It refers to a passage of Haggai (ii. 23), where God has promised that he will make Zerubbabel his signet. It has the same symbolic meaning as is given to its synonym the "Signet of Truth," because Zerubbabel, as the head of the second Temple, was the symbol of the searcher after truth. But something may be said of the incorrect form in which it is found in many Chapters. At least from the time when Cross presented an engraving of this signet in his *Hieroglyphic Chart,* and perhaps from a much earlier period, for he may possibly have only perpetuated the blunder, it has been represented in most Chapters by a triangular plate of metal. Now, an unattached plate of metal, in any shape whatsoever, is about as correct a representation of a signet as a walking-cane is of a piece of money. The signet is and always has been a finger-ring, and so it should be represented in the ceremonies of the Chapter. What the peculiar device of this signet was—for every signet must have a device—we are unable to show, but we may suppose that it was the Tetragrammaton, perhaps in its well-known abbreviated form of a *yod within a triangle.* Whether this was so or not, such a device would be most appropriate to the symbolism of the Royal Arch ritual.

Silver Cord. In the beautiful and affecting description of the body of man suffering under the infirmities of old age given in the twelfth chapter of Ecclesiastes, we find the expression "or ever the silver cord be loosed, or the golden bowl be broken, or the pitcher be broken at the fountain, or the wheel broken at the cistern: then shall the dust return to the earth as it was, and the spirit shall return to God who gave it." Dr. Clarke thus explains these beautiful metaphors. The silver cord is the spinal marrow; its loosening is the cessation of all nervous sensibility; the golden bowl is the brain, which is rendered unfit to perform its functions by the approach of death; the pitcher means the great vein which carries the blood to the right ventricle of the heart, here called the fountain; by the wheel is meant the great artery which receives the blood from the left ventricle of the heart, here designated as the cistern. This collection of metaphors is a part of the Scripture reading in the Third Degree, and forms an appropriate introduction to those sublime ceremonies whose object is to teach symbolically the resurrection and life eternal.

Shekel. In the Fourth or Mark Master's Degree, it is said that the value of a mark is "a Jewish half-shekel of silver, or twenty-five cents in the currency of this country." The shekel of silver was a weight of great antiquity among the Jews, its value being about a half-dollar. In the time of Solomon, as well as long before and long after, until the Babylonish exile, the Hebrews had no regularly stamped money, but generally used in traffic a currency which consisted of uncoined shekels, which they weighed out to one another. The earliest specimens of the coined shekel which we know are of the coinage of Simon Maccabeus, issued about the year 144 B.C. Of these, we generally find on the obverse the sacred pot of manna, with the inscription, "Shekel Israel," in the old Samaritan character; on the reverse, the rod of Aaron, having three buds, with the inscription, "Ierushalem Kadoshah," or Jerusalem the Holy, in a similar character.

Shekinah. Heb., שבינה, derived from SHAKAN, to dwell. A term applied by the Jews, especially in the Targums, to the Divine glory which dwelt in the tabernacle and the Temple, and which was manifested by a visible cloud resting over the mercy-seat in the Holy of Holies. It first appeared over the ark when Moses consecrated the tabernacle; and was afterward, upon the consecration of the Temple by Solomon, translated thither, where it remained until the destruction of that building.

The Shekinah disappeared after the destruction of the first Temple, and was not present in the second. Mr. Christie, in his learned treatise on the *Worship of the Elements,* says that "the loss of the Shekinah, that visible sign of the presence of the Deity, induced an early respect for solar light as its substitute." Now there is much that is significative of Masonic history in this brief sentence. The sun still remains as a prominent symbol in the Masonic system. It has been derived by the Masons from those old sun-worshipers. But the idea of Masonic light is very different from their idea of solar light. The Shekinah was the symbol of the Divine glory; but the true glory of divinity is *Truth,* and Divine Truth is therefore the Shekinah of Masonry. This is symbolized by light, which is no longer used by us as a "substitute" for the Shekinah, or the Divine glory, but as its symbol—the physical expression of its essence.

Shock of Enlightenment. A ceremony used in all the degrees of Symbolic Masonry. By it we seek to symbolize the idea of the birth of material light, by the representation of the circumstances that accompanied it, and their reference to the birth of intellectual or Masonic light. The one is the type of the other; and hence the illumination of the candidate is attended with a ceremony that may be supposed to imitate the primal illumination of the universe—most feebly, it is true, and yet not altogether without impressiveness.

The *Shock of Enlightenment* is, then, a symbol of the change which is now taking place in the intellectual condition of the candidate. *It is the symbol of the birth of the candidate.*

Shem, Ham, Japheth. The three sons of Noah, who assisted him in the construction of the ark of safety, and hence they became significant words in the Royal Arch Degree according to the American system. The interpolation of *Adoniram* in the place of one of these names, which is sometimes met with, is a blunder of some modern, ignorant ritual maker.

Shewbread. The twelve loaves which were placed upon a table in the sanctuary of the Temple, and which were called the shewbread or bread of the presence, are represented among the paraphernalia of a Lodge of Perfection in the Ancient and Accepted Rite. Bähr (*Symbolik*) says that the shewbread was a symbol of the bread of life—of the eternal life by which we are brought into the presence of God and know him; an interpretation that is equally applicable to the Masonic symbolism.

Skull. The skull as a symbol is not used in Masonry except in Masonic Templarism, where it is a symbol of mortality. Among the articles of accusation sent by the Pope to the bishops and papal commissaries upon which to examine the Knights Templar, those from the forty-second to the fifty-seventh refer to the human skull, "cranium humanum," which the Templars were accused of using in their reception, and worshiping as an idol. It is possible that the Old Templars made use of the skull in their ceremony of reception; but Modern Templars will readily acquit their predecessors of the crime of idolatry, and find in their use of a skull a symbolic design. (See *Baphomet.*)

Slander. Inwood, in his sermon on "Union Amongst Masons," says: "To defame our brother, or suffer him to be defamed, without interesting ourselves for the preservation of his name and character, there is scarcely the shadow of an excuse to be formed. Defamation is always wicked. Slander and evil speaking are the pests of civil society, are the disgrace of every degree of religious profession, are the poisonous bane of all brotherly love."

Spes mea in Deo est. (My hope is in God.) The motto of the Thirty-second Degree of the Ancient and Accepted Scottish Rite.

Spiritual Temple. The French Masons say: "We erect temples for virtue and dungeons for vice"; thus referring to the great Masonic doctrine of a spiritual temple. There is no symbolism of the Order more sublime than that in which the Speculative Mason is supposed to be engaged in the construction of a spiritual temple, in allusion to that material one which was erected by his operative predecessors at Jerusalem. Indeed, the difference, in this point of view, between Operative and

Speculative Masonry is simply this: that while the former was engaged in the construction, on Mount Moriah, of a material temple of stones and cedar, and gold and precious stones, the latter is occupied, from his first to his last initiation, in the construction, the adornment, and the completion of the spiritual temple of his body. The idea of making the temple a symbol of the body is not, it is true, exclusively Masonic. It had occurred to the first teachers of Christianity. Christ himself alluded to it when he said, "Destroy this temple, and in three days I will raise it up"; and St. Paul extends the idea, in the first of his Epistles to the Corinthians, in the following language: "Know ye not that ye are the temple of God, and that the spirit of God dwelleth in you?" (iii. 16.) And again, in a subsequent passage of the same Epistle, he reiterates the idea in a more positive form: "What, know ye not that your body is the temple of the Holy Ghost which is in you, which ye have of God, and ye are not your own?" (vi. 19.)

But the mode of treating this symbolism by a reference to the particular Temple of Solomon, and to the operative art engaged in its construction, is an application of the idea peculiar to Freemasonry. Hitchcock, in his *Essay on Swedenborg,* thinks that the same idea was also shared by the Hermetic philosophers. He says: "With perhaps the majority of readers, the Temple of Solomon, and also the tabernacle, were mere buildings—very magnificent, indeed, but still mere buildings—for the worship of God. But some are struck with many portions of the account of their erection admitting a moral interpretation; and while the buildings are allowed to stand (or to have stood, once,) visible objects, these interpreters are delighted to meet with indications that Moses and Solomon, in building the Temples, were wise in the knowledge of God and of man; from which point it is not difficult to pass on to the moral meaning altogether, and affirm that the building, which was erected without the noise of a 'hammer, nor ax, nor any tool of iron' (1 Kings vi. 7,) was altogether a moral building—a building of God, not made with hands. In short, many see in the story of Solomon's Temple, a symbolical representation of MAN as the temple of God, with its HOLY OF HOLIES deep seated in the centre of the human heart."

Step. The *step* can hardly be called a mode of recognition, although Apuleius informs us that there was a peculiar step in the Osiriac initiation which was deemed a sign. It is in Freemasonry rather an esoteric usage of the ritual. The *steps* can be traced back as far as to at least the middle of the last century, in the rituals of which they are fully described. The custom of advancing in a peculiar manner and form, to some sacred place or elevated personage, has been preserved in the customs of all countries, especially among the Orientalists, who resort even to prostrations of the body when approaching the throne of the sovereign or the holy part of a religious edifice. The steps of Masonry are symbolic of respect and veneration for the altar, whence Masonic light is to emanate.

It must be evident to every Master Mason, without further explanation, that the three steps are taken from the place of darkness to the place of light, either figuratively or really over a coffin, the symbol of death, to teach symbolically that the passage from the darkness and ignorance of this life is through death to the light and knowledge of the eternal life. And this, from the earliest times, was the true symbolism of the step.

Stone of Foundation. The Stone of Foundation constitutes one of the most important and abstruse of all the symbols of Freemasonry. It is referred to in numerous legends and traditions not only of the Freemasons, but also of the Jewish Rabbis, the Talmudic writers, and even the Mussulman doctors. Many of these, it must be confessed, are apparently puerile and absurd; but most of them, and especially the Masonic ones, are deeply interesting in their allegorical signification.

The Stone of Foundation is, properly speaking, a symbol of the higher degrees. It makes its first appearance in the Royal Arch, and forms indeed the most important symbol of that degree. But it is so intimately connected, in its legendary history, with the construction of the Solomonic Temple, that it must be considered as a part of Ancient Craft Masonry, although he who confines the range of his investigations to the first three degrees will have no means, within that narrow limit, of properly appreciating the symbolism of the Stone of Foundation.

As preliminary to the inquiry, it is necessary to distinguish the Stone of Foundation, both in its symbolism and its legendary history, from other stones which play an important part in the Masonic ritual, but which are entirely distinct from it. Such are the *cornerstone,* which was always placed in the northeast corner of the building about to be erected, and to which such a beautiful reference is made in the ceremonies of the Frst Degree; or the *keystone,* which constitutes an interesting part of the Mark Master's Degree; or, lastly, the *cape-stone,* upon which all the ritual of the Most Excellent Master's Degree is founded. There are all, in their proper places, highly interesting and instructive symbols, but have no connection whatever with the Stone of Foundation, whose symbolism it is our present object to discuss. Nor, although the Stone of Foundation is said, for peculiar reasons, to have been of a cubical form, must it be confounded with that stone called by the continental Masons the *cubical stone*—the *pierre cubique* of the French and the *cubik stein* of the German Masons but which in the English system is known as the *perfect ashlar.*

The Stone of Foundation has a legendary history and a symbolic signification which are peculiar to itself, and which differ from the history and meaning which belong to these other stones. I propose first to define this Masonic Stone of Foundation, then to collate the legends which refer to it, and afterward to investigate its significance as a symbol. To the Mason who takes a pleasure in the study of the mysteries of his Institution, the investigation cannot fail to be interesting, if it is conducted with any ability.

But in the very beginning, as a necessary preliminary to any investigation of this kind, it must be distinctly understood that all that is said of this Stone of Foundation in Masonry is to be strictly taken in a mythical or allegorical sense. Dr. Oliver, while undoubtedly himself knowing that it was simply a symbol, has written loosely of it as though it were a substantial reality; and hence, if the passages in his *Historical Landmarks,* and in his other works which refer to this celebrated stone, are accepted by his readers in a literal sense, they will present absurdities and puerilities which would not occur if the Stone of Foundation was received, as it really is, as a myth conveying a most profound and beautiful symbolism. It is as such that it is to be treated here; and, therefore, if a legend is recited or a tradition related, the reader is requested on every occasion to suppose that such legend or tradition is not intended as the recital or relation of what is deemed a fact in Masonic history, but to wait with patience for the development of the symbolism which it conveys. Read in this spirit, as all the legends of Masonry should be read, the legend of the Stone of Foundation becomes one of the most important and interesting of all the Masonic symbols.

The Stone of Foundation is supposed, by the theory which establishes it, to have been a stone placed at one time within the foundations of the Temple of Solomon, and afterward, during the building of the second Temple, transported to the Holy of Holies. It was in form a perfect cube, and had inscribed upon its upper face, within a delta or triangle, the sacred Tetragrammaton, or ineffable name of God. Oliver, speaking with the solemnity of an historian, says that Solomon thought that he had rendered the house of God worthy, so far as human adornment could effect, for the dwelling of God, "when he had placed the celebrated Stone of Foundation, on which the sacred name was mystically engraven, with solemn ceremonies, in that sacred depository on Mount Moriah, along with the foundations of Dan and Asher, the centre of the Most Holy Place, where the ark was overshadowed by the shekinah of God." The Hebrew Talmudists, who thought as much of this stone, and had as many legends concerning it, as the Masonic Talmudists, called it *eben shatijah,* or "Stone of Foundation," because, as they said, it had been laid by Jehovah as the foundation of the world, and hence the apocryphal Book of Enoch speaks of the "stone which supports the corners of the earth."

This idea of a foundation-stone of the world was most probably derived from that magnificent passage of the Book of Job (ch. xxxviii. v. 4–7) in which the Almighty demands of Job,

"Where wast thou, when I laid the foundation
of the earth?

Declare, since thou hast such knowledge!
Who fixed its dimensions, since thou knowest!
Or who stretched out the line upon it?
Upon what were its foundations fixed?
And who laid its corner-stone,
When the morning stars sang together,
And all the sons of God shouted for joy?"

Noyes, whose translation I have adopted as not materially differing from the common version, but far more poetical and more in the strain of the original, thus explains the allusions to the foundation-stone: "It was the custom to celebrate the laying of the corner-stone of an important building with music, songs, shouting, etc. Hence the morning stars are represented as celebrating the laying of the corner-stone of the earth."

Upon this meager statement has been accumulated more traditions than appertain to any other Masonic symbol. The Rabbis, as has already been intimated, divide the glory of these apocryphal histories with the Masons; indeed, there is good reason for a suspicion that nearly all the Masonic legends owe their first existence to the imaginative genius of the writers of the Jewish Talmud. But there is this difference between the Hebrew and the Masonic traditions: that the Talmudic scholar recited them as truthful histories, and swallowed, in one gulp of faith, all their impossibilities and anachronisms; while the Masonic scholar has received them as allegories, whose value is not in the facts, but in the sentiments which they convey.

With this understanding of their meaning, let us proceed to a collation of these legends.

In that blasphemous work, the *Toldoth Jeshu,* or *Life of Jesus,* written, it is supposed, in the thirteenth or fourteenth century, we find the following account of this wonderful stone:

"At that time [the time of Jesus] there was in the House of the Sanctuary [that is, the Temple] a stone of foundation, which is the very stone that our father Jacob anointed with oil, as it is described in the twenty-eighth chapter of the Book of Genesis. On that stone the letters of the Tetragrammaton were inscribed, and whosoever of the Israelites should learn that name would be able to master the world. To prevent, therefore, any one from learning these letters, two iron dogs were placed upon two columns in front of the Sanctuary. If any person, having acquired the knowledge of these letters, desired to depart from the Sanctuary, the barking of the dogs, by magical power, inspired so much fear that he suddenly forgot what he had acquired."

This passage is cited by the learned Buxtorf in his *Lexicon Talmudicum;* but in my copy of *Toldoth Jeshu,* I find another passage, which gives some additional particulars, in the following words:

"At that time there was in the Temple the ineffable name of God, inscribed upon the Stone of Foundation. For when King David was digging the foundation for the Temple, he found in the depths of the excavation a certain stone on which the name of God was inscribed. This stone he removed and deposited it in the Holy of Holies."

The same puerile story of the barking dogs is repeated still more at length. It is not pertinent to the present inquiry, but it may be stated, as a mere matter of curious information, that this scandalous book, which is throughout a blasphemous defamation of our Savior, proceeds to say, that he cunningly obtained a knowledge of the Tetragrammaton from the Stone of Foundation, and by its mystical influence was enabled to perform his miracles.

The Masonic legends of the Stone of Foundation, based on these and other rabbinical reveries, are of the most extraordinary character, if they are to be viewed as histories, but readily reconcilable with sound sense, if looked at only in the light of allegories. They present an uninterrupted succession of events, in which the Stone of Foundation takes a prominent part, from Adam to Solomon, and from Solomon to Zerubbabel.

Thus, the first of these legends, in order of time, relates that the Stone of Foundation was possessed by Adam while in the Garden of Eden; that he used it as an altar, and so reverenced it that, on his expulsion from Paradise, he carried it with him into the world in which he and his descendants were afterward to earn their bread by the sweat of their brow.

Another legend informs us that from Adam the Stone of Foundation descended to Seth. From Seth it passed by regular succession to Noah, who took it with him into the ark, and after the subsidence of the deluge made on it his first thank-offering. Noah left it on Mount Ararat, where it was subsequently found by Abraham, who removed it, and constantly used it as an altar of sacrifice. His grandson Jacob took it with him when he fled to his uncle Laban in Mesopotamia, and used it as a pillow when, in the vicinity of Luz, he had his celebrated vision.

Here there is a sudden interruption in the legendary history of the stone, and we have no means of conjecturing how it passed from the possession of Jacob into that of Solomon. Moses, it is true, is said to have taken it with him out of Egypt at the time of the exodus, and thus it may have finally reached Jerusalem. Dr. Adam Clarke repeats, what he very properly calls "a foolish tradition," that the stone on which Jacob rested his head was afterward brought to Jerusalem, thence carried after a long lapse of time to Spain, from Spain to Ireland, and from Ireland to Scotland, where it was used as a seat on which the kings of Scotland sat to be crowned. Edward I., we know, brought a stone to which this legend is attached from Scotland to Westminster Abbey, where, under the name of Jacob's Pillow, it still remains, and is always placed under the chair upon which the British sovereign sits to be crowned; because there is an old distich which declares that wherever this stone is found the Scottish kings shall reign.

But this Scottish tradition would take the Stone of Foundation away from all its Masonic connections, and therefore it is rejected as a Masonic legend.

The legends just related are in many respects contradictory and unsatisfactory, and another series, equally as old, is now very generally adopted by Masonic scholars as much better suited to the symbolism by which all these legends are explained.

This series of legends commences with the patriarch Enoch, who is supposed to have been the first consecrator of the Stone of Foundation. The legend of Enoch is so interesting and important in this connection as to excuse its repetition in the present work.

The legend in full is as follows: Enoch, under the inspiration of the Most High, and in obedience to the instructions which he had received in a vision, built a temple underground on Mount Moriah, and dedicated it to God. His son, Methuselah, constructed the building, although he was not acquainted with his father's motives for the erection. This temple consisted of nine vaults, situated perpendicularly beneath each other, and communicating by apertures left in each vault.

Enoch then caused a triangular plate of gold to be made, each side of which was a cubit long; he enriched it with the most precious stones, and encrusted the plate upon a stone of agate of the same form. On the plate he engraved the true name of God, or the Tetragrammaton, and placing it on a cubical stone, known thereafter as the Stone of Foundation, he deposited the whole within the lowest arch.

When this subterranean building was completed, he made a door of stone, and attaching to it a ring of iron, by which it might be occasionally raised, he placed it over the opening of the uppermost arch, and so covered it that the aperture could not be discovered. Enoch, himself, was permitted to enter it but once a year; and on the deaths of Enoch, Methuselah, and Lamech, and the destruction of the world by the deluge, all knowledge of the vault or subterranean temple and of the Stone of Foundation, with the sacred and ineffable name inscribed upon it, was lost for ages to the world.

At the building of the first Temple of Jerusalem, the Stone of Foundation again makes its appearance. Reference has already been made to the Jewish tradition that David, when digging the Foundations of the Temple, found in the excavation which he was making a certain stone, on which the ineffable name of God was inscribed, and which stone he is said to have removed and deposited in the Holy of Holies. That King David laid the foundations of the Temple upon which the superstructure was subsequently erected by Solomon, is a favorite theory of the legend-mongers of the Talmud.

The Masonic tradition is substantially the same as the Jewish, but it substitutes Solomon for David, thereby giving a greater air of probability to the narrative, and it supposes that the stone thus discovered by Solomon was the identical one that had been deposited in his secret vault by Enoch. This Stone of Foundation, the tradition states, was subsequently removed by King Solomon and, for wise purposes, deposited in a secret and safer place.

In this the Masonic tradition again agrees with the Jewish, for we find in the third chapter of the *Treatise on the Temple,* the following narrative:

"There was a stone in the Holy of Holies, on its west side, on which was placed the ark of the covenant, and before the pot of manna and Aaron's rod. But when Solomon had built the Temple, and foresaw that it was at some future time to be destroyed, he constructed a deep and winding vault under ground, for the purpose of concealing the ark, wherein Josiah afterwards, as we learn in the Second Book of Chronicles, xxxv. 3, deposited it with the pot of manna, the rod of Aaron, and the oil of anointing."

The Talmudical book *Yoma* gives the same tradition, and says that "the ark of the covenant was placed in the centre of the Holy of Holies, upon a stone rising three fingers' breadth above the floor, to be as it were a pedestal for it." This stone, says Prideaux, in his *Old and New Testament Connected* (vol. i., p. 148), "the Rabbins call the Stone of Foundation, and give us a great deal of trash about it."

There is much controversy as to the question of the existence of any ark in the second Temple. Some of the Jewish writers assert that a new one was made; others that the old one was found where it had been concealed by Solomon; and others again contend that there was no ark at all in the temple of Zerubbabel, but that its place was supplied by the Stone of Foundation on which it had originally rested.

Royal Arch Masons well know how all these traditions are sought to be reconciled by the Masonic legend, in which the substitute ark and the Stone of Foundation play so important a part.

In the Thirteenth Degree of the Ancient and Accepted Rite, the Stone of Foundation is conspicuous as the resting-place of the sacred delta.

In the Royal Arch and Select Master's degrees of the American Rite, the Stone of Foundation constitutes the most important part of the ritual. In both of these it is the receptacle of the ark, on which the ineffable name is inscribed.

Lee, in his *Temple of Solomon,* has devoted a chapter to this Stone of Foundation, and thus recapitulates the Talmudic and Rabbinical traditions on the subject:

"Vain and futilous are the feverish dreams of the ancient Rabbins concerning the Foundation-Stone of the Temple. Some assert that God placed this stone in the centre of the world, for a future basis and settled consistency for the earth to rest upon. Others held this stone to be the first matter out of which all the beautiful visible beings of the world have been hewn forth and produced to light. Others relate that this was the very same stone laid by Jacob for a pillow under his head, in that night when he dreamed of an angelic vision at Bethel, and afterwards anointed and consecrated it to God. Which when Solomon had found (no doubt by forged revelation or some tedious search like another Rabbi Selemoh) he durst not but lay it sure, as the principal Foundation-Stone of the Temple. Nay, they say further, he caused to be engraved upon it the Tetragrammaton, or the ineffable name of Jehovah."

It will be seen that the Masonic traditions on the subject of the Stone of Foundation do not differ very materially from these Rabbinical ones, although they add a few additional circumstances.

In the Masonic legend, the Foundation-Stone first makes its appearance, as we have already said, in the days of Enoch, who placed it in the bowels of Mount Moriah. There it was subsequently discovered by King Solomon, who deposited it in a crypt of the first Temple, where it remained concealed until the foundations of the second Temple were laid, when it was discovered and removed to the Holy of Holies. But the most important point of the legend of the Stone of Foundation is its intimate and constant connection with the Tetragrammaton or ineffable name. It is this name, inscribed upon it within the sacred and symbolic delta, that gives to the stone all its Masonic value and significance. It is upon this fact, that it was so inscribed, that its whole symbolism depends.

Looking at these traditions in anything like the light of historical narratives, we are compelled to consider them, to use the plain language of Lee, "but as so many idle and absurd conceits." We must go behind the legend, which we acknowledge at once to be only an allegory, and study its symbolism.

The following facts can, I think, be readily established from history. First, that there was a very general prevalence among the earliest nations of antiquity of the worship of stones as the representatives of Deity; secondly, that in almost every ancient temple there was a legend of a sacred or mystical stone; thirdly, that this legend is found in the Masonic system; and lastly, that the mystical stone there has received the name of the "Stone of Foundation."

Now, as in all the other systems the stone is admitted to be symbolic, and the traditions connected with it mystical, we are compelled to assume the same predicates of the Masonic stone. It, too, is symbolic, and its legend a myth or an allegory.

Of the fable, myth, or allegory, Bailly has said that, "subordinate to history and philosophy, it only deceives that it may the better instruct us. Faithful in preserving the realities which are confided to it, it covers with its seductive envelop the lessons of the one and the truths of the other." It is from this standpoint that we are to view the allegory of the Stone of Foundation, as developed in one of the most interesting and important symbols of Masonry.

The fact that the mystical stone in all the ancient religions was a symbol of the Deity, leads us necessarily to the conclusion that the Stone of Foundation was also a symbol of Deity. And this symbolic idea is strengthened by the Tetragrammaton, or sacred name of God, that was inscribed upon it. This ineffable name sanctifies the stone upon which it is engraved as the symbol of the Grand Architect. It takes from it its heathen signification as an idol, and consecrates it to the worship of the true God.

The predominant idea of the Deity, in the Masonic system, connects him with his creative and formative power. God is to the Freemason *Al Gabil,* as the Arabians called him, that is, *The Builder;* or, as expressed in his Masonic title, the *Grand Architect of the Universe,* by common consent abbreviated in the formula G A O T U. Now, it is evident that no symbol could so appropriately suit him in this character as the Stone of Foundation, upon which he is allegorically supposed to have erected his world. Such a symbol closely connects the creative work of God, as a pattern and exemplar, with the workman's erection of his temporal building on a similar foundation-stone.

But this Masonic idea is still further to be extended. The great object of all Masonic labor is *Divine truth.* The search for the *lost word* is the search for truth. But Divine truth is a term synonymous with God. The ineffable name is a symbol of truth, because God, and God alone, is truth. It is properly a Scriptural idea. The Book of Psalms abounds with this sentiment. Thus it is said that the truth of the Lord "reacheth unto the clouds," and that "his truth endureth unto all generations." If, then, God is truth, and the Stone of Foundation is the Masonic symbol of God, it follows that it must also be the symbol of Divine truth.

When we have arrived at this point in our speculations, we are ready to show how all the myths and legends of the Stone of Foundation may be rationally explained as parts of that beautiful "science of morality, veiled in allegory and illustrated by symbols," which is the acknowledged definition of Freemasonry.

In the Masonic system there are two temples: the first temple, in which the degrees of Ancient Craft Masonry are concerned, and the second temple, with which the higher degrees, and especially the Royal Arch, are related. The first temple is symbolic of the present life; the second temple is symbolic of the life to come. The first temple, the present life, must be destroyed; on its foundations the second temple, the life eternal, must be built.

But the mystical stone was placed by King Solomon in the foundations of the first Temple. That is to say, the first temple of our present life must be built on the sure foundation of Divine truth, "for other foundation can no man lay."

But although the present life is necessarily built upon the foundation of truth, yet we never thoroughly attain it in this sublunary sphere. The Foundation-Stone is concealed in the first temple, and the Master Mason knows it not. He has not the true word. He receives only a substitute.

But in the second temple of the future life, we have passed from the grave which had been the end of our labors in the first. We have removed the rubbish, and have found that Stone of Foundation which had been hitherto concealed from our eyes. We now throw aside the substitute for truth which had contented us in the former temple, and the brilliant effulgence of the Tetragrammaton and the Stone of Foundation are discovered, and thenceforth we are the possessors of the true word—of Divine truth. And in this way, the Stone of Foundation, or Divine truth, concealed in the first temple, but discovered and brought to light in the second, will explain that passage of the Apostle: "For now we see through a glass darkly; but then, face to face: now I know in part; but then I shall know face to face."

And so the result of this inquiry is, that the Masonic Stone of Foundation is a symbol of Divine truth, upon which all speculative Masonry is built, and the legends and traditions which refer to it are intended to describe, in an allegorical way, the progress of truth in the soul, the search for which is a Mason's labor, and the discovery of which in his reward.

Stone-Masons of the Middle Ages. The history of the origin and progress of the Brotherhood of Stone-Masons in Europe, during the Middle Ages, is of great importance, as a study, to the Masonic scholar, because of the intimate connection that existed between that Brotherhood and the Fraternity of Freemasons. Indeed, the history of the one is but the introduction to the history of the other. In an historical excursus, we are compelled to take up the speculative science where we find it left by the operative art. Hence, whoever shall undertake to write a history of Freemasonry, must give, for the completion of his labor, a very full consideration to the Brotherhood of Stone-Masons.

In the year 1820, there issued from the press of Leipsic, in Germany, a work, by Dr. Christian Ludwig Steiglitz, under the title of *Von Altdeutscher Baukunst,* that is, "An Essay on the Old German Architecture," published in 1820. In this work the author traces, with great exactness, the rise and the progress of the fraternities of Stone-Masons from the earliest times, through the Middle Ages, until their final absorption into the associations of Freemasons. From the labors of Dr. Steiglitz, collated with some other authorities in respect to matters upon which he is either silent or erroneous, I have compiled the following sketch.

It is universally admitted that, in the early ages of Christianity, the clergy were the most important patrons of the arts and sciences. This was because all learning was then almost exclusively confined to ecclesiastics. Very few of the laity could read or write, and even kings affixed the sign of the cross, in the place of their signatures, to the charters and other documents which they issued, because, as they frankly confessed, of their inability to write their names; and hence comes the modern expression of *signing* a paper, as equivalent to subscribing the name.

From the time of Charlemagne, in the eighth century, to the middle of the twelfth, all knowledge and practise of architecture, painting, and sculpture were exclusively confined to the monks; and bishops personally superintended the erection of the churches and cathedrals in their dioceses, because not only the principles, but the practise of the art of building were secrets scrupulously maintained within the walls of cloisters, and utterly unknown to laymen.*

Many of the founders of the Monastic Orders, and especially among these St. Benedict, made it a peculiar duty for the brethren to devote themselves to architecture and church building. The English monk Winfrid, better known in ecclesiastical history as St. Boniface, and who, for his labors in Christianizing that country, has been styled the Apostle of Germany, followed the example of his predecessors in the erection of German monasteries. In the eighth century he organized an especial class of monks for the practise of building, under the name of *Operarii*, or Craftsmen, and *Magistri Operum*, or Masters of the Works. The labors and duties of these monks were divided. Some of them designed the plan of the building; others were painters and sculptors; others were occupied in working in gold and silver and embroidery; and others again, who were called *Cæmentarii*, or Stone-Masons, undertook the practical labors of construction. Sometimes, especially in extensive buildings, where many workmen were required, laymen were also employed, under the direction of the monks. So extensive did these labors become, that bishops and abbots often derived a large portion of their revenues from the earnings of the workmen in the monasteries.

Among the laymen who were employed in the monasteries as assistants and laborers, many were of course possessed of superior intelligence. The constant and intimate association of these with the monks in the prosecution of the same design led to this result, that in process of time, gradually and almost unconsciously, the monks imparted to them their art secrets and the esoteric principles of architecture. Then, by degrees, the knowledge of the arts and sciences went from these monkish builders out into the world, and the laymen architects, withdrawing from the ecclesiastical fraternities, organized brotherhoods of their own. Such was the beginning of the Stone-Masons in Germany, and the same thing occurred in other countries. These brotherhoods of Masons now began to be called upon, as the monks formerly had been, when an important

* This view was long held, but is by no means correct, for we now know that there were many scholarly architects during this period of supposed darkness. [E. E. C.]

building, and especially a church or a cathedral, was to be erected. Eventually they entirely superseded their monkish teachers in the prosecution of the art of building about the beginning of the twelfth century. To their knowledge of architecture they added that of the other sciences, which they had learned from the monks. Like these, too, they devoted themselves to the higher principles of the art, and employed other laymen to assist their labors as stone-masons. And thus the union of these architects and stone-masons presented, in the midst of an uneducated people, a more elevated and intelligent class, engaged as an exclusive association in building important and especially religious edifices.

But now a new classification took place. As formerly, the monks, who were the sole depositaries of the secrets of high art, separated themselves from the laymen, who were entrusted with only the manual labor of building; so now the more intelligent of the laymen, who had received these secrets from the monks, were distinguished as architects from the ordinary laborers, or common masons. The latter knew only the use of the trowel and mortar, while the former were occupied in devising plans for building and the construction of ornaments by sculpture and skilful stone-cutting.

These brotherhoods of high artists soon won great esteem, and many privileges and franchises were conceded to them by the municipal authorities among whom they practised their profession. Their places of assembly were called *Hutten, Logen,* or *Lodges,* and the members took the name of *Steinmetzen.* Their patron saint was St. John the Baptist, who was honored by them as the mediator between the Old and the New Covenants, and the first martyr of the Christian religion. To what condition of art these Freemasons of the Middle Ages had attained, we may judge from what Hallam says of the edifices they erected—that they "united sublimity in general composition with the beauties of variety and form, skilful or at least fortunate effects of shadow and light, and in some instances extraordinary mechanical science." (*Mid. Ages,* iv., 280.) And he subsequently adds, as an involuntary confirmation of the truth of the sketch of their origin just given, that the mechanical execution of the buildings was "so far beyond the apparent intellectual powers of those times, that some have ascribed the principal ecclesiastical structures to the Fraternity of Freemasons, depositaries of a concealed and traditionary science. There is probably some ground for this opinion, and the earlier archives of that mysterious association, if they existed, might illustrate the progress of Gothic architecture, and perhaps reveal its origin." (*Ib.*, 284.) These archives do exist, or many of them; and although unknown to Mr. Hallam, because they were out of the course of his usual reading, they have been thoroughly sifted by recent Masonic scholars, especially by our German and English brethren; and that which the historian of the Middle Ages had only assumed as a plausible conjecture has, by their researches, been proved to be a fact.

The prevalence of Gnostic symbols—such as lions, serpents, and the like—in the decorations of churches of the Middle Ages, have led some writers to conclude that the Knights Templar exercised an influence over the architects, and that by them the Gnostic and Ophite symbols were introduced into Europe. But Dr. Steiglitz denies the correctness of this conclusion. He ascribes the existence of Gnostic symbols in the church architecture to the fact that, at an early period in ecclesiastical history, many of the Gnostic dogmas passed over into Christendom with the Oriental and Platonic philosophy, and he attributes their adoption in architecture to the natural compliance of the architects or Masons with the predominant taste in the earlier periods of the Middle Ages for mysticism, and the favor given to grotesque decorations, which were admired without any knowledge of their actual import.

Steiglitz also denies any deduction of the Builders' Fraternities, or Masonic Lodges, of the Middle Ages from the Mysteries of the old Indians, Egyptians, and Greeks; although he acknowledges that there is a resemblance between the organizations. This, however, he attributes to the fact that the Indians and Egyptians preserved all the sciences, as well as the principles of architecture, among their secrets, and because, among the Greeks, the artists were initiated into their mysteries, so that, in the old as well as in the new brother-hoods, there was a purer knowledge of religious truth, which elevated them as distinct associations above the people. In like manner, he denies the descent of the Masonic fraternities from the sect of Pythagoreans, which they resembled only in this: that the Samian sage established schools which were secret, and were based upon the principles of geometry.

But he thinks that those are not mistaken who trace the associations of Masons of the Middle Ages to the Roman Colleges, the *Collegia Cæmentariorum,* because these colleges appear in every country that was conquered and established as a province or a colony by the Romans, where they erected temples and other public buildings, and promoted the civilization of the inhabitants. They continued until a late period. But when Rome began to be convulsed by the wars of its decline, and by the incursions of hordes of barbarians, they found a welcome reception at Byzantium, or Constantinople, whence they subsequently spread into the west of Europe, and were everywhere held in great estimation for their skill in the construction of buildings.

In Italy the associations of architects never entirely ceased, as we may conclude from the many buildings erected there during the domination of the Ostrogoths and the Longobards. Subsequently, when civil order was restored, the Masons of Italy were encouraged and supported by popes, princes, and nobles. And Muratori tells us, in his *Historia d'Italia,* that under the Lombard kings the inhabitants of Como were so superior as masons and bricklayers, that the appellation of Magistri

Comacini, or Masters from Como, became generic to all those of the profession. (See *Comacine Masters.*)

In England, when the Romans took possession of it, the corporations, or colleges of builders, also appeared, who were subsequently continued in the Fraternity of Freemasons, probably established, as Steiglitz thinks, about the middle of the fifth century, after the Romans had left the island. The English Masons were subjected to many adverse difficulties, from the repeated incursions of Scots, Picts, Danes, and Saxons, which impeded their active labors; yet were they enabled to maintain their existence, until, in the year 926, they held that General Assembly at the city of York which framed the Constitutions that governed the English Craft for eight hundred years, and which is claimed to be the oldest Masonic record now extant. It is but fair to say that the recent researches of Bro. Hughan and other English writers have thrown a doubt upon the authenticity of these Constitutions, and that the very existence of this York assembly has been denied and practically confirmed.

In France, as in Germany, the Fraternities of Architects originally sprang out of the connection of lay builders with the monks in the era of Charlemagne. The French Masons continued their fraternities throughout the Middle Ages, and erected many cathedrals and public buildings.

We have now arrived at the middle of the eleventh century, tracing the progress of the fraternities of Stone-Masons from the time of Charlemagne to that period. At that time all the architecture of Europe was in their hands. Under the distinctive name of *Traveling Freemasons* they passed from nation to nation, constructing churches and cathedrals wherever they were needed. Of their organization and customs, Sir Christopher Wren, in his *Parentalia,* gives the following account:

"Their government was regular, and where they fixed near the building in hand, they made a camp of huts. A surveyor governed in chief; every tenth man was called a warden, and overlooked each nine."

Mr. Hope, who, from his peculiar course of studies, was better acquainted than Mr. Hallam with the history of these Traveling Freemasons, thus speaks, in his *Essay on Architecture,* of their organization at this time, by which they effected an identity of architectural science throughout all Europe:

"The architects of all the sacred edifices of the Latin Church, wherever such arose,—north, south, east, or west—thus derived their science from the same central school; obeyed in their designs the dictates of the same hierarchy; were directed in their constructions by the same principles of propriety and taste; kept up with each other, in the most distant parts to which they might be sent, the most constant correspondence; and rendered every minute improvement the property of the whole body, and a new conquest of the art."

Working in this way, the Stone-Masons, as corporations of builders, daily increased in numbers and in power. In the thirteenth century they assumed a new organization, which allied them more closely than ever with that Brotherhood of Speculative Freemasons into which they were finally merged in the eighteenth century, in England, but not in Germany, France, or Italy.

These fraternities or associations became at once very popular. Many of the potentates of Europe, and among them the Emperor Rudolph I., conceded to them considerable powers of jurisdiction, such as would enable them to preserve the most rigid system in matters pertaining to building, and would facilitate them in bringing master builders and stone-masons together at any required point. Pope Nicholas III. granted the Brotherhood, in 1278, letters of indulgence, which were renewed by his successors, and finally, in the next century, by Pope Benedict XII.

The Steinmetzen, as a fraternity of Operative Masons, distinguished from the ordinary masons and laborers of the craft, acquired at this time great prominence, and were firmly established as an association. In 1452 a general assembly was convened at Strasburg, and a new constitution framed, which embraced many improvements and modifications of the former one. But seven years afterward, in 1459,* Jost Dotzinger, then holding the position of architect of the Cathedral of Strasburg, and, by virtue of his office, presiding over the Craft of Germany, convened a general assembly of the Masters of all the Lodges at the city of Ratisbon. There the code of laws which had been adopted at Strasburg in 1452, under the title of "Statutes and Regulations of the Fraternity of Stone-Masons of Strasburg," was fully discussed and sanctioned. It was then also resolved that there should be established four Grand Lodges—at Strasburg, at Vienna, at Cologne, and at Zurich; and they also determined that the master workman, for the time being, of the Cathedral of Strasburg should be the Grand Master of the Masons of Germany. These constitutions or statutes are still extant, and are older than any other existing Masonic record of undoubted authenticity, except the manuscript of Halliwell. They were "kindly and affably agreed upon," according to their preamble, "for the benefit and requirements of the Masters and Fellows of the whole Craft of Masonry and Masons in Germany."

General assemblies, at which important business was transacted, were held in 1464 at Ratisbon, and in 1469 at Spire, while provincial assemblies in each of the Grand Lodge jurisdictions were annually convened.

In consequence of a deficiency of employment, from political disturbances and other causes, the Fraternity now for a brief period de-

* Besides the Strasburg Constitution of 1459 there are two other very important documents of the Steinmetzen of Germany: The Torgau Ordinances of 1462 and the Brothers' Book of 1563. [E. E. C.]

clined in its activity. But it was speedily revived when, in October, 1498, the Emperor Maximilian I. confirmed its statutes, as they had been adopted at Strasburg, and recognized its former rights and privileges. This act of confirmation was renewed by the succeeding emperors, Charles V. and Ferdinand I. In 1563 a general assembly of the Masons of Germany and Switzerland was convened at the city of Basle by the Grand Lodge of Strasburg. The Strasburg constitutions were again renewed with amendments, and what was called the Stone-Masons' Law (*das Steinwerkrecht*) was established. The Grand Lodge of Strasburg continued to be recognized as possessing supreme appellate jurisdiction in all matters relating to the Craft. Even the Senate of that city had acknowledged its prerogatives, and had conceded to it the privilege of settling all controversies in relation to matters connected with building; a concession which was, however, revoked in 1620, on the charge that the privilege had been misused.

Thus the Operative Freemasons of Germany continued to work and to cultivate the high principles of a religious architectural art. But on March 16, 1707, up to which time the Fraternity had uninterruptedly existed, a decree of the Imperial Diet at Ratisbon dissolved the connection of the Lodges of Germany with the Grand Lodge of Strasburg, because that city had passed into the power of the French. The head being now lost, the subordinate bodies began rapidly to decline. In several of the German cities the Lodges undertook to assume the name and exercise the functions of Grand Lodges; but these were all abolished by an imperial edict in 1731, which at the same time forbade the administration of any oath of secrecy, and transferred to the government alone the adjudication of all disputes among the Craft. From this time we lose sight of any national organization of the Freemasons in Germany until the restoration of the Order, in the eighteenth century, through the English Fraternity.* But in many cities—as in Basle, Zurich, Hamburg, Dantzic, and Strasburg—they preserved an independent existence under the statutes of 1559, although they lost much of the profound symbolical knowledge of architecture which had been possessed by their predecessors.

Before leaving these German Stone-Masons, it is worth while to say something of the symbolism which they preserved in their secret teachings. They made much use, in their architectural plans, of mystical numbers, and among these five, seven, and nine were especially prominent. Among colors, gold and blue and white possessed symbolic meanings. The foot rule, the compasses, the square, and the gavel, with some other implements of their art, were consecrated with a spiritual signification. The east was considered as a sacred point; and many allusions were made to Solomon's Temple, especially to the pillars of the porch, representations of which are to be found in several of the cathedrals.

* Thus we see that the great order of the Steinmetzen of Germany took no part in the formation of the Speculative Freemasons. [E. E. C.]

In France the history of the Free Stone-Masons was similar to that of their German brethren. Originating, like them, from the cloisters, and from the employment of laymen by the monkish architects, they associated themselves together as a brotherhood superior to the ordinary stone-masons. The connection between the Masons of France and the Roman Colleges of Builders was more intimate and direct than that of the Germans, because of the early and very general occupation of Gaul by the Roman legions: but the French organization did not materially differ from the German. Protected by popes and princes, the Masons were engaged, under ecclesiastical patronage, in the construction of religious edifices. In France there was also a peculiar association, the *Pontifices,* or *Bridge Builders,* closely connected in design and character with the Masonic Fraternity, and the memory of which is still preserved in the name of one of the degrees of the Scottish Rite, that of "Grand Pontiff." The principal seat of the French Stone-Masonry was in Lombardy, whence the Lodges were disseminated over the kingdom, a fact which is thus accounted for by Mr. Hope: "Among the arts exercised and improved in Lombardy," he says, "that of building held a pre-eminent rank, and was the more important because the want of those ancient edifices to which they might recur for materials already wrought, and which Rome afforded in such abundance, made the architects of these more remote regions dependent on their own skill and free to follow their own conceptions." But in the beginning of the sixteenth century, the necessity for their employment in the further construction of religious edifices having ceased, the Fraternity began to decline, and the Masonic corporations were all finally dissolved, with those of other workmen, by Francis I., in 1539. Then originated that system which the French call *Compagnonage,* a system of independent gilds or brotherhoods, retaining a principle of community as to the art which they practised, and with, to some extent, a secret bond, but without elevated notions or general systematic organizations. The societies of *Compagnons* were, indeed, but the *débris* of the Building Masons. Masonry ceased to exist in France as a recognized system until its revival in the eighteenth century.

We see, then, in conclusion, that the Stone-Masons—coming partly from the Roman Colleges of Architects, as in England, in Italy, and in France, but principally, as in Germany, from the cloistered brotherhoods of monks—devoted themselves to the construction of religious edifices. They consisted mainly of architects and skilful operatives; but—as they were controlled by the highest principles of their art, were in possession of important professional secrets, were actuated by deep sentiments of religious devotion, and had united with themselves in their labors men of learning, wealth, and influence—to serve as a proud distinction between themselves and the ordinary laborers and uneducated workmen, many of whom were of servile condition.

Subsequently, in the beginning of the eighteenth century, they threw off the operative element of their institution, and, adopting an entirely speculative character, they became the Freemasons of the present day, and established on an imperishable foundation that sublime Institution which presents over all the habitable earth the most wonderful system of religious and moral symbolism that the world ever saw.

Stone, Rejected. St. Matthew records (xxi. 42) that our Lord said to the chief priests and elders, "Did ye never read in the Scriptures, The stone which the builders rejected, the same is become the head of the corner?" Commenting on this, Dr. Adam Clarke says: "It is an expression borrowed from masons, who, finding a stone which, being tried in a particular place, and appearing improper for it, is thrown aside and another taken; however, at last, it may happen that the *very stone* which had been before *rejected* may be found the most suitable as *the head stone of the corner.*" This is precisely the symbolism of the Mark Master or Fourth Degree of the American Rite, where the *rejected stone* is suggested to the neophyte "as a consolation under all the frowns of fortune, and as an encouragement to hope for better prospects." Bro. G. F. Yates says that the symbolism of the rejected stone in the present Mark Degree is not in the original Master Mark Mason's Degree, out of which Webb manufactured his ritual, but was introduced by him from some other unknown source.

Strength. This is said to be one of the three principal supports of a Lodge, as the representative of the whole Institution, because it is necessary that there should be Strength to support and maintain every great and important undertaking, not less than there should be Wisdom to contrive it, and Beauty to adorn it. Hence, Strength is symbolized in Masonry by the Doric column, because, of all the orders of architecture, it is the most massive; by the Senior Warden, because it is his duty to strengthen and support the authority of the Master; and by Hiram of Tyre, because of the material assistance that he gave in men and materials for the construction of the Temple.

Supreme Authority. The supreme authority in Masonry is that dogmatic power from whose decisions there is no appeal. At the head of every Rite there is a supreme authority which controls and directs the acts of all subordinate bodies of the Rite. In the United States, and in the American Rite which is there practised, it would, at the first glance, appear that the supreme authority is divided. That of symbolic Lodges is vested in Grand Lodges, of Royal Arch Chapters in Grand Chapters, of Royal and Select Councils in Grand Councils, and of Commanderies of Knights Templar in the Grand Encampment. And so far as ritualistic questions and matters of internal arrangement are concerned, the supreme authority is so divided. But the supreme authority of Masonry in each State is actually vested in the Grand Lodge of that State. It is universally recognized as Masonic law that a Mason expelled or suspended by the Grand Lodge, or by a subordinate Lodge with the approval and confirmation of the Grand Lodge, thereby stands expelled or suspended from Royal Arch, from Cryptic, and from Templar Masonry. The same rules apply to the A. and A. S. Rite. Nor can he be permitted to visit any of the bodies in either of these divisions of the Rite so long as he remains under the ban of expulsion of the Grand Lodge. So the status or condition of every Mason in the jurisdiction is controlled by the Grand Lodge, from whose action on that subject there is no appeal. The Masonic life and death of every member of the Craft, in every class of the Order, is in its hands, and thus the Grand Lodge becomes the real supreme authority of the jurisdiction.

Supreme Council. The Supreme Masonic authority of the Ancient and Accepted Scottish Rite is called a Supreme Council. A Supreme Council claims to derive the authority for its existence from the Constitutions of 1786.* I have no intention here of entering into the question of the authenticity of that document. The question is open to the historian, and has been amply discussed, with the natural result of contradictory conclusions. But he who accepts the Ancient and Accepted Scottish Rite as genuine Freemasonry, and owes his obedience as a Mason to its constituted authorities, is compelled to recognize those Constitutions wherever or whenever they may have been enacted as the fundamental law—the constitutional rule of his Rite. To their authority all the Supreme Councils owe their legitimate existence.

Dr. Frederick Dalcho, who, I think, may very properly be considered as the founder in the United States, and therefore in the world, of the Ancient and Accepted Scottish Rite in its present form as the legitimate successor of the Rite of Perfection or of Herodem, has given in the *Circular* written by him, and published December 4, 1802, by the Supreme Council at Charleston, the following account of the establishment of Supreme Councils:

"On the 1st of May, 1786, the Grand Constitution of the thirty-third degree, called the Supreme Council of Sovereign Grand Inspectors General, was finally ratified by his Majesty the King of Prussia, who, as Grand Commander of the Order of Prince of the Royal Secret, possessed the Sovereign Masonic power over all the Craft. In the new Constitution, this high power was conferred on a Supreme Council of nine brethren in each nation, who possess all the Masonic prerogatives, in their own district, that his Majesty individually possessed, and are *Sovereigns of Masonry.*"

The law for the establishment of a Supreme Council is found in the following words in the Latin Constitutions of 1786: "The first degree will be subordinated to the second, that to the third, and so in order to the sublime, Thirty-third, and last, which will watch over all the others, will correct their errors and will govern them, and whose congregation

* See *Constitutions of 1786.*

or convention will be a dogmatic *Supreme Grand Council*, the Defender and Conservator of the Order, which it will govern and administer according to the present Constitutions and those which may hereafter be enacted."

But the Supreme Council at Charleston derived its authority and its information from what are called the French Constitutions; and it is in them that we find the statement that Frederick invested the Supreme Council with the same prerogatives that he himself possessed, a provision not contained in the Latin Constitutions. The twelfth article says: "The Supreme Council will exercise all the Masonic sovereign powers of which his Majesty Frederick II., King of Prussia, was possessed." *

These Constitutions further declare (Art. 5) that "every Supreme Council is composed of nine Inspectors-General, five of whom should profess the Christian religion." In the same article it is provided that "there shall be only one Council of this degree in each nation or kingdom in Europe, two in the United States of America as far removed as possible the one from the other, one in the English islands of America, and one likewise in the French islands."

It was in compliance with these Constitutions that the Supreme Council at Charleston, South Carolina, was instituted. In the *Circular,* already cited, Dalcho gives this account of its establishment:

"On the 31st of May, 1801, the Supreme Council of the thirty-third degree for the United States of America was opened, with the high honors of Masonry, by Brothers John Mitchell and Frederick Dalcho, Sovereign Grand Inspectors-General; and in the course of the present year, [1802,] the whole number of Grand Inspectors-General was completed, agreeably to the Grand Constitutions."

This was the first Supreme Council of the Ancient and Accepted Scottish Rite ever formed; from it has emanated either directly or indirectly all the other Councils which have been since established in America or Europe; and although it now exercises jurisdiction only over a part of the United States under the title of the Supreme Council for the Southern Jurisdiction of the United States, it claims to be and is recognized as "the Mother Council of the World."

Under its authority a Supreme Council, the second in date, was established by Count de Grasse in the French West Indies, in 1802; a third in France, by the same authority, in 1804; and a fourth in Italy in 1805. In 1813 the Masonic jurisdiction of the United States was divided; the Mother Council establishing at the city of New York a Supreme Council for the Northern Jurisdiction, and over the States north of the Ohio and east of the Mississippi, reserving to itself all the remainder of the territory of the United States. The seat of the Northern Council is now at

* This shows the difference in the sources of authority between the A. and A. S Rite and Symbolic Masonry. The former is monarchical, while the latter is supposed to be democratic. [E. E. C.]

Boston; and although the offices of the Grand Commander and Secretary-General of the Southern Council are now in the city of Washington, whence its documents emanate, its seat is still constructively at Charleston.

On their first organization, the Supreme Councils were limited to nine members in each. That rule continued to be enforced in the Mother Council until the year 1859, when the number was increased to thirty-three. Similar enlargements have been made in all the other Supreme Councils except that of Scotland, which still retains the original number.

The officers of the original Supreme Council at Charleston were: a Most Puissant Sovereign Grand Commander, Most Illustrious Lieutenant Grand Commander, Illustrious Treasurer-General of the Holy Empire, Illustrious Secretary-General of the Holy Empire, Illustrious Grand Master of Ceremonies, and Illustrious Captain of the Guards.

In 1859, with the change of numbers in the membership, there was also made a change in the number and titles of the officers. These now in the Mother Council, according to its present Constitution, are: 1. Sovereign Grand Commander; 2. Lieutenant Grand Commander; 3. Secretary-General of the Holy Empire; 4. Grand Prior; 5. Grand Chancellor; 6. Grand Minister of State; 7. Treasurer-General of the Holy Empire; 8. Grand Auditor; 9. Grand Almoner; 10. Grand Constable; 11. Grand Chamberlain; 12. First Grand Equerry; 13. Second Grand Equerry; 14. Grand Standard-Bearer; 15. Grand Sword-Bearer; 16. Grand Herald. The Secretary-General is properly the seventh officer, but by a decree of the Supreme Council he is made the third officer in rank "while the office continues to be filled by Bro. Albert G. Mackey, the present incumbent, who is the Dean of the Supreme Council." Dr. Mackey held this position until his death.

The officers somewhat vary in other Supreme Councils, but the presiding and recording officers are everywhere a Sovereign Grand Commander and a Secretary-General of the Holy Empire.

Supreme Councils, A. A. Scottish Rite. These Councils are organized in almost every country of the world, a number being under royal patronage, and in many nations are the governing power over all existing Masonry. A synoptical history of all the Supreme Councils that have ever existed, with the manner of their formation in chronological order, is published in the *Proceedings of the Supreme Council for the Northern Masonic Jurisdiction for 1908.* From this article is taken the following list (on p. 742), giving the Supreme Councils which have received general recognition.

The following Supreme Councils have been formed, but have not received formal recognition and the courtesy of an exchange of representation: Florence, Hungary, Luxembourg, Naples, Palerno, Rome, and Turkey. The number of these Supreme Bodies accomplishes 33.

On the 22d of September, 1875, a congress of the various Supreme Councils was convened at Lausanne, Switzerland, to consider such matters as might then and there be submitted for consideration and united action, and be deemed for the general benefit of the Rite. Much speculation and lack of confidence was the result among many of the invited participants lest they might be committed by uniting in the conference. The Congress, however, was held, and a declaration of principles set forth. There was also stipulated and agreed upon a treaty, involving highly important measures, embraced within twenty-three articles, which was concluded September 22, 1875. "The intimate alliance and confederation of the contracting Masonic powers extended and extends under their auspices to all the subordinates and to all true and faithful Masons of their respective jurisdictions." "Whoever may have illegitimately and irregularly received any Degree of the A. A. Scottish Rite can nowhere enjoy the prerogatives of a Freemason until he has been lawfully healed by the regular Supreme Council of his own country." The confederated powers again recognized and proclaimed as Grand Constitutions of the A. A. Scottish Rite, the constitutions and statutes adopted May 1, 1876, with the modifications and "Tiler" adopted by the Congress of Lausanne, the 22d of September, 1875.

The declaration and articles were signed by representatives of eighteen Supreme Councils, who recognized the territorial jurisdictions of the following Supreme Councils, to wit:

Northern Jur., U. S.
Southern Jur., U. S.
Central America,
England,
Belgium,
Canada,
Chili,
Colon,
Scotland,
U. S. of Colombia,
France,
Greece,
Hungary,
Ireland,
Italy,
Mexico,
Peru,
Portugal,
Argentine Republic,
Switzerland,
Uruguay.
Venezuela.

The same delegates, by virtue of the plenary powers they held, and by which they were justified, promised, for their principals, to maintain and defend with all their power, to preserve, and cause to be observed and respected, not only the territorial jurisdiction of the Confederated Supreme Councils represented in the said Congress at Lausanne, and the parties therein contracting, but also the territorial jurisdiction of the other Supreme Councils named in the foregoing table.

It is not possible to give statistics as to the number of the A. A. Scottish Rite Masons in the world, but calculating those, of whatever degree, who are governed by Supreme Councils in the different nations, it is but reasonable to presume one-half of the entire Fraternity is of that Rite, and as a matter of extensiveness, it is *par excellence* the Universal Rite. In many nations there is no other Rite known, and therein it confers all the degrees of its system, including the first three. Among the English-speaking Masons, it builds its structure upon the York or the American system of three degrees.

In the United States the number of this Rite, enrolled and unenrolled, will approximate one hundred and fifty thousand in the two Jurisdictions. Its organizations are to be found in every prominent city and many towns, and in numerous instances possessing and occupying temples built specially to accommodate its own peculiar forms, elegant of structure and in appointments, and of great financial value.

The progress of this Rite in the last half century has been most remarkable, and its future appears without a cloud.

The Supreme Council of the Ancient and Accepted Scottish Rite in the United States have adopted the custom of electing honorary members, who are sometimes called Honorary Thirty Thirds. They possess none of the rights of the Inspectors General, or Active Members, except that of being present at the meetings of the Council, taking part to a limited extent in its deliberations, except when it holds an Executive Session.

The original number of Honorary Members in the United States of America was nine Sovereign Grand Inspectors General comprising a Supreme Council. The additional Thirty Third Degree Members were made only by vacancies occasioned by the death of one of the original nine.

As time passed, the organization of Supreme Councils proceeded, the number of Thirty Thirds grew. Thirty-three active members was the number set for a Supreme Council.

The Supreme Council, Ancient and Accepted Scottish Rite, Southern Jurisdiction has its See in the City of Charleston, South Carolina, but its active domicil is in the City of Washington, U. S. A. The Supreme Council for the Northern Jurisdiction, U. S. A., is in the city of Boston, U. S. A.

The place where business meetings are held is called the Senatorial Chamber.

Sun. Hardly any of the symbols of Masonry are more important in their signification or more extensive in their application than the sun. As the source of material light, it reminds the Mason of that intellectual light of which he is in constant search. But it is especially as the ruler of the day, giving to it a beginning and end, and a regular course of hours, that the sun is presented as a Masonic symbol. Hence, of the three lesser lights, we are told that one represents or symbolizes the sun, one the moon, and one the Master of the Lodge, because, as the sun rules the day and the moon governs the night, so should the Worshipful Master rule and govern his Lodge with equal regularity and precision. And this is in strict analogy with other Masonic symbolisms. For if the Lodge is a symbol of the world, which is thus governed in its changes of times and seasons by the sun, it is evident that the Master who governs the Lodge, controlling its time of opening and closing, and the work which it should do, must be symbolized by the sun. The heraldic definition of the sun as a bearing fits most appositely to the symbolism of the sovereignty of the Master. Thus Gwillim says: "The sun is the symbol of sovereignty, the hieroglyphic of royalty; it doth signify absolute authority." This representation of the sun as a symbol of authority, while it explains the reference to the Master, enables us to amplify its meaning, and apply it to the three sources of authority in the Lodge, and accounts for the respective positions of the officers wielding this authority. The Master, therefore, in the East is a symbol of the rising sun; the Junior Warden in the South, of the Meridian Sun; and the Senior Warden in the West, of the Setting Sun.

Superexcellent Master. A degree which was originally an honorary or side degree conferred by the Inspectors-General of the Ancient and Accepted Scottish Rite at Charleston. It has since been introduced into some of the Royal and Select Councils of the United States, and there conferred as an additional degree. This innovation on the regular series of Cryptic degrees, with which it actually has no historical connection, met with great opposition; so that the convention of Royal and Select Masters, which met at New York in June, 1873, resolved to place it in the category of an honorary degree, which might or might not be conferred at the option of a Council, but not as an integral part of the Rite. Although this body had no dogmatic authority, its decision will doubtless have some influence in settling the question. The degree is simply an enlargement of that part of the ceremonies of the Royal Arch which refer to the Temple destruction. To that place it belongs, if it belongs anywhere, but has no more to do with the ideas inculcated in Cryptic Masonry, than have any of the degrees lately invented for modern secret societies.

Whence the degree originally sprang, it is impossible to tell. It could hardly have had its birth on the Continent of Europe; at least, it does not appear to have been known to European writers. Neither Gädicke nor Lenning mention it in their *Encyclopedias;* nor is it found in the catalogue of more than seven hundred degrees given by Thory in his *Acta Latomorum;* nor does Ragon allude to it in his *Tuileur Général,* although he has there given a list of one hundred and fifty-three degrees or modifications of the *Master.* Oliver, it is true, speaks of it, but he evidently derived his knowledge from an American source. It may have been manufactured in America, and possibly by some of those engaged in founding the Scottish Rite. The only Cahier that I ever saw of the original ritual, which is still in my possession, is in the handwriting of Alexander McDonald, a very intelligent and enthusiastic Mason, who was at one time the Grand Commander of the Supreme Council for the Southern Jurisdiction.

The Masonic legend of the degree of Superexcellent Master refers to circumstances which occurred on the last day of the siege of Jerusalem by Nebuzaradan, the captain of the Chaldean army, who had been sent by Nebuchadnezzar to destroy the city and Temple, as a just punishment of the Jewish king Zedekiah for his perfidy and rebellion. It occupies, therefore, precisely that point of time which is embraced in that part of the Royal Arch Degree which represents the destruction of the Temple, and the carrying of the Jews in captivity to Babylon. It is, in fact, an exemplification and extension of that part of the Royal Arch Degree.

As to the symbolic design of the degree, it is very evident that its legend and ceremonies are intended to inculcate that important Masonic virtue—fidelity to vows. Zedekiah, the wicked King of Judah, is, by the modern ritualists who have symbolized the degree, adopted very appropriately as the symbol of perfidy; and the severe but well-deserved punishment which was inflicted on him by the King of Babylon is set forth in the lecture as a great moral lesson, whose object is to warn the recipient of the fatal effects that will ensue from a violation of his sacred obligations.

Super-Excellent Master. This was originally an honorary Degree conferred by the Inspectors-General of the Ancient and Accepted Scottish Rite at Charleston. It has since been introduced into some of the Royal and Select Councils of the United States, and there conferred as an additional Cryptic Degree. The legend of the Degree refers to circumstances which occurred on the last day of the siege of Jerusalem by Nebuzaradan, the Captain of the Chaldean army, who had been sent by Nebuchadnezzar to destroy the city and Temple, as a just punishment for the Jewish King Zedekiah for his perfidy and rebellion. It refers to that part of the Royal Arch Degree which represents the destruction of the Temple, and the carrying of the Jews into captivity to Babylon. As to the symbolic design of the Degree, it is evident that its legend and ceremonies inculcate that important Masonic virtue—fidelity to vows. The severe but well deserved punishment inflicted on King Zedekiah, by the King of Babylon is set forth in the lecture as a great moral lesson, the idea being to warn the recipient of the fatal effects that will ensue from a violation of his obligations.

Sword. The sword is in chivalry the ensign or symbol of knighthood.

So important an ensign of knighthood as the sword must have been accompanied with some symbolic meaning, for in the Middle Ages symbolism was referred to on all occasions.

But there is a still better definition of the symbolism of the sword of knighthood in an old MS. in the library of the London College of Arms to the following effect:

"Unto a knight, which is the most honorable office above all other, is given a sword, which is made like unto a crosse for the redemption of mankynde in signifying that like as our Lord God died uppon the crosse for the redemption of mankynde, even so a knight ought to defend the crosse and to overcome and destroie the enemies of the same; and it hath two edges in tokening that with the sword he ought to mayntayne knighthood and justice."

Hence in Masonic Templarism we find that this symbolism has been preserved, and that the sword with which the modern knight is created is said to be endowed with the qualities of justice, fortitude, and mercy.

The charge to a Knights Templar, that he should never draw his sword unless convinced of the justice of the cause in which he is engaged, nor to sheathe it until his enemies were subdued, finds also its origin in the custom of the Middle Ages. Swords were generally manufactured with a legend on the blade. Among the most common of these legends was that used on swords made in Spain, many examples of which are still to be found in modern collections. That legend is: "No me saques sin rason. No me embaines sin honor"; i. e., *Do not draw me without justice. Do not sheathe me without honor.*

In Masonry, the use of the sword as a part of the Masonic clothing is confined to the high degrees and the degrees of chivalry, when, of course, it is worn as a part of the insignia of knighthood. In the symbolic degrees its appearance in the Lodge, except as a symbol, is strictly prohibited. The Masonic prints engraved in the last century, when the sword, at least as late as 1780, constituted a part of the dress of every gentleman, show that it was discarded by the members when they entered the Lodge. The official swords of the Tiler and the Pursuivant or Sword-Bearer are the only exceptions. This rule is carried so far, that military men, when visiting a Lodge, are required to divest themselves of their swords, which are to be left in the Tiler's room.

Symbolic Degrees. The first three degrees of Freemasonry, namely, those of Entered Apprentice, Fellow-Craft, and Master Mason, are known, by way of distinction, as the "symbolic degrees." This term is never applied to the degrees of Mark, Past, and Most Excellent Master, and the Royal Arch, which, as being conferred in a body called a Chapter, are generally designated as "capitular degrees"; nor to those of Royal and Select Master, which, conferred in a Council, are, by an excellent modern usage, styled "cryptic degrees," from the crypt or vault which plays so important a part in their ritual. But the term "symbolic" is exclusively confined to the degrees conferred in a Lodge of the three primitive degrees, which Lodge, therefore, whether opened on the First, the Second or the Third Degree, is always referred to as a "symbolic Lodge." As this distinctive term is of constant and universal use, it may be considered not altogether useless to inquire into its origin and signification.

The germ and nucleus of all Freemasonry is to be found in the three primitive degrees—the Apprentice, the Fellow-Craft, and the Master Mason. They were at one time (under a modification, however, which included the Royal Arch) the only degrees known to or practised by the Craft, and hence they are often called "Ancient Craft Masonry," to distinguish them from those comparatively modern additions which constitute what are designated as the "high degrees," or, by the French, *"les hautes grades."* The striking peculiarity of these primitive degrees is that their prominent mode of instruction is by symbols. Not that they are without legends. On the contrary, they have each an abundance of legends; such, for instance, as the details of the building of the Temple; of the payment of wages in the middle chamber, or of the construction of the pillars of the porch. But these legends do not perform any very important part in the constitution of the degree. The lessons which are communicated to the candidate in these primitive degrees are conveyed, principally, through the medium of symbols, while there is (at least in the working of the degrees) but little tradition or legendary teaching, with the exception of the great legend of Masonry, the "GOLDEN LEGEND" of the Order, to be found in the Master's Degree, and which is, itself, a symbol of the most abstruse and solemn signification. But even in this instance, interesting as are the details of the legend, they are only subordinate to the symbol. Hiram the Builder is the profound symbol of manhood laboring for immortality, and all the different points of the legend are simply clustered around it, only to throw out the symbol in bolder relief. The legend is of itself inert—it is the symbol of the Master Workman that gives it life and true meaning.

Symbolism is, therefore, the prevailing characteristic of these primitive degrees; and it is because all the science and philosophy and religion of Ancient Craft Masonry is thus concealed from the profane but unfolded to the initiates in symbols, that the first three degrees which comprise it are said to be symbolic.

Now, nothing of this kind is to be found in the degrees above and beyond the third, if we except the Royal Arch, which, however, as I have already intimated, was originally a part of Ancient Craft Masonry, and was unnaturally torn from the Master's Degree, of which it, as every Masonic student knows, constituted the complement and consummation. Take, for example, the intermediate degrees of the American Chapter, such, for instance, as the Mark and Most Excellent Master. Here we find the symbolic feature ceasing to predominate, and the traditional or legendary taking its place. It is true that in these capitular degrees the use of symbols is not altogether abandoned. This could not well be, for the symbol constitutes the very essence of Freemasonry. The symbolic element is still to be discovered in these degrees, but only in a position subordinate to legendary instruction. As an illustration, let us consider the keystone in the Mark Master's Degree. Now, no one will deny that this is, strictly speaking, a symbol, and a very important and beautiful one, too. It is a symbol of a fraternal convenant between those who are engaged in the common search after Divine truth. But, in the *rôle* which it plays in the ritual of this degree, the symbol, however beautiful and appropriate it may be, is in a manner lost sight of, and the keystone derives almost all its importance and interest from the traditional history of its construction, its architectural design, and its fate. It is as the subject of a legend, and not as a symbol, that it attracts attention. Now, in the Third or Master's Degree we find the trowel, which is a symbol of almost precisely the same import as the keystone. They both refer to a Masonic covenant. But no legend, no tradition, no history, is connected with the trowel. It presents itself simply and exclusively as a symbol. Hence we learn that symbols do not in the capitular, as in the primitive, degrees of Masonry strike the eye, and inform the mind, and teach the heart, in every part of the Lodge, and in every part of the ceremonial initiation. On the contrary, the capitular degrees are almost altogether founded on and composed of a series of events in Masonic history. Each of them has attached to it some tradition or legend which it is the design of the degree to illustrate, and the memory of which is preserved in its ceremonies and instructions. That most of these legends are themselves of symbolic signification is not denied. But this is their interior sense. In their outward and ostensible meaning, they appear before us simply as legends. To retain these legends in the memory of Masons appears to have been the primary design of the establishment of the higher degrees, and as the information intended to be communicated in these degrees is of an historical character, there can of course be but little room for symbols or for symbolic instruction, the profuse use of which would rather tend to an injury than to a benefit, by complicating the purposes of the ritual and confusing the mind of the aspirant.

The celebrated French writer, Ragon, objects to this exclusive application of the term "symbolic" to the first three degrees as a sort of unfavorable criticism on the higher degrees, and as if implying that the latter are entirely devoid of the element of symbolism. But he has mistaken the true import and meaning of the application. It is not because the higher or capitular and cryptic degrees are altogether without symbols—for such is not the case—that the term symbolic is withheld from them, but because symbolic instruction does not constitute their predominating characteristic, as it does of the first three degrees.

And hence the Masonry taught in these three primitive degrees is very properly called *Symbolic Masonry,* and the Lodge in which this Masonry is taught is known as a *Symbolic Lodge.*

Symbolic Lectures. The lectures appropriated to the First, Second, and Third degrees are sometimes called Symbolic lectures; but the term is more properly applied to any lecture which treats of the meaning of Masonic symbols, in contradistinction to one which discusses only the history of the Order, and which would, therefore, be called an Historical Lecture. But the English Masons have a lecture called "the symbolical lecture," in which is explained the forms, symbols, and ornaments of Royal Arch Masonry, as well as its rites and ceremonies.*

Symbolic Lodge. A Lodge of Master Masons, with the Fellow-Craft and Apprentice Lodge worked under its Constitution, is called a Symbolic Lodge, because in it the Symbolic degrees are conferred. (See *Symbolic Degrees.*)

Symbolic Masonry. The Masonry that is concerned with the first three degrees in all the Rites. This is the technical meaning. But in a more general sense, Symbolic Masonry is that Masonry, wherever it may be found, whether in the primary or in the high degrees, in which the lessons are communicated by symbols. (See *Symbolic Degrees.*)

Symbolism, The Science of. The science which is engaged in the investigation of the meaning of symbols, and the application of their interpretation to moral, religious, and philosophical instruction. In this sense, Freemasonry is essentially a science of symbolism. The English lectures define Freemasonry to be "a peculiar system of morality veiled in allegory and illustrated by symbols." The definition would be more correct were it in these words: *Freemasonry is a system of morality developed and inculcated by the science of symbolism.* It is this peculiar character as a symbolic institution, this entire adoption of the method of instruction by symbolism, which gives its whole identity to Freemasonry and has caused it to differ from every other association that the ingenuity of man has devised. It is this that has bestowed upon it that attractive form which has always secured the attachment of its disciples and its own perpetuity.

The Roman Catholic Church is, perhaps, the only contemporaneous institution which continues to cultivate, in any degree, the beautiful system of symbolism. But that which, in the Catholic Church, is, in a great measure, incidental, and the fruit of development, is, in Freemasonry, the very life-blood and soul of the Institution, born with it at its birth, or, rather, the germ from which the tree has sprung, and still giving it support, nourishment, and even existence. Withdraw from Freemasonry its Symbolism, and you take from the body its soul, leaving behind nothing but a lifeless mass of effete matter, fitted only for a rapid decay.

Since, then, the science of symbolism forms so important a part of the system of Freemasonry, it will be well to commence any discussion of that subject by an investigation of the nature of symbols in general.

There is no science so ancient as that of symbolism, and no mode of

* It is unfortunate that the Historical Lecture usually given in the Master's Degree is often absurd from any known historical or Masonic basis. This is misleading to those who have every reason to expect a different treatment at our hands, and efforts should be made to correct this error. [E. E. C.]

instruction has ever been so general as was the symbolic in former ages. "The first learning in the world," says the great antiquary, Dr. Stukely, "consisted chiefly of symbols. The wisdom of the Chaldeans, Phœnicians, Egyptians, Jews, of Zoroaster, Sanchoniathon, Pherecydes, Syrus, Pythagoras, Socrates, Plato, of all the ancients that is come to our hand, is symbolic." And the learned Faber remarks, that "allegory and personification were peculiary agreeable to the genius of antiquity, and the simplicity of truth was continually sacrificed at the shrine of poetical decoration."

In fact, man's earliest instruction was by symbols. The objective character of a symbol is best calculated to be grasped by the infant mind, whether the infancy of that mind be considered *nationally* or *individually*. And hence, in the first ages of the world in its infancy, all propositions, theological, political, or scientific, were expressed in the form of symbols. Thus the first religions were eminently symbolical, because, as that great philosophical historian, Grote, has remarked, "At a time when language was yet in its infancy, visible symbols were the most vivid means of acting upon the minds of ignorant hearers."

Even in the very formation of language, the medium of communication between man and man, and which must hence have been an elementary step in the progress of human improvement, it was found necessary to have recourse to symbols, for words are only and truly certain arbitrary symbols by which and through which we give an utterance to our ideas. The construction of language was, therefore, one of the first products of the science of symbolism.

We must constantly bear in mind this fact of the primary existence and predominance of symbolism in the earliest times, when we are investigating the nature of the ancient religions, with which the history of Freemasonry is so intimately connected. The older the religion, the more the symbolism abounds. Modern religions may convey their dogmas in abstract propositions; ancient religions always conveyed them in symbols. Thus there is more symbolism in the Egyptian religion than in the Jewish, more in the Jewish than in the Christian, more in the Christian than in the Mohammedan, and, lastly, more in the Roman than in the Protestant.

But symbolism is not only the most ancient and general, but it is also the most practically useful, of sciences. We have already seen how actively it operates in the early stages of life and of society. We have seen how the first ideas of men and of nations are impressed upon their minds by means of symbols. It was thus that the ancient peoples were almost wholly educated.

"In the simpler stages of society," says one writer on this subject, "mankind can be instructed in the abstract knowledge of truths only by symbols and parables. Hence we find most heathen religions becoming mythic, or explaining their mysteries by allegories, or instructive incidents. Nay, God himself, knowing the nature of the creatures formed by him, has condescended, in the earlier revelations that he made of himself, to teach by symbols; and the greatest of all teachers instructed the multitudes by parables. The great exemplar of the ancient philosophy and the grand archetype of modern philosophy were alike distinguished by their possessing this faculty in a high degree, and have told us that man was best instructed by similitudes.''

Such is the system adopted in Freemasonry for the development and inculcation of the great religious and philosophical truths, of which it was, for so many years, the sole conservator. And it is for this reason that I have already remarked, that any inquiry into the symbolic character of Freemasonry, must be preceded by an investigation of the nature of symbolism in general, if we would properly appreciate its particular use in the organization of the Masonic Institution.

Symbol of Glory. In the old lectures of the last century, the Blazing Star was called ''the glory in the centre''; because it was placed in the centre of the floor-cloth or tracing-board, and represented hieroglyphically the glorious name of God. Hence Dr. Oliver has given to one of his most interesting works, which treats of the symbolism of the Blazing Star, the title of *The Symbol of Glory.*

Tau Cross. A cross of three limbs, so called because it presents the figure of the Greek letter T. (See *Tau.*)

Team. Royal Arch Masons in America apply this word rather inelegantly to designate the three candidates upon whom the degree is conferred at the same time.

Tears. In the Master's Degree in some of the continental Rites, and in all the high degrees where the legend of the degree and the ceremony of reception are intended to express grief, the hangings of the Lodge are black strewn with tears. The figures representing tears are in the form depicted in the annexed cut. The symbolism is borrowed from the science of heraldry, where these figures are called *guttes,* and are defined to be ''drops of anything that is by nature liquid or liquefied by art.'' The heralds have six of these charges, viz., *yellow,* or drops of liquid gold; *white,* or drops of liquid silver; *red,* or drops of blood; *blue,* or drops of tears; *black,* or drops of pitch; and *green,* or drops of oil. In funeral hatchments, a black velvet cloth, sprinkled with these ''drops of tears,'' is placed in front of the house of a deceased nobleman and thrown over his bier; but there, as in Masonry, the *guttes de larmes,* or drops of tears, are not painted blue, but white.

Tebeth. טבת. The fourth month of the Hebrew civil year, corresponding to the months December and January, beginning with the new moon of the former.

Telamones. See *Caryatides.*

Tempelorden or **Tempelherrenorden.** The title in German of the Order of Knights Templar.

Temperance. One of the four cardinal virtues, the practise of which is inculcated in the First Degree. The Mason who properly appreciates the secrets which he has solemnly promised never to reveal, will not, by yielding to the unrestrained call of appetite, permit reason and judgment to lose their seats, and subject himself, by the indulgence in habits of excess, to discover that which should be concealed, and thus merit and receive the scorn and detestation of his brethren. And lest any brother should forget the danger to which he is exposed in the unguarded hours of dissipation, the virtue of temperance is wisely impressed upon his memory, by its reference to one of the most solemn portions of the ceremony of initiation. Some Masons, very properly condemning the vice of intemperance and abhorring its effects, have been unwisely led to confound temperance with total abstinence in a Masonic application, and resolutions have sometimes been proposed in Grand Lodges which declare the use of stimulating liquors in any quantity a Masonic offense. But the law of Masonry authorizes no such regulation. It leaves to every man the indulgence of his own tastes within due limits, and demands not abstinence, but only moderation and temperance, in anything not actually wrong.

Templar. See *Knights Templar.*

Templarius. The Latin title of a Knights Templar. Constantly used in the Middle Ages.

Templar Land. The Order of Knights Templar was dissolved in England, by an act of Parliament, in the seventeenth year of the reign of Edward II., and their possessions transferred to the Order of St. John of Jerusalem, or Knights Hospitalers. Subsequently, in the thirty-second year of the reign of Henry VIII., their possessions were transferred to the king. One of the privileges possessed by the English Templars was that their lands should be free of tithes; and these privileges still adhere to these lands, so that a farm being what is termed "Templar land," is still exempt from the imposition of tithes, if it is occupied by the owner; an exemption which ceases when the farm is worked under a lease.

Templar Origin of Masonry. The theory that Masonry originated in the Holy Land during the Crusades, and was instituted by the Knights Templar, was first advanced by the Chevalier Ramsay, for the purpose, it is supposed, of giving an aristocratic character to the association. It was subsequently adopted by the College of Clermont, and was accepted by the Baron von Hund as the basis upon which he erected his Rite of Strict Observance. The legend of the Clermont College is thus detailed by M. Berage in his work entitled *Les Plus Secrets Mystéres des Hauts Grades* (iii., 194). "The Order of Masonry was instituted by Godfrey de Bouillon, in Palestine in 1330, after the defeat of the Christian armies, and was communicated only to a few of the French Masons, sometime afterwards, as a reward for the services which they had rendered to the English and Scottish Knights. From these latter true Masonry is derived. Their Mother Lodge is situated on the mountain of Heredom, where the first Lodge in Europe was held, which still exists in all its splendor. The Council General is always held there, and it is the seat of the Sovereign Grand Master for the time being. This mountain is situated between the west and the north of Scotland, sixty miles from Edinburgh.

"There are other secrets in Masonry which were never known among the French, and which have no relation to the Apprentice, Fellow Craft, and Master—degrees which were constructed for the general class of Masons. The high degrees, which developed the true design of Masonry and its true secrets, have never been known to them.

"The Saracens having obtained possession of the holy places in Palestine, where all the mysteries of the Order were practised, made use of them for the most profane purposes. The Christians then leagued together to conquer this beautiful country, and to drive these barbarians from the land. They succeeded in obtaining a footing on these shores under the protection of the numerous armies of Crusaders which had been sent there by the Christian princes. The losses which they subsequently experienced put an end to the Christian power, and the Crusaders who remained were subjected to the persecutions of the Saracens, who massacred all who publicly proclaimed the Christian faith. This induced Godfrey de Bouillon, towards the end of the third century, to conceal the mysteries of religion under the veil of figures, emblems, and allegories.

"Hence the Christians selected the Temple of Solomon because it has so close a relation to the Christian Church, of which its holiness and its magnificence make it the true symbol. So the Christians concealed the mystery of the building up of the Church under that of the construction of the Temple, and gave themselves the title of Masons, Architects, or Builders, because they were occupied in building the faith. They assembled under the pretext of making plans of architecture to practise the rites of their religion, with all the emblems and allegories that Masonry could furnish, and thus protect themselves from the cruelty of the Saracens.

"As the mysteries of Masonry were in their principles, and still are only those of the Christian religion, they were extremely scrupulous to confide this important secret only to those whose discretion had been tried, and who had been found worthy. For this purpose they fabricated degrees as a test of those to whom they wished to confide it, and they gave them at first only the symbolic secret of Hiram, on which all the mystery of Blue Masonry is founded, and which is, in fact, the only secret of that Order which has no relation to true Masonry. They explained nothing else to them as they were afraid of being betrayed, and they conferred these degrees as a proper means of recognizing each other, surrounded as they were by barbarians. To succeed more effectually in this, they made use of different signs and words for each degree, so as not only to distinguish themselves from the profane Saracens, but to designate the different degrees. These they fixed at the number of seven, in imitation of the Grand Architect, who built the Universe in six days and rested on the seventh; and also because Solomon was seven years in constructing the Temple, which they had selected as the figurative basis of Masonry. Under the name of Hiram they gave a false application to the Masters, and developed the true secret of Masonry only to the higher degrees."

Such is the theory of the Templar origin of Masonry, which, mythical as it is, and wholly unsupported by the authority of history, has exercised a vast influence in the fabrication of high degrees and the invention of continental Rites. Indeed, of all the systems propounded during the eighteenth century, so fertile in the construction of extravagant systems, none has played so important a part as this in the history of Masonry. Although the theory is no longer maintained, its effects are everywhere seen and felt.

Templars of England. An important change in the organization of Templarism in England and Ireland took place in 1873. By it a union took place of the Grand Conclave of Masonic Knights Templar of England and the Grand Conclave of High Knights Templar of Ireland into one body, under the title of the "Convent General of the United Religious and Military Orders of the Temple and of St. John of Jerusalem, Palestine, Rhodes, and Malta." The following is a summary of the statutes by which the new Order is to be governed, as given by Sir Knight W. J. B. McLeod Moore, Grand Prior, in his circular to the Preceptors of Canada:

"1. The existing Grand Masters in the Empire are to be termed Great Priors, and Grand Conclaves or Encampments, Great Priories, under and subordinate to one Grand Master, as in the early days of the Order, and one Supreme Governing Body, the Convent General.

"2. The term Great is adopted instead of Grand, the latter being a French word; and grand in English is not grand in French. Great is the proper translation of 'Magnus' and 'Magnus Supremus.'

"3. The Great Priories of each nationality—England, Scotland, and Ireland, with their dependencies in the Colonies—retain their internal government and legislation, and appoint their Provincial Priors, doing nothing inconsistent with the supreme statutes of the Convent General.

"4. The title Masonic is not continued; the Order being purely Christian, none but Christians can be admitted; consequently it cannot be considered strictly as a Masonic body: Masonry, while inculcating the highest reverence for the Supreme Being, and the doctrine of the immortality of the soul, does not teach a belief in one particular creed, or unbelief in any. The connection with Masonry is, however, strengthened still more, as a candidate must now be two years a Master Mason, in addition to his qualification as a Royal Arch Mason.

"5. The titles Eminent 'Commander' and 'Encampment' have been discontinued, and the original name 'Preceptor' and 'Preceptory' substituted, as also the titles 'Constable' and 'Marshal' for 'First' and 'Second Captains.' 'Encampment' is a modern term, adopted probably when, as our traditions inform us, 'at the suppression of the ancient Military Order of the Temple, some of their number sought refuge and held conclaves in the Masonic Society, being independent small bodies, without any governing head.' 'Prior' is the correct and original title for the head of a langue or nationality, and 'Preceptor' for the subordinate bodies. The Preceptories were the ancient 'Houses' of the Templar Order; 'Commander' and 'Commanderies' was the title used by the Order of St. John, commonly known as Knights of Malta.

"6. The title by which the Order is now known is that of 'The United Religious and Military Orders of the Temple and of St. John of Jerusalem, Palestine, Rhodes, and Malta.' The Order of the Temple originally had no connection with that of Malta or Order of St. John; but the combined title appears to have been adopted in commemoration of the union which took place in Scotland with 'The Temple and Hospital of St. John,' when their lands were in common, at the time of the Reformation. But our Order of 'St. John of Jerusalem, Palestine, Rhodes, and Malta,' has no connection with the present Knights of Malta in the Papal States, or of the Protestant branches of the Order, the lineal successors of the ancient Knights of St. John, the sixth or English langue of which is still in existence, and presided over, in London, by His Grace the Duke of Manchester. The Order, when it occupied the Island of Malta as a sovereign body, was totally unconnected with Freemasonry.

"7. Honorary past rank is abolished, substituting the chivalric dignities of 'Grand Crosses' and 'Commanders,' limited in number, and confined to Preceptors. These honors to be conferred by His Royal Highness the Grand Master, the Fountain of Grace and Dignity; and it is contemplated to create an Order of Merit, to be conferred in like manner, as a reward to Knights who have served the Order.

"8. A Preceptor holds a degree as well as rank, and will always retain his rank and privileges as long as he belongs to a Preceptory.

"9. The abolition of honorary past rank is not retrospective, as their rank and privileges are reserved to all those who now enjoy them.

"10. The number of officers entitled to precedence has been reduced to seven; but others may be appointed at discretion, who do not, however, enjoy any precedence.

"11. Equerries, or serving brethren, are not to receive the accolade, or use any but a brown habit, and shall not wear any insignia or jewel: they are to be addressed as 'Frater,' not Sir Knight. In the early days of the Order they were not entitled to the accolade, and, with the esquires and men-at-arms, wore a dark habit, to distinguish them from the Knights, who wore white, to signify that they were bound by their vows to cast away the works of darkness and lead a new life.

"12. The apron is altogether discontinued, and a few immaterial alterations in the insignia will be duly regulated and promulgated: they do not, however, affect the present, but only apply to future, members of the Order. The apron was of recent introduction, to accord with Masonic usage: but reflection will at once show that, as an emblem of care and toil, it is entirely inappropriate to a Military Order, whose badge is the sword. A proposition to confine the wearing of the star to the Preceptors was negatived; the star and ribbon being in fact as much a part of the ritual as of the insignia of the Order.

"13. From the number of instances of persons totally unfitted having obtained admission into the Order, the qualification of candidates has been increased. A declaration is now required, to be signed by every candidate, that he is of the full age of twenty-one years, and in addition to being a Royal Arch Mason, that he is a Master Mason of two years' standing, professing the doctrines of the Holy and Undivided Trinity, and willing to submit to the statutes and ordinances, present and future, of the Order."

Templars of Scotland. *The Statutes of the Grand Priory of the Temple* of Scotland prescribe for the Order of Knights Templar in that kingdom an organization very different from that which prevails in other countries.

"The Religious and Military Order of the Temple" in Scotland consists of two classes: 1. Novice and Esquire; 2. Knight Templar. The Knights are again divided into four classes: 1. Knights created by Priories; 2. Knights elected from the companions on memorial to the Grand Master and Council, supported by the recommendation of the Priories to which they belong; 3. Knights Commanders; 4. Knights Grand Crosses, to be nominated by the Grand Master.

The supreme legislative authority of the Order is the Chapter General, which consists of the Grand Officers, the Knights Grand Crosses, and the Knights Commanders. One Chapter is held annually, at which the Grand Master, if present, acts as President. The anniversary of the death of James de Molay, March 11th, is selected as the time of this meeting, at which the Grand Officers are elected.

During the intervals of the meetings of the Chapter General, the affairs of the Order, with the exception of altering the Statutes, is entrusted to the Grand Master's Council, which consists of the Grand Officers, the Grand Priors of Foreign Langues, and the Knights Grand Crosses.

The Grand Officers, with the exception of the Past Grand Masters, who remain so for life, the Grand Master, who is elected triennially, and the Grand Aides-de-Camp, who are appointed by him and removed at his pleasure, are elected annually. They are as follows:

Grand Master,
Past Grand Masters,
Grand Seneschal,
Preceptor and Grand Prior of Scotland,
Grand Constable and Mareschal,
Grand Admiral,
Grand Almoner or Hospitaler,
Grand Chancellor,
Grand Treasurer,
Grand Registrar,
Primate or Grand Prelate,
Grand Provost or Governor-General,
Grand Standard-Bearer or Beaucennifer,
Grand Bearer of the Vexillum Belli,
Grand Chamberlain,
Grand Steward,
Two Grand Aides-de-Camp.

A Grand Priory may be instituted by the Chapter General in any nation, colony, or langue, to be placed under the authority of a Grand Prior, who is elected for life, unless superseded by the Chapter General.

A Priory, which is equivalent to our Commanderies, consists of the following officers:

Prior,
Subprior,
Mareschal or Master of Ceremonies,
Hospitaler or Almoner,
Chancellor,
Treasurer,
Secretary,
Chaplain and Instructor,
Beaucennifer, or Bearer of the Beauseant,
Bearer of the Red Cross Banner, or Vexillum Belli,
Chamberlain,
Two Aides-de-Camp.

The Chapter General or Grand Priory may unite two or more Priories into a Commandery, to be governed by a Provincial Commander, who is elected by the Chapter General.

The costume of the Knights, with the exception of a few slight variations to designate difference of rank, is the same as the ancient costume.

Templar Statistics. See *Statistics of the Order of the Temple.*

Temple. The symbolism of Speculative Masonry is so intimately connected with temple building and temple worship, that some notice of these edifices seems necessary. The Hebrews called a temple *beth,* which literally signifies a house or dwelling, and finds its root in a word which signifies "to remain or pass the night," or *hecal,* which means a palace, and comes from an obsolete word signifying "magnificent." So that they seem to have had two ideas in reference to a temple. When they called it *beth Jehovah,* or the "house of Jehovah" they referred to the continued presence of God in it; and when they called it *hecal Jevohah,* or the "palace of Jehovah," they referred to the splendor of the edifice which was selected as his residence. The Hebrew idea was undoubtedly borrowed from the Egyptian, where the same hieroglyphic ▭ I signified both a house and a temple. Thus, from an inscription at Philæ, Champollion (*Dict. Egyptienne*) cites the sentence, "He has made his devotions in the house of his mother Isis."

The classical idea was more abstract and philosophical. The Latin word *templum* comes from a root which signifies "to cut off," thus referring to any space, whether open or occupied by a building, which was cut off, or separated for a sacred purpose, from the surrounding profane ground. The word properly denoted a sacred enclosure where the omens were observed by the augurs. Hence Varro (*De Ling. Lat.*, vi., 81) defines a temple to be "a place for auguries and auspices." As the same practise of worshiping under the sky in open places prevailed among the northern nations, we might deduce from these facts that the temple of the sky was the Aryan idea, and the temple of the house the Semitic. It is true, that afterward, the augurs having for their own convenience erected a tent within the enclosure where they made their observations, or, literally, their *contemplations,* this in time gave rise among the Greeks and the Romans to permanent edifices like those of the Egyptians and the Hebrews.

Masonry has derived its temple symbolism, as it has almost all its symbolic ideas, from the Hebrew type, and thus makes the temple the symbol of a Lodge. But of the Roman temple worship it has not been neglectful, and has borrowed from it one of the most significant and important words in its vocabulary. The Latin word *speculor* means to observe, to look around. When the augur, standing within the sacred precincts of his open temple on the Capitoline hill, watched the flight of birds, that from it he might deduce his auspices of good or bad fortune, he was said, *speculari,* to speculate. Hence the word came at length to denote, like *contemplate* from *templum,* an investigation of sacred things, and thus we got into our technical language the title of "Speculative Masonry," as distinguished by its religious design from Operative or Practical Masonry, which is devoted to more material objects. The EGYPTIAN TEMPLE was the real archetype of the Mosaic tabernacle, as that was of the temple of Jerusalem. The direction of an Egyptian temple was usually from east to west, the entrance being at the east. It was a quadrangular building, much longer than its width, and was situated in the western part of a sacred enclosure. The approach through this enclosure to the temple proper was frequently by a double row of sphinxes. In front of the entrance were a pair of tall obelisks, which will remind the reader of the two pillars at the porch of Solomon's Temple. The temple was divided into a spacious hall, the sanctuary where the great body of the worshipers assembled. Beyond it, in the western extremity, was the cell or sekos, equivalent to the Jewish Holy of Holies, into which the priests only entered; and in the remotest part, behind a curtain, appeared the image of the god seated on his shrine, or the sacred animal which represented him.

GRECIAN TEMPLES, like the Egyptian and the Hebrew, were placed within an enclosure, which was separated from the profane land around it, in early times, by ropes, but afterward by a wall. The temple was usually quadrangular, although some were circular in form. It was divided into two parts, the πρόναος, porch or vestibule, and the νάος, or cell. In this latter part the statue of the god was placed, surrounded by a balustrade. In temples connected with the mysteries, the cell was called the ἄδυτον (Lat. *adytum*), and to it only the priests and the initiates had access; and we learn from Pausanias that various stories were related of calamities that had befallen persons who had unlawfully ventured to cross the threshold. Vitruvius says that the entrance of Greek temples was always toward the west; but this statement is contradicted by the appearance of the temples still partly existing in Attica, Ionia, and Sicily.

ROMAN TEMPLES, after they emerged from their primitive simplicity, were constructed much upon the model of the Grecian. There were the same vestibule and cells, or adytum, borrowed, as with the Greeks, from the holy and the most holy place of the Egyptians. Vitruvius says that the entrance of a Roman temple was, if possible, to the west, so that the worshipers, when they offered prayers or sacrifices, might look toward the east; but this rule was not always observed.

It thus appears, notwithstanding what Montfaucon (*Antiq.*, ii., 1. ii., ch. 2) says to the contrary, that the Egyptian form of a temple was the type from which other nations borrowed their idea.

This Egyptian form of a temple was borrowed by the Jews, and with some modifications adopted by the Greeks and Romans, whence it passed over into modern Europe. The idea of a separation into a holy and a most holy place has everywhere been preserved. The same idea is maintained in the construction of Masonic Lodges, which are but imitations, in spirit, of the ancient temples. But there has been a transposition of parts, the most holy place, which with the Egyptians and the Jews was in the west, being placed in Lodges in the east.

Temple, Grand Commander of the. (*Grand Commandeur du Temple.*) The Fifty-eighth Degree of the collection of the Metropolitan Chapter of France. It is the name of the Knight Commander of the Temple of the Scottish Rite.

Temple of Ezekiel. An ideal temple seen by the prophet Ezekiel, in the twenty-fifth year of the captivity, while residing in Babylon. It is supposed by Calmet, that the description given by the prophet was that of the Temple of Solomon, which he must have seen before its destruction. But an examination of its admeasurements will show that this could not have been the fact, and that the whole area of Jerusalem would not have been sufficient to contain a building of its magnitude. Yet, as Mr. Ferguson observes (*Smith Dict.*), the description, notwithstanding its ideal character, is curious, as showing what were the aspirations of the Jews in that direction, and how different they were from those of other nations; and also because it influenced Herod to some extent in his restoration of the temple of Zerubbabel. Between the visionary temple of Ezekiel and the symbolic city of the New Jerusalem, as described by the Evangelist, there is a striking resemblance, and hence it finds a place among the symbols in the Apocalyptic degrees. But with Symbolic or with Royal Arch Masonry it has no connection.

Temple of Herod. This was not the construction of a third temple, but only a restoration and extensive enlargement of the second, which had been built by Zerubbabel. To the Christian Mason it is interesting, even more than that of Solomon, because it was the scene of our Lord's ministrations, and was the temple from which the Knights Templar derived their name. It was begun by Herod 7 B.C., finished A.D. 4, and destroyed by the Romans in A.D. 70, having subsisted only seventy-seven years.

Temple of Solomon. The first Temple of the Jews was called *hecal Jehovah* or *beth Jehovah,* the palace or the house of Jehovah, to indicate its splendor and magnificence, and that it was intended to be the perpetual dwelling-place of the Lord. It was King David who first proposed to substitute for the nomadic tabernacle a permanent place of worship for his people; but although he had made the necessary arrangements, and even collected many of the materials, he was not permitted to commence the undertaking, and the execution of the task was left to his son and successor, Solomon.

Accordingly, that monarch laid the foundations of the edifice in the fourth year of his reign, 1012 B.C., and, with the assistance of his friend and ally, Hiram, King of Tyre, completed it in about seven years and a half, dedicating it to the service of the Most High in 1004 B.C. This was the year of the world 3000, according to the Hebrew chronology; and although there has been much difference among chronologists in relation to the precise date, this is the one that has been generally accepted, and it is therefore adopted by Masons in their calculations of different epochs.

The Temple stood on Mount Moriah, one of the eminences of the ridge which was known as Mount Zion, and which was originally the property of Ornan the Jebusite, who used it as a threshing-floor, and from whom it was purchased by David for the purpose of erecting an altar on it.

The Temple retained its original splendor for only thirty-three years. In the year of the world 3033, Shishak, King of Egypt, having made war upon Rehoboam, King of Judah, took Jerusalem, and carried away the choicest treasures. From that time to the period of its final destruction, the history of the Temple is but a history of alternate spoliations and repairs, of profanations to idolatry and subsequent restorations to the purity of worship. One hundred and thirteen years after the conquest of Shishak, Joash, King of Judah, collected silver for the repairs of the Temple, and restored it to its former condition in the year of the world 3148. In the year 3264, Ahaz, King of Judah, robbed the Temple of its riches, and gave them to Tiglath-Pileser, King of Assyria, who had united with him in a war against the Kings of Israel and Damascus. Ahaz also profaned the Temple by the worship of idols. In 3276, Hezekiah, the son and successor of Ahaz, repaired the portions of the Temple which his father had destroyed, and restored the pure worship. But fifteen years after he was compelled to give the treasures of the Temple as a ransom to Sennacherib, King of Assyria, who had invaded the land of Judah. But Hezekiah is supposed, after his enemy had retired, to have restored the Temple.

Manasseh, the son and successor of Hezekiah, fell away to the worship of Sabianism, and desecrated the Temple in 3306 by setting up altars to the host of heaven. Manasseh was then conquered by the King of Babylon, who in 3328 carried him beyond the Euphrates. But subsequently repenting of his sins he was released from captivity, and having returned to Jerusalem he destroyed the idols, and restored the altar of burnt-offerings. In 3380, Josiah, who was then King of Judah, devoted his efforts to the repairs of the Temple, portions of which had been demolished or neglected by his predecessors, and replaced the ark in the sanctuary. In 3398, in the reign of Jehoiakim, Nebuchadnezzar, King of Chaldea, carried a part of the sacred vessels to Babylon. Seven years afterward, in the reign of Jechoniah, he took away another portion; and finally, in 3416, in the eleventh year of the reign of Zedekiah, he took the city of Jerusalem, and entirely destroyed the Temple, and carried many of the inhabitants captives to Babylon.

The Temple was originally built on a very hard rock, encompassed with frightful precipices. The foundations were laid very deep, with immense labor and expense. It was surrounded with a wall of great height, exceeding in the lowest part four hundred and fifty feet, constructed entirely of white marble.

The body of the Temple was in size much less than many a modern parish church, for its length was but ninety feet, or, including the porch, one hundred and five, and its width but thirty. It was its outer court, its numerous terraces, and the magnificence of its external and internal decorations, together with its elevated position above the surrounding dwellings which produced that splendor of appearance that attracted the admiration of all who beheld it, and gives a color of probability to the legend that tells us how the Queen of Sheba, when it first broke upon her view, exclaimed in admiration, "A most excellent master must have done this!"

The Temple itself, which consisted of the porch, the sanctuary, and the Holy of Holies, was but a small part of the edifice on Mount Moriah. It was surrounded with spacious courts, and the whole structure occupied at least half a mile in circumference. Upon passing through the outer wall, you came to the first court, called the court of the Gentiles, because the Gentiles were admitted into it, but were prohibited from passing farther. It was surrounded by a range of porticoes or cloisters, above which were galleries or apartments, supported by pillars of white marble.

Passing through the court of the Gentiles, you entered the court of the children of Israel, which was separated by a low stone wall, and an ascent of fifteen steps, into two divisions, the outer one being occupied by the women, and the inner by the men. Here the Jews were in the habit of resorting daily for the purposes of prayer.

Within the court of the Israelites, and separated from it by a wall one cubit in height, was the court of the priests. In the center of this court was the altar of burnt-offerings, to which the people brought their oblations and sacrifices, but none but the priests were permitted to enter it.

From this court, twelve steps ascended to the Temple, strictly so called, which, as I have already said, was divided into three parts, the porch, the sanctuary, and the Holy of Holies.

The PORCH of the Temple was twenty cubits in length, and the same in breadth. At its entrance was a gate made entirely of Corinthian brass, the most precious metal known to the ancients. Beside this gate there were the two pillars Jachin and Boaz, which had been constructed by Hiram Abif, the architect whom the King of Tyre had sent to Solomon.

From the porch you entered the SANCTUARY by a portal, which, instead of folding doors, was furnished with a magnificent veil of many colors, which mystically represented the universe. The breadth of the sanctuary was twenty cubits, and its length forty, or just twice that of the porch and Holy of Holies. It occupied, therefore, one-half of the body of the Temple. In the sanctuary were placed the various utensils necessary for the daily worship of the Temple, such as the altar of incense, on which incense was daily burnt by the officiating priest; the ten golden candlesticks; and the ten tables on which the offerings were laid previous to the sacrifice.

THE HOLY OF HOLIES, or innermost chamber, was separated from the sanctuary by doors of olive, richly sculptured and inlaid with gold, and covered with veils of blue, purple, scarlet, and the finest linen. The size of the Holy of Holies was the same as that of the porch, namely, twenty cubits square. It contained the Ark of the covenant, which had been transferred into it from the tabernacle, with its overshadowing Cherubim and its mercy-seat. Into the most sacred place, the high priest alone could enter, and that only once a year, on the day of atonement.

The Temple, thus constructed, must have been one of the most magnificent structures of the ancient world. For its erection, David had collected more than four thousand millions of dollars, and one hundred and eighty-four thousand six hundred men were engaged in building it for more than seven years; and after its completion it was dedicated by Solomon with solemn prayer and seven days of feasting; during which a peace-offering of twenty thousand oxen and six times that number of sheep was made, to consume which the holy fire came down from heaven.

In Masonry, the Temple of Solomon has played a most important part. Time was when every Masonic writer subscribed with unhesitating faith to the theory that Masonry was there first organized; that there Solomon, Hiram of Tyre, and Hiram Abif presided as Grand Masters over the Lodges which they had established; that there the Symbolic degrees were instituted and systems of initiation were invented; and that from that period to the present Masonry had passed down the stream of Time in unbroken succession and unaltered form. But the modern method of reading Masonic history has swept away this edifice of imagination with as unsparing a hand, and as effectual a power, as those with which the Babylonian king demolished the structure upon which they are founded. No writer who values his reputation as a critical historian would now attempt to defend this theory. Yet it has done its work. During the long period in which the hypothesis was accepted as a fact, its influence was being exerted in molding the Masonic organizations into a form closely connected with all the events and characteristics of the Solomonic Temple. So that now almost all the Symbolism of Freemasonry rests upon or is derived from the "House of the Lord" at Jerusalem. So closely are the two connected, that to attempt to separate the one from the other would be fatal to the further existence of Masonry. Each Lodge is and must be a symbol of the Jewish Temple; each Master in the chair a representative of the Jewish king; and every Mason a personation of the Jewish workman.

Thus must it ever be while Masonry endures. We must receive the myths and legends that connect it with the Temple, not indeed as historic facts, but as allegories; not as events that have really transpired, but as symbols; and must accept these allegories and these symbols for what their inventors really meant that they should be—the foundations of a science of morality.

Temple of Zerubbabel. For the fifty-two years that succeeded the destruction of Jerusalem by Nebuchadnezzar that city saw nothing but the ruins of its ancient Temple. But in the year of the world 3468 and 536 B.C., Cyrus gave permission to the Jews to return to Jerusalem, and there to rebuild the Temple of the Lord. Forty-two thousand three hundred and sixty of the liberated captives returned under the guidance of Joshua, the High Priest, Zerubbabel, the Prince or Governor, and Haggai, the Scribe, and one year after they laid the foundations of the second Temple. They were, however, much disturbed in their labors by the Samaritans, whose offer to unite with them in the building they had rejected. Artaxerxes, known in profane history as Cambyses, having succeeded Cyrus on the throne of Persia, forbade the Jews to proceed with the work, and the Temple remained in an unfinished state until the death of Artaxerxes and the succession of Darius to the throne. As in early life there had been a great intimacy between this sovereign and Zerubbabel, the latter proceeded to Babylon, and obtained permission from the monarch to resume the labor. Zerubbabel returned to Jerusalem, and notwithstanding some further delays, consequent upon the enmity of the neighboring nations, the second Temple, or, as it may be called by way of distinction from the first, the Temple of Zerubbabel, was completed in the sixth year of the reign of Darius, 515 B.C., and just twenty years after its commencement. It was then dedicated with all the solemnities that accompanied the dedication of the first.

The general plan of this second Temple was similar to that of the first. But it exceeded it in almost every dimension by one-third. The decorations of gold and other ornaments in the first Temple must have far surpassed those bestowed upon the second, for we are told by Josephus (*Antiq.*, xi., 4) that "the Priests and Levites and Elders of families were disconsolate at seeing how much more sumptuous the old Temple was than the one which, on account of their poverty, they had just been able to erect."

The Jews also say that there were five things wanting in the second Temple which had been in the first, namely, the Ark, the Urim and Thummin, the fire from heaven, the Divine presence or cloud of glory, and the spirit of prophecy and power of miracles.

Such are the most important events that relate to the construction of this second Temple. But there is a Masonic legend connected with it which, though it may have no historical foundation, is yet so closely interwoven with the Temple system of Masonry, that it is necessary it should be recounted. It was, says the legend, while the workmen were engaged in making the necessary excavations for laying the foundation, and while numbers continued to arrive at Jerusalem from Babylon, that three worn and weary sojourners, after plodding on foot over the rough and devious roads between the two cities, offered themselves to the Grand Council as willing participants in the labor of erection. Who these sojourners were, we have no historical means of discovering; but there is a Masonic tradition (entitled, perhaps, to but little weight) that they were Hananiah, Mishael, and Azariah, three holy men, who are better known to general readers by their Chaldaic names of Shadrach, Meshach, and Abed-nego, as having been miraculously preserved from the fiery furnace of Nebuchadnezzar.

Their services were accepted, and from their diligent labors resulted that important discovery, the perpetuation and preservation of which constitute the great end and design of the Royal Arch Degree.

As the symbolism of the first or Solomonic Temple is connected with and refers entirely to the Symbolic degrees, so that of the second, or Temple of Zerubbabel, forms the basis of the Royal Arch in the York and American Rites, and of several high degrees in other Rites.

Temple, Order of the. When the Knights Templar had, on account of their power and wealth, excited the fears and the cupidity of Pope Clement V., and King Philip the Fair, of France, the Order was soon compelled to succumb to the combined animosity of a spiritual and a temporal sovereign, neither of whom was capable of being controlled by a spirit of honor or a dictate of conscience. The melancholy story of the sufferings of the Knights, and of the dissolution of their Order, forms a disgraceful record, with which the history of the fourteenth century begins.

On the 13th of March, in the year 1314, and in the refined city of Paris, James de Molay, the last of a long and illustrious line of Grand Masters of the Order of Knights Templar, testified at the stake his fidelity to his vows; and eleven years of service in the cause of religion were terminated, not by the sword of a Saracen, but by the iniquitous sentence of a Catholic pope and a Christian king.

The manufacturers of Masonic legends have found in the death of de Molay and the dissolution of the Order of Templars a fertile source from which to draw materials for their fanciful theories and surreptitious documents. Among these legends there was, for instance, one which maintained that during his captivity in the Bastile the Grand Master of the Templars established four Chiefs of the Order in the north, the south, the east, and the west of Europe, whose seats of government were respectively at Stockholm, Naples, Paris, and Edinburgh. Another invention of these Masonic speculators was the forgery of that document so well known as the Charter of Larmenius, of which I shall presently take notice. Previously, however, to any consideration of this document, I must advert to the condition of the Templar Order in Portugal, because there is an intimate connection between the society there organized and the Order of the Temple in France, which is more particularly the subject of the present article.

Surprising as it may appear, it is nevertheless true, that the Templars did not receive that check in Portugal to which they were subjected in France, in England, and some other countries of Europe. On the contrary, they were there maintained by King Denis in all their rights and privileges; and although compelled, by a bull of Clement V., to change their names to that of the Knights of Christ, they continued to be governed by the same rules and to wear the same costume as their predecessors, excepting the slight addition of placing a white Latin cross in the center of the usual red one of the ancient Order; and in the decree of establishment it was expressly declared that the king, in creating this new Order, intended only to effect a reform in that of the Templars. In 1420, John I., of Portugal, gave the Knights of Christ the control of the possessions of Portugal in the Indies, and succeeding monarchs granted them the proprietorship of all countries which they might discover, reserving, of course, the royal prerogative of sovereignty. In process of time the wealth and the power of the Order became so great, that the kings of Portugal found it expedient to reduce their rights to a considerable extent; but the Order itself was permitted to continue in existence, the Grand Mastership, however, being for the future vested in the sovereign.

We are now prepared to investigate understandingly the history of the Charter of Larmenius, and of the Order of the Temple at Paris, which was founded on the assumed authenticity of that document. The writings of Thory, of Ragon, and of Clavel, with the passing remarks of a few other Masonic writers, will furnish us with abundant materials for this narrative, interesting to all Freemasons, but more especially so to Masonic Knights Templar.

In the year 1682, and in the reign of Louis XIV., a licentious society was established by several young noblemen, which took the name of "La Petite Resurrection des Templiers," or "*The Little Resurrection of the Templars.*" The members wore concealed upon their shirts a decoration in the form of a cross, on which was embossed the figure of a man trampling on a woman, who lay prostrate at his feet. The emblematic signification of this symbol was, it is apparent, as unworthy of the character of man as it was derogatory to the condition and claims of woman; and the king, having been informed of the infamous proceedings which took place at the meetings, dissolved the society (which it was said was on the eve of initiating the dauphin); caused its leader, a prince of the blood, to be ignominiously punished, and banished the members from the court; the heaviest penalty that, in those days of servile submission to the throne, could be inflicted on a courtier.

In 1705, Philip of Orleans, who was subsequently the regent of France during the minority of Louis XV., collected together the remnants of this society, which still secretly existed, but had changed its object from a licentious to one of a political character. He caused new statutes to be constructed; and an Italian Jesuit, by name Father Bonani, who was a learned antiquary and an excellent designer, fabricated the document now known as the Charter of Larmenius, and thus pretended to attach the new society to the ancient Order of the Templars.

As this charter is not the least interesting of those forged documents with which the history of Freemasonry unfortunately abounds, a full description of it here will not be out of place.

The theory of the Duke of Orleans and his accomplice Bonani was (and the theory is still maintained by the Order of the Temple at Paris) that when James de Molay was about to suffer at the stake, he sent for Larmenius, and in prison, with the consent and approbation of such of his knights as were present, appointed him his successor, with the right of making a similar appointment before his death. On the demise of de Molay, Larmenius accordingly assumed the office of Grand Master, and ten years after issued this charter, transmitting his authority to Theobaldus Alexandrinus, by whom it was in like manner transmitted through a long line of Grand Masters, until in 1705 it reached Philip, Duke of Orleans. It will be seen hereafter that the list was subsequently continued to a later period.

The signatures of all these Grand Masters are affixed to the charter, which is beautifully executed on parchment, illuminated in the choicest style of Medieval chirography, and composed in the Latin language, but written in the Templar cipher. From the copy of the document given by Thory in his *Acta Latomorum* (ii., 145), I make the following translation:

"I, Brother John Mark Larmenius, of Jerusalem, by the grace of God and the secret decree of the most venerable and holy martyr, the Grand Master of the Soldiery of the Temple, (to whom be honor and glory,) confirmed by the common council of the brethren, being endowed with the Supreme Grand Mastership of the whole Order of the Temple, to every one who shall see these letters decretal thrice greeting:

"Be it known to all, both present and to come, that the failure of my strength, on account of extreme age, my poverty, and the weight of government being well considered, I, the aforesaid humble Master of the Soldiery of the Temple, have determined, for the greater glory of God and the protection and safety of the Order, the brethren, and the statutes, to resign the Grand Mastership into stronger hands.

"On which account, God helping, and with the consent of a Supreme Convention of Knights, I have conferred, and by this present decree do confer, for life, the authority and prerogatives of Grand Master of the Order of the Temple upon the Eminent Commander and very dear brother, Francis Thomas Theobald Alexandrinus, with the power, according to time and circumstances, of conferring the Grand Mastership of the Order of the Temple and the supreme authority upon another brother, most eminent for the nobility of his education and talent and decorum of his manners: which is done for the purpose of maintaining a perpetual succession of Grand Masters, an uninterrupted series of successors, and the integrity of the statutes. Nevertheless, I command that the Grand Mastership shall not be transmitted without the consent of a general convention of the fellow-soldiers of the Temple, as often as that Supreme Convention desires to be convened; and, matters being thus conducted, the successor shall be elected at the pleasure of the knights.

"But, lest the powers of the supreme office should fall into decay, now and for ever let there be four Vicars of the Grand Master, possessing supreme power, eminence, and authority over the whole Order, with the reservation of the rights of the Grand Master; which Vicars of the Grand Masters shall be chosen from among the elders, according to the order of their profession. Which is decreed in accordance with the above-mentioned wish, commended to me and to the brethren by our most venerable and most blessed Master, the martyr, to whom be honor and glory. Amen.

"Finally, in consequence of a decree of a Supreme Convention of the brethren, and by the supreme authority to me committed, I will, declare, and command that the Scottish Templars, as deserters from the Order, are to be accursed, and that they and the brethren of St. John of Jerusalem, (upon whom may God have mercy,) as spoliators of the domains of our soldiery, are now and hereafter to be considered as beyond the pale of the Temple.

"I have therefore established signs, unknown to our false brethren, and not to be known by them, to be orally communicated to our fellow-soldiers, and in which way I have already been pleased to communicate them in the Supreme Convention.

"But these signs are only to be made known after due profession and knightly consecration, according to the statutes, rites, and usages of the fellow-soldiery of the Temple, transmitted by me to the above-named Eminent Commander as they were delivered into my hands by the venerable and most holy martyr, our Grand Master, to whom be honor and glory. Let it be done as I have said. So mote it be. Amen.

"I, John Mark Larmenius, have done this on the thirteenth day of February, 1324.

"I, Francis Thomas Theobaldus Alexandrinus, God helping, have accepted the Grand Mastership, 1324."

And then follow the acceptances and signatures of twenty-two succeeding Grand Masters—the last, Bernard Raymund Fabré, under the date of 1804.*

The society, thus organized by the Duke of Orleans in 1705, under this Charter, which purported to contain the signatures *manu propria* of eighteen Grand Masters in regular succession, commencing with Larmenius and ending with himself, attempted to obtain a recognition by the Order of Christ, which we have already said was established in Portugal as the legitimate successor of the old Templars, and of which King John V. was at that time the Grand Master. For this purpose the Duke of Orleans ordered two of his members to proceed to Lisbon, and there to

* After having disappeared for many years, the original of this Charter was rediscovered and purchased by Bro. F. J. W. Crowe, of Chichester, England, who thought it too important and valuable to remain in private hands, and it is now in the possession of the Great Priory of England. A transcript of the document, differing slightly from that given above, has been published by Bro. Crowe in *Ars Quatuor Coronatorum*, vol. 24. [E. L. H.]

open negotiations with the Order of Christ. The king caused inquiries to be made of Don Luis de Cunha, his ambassador at Paris, upon whose report he gave orders for the arrest of the two French Templars. One of them escaped to Gibraltar; but the other, less fortunate, after an imprisonment of two years, was banished to Angola, in Africa, where he died.

The society, however, continued secretly to exist for many years in France, and is supposed by some to have been the same which, in 1789, was known by the name of the *Societé d'Aloyau,* a title which might be translated into English as the "Society of the Sirloin"—a name much more appropriate to a club of *bons vivants* than to an association of knights. The members of this society were dispersed at the time of the French Revolution, the Duke of Casse Brissac, who was massacred at Versailles in 1792, being its Grand Master at the period of its dispersion. Thory says that the members of this association claimed to be the successors of the Templars, and to be in possession of their charters.

A certain Bro. Ledru, one of the sons of the learned Nicholas Philip Ledru, was the physician of Casse Brissac. On the death of that nobleman and the sale of his property, Ledru purchased a piece of furniture, probably an escritoire, in which was concealed the celebrated Charter of Larmenius, the manuscript statutes of 1705, and the journal of proceedings of the Order of the Temple. Clavel says that about the year 1804, Ledru showed these articles to two of his friends—de Saintot and Fabré Palaprat; the latter of whom had formerly been an ecclesiastic. The sight of these documents suggested to them the idea of reviving the Order of the Temple. They proposed to constitute Ledru the Grand Master, but he refused the offer, and nominated Claudius Matheus Radix de Chevillon for the office, who would accept it only under the title of Vicar; and he is inscribed as such on the list attached to the Charter of Larmenius, his name immediately following that of Casse Brissac, who is recorded as the last Grand Master.

These four restorers of the Order were of opinion that it would be most expedient to place it under the patronage of some distinguished personage; and while making the effort to carry this design into execution, Chevillon, excusing himself from further official labor on account of his advanced age, proposed that Fabré Palaprat should be elected Grand Master, but for one year only, and with the understanding that he would resign the dignity as soon as some notable person could be found who would be willing to accept it. But Fabré, having once been invested with the Grand Mastership, ever afterward refused to surrender the dignity.

Among the persons who were soon after admitted into the Order were Decourchant, a notary's clerk; Leblond, an official of the imperial library; and Arnal, an ironmonger, all of whom were entrusted with the secret of the fraud, and at once engaged in the construction of what have since been designated the "Relics of the Order." Of these relics, which are preserved in the treasury of the Order of the Temple at Paris, an inventory was made on the 18th day of May, 1810, being, it is probable, soon after their construction. Dr. Burnes, who was a firm believer in the legitimacy of the Parisian Order and in the authenticity of its archives, has given in his *Sketch of the History of the Knights Templars* (App., p. xii.) a copy of this inventory in the original French. Thory gives it also in his *Acta Latomorum* (ii., 143). A brief synopsis of it may not be uninteresting. The *relics* consist of twelve pieces—"a round dozen"—and are as follows:

1. The Charter of Larmenius, already described. But to the eighteen signatures of Grand Masters in the Charter, which was in 1705 in possession of Philip, Duke of Orleans, are added six more, carrying the succession on from the last-named to Fabré Palaprat, who attests as Grand Master in 1804.
2. A volume of twenty-seven paper sheets, in folio, bound in crimson velvet, satin, and gold, containing the statutes of the Order in manuscript, and signed "Philip."
3. A small copper reliquary, in the shape of a Gothic church, containing four fragments of burnt bones, wrapped in a piece of linen. These are said to have been taken from the funeral pile of the martyred Templars.
4. A sword, said to be one which belonged to James de Molay.
5. A helmet, supposed to have been that of Guy, Dauphin of Auvergne.
6. An old gilt spur.
7. A bronze patina, in the interior of which is engraved an extended hand, having the ring and little fingers bent in upon the palm, which is the form of the episcopal benediction in the Roman Church.
8. A pax in gilt bronze, containing a representation of St. John, under a Gothic arch. The pax is a small plate of gold, silver, or other rich material, carried round by the priest to communicate the "kiss of peace."
9. Three Gothic seals.
10. A tall ivory cross and three miters, richly ornamented.
11. The beauseant, in white linen, with the cross of the Order.
12. The war standard in white linen, with four black rays.

Of these "relics," Clavel, who, as being on the spot, may be supposed to know something of the truth, tells us that the copper reliquary, the sword, the ivory cross, and the three miters were bought by Leblond from an old iron shop in the market of St. Jean, and from a maker of church vestments in the suburbs of Paris, while the helmet was taken by Arnal from one of the government armories.

Francisco Alvaro da Sylva Freyre de Porto, a knight of the Order of Christ, and a secret agent of John VI., King of Portugal, was admitted into the Order in 1805, and continued a member until 1815. He was one of the few, Clavel says, whom Fabré and the other founders admitted into their full confidence, and in 1812 he held the office of Grand Master's

Secretary. Fabré having signified to him his desire to be recognized as the successor of James de Molay by the Grand Master of the Order of Christ, Da Sylva sent a copy of the Charter of Larmenius to John VI., who was then in Brazil; but the request for recognition was refused.

The Order of the Temple, which had thus been ingeniously organized by Fabré Palaprat and his colleagues, began now to assume high prerogatives as the only representative of Ancient Templarism. The Grand Master was distinguished by the sounding titles of "Most Eminent Highness, Very Great, Powerful, and Excellent Prince, and Most Serene Lord." The whole world was divided into different jurisdictions, under the names of provinces, bailiwicks, priories, and commanderies, all of which were distributed among the members; and proofs of nobility were demanded of all candidates; but if they were not able to give these proofs, they were furnished by the Grand Master with the necessary patents.

The ceremonies of initiation were divided into three houses, again subdivided into eight degrees, and were as follows:

I. House of Initiation.

1. *Initiate.* This is the Entered Apprentice's Degree of Freemasonry.
2. *Initiate of the Interior.* This is the Fellow-Craft.
3. *Adept.* This is the Master Mason.
4. *Adept of the East.* The Elu of Fifteen of the Scottish Rite.
5. *Grand Adept of the Black Eagle of St. John.* The Elu of Nine of the Scottish Rite.

II. House of Postulance.

6. *Postulant of the Order.* The Rose Croix Degree.

III. Council.

7. *Esquire.* Merely a preparation for the Eighth Degree.
8. *Knight,* or *Levite of the Interior Guard.* The Philosophical Kadosh.

At first the members of the Order professed the Roman Catholic religion, and hence, on various occasions, Protestants and Jews were denied admission. But about the year 1814, the Grand Master having obtained possession of a manuscript copy of a spurious Gospel of St. John, which is supposed to have been forged in the fifteenth century, and which contradicted in many particulars the canonical Gospel, he caused it to be adopted as the doctrine of the Order; and thus, as Clavel says, at once transformed an Order which had always been perfectly orthodox into a schismatic sect. Out of this spurious Gospel and an introduction and commentary called the "Levitikon," said to have been written by Nicephorus, a Greek monk of Athens, Fabré and his colleagues composed a liturgy, and established a religious sect to which they gave the name of "Johannism."

The consequence of this change of religious views was a schism in the Order. The orthodox party, however, appears to have been the stronger; and after the others had for a short time exhibited themselves as *soi-disant* priests in a Johannite church which they erected, and in which they publicly chanted the liturgy which they had composed, the church and the liturgy were given up, and they retired once more into the secrecy of the Order.

Such is the brief history of the rise and progress of the celebrated Order of the Temple, which still exists at Paris, with, however, a much abridged exercise, if not with less assumption of prerogative. It still claims to be the only true depository of the powers and privileges of the ancient Order of Knights Templar, denouncing all other Templars as spurious, and its Grand Master proclaims himself the legal successor of James de Molay; with how much truth the narrative already given will enable every reader to decide.

The question of the legality of the "Order of the Temple," as the only true body of Knights Templar in modern days, is to be settled only after three other points have been determined: First, was the Charter of Larmenius, which was brought for the first time to light in 1705 by the Duke of Orleans, an authentic or a forged document? Next, even if authentic, was the story that Larmenius was invested with the Grand Mastership and the power of transmission by de Molay a fact or a fable? And, lastly, was the power exercised by Ledru, in reorganizing the Order in 1804, assumed by himself or actually derived from Casse Brissac, the previous Grand Master? There are many other questions of subordinate but necessary importance to be examined and settled before we can consent to give the Order of the Temple the high and, as regards Templarism, the exclusive position that it claims.

Temple, Second. The Temple built by Zerubbabel is so called. See *Temple of Zerubbabel.*

Temple, Symbolism of the. Of all the objects which constitute the Masonic science of symbolism, the most important, the most cherished by Masons, and by far the most significant, is the Temple of Jerusalem. The spiritualizing of the Temple is the first, the most prominent, and the most pervading of all symbols of Freemasonry. It is that which most emphatically gives it its religious character. Take from Freemasonry its dependence on the Temple; leave out of its ritual all reference to that sacred edifice, and to the legends and traditions connected with it, and the system itself would at once decay and die, or at best remain only as some fossilized bone, serving merely to show the nature of the once living body to which it had belonged.

Temple worship is in itself an ancient type of the religious sentiment in its progress toward spiritual elevation. As soon as a nation emerged out of Fetishism, or the worship of visible objects, which is the most degraded form of idolatry, its people began to establish a priesthood, and to erect temples. The Goths, the Celts, the Egyptians, and the Greeks, however much they may have differed in the ritual, and in the objects of their polytheistic worship, were all in the possession of priests and of temples. The Jews, complying with this law of our religious nature, first constructed their tabernacle, or portable temple, and then, when time and opportunity permitted, transferred their monotheistic worship to that more permanent edifice which towered in all its magnificence above the pinnacle of Mount Moriah. The mosque of the Mohammedan and the church or chapel of the Christian is but an embodiment of the same idea of temple worship in a simpler form.

The adaptation, therefore, of the Temple of Jerusalem to a science of symbolism, would be an easy task to the mind of those Jews and Tyrians who were engaged in its construction. Doubtless, at its original conception, the idea of this temple symbolism was rude and unembellished. It was to be perfected and polished only by future aggregations of succeeding intellects. And yet no Biblical nor Masonic scholar will venture to deny that there was, in the mode of building and in all the circumstances connected with the construction of King Solomon's Temple, an apparent design to establish a foundation for symbolism.

The Freemasons have, at all events, seized with avidity the idea of representing in their symbolic language the interior and spiritual man by a material temple. They have the doctrine of the great Apostle of the Gentiles, who has said, "Know ye are the temple of God, and that the spirit of God dwelleth in you." The great body of the Masonic Craft, looking only to this first Temple erected by the wisdom of King Solomon, make it the symbol of life; and as the great object of Masonry is the search after truth, they are directed to build up this temple as a fitting receptacle for truth when found, a place where it may dwell, just as the ancient Jews built up their great Temple as a dwelling-place for Him who is the author of all truth.

To the Master Mason, this Temple of Solomon is truly the symbol of human life; for, like life, it was to have its end. For four centuries it glittered on the hills of Jerusalem in all its gorgeous magnificence; now, under some pious descendant of the wise King of Israel, the spot from whose altars arose the burnt-offerings to a living God, and now polluted by some recreant monarch of Judah to the service of Baal; until at length it received the Divine punishment through the mighty King of Babylon, and, having been despoiled of all its treasures, was burnt to the ground, so that nothing was left of all its splendor but a smoldering heap of ashes. Variable in its purposes, evanescent in its existence, now a gorgeous pile of architectural beauty, and anon a ruin over which the resistless power of fire has passed, it becomes a fit symbol of human life occupied in the search after Divine truth, which is nowhere to be found;

now sinning and now repentant; now vigorous with health and strength, and anon a senseless and decaying corpse.

Such is the symbolism of the first Temple, that of Solomon, as familiar to the class of Master Masons. But there is a second and higher class of the Fraternity, the Masons of the Royal Arch, by whom this temple symbolism is still further developed.

This second class, leaving their early symbolism and looking beyond this Temple of Solomon, find in Scriptural history another Temple, which, years after the destruction of the first one, was erected upon its ruins; and they have selected the second Temple, the Temple of Zerubbabel, as their prominent symbol. And as the first class of Masons find in their Temple the symbol of mortal life, limited and perishable, they, on the contrary, see in this second Temple, built upon the foundations of the first, a symbol of life eternal, where the lost truth shall be found, where new incense shall arise from a new altar, and whose perpetuity their great Master had promised when, in the very spirit of symbolism, he exclaimed, "Destroy this temple, and in three days I will raise it up."

And so to these two classes or Orders of Masons the symbolism of the Temple presents itself in a connected and continuous form. To the Master Mason, the Temple of Solomon is the symbol of this life; to the Royal Arch Mason, the Temple of Zerubbabel is the symbol of the future life. To the former, his Temple is the symbol of the search for truth; to the latter, his is the symbol of the discovery of truth; and thus the circle is completed and the system made perfect.

Three. Everywhere among the ancients the number three was deemed the most sacred of numbers. A reverence for its mystical virtues is to be found even among the Chinese, who say that numbers begin at one and are made perfect at three, and hence they denote the multiplicity of any object by repeating the character which stands for it three times. In the philosophy of Plato, it was the image of the Supreme Being, because it includes in itself the properties of the two first numbers, and because, as Aristotle says, it contains within itself a beginning, a middle, and an end. The Pythagoreans called it perfect harmony. So sacred was this number deemed by the ancients, that we find it designating some of the attributes of almost all the gods. The thunderbolt of Jove was three-forked; the scepter of Neptune was a trident; Cerberus, the dog of Pluto, was three-headed; there were three Fates and three Furies; the sun had three names, Apollo, Sol, and Liber; and the moon three also, Diana, Luna, and Hecate. In all incantations, three was a favorite number, for, as Virgil says, "numero Deus impari gaudet," God delights in an odd number. A triple cord was used, each cord of three different colors, white, red, and black; and a small image of the subject of the charm was carried thrice around the altar.

In Freemasonry, the ternary is the most sacred of all the mystical numbers. Beginning with the old axiom of the Roman Artificers, that *tres faciunt collegium,* or it requires three to make a college, they have established the rule that not less than three shall congregate to form a Lodge. Then in all the Rites, whatever may be the number of superimposed grades, there lie at the basis the three Symbolic degrees. There are in all the degrees three principal officers, three supports, three greater and three lesser lights, three movable and three immovable jewels, three principal tenets, three working-tools of a Fellow-Craft, three principal orders of architecture, three chief human senses, three Ancient Grand Masters. In fact, everywhere in the system the number three is presented as a prominent symbol. So much is this the case, that all the other mystical numbers depend upon it, for each is a multiple of three, its square or its cube, or derived from them. Thus, 9, 27, 81, are formed by the multiplication of three, as $3 \times 3 = 9$, and $3^2 \times 3 = 27$, and $3^2 \times 3^2 = 81$.

But in nothing is the Masonic signification of the ternary made more interesting than in its connection with the sacred delta, the symbol of Deity.

Three Points. Three points in a triangular form (.˙.) are placed after letters in a Masonic document to indicate that such letters are the initials of a Masonic title or of a technical word in Masonry, as G.˙. M.˙. for Grand Master, or G.˙. L.˙. for Grand Lodge. It is not a symbol, but simply a mark of abbreviation. The attempt, therefore, to trace it to the Hebrew three yods, a Kabbalistic sign of the Tetragrammaton, or any other ancient symbol, is futile. It is an abbreviation, and nothing more; although it is probable that the idea was suggested by the sacred character of the number three as a Masonic number, and these three dots might refer to the position of the three officers in a French Lodge. Ragon says (*Orthod. Maçon.*, p. 71) that the mark was first used by the Grand Orient of France in a circular issued August 12, 1774, in which we read "G.˙. O.˙. de France." The abbreviation is now constantly used in French documents, and, although not accepted by the English Masons, has been very generally adopted in other countries. In the United States, the use of this abbreviation is gradually extending.

Three Sacred Utensils. These were the vessels of the Tabernacle as to which the Rev. Joseph Barclay, LL.D., makes the following quotation: "Rabbi José, son of Rabbi Judah, said a fiery ark, and a fiery table, and a fiery candlestick descended from heaven. And Moses saw them, and made according to their similtude"; and thus comments: "They also think that the Ark of the Covenant is concealed in a chamber under the Temple Enclosure, and that it and all the holy vessels will be found at the coming of the Messiah." The Apocrypha, however, informs us that Jeremiah laid the Tabernacle, and the Ark, and the Altar of Incense in a "hollow cave, in the mountain, where Moses climbed up and saw the heritage of God. And the place shall be unknown until the time that God gather his people again together, and receive them into Mercy." (2 Mac.

ii. 4–7.) The sacred vessels, which were taken to Rome after the destruction of Jerusalem in A.D. 70, and are now seen sculptured on the Arch of Titus, were carried off to Africa by the Vandals under Genseric. Belisarius took them to Constantinople in A.D. 520. They were afterward sent back to Jerusalem, and thence they are supposed to have been carried to Persia, when Chosroes plundered the Holy City, in June, 614.

Three Senses. Of the five human senses, the three which are the most important in Masonic symbolism are Seeing, Hearing, and Feeling, because of their respective reference to certain modes of recognition, and because, by their use, Masons are enabled to practise that universal language the possession of which is the boast of the Order.

Token. The word token is derived from the Anglo-Saxon *tacn,* which means a sign, presage, type, or representation, that which points out something; and this is traced to *tæcan,* to teach, show, or instruct, because by a token we show or instruct others as to what we are. Bailey, whose *Dictionary* was published soon after the revival, defines it as "a sign or mark"; but it is singular that the word is not found in either of the dictionaries of Phillips or Blount, which were the most popular glossaries in the beginning of the last century. The word was, however, well known to the Fraternity, and was in use at the time of the revival with precisely the same meaning that is now given to it as a mode of recognition.

The Hebrew word אות, *ōth,* is frequently used in Scripture to signify a sign or memorial of something past, some covenant made or promise given. Thus God says to Noah, of the rainbow, "it shall be for a *token* of a covenant between me and the earth"; and to Abraham he says of circumcision, "it shall be a *token* of the covenant betwixt me and you." In Masonry, the grip of recognition is called a token, because it is an outward sign of the covenant of friendship and fellowship entered into between the members of the Fraternity, and is to be considered as a memorial of that covenant which was made, when it was first received by the candidate, between him and the Order into which he was then initiated.

Triangle. There is no symbol more important in its signification, more various in its application, or more generally diffused throughout the whole system of Freemasonry, than the triangle. An examination of it, therefore, cannot fail to be interesting to the Masonic student.

The *equilateral triangle* appears to have been adopted by nearly all the nations of antiquity as a symbol of the Deity, in some of his forms or emanations, and hence, probably, the prevailing influence of this symbol was carried into the Jewish system, where the yod within the triangle was made to represent the Tetragrammaton, or sacred name of God.

The equilateral triangle, "viewed in the light of the doctrines of those who gave it currency as a divine symbol, represents the Great First Cause, the creator and container of all things, as one and indivisible, manifesting himself in an infinity of forms and attributes in this visible universe."

Among the Egyptians, the darkness through which the candidate for initiation was made to pass was symbolized by the trowel, an important Masonic implement, which in their system of hieroglyphics has the form of a triangle. The equilateral triangle they considered as the most perfect of figures, and a representative of the great principle of animated existence, each of its sides referring to one of the three departments of creation, the animal, vegetable, and mineral.

The equilateral triangle is to be found scattered throughout the Masonic system. It forms in the Royal Arch the figure within which the jewels of the officers are suspended. It is in the ineffable degrees the sacred delta, everywhere presenting itself as the symbol of the Grand Architect of the Universe. In Ancient Craft Masonry, it is constantly exhibited as the element of important ceremonies. The seats of the principal officers are arranged in a triangular form, the three lesser lights have the same situation, and the square and compass form, by their union on the greater light, two triangles meeting at their bases. In short, the equilateral triangle may be considered as one of the most constant forms of Masonic symbolism.

The *right-angled triangle* is another form of this figure which is deserving of attention. Among the Egyptians, it was the symbol of universal nature; the base representing Osiris, or the male principle; the perpendicular, Isis, or the female principle; and the hypotenuse, Horus, their son, or the product of the male and female principle.

This symbol was received by Pythagoras from the Egyptians during his long sojourn in that country, and with it he also learned the peculiar property it possessed, namely, that the sum of the squares of the two shorter sides is equal to the square of the longest side—symbolically expressed by the formula, that the product of Osiris and Isis is Horus. This figure has been adopted in the Third Degree of Masonry, and will be there recognized as the forty-seventh problem of Euclid.

Triangle and Square. As the Delta was the initial letter of Deity with the ancients, so its synonym is among modern nations. It is a type of the Eternal, the All-Powerful, the Self-Existent.

The material world is typified by the "square" as passive matter, in opposition to force symbolized by the triangle.

The Square is also an emblem of humanity, as the Delta or Triangle typifies Deity.

The Delta, Triangle, and Compasses are essentially the same. The raising one point, and then another, signifies that the Divine or higher portion of our nature should increase in power, and control the baser tendencies. This is the real, the practical "journey toward the East."

The interlacing triangles or deltas symbolize the union of the two principles or forces, the active and passive, male and female, pervading the universe.

The two triangles, one white and the other black, interlacing, typify the mingling of the two apparent powers in nature, darkness and light, error and truth, ignorance and wisdom, evil and good, throughout human life.

The triangle and square together form the pyramid, as seen in the Entered Apprentice's apron. In this combination the pyramid is the metaphor for unity of matter and force, as well as the oneness of man and God. The numbers 3, 5, 7, 9, have their places in the parts and points of the square and triangle when in pyramidal form, and imply Perfection.

Triangle, Radiated. A triangle placed within and surrounded by a circle of rays. This circle is called, in Christian art, "a glory." When this glory is distinct from the triangle, and surrounds it in the form of a circle, it is then an emblem of God's eternal glory. This is the usual form in religious uses. But when, as is most usual in the Masonic symbol, the rays emanate from the center of the triangle, and, as it were, enshroud it in their brilliancy, it is symbolic of the Divine Light. The perverted ideas of the Pagans referred these rays of light to their sun-god and their Sabian worship.

But the true Masonic idea of this glory is, that it symbolizes that Eternal Light of Wisdom which surrounds the Supreme Architect as a sea of glory, and from Him as a common center emanates to the universe of His creation.

Triangle, Triple. The *pentalpha,* or triangle of Pythagoras, is usually called also the triple triangle, because three triangles are formed by the intersection of its sides. But there is another variety of the triple triangle which is more properly entitled to the appellation, and which is made in the annexed form.

It will be familiar to the Knights Templar as the form of the jewel worn by the Prelate of his Order. Like every modification of the triangle, it is a symbol of the Deity; but as the degree of Knights Templar appertains exclusively to Christian Masonry, the triple triangle there alludes to the mystery of the Trinity. In the Scottish Rite Degree of Knight of the East the symbol is also said to refer to the triple essence of Deity; but the symbolism is made still more mystical by supposing that it represents the sacred number 81, each side of the three triangles being equivalent to 9, which again is the square of 3, the most sacred number in Freemasonry. In the Twentieth Degree of the Ancient and Accepted Scottish Rite, or that of "Grand Master of all Symbolic Lodges," it is said that the number 81 refers to the triple covenant of God, symbolized by a triple triangle said to have been seen by Solomon when he consecrated the Temple. Indeed, throughout the ineffable and the philosophic degrees, the allusions to the triple triangle are much more frequent than they are in Ancient Craft Masonry.

Toleration. The grand characteristic of Masonry is its toleration in religion and politics. In respect to the latter, its toleration has no limit. The question of a man's political opinions is not permitted to be broached in the Lodge; in reference to the former, it requires only that, to use the language of the *Old Charge,* Masons shall be of "that religion in which all men agree, leaving their particular opinions to themselves." (*Constitutions,* 1723, p. 50.) The same *Old Charges* say, "No private piques or quarrels must be brought within the door of the Lodge, far less any quarrels about religion, or nations, or state policy, we being only, as Masons, of the Universal religion above-mentioned; we are also of all nations, tongues, kindreds, and languages, and are resolved against all politics, as what never yet conduced to the welfare of the Lodge, nor ever will."

Triple Alliance. An expression in the high degrees, which, having been translated from the French rituals, should have more properly been the triple covenant. It is represented by the triple triangle, and refers to the covenant of God with his people, that of King Solomon with Hiram of Tyre, and that which binds the fraternity of Masons.

Triple Tau. The tau cross, or cross of St. Anthony, is a cross in the form of a Greek T. The triple tau is a figure formed by three of these crosses meeting in a point, and therefore resembling a letter T resting on the traverse bar of an H. This emblem, placed in the center of a triangle and circle—both emblems of the Deity—constitutes the jewel of the Royal Arch as practised in England, where it is so highly esteemed as to be called the "emblem of all emblems," and "the grand emblem of Royal Arch Masonry." It was adopted in the same form as the Royal Arch badge, by the General Grand Chapter of the United States in 1859; although it had previously been very generally recognized by American Masons. It is also found in the capitular Masonry of Scotland. (See *Royal Arch Badge.*)

The original signification of this emblem has been variously explained. Some suppose it to include the initials of the Temple of Jerusalem, T. H., *Templum Hierosolymæ;* others, that it is a symbol of the mystical union of the Father and Son, H signifying Jehovah, and T, or the cross, the Son. A writer in *Moore's Magazine* ingeniously supposes it to be a representation of three T squares, and that it alludes to the three jewels of the three ancient Grand Masters. It has also been said that it is the monogram of Hiram of Tyre; and others assert that it is only a modification of the Hebrew letter *shin,* ש, which was one of the Jewish abbreviations of the sacred name. Oliver thinks, from its connection with the circle and triangle in the Royal Arch jewel, that it was intended to typify the sacred name as the author of eternal life. The English Royal Arch lectures say that "by its intersection it forms a given number of angles that may be taken in five several combinations; and, reduced, their amount in right angles will be found equal to the five Platonic bodies which represent the four elements and the sphere of the Universe." Amid so many speculations, I need not hesitate to offer one of my own. The Prophet Ezekiel speaks of the *tau* or tau cross as the mark distinguishing those who were to be saved, on account of their sorrow for their sins, from those who, as idolaters, were to be slain. It was a mark or sign of favorable distinction; and with this allusion we may, therefore, suppose the triple tau to be used in the Royal Arch Degree as a mark designating and separating those who know and worship the true name of God from those who are ignorant of that august mystery.

Twelve. Twelve being composed of the mystical numbers 7 + 5 or of 3 × 4, the triad multiplied by the quaternion, was a number of considerable value in ancient systems. Thus there were twelve signs of the zodiac, twelve months in the year, twelve tribes of Israel, twelve stones in the pectoral, and twelve oxen supporting the molten sea in the Temple. There were twelve apostles in the new law, and the New Jerusalem has twelve gates, twelve foundations, is twelve thousand furlongs square, and the number of the sealed is twelve times twelve thousand. Even the Pagans respected this number, for there were in their mythology twelve superior and twelve inferior gods. There were also twelve Fellow-Crafts.

United Grand Lodge of England. The present Grand Lodge of England assumed that title in the year 1813, because it was then formed by the union of the Grand Lodge of the *Ancients,* called the "Grand Lodge of Free and Accepted Masons of England according to the Old Institutions," and the Grand Lodge of *Moderns,* called the "Grand Lodge of Free and Accepted Masons under the Constitution of England." The body thus formed, by which an end was put to the dissensions of the Craft which had existed in England for more than half a century, adopted the title, by which it has ever since been known, of the "United Grand Lodge of Ancient Freemasons of England."

United States of America. The history of the introduction of Freemasonry into the United States of America is discussed in this work under the titles of the different States into which the Union is divided, and to which therefore the reader is referred.

It may, however, be necessary to say, in a general view of the subject, that the first notice we have of Freemasonry in the United States is in 1729, in which year, during the Grand Mastership of the Duke of Norfolk, Mr. Daniel Coxe was appointed Provincial Grand Master for New Jersey. I have not, however, been able to obtain any evidence that he exercised his prerogative by the establishment of Lodges in that province, although it is probable that he did. In the year 1733, the "St. John's Grand Lodge" was opened in Boston, in consequence of a Charter granted, on the application of several brethren residing in that city, by Lord Viscount Montague, Grand Master of England. From that time Masonry was rapidly disseminated throughout the country by the establishment of

Provincial Grand Lodges, all of which after the Revolutionary War, which separated the colonies from the mother country, assumed the rank and prerogatives of independent Grand Lodges. The history of these bodies being treated under their respective titles, the remainder of this article may more properly be devoted to the character of the Masonic organization in the United States.

The Rite practised in this country is most correctly called the American Rite. This title, however, has been adopted within only a comparatively recent period. It is still very usual with Masonic writers to call the Rite practised in this country the York Rite. The expression, however, is wholly incorrect. The Masonry of the United States, though founded, like that practised in every other country, upon the three Symbolic degrees which alone constitute the true York Rite, has, by its modifications and its adoption of high degrees, so changed the Rite as to give it an entirely different form from that which properly constitutes the pure York Rite. (See *American Rite.*)

In each State of the Union, and in most of the Territories, there is a Grand Lodge which exercises jurisdiction over the Symbolic degrees. The jurisdiction of the Grand Lodge, however, is exercised to a certain extent over what are called the higher bodies, namely, the Chapters, Councils, and Commanderies. For by the American construction of Masonic law, a Mason expelled by the Grand Lodge forfeits his membership in all of these bodies to which he may be attached. Hence a Knights Templar, or a Royal Arch Mason, becomes *ipso facto* suspended or expelled by his suspension or expulsion by a Symbolic Lodge, the appeal from which action lies only to the Grand Lodge. Thus the Masonic standing and existence of even the Grand Commander of a Grand Commandery is actually in the hands of the Grand Lodge, by whose decree of expulsion his relation with the body over which he presides may be dissevered.

Royal Arch Masonry is controlled in each State by a Grand Chapter. Besides these Grand Chapters, there is a General Grand Chapter of the United States, which, however, exercises only a moral influence over the State Grand Chapters, since it possesses "no power of discipline, admonition, censure, or instruction over the Grand Chapters." In Territories where there are no Grand Chapters, the General Grand Chapter constitutes subordinate Chapters, and over these it exercises plenary jurisdiction.

The next highest branch of the Order is Cryptic Masonry, which, although rapidly growing, is not yet as extensive as Royal Arch Masonry. It consists of two degrees, Royal and Select Master, to which is sometimes added the Superexcellent, which, however, is considered only as an honorary degree. These degrees are conferred in Councils which owe their obedience to Grand Councils. Only one Grand Council can exist in a State or Territory, as is the case with a Grand Lodge, a Grand Chapter, or a Grand Commandery. Grand Councils exist in many of the States, and in any State where no such body exists, the Councils are established by Charters emanating from any one of them. There is no General Grand Council. Efforts have been repeatedly made to establish one, but the proposition has not met with a favorable response from the majority of Grand Councils.

Templarism is governed by a Supreme body, whose style is the Grand Encampment of the United States, and this body, which meets triennially, possesses sovereign power over the whole Templar system in the United States. Its presiding officer is called Grand Master, and this is the highest office known to American Templarism. In most of the States there are Grand Commanderies, which exercise immediate jurisdiction over the Commanderies in the State, subject, however, to the superintending control of the Grand Encampment. Where there are no Grand Commanderies, Charters are issued directly to subordinate Commanderies by the Grand Encampment.

The Ancient and Accepted Scottish Rite is very popular in the United States. There are two Supreme Councils—one for the Southern Jurisdiction, which is the Mother Council of the world. Its nominal Grand East is at Charleston, South Carolina; but its Secretariat has been removed to Washington City since the year 1870. The other Council is for the Northern Jurisdiction. Its Grand East is at Boston, Massachusetts; but its Secretariat is at New York City. The Northern Council has jurisdiction over the States of Maine, Vermont, New Hampshire, Massachusetts, Connecticut, Rhode Island, New York, Pennsylvania, New Jersey, Delaware, Ohio, Indiana, Illinois, and Wisconsin. The Southern Supreme Council exercises jurisdiction over all the other States and Territories of the United States.

Unity of God. In the popular mythology of the ancients there were many gods. It was to correct this false opinion, and to teach a purer theogony, that the initiations were invented. And so, as Warburton says, "the famous secret of the mysteries was the unity of the Godhead." This, too, is the doctrine of Masonic initiation, which is equally distant from the blindness of atheism and the folly of polytheism.

Uniformity of Work. An identity of forms in opening and closing, and in conferring the degrees, constitutes what is technically called uniformity of work. The expression has no reference, in its restricted sense, to the working of the same degrees in different Rites and different countries, but only to a similarity in the ceremonies practised by Lodges in the same Rite, and more especially in the same jurisdiction. This is greatly to be desired, because nothing is more unpleasant to a Mason, accustomed to certain forms and ceremonies in his own Lodge, than on a visit to another to find those forms and ceremonies so varied as to be sometimes scarcely recognizable as parts of the same Institution. So anxious are the dogmatic authorities in Masonry to preserve this uniformity, that in the charge to an Entered Apprentice he is instructed never to "suffer an infringement of our rites, or a deviation from established usages and customs." In the act of union in 1813, of the two Grand Lodges of England, in whose systems of working there were many differences, it was provided that a committee should be appointed to visit the several Lodges, and promulgate and enjoin one system, "that perfect reconciliation, unity of obligation, law, working, language, and dress, might be happily restored to the English Craft." (Article XV.) A few years ago, a writer in *C. W. Moore's Magazine,* proposed the appointment of delegates to visit the Grand Lodges of England, Scotland, and Ireland, that a system of work and lectures might be adopted, which should thereafter be rigidly enforced in both hemispheres. The proposition was not popular, and no delegation was ever appointed. It is well that it was so, for no such attempt could have met with a successful result.

It is a fact, that uniformity of work in Masonry, however much it may be desired, can never be attained. This must be the case in all institutions where the ceremonies, the legends, and the instructions are oral. The treachery of memory, the weakness of judgment, and the fertility of imagination, will lead men to forget, to diminish, or to augment, the parts of any system which are not prescribed within certain limits by a written rule. The Rabbis discovered this when the Oral Law was becoming perverted, and losing its authority as well as its identity by the interpretations that were given to it in the schools of the Scribes and Prophets. And hence, to restore it to its integrity, it was found necessary to divest it of its oral character and give to it a written form. To this are we to attribute the origin of the two Talmuds which now contain the essence of Jewish theology. So, while in Masonry we find the esoteric ritual continually subjected to errors arising mainly from the ignorance or the fancy of Masonic teachers, the monitorial instructions—few in Preston, but greatly enlarged by Webb and Cross—have suffered no change.

It would seem from this that the evil of non-conformity could be removed only by making all the ceremonies monitorial; and so much has this been deemed expedient, that a few years since the subject of a written ritual was seriously discussed in England. But the remedy would be worse than the disease. It is to the oral character of its ritual that Masonry is indebted for its permanence and success as an organization. A written, which would soon become a printed, ritual would divest Symbolic Masonry of its attractions as a secret association, and would cease to offer a reward to the laborious student who sought to master its mystical science. Its philosophy and its symbolism would be the same, but the books containing them would be consigned to the shelves of a Masonic library, their pages to be discussed by the profane as the common property of the antiquary, while the Lodges, having no mystery within their portals, would find but few visitors, and certainly no workers.

It is, therefore, a matter of congratulation that uniformity of work, however desirable and however unattainable, is not so important and essential as many have deemed it. Oliver, for instance, seems to confound in some of his writings the ceremonies of a degree with the landmarks of the Order. But they are very different. The landmarks, because they affect the identity of the Institution, have long since been embodied in its written laws, and unless by a wilful perversion, as in France, where the Grand Mastership has been abolished, can never be changed. But variations in the phraseology of the lectures, or in the forms and ceremonies of initiation, so long as they do not trench upon the foundations of symbolism on which the science and philosophy of Masonry are built, can produce no other effect than a temporary inconvenience. The errors of an ignorant Master will be corrected by his better instructed successor. The variation in the ritual can never be such as to destroy the true identity of the Institution. Its profound dogmas of the unity of God, and the eternal life, and of the universal brotherhood of man, taught in its symbolic method, will forever shine out preeminent above all temporary changes of phraseology. Uniformity of work may not be attained, but uniformity of design and uniformity of character will forever preserve Freemasonry from disintegration.

Universality of Masonry. The boast of the Emperor Charles V., that the sun never set on his vast empire, may be applied with equal truth to the Order of Freemasonry. From east to west, and from north to south, over the whole habitable globe, are our Lodges disseminated. Wherever the wandering steps of civilized man have left their footprints, there have our temples been established. The lessons of Masonic love have penetrated into the wilderness of the West, and the red man of our soil has shared with his more enlightened brother the mysteries of our science; while the arid sands of the African desert have more than once been the scene of a Masonic greeting. Masonry is not a fountain, giving health and beauty to some single hamlet, and slaking the thirst of those only who dwell upon its humble banks; but it is a mighty stream, penetrating through every hill and mountain, and gliding through every field and valley of the earth, bearing in its beneficent bosom the abundant waters of love and charity for the poor, the widow, and the orphan of every land.

Untempered Mortar. In the lecture used in the United States in the early part of the present century, and in some parts of the country almost as recently as the middle of the century, the apprentices at the Temple were said to wear their aprons in the peculiar manner characteristic of that class that they might preserve their garments from being defiled by "untempered mortar." This is mortar which has not been properly mixed for use, and it thus became a symbol of passions and appetites not duly restrained. Hence the Speculative Apprentice was made to wear his apron in that peculiar manner to teach him that he should not allow his soul to be defiled by the "untempered mortar of unruly passions."

Vault, Secret. As a symbol, the Secret Vault does not present itself in the primary degrees of Masonry. It is found only in the high degrees, such as the Royal Arch of all the Rites, where it plays an important part. Dr. Oliver, in his *Historical Landmarks* (vol. ii., p. 434), gives, while referring to the building of the second Temple, the following general detail of the Masonic legend of this vault:

"The foundations of the Temple were opened, and cleared from the accumulation of rubbish, that a level might be procured for the commencement of the building. While engaged in excavations for this purpose, three fortunate sojourners are said to have discovered our ancient stone of foundation, which had been deposited in the secret crypt by Wisdom, Strength, and Beauty, to prevent the communication of ineffable secrets to profane or unworthy persons. The discovery having been communicated to the prince, prophet, and priest of the Jews, the stone was adopted as the chief corner-stone of the re-edified building, and thus became, in a new and more expressive sense, the type of a more excellent dispensation. An avenue was also accidentally discovered, supported by seven pairs of pillars, perfect and entire, which, from their situation, had escaped the fury of the flames that had consumed the Temple, and the desolation of war that had destroyed the city. The secret vault, which had been built by Solomon as a secure depository for certain secrets that would inevitably have been lost without some such expedient for their preservation, communicated by a subterranean avenue with the king's palace; but at the destruction of Jerusalem the entrance having been closed by the rubbish of falling buildings, it had been discovered by the appearance of a keystone amongst the foundations of the sanctum sanctorum. A careful inspection was then made, and the invaluable secrets were placed in safe custody."

To support this legend, there is no historical evidence and no authority except that of the Talmudic writers. It is clearly a mythical symbol, and as such we must accept it. We cannot altogether reject it, because it is so intimately and so extensively connected with the symbolism of the Lost and the Recovered Word, that if we reject the theory of the Secret Vault, we must abandon all of that symbolism, and with it the whole of the science of Masonic symbolism. Fortunately, there is ample evidence in the present appearance of Jerusalem and its subterranean topography, to remove from any tacit and, as it were, conventional assent to the theory, features of absurdity or impossibility.

Considered simply as an historical question, there can be no doubt of the existence of immense vaults beneath the superstructure of the original Temple of Solomon. Prime, Robison, and other writers who in recent times have described the topography of Jerusalem, speak of the existence of these structures, which they visited and, in some instances, carefully examined.

After the destruction of Jerusalem by Titus, the Roman Emperor Hadrian erected on the site of the "House of the Lord" a temple of Venus, which in its turn was destroyed, and the place subsequently became a depository of all manner of filth. But the Calif Omar, after his conquest of Jerusalem, sought out the ancient site, and, having caused it to be cleansed of its impurities, he directed a mosque to be erected on the rock which rises in the center of the mountain. Fifty years afterward the Sultan Abd-el-Meluk displaced the edifice of Omar, and erected that splendid building which remains to this day, and is still incorrectly called by Christians the mosque of Omar, but known to Mussulmans as Elkubbet-es-Sukrah, or the Dome of the Rock. This is supposed to occupy the exact site of the original Solomonic Temple, and is viewed with equal reverence by Jews and Mohammedans, the former of whom, says Mr. Prime (*Tent Life in the Holy Land,* p. 183), "have a faith that the ark is within its bosom now."

Bartlett (*Walks about Jerusalem,* p. 170), in describing a vault beneath this mosque of Omar, says: "Beneath the dome, at the southeast angle of the Temple wall, conspicuous from all points, is a small subterraneous place of prayer, forming the entrance to the extensive vaults which support the level platform of the mosque above."

Dr. Barclay (*City of the Great King*) describes, in many places of his interesting topography of Jerusalem, the vaults and subterranean chambers which are to be found beneath the site of the old Temple.

Conformable with this historical account is the Talmudical legend, in which the Jewish Rabbis state that, in preparing the foundations of the Temple, the workmen discovered a subterranean vault sustained by seven arches, rising from as many pairs of pillars. This vault escaped notice at the destruction of Jerusalem, in consequence of its being filled with rubbish. The legend adds that Josiah, foreseeing the destruction of the Temple, commanded the Levites to deposit the Ark of the Covenant in this vault, where it was found by some of the workmen of Zerubbabel at the building of the second Temple.

In the earliest ages, the cave or vault was deemed sacred. The first worship was in cave temples, which were either natural or formed by art to resemble the excavations of nature. Of such great extent was this practise of subterranean worship by the nations of antiquity, that many of the forms of heathen temples, as well as the naves, aisles, and chancels of churches subsequently built for Christian worship, are said to owe their origin to the religious use of caves.

From this, too, arose the fact, that the initiation into the ancient mysteries was almost always performed in subterranean edifices; and when the place of initiation, as in some of the Egyptian temples, was really above ground, it was so constructed as to give to the neophyte the appearance, in its approaches and its internal structure, of a vault. As the great doctrine taught in the mysteries was the resurrection from the dead—as *to die* and *to be initiated* were synonymous terms—it was deemed proper that there should be some formal resemblance between a descent into the grave and a descent into the place of initiation. "Happy is the man," says the Greek poet Pindar, "who descends beneath the hollow earth having beheld these mysteries, for he knows the end as well as the divine origin of life"; and in a like spirit Sophocles exclaims, "Thrice happy are they who descend to the shades below after having beheld the sacred rites, for they alone have life in Hades, while all others suffer there every kind of evil."

The vault was, therefore, in the ancient mysteries, symbolic of the grave; for initiation was symbolic of death, where alone Divine Truth is to be found. The Masons have adopted the same idea. They teach that death is but the beginning of life; that if the first or evanescent temple of our transitory life be on the surface, we must descend into the *secret vault* of death before we can find that sacred deposit of truth which is to adorn our second temple of eternal life. It is in this sense of an entrance through the grave into eternal life that we are to view the symbolism of the secret vault. Like every other myth and allegory of Masonry, the historical relation may be true or it may be false; it may be founded on fact or be the invention of imagination; the lesson is still there, and the symbolism teaches it exclusive of the history.

Vacancies in Office. Every Masonic officer is elected and installed to hold his office for the time for which he has been elected, and until his successor shall be installed. This is in the nature of a contract between the officer and the Lodge, Chapter, or other body which has elected him, and to its terms he signifies his assent in the most solemn manner at the time of his installation. It follows from this that to resign the office would be on his part to violate his contract. Vacancies in office, therefore, can only occur by death. Even a removal from the jurisdiction, with the intention of permanent absence, will not vacate a Masonic office, because the person removing might change his intention, and return. For the reasons why neither resignation nor removal can vacate an office, see *Succession to the Chair.*

Vagao or **Bagaos.** Found in the Fourth Degree of the French Rite of Adoption.

Vale or **Valley.** The vale or valley was introduced at an early period into the symbolism of Masonry. A catechism of the beginning of the last century says that "the Lodge stands upon holy ground, or the highest hill or lowest vale, or in the vale of Jehoshaphat, or any other secret place." And Browne, who in the beginning of the present century gave a correct version of the Prestonian lectures, says that "our ancient brethren met on the highest hills, the lowest dales, even in the valley of Jehoshaphat, or some such secret place."

Hutchinson (*Sp. of Mas.*, p. 94) has dilated on this subject, but with a mistaken view of the true import of the symbol. He says: "We place the spiritual Lodge in the vale of Jehoshaphat."

War, Masonry in. The question how Masons should conduct themselves in time of war, when their own country is one of the belligerents, is an important one. Of the political course of a Mason in his individual and private capacity there is no doubt. The Charges declare that he must be "a peaceable subject to the civil powers, and never be concerned in plots and conspiracies against the peace and welfare of the nation." (*Constitutions*, 1723, p. 50.) But so anxious is the Order to be unembarrassed by all political influences, that treason, however discountenanced by the Craft, is not held as a crime which is amenable to Masonic punishment. For the same charge affirms that "if a brother should be a rebel against the State, he is not to be countenanced in his rebellion, however he may be pitied as an unhappy man; and if convicted of no other crime, though the loyal brotherhood must and ought to disown his rebellion and give no umbrage or ground of political jealousy to the government for the time being, they cannot expel him from the Lodge, and his relation to it remains indefeasible."

The Mason, then, like every other citizen, should be a patriot. He should love his country with all his heart; should serve it faithfully and cheerfully; obey its laws in peace; and in war should be ever ready to support its honor and defend it from the attacks of its enemies. But even then the benign principles of the Institution extend their influence, and divest the contest of many of its horrors. The Mason fights, of course, like every other man, for victory; but when the victory is won, he will remember that the conquered foe is still his brother.

On the occasion, many years ago, of a Masonic banquet given immediately after the close of the Mexican War to General Quitman by the Grand Lodge of South Carolina, that distinguished soldier and Mason remarked that, although he had devoted much of his attention to the nature and character of the Masonic institution, and had repeatedly held the highest offices in the gift of his brethren, he had never really known what Masonry was until he had seen its workings on the field of battle.

But as a collective and organized body—in its Lodges and its Grand Lodges—it must have nothing to do with war. It must be silent and neutral. The din of the battle, the cry for vengeance, the shout of victory, must never penetrate its portals. Its dogmas and doctrines all teach love and fraternity; its symbols are symbols of peace; and it has no place in any of its rituals consecrated to the inculcation of human contention.

Bro. C. W. Moore, in his *Biography of Thomas Smith Webb*, the great American ritualist, mentions a circumstance which occurred during the period in which Webb presided over the Grand Lodge of Rhode Island, and to which Moore, I think, inconsiderately has given his hearty commendation.

The United States was at that time engaged in a war with England. The people of Providence having commenced the erection of fortifications, the Grand Lodge volunteered its services; and the members, marching in procession as a Grand Lodge to the southern part of the town, erected a breastwork, to which was given the name of Fort Hiram. (See *Fort Masonic.*) I doubt the propriety of the act. While (to repeat what has been just said) every individual member of the Grand Lodge, as a Mason, was bound by his obligation to be "true to his government," and to defend it from the attacks of its enemies, it was, I think, unseemly, and contrary to the peaceful spirit of the Institution, for any organized body of Masons, organized as such, to engage in a warlike enterprise. But the patriotism, if not the prudence of the Grand Lodge, cannot be denied.

Since writing this paragraph, I have met in Bro. Murray Lyon's *History of the Lodge of Edinburgh* (p. 83) with a record of the Grand Lodge of Scotland, a century ago, which sustains the view that I have taken. In 1777, recruits were being enlisted in Scotland for the British army, which was to fight the Americans in the war of the Revolution, which had just begun. Many of the Scotch Lodges offered, through the newspapers, bounties to all who should enlist. But on February 2, 1778, the Grand Lodge passed a resolution, which was published on the 12th, through the Grand Secretary, in the following circular:

"At a quarterly meeting of the Grand Lodge of Scotland, held here the second instant, I received a charge to acquaint all the Lodges of Scotland holding of the Grand Lodge that the Grand Lodge has seen with concern advertisements in the public newspapers, from different Lodges in Scotland, not only offering a bounty to recruits who may enlist in the new levies, but with the addition that all such recruits shall be admitted to the freedom of Masonry. The first of these they consider as an improper alienation of the funds of the Lodge from the support of their poor and distressed brethren; and the second they regard as a prostitution of our Order, which demands the reprehension of the Grand Lodge. Whatever share the brethren may take as individuals in aiding these levies, out of zeal to serve their private friends or to promote the public service, the Grand Lodge considered it to be repugnant to the spirit of our Craft that any Lodge should take a part in such a business as a collective body. For Masonry is an Order of Peace, and it looks on all mankind to be brethren as Masons, whether they be at peace or at war with each other as subjects of contending countries. The Grand Lodge therefore strongly enjoins that the practice may be forthwith discontinued. By order of the Grand Lodge of Scotland. W. Mason, Gr. Sec."

Of all human institutions, Freemasonry is the greatest and purest Peace Society. And this is because its doctrine of universal peace is founded on the doctrine of a universal brotherhood.

West. Although the west, as one of the four cardinal points, holds an honorable position as the station of the Senior Warden, and of the pillar of Strength that supports the Lodge, yet, being the place of the sun's setting and opposed to the east, the recognized place of light, it, in Masonic symbolism, represents the place of darkness and ignorance. The old tradition, that in primeval times all human wisdom was confined to the eastern part of the world, and that those who had wandered toward the west were obliged to return to the east in search of the knowledge of their ancestors, is not confined to Masonry. Creuzer (*Symbolik*) speaks of an ancient and highly instructed body of priests in the East, from whom all knowledge, under the veil of symbols, was communicated to the Greeks and other unenlightened nations of the West. And in the "Legend of the Craft," contained in the old Masonic Constitutions, there is always a reference to the emigration of the Masons from Egypt eastward to the "land of behest," or Jerusalem. Hence, in the modern symbolism of Speculative Masonry, it is said that the Mason during his advancement is *traveling from the West to the East in search of light.*

White. White is one of the most ancient as well as most extensively diffused of the symbolic colors. It is to be found in all the ancient mysteries, where it constituted, as it does in Masonry, the investiture of the candidate. It always, however, and everywhere has borne the same signification as the symbol of purity and innocence.

In the religious observances of the Hebrews, white was the color of one of the curtains of the tabernacle, where, according to Josephus, it was a symbol of the element of earth; and it was employed in the construction of the ephod of the high priest, of his girdle, and of the breastplate. The word לבן, *laban,* which in the Hebrew language signifies "to make white," also denotes "to purify"; and there are to be found throughout the Scriptures many allusions to the color as an emblem of purity. "Though thy sins be as scarlet," says Isaiah, "they shall be as white as snow." Jeremiah, describing the once innocent condition of Zion, says, "her Nazarites were purer than snow, they were whiter than milk." "Many," says Daniel, "shall be purified and made white." In Revelation, a *white stone* was the reward promised by the Spirit to those who overcame; and again, "he that overcometh, the same shall be clothed in white garments"; and in another part of the same book the Apostle is instructed to say that fine linen, clean and white, is the righteousness of the saints. The ancient prophets always imagined the Deity clothed in white, because, says Portal (*Des Couleurs Symboliques,* p. 35), "white is the color of absolute truth, of Him who is; it alone reflects all the luminous rays; it is the unity whence all the primitive colors emanate." Thus Daniel, in one of his prophetic visions, saw the Ancient of days, "whose garment was white as snow, and the hair of his head like pure wool." Here, the whiteness of the garment "noted the splendor and purity of God in all the administrations of his justice."

Among the Gentile nations, the same reverence was paid to this color. The Egyptians decorated the head of their deity, Osiris, with a white tiara. In the school of Pythagoras, the sacred hymns were chanted in white robes. The Druids clothed their initiates who had arrived at the ultimate degree, or that of perfection, in white vestments. In all the mysteries of other nations of antiquity, the same custom was observed. White was, in general, the garment of the Gentile as well as of the Hebrew priests in the performance of their sacred rites. As the Divine power was supposed to be represented on earth by the priesthood, in all nations the sovereign pontiff was clad in white. Aaron was directed to enter the sanctuary only in white garments; in Persia, the Magi wore white robes, because, as they said, they alone were pleasing to the Deity; and the white tunic of Ormuzd is still the characteristic garment of the modern Parsees.

White, among the ancients, was consecrated to the dead, because it was the symbol of the regeneration of the soul. On the monuments of Thebes the manes or ghosts are represented as clothed in white; the Egyptians wrapped their dead in white linen; Homer (*Iliad,* xviii., 353) refers to the same custom when he makes the attendants cover the dead body of Patroclus, φάρέι λεύκῳ, with a white pall; and Pausanias tells us that the Messenians practised the same customs, clothing their dead in white, and placing crowns upon their heads, indicating by this double symbolism the triumph of the soul over the empire of death.

The Hebrews had the same usage. St. Matthew (xxvii. 59) tells us that Joseph of Arimathea wrapped the dead body of our Lord "in a clean linen cloth." Adopting this as a suggestion, Christian artists have, in their paintings of the Savior after his resurrection depicted him in a white robe. And it is with this idea that in the Apocalypse white vestments are said to be the symbols of the regeneration of souls, and the reward of the elect. It is this consecration of white to the dead that caused it to be adopted as the color of mourning among the nations of antiquity. As the victor in the games was clothed in white, so the same color became the symbol of the victory achieved by the departed in the last combat of the soul with death. "The friends of the deceased wore," says Plutarch, "his livery, in commemoration of his triumph." The modern mourning in black is less philosophic and less symbolic than this ancient one in white.

In Speculative Masonry, white is the symbol of purity. This symbolism commences at the earliest point of initiation, when the white apron is presented to the candidate as a symbol of purity of life and rectitude of conduct. Wherever in any of the subsequent initiations this color appears, it is always to be interpreted as symbolizing the same idea. In the Thirty-third Degree of the Ancient and Accepted Scottish Rite, the Sovereign Inspector is invested with a white scarf as inculcating that virtuous deportment above the tongue of all reproach which should distinguish the possessors of that degree, the highest in the Rite.

This symbolism of purity was most probably derived by the Masons from that of the primitive church, where a white garment was placed on the catechumen who was about to be baptized, as a token that he had put off the lusts of the flesh, and, being cleansed from his former sins, had obliged himself to maintain an unspotted life. The ancient symbolism of regeneration which appertained to the ancient idea of the color white has not been adopted in Masonry; and yet it would be highly appropriate in an Institution one of whose chief dogmas is the resurrection.

White Stone. A symbol in the Mark Degree referring to the passage in the Apocalypse (ii. 17): "To him that overcometh will I give to eat of the hidden manna, and will give him a white stone, and in the stone a new name written, which no man knoweth, saving he that receiveth it." In this passage it is supposed that the Evangelist alluded to the stones or tesseræ which, among the ancients and the early Christians, were used as tokens of alliance and friendship. Hence in the Mark Degree, the white stone and the new name inscribed upon it is a symbol of the covenant made between the possessors of the degree, which will in all future time, and under every circumstance of danger or distress, secure the kind and fraternal assistance of all upon whom the same token has been bestowed. In the symbolism of the degree the candidate represents that white stone upon whom the new name as a Mark Master is to be inscribed.

Word. When emphatically used, the expression, "the Word," is in Masonry always referred to the Third Degree, although there must be a word in each degree. In this latter and general sense, the Word is called by French Masons "la parole," and by the Germans "ein Worterzeichen." The use of a word is of great antiquity. We find it in the ancient mysteries. In those of Egypt it is said to have been the Tetragrammaton. The German Stone-Masons of the Middle Ages had one, which, however, was probably only a password by which the traveling Companion might make himself known in his professional wanderings. Lyon (*Hist. of the L. of Edinb.*, p. 22) shows that it existed, in the sixteenth and subsequent centuries, in the Scotch Lodges, and he says that "the Word is the only secret that is ever alluded to in the minutes of Mary's Chapel, or in those of Kilwinning, Atcheson's Haven, or Dunblane, or any other that we have examined of a date prior to the erection of the Grand Lodge." Indeed, he thinks that the communication of this Word constituted the only ceremony of initiation practised in the Operative Lodges. At that time there was evidently but one Word for all the ranks of Apprentices, Craftsmen, and Masters. He thinks that this communication of the Mason Word to the Apprentices under oath constituted the germ whence has sprung the Symbolical Masonry. But it must be remembered that the learned and laborious investigations of Bro. Lyon refer only to the Lodges of Scotland. There is no sufficient evidence that a more extensive system of initiation did not prevail at the same time, or even earlier, in England and Germany. Indeed, Findel has shown that it did in the latter country; and it is difficult to believe that the system, which we know was in existence in 1717, was a sudden development out of a single Word, for which we are indebted to the inventive genius of those who were engaged in the revival of that period. Be this as it may, the evidence is conclusive that everywhere, and from the earliest times, there was a Word. This at least is no modern usage.

But it must be admitted that this Word, whatever it was, was at first a mere mark of recognition. Yet it may have had, and probably did have, a mythical signification, and had not been altogether arbitrarily adopted. The word given in the Sloane MS., No. 3329 which Bro. Hughan places at a date not posterior to 1700, is undoubtedly a corrupted form of that now in use, and with the signification of which we are well acquainted. Hence we may conclude that the legend and the symbolism connected with it, also existed at the same time, but only in a nascent and incomplete form.

The modern development of Speculative Masonry into a philosophy has given a perfected form to the symbolism of the Word no longer confined to use as a means of recognition, but elevated, in its connection with the legend of the Third Degree, to the rank of a symbol.

So viewed, and by the scientific Mason it is now only so viewed, the Word becomes the symbol of Divine Truth, the loss of which and the search for it constitute the whole system of Speculative Masonry. So important is this Word, that it lies at the very foundation of the Masonic edifice. The Word might be changed, as might a grip or a sign, if it were possible to obtain the universal consent of the Craft, and Masonry would still remain unimpaired. But were the Word abolished, or released from its intimate connection with the Hiramic legend, and with that of the Royal Arch, the whole symbolism of Speculative Masonry would be obliterated. The Institution might withstand such an innovation, but its history, its character, its design, would belong to a newer and a totally different society. The Word is what Dermott called the Royal Arch, "the marrow of Masonry."

Word, Lost. See *Lost Word.*

Working Tools—Royal Arch Mason. The Working Tools of The Royal Arch Mason are the Pick Ax and the Shovel.

The Pick Ax is an instrument to loosen the soil and prepare it for digging. It symbolically teaches the Mason to loosen from his heart the hold of evil habits. The Shovel is an instrument to remove rubbish and symbolically teaches the Mason to remove the rubbish of passions and prejudices, that he may be fitted, when he thus escapes from the captivity of sin, for the search and the reception of Eternal Truth and Wisdom.

Workmen at the Temple. We have no historical book, except the meager details in the Books of Kings and Chronicles, of the number or classification of the workmen at the Temple of Solomon. The subject has, however, afforded a fertile theme for the exercise of the inventive genius of the ritualists. Although devoid of interest as an historical study, an acquaintance with these traditions, especially the English and American ones, and a comparison of them with the Scriptural account and with that given by Josephus, are necessary as a part of the education of a Masonic student. I furnish the legends, therefore, simply as a matter of curiosity, without the slightest intention to vouch for their authenticity, at the same time trusting that the good sense and common fairness of the reader will prevent him from including such unauthenticated matter in lectures usually given in the Third Degree and often with much pretense to learning.

In the 2d Book of Chronicles, chap. ii., verses 17 and 18, we read as follows:

"And Solomon numbered all the strangers that were in the land of Israel, after the numbering wherewith David his father had numbered them; and they were found an hundred and fifty thousand and three thousand and six hundred.

"And he set threescore and ten thousand of them to be bearers of burdens, and fourscore thousand to be hewers in the mountain, and three thousand and six hundred overseers to set the people a-work."

The same numerical details are given in the second verse of the same chapter. Again, in the 1st Book of Kings, chap. v., verses 13 and 14, it is said:

"And King Solomon raised a levy out of all Israel; and the levy was thirty thousand men.

"And he sent them to Lebanon, ten thousand a month by courses: a month they were in Lebanon, and two months at home: and Adoniram was over the levy."

The succeeding verses make the same enumeration of workmen as that contained in the Book of Chronicles quoted above, with the exception that, by omitting the three hundred Harodim, or rulers over all, the number of overseers is stated in the Book of Kings to be only three thousand three hundred.

With these authorities, and the assistance of Masonic traditions, Anderson, in the *Book of Constitutions* (2d ed., p. 11), constructs the following table of the Craftsmen at the Temple:

Harodim, Princes, Rulers, or Provosts		300
Menatzchim, Overseers, or Master Masons		3,300
Ghiblim, Stone-Squarers	All Fellow-Crafts	80,000
Ischotzeb, Hewers		
Benai, Builders		
The levy out of Israel, who were timber-cutters		30,000
All the Freemasons employed in the work of the Temple, exclusive of the two Grand Wardens		113,600

Besides the *Ish Sabal*, or men of burden, the remains of the old Canaanites, amounting to 70,000, who are not numbered among the Masons.

In relation to the classification of these workmen, Anderson says: "Solomon partitioned the Fellow Crafts into certain Lodges, with a Master and Wardens in each, that they might receive commands in a regular manner, might take care of their tools and jewels, might be paid regularly every week, and be duly fed and clothed; and the Fellow Crafts took care of their succession by educating Entered Apprentices."

Josephus makes a different estimate. He includes the 3,300 Overseers in the 80,000 Fellow-Crafts, and makes the number of Masons, exclusive of the 70,000 bearers of burden, amount to only 110,000.

A work published in 1764, entitled *The Masonic Pocket-Book,* gives a still different classification. The number, according to this authority, was as follows:

Harodim	300
Menatzchim	3,300
Ghiblim	83,000
Adoniram's men	30,000
Total	116,600

which, together with the 70,000 Ish Sabal, or laborers, will make a grand total of 186,600 workmen.

According to the statement of Webb, which has been generally adopted by the Fraternity in the United States, there were:

Grand Masters	3
Overseers	3,300
Fellow-Crafts	80,000
Entered Apprentices	70,000

This account makes no allusion to the 300 Harodim, nor to the levy of 30,000; it is, therefore, manifestly incorrect. Indeed, no certain authority can be found for the complete classification of the workmen, since neither the Bible nor Josephus gives any account of the number of Tyrians employed. Oliver, however, in his *Historical Landmarks,* has collected from the Masonic traditions an account of the classifications of the workmen, which I shall insert, with a few additional facts taken from other authorities.

According to these traditions, the following was the classification of the Masons who wrought in the quarries of Tyre:

Superexcellent Masons	6
Excellent Masons	48
Grand Architects	8
Architects	16
Master Masons	2,376
Mark Masters	700
Markmen	1,400
Fellow-Crafts	53,900
Total	58,454

These were arranged as follows: The six Superexcellent Masons were divided into two Grand Lodges, with three brethren in each to superintend the work. The Excellent Masons were divided into six Lodges of nine each, including one of the Superexcellent Masons, who presided as Master. The eight Grand Architects constituted one Lodge, and the sixteen Architects another. The Grand Architects were the Masters, and the Architects the Wardens, of the Lodges of Master Masons, which were eight in number, and consisted, with their officers, of three hundred in each. The Mark Masters were divided into fourteen Lodges of fifty in each, and the Markmen into fourteen Lodges also, of one hundred in each. The Mark Masters were the Masters, and the Markmen the Wardens, of the Lodges of Fellow-Crafts, which were seven hundred in number, and with their officers consisted of eighty in each.

The classification of the workmen in the forest of Lebanon was as follows:

Superexcellent Masons	3
Excellent Masons	24
Grand Architects	4
Architects	8
Master Masons	1,188
Mark Masters	300
Markmen	600
Fellow-Crafts	23,100
Entered Apprentices	10,000
Total	35,227

These were arranged as follows: The three Superexcellent Masons formed one Lodge. The Excellent Masons were divided into three Lodges of nine each, including one of the Superexcellent Masons as Master. The four Grand Architects constituted one Lodge, and the eight Architects another, the former acting as Masters and the latter as Wardens of the Lodges of Master Masons, which were four in number, and consisted, with their officers, of three hundred in each. The Mark Masters were divided into six Lodges of fifty in each, and the Markmen into six Lodges also, of one hundred in each. These two classes presided, the former as Masters and the latter as Wardens, over the Lodges of Fellow-Crafts, which were three hundred in number, and were composed of eighty in each, including their officers.

After three years had been occupied in "hewing, squaring, and numbering" the stones, and in "felling and preparing" the timbers, these two bodies of Masons, from the quarries and the forest, united for the purpose of properly arranging and fitting the materials, so that no metallic tool might be required in putting them up, and they were then carried up to Jerusalem. Here the whole body was congregated under the superintending care of Hiram Abif, and to them were added four hundred and twenty Lodges of Tyrian and Sidonian Fellow-Crafts, having eighty in each, and the twenty thousand Entered Apprentices of the levy from Israel, who had heretofore been at rest, and who were added to the Lodges of their degree, making them now consist of three hundred in each, so that the whole number then engaged at Jerusalem amounted to two hundred and seventeen thousand two hundred and eighty-one, who were arranged as follows:

9 Lodges of Excellent Masons, 9 in each, were................	81
12 Lodges of Master Masons, 300 in each, were..............	3,600
1,000 Lodges of Fellow-Crafts, 80 in each, were..............	80,000
420 Lodges of Tyrian Fellow-Crafts, 80 in each, were.........	33,600
100 Lodges of Entered Apprentices, 300 in each, were........	30,000
70,000 Ish Sabal, or laborers............................	70,000
Total	217,281

Such is the system adopted by our English brethren. The American ritual has greatly simplified the arrangement. According to the system now generally adopted in this country, the workmen engaged in building King Solomon's Temple are supposed to have been classified as follows:

3 Grand Masters.

300 Harodim, or Chief Superintendents, who were Past Masters.

3,300 Overseers, or Master Masons, divided into Lodges of three in each.

80,000 Fellow-Crafts, divided into Lodges of five in each.

70,000 Entered Apprentices, divided into Lodges of seven in each.

According to this account, there must have been eleven hundred Lodges of Master Masons; sixteen thousand of Fellow-Crafts; and ten thousand of Entered Apprentices. No account is here taken of the levy of thirty thousand who are supposed not to have been Masons, nor of the builders sent by Hiram, King of Tyre, whom the English ritual places at thirty-three thousand six hundred, and most of whom we may suppose to have been members of the Dionysiac Fraternity of Artificers, the institution from which Freemasonry, according to legendary authority, took its origin.

On the whole, the American system seems too defective to meet all the demands of the inquirer into this subject—an objection to which the English is not so obnoxious. But, as I have already observed, the whole account is mythical, and is to be viewed rather as a curiosity than as having any historical value.

Year of the Discovery. An era adopted by Royal Arch Masons, and refers to the time when certain secrets were made known to the Craft at the building of the second Temple. (See *Anno Inventionis.*)

Year of the Order. The date used in documents connected with Masonic Templarism. It refers to the establishment of the Order of Knights Templar in the year 1118. (See *Anno Ordinis.*)

Year of the World. This is the era adopted by the Ancient and Accepted Scottish Rite and is borrowed from the Jewish computation. The Jews formerly used the era of contracts, dated from the first conquests of Seleucus Nicator in Syria. But since the fifteenth century they have counted from the creation, which they suppose to have taken place in September, 3760 before Christ. (See *Anno Mundi.*)

Year of Light. *Anno Lucis,* in the year of light, is the epoch used in Masonic documents of the Symbolic degrees. This era is calculated from the creation of the world, and is obtained by adding four thousand to the current year, on the supposition that Christ was born four thousand years after the creation of the world. But the chronology of Archbishop Usher, which has been adopted as the Bible chronology in the authorized version, places the birth of Christ in the year 4004 after the creation. According to this calculation, the Masonic date for the "year of light" is four years short of the true date, and the year of the Lord 1874, which in Masonic documents is 5874, should correctly be 5878. The Ancient and Accepted Masons in the beginning of this century used this correct or Usherian era, and the Supreme Council at Charleston dated their first circular, issued in 1802, as 5806. Dalcho (*Ahim. Rez.,* 2d ed., p. 37) says: "If Masons are determined to fix the origin of their Order at the time of the creation, they should agree among themselves at what time before Christ to place that epoch." At that agreement they have

Yellow. Of all the colors, yellow seems to be the least important and the least general in Masonic symbolism. In other institutions it would have the same insignificance, were it not that it has been adopted as the representative of the sun, and of the noble metal gold. Thus, in colored blazonry, the small dots, by which the gold in an engraved coat of arms is designated, are replaced by the yellow color. La Colombiere, a French heraldic writer, says (*Science Heroique,* p. 30), in remarking on the connection between gold and yellow, that as yellow, which is derived from the sun, is the most exalted of colors, so gold is the most noble of metals. Portal (*Des Couleurs Symboliques,* p. 64) says that the sun, gold, and yellow are not synonymous, but mark different degrees which it is difficult to define. The natural sun was the symbol of the spiritual sun, gold represented the natural sun, and yellow was the emblem of gold. But it is evident that yellow derives all its significance as a symbolic color from its connection with the hue of the rays of the sun and the metal gold.

Among the ancients, the Divine light or wisdom was represented by yellow, as the Divine heat or power was by red. And this appears to be about the whole of the ancient symbolism of this color.

In the old ritual of the Scottish and Hermetic degree of Knight of the Sun, yellow was the symbol of wisdom darting its rays, like the yellow beams of the morning, to enlighten a waking world. In the Prince of Jerusalem, it was also formerly the characteristic color, perhaps with the same meaning, in reference to the elevated position that that degree occupied in the Rite of Perfection, and afterward in the Ancient and Accepted Rite.

Thirty or forty years ago, yellow was the characteristic color of the Mark Master's Degree, derived, perhaps, from the color of the Princes of Jerusalem, who originally issued charters for Mark Lodges; for it does not seem to have possessed any symbolic meaning.

In fact, as has been already intimated, all the symbolism of yellow must be referred to and explained by the symbolism of gold and of the sun, of which it is simply the representative.

Yod. The Hebrew letter י, equivalent in sound to I or Y. It is the initial letter of the word יהוה, or Jehovah, the Tetragrammaton, and hence was peculiarly sacred among the Talmudists. Basnage (lib. iii., c. 13), while treating of the mysteries of the name Jehovah among the Jews, says of this letter:

"The *yod* in Jehovah is one of those things which eye hath not seen, but which has been concealed from all mankind. Its essence and matter are incomprehensible; it is not lawful so much as to meditate upon it. Man may lawfully revolve his thoughts from one end of the heavens to the other, but he cannot approach that inaccessible light, that primitive existence, contained in the letter *yod;* and indeed the masters call the letter thought or idea, and prescribe no bounds to its efficacy. It was this letter which, flowing from the primitive light, gave being to emanations. It wearied itself by the way, but assumed a new vigor by the sense of the letter ה, which makes the second letter of the Ineffable Name."

In Symbolic Masonry, the *yod* has been replaced by the letter G. But in the high degrees it is retained, and within a triangle, thus, ◬ constitutes the symbol of the Deity.

York Rite of Freemasonry, The. The oldest and perhaps the purest form of Ancient-Craft Masonry takes its name from the City of York, in the north of England.

It was there in the year A.D. 926 that we find Masonry adopting its first recorded Constitution. It is recorded in many very ancient manuscripts that during the reign of the good King Athelstan he granted a patent to (his nephew) Prince Edwin, under authority of which an assembly of divers lords, dukes, barons, knights, squires, great burgesses of cities and many more, all Masons, convened in the City of York and adopted a Constitution of fifteen Articles for the future government of the Craft.

An account of this historical incident is fully recorded in the Halliwell Manuscript which dates from the year A.D. 1390. In the Cook Manuscript whose date is placed at A.D. 1490, three hundred and twenty-seven years before the organization of the Grand Lodge of England, the York meeting was again described.

That Masonry existed in England before the reign of good King Athelstan, we find in historical Lansdowne MS. written in 1560 A.D. from which is quoted the following:

"Soon after the decease of St. Albans, there came divers warrs into England out of divers nations, so that the good rule of Masons was disturbed and put down until the tyme of King Athelstan. In his tyme he brought this land into good rest and he builded many great works and buildings, therefore he loved Masons well for he had a (nephew) called Edwin, the which loved Masons much, * * * and he was soe practized in Geometry that he delighted so much to come and talke with Masons and to learn of them the Craft, and after, for the love he had to Masons and to the Craft, he was made a Mason at Windsor and got from the King, * * * a charter and commission once every year to have assembly within the Realm and to correct within themselves faults and trespasses that were done as touching the craft and he held them an Assembly, and there he made Masons and gave them charges, and taught them the Manners and comande the same to be kept ever afterwards."

Prince Edwin called upon all members old and young to bring in any writings to be found concerning "Masonrie." There were some found in Greek, some in Hebrew and some in English and some in other languages, some of them hundreds of years old, and when they were read "and overseen well, the intent of them was understood to be *all one,*" and then he caused a book to be made thereof how this worthy craft of Masonrie was first founded. "* * * And from that, until this day manners of Masons have been kept in this manner and forme."

Based upon the older manuscripts named, Dr. Anderson, in A.D. 1723, published the first edition of the *Book of Constitutions,* in which the history of the fraternity of Free Masons is, he says, "collected from their general records and their faithful traditions of many ages." The history, as narrated herein, is repeated by Dr. Anderson and subsequently by Preston, author of the first Masonic Monitor.

The degrees recognized by the Grand Lodge of England at the revival in 1717 A.D. were as follows:

"Pure ancient Masonry consists of three degrees, no more; viz: those of the Entered Apprentice, the Fellow Craft, and the Master Mason, including the Supreme Order of the Holy Royal Arch."

It is therefore seen that the Royal Arch Degree was once a part of the Master's Degree. It was the crowning feature and glorious completion of Ancient-Craft Masonry. The Grand Lodge of England to this day exercises jurisdiction over the "Holy Royal Arch."

There was a schism in the Grand Lodge of England in 1738 A.D., at which time a rival Grand Lodge was organized by the schismatics. This situation continued for a period of seventy-five years. In 1813 the breach was healed by the reconciliation and union of the two Grand Lodges.

During the rivalry of the two Grand Lodges both granted charters to form Lodges in the American Colonies. The jurisdiction over the Degrees underwent some changes in this country, resulting finally in organizing separate Grand Bodies which took over what are now called the Chapter Degrees. The organization of the General Grand Royal Arch Chapter was begun shortly after the Revolutionary War and in the year 1806 A.D. was finally completely organized.

While under the system in vogue in the United States, the Capitular degrees are severed from the Blue Lodge, yet, they should be regarded as an *integral part,* and necessary to the *completion* of Ancient-Craft Masonry. They are essential to a full understanding of the *system as a whole.*

Thus, you have a brief but authentic historical sketch of Ancient-Craft Masonry extending backward a thousand years. The traditional history extends back much further. Well informed Masons are familiar with the traditions concerning its origin. I will offer some additional evidence hereinafter in support of the sound basis on which rests securely, the verity of these traditions.

The York Rite System in the United States

The York Rite System of Freemasonry in the United States is composed of four Grand Divisions as follows:

The Degrees of Entered Apprentice, Fellow-Craft and Master Mason constitute what is termed the "Blue Lodge degrees." They are conferred in Lodges holding a warrant or charter from the Grand Lodge.

There is a separate Grand Lodge in each state of the Union, and in the District of Columbia. Each exercises exclusive sovereign jurisdiction over the Blue Lodges in its own territory. The Blue Lodge degrees are called "Symbolic Degrees" and the Lodge, while conferring a degree, is termed the "Symbolic Lodge." The reason therefor will be hereafter explained.

Capitular Masonry

The second Grand Division of the York Rite System is called "The Capitular Degrees," composed of four degrees, namely: Mark Master, Past Master, Most Excellent Master, and the Royal Arch. These degrees are conferred in what is commonly called the "Royal Arch Chapter."

The subordinate Chapters receive their charters from the Grand Royal Arch Chapter of their state which is the exclusive and highest authority over the Capitular degrees as hereinbefore pointed out. The Capitular degrees, when taken in connection with the Blue Lodge, or Symbolic degrees, completes what is termed "Ancient-Craft Masonry."

The word "Capitular" is derived from the Latin word *"Capitulum,"* which means "of, or pertaining to a Chapter."

"Cryptic Degrees"

The third Grand Division of the York Rite System is called the "Cryptic or Council Degrees." The word "Cryptic" is derived from the Latin word *"Crypta,"* and means, literally, "to hide, hidden, secret." The Cryptic Rite is composed of the Degrees of "Royal Master" and "Select Master," with a third degree, conferred on special occasions, called the "Super-Excellent Master." These degrees are conferred in subordinate Councils which hold charters from the Grand Council of Royal and Select Masters of the state.

While the Cryptic, or Council, Degrees were not, originally, an integral part of Ancient-Craft Masonry, the historical and ethical truths taught therein are deemed complementary and necessary to a full exposition of them, for the light they throw on certain historical sections of Ancient Craft Masonry. They are deemed of such beauty and importance, that each petitioner for the Capitular degrees should also, petition for the Council degrees.

Knights Templar

The fourth and final division of the York Rite System is composed of the Illustrious Order of the Red Cross, Knights of Malta, and Knights Templar. These orders are conferred in a constituent body called the "Commandery." Commanderies are chartered by the Grand Commandery of the State, which in turn is chartered by the Supreme authority over Templar Masonry called "The Grand Encampment of Knights Templar of the United States of America." The Grand Encampment is the only nation-wide Masonic Grand body which exercises any authority or jurisdiction within the state.

Differing from all the previous degrees in the York Rite System, the Order of Knights Templar is an Order composed of Masons professing the Christian faith. It makes no claim to being a part of "Ancient-Craft Masonry," as that term is commonly understood by Masons, although some of the symbolism of the Ancient rite is carried into and impressively exemplified in their beautiful rites.

The probable reason why the Valiant and Magnanimous Order of the Temple has been included in the system of York Rite Masonry, is, perhaps, due to the fact that it requires, as a prerequisite to membership, that each petitioner must be a Mason in good standing in the Blue Lodge and Royal Arch Chapter. In this respect, the Knights Templar require an applicant to possess the full qualifications of "an Ancient-Craft Mason" as well as to be of the Christian faith, in order to be eligible to petition for the Orders of Christian Knighthood.

The Grand Encampment of Knights Templar was organized in this country on June 22, 1816. While, like the Grand Priory of England and Canada, it is comparatively a modern Order, yet, it has for its model and foundation those heroic and valiant Orders of Knighthood founded in the year 1118 A.D., and which, for 200 years, led the Crusades in an effort to expel the Saracens from the Holy Land.

The old Order of Christian Knighthood was suppressed in the year A.D. 1313 by the Edicts of a French King, aided and abetted by a Pope of the Roman Church. The suppression was accomplished by the arbitrary use of dictatorial power similar to that exercised by the Dictators of Germany, Russia and Italy in recent times.

There is much historical authority to show that the old Orders of Knighthood perpetuated themselves under other names, in Scotland and other countries, for 400 years until the Revival of Masonry in England in A.D. 1717. The limits of this brochure will not permit us entering further into that field. Suffice it to say that for those Masons of the Christian faith, the beautiful and impressive rites of the Order of the Temple, is, in every respect, worthy to be accorded a place in the Grand system of York Rite Masonry.

Rite

The word "Rite" as employed in connection with a system of Masonry, is derived from the Latin word *"ritus,"* signifying "an approved usage or custom. It is also traceable to a Greek verb, whence literally it signifies "a trodden path." As a Masonic term, its application is therefore apparent. It signifies a method of conferring Masonic light by a collection of degrees of a long-followed custom.

Internal Evidence of the Antiquity of Ancient-Craft Masonry

The highest internal evidence we have of the ancient origin and antiquity of Ancient-Craft Masonry, aside from its historical records, is found in the form of its structure, and the method it employs in imparting to its Initiates the truths embodied in its sublime rites and beautiful ceremonies.

Prior to the Christian era, there were no schools or churches as we know them. The children of the nobility and the rich received instruction from private tutors, while the children of the poor and lower classes were allowed to grow up in ignorance, without schooling or learning in the arts or sciences. They could neither read nor write and were a prey to all the superstitious fears and idolatry which can be imposed upon the illiterate and ignorant masses.

In every ancient country were to be found splendid temples erected to the God of their faith. Worship of their Deities was carried on by certain established rites and ceremonies. Admission into these ceremonies was obtained only through *"initiation."* Only men of known probity and good moral character were initiated into the mysteries of their religion. Moreover, the rites of the ancient temples were organized into three grades or degrees. The Neophyte, after his initiation into the first degree, had to apply himself for several years in mastering the knowledge imparted to him, and in improving his intellectual, moral and spiritual character before he could be advanced. If he proved in every respect trustworthy, and made satisfactory progress, he was advanced. Eventually, after strict trials to test his fidelity, zeal, moral and intellectual attainments, he might be, finally, initiated into the Inner Sanctuary, where full explanations and interpretations of their sacred writings, symbols and allegories were made known to him. These would include all the knowledge possessed concerning moral and spiritual truths; the laws of nature; the phenomena of the celestial world; the true form of the earth; the revolutions and orbits of the planets, the apparent movement of the sun between the tropics; the constellations of the Zodiac; and the known secrets of the liberal arts and sciences, particularly of Grammar, Rhetoric, Logic, Arithmetic, Geometry, Music and Astronomy, as well as other vital knowledge.

All these things were carefully guarded from the profane, or uninitiated. A penalty of death was inflicted for unlawfully revealing the secrets of the sanctuary. To be deemed worthy of the privilege of initiation was the most valued and highly prized honor to which one could aspire.

They taught their truths through the use of signs, symbols and allegories, each of which was carefully chosen by their wisest sages and seers, and had the virtue of being capable of more than one interpretation. For example, the compasses might be used to teach the beginner a moral lesson, illustrated by drawing a circle and instructing him that he should, likewise, circumscribe his appetites and desires, and keep all the passions engendered by the five senses within due bounds, thus obtaining mastery over himself, and thereby to improve his moral nature. The moral interpretation would probably be the extent of the explanation given the beginner. So, if he became remiss in his duty and fealty, or fell by the wayside, or was not deemed worthy of advancement, he would possess no knowledge, which if disclosed to the profane, would betray the profounder secrets of the temple. To the advanced Initiate, other significations of the compasses would be unfolded. It would, perhaps, be exhibited in its relation to the sciences of Geometry and Astronomy. The candidate would be enlightened on all the secrets of science known to the Priests and Sages of their time.

The Supreme light, finally diffused, taught him that the universe was created by the Grand Architect of the Universe; that it is sustained and preserved by Divine laws enacted by Him for its government; that man is more than a mere animal; that he is an immortal soul that will live beyond the change we call death; that his body is a true temple created for the indwelling of the spirit of God which dwelleth in man. St. John revealed one of the great secrets of the Sanctuary when he proclaimed, "Know ye not that ye are the Temple of God and *that* the spirit of God dwelleth in you."

In all the ancient temples, much stress was placed upon obedience to the "Moral Law," because they believed that without it, no man could develop those virtues, whose excellence will befit him to receive the loftier truths of science and of the spirit, which they reserved for those who proved themselves by long service and devotion, to be worthy and well qualified to receive, safeguard, and cherish them.

The Sages and Seers of the ancient mysteries were careful to show their highest initiates that every thing in the universe is governed by divine laws. They unfolded the method by which the laws of attraction and repulsion enabled the sun to fix the planets in orbits, and compel them to revolve in such orbits about it. They demonstrated how these movements brought about changes in seasons, producing our spring, summer, fall and winter. How these seasons affected the vegetable and animal kingdoms. In fact, how all nature, of necessity, must adapt itself to these constant changes, and taught them the natural laws, by which all these changes are accomplished. These carefully guarded secrets of the Sanctuary of the Temples extended into the realm of moral and spiritual laws, which, likewise, govern the physical, intellectual, moral and spiritual growth and development of man himself.

Initiation

It will therefore be seen and understood that the word "initiation" had a different significance in ancient times than is commonly accorded it in modern times. "Initiation" in modern times is commonly understood to mean, when applied to receiving degrees, "as the ceremonial progress through the work of the Rite." When that is completed, the charge given, and the candidate is invited to "find a seat among the brethren"; he is presumed to be through; a graduate of the system; and believes himself in possession of all the light and knowledge necessary to be obtained.

Laboring under such a delusion, the proud candidate usually blossoms forth the next day with the emblem of the *Master* upon the lapel of his coat, justly and pardonably happy in the feeling that he had reached the summit of his ambition.

It might be helpful if we put ourselves in mind, ever so often, of the real meaning of the word *"initiation"* as it was understood, when applied to the ceremony of reception into the mysteries of the ancient temples. With them it was understood to merely be a beginning and not a completion; the taking of the first step, and not the last one; the starting of something, and not the finish; the first move in a great enterprise, and not its final consummation. It required a lifetime of work, study, meditation, reflection and application to attain the true title of "a Master."

Initiation into the mysteries was held in loftiest esteem by the wisest men of olden times. Plato said that the "object of initiation into the mysteries of the Temple was to re-establish the soul in its primitive purity, and in that state of perfection which it had *lost.*" Epictetus said, "whatever is met with therein has been instituted by our Masters, for the instruction of Man, and the correction of Morals."

St. Clemens of Alexandria, one of the early Bishops of the Christian Church in Egypt, and himself, perhaps, an Initiate, says, "that that was taught in the great Mysteries concerned the universe, and was the completion of all instruction; wherein things were seen as they were, and nature and her works were made known."

"It seems to me," says the great Orator, philosopher and moralist, Cicero, "that Athens, among many excellent inventions, divine and very useful to the human family, has produced none comparable to the mysteries, which for a wild and ferocious life have substituted humanity and urbanity of manners. It is with good reason the use of the term *initiation;* for it is through them that we in reality have learned the first principles of life; and they not only teach us to live in a manner more consoling and agreeable, but they soften the pains of death by the hope of a better life hereafter."

Masonry, the successor of the ancient temple-mysteries, still follows the ancient manner of teaching. The deeper and more important truths of nature, of science, of philosophy, and wisdom, are "veiled in allegory and illustrated by symbols." The esoteric lectures and monitorial instruction, beautiful and impressive as they are, are designed to be merely the beginning; the first steps; the starting; the first movement toward "more light" and the "further light" it has so deftly veiled in its beautiful and impressive symbols.

A great Masonic scholar and savant has truly said: "He, who would become an accomplished Mason, must not be content merely to hear, or even to understand, the lectures; he must, aided by them, and they having, as it were, marked out the way for him, study, interpret, and develop these symbols for himself."

Ancient-Craft Masonry does not expound the *inner* meanings of its symbols and allegories. It merely displays them, with a brief allusion to their *moral* signification, and leaves their other meanings to be *discovered* by the industry, meditation and contemplation of the initiate.

One often hears the questions asked, "How then are we to discover the truth?" "By what method are we to understand the symbolic meaning of our ancient symbols?" "Where do we begin in order to unravel this Mystic Science and Royal Art?" These are legitimate questions and are deserving of an answer that will point a direction, through which others have found a pathway, that inevitably leads toward the light.

Ancient-Craft Masonry has been described as a "beautiful *system* of morality, veiled in allegory and illustrated by symbols." This definition is the most restricted one which can describe it. A more comprehensive definition would be as follows: "Masonry is a beautiful *system* of Moral Philosophy; Divine Science and Royal Art; heavily veiled in Allegories; illuminated and illustrated by significant symbols."

By this expression we learn that "Ancient-Craft Masonry" is a *system* of some sort. It will, perhaps, aid us, if we understand more clearly just what is meant by the word "*system.*" The word "system" may be defined as "an assemblage of degrees arranged in regular subordination, after some distinct method, usually logical or scientific. A complete exhibition of essential principles or facts, arranged in rational dependence or connection. A regular union of principles or parts forming *one entire thing.* A natural combination, or organization of part to part, conceived as formed by a process of growth, or due to the nature of the objects connected; an organic whole; as a railway system; a system of philosophy; of government; a solar system; a system of morality; a system of natural laws."

Since Ancient-Craft Masonry, as a system, embraces the Blue Lodge and Capitular degrees a knowledge of *all* these degrees is believed to be essential for a thorough understanding of the system as a *whole.* A knowledge of only a part of the system will not reveal the Divine plan, as a *whole,* as, it is claimed, to be embodied in the completed structure. A visitation to the ground floor and middle chamber of King Solomon's Temple never revealed what was deposited in the Sanctum Sanctorum or Holy of Holies.

If, therefore, Ancient-Craft Masonry is truly a *system* of some kind, which is "veiled in allegory and illustrated by symbols," the next logical step will be to consider the nature and functions of *symbols* and *allegories,* and the manner in which they may be employed to conceal, as well as to reveal, divine truth. We must ever bear in mind that symbols were primarily designed to *conceal* rather than to *reveal.*

Symbols

A symbol differs materially from an allegory. The word "symbol" is derived from a Greek word which signifies "to compare one thing with another"; and hence a symbol is the expression of an idea which is derived from the comparison or contrast of some object with a moral conception or attribute. A symbol is an emblem selected, arbitrarily and by agreement, because by its nature or qualities, it is capable of reflecting some higher truth or idea.

Since every virtue springs out of the moral law, the symbolic degrees of the Blue Lodges in their first aspects, are chiefly concerned in expounding the moral laws and virtues. They are a necessary prelude and preparation for the unfolding, through symbols and allegories, of its more profound and important scientific and spiritual laws.

In illustrating a virtue some specific emblem or symbol is selected, arbitrarily, which bears in its own nature, some inherent quality or characteristic that is comparable to the nature of the virtue to be illustrated. For illustration: To inculcate the moral quality of "Rectitude," the figure of a Plumb may be exhibited, because it is upright and cannot be employed otherwise. Likewise, "Equality" is illustrated by the level. As an appropriate symbol of "Industry" and orderly government, a Beehive may be used; "immortality" is well illustrated by a sprig of evergreen, etc., etc.

The Plumb thus becomes to the Mason after he has once been taught its symbolic meaning, forever afterwards, the visible representation or expression of the idea of rectitude or uprightness of conduct.

To study and compare these visible emblems—to elicit from them the moral and other ideas which they are intended to express—is to make one's self acquainted with the symbolism of Masonry.

This action will put the feet of the searcher after "more light," upon the path that leads to profounder knowledge and wisdom.

In addition to being a beautiful system of moral laws, Masonry also lays claim to a "Divine Science and a Royal Art." We would, therefore, expect to find among our symbols some that embody the truths of Divine Science. For example: A point within a circle is generally accepted as a fitting symbol of circumscribed desires and habits, necessary to upright and moral conduct. In a deeper sense it is an appropriate symbol of the sun in the center of our solar system, extending its power and influence through the immensity of space, controlling the movements of the planets and of comets, and holding them steadfast in their stupendous orbits.

The scientific fact that the sun, and not the earth, is the center of our solar system was not known to the profane world until proclaimed by Copernicus and Galileo in comparatively modern times.

The point within a circle may also be employed to reflect a still deeper symbolism. It is a fitting symbol of the Great Architect of the Universe in the center of the Cosmos, animating, sustaining and permeating it to the outermost reaches of illimitable space. "The heavens declare the glory of God and the firmament sheweth his handiwork."

Allegories

Since the truths of the Ancient Temples are also said to be "veiled in allegories," it might aid to a clearer understanding of the system to set forth, briefly, an explanation of that term.

An *allegory* is a discourse, narrative or legend, in which there are two or more meanings, one literal and the other figurative. The discourse may have as its subject an historical event, such as the building of the

Temple. The narrative may describe, in detail, all the operations, from the laying of the foundation to the final completion of the structure. On its surface the narration may have the appearance, only, of detailing an ordinary historical event connected with the erection of a building. If the historical event is employed as an allegory, it will be detailed in such a manner, and in such language, that a second narrative can be read *between* the lines. The truths veiled in this manner carry the more important information. The unreflecting mind will see only the historical fact detailed, but the more thoughtful and discerning mind may, upon meditation and reflection, discern the *veiled* truths intended to be veiled and preserved, against revelation to idle curiosity, impostors or the profane.

A French poet has given us a very good definition of the word, he says: "Allegory lives in a transparent palace." All the legends of ancient mythologies are generally viewed as allegories. In the twelve labors of Hercules, may be read inner truths not at once apparent in the stories as told.

Bunyan's "Pilgrim's Progress," Spenser's "Fairie Queen," and Dante's "Divine Comedy" are notable examples of allegorical writings.

The story of Sampson and Delilah may well serve to illustrate the point: When Sampson was shorn of his long hair by Delilah, he is said to have lost his strength and languished in weakness and impotence until his hair grew long again, when he was restored to his former invincible strength.

If the story is viewed as an allegory the legend will be seen to *veil* a great law of nature. When the sun sinks far to the south at the feast day of St. John the Evangelist, December 27th, its rays lose their strength and power in the northern hemisphere. The cold winds, snows and ice appear. Vegetation is destroyed, trees shed their leaves and all the vegetable kingdom seems to die or become dormant. When the sun begins its return journey northward, its rays, represented by the hair of Sampson, begin to grow in length. The days become longer and longer, the rays gain in strength and power, and by the feast day of St. John the Baptist, June 24th, they have reached their fullest length, strength and power. The cold and icy winds have been driven into the Arctic, nature is fully revived and the flowers, fruits and harvest glorify the vegetable kingdom. Thus it may be seen how a historical or Biblical narrative may be utilized to veil a scientific law. In the allegory, Sampson is made to personify the Sun in its apparent movements between two of the great cardinal points.

Every degree of Ancient-Craft Masonry contains important allegories, a knowledge and understanding of which will bring "more light" and "further light" as they are unveiled in their transcendent beauty and glory. The building of the Temple; the Holy place; the most Holy Place; Jacob's Ladder; and the sublime legend of the Second Section of the Master's Degree may also be considered as allegories, which veil the most profound truths of divine science and of moral and spiritual laws, found in the symbolic Lodge.

The same is true of the Capitular and Cryptic Degrees. A full comprehension of the system of Ancient-Craft Masonry and its supernal light, can only be attained with a knowledge and *understanding* of the Capitular and Cryptic degrees. They illustrate the Temple completed in all its parts. The placing of the keystone is necessary to bind the final arch.

Teaching truths by parables or allegories was the favorite method employed by Jesus. The parables of the sower; the talents; the wise and foolish virgins and the Good Samaritan; are each a splendid example of concealing, as well as teaching, great fundamental truths by allegory.

The foregoing hints should suffice to point the way whereby more light may be attained, and our minds illuminated, by a richer knowledge of the divine wisdom concealed in the symbols and allegories of the system of Ancient Craft-Masonry.

One must study each symbol displayed for all of its possible meanings, and search each allegory for its inner truths, if one is to really advance toward a brighter and more abundant knowledge of the sublime system of this wonderful Institution. When this is accomplished there will be so much light upon the pathway that there will be little or no need for other suggestions to point the way. The question may be asked: "In this day of enlightenment and freedom, where there is such a wide diffusion of knowledge of the laws of nature and of science, of moral, spiritual and intellectual sciences, why is it necessary to delve into the hidden meanings of ancient symbols of vanished temples?"

In answer, one needs only to point to the fact that seven great civilizations have risen, flourished and disappeared since the beginning of written history. Following each of these catastrophes the world, invariably, lapsed into extended eras of darkness, ignorance and brutal savagery. The influence of the ancient wisdom, preserved in faithful breasts by the loyal few, has always been instrumental in leading mankind out of the darkness into the light of a new civilization. The blessings of the enlightened civilization which we enjoy today may be traced to such a system.

In our own day and generation we have witnessed the recurrence of the experiences of history. The rise of dictatorial power in many quarters of the world is being employed to overthrow freedom; is engaged in the destruction of the temples of faith; the grinding of human beings into economic, social, moral and religious serfdom. If the present trend is not checked and its course reversed, another of the world's great civilizations may be destined to crumble into ruins.

If we are conscious of any duty or obligation to the past, a past which safeguarded and transmitted to us the fundamentals of our precious civilization, then, do we not owe a similar debt to posterity, to preserve and transmit to it, unimpaired, the glorious heritage which we received from the strong minds and devoted hearts of the fathers of ancient days?

When one has received the degrees of the "symbolic" or "Blue Lodge," he has taken the first step over the threshold of Ancient-Craft Masonry. The first step toward the inner sanctuary and heart of the Temple. He is on the path that leads up the slope of the Mountain of Faith. It depends upon his interest, zeal and industry, whether he will advance or be content to *remain stationary.*

The system of Ancient-Craft Masonry was not designed in a manner so that the full scope of its Divine Science and Royal Art should be expounded, and fully inculcated, in the three symbolic degrees as now constituted. *Ancient-Craft Masonry* is completed only in the Capitular and Cryptic degrees of the Chapter and Council. It was designed to be that way. Something was left lacking in the symbolic degrees. Something was *lost* and never *recovered* therein. Mackey, one of our most eminent Masonic scholars, wrote: "Whosoever carefully studies the Master's degree in its *symbolic signification,* will be convinced that it is imperfect and unfinished in its history, and that, terminating abruptly in its symbolism, it leaves the mind still waiting for something that is necessary to its completeness. This deficiency is supplied by the *Royal Arch Degree.*"

Capitular Masonry

The degrees of the Royal Arch Chapter, as before stated, are designated as "Capitular Degrees" and its four degrees are named, Mark Master, Past Master, Most Excellent Master and Royal Arch.

The *system* of ceremonies established in the Symbolic Lodges extends into the Royal Arch Chapter, expanding their scope and unfolding their truths into ever increasing Masonic light and knowledge.

This fact illustrates the intimate connection which has always existed between the Blue Lodges and Chapters from time immemorial.

The fourth Degree in Masonry (the first in the Chapter) is designated the "Mark Master's Degree." "The tradition of the degree made it of great historical importance, since by them we are informed that by its influence, each Operative Mason at the building of the Temple was known and distinguished, and the disorder and confusion which might otherwise have attended so immense an undertaking was completely prevented. Not less useful is its *symbolic signification.*" A highly important and significant part of the Mark Masters Degree was once a part of the Fellow-Craft Degree. "If the Fellow-Craft's Degree is devoted to the inculcation of learning, that of the Mark Master is intended to instruct us how this learning can most usefully and judiciously be employed for our honor and the profit of others. * * * The true Mark Master is a type of that man mentioned in the sacred parable who received from his master this approving language: 'Well done, good and faithful servant;

thou has been faithful over a few things, I will make thee ruler over many things; enter thou into the joys of thy Lord.' "

The fifth and sixth degrees of York Rite Masonry are designated "Past Master," and "Most Excellent Master." In these degrees many important truths are illustrated and inculcated.

The seventh degree is the "Royal Arch." It is known as the Chapter, while the Mark Master, Past Master and Most Excellent Masters' degrees are conferred in Lodges of those names within the Chapter.

Of the Royal Arch Degree it may be said, "If we except the Master's, there is no other degree in Masonry that has been so extensively diffused, or is as important in its *historical* and *symbolic* import, as the Royal Arch, or, as it has been called, on account of its sublime significance, the 'Holy Royal Arch.' "

Dermott calls it "the root, heart and marrow of Masonry." Oliver says that it is indescribably more august, sublime, and important than any which precede it, and is, in fact, the summit and perfection of ancient Masonry."

It is unnecessary that anything be added to the opinions expressed by these eminent Masonic authorities, further than to observe that it requires these additional degrees to amplify and complete the *beautiful system of Ancient-Craft Masonry* and bring the searcher for truth into a situation rendering it possible to obtain the full glory of Masonic *light* and *knowledge.*

These degrees, supplemented by the Cryptic dgrees of the Council, together with a knowledge of their wonderful system of historical, philosophical, scientific, moral and spiritual truths, complete the grand plan devised by the Grand Masters of the Ancient Temple, through which the light will ever continue to shine in effulgent and refulgent splendor, "Seek and ye shall find, knock and it shall be opened unto you."

Albert Pike, one of Masonry's greatest savants, has written: "He who desires to understand the harmonious and beautiful proportions of Freemasonry must read, study, reflect, digest and discriminate. The true Mason is an ardent seeker after knowledge; and he knows that both books and the antique symbols of Masonry are *vessels* which come down to us full-freighted with the intellectual riches of the past; and that in the lading of these argosies, is much that sheds light on the history of Masonry, and proves its claim to be acknowledged the benefactor of mankind, born in the very cradle of the race."

In conclusion, permit me to observe that the object of Masonry, primarily, is to teach men a better way of life. To instruct him of the most orderly way to develop character, mentality and spirituality, in order that he may prepare himself as a living stone in that mighty spiritual temple which is slowly rising in the earth and shall stand at last eternal in the Heavens. In this respect the grand design is to make men wiser, freer, better and consequently happier men.

But the beautiful system does not end there. It has much more to teach than mere *human behavior*. The divine laws of nature were not at first written in books. They were displayed in the wonderful symbols created by wisdom of God, and displayed by Him in the Heavens; the earth; and beneath the waters of the sea.

Mankind had to discover them by observation, meditation and revelation.

If in the beautiful and significant degrees of Ancient-Craft Masonry we have seen only a series of unmeaning rites; if the spirit of Truth has not impressed upon our hearts the moral laws embodied in them; if they have failed to stir within us a desire to search further for its inexhaustible riches; then indeed have we labored in vain and you have spent your strength for naught.

*"If ye fulfil the royal law according to the scripture, Thou shalt love thy neighbor as thyself, ye do well. * * * Even so, faith without works, is dead, being alone * * * For as the body without the spirit is dead, so faith without works is dead also."*

—James 2:8, 17, 26.

Zabud. An historical personage at the court of King Solomon, whose name appears in several of the high degrees. In that of Select Master in the American Rite, it has been corrupted into *Izabud.* He is mentioned in 1 Kings iv. 5, where he is described in the authorized version as being "principal officer and the king's friend." The original is *Zabud ben Nathan cohen regneh hahmelek,* which is literally "Zabud, son of Nathan, a priest, the friend of the king." Adam Clarke says he was "the king's chief favorite, his confidant." Smith (*Dict. Bib.*) says: "This position, if it were an official one, was evidently distinct from that of counsellor, occupied by Ahithophel under David, and had more of the character of private friendship about it." Kitto (*Cyclopæd. Bib. Lit.*) says of Zabud and of his brother Azariah, that their advancement in the household of King Solomon "may doubtless be ascribed not only to the young king's respect for the venerable prophet (their father), who had been his instructor, but to the friendship he had contracted with his sons during the course of education. The office, or rather honor, of 'friend of the king,' we find in all the despotic governments of the East. It gives high power, without the public responsibility which the holding of a regular office in the state necessarily imposes. It implies the possession of the utmost confidence of, and familiar intercourse with, the monarch, to whose person 'the friend' at all times has access, and whose influence is therefore often far greater, even in matters of state, than that of the recognized ministers of government."

This has been fully carried out in the legend of the Select Master's Degree.

Zadok. A personage in some of the Ineffable degrees of the Scottish Rite. In Scripture he is recorded as having been one of the two chief priests in the time of David, Abiathar being the other. He subsequently, by order of David, anointed Solomon to be king, by whom he was rewarded with the post of high priest. Josephus (*Ant.*, x., 8, § 6) says that "Sadoc, the high priest, was the first high priest of the Temple which Solomon built." Yet it has been supposed by some authors, in consequence of his name not being mentioned in the detailed account of the dedication, that he had died before the completion of the Temple.

PRONOUNCING MASONIC DICTIONARY

VOWELS, REGULAR LONG AND SHORT SOUNDS.

ā (long), as in *āle*	ē (long), as in *ēve*	ĭ (short), as in *ĭll*	ū (long), as in *ūse*
ă (short), as in *ădd*	ĕ (short), as in *ĕnd*	ō (long), as in *ōld*	ŭ (short), as in *ŭs*
ä (Italian), as in *ärm*	ī (long), as in *īce*	ŏ (short), as in *ŏdd*	ȳ (long), as in *mȳ*

The above simple process is adopted, omitting instruction relating to diphthongs or tripthongs, occasional sounds, or references to consonants.

ACCENT.—When a word has two accents, the principal accent is denoted by a heavy mark; the secondary, by a lighter mark, as in *Ab'ra-ca-dab'ra.* When a word has only one accent, the lighter accent mark is used for the principal accent. In the division of words into syllables, these marks also supply the place of the hyphen.

Ab (ăb). Heb. Father; 11th Hebraic month.
abaciscus (ă'bă-cis'cŭs). Flooring blocks.
abacus (ăb'a-cŭs). A drawing-board—a tray.
Abaddon (a-băd'don). The destroyer, or angel of darkness.
Abazar (ă'bă-zăr). Master of Ceremonies of 6th Degree.
Abchal (ăb'chăl).
Abda (ăb'dă). Father of Adoniram.
abdamon (ăb'dă'mŏn). To serve.
Abdiel (ăb'dīel). Servant of God.
abditorium (ăb'dī-to'rī-ŭm). A secret place for deposit of records.
Abelites (ā'bel-ītes). A secret order of the 18th century.
Abib (ăb'īb). Seventh Jewish month.
Abibala (ăb'i-bă-lă). Derived from Hebrew Abi and Balah.
Abibalk (ăb'ī-bălk). Chief of the three assassins.
Abif (ăb-īf'). Literally, his father.
Abihael (a-bi'ha-ĕl). Father of Strength.
Abihu (ăb'i-hū). A son of Aaron.
Abiram (ăb-ī'răm). Abiram Akisop, traitorous craftsman.
ablution (ăb-lū'shun). Washing, baptizing.
Abrac (ăb-răc'). Acquiring the science of Abrac.
abracadabra (ăb'ră-că-dăb'ră). A term of incantation.
Abraxas (a-brăx'as). A symbol of the year.
Acacia (a-că'ci-ă). Symbolic of the soul's immortality.
Acanthus (a-căn'thus). A part of the Corinthian capital.
accessory (ak-ses'so-rī). Private companionship.
accolade (ăc'co-lāde'). The welcome into knighthood.
Aceldama (ă-cĕl'da-mă). Field of blood.
Achad (ă-chăd; ă-kăd).
Acharon Schilton (ă'chă-rŏn schil-tŏn; ă'kă-rŏn schil-ton).
Achias (ă-chī'as; ă-kē-as).
Achishar (ăc-hī'shar). One over the household of Solomon.
Achmetha (ăch'mē-thă). Name of a Hebrew city.
Achtariel (ăch-tă'rī-el). Kabbalistic name of God.
acolyte (ak'ō-līte). Candle bearer. Church servant.
Acousmatici (ă'coŭs-mă-tī'cī; ă-coos'mate'cē).
Adah (ā'dă). Jephtha's daughter.
Adar (ā'dar). The twelfth Jewish month.
Adarel (ă'dă-rĕl). Angel of fire.
adept (ă-dept'). An expert.
Adeptus Coronatus (ăd-ept'us cōrō-na'tus). Seventh Degree of the Swedish Rite.

adhere (ad-hēre'). Cling to.
adjudicate (ad-jū'di-kāte). To determine.
Admah (ăd'mä). A Hebrew city.
Ad Majorum Dei Gloriam (ăd mä-jō-rum dā-ē glō-ri-ām). To the greater glory of God.
Adonai (ă'dō-nă'ī; ă-dō-näh'e). The Lord.
Adonhiram (ăd'on-hī'ram). Signifying the master who is exalted.
Adoniram (ăd'ō-nī'ram). Son of Abda.
Adonis (ăd-ō'nis). Son of Myrrha and Cinyras.
adult (ă-dult'). Of full age.
ad vitam (ad vē-tăm). For life.
adytum (ăd'y-tum). A retired part of the ancient temples.
Æneid (æ-nē'id). A creation of Virgil.
Æon (æ-ōn; ē'on). Age or duration of anything.
affiliate (af-fil'e-āte). An adopted one.
Agapæ (ăg'a-pæ; ag'a-pe). Love feasts.
agate (ăg'it). The eighth stone in the breastplate.
Agathopades (ă'gă-thō-pă'des). Ecclesiastical Order of 16th century.
age (āje). Of a given number of years.
agenda (ă-jĕn'da). Order of business. Book of precepts.
Agla (ăg'lă). One of the Kabbalistic names of God.
Agnus Dei (ăg'nus dē'ī; ag'nŭs dā'ē). Lamb of God.
Ahad (ä'had). A name of God.
Ahabath Olam (ă'hă-băth ō'lăm). Eternal love.
Ahashuerus (a-hăs'-u-ē'rus). Name of a Persian king.
Ahel (ä'hel). A curtain of the Tabernacle.
Ahiah (ă-hī'äh; ă-hē'ă). One of the scribes of Solomon.
Ahilud (ă-hīl'ud). The father of Josaphat.
Ahiman Rezon (ă-hī'man rē-zōn'). The will of selected brethren.
Ahinadab (a-hĭn'a-dăb). The son of Jetdo.
Ahisamach (a-hĭs'a-măk). The father of Aholiab.
Ahisar (a-hī'săr; ă-hī'săr).
Aheshar (ă-hī'shar). An officer over Solomon's household.
Aholiab (ă-hō'li-ăb). A skilful artificer.
Ahriman (ăh'rī-man). Principle of evil in Zoroaster system.
Aichmalotarch (ăĭch-mal'ō-tarch). The Prince of Captivity.
Aixlachapelle (āks'-lă-shă'pel'). A city of Germany.
Akar (ă'kär). Or Achar, a password.
Akirop (ă-kī'rop). One of the ruffians of the Third Degree.
Alapa (ă-lă-pă). A symbol of manumission.
alchemy (ăl'-ki-my). The science of Chemistry.
Aldebaran (ăl-deb'a-ran). A star of the first magnitude.
Aleppo (ă-lĕp'pō). A town in northern Syria.
Alethophile (ă-lē'thō-phile). Lover of Truth.
Alfader (ăl-fă'der). Chief God of the Scandinavians.
Algabil (ăl'gă-bĭl). Signifying The Builder.
Allah (ăl'ä). The God of the Moslem.
allegiance (ăl-lē'jance). Fealty.
allegory (ăl'lĕ-gō-ry). A fable, or figurative expression.
Allelujah (ăl-le-lū'yä). Praise Jehovah.
alleviate (ăl-lē've-āte). To relieve.
Allies (al-līz'). Companions in enterprise.
allocution (ăl-lō-kū'shun). The official opening address.
almoner (ăl'mō-ner). Dispenser of alms.
alms (āmz). Charitable gifts.
Al-om-Jah (ăl-ōm-jăh). A name of the Supreme Being.
alpha (ăl'fä). Greek letter A.
Alpina (ăl-pī-nă). Name of Grand Lodge of Switzerland.
Als (älz). The All-powerful God.
Al Shaddai (ăl-shăd'dă-e). The second sanctified name of God.
al-sirat (ăl' sī-răt'). The path.
Alycuber (ăl-e-kū'ber). Master of the Tribe of Manasseh.
Amal-Sagghi (ămăl-săg'ghī). Fifth step of Kadosh ladder.
Amar-jah (ă'măr-jăh). God spake.
Amboth (ăm'bōth). A country in Syria.
Amenti (ă-men'-tī). Place of Judgment of the Dead.
Ameth (ă'mĕth). See *Emeth.*
amethyst (ăm'e-thist). A stone in the breastplate.
Amicists (ă'mi-cists). Association of students of Germany.
Aminidab (ă-mĭn'a-dăb). One of the Chiefs of Israel.
Amis Reunis (ămĭs re'ūnis; ă'mē re'u-nē).
Ammonites (ăm'mon-ītz). Descendants of Lot.
amshaspands (ăm-shăs'pands). Principle of good among Persians.
amulets (ăm'u-lets). Mystic gems.
Amun (ă'mŭn). The Supreme God of the Egyptians.
anachronism (an-a'chrō-nĭsm). An error in computing time.
anakim (ăn'a-kĭm). Giants.
Ananias (ăn-a-nī'as). Sapphira's conspirator.
ancient (ăn'shunt). Indefinite time.
Andre (an'drĕ). Christopher Karl André.
Andrea (an'drĕă). John Valentine Andreă.
androgynous (an-drŏg'-ŷnous; an-drŏg-ē-nous). Side degrees.
angel (ăn'jel). Messenger.

Angerona (an'ge-rō-nă). A pagan deity of the Romans.
anima mundi (ăn'ĭ-ma mŭn'dī). Soul of the World.
annihilate (ăn-ni'he-late). Destroy finally.
anno depositionis (ăn'nō de'pō-sĭ'-tio'nĭs). In the year of the Deposite.
anno domini (ăn'nō dŏm'ĭn-ī). The year of the Lord.
anno hebraico (ăn'nō he'bră'ĭ-co). In the Hebrew year.
anno inventionis (ăn'nō in-ven'she-ō-nĭs). The year of discovery.
anno lucis (ăn'nō lū'cis). In the year of light.
anno mundi (ăn'nō mūn'dī). The year of the world.
anno ordinis (ăn'nō or'di-nis). In the year of the Order.
annuaire (ăn'nū-ăīre). French annual record of proceedings.
Ansyreeh (ăn'sȳ-rēĕh). A sect of northern Syria.
antarctic (ănt-ark'tic). Opposite to the northern circle.
antepenult (ăn-tē-pē-nult'). The last syllable except two.
antipodeans (ăn'tĭ-pō-dē'ans). Les Antipodiens.
antipodes (ăn-tip'o-dēz). Opposite sides of the globe.
Anubis or **Anepu** (ăn-ū-bis or ăn-ē-pū). Egyptian deity. Son of Osiris and Nephthys.
Apame (ăp'a-me). Wife of King Darius.
aphanism (ăph'an-ism). Concealing of the body.
Apharsathchites (ă-phăr'sath-chītes). A Persian tribe.
Apocalypse (ā-pŏk'a-līps). Book of Revelation.
Apollo (ă-pol'o). A Greek deity.
aporrheta (a'pŏrr-hē'tă). Intelligible to the initiated.
apostle (ā-pŏs'l). A deputed agent.
apotheosis (ăp-ō-the'ō-sis). Deification.
apparent (ăp-păr'ent). Evident.
apprentice (ăp-pren'tis). The servitor of a mechanic.
apron (ā'prun). Badge of a Mason.
Aquarius (ā-quā'ri-us). Water-bearer. Zodiac.
Arab (ăr'ab or ā'rab). Inhabitant of Arabia.
arabici (ă'ră-bĭ'cī). Pertaining to the Wilderness.
Aral (ā'rĕl). "Lion of God."
Aranyaka (ă'ran-yă'kă). An appendage to the Veda of the Indians.
Araunah (ă-rău'năh). See *Ornan*.
Arbroath (ăr-brōath). Abbey of England, 12th century.
arcana (ăr-kā'na). Secrets, mystery.
archangel (ărk-ān'jel). An angel of the highest order.
archbishop (arch-bish'op). A church dignitary.
archetype (är'ke-tīp). An original model.
Archimagus (ăr'chī-mă'gŭs). Chief Ruler.
archipelago (är-kī-pel'a-go). Group of islands.
architect (ăr'kī-tect). Skilled in the art of building.
architectonicus (ăr'chi-tĕc-ton'ĭ-cus). Relating to Architecture.
archives (är'kīvz). Place for records.
archiviste (ăr'chi-vīste). An officer in charge of the archives.
Arctic (ärk'tik). A northern circle of space.
arduous (är'dū-us). With difficulty.
area (ā're-a). The given surface.
arelim (ăr'ē-lim). Literally, valiant, heroic.
Areopagus (ă're-ŏp'a-gus). A tribunal.
Arianism (ā'rī-an-ĭsm). The doctrine of Arius.
arid (ăr'id). Exhausted of moisture.
Aries (ā'riez). The sign Ram in the Zodiac.
armenbuchse (ăr'men-būchse). The poor box.
armistice (är'mis-tis). Temporary truce.
aroba (ă-rō'bă). Pledge, covenant.
aroma (ā-rō'ma). An agreeable odor.
arrogant (ăr'rō-gant). Overbearing.
Artaban (är'ta-băn). A Scribe in the Scottish Rite.
Artaxerxes (är'tag-zerk'zez). A Persian king.
artificer (är-tif'i-ser). Designer of buildings.
Aryan (ā'ry-an). One of three historical divisions of religion.
asarota (ă'să-rō'ta). A variegated pavement.
Asher (ăsh'er). A tribe of Israel.
ashlar (ăsh'lar). Stone as taken from the quarry.
Asia (ā'shī-a). An Eastern continent.
Asnapper (as-nap'per).
aspirant (ăs-pir'ant). One who aspires.
associate (ăs-so'shī-at). Companion with.
Assur (ăs'sur). Assyria.
Astarte (ăs-tär'te). Female deity of the Phœnicians.
Astræa (ăs'trā-ēā). The Grand Lodge of Russia.
asylum (ă-sī'lum). Place of retreat.
atelier (ă'tĕl-ier). A workshop where workmen are assembled.
athenæum (ăth-e-ne'um). A building for philosophic instruction.
Atossa (ă-tos'să). Daughter of Cyrus.
attacked (ăt-takt'). Assailed, assaulted.
Atthakatha (ăt'thă-kă'thă). Commentary on Canonical books of Buddhism.
attouchement (ă-tou'sh-măn; ăt-toūch'-emĕnt).
Atys (ăt'is). The Phrygian god.
audacious (äw-dā'shus). Contemning law.
audience (äu'dī-ence). An assembly of hearers.
aude, vide, tace (ău-dī, vī-de, tă-cē). Hear, see, and be silent.
aufseher (ăŭf'sē-her). Inspector, overseer.
Auriel (äu'rī-el). Angel of Fire.
Aurim (äu'rim). Or Urim.

auserwahlter (ăŭs'er-wăhl-ter). Chosen, selected.
Aum or **Om** (ăŭm; ŏm). God of the Hindus.
aut mori (äut mō'rī). **aut vincere** (aut vĭn'cē-rē). Either conquer or die.
avatar (ă'vă-tăr). The descent of a Hindu deity.
Avis (ă'vĭs).
axiom (ak'sĭ-um). Self-evident truth.
aye (ā). An affirmative vote.
Aynon (ăy'nŏn). Agnon, Ajuon.
Azariah (ăz-ā-rĕ'ă). Solomon's Captain of the Guards.
Azazel (ă-ză'zel). "Scapegoat," the demon of dry places.

Baal (ba'ăl; ba-a'lim). Master.
Baana (bā-an'ä). Son of grief.
Babylon (băb'e-lon). Gate of Bel. A kingdom.
Bactylea (băc'tyl-ĕ'ă).
baculus (bă'cu-lus). The pastoral staff carried by a bishop.
Bafomet (ba'fō-mĕt). See *Baphomet.*
bagulkal (ba'gŭl-kăl). Guardian of the sacred ark.
baldachin (băl'dă-chin). A canopy supported by pillars.
baldric (băl'drik). A ribbon worn from shoulder to hip.
balm (bäm). A medicinal gum.
Balsamo (băl-sa'mō). Joseph Balsamo. See *Cagliostro.*
baluster (băl'us-ter). The support of a stair-rail.
Banacas (bān'a-käs). A Captain of Guards.
Baphomet (băf'ō-met). An imaginary idol or symbol.
Barabbas (ba-răb'bas). A father's son. Son of Abba or Father.
barbarous (băr'bā-rus; not băr-ba'ri-ous).
Barbati Fratres (băr-bă'tī fră'tres). Bearded Brothers.
bar mitzvah (băr mĭtz'vah). Son of Commandment.
Barruel, Abbé (bar'ruel, ab'bĕ). Augustin Barruel.
basmoth (băs'moth). Fragrant, spicy.
basilica (ba-sil'ĭ-că). Court-room for administration of laws.
bath kol (băth kŏl). A voice from the Shekinah.
bea macheh (bē-ä măk'-ä). To be with God.
beaucenifer (beau-cĕn'ĭ-fer). To carry.
Beauchaine (beau-chaine; bō-shā'ne).
beauseant (beau'se-ănt). A war banner.
begone (be-gon'; not be-gawn').
Bel (bĕl). A contraction of Baal.
Belenus (bĕ-le'nus). The Baal of Scripture.
Belshazzar (bel-shăz'zar). King of Babylon.
Belus (bē'lus). Corruption of Baal. Lord. A temple.
Benac (bē'năc). See *Macbenac.*
Benai (be-nă'ĭ). The Intelligent God.
Bendekar (ben'dĕ-kăr). One of the Princes of Solomon.
Benjamin (ben'ja-min). Youngest son of Jacob.
benkhurim (ben-ku'rim). Free since birth.
Benyah (ben'yăh). The son of Jah.
bereth (bē-rith). Alliance.
beryl (bĕr'il). Chrysolite, topaz.
Bethlehem (bĕth'le-em). Literally, Place of food. Of Judah.
Beyerle (bey'er-le). François Louis de Beyerle.
beyond (be-yond'; not be-yund').
Bezaleel (be-zăl'e-el). A builder of the Ark of the Covenant.
biennial (bī-en'ni-al; not bī-en'yal).
Binah (bī'na). The mother of understanding.
blatant (blā'tant; not blăt'ant).
blessed (bless-ed; not blest).
Boaz (bo'ăz). Literally, fleetness, strength.
Bochim (bō'chĭm; bō'kim). The weepers.
Boeber (bō-e'ber). Johann Boeber.
Boehmen (bōeh'men). Jacob Boehmen.
Bonaim (bō-nă'im; bō-nah'im).
Bone (bōne'). Boneh, a builder.
Bosonian (bō-sō'nĭ-an). Fourth Degree of African Architects.
bourn (bōurn). Bound, limit.
Bramin (bră'min). Corruption of Brahman.
brethren (breth'ren; not breth'er-en).
Buddha (bū'dä). A Hindu god.
Buh (būh). A corruption of the word Bel.
Buhle (būhle). Johann Gottlieb Buhle.
Bul (būl). The rain-god.
Buri or **Bure** (bū'ri or bū're). The first god of Norse mythology.
Byblos (byb'los). An ancient city of Phœnicia.
Byzantine (biz'an-tin). An art from the days of Constantine.

Caaba or **Kaaba** (că-ă'bă or kă-ă'bă). Square building or temple in Mecca.
cabala (că-bă'lă). Kabbala. Mystical philosophy or theosophy of Jews.
cabiric (că'bir-ic). Dry, sandy.
cable-tow (kā'ble-tō). A man's reasonable ability.
Cabul (că'bul). A district containing twenty cities.
caduceus (că'dū'ce-us). Peace, power, wisdom.
cæmentarius (ca'ē-men-ta'ri-us). A builder of walls.
Cagliostro (căg'li-os'tro). A Masonic charlatan.
cahier (căh'ier). Sheets of paper or parchment fastened together.
cairns (căirns). Heaps of stones of a conical form.
Calatrava (căl'ă-tră'vă). Military Order, instituted 1158.

Calid (căl'ĭd). A sultan of Egypt about 1110.
Callimachus (căl-lim'ă-chŭs). Noted Grecian artist.
calm (käm). Tranquil, serene.
Cama (kä'mä). A Hindu god.
Canaanite (kā'năn-īte). Descendants of Canaan.
candelabra (kăn-del-ā'brā). A branched candlestick.
cantilever (căn'ti-lĕv'er). A projecting block or bracket.
Capella (kă-pĕl'la). The name of a star.
capitular (kă-pĭt'u-lar). Pertaining to a Chapter.
Capricornus (kăp-ri-korn'us). A Zodiacal sign, the Goat.
Capuchin (că-pū'chĭn). A monk of the Order of St. Francis.
caravan (kăr'a-van; not kăr-a-van'). Company of merchants.
Carbonarism (căr'bō-nar-ism). A secret society of Italy.
carbuncle (kär'bun-kĕl). A stone in the breastplate.
Carmel (kär'mel). Literally, a fruitful place.
Caryatides (căr'y-ăt'i-dēs). The women of Caryæ.
Casmaran (căs'mă-răn). The angel of air.
catacombs (kat'a-kōmbs). A cave for the burial of the dead.
catechumen (căt'ē-chū'men). A novice in religious rites.
Cathari (căth'ăr-ī). Italian heretical society, 12th century.
cement (sem'ent or sē-ment'). The noun. The bond of union.
cement (se-ment'). The verb. To bind together.
cemetery (sem'e-tĕr-ĭ). A place of burial.
Cenephorus (cĕn'ē-phō'rus). Officer in charge of sacred implements.
Centaine (cĕn'tāine). A mystical society of 19th century.
centenary (sen'te-na-rĭ; not sen-ten'a-rĭ). A century.
censer (sĕn'ser). An incense cup or vase.
Cephas (sē'fas). A Syrian name. Literally, a stone.
Ceres (sē'rēs). The goddess of corn.
Ceridwen (cē-rid'wen). The Isis of the Druids.
cerneau (cĕr'neau; cĕr'no).
cerulean (sē-ru'le-an). The color of the sky.
Chaldea (chăl-dē'ă). A country along the Euphrates and Tigris rivers.
chalice (chăl'is). A cup or bowl.
chamber (chām'ber). An enclosed place.
chaos (ka'os; not ka'us). A confused mass.
chapeau (chăp'eau; shăpo').
chapiters (chăp'e-tĕrz). The capital of a column.
Chasidim (chă'sĭd-im). A sect in the time of the Maccabees.
chasm (kazm; not kaz'um). A void space.
Chastanier (chăs'tan-ī'er). Benedict Chastanier.
chasuble (chăs'ū-ble). An outer dress in imitation of the Roman toga.
chef-d'œuvre (chef-d'œuvre'; she-deū'vr).
cherubim (chĕr'u-bim). Literally, those held fast.
Chesed (chĕ'sĕd). Signifying mercy.
Chesvan (chēs'van). Name of the second Jewish month.
Cheth (chĕth). A city of Palestine.
chibbelum (chĭb'bē-lum). A worthy Mason.
chisel (chiz'el). An instrument used by a mason or carpenter.
chivalric (shiv-ăl'rik). Pertaining to chivalry.
chochmah (chŏk'māh). Heb., Wisdom.
Chrisna (krish'nä). The Hindu God.
chrysolite (krĭs'o-līte). A stone in the breastplate.
clandestine (klăn-des'tĭn). Illegal.
cleche (klēēch). A cross charged with another cross.
clothed (klōthd). Invested with raiment.
Cœur de Lion (kūr de lī'on). Surname of Richard I. of England.
cochleus (cōch'lē-us). A winding staircase.
coetus (cō'e-tŭs). An assembly.
coexist (ko-egz-ist'). Living at the same time.
coffin (kŏf'in; not kawf'in). Casket for the dead.
cognizant (kog'nĭ-zant). Within the knowledge.
collation (kol-la'shun; not co-la'shun). Luncheon.
collocatio (cŏl'lō-că'ti-o; cŏl-lo-că'sheo).
column (kŏl'um; not kol'yoōm). A pillar.
comment (kom'ment). To explain, to expound.
commiserate (kom-miz'er-āt). Compassion for, to pity.
compagnon (cŏm-păn'ion). A French term for Fellow-Craft.
composite (kom-pŏs'ĭt). An order of Architecture.
conclave (kŏn'klāve). An assemblage of Templars.
condemner (kon-dem'ner; not kon-dem'er). One who censures.
condolence (kon-do'lence; not kon'do-lence). Sympathy.
confidant (kon-fĭ-dant'; not kon'fĭ-dant). A bosom friend.
consistory (kon-sis'to-ry). An assemblage of brethren of the R. Secret.
consummatum (cŏn'sum-mă'tum). It is finished.
conspiracy (kon-spĭr'a-sĭ). A combination for evil purpose.
constans (kŏn'stănz). Unwavering, constant.

contemplating (con'tem-pla-ting). Looking around carefully on all sides.
convocation (kŏn'vo-kā'shun). An assemblage of Royal Arch Masons.
corde gladio potens (kŏr'dā glă'dĭ-o pō'tĕnz). Powerful in heart and with the sword.
cordon (kŏr'don). A ribbon of honor.
Corinthian (kŏr-in'thi-an). An order in Architecture.
corybantes (cŏr'y-ban'tes). Rites in honor of Atys.
costume (kos'tūm). A manner of dress.
Cottyto (cō-tȳt'ō). Mysteries of. Rites of the Bona Dea.
Coustos (coūs'tos). John Coustos.
couverur (coū'vrier; kū'vrir).
covenant (kŭv'e-nant). An agreement, a contract.
cowans (kŏw'anz). Pretenders, dry dikers, intruders.
cowls (kowls). The hood of the mantle.
Crata Repoa (crā'tă re-pō'ă). An Egyptian rite of seven degrees.
credence (krē'dence; not krĕd'ence). Reliance on evidence.
cresset (crĕs'set). Symbol of Light and Truth, open lamp.
Crete (krēte). An island in the Mediterranean.
cromlech (crŏm'lĕch). A large stone resting on two or more stones.
crosier (krō'zher). The staff of the Prelate.
Crotona (crō-tō'nă). A city of Greek colonists in Italy.
cryptic (krĭp'tic). Pertaining to Royal and Select Masonry.
crux ansata (crŭx ăn-să'tă). The cross with a handle.
cum civi (kūm sĭvĭ). Arise and kneel.
cupola (kū'pō-la; not kū'pa-lo). A surmounting dome.
Curetes (cū-rē'tēs). Priests of ancient Crete.
custos arcani (kŭs'tŏs ar-cā'ni). The guardian of the treasury.
cynocephalus (cyn'ō-cĕph'a-lŭs). Figure of a man with head of a dog.
cynosure (sĭn'ō-shōōr). The center of attraction.
Cyrene (cy-rē'nĕ). Ancient city of North Africa.
Cyrus (si'rŭs). A King of Persia.

dabir (dā-bēr'). Most sacred.
Dactyli (dăc'ty-li). Priests of Cybele.
daduchos (dă'dū-chŏs). A torch-bearer.
Dædalus (dæd'a-lus). A famous artist and mechanician.
dais (dă'is). A canopy.
dambool (dăm-bool). Rock temple of Buddhists of Ceylon.
dao (dă'ō). From Daer, to shine.
darakiel (dā-ră-kĭel'). By direction of God.
Darius (dā-rĭ'us). A King of Persia.
Dathan (dă'than). A Reubenite who revolted against Moses.
Dazard (dă'zard). Michel François Dazard.
decrepit (de-crep'ĭt). Wasted by age.
deiseil (dĕ-is'ēil). Southward, following the course of the sun.
Delalande (dĕ-lă-lan'de). Joseph Jérôme François.
Delaunay (dĕ-lău'nāy). François H. Stanislaus Delaunay.
delineated (de-lin'e-ā-ted). Marked, described.
delta (dĕl'tä). Fourth letter of Greek alphabet.
Demeter (dĕ-me'ter). Greek name of Ceres.
demit (de-mĭt'). Release.
Denderah (dĕn-dĕ'răh). A ruined town of Upper Egypt.
depths (depths; not deps nor debths). Profundity.
derogate (dĕr'o-gāte). Degrade.
Desaguliers (dĕ-să-gū'liērs). John Theophilus Desaguliers.
design (de-sīn'). A preliminary sketch.
dessert (dez-zert'). The last course of a feast.
deuchar charters (deū-chăr' chărters). Working warrants.
deus meumque jus (dĕ'us mē-ŭm'que jus). God and my right.
devoir (dĕ'voir; dĕ'vōa).
dew (dū). Atmospheric moisture.
dieseal (dĭ-es-ē'al). A Druidic term.
Dieu et mon droit (dieu ĕt mŏn droit; dĭeū ă mon droa).
Dieu le veut (dieu lĕ veūt; dĭeū lĕ veu-t).
different (dif'fer-ent; not dif'rent). Distinct, separate.
Dionysian (dĭ'o-nys'ĭan). Celebrations by which the years were numbered.
Dionysus (dĭ'o-nys'us). Greek name of Bacchus.
diploma (dĭ-plo'ma; not dī-plo-ma). A sealed writing.
dislodge (dis-lŏdge'). To drive from a place of rest.
disloyal (dis-loy'al). Faithless.
dissolve (diz-zolv'). Separation into component parts.
district (dis'trikt). A portion of territory.
Diu (dĭ'ū). The "Shining Light of Heaven."
divest (dĭ-vest'). Deprive of, remove.
divulge (dĭ-vulj'). To make publicly known.
Domino Deus Meus (dŏm'i-nĕ dā'us mā'us). O Lord, my God.
Domitian (do-mĭsh'i-an). A Roman Emperor.
donats (dō'năts). Wearers of the demi-cross.
Doric (dŏr'ik). An order in Architecture.
doth (duth; not dŏth). Third person of do.
drachma (drăk'mă). A coin, a weight.

Dræseke (drā'e-sēke). Johann Heinrich Bernhardt Dræseke.
Druid (drōō'id). A Celtic priest.
Druses (drū'sēs). A sect of religionists in Syria.
duad (dū'ad). Number two in Pythagorean system.
due guard (dū' gärd). Mode of recognition.
Dupaty (du'pă-ty). Louis Emanuel Charles M. Dupaty.
Dyaus (dy'aus). Sanskrit for sky. Bright, exalted.
Dyena Sore (dy'ē-nă so-ré). A Masonic romance by Van Meyern.

eastward (east'ward; not east'ard). Direction of the East.
Ebal (ĕ'băl). Literally, bare. Son of Shobal.
Eban Bohan (ĕ'băn bō'hăn). A witness stone set up by Bohan.
Eblis (ĕb'lis). Arabic for Prince of Apostate Angels.
Ecbatana (ĕc-băt'ă-nă). Capital of Media.
ecossais (ĕ'cŏs-sāis; ā'cōs-sais).
ecossism (ĕ'cŏs-sĭsm).
edicts (ē'dikts). Decrees by an authority.
eheyeh (ĕ-hĕ'yĕh). I am that I am.
Elai beni almanah (ĕ'lă-ī bĕn-i ăl-mă'năh). Third Degree A. A. Scottish Rite.
Elchanan (ĕl-chăn'ăn; āl-kănă'n).
Eleazar (ĕl-e-ā'zar). Son of Aaron.
Electa (e-lĕk'tā). An eminent woman of Judea.
eleemosynary (el-e-moz'ĭ-na-rĭ). Relating to charity.
Eleham (ĕl'ĕ-ham). See *Elchanan*.
Elephanta (ĕl-ē-phăn'ta). Ancient temple in Gulf of Bombay.
Eleusinian (ĕ'leū-sĭn'ĭ-an). Mysteries of ancient Athenian religion.
Eleusis (e-lū'sis). An ancient Grecian city.
Eliasaph (e-lī'a-saf). A Levite.
Elihoreph (ĕlĭ-hŏ'rĕph). One of Solomon's secretaries.
Elohim (ĕl-ō'hĭm). The Creator.
El Shaddai (el shād'dā-ē). The second name of God in the Bible.
elu (ĕl'u). See *Elus*.
Elul (ĕl'ŭl). Twelfth civil month of Jewish year.
elus (ĕl'ūs). Elected.
Elysium (e-lizh'ĭ-um). A place of happiness.
emeritus (ĕ-mĕr'ĭ-tŭs). One who has served out his time.
emeth (ĕ'mĕth). Integrity, fidelity, firmness.
Emir (a'mĭr). An Arabic counselor.
emounah (ĕ-mou'năh). Fidelity, truth.
empyrean (em-pĭ'rē-an). The highest Heaven.
emunah (ĕ-mū'năh). Fidelity to one's promises.
encyclical (ĕn-cy'clĭ-cal). Circular, sent to many places and persons.
en famille (ĕn fă-mĭlle'; en fă-meēl).
enochian (ĕ-nō'chi-an; ĕ-nō'kee-an). Relating to Enoch.
En Soph (ĕn' sŏph).
ephod (ĕ'phŏd). Sacred vestment of the high priest.
eons (e'ŏns). Divine spirits in intermediate state.
Eostre (e-os'tre). Easter.
Ephesus (ĕf'ē-sus). An ancient city of Asia.
Ephraim (ē'fra-im). A tribe of Israel.
epistle (ē-pis'l). A letter, a missive.
epitome (ē-pĭt'o-me). A summary.
epopt (e'pŏpt). An eye-witness.
eques (ĕ'quēs). Signifying knight.
equitas (ĕk'wĭ-tās). Equity.
Eranoi (e'ră-nŏ'ĭ). Friendly societies among the Greeks.
erica (e-rī'că). A sacred plant among the Egyptians.
Erosch (a-rōsh'). The Celestial Raven.
errand (ĕr'rand). A commission.
erratum (ĕr-ra'tum). An error in writing.
Esar Haddon (ē-sar hăd'don). A king of Assyria.
esoteric (ĕs'o-tĕr'ic). That which is taught to a select few.
esperance (ĕs'pē-rănce; ĕs'pē-rănse).
esquire (es-kwīr'). An armor-bearer.
esrim (ĕz'rim). The Hebrew number twenty.
Essenes (ĕs'sĕn-ēs; es'sen-ēes). A Jewish sect.
Esther (ĕs'ter). Wife of King Ahasuerus.
Ethanim or Tishri (ĕth'a-nĭm). The seventh Hebrew month.
Eumolpus (eū-mōl'pūs). A king of Eleusis.
eunuch (eū'nŭch). Prohibited candidates.
eureka (ū-rē'ka). I have found it.
European (ū-rŏ-pe'an). Relating to Europe.
Evates (ē-vă'tes). 2d Degree in the Druidical system.
Eveilles, Secte des (ē-vĕil-lĕs, sĕct-e dĕs; ē-vā-ēā). Bright, enlightened.
Evergeten Bundder (ē'vĕr-gē'ten būnd'dĕr). Secret order similar to the *Illuminati*.
Evora (ē-vŏ-ră). Knights of. A military order.
exalt (egz-awlt). To elevate.
examine (egz-am'ĭn). To scrutinize.
example (egz-am'pl). To be imitated.
Excalibar (ex-căl'i-băr). King Arthur's famous sword.
excellent (eks-sel-lent). Admirable.
executive (egz-ek'ū-tiv). An executor of the laws.
exempt (egz-emt'). Not subject.
exist (egz-ist'). The state of being.
exordium (egz-or'dĭ-um). The introduction.
exoteric (ĕx'o-tĕr'ic). Public, not secret.
expert (eks'pert). An experienced person.
expiration (eks-pĭ-rā'shun). A breathing out.

extempore (eks-tem'pō-re). Without previous study.
Ezekiel (ē-zē'ki-el). A Hebrew prophet.
ezel (ĕ'zĕl). Division, separation.

Familien Logen (fă-mil'ĭ-en lōgen). A family lodge, private.
Fanor (făn'or). Name given to the Syrian Mason.
fasces (făs'cēs). Speeches or records done up in a roll.
fealty (fē'al-ty). Loyalty.
February (feb'rōō-a-rĭ). Second month in the Calendar.
Feix-Feax (fe-ĭx'-fe-ăx'). Signifying School of Thought.
fendeurs (fĕn-deūrs; făn-deūr).
fervency (fūr'ven-cy). Devotion.
feuillants (feu-ĭl-lănts; feu-iăn-ts).
fiat lux (fē'at lux). Let there be light.
fiat justitia ruat cœlum (fē'at jŭs-tĭ-shĭ-a rū'ăt sē-lŭm). Let justice be done though the heavens fall.
fidelity (fĭ-del'ĭ-tĭ). Faithfulness.
Fides (fī'dēs). A Roman goddess. Faith.
fiducial (fĭ-dū'cĭ-al). Confiding trust.
fillet (fĭl'let). Head-band.
finance (fĭ-nănce'). Revenue of a person or state.
forehead (fŏr'ed). The front of the skull.
forest (fŏr'est; not for'ist). A large tract of wood.
frankincense (frănk'in-sĕnse). An odorous resin.
frater (frā'ter). Latin for Brother.
freimaurer (freī-maur'ĕr; fri-mou'rer). A builder of walls.
Frères Pontives (frĕres pŏn-tives; frāres pŏn-tives).
friendship (frend'ship). Personal attachment.
frieze (freez). The entablature, between architrave and cornice.
fylfot (fȳl'fŏt). An ancient symbol.

gabaon (gă'bā-ōn). A high place.
gabor (gă'bor). Strong.
Gabriel (ga'bri-el). An archangel.
Gaedicke (găed'ĭcke). Johann Christian Gădicke.
Galahad (gă'lă-hăd). A corruption of Gilead.
G. A. O. T. U. (G. A. O. T. U.). Great Architect of the Universe.
Gareb (gă'reb). A Hebrew engraver.
Garimout (găr'i-mŏut). Corruption of Garimond or Garimund.
garinus (gă'rĭ-nus). A standard-bearer.
gavel (găv'el). A working tool of an Entered Apprentice.
Gebal (gē'băl). A city of Phœnicia. Border, hilly.
Gedaliah (gē-dal'iăh). Son of Pashur.
Gemara (gē-mă'ră). See *Talmud*.
generalissimo (gen-ĕr-al-ĭs'si-mō). Second officer in command of K. T.
geometry (je-om'ē-trē). A science of magnitudes.
Gethsemane (geth-sem'a-nĕ). A garden near Jerusalem.
Gershon (gūr'shon). A son of Levi.
ghemoul (gē'mul). A step of the Kadosh ladder.
ghemoul binah thebounah (ghe'moul bĭ'-nah thē-boū'nah). Prudence in the midst of vicissitude.
gibeah (gĭb'e-ah). Literally, height.
giblim (gib'lim). Stonesquarer.
Gilead (gĭl'e-ad). The Syrian mountains.
gnostics (gnŏs'tics; nŏs'tiks). Superior or celestial knowledge.
God (God; not Gawd).
Godfrey de St. Aldemar (god'fry de san aldemar). One of the founders of ancient Knights Templarism.
Goethe (gōe'thē). John Wolfgang von Goethe.
goetia (gō-e'tiă; go-ē'sha).
Golgotha (gol'go-tha). Name given to Calvary by the Jews.
gomel (gō'mĕl). Reward.
Gormogons (gōr'mō-gons). A society opposing Freemasonry.
Gomorrah (gom-ŏr'ra). Name of a Hebrew city.
gonfalon (gŏn'făl-ŏn'). Ecclesiastical banner.
Gordian (gor'dĭ-an; not gord'yan).
gorgeous (gor'jus). Magnificent.
Gothic (gŏth'ic). A style of Architecture.
Gravelot (grăv'ē-lot). One of the three ruffians.
Gugomos (gū'gō-mŏs). Baron von Gugomos.
Guibs (gibz). A ruffian in the Scottish Rite.
guillemain (guil'lĕ-māin; gē'ye-māin).
guttural (gŭt'tūr-ăl). Pertaining to the throat.
gymnosophists (gȳm-nŏs'ō-phists). Signifying "naked sages."

Habakkuk (hăb'ak-kŭk). Love's embrace. A Jewish prophet.
Habin (hăb'ĭn). Initiate of 4th Degree, Mod. Fr. R.
Habramah (hăb'ră-măh). Used only in France.
Hadeases (hă-dēes'ēs). Traditions handed down by Mohammed.
Hafedha (hăf'ĕd-hă). Second of four gods of Arab tribe of Ad.
Haggai (hăg'gā-ī). A Hebrew prophet.
hah (hăh'). Hebrew definite article "the."
hail (hāil). Whence do you hail?
hale (hāle'). To hide.
Hallelujah (hăl-le-lū'yă). Praise ye Jehovah.
Hamaliel (hăm-ă'lĭ-el). The angel of Venus.
Haphtziel (hăpht'zĭ-el; hăf-zi-el).

Harnouester (hărn-ouest-er; harn-west-er).
Harodim (har'ō-dīm). Princes in Masonry.
haruspices (hă'rŭs-pī'cēs). Implying a soothsayer or aruspice.
haupt-hutte (hăupt-hŭtte; hoŭt-hŭte).
hautes grades (hăutes grades; hō-gră-d).
heal (hēal'). To make legal.
heaven (hĕv'n). The abode of bliss.
hecatomb (hĕc'ă-tŭm). A sacrifice of a hundred oxen.
heptagon (hĕp'ta-gŏn). A plane figure of seven equal sides.
Hermaimes (hĕr-măimes). A corruption of Hermes.
Hermandad (hĕr-măn-dăd). "Spanish Brotherhood."
Hermes (hĕr'mēz). The Greek God, Mercury.
Herodoin (hĕr'ō-dŏin). Mythical mountain in Scotland.
hesed (he'sĕd). Literally, kindness.
hibbut-hakkeber (hĭb'bŭt-hăk'kē-ber). Beating of the sepulcher.
Hieronymites (hī'e-rŏn'y-mītes). Hermit Order of the 14th century.
Hierophylax (hi'ē-ro-phy'lăx). Guardian of the holy vessels and vestments.
Hindu (hĭn'du). A native of Hindustan.
Hiram Abba (hī'ram ab'bā; not Abi). Hiram the Master, Father.
Hiram-Abif (hiram-ăb-ĭf'). A widow's son of the tribe of Naphtali.
ho la tai (hō lä tä-e). He has suffered.
homage (hŏm'ăj). Reverential worship.
Hor (hŏr). The mountain on which Aaron died.
Horeb (hō'rĕb). The Mount Sinai range.
horizon (hō-ri'zun; not hor'i-zŏn). Visible boundary of earth.
hoschea (hŏs-chē-a). A corruption of the word huzza.
Hospitalers (hŏs'pĭ-tal-erz). A branch of the Templar Knighthood.
humble (hum'bl). Lowly of mind.
huzza (hŭz-ză'). Acclamation.
hypotenuse (hi-pot'e-nŭs). The longest side of a right angle triangle.
Hystaspes (his-tăs'pēz). Father of the Persian King, Darius.
hyssop (hĭs'up). A species of caper.

iatric (ī-ăt'ric). Searchers after universal medicine.
i-colm-kill (ic'ŏlm-kill'; ik'ŏm-kil').
iconoclasts (ī-cŏn'ō-clăsts). Image-breakers.
iconology (ī'con-ŏl'o-gy). Teaching the doctrine of images.
Iesus Hominum Salvator (yā'sŭs hom'e-nŭm säl-vā'tor). Jesus, savior of men.
Iesus Nazerenus Rex Judaeorum (yā'sŭs nä-ză-ră-nŭs rĕx jū-dē-ō-rŭm). Jesus of Nazareth, King of the Jews.
ih-ho (ĭh-hō). See *Ho-hi.*
Ijar (ī-jăr). Eighth month of the Hebrew year.
illuminati (ĭl-lū'mi-nă'tī). Immaculate.
imaum (ĭm'aum; im'ŏm).
Immanuel (im-man'u-el). God with us.
immortality (im-mor-tal'ĭ-tĭ). Unending existence.
impious (im'pĭ-us). Profane, wicked.
impostor (im-pŏs'tor; not im-paw'stor). A deceiver.
incomparable (in-kŏm'pa-ra-bl). Transcendent, peerless.
Indian (in'dĭ-an). Pertaining to the Indies.
ineffable (in-ĕf'fă-bl). Unutterable.
inexplicable (in-eks'plĭ-ka-bl). Without explanation.
in hoc signo vinces (in hŏk sĭg'nō vĭn'sēz). By this sign thou shalt conquer.
initiate (in-ĭ'shē-ăt). Performing the first rite.
inquiry (in-kwī'rĭ). Search for information.
institute (in'stĭ-tūt). Erect, establish.
interesting (ĭn'ter-ĕst-ing). Engaging the attention or curiosity.
Ionic (I-on'ic). A style of Architecture.
irrevocable (ir-rev'ō-ca-bl). Incapable of being recalled.
Ischngi (ĭsch'n-gī). One of the five masters of Solomon.
ish chotzeb (ĭsh-chōtzĕb). Literally, hewers.
Ishmael (ĭsh-ma'ĕl). God is hearing.
ish sabal (ĭsh-să'băl). Men of burden.
ish sodi (ĭsh-sŏ'dĭ). A select master.
isiac tables (ĭs'ĭ-ăc tă'bles). A flat rectangular bronze plate.
Islamism (ĭz'lam-ĭzm). The Moslem faith.
isolate (ĭz'ō-lāte). Place by itself.
Israfeel (ĭs'ră-fēel). Trumpeting Angel of Resurrection.
Isis (ī-sis). Sister of Osiris. Beneficent Goddess of Egypt.
Ithamar (ĭth'ă-măr). Youngest son of Aaron.
Itratics (ī-tră'tics). A society of adepts.
Izads (ĭz'ăds). The twenty-eight creations of Ormudz.

jaaborou hammain (jă-ăb'ō-rōu hăm-mă'ĭn). A word of covered significance.
jabesh (jä'băsh). Dry place.
jabescheh (jă-bĕs'chĕh). The dry soil.
Jabulum (jă'bū-lŭm). Corruption of Jū-bē-lŭm'.
jachin (jă'kĭn). To establish. A pillar in Solomon's temple.
Jachinai (jă'chĭn-ăĭ; jă'kin-ăhĭ). Corruption of Shekinah.
jacinth (jă'sinth). A mineral gem of value.
Jacques de Molay (shăk' dā mō-lăy'). Past Grand Master of the Templars.
Jafuhar (jă'fū-hăr). Synonym for Thor.
Jah (jăh). Triliteral name of God.
jaina (jă-ĭ'nă). A cross adopted by the Jainas.

Jamblichus (jăm'blĭ-chus). A Neoplatonic philosopher.
James de Molay (james dē mōlāy). Last Grand Master of ancient K. T.
Jared (jä'red). Descendant of Seth. Lived 962 years.
jasher (jă'sher). Upright.
jasper (jăs'per). Fourth stone in the breastplate.
Jebusites (jeb'ū-sites). Natives of Jebus (afterward Jerusalem).
Jehoshaphat (jē-hŏsh'a-făt). A valley east of Jerusalem.
Jeksan (jĕk'săn). Son of Abraham and Keturah.
Jeroboam (jĕr-o-bō'am). First king of the ten tribes.
Jetzirah Sepher (jĕt-zī'rah sē'pher). A traditional document.
Jeva. Jova. Jua. (jă'vä. jō'vä. jū-ä.). Abbreviations and corruptions of Jehovah.
Jezeeds (jĕz' ēēds). Jah is honor.
Joabert (jō-ă'bert). The chief favorite of Solomon.
Joah (jō'ah). Jah is brother.
Jobel (jō'bĕl). A name of God.
Jochebed (jō-che'bĕd; jō-kē'bĕd). Jah is honor.
Jod he vau he (yŏd hā vau hē). Hebrew letters spelling Jehovah.
Joha (jō'ha). Jah is living.
Jo-ha-ben (yō-hä'ben). A mystical word.
Jokshan (jŏk'shăn). Fowler. Second son of Abraham.
Joppa (jŏp'pa). Seacoast city, 37 miles from Jerusalem.
Jordan (jŏr'dan). A tortuous river of Palestine.
Josedech (jō'sē-dek). Jah is righteous. Father of Jeshua.
Joshua (josh'u-a). High priest who rebuilt the temple.
Jua (jū'a). Corrupted form of Tetragrammaton.
Jubal (jū'bal). Shout, blow. Son of Adah.
Jubalcain (jū'bal-cāīn). Founder of the science of music.
Jubala (jū-bē-lă'). First ruffian.
Jubalo (jū-bē-lō'). Second ruffian.
jubela-o-m (jū-bē-lă'ō'm'). Assassins.
Jubelum (jū-bē-lŭm). Third ruffian.

Kaaba (kă-ă'bă; kă-ăr'bar). Holy temple of Mecca.
kabbala (kăb'bă-lă'). A mystical philosophy of the Jews.
kabbalistic (kab'bal-is-tic). Pertaining to the mysteries.
kadosh (kă'dosh). Holy. Same as *Kedesh*.
Kadiri (kă'dĭ-rĭ). An Arabian secret society.
kamea (kă'mē-ă). An amulet.
Karmatians (kăr-mă'tiăns). A Mohammedan sect.
Kasideans (kă'sĭ-dē'ans). Latinized spelling of Chasidim.
Katharsis (kă-thăr'sis). Ceremony of purification.
Khem (khĕm). The Egyptian deity, Amon.
Khepra (khē'pră). An Egyptian deity.
kher-heb (khĕr'hĕb). Master of Ceremonies.
Khesvan (khĕs'văn). Second month of Jewish civil year.
Khetem el Nabiim (khē'tĕm el năb-īim; kē'-tĕm el nahb-īim).
khon (khŏn). The dead. Subject to examination.
khotbah (khŏt'băh). Mohammedan Confession of Faith.
Khurum-Abba (khū-rŭm-ăb'bă). Hiram Abba.
ki (kī). In old Ritual of A. A. Scottish Rite.
Kidron (kĭd'ron). Turbid water. A brook near Mount of Olives.
Kislev (kĭs'lev). The third Hebrew month.
Knewt-neb-s (knewt'nĕb-s; nūte'nĕbs).
Kohath (kō'hăth). Assembly. Ancestor of Moses.
Kojiki (kŏ'jĭ'ki). The ancient religion of Japan.
konx ompax (kŏnx ŏm'păx). Definition uncertain.
Korah (kō'răh). Baldness. A son of Esau.
Koran (kō'răn). The reading. The Moslem Bible.
Krishna (krĭsh'nă). A Trimurti in Hindu religious system.
Kulma (kŭl'mă). Hindustani Confession of Faith.
kum kivi (kūm kĭ-vĭ). Arise! and kneel!
kun (kūn). The creative fiat of God.

laanah (lă'a-năh). Wormwood.
Labarum (lă'bă-rum). Monogram of Christ.
laborare est orare (lă'bō-ră'rē est ō-ră'rē). To labor is to pray.
lacorne (lā-corne'; lă'kor'nă').
lakak deror pessah (lă'kăk dĕr'or pĕs'săh). Liberty of passage and thought.
Lalande (lă'lănde'). See *Delalande*.
Lamaism (lă'mă-ism). Religion of Tibet and Mongolia.
Lamma Sabactani (lăm'mă să'băc-tă'nĭ). Used in French Rite of Adoption.
Lanturelus (lăn'tū-rē'lŭs). Instituted in 1771.
lapicida (lă'pĭ-cī'dă). A stone-cutter.
Larudan, Abbé (lă'rū-dan, ăb'bē). Author of a libellous work.
latomia (lă'tō-mē'ă). A stone quarry.
latres (lă-trĕs'). A brick.
Laus Deo (läw-ŭs dā'ō). God be praised.
laurel (lŏr'el). An evergreen shrub.

Lebanon (lĕb'a-non). The forest mountains in Syria.
lechangeur (lĕ-chăn'geur).
Lefranc (lĕ-frănc'). A bitter enemy of Freemasonry.
legate (lĕg'ate). An embassador.
legend (lĕj'end). A fable.
Lehrling (lĕhr'ling). German for Entered Apprentice.
Lemanceau (lĕ-man-ceău'; lā-man-so').
leontica (lē-on'tĭ-că). Ancient sacrifices in honor of the sun.
lepage (lĕ-pāge'; lĕ-pa'j).
leucht (leūcht). A Masonic charlatan.
level (lĕv'el). An instrument to find a horizontal line.
Levitikon (lĕ-vit'ĭ-kŏn). The spurious Gospel of St. John.
Libanus (lĭ-bă'nus). The Latin for Lebanon.
libation (lī-bā'shun). A pouring out of liquor.
Liber (lī'bĕr). The Book.
libertas (lib-er-tas'). Liberty.
libertine (lĭb'er-tīn). A dissolute, licentious person.
licht (lĭcht). Light.
Lichtseher (lĭcht'sē-hĕr). A mystical sect of the 16th century.
linear triad (lĭn'ē-ăr trī'ad). A figure in some old floor cloths.
listen (lis'n). To attend and hear.
Livre d'Architecture (lī'vre d'ăr'chi-tec-tur; lī'vr d'ar'she-tek-tū-r).
Livre d'Or (lī'vre d'or; lē'vr-d'or). The Book of Gold.
lodge (lŏdg). A place of shelter.
logos (lŏg'ŏs). The word.
Loki (lō'kī).
lotos (lō'tus). An Egyptian aquatic plant.
Louveteau (loū-vĕ-teău'; loū-v-to').
loyal (loi-al). Devoted, faithful.
Lubec (lū'bĕk). A town in Germany.
Lumiere la Grande (lū'mīere lă grăndē). The Grand Light.
lux e tenebris (lŭx ē ten'ē-bris). Light out of darkness.
lux fiat et lux fit (lŭx fī'at ĕt lŭx fit). Let there be light, and there was light.
luz (lŭz). Literally, bending, curve.

Maacha (mă-ă-chă; mă-ăr'kă).
Macbenac (măc-bē-năc). See *Mac.*
Maccabees (măc'că-bēēs). A heroic Jewish family.
macconniere rouge (mă-çŏn'nē-rie rouge; mă-sŏn-nē-rē rūge).
Macconnieke Societeiten (mă-çon'niē-ke sŏ-ci'e-teī'ten). Dutch Masonic clubs.
macerio (mă'ce-rī'ō). This word is now obsolete.
macio (mă'cī-o; mă'she-o).
maconetus (mă'cŏn-ē'tŭs; mă'son-e-tus).
maconne (mă'çon-ne; ma-son-e).
macrocosm (măc'ro-cŏsm; ma'cro-cŏsm). Creating the universe.
maczo (măc'zō). A mason, a constructor of walls.
Magi (mă'gī; mă'ji). Wise Men of Persia.
magna est veritas et praevalebit (măg'nă ĕst vĕr'e-tas ĕt prē'vā-lā-bĭt). Truth is mighty and will prevail.
magus (mă'gŭs; mă-gŭs).
mah (mäh). Hebrew pronoun what.
Mahabharata (mă'hă-bhă'ră-tă). A Sanskrit poem.
Mahadeva (mă'hă-dē'vă). "The Great God."
Mahakasyapa (mă'hă-kă'sy-ă-pă'). Disciple of Buddha Sakyamuni.
maher-shalal-hash-baz (mă'hĕr shă-lăl hăsh-baz). Make haste to the prey, fall upon the spoil.
Mahomet (mă-hŏm'et). The Moslem prophet.
mah shim (mä'shēm). A standard-bearer.
Maitre Macon (māī'trĕ mă-cōn'; mē'tr mă-sŏn').
maitresse agissante (māī'trĕsse). Acting mistress.
maitrise (māī'trīse). Without an English equivalent.
Malach (mă-lăch'). An angel.
Malachi (măl-ă'chī). Messenger of Job.
Malakoth (măl'a-kŏth). The angelic messenger.
Malek Adhel Sayfeddia (mă'lek' ăd-ĕl săf-ĕd-dĭa). The just king who holds the Sword of Faith.
Malta (măl'tă). An island in the Mediterranean Sea.
Manasseh (ma-năs'să). A tribe of Israel.
manes (mă'nēs). Souls of the dead.
Manichaeans (măn'i-chē'ans). Also termed Gnostics.
Manu (măn'ū). Corresponding to the word West.
Marchesvan (măr-kesh'van). The second Jewish month.
Marduk (măr'duk). A victorious warrior-god.
Masora (măs-ŏ'ră). A Hebrew work on the Bible.
Masoretic points (mă'sŏ-rĕt'ic points). Vowel signs.
Massonus (măs-sŏ'nŭs). Mason.
Master (măs-ter). Lord, Chief, Prince.
mathoc (mă'thŏc). Amiability.
mausoleum (mau-sŏ-lē'ŭm). A stately sepulcher.
maut (măut). Mort.
megacosm (mĕg'a-cŏsm). An intermediate world.
mehen (mē'hĕn or, may-hĕn).
mehour (mē'hoūr or, may-hūre).
meister (meīst'ĕr). German for master.
Melchizedek (mĕl-chīz'ē-dĕk). King of Salem.

Melech (mĕ'lĕck; mă'lak).
Melesino, Rite of (mĕl'es-ĭ'nō). Scarcely known out of Russia.
Melita (mĕl-ĭ'tă). Ancient name of island of Malta.
memento mori (mē-mĕn'tō mō-re). Remember death.
memory (mem'ō-re not mem'ry). Mental power to reproduce thoughts.
Menatzchim (mĕ-năt'chim). Expert Master Masons.
Menu (mĕ'nū). Son of Brahma.
Merari (mē-rä're). Heb., Bitter. Youngest son of Levi.
mer-sker (mĕr' skĕr). Space in which the sun moves.
Meshia Meshiane (mĕsh'ĭ-a mĕsh'ĭ-āne). Corresponding to Adam and Eve.
Mesopolyte (mĕs'ō-pō-ly'te). 4th Degree of German Union of XXII.
mesouraneo (mĕ'sōu-ră-nĕ'ō). I am the center of heaven.
Metusael (mĕ-tu'să-el). Heb. quarryman, one of the assassins.
mezuza (mĕz'ū-ză). Third principle of Judaism.
microcosm (mī-crō-cosm). See *Man*.
Minos (mī'nos). The lawgiver of Crete.
mistletoe (mĭz'l-tō). An evergreen plant.
Mithras (mĭth'răs). The principal deity of the Persians.
miter (mī'ter). The covering of a bishop's head.
Mizeph (mĭz'pĕ). A city in Gilead.
Mizraim (mĭz'raim). Rite of, originated at Milan in 1805.
Moabon (mō-ă'bŏn; mō-ah'bŏn).
Moloch (mŏl'ok). The deity of the Ammonites.
Montfauçon, Prior of (mont'fău-çon', prior of). One of the two traitors.
monument (mon'ū-ment). A memorial.
Mopses (mŏp'sĕs). A pretended name for Masonry.
Moriah (mō-rī-ă). The hill on which the Temple was built.
mortal (mor'tal). Subject to death.
mosaic (mō-să-ĭc). Variegated, tessellated.
Moslem (mŏz'lem). Mohammedan.
Mot de Semestre (mōt' dĕ se-mes'tre; mō' de se-mest-r).
murderer (mur'der-er not murd'rer). Assassin.
mystagogue (mȳs'tă-gŏgue'). One who makes or conducts an initiate.
mystes (mys'tĕs). To shut the eyes.
mythology (mī-thol'ō-ji). The science of myths.

Naamah (nă-ă'măh). The daughter of Lamech.
Nabaim (nă'bă-im). See *Schools of the Prophets*.
Nadab (nā'dăb). High priest of the Persians.
naked (nă'kĕd). Unclothed, defenseless.
Naphthali (năf'ta-lī). One of Jacob's sons.
narbonne (năr-bonne).
Naymus Grecus (nāy'mūs grē'cūs). Possible corruption of Magna Græcia.
Nazarene (năz'ă-rene). An inhabitant of Nazareth.
Nebuchadnezzar (nĕb-uk-ăd-nĕz'zar). A King of Babylon.
Nebuzaradan (nēb-ū-zăr'ă-dăn). An officer under Nebuchadnezzar.
necum (nē'kōōm). Vengeance.
nec proditur, nec proditur, innocens ferat (nĕk prō'dĭ-tor, nĕk prō'dĭ-tor, ĭn-nō-sĕnz fē-răt). Not the traitor, not the traitor, let the innocent bear it.
neder (nā'dĕr). Promise.
Neith (nĕĭth). Egyptian synonym for Greek Athené.
nekam (nĕ'kăm). Signifying vengeance.
nekamah (nĕ'kă-măh). Same as nekam.
neocorus (nē'ō-cō'rūs). The Guardian of the Temple.
ne plus ultra (nā plus ŭl'trä). Nothing beyond.
ne varietur (nā vă-rī-e'tūr). Unless changed.
nicotiates (nĕ-cō'tĭ-a'tes; nĕ-cō'tĭ-ah'tes).
Nihongi (nī-hon'gī). Chronicles of Nihon.
nil nisi clavis (nĭl nīsī clăvis). Nothing but the key is wanting.
Nisan (nī'san). First month of Jewish year.
noachidæ (nō-ach'ĭ-dæ). Descendants of Noah.
noffodeli (nŏf'fō-dĕl'). An apostate Templar.
nonage (nŏn'aj). Under lawful age.
nonesynches (nŏnĕ-sȳn-chĕs). A corruption of Noonshun (luncheon).
nonis (nō'nĭs). A mystic word.
non nobis, Domine, non nobis, sed nomini tuo da gloriam (nŏn nō-bis, dŏm-ĭ-nē, nŏn nōbis, sĕd nŏm-in-ē tū-ō dă glō-rĭ-ăm). Not to us, O Lord! not to us, but to Thy name give the glory.
nornæ (nŏr'næ). Signifying Past, Present and Future.
notuma (nō-tūm). Anagram of Aumont.
Novice Maçonne (nŏvice ma-çon'ne; novice má-sŏn-né).
novitiate (nō-vish'e-āte). A person under probation.
nuk-pe-nuk (nŭk'pĕ-nŭk). "I am that I am."
Nyaya (nȳ-ă'yă). A system of ancient Hindu philosophy.
Nyctazontes (nȳc'tă-zŏn'tes). An ancient sect.

Oannes (ō-ăn'nes).
oath (ōth). Solemn affirmation.

obligatory (ob'lĭgā-to-rȳ). Binding in law or conscience.
obsequies (ob'sē-kwiz). Funeral rites or solemnities.
occult (ok-kult'). Secret, unknown.
odious (o'dĭ-us). Deserving hatred.
off (off not awf). Away from.
offer (of'fer not aw'fer). Present for acceptance.
office (of'fis not aw'fis). Assumed duties or business.
officiate (of-fish'ĭ-āt). To act as an officer.
often (of'n not of'ten). Frequent.
oheb Eloah (ō-hĕb e-lō'ā). Love of God.
oheb karobo (ō-hĕb kā-rō'bō). Love of neighbor.
olibanum (ol-ĭ-bā'num). An aromatic sap, frankincense.
omega (ō-mē'gā). Last letter of Greek alphabet.
omer (ō'mĕr). A Hebrew measure.
omnia tempus alit (ŏm'nĭ-ă tĕm'pŭs ă'lĭt). Time heals all things.
On (ŏn'). A name for Jehovah among Egyptians.
Onech (ō'nĕch). After Enoch or Phenoch (the Phenix).
onyx (ō'nix). A stone of the breastplate.
Ophites (ō'phītes). Brotherhood of the Serpent.
oral (ō'ral). Verbal, by word of mouth.
ordo ab chao (ŏr'dō ăb chā'o). Order out of chaos.
oriflamme (ō'rĭ-flamme). Ancient banner of the Counts of Vezin.
Orion (o-rī'un). One of the constellation of stars.
ormudz and ahriman (ŏrmŭdz and ăh-rĭ-măn). Good and evil. Darkness and light.
Ornan (ŏr'nan). Strong. Whose threshing floor became David's altar.
Osiris (ō-sī'ris). Chief god of old Egyptian mythology.
Oterfut (ō'ter-fŭt). The assassin at the west gate.
Otreb (ō'trĕb). Pseudonym of Rosicrucian Michel Mayer.
ouriel (ou'rĭ-ĕl).
overseer (o-ver-sēr). Nutsach. One who inspects.
ozee (ō'zēē). Acclamation.
Oziah (o'zi-āh). A Prince of Judah.

Pachacamac (păch'ā-cā'măc). Peruvian for Creator of the Universe.
Paganis, Hugo de (pă-gă'nĭs, hŭgō de). Latinized name of Hugh de Payens.
Palestine (pal-es'tīne). Commonly called The Holy Land.
palladium (pal-lā'di-um). That which is an effectual defense.
Paracelsus (pă-ră-cĕl'sŭs). Degree in MSS. collections of Peuvret.
parent (păr'ent). One who begets offspring.
parian (pā'ri-an). A fine quality of marble.
Parikchai Agrouchada (pa'rĭk-chă'ĭ a'groŭ-chă'dă). An occult scientific work of Brahmans.
parlirer (păr'lĭr-er). Spokesmen.
Parsees (pär'sēz). Followers of Zoroaster.
pas perdus (pás' pĕr-dŭs'). French name for room for visitors.
pastophori (păs'tō-phō'rī). Couch or shrine bearers.
pastos (păs'tos). Greek for couch.
patent (pat'ent). A letter securing certain rights.
pax vobiscum (pax vō-bes'cŭm). Peace be with you.
pectoral (pĕk'tō-ral). Pertaining to the breast.
pedal (pē'dal). Pēdes, the feet.
pedum (pē'dŭm). Literally, a shepherd's crook.
peetash (peēt'ăsh). The Demon of Calumny.
Peleg or Phaleg (pē'leg or fā'leg). Division. A son of Eber.
penance (pen'ance). Suffering as evidence of repentance.
pentacle (pĕn'tā-kl). Two intersecting triangles.
Pentateuch (pĕn'tā-tŭk). The five books of Moses.
perambulate (per-ăm'bu-lāte). To walk over.
periclyte (pĕr'ĭ-clȳte).
Perignan (pĕr'ig-năn). See *Elect of Perignan.*
Persian (per'shan). A country in Western Asia.
pestle (pes'tl). An instrument for pounding.
phaal chol (fā'äl kōl). Separated, driven apart.
Phainoteletian Society (phāi'nō-tē-le'tian). Founded at Paris in 1840.
pharaxal (phă'răx-ăl). Division and subsequent reunion.
Pharaoh (fā'ra-ō). A king, a sovereign.
pharaoschol (fā-rā-ōs'kōl). Congregated, reassembled.
Philalethes (phĭ'lā-lē'thēs). Literally, Friends of Truth.
Philistine (fĭ-lis'tĭn). An inhabitant of Philistia.
Philocoreites, Order of (phĭ'lō-cō-re'ĭ-tes). Established in French army in Spain in 1808.
phylacteries (phȳ-lac'ter-ies). Ornaments.
Picart's Ceremonies (pĭ'cart). By Bernard Picart.
pilaster (pĭ-las'ter). A partly projecting column.
pilier (pĭl'iĕr). A pillar or support of an edifice.
pinceau (pĭn'ceău; pin-so). To act as secretary.
Pirlet (pĭr'let). Organizer of Council of Knights of the East.
Pitaka (pĭt'a-ka). The Bible of Buddhism.

Pitris (pĭt'rĭs). Spirits.
planche tracee (plan'che trā-cēe). Designation for minutes in French Lodges.
pleiades (pley'a-dēz). A group of seven stars.
polkal (pŏl'kăl). Altogether separated.
Polycronicon (pŏlȳ-crŏn'i-cŏn). Latin Chronicle by Ranulf Higden.
pomegranate (pŏme'gran-ate). Adopted as the symbol of plenty.
Pomme Verte (pōmme vĕrtē; pō-m vĕr-t).
poniard (pŏn'yard). A small dagger.
pontifes frères (pŏn'ti-fēs frēres; pon'te-fēes frāres).
pontiff (pŏn'tiff). A high priest.
porch (porch not pawrch). A gate or entrance.
position (po-zish'un). Situation, station.
postulant (pŏs'tŭ-lănt). From Latin postulans —asking for.
potens (pō'tĕnz). Powerful.
potentate (pō'ten-tāt). One of high authority.
poursuivant (pour-su'ī-vănt; poor-su'e-van).
Praxoeans (prăx'ō-ēans). Followers of Praxeas.
prelate (prĕl'ate). A dignitary of the church.
precept (pre'sept). An injunction, mandate.
presentation (prĕz-en-ta'shun). Setting forth, a gift.
princeps (prĭn'cĕps). Chief.
progress (prog'res). Advancement.
proponenda (prō'pō-nen'dă). Subjects to be proposed.
propylæum (prŏp'y-lae'um). Court or vestibule in front of an edifice.
pro tempore (prō tĕm'pō-rē). For the present time.
protean (pro'tē-an). Assuming different shapes.
protocol (prō'tō-kŏl). The original writing.
provost (prŏv'ust). A presiding officer.
prudence (prū'dence). Wisdom applied to practice.
Psalms (sămz). A sacred song.
Psaterians (psăt-ē'rians). A sect of Arians.
pseudonym (pseū-dō-nym; sū'do-nim). False or fictitious name.
puissant (pū-is'sant). Powerful.
pulsanti operietur (pul-san'ti ōpē-rī-ē-tur). To him who knocks it shall be opened.
punjaub (pun-jaub'; pun-jawb).
puranas (pū-ră'nas). Text-books of worshipers of Vishnu.
Pursuivant (pŭr'sui-vant; per'swē-vant). Messenger.
Pythagoras (py-thag'o-ras). School of, supposed model of Masonry.

quadrivium and trivium (quăd-rĭv'i-um; triv'ī-um).
quaternion (quă-ter'nī-ŏn). The number four.
quetzialcoatl (quet'zi-ăl'coatl; kĕt'ze-al'cotl).

Rabbanaim (răb'bă-nă'ĭm). Chief of the architects.
rabbi (răb'bē). An eminent teacher.
rabbinism (răb'bĭn-ism). A Jewish system of philosophy.
rabboni (răb-bŏ'nī). My Rabbi. A most excellent Master.
Ragon (ră'gŏn). A noted Masonic writer of France.
Rahab (rä'ab). A name of Egypt.
Ramayana (ră'ma-yă'na). The great epic of ancient India.
raphodom (răf'ō-dŏm). A mystic word.
Ratisbon (răt'is-bon). A city of Bavaria.
razahbelsijah (rä-zäbĕl-sī'yă). A mystic word.
recognize (rĕk'ŏg-nīz). To know again.
recovery (rē-kuv'er-ī). Restoration.
rectitude (rek'tī-tūd). Straightness, justice.
recusant (rē-cū'sant). Insubordinate.
Rehoboam (rē-hō-bō'am). Son and successor of Solomon.
Rehum (rē-hŭm). A Persian officer.
rendezvous (ren'de-vōō). An appointed place.
requiem (re'kwī-em). A hymn for the dead.
research (re-serch'). Investigation, examination.
resplendens (rē-splen'danz). Resplendent.
restoravit pacem patri (re-stō-răv'it pă-sĕm pătrī). He restored peace to his country.
reverent (rev'er-ent). Expressing veneration.
revestiary (re-vĕst'ī-a-ry). Wardrobe, place for sacred vestments.
rex regum dominus dominorum (rex regum dŏm-ī-nŭs dominōrum). King of Kings and Lord of Lords.
Robelot (rō'bē-lŏt). A distinguished French Mason.
rose croix (rōse croīx; roz-crwa). Literally, Rose Cross.
Rosenkreuz, Christian (rō'sen-kreuz). See *Rosicrucianism*.
Rosicrucians (rŏs'i-crū'cians). A Brotherhood of the 14th century.
route (root). The course or way.
ruchiel (rūch'ī-el; rōōsh'e-el).

saadh (să'ădh). Literally, hosts.
sabaism (săb'a-ism). Worship of the sun, moon, and stars.
Sabaoth (să-bă'ōth). Jehovah of Hosts.
sabbal (săb-bal'). Mystic word, Scottish Rite.
Sabianism (săb'ī-an-ism). Same as *Sabaism*.
sacellum (să-cĕl'lum). A walled enclosure without roof.
sacerdotal (sas-er-dō'tal). Pertaining to the order of priests.
sacrifice (săk'rī-fīz). An offering.
Sadoc (să'dok). Heb., just. Father of Achim, ancestor of Jesus.

sadonias (sa-dŏ'ne-as). Significant word in the higher degrees.
sagitta (să-git'ta). The keystone of an arch.
Saint Adhabell (saint ad'hă-bell). Evidently meaning St. Amphibalus.
Saint Amphibalus (saint am'phĭ-bal'us).
Saint Nicaise (saint nĭ-caise). Title of a sensational Masonic work.
Sakinat (să'kĭ-năt). The Divine presence.
Sakti (săk'tĭ). The female energy of Siva.
Salah-eddin (să-läh-ed-deen'). King of Kings.
salix (săl'ĭx). Initials forming part of a sentence.
Salle des Pas Perdus (sällĕ des păs' per-dūs'). The Hall of the Last Steps.
Salsette (săl-sĕtte'). An island in the Bay of Bombay.
salute (sa-lūt'). To greet, to hail.
salutem (sal-ū'tĕm). Health, a Roman greeting.
Samaritan (sa-măr'ĭ-tan). Of the principal city of the Ten Tribes.
Samothracian (să-mŏ-thrā'cĭ-an). See *Mysteries of Cabiri.*
sanctum sanctorum (sănk'tūm sănk-tŏ-rūm). Holy of Holies.
san graal (săn grāăl). An emerald dish.
Sanhedrim (săn-he-drĭm). Highest judicial tribunal of the Jews.
sapicole (să'pĭ-cōle). Cited in the nomenclature of Fustier.
Saracens (săr'a-cens). Arabic followers of Mohammed.
sardius (sär'de-us). A precious stone of the breastplate.
sarsena (sar-sĕ'nă). Pretended exposition of Freemasonry.
Sat B'hai (săt b'hăi'; sot-b-hoi').
satrap (săt'rap or sa'trap). A local Eastern ruler.
scarabæus (skăr'ă-bē-us). An insect with wings cased.
schism (sizm). Division, separation.
schismatic (schĭs-măt'ĭc). Insubordinate Masons.
Schor-Laban (schor-lăban'). White Ox, or Innocence.
secretary (sek're-tă-rĭ). A superintending officer of records.
Sefidd Schamagan (sĕ-fĭdd schă'mă-gan). A secret Moslem society.
Sejjin (sĕj'jin). Arabic register of all the wicked.
selah (sĕ'lăh). A pause or musical note.
Selamu Aleikum (sĕ-la'mū ă'lĕi-kūm; selă'moo a'lĭ-koom).
semester (sĕ-mĕs'ter). Semi-annual word used only in France.
seneschal (sĕn'e-shal). A steward.
seniority (seen-yŏr'ĭ-ty). Priority, or superiority in rank.
sephiroth (sĕph'i-rŏth). From Saphiri—splendid.
seraphim (sĕr'ă-fim). An angel of the highest order.
serai (se-rä'e). A rest house.
Serapis (se-rä'pis). An Egyptian deity.
Sesh Bazzar (sĕsh baz-zär'). A name of Zerubbabel.
Sethos (sĕ'thŏs). A popular work published in 1731.
Shaddai (shăd-dă-ĭ). One of the names of God.
shalal shalom aba (shăl'äl shăl'ōm ăb'ba). He restored peace to his father.
shalash esrim (shăl'ăsh ĕz-rem). Twenty-third.
shamir (shăm'ĭr). The worm used for building the Temple.
Shastras (shăs'trăs). The sacred book of the Hindus.
Shaveh (shä'vä). A valley in Palestine.
Shealtiel (shē-ăl'te-el). Father of Zerubbabel, who led back the Jews from Babylon.
Shebat (shē-băt). Fifth month of Hebrew civil year.
shekel (shĕk'l). A Jewish coin. Value about 62 cents.
shekinah (shē-kĭ-năh). To dwell.
shelomoth (she'lŏ-mŏth). Peacefulness.
shelum lecka (shē-lūm leck'ă). Password of the Order of Felicity.
shem ham phorash (shem hăm fō'răsh). The unsolved mystery. The name.
shemitic (shĕm-it'ic). An historical religious division.
shesha (shĕ'shă). Free, noble.
shetharboznai (shē-thar-bŏz'nă-ĭ). See *Tatnai.* A Persian officer.
shibboleth (shĭb-bŏ'leth). An ear of corn. Stream of water.
shimshai (shims-shaĭ).
Shinar (shĭ'năr). Babylonia in its fullest extent.
shoulkain (shōul'kain). Stolkin, mentioned in A. A. S. R.
shrine (shrīn). A hallowed place.
shrub (shrub; not srub). A dwarf tree.
Shushan (shū'shan). The ancient capital of Persia.
sic transit gloria mundi (sĭk trăns'ĭt glōr'ia mūndĭ). Thus passes the glory of the world.
Sijel Al (sĭg'el ăl). Recording Angel in Islam.
Simeon (sĭm'e-on). One of the tribes of Israel.
Simorgh (sĭm'orgh). Guardian of the Persian mysteries.
Sinai (sĭ'năĭ). A mountain of Arabia.
sirat (sĭ'răt).
siroc (sĭ'rŏc). Signifies a shoe-latchet.
Sivan (sĭv'ăn). The ninth Hebrew month.

Smaragdine (sma-răg'dīne). Foundation of Hermetic knowledge.
Socius (sō'cī-ŭs). 6th Deg. of Order of Strict Observance.
Sofism (sō'fism). A mystical religious sect of Persia.
sojourn (sō'jurn). Temporary residence.
solemn (sŏl'em). Reverential, devout.
Solomon (sŏl'ō-mon). King of Israel.
solstice (sŏl'stis). The apparent stoppage of the sun.
solus (so'lus). Latin, alone.
Sorbonne (sŏr'bonne). College of theological professors in Paris.
southerly (sŭth'er-le). Toward the South.
spes mea in Deo est (spĕs me'a in deo' ĕst). My hope is in God.
squarmen (squăr'men). Companies of wrights, slaters, in Scotland.
sruti (srū'tī). Revelation.
stauros (stou'rus). A stake. Cross.
stibium (stĭb'i-um). Antimony.
Steinmetz (stĕin'mĕtz). German for stonemason.
St. Jean d'Acre (shăn dä'ker). The city Acca, taken by Richard I. in 1191 and given the new name.
stolkin (stŏl'kin). Inspector of the Tribe of Benjamin.
strength (strength; not strenth). Force, vigor.
Succoth (suc-kōth'). Heb., Booths. A place east of Jordan.
sultan (sŭl'tan). A Turkish sovereign.
superficies (sū'per-fĭsh-ēz). The surface, the face of a thing.
summoned (sŭm'mund; not sum'manzd). Commanded.
sword (sōrd; not sword). Military officer's weapon.
symbolic (sim-bŏl-ik). Relating to symbols.
synagogue (sĭn'a-gŏg). Place of Jewish worship.
synod (syn'od). A meeting, convention or council.
Syria (sĭr'i-ă). Heb., Aram. East of the Mediterranean.
systyle (sy̆s'ty̆le). An arrangement of columns.

Tabaor (tă'bā-or). A name of Edom.
tabernacle (tab'er-nă-kl). A temporary habitation.
tableau (tab'lō). A vivid representation.
Tadmor (tăd'mŏr). City of Palms.
talisman (tăl'iz-man). Magical charm.
talith (tăl'ĭth). An oblong shawl.
taljahad (tăl-jăh'ad). Angel of water.
Talmud (tăl'mud). The Hebrew laws and traditions.
Tamuz (tă'mūz). The tenth Jewish month.
tapestry (tap'es-trē). Woven hangings.
tarshatha (tăr-shă'thă). See *Tirshatha*.
tassel (tăs'sĕl). A pendant ornament.
tatnai (tăt'nā-ī). A Persian officer.
tau (täu). The last letter of Hebrew alphabet.
Taurus (täu'rŭs). Bull. A sign of the Zodiac.
tchandalas (tchăn'dăl-as). A class of pariahs.
Tebet (ta'bet). The fourth Jewish month.
tebeth (te'bĕth). Literally, winter.
Templum Hierosolymæ (tĕm'plum hī'ē-rō-sŏl'y-mæ). Latin for Temple of Jerusalem.
tenets (tĕn'ets). Dogmas, doctrines and principles.
tengu (tĕn-gū). Initials of a sentence.
Tensio-Dai-Sin (ten'sī-o-daī'-sĭn). A deity held in adoration by Japanese.
teraphim (tĕr'ă-fĭm). Household deities.
tessellated (tĕs'se-lā-ted). Ornament of a lodge.
tessera (tĕs'sĕ-ră). Tessera Hospitalis, token of the guest.
tetractys (tē-trăc'ty̆s). The number four.
tetradites (tĕt'ră-dītes). Believers in a Godhead of four persons.
tetragram (tĕt'ra-grăm). A four-letter word.
tetragrammaton (tet'ra-gram-ma-ton). Signifies a word of four letters.
Teutonic (tū-ton'ĭk). Relating to the ancient Germans.
Thammuz (thăm'mūz). Syrian god Adonis.
Thebet (thă'bet). Same as *Tebet*, above.
thebounah (the-bū'nă). A mystic word in Kadosh.
Theopaschites (thē'o-pas'chītes). Followers of Peter the Fuller.
theoricus (thē-or'ĭ-cŭs). 12th Degree of German Rose Croix.
Therapeutæ (thĕr'a-peū'tæ). Ascetic sect of Jews in first A. D.
theriog (thē'rī-ŏg).
theurgy (thē-ŭr'gy). Magic operated by celestial means.
thokath (thō'kăth). Strength.
thummim (thum'mim). See *Urim and Thummim*. Truth.
tiara (te-ā'rä). A crown. The Pope's triple crown.
Tiberius (tī-be're-ŭs). A city of Palestine.
tiluk (tī'lŭk). Impress upon forehead of Brahman.
timbre (tĭm'brē). Name given in France to a stamp.
tirshatha (tĭr-shă'thă). Title of Persian governors of Judea.
Tisri (tĭs'rī). The first Hebrew month.
Tito (tī-tō). A favorite of the King of Israel.
Torgau (tŏr-gău). A fortified town on the Elbe.
tortuous (tŏrt'ū-us). Deviating from rectitude.
traveler (trăv'el-er). One who journeys.
tredic (trĕd'ic). The ranking king in Scan. Mysteries.

trestle (trĕs'sel). The designing board.
triad (trī'ăd). The union of three objects.
tribute (trĭb'ūte). A subsidy or tax.
triglyphs (trī'glifs). An ornament in the Doric Order.
Triliteral (trī-lit'e-ral). Sacred name of God among Hindus.
Trimurti (trī-mŭr'tē). The Hindu Trinity.
Trinosophs (trī'nō-sophs). A lodge instituted at Paris in 1816.
Tripitaka (trī-pit'ă-kă). Canonical book of the Buddhists.
triune (trī'ūn). Three in one.
Tsaphiel (tsă'phī-el; să'fē-ĕl). The Luna angel.
tsedakah (tse-dă-kăh). First step of the mystical ladder.
tsidoni (tsī-dō-ni). An enquirer.
Tsoim (tsō'ĭm; sō-ĭm).
tuapholl (tū-ă-pholl). A term used by the Druids.
Tubal Cain (tū-băl cā'ĭn). Son of Lamech and Zillah.
tunic (tū'nĭk). The long undergarment of the clergy.
turcopolier (tŭr'cō-pō-li'er). Commander of cavalry.
Turquoise (tŭr-quōīse; tur-koă-z). A stone in breastplate.
Tuscan (tŭs'căn). An order of Architecture.
Typhon (tī'fōn). The Egyptian evil deity.
Tyrian (tĭr'e-an). Relating to Tyre.

unaffiliated (ŭn-af-fil'ē-ā-ted). Not a member.
unhele (ŭn-hele'). To uncover or reveal.
unison (yū'ne-sun). Harmony, concord.
upadevas (ū'pă-de'văs).
Upanishad (ū'păn-ĭsh-ăd). Name for certain Sanskrit works.
ur (ūr). Fire, light, or spirit.
Uri (ū'rī). Heb., Enlightened. Son of Hur.
Uriel (ū'ri-el). God is light.
urim (ū'rĭm). Lights.
usage (yū'zij). Custom, use, habit.
Utopia (ū-tō'pe-a). Ideal perfection.
usurp (ū-zŭrp'). Seize and hold possession.

Vagao (vă'gă-ō). Found in French Rite of Adoption.
valorous (văl'or-oŭs). Brave, courageous.
vase (văz). An ornamental vessel.
Vashti (văsh'tē). Wife of Ahasuerus.
Veadar (vē'ă-dar). That is, the second Adar.
Vedas (vē'dăs). Sacred canon of the Hindus.
Vehm-gericht (vĕhm'-gĕr-ĭcht'). See *Secret Tribunal of Westphalia.*
verger (vĕr'jer). An attendant upon a dignitary.
veritas (ver'i-tas). Truth.
vesica pisces (vĕs'ī-ca pĭs-cis). The air-bladder of a fish.
Vespasian (ves-pa'sian).
vexillum belli (vĕx-il'lum bellī). A war flag.
vicegerent (vīs'gē-rent). An officer authorized to act for another.
Vielle-Bru (vī'elle brū). V-ie-l Brū, Rite of, established 1748.
vincere aut mori (vĭn'cé-rē ăut mori). To conquer or to die.
vineyards (vĭn'yărdz). A plantation of vines.
Vitra (vī'tră). A Mohammedan sect, established 1740.
viva voce (vē'vă vō'să). By word of mouth.
vivat (vī'văt). Vivat! vivat! vivat! Acclamation.
voishnuvus (vō-ĭsh'nū-vŭs).
volutes (vō'lūtz). A spiral ornament in Architecture.
vouch (vouch). To attest or bear witness.

Wahabites (wă'hă-bītes). Represents the opponents of Masonry.
warrant (wŏr'rant). Commission, authority.
Westward (west'ward; not west'urd). Toward the West.
Wilhelmsbad (wil'helms-băd). A city of Germany.
Wolfenbuttel (wōl-fen-bŭttel). A city of Lower Saxony.
worship (wŭr'ship). Title of honor. To adore.
worthy (wŭr'the). Estimable, possessing merit.

xerophagists (xē'ro-pha'gĭsts). Eaters of dry food.
Xinxe (xĭn'xe). The seat of the soul.
xysuthrus (xys'ū-thrŭs; zīs'ū-thrŭs).

Yah, Yeva, Yod (yā, yăvä, yŏd). Corrupt names of the Deity.
Yaksha (yăk'shă). Hindu deity.
yaveron hamaim (yă've-rōn hă'măim). The passage of the river.
Yezdegerdian (yĕz'dē-gĕr'dĭan). Pertaining to the era of Yezdegerd.
Yezidee (yĕz'i-dēe). A sect bordering on the Euphrates.
Yggdrasil (ygg-dră'sil). Sacred tree, Scandinavian mythology.
Y-ha-ho (y-hă'hō). Signifying the Eternal God.
Yod (yŏd). A Hebrew letter.
Yoni (yō'nī). A female symbol of the Orientalists.

Zabud (ză-bŭd). An historical personage at Solomon's court.
Zabulon (ză'bū-lōn). Tenth son of Jacob.
Zadok (ză'dŏk). Righteous. Son of Ahitub, a priest.
Zadki-el (zăd'kī-el). Angel of the planet Jupiter.
Zaherlaherbon (ză-her'lă-her-bon').

Zaphnath-paaneah (zăph-năth-paa'ne'ăh). Savior of the world.

Zarathustra (ză'ra-thŭs-tră). Name of Zoroaster in Zend language.

Zarriel (zăr'rī-el). The angel that governs the sun.

Zarthan (zăr'thăn). See *Zeredatha*.

Zebedee (zĕb'e-dē; zeb-ē'de). Jah is gift. Husband of Salome.

Zedekiah (zĕd'e-kī'ă). Jah is might. A false prophet.

Zend-Avesta (zĕnd-ă-vĕs'tă). Persian Bible in Zend language.

zennaar (zĕn'na͝ar). Sacred cord used in Hindustanee initiation.

Zeraias (zē-răi'ăs).

Zerbal (zĕr'băl). King Solomon's Captain of Guards.

Zeredatha (ze-rĕd'ă-tha). See *Clay Ground*.

Zerubbabel (zē-rŭb-ba'bel). A prince of the House of Judah.

Zeus (zē'ŭs). The chief deity of the Greeks.

Zicu (zī'cū).

Zif (zĭf). Blossom. The second Jewish month.

Zipporah (zĭp-pō'ră). Little bird. Wife of Moses.

zithern (zĭth'ern). A musical instrument of 28 strings.

zizon (ze'zŏn). Balustrade.

zodiac (zō'de-ak). An imaginary belt in the heavens.

zohar (zō'hăr). Distinction, nobility.

zohariti (zō'ha-rī'tī). Nobility.

Zoroaster (zō-rō-as'ter). Founder of the Parsee religion.

Zschokke (zschŏk'kē). An eminent German Masonic authority.

Zuni (zū'nī). Indian tribe of New Mexico.

Zurthost (zŭr-thōst). Modern Parsee name for Zoroaster.

Zuzim (zū'zĭm). Strong. A primitive race.

INDEX

D

F

G

J

S

U

PARTIAL LIST OF AUTHORITIES QUOTED

Abarbanel
Abbe Barruel
Abbie Grandidier
Abeille Maconnique
Aben Azra
Abraham Ben David Halevi
Abuse and Use of Freemasonry
Adams, John Quincy, Letters to
Adhering Mason
Ahiman Rezon
Alaophamus Lobeck
Albanus
Albert Pike
Anderson
Anderson's Constitutions
Annales Archeologiques
Anti-Masonic books, catalogue of
Architecture, Essay of Old German
Aristotle
Ashmole, Elias, Life of
Bailey
Barruel
Bazot
Bechai, Rabbi
Beracoth
Berage
Bestiary
Beweiss dass die Freimaurer-Gesellschaft in allen Staaten, u. s. w.
Biblical Cyclopedia
Bibliography of Freemasonry
Biographie Universalle
Birkhead, Matthew
Bishop of Utrecht
Blaney, Lord
Blount
Bochart
Book of the Conversation of God with Moses on Mount Sinai
Boston Magazine
British Archoeologia
British Magazine
Brown's Master key
Burns, Robert
Buxtorf
Calcott
Callimachus
Calmet
Capellus
Carausius
Cardinal Firrao
Carey, Henry
Carlile, Richard
Catalogue of Anti-Masonic books
Catalogue of Books on Masonic Institution
Cawthorn
Chambers
Chambers, in Scottish Biography
Chart, Cross's Hieroglyphic
Cicero
Clark
Clarke, G. C.
Clarke, Dr.
Clavel
Clavis Symbolica
Clemens Alexandrinus
Cole
Conversation-Lexicaon
Cooke
Count de Gebelin
Creuzer
Cross, Hieroglyphic Chart
Cross, Jeremy
Cureton, Rev. W.
Dalcho
Davies, John
Defense of Masonry, A
De Hominis Dignitate
De Idolatria
Dermott, Laurence
Desaguliers, John Theophilus
Detection of Dr. Plots' Account of the Freemason
de Thaun, Philip
Dibdin
Dictionary of Masonry
Didron, M.
Diodorus
Dotzinger, Jost
Dowland, M.
Drake, George
Drummond, Sir William
Du Cange
Dudley
Dunckerley
DuPauw
Ellmaker, Amos
Enfield
Enoch Brother
Entick
Ernst und Falk
Erwin of Steinbach

Essai sur les Illumines
Essay on Architecture
Essay on Old German Architecture
Essay on Swedenborg
Euripides
European Magazine
Eusebius
Faber
Feller, Dr.
Festus
Findel
Firrao, Cardinal
Flammel, Nicolas
Fludd
Freemason's Library
Freemason's Monitor
Freemasonry, Abuse and Use of
Gassett, Henry
Gebelin, Count de
Geber
Gesenius
Gibson
Godwin, George
Golden Remains of the Early Masonic Writers, Oliver's
Gould
Greinemann, Ludwig
Gridley, Richard
Guillemain, de St. Victor
Gwillim
Hallam
Hardynge
Harris, Dr. T. M.
Hemming, Dr.
Herodotus
Hieroglyphic Chart, Cross's
Higgins, Godfrey
Hiram, or the Grand Master Key
Histoire Pittoresque de la Franc-Maconnerie
Historia
Historical Essay on Architecture
Hitchcock
Homer
Hope, Mr.
Horace
Horapollo
Hughan, Bro. Wm. J.
Hure
Hutchinson
Illustrations of Masonry, Preston
Inwood
Irenaeus
Jameson, Mrs.
Jamieson, Scottish Dictionary
Jerome
Josephus
Justin
Kaempfer
Kallisch
Kip
Kitto
Kloss
Koran
Krause
Kyd
Lalande
Lambertus, Ardensis
Lawrie
Lee, Samuel
Leslie
Lessing
Lettres Maconniques
Letters on Masonic Institution
Letters on Masonry and Anti-Masonry
Letters to Hon. John Quincy Adams
Leusden
Le Vrai Franc-Macon
Literary Anecdotes
Lobeck Alaophamus
Locke, Mr.
London Freemasons Quarterly
Louffton
Lynch, Lieutenant
Mackay, Charles
Macrobius
Maimonides
Marquis Luchets
Masonry, A Defense of
Masonry Dissected, Samuel Prichard
Masonry the Turnpike-Road to Happiness
Masonry the Way to Hell
Matthew, Thomas
Memoires pour servir a l'Histore du Jacobinisme
Menasseh Ben Israel
Mendelssohn
Metrical Chronicle of England
Midrashes
Mirandola, Picus of
Mirror of the Johannite Masons, A
Monitor, Freemasons
Moore, C. W.
Morris
Mosaica Philosophia
Natural History of Staffordshire, The, Dr. Robert Plot
Naturales, Quoestiones
Nichols
Nicolai
Notes and Queries
Odiorne, James C.
Oliver, Dr.
Origen
Ovid

Paley
Papworth
Parentalia
Parsee, the Zendavesta
Patrick, Bishop
Payne, George
Phillips
Philo Byblius
Philosphia Mosaica
Picus of Mirandola
Pike, Albert
Pernetty
Plato
Pliny
Plot, Dr. Robert
Plutarch
Porter, Robert Ker
Potter, Dr.
Preston
Prichard, Samuel, Masonry Dissected
Prideaux
Proeparatio Evangelica
Proofs of a Conspiracy, John Robison
Properitus
Rabbi Bechai
Ragon
Ramsay, Chevalier
Raphael
Raphall, Dr.
Rebold
Recueil Precieux
Reghellini
Richardson
Robison
Rockwell, William S.
Sanconiatho
Savage, Abraham
Schiller
Schwarz, Rabbi Joseph
Scottish Biography, Chambers
Selden
Seneca
Simpson, James
Smith, Capt. George
Sophocles
Spence
Spencer
Steiglitz, Christian Ludwig
Steinbach, Erwin of
Stephens
Stillingfleet, Bishop
Stone, William L.
Suarez
Suetonius
Summa Totalis
Tacitus
Talmud
Taylor, Robert
Tertullian
Thacher, J. M.
Thornburgh, Geo.
Three Distinct Knocks, The
Tournon
Towne, Rev. Salem
Tschoudy, Baron
Tucker, Philip S.
Turner, Robert
Use and Abuse of Freemasonry
Van Paun, Cornelius

CPSIA information can be obtained at www.ICGtesting.com
Printed in the USA
BVOW051606160112

280662BV00004B/30/A

9 780766 126244